Causal Inference for Heterogeneous Data and Information Theory

Causal Inference for Heterogeneous Data and Information Theory

Editor

Kateřina Hlaváčková-Schindler

MDPI • Basel • Beijing • Wuhan • Barcelona • Belgrade • Manchester • Tokyo • Cluj • Tianjin

Editor
Kateřina Hlaváčková-Schindler
University of Vienna
Wien
Austria

Editorial Office
MDPI
St. Alban-Anlage 66
4052 Basel, Switzerland

This is a reprint of articles from the Special Issue published online in the open access journal *Entropy* (ISSN 1099-4300) (available at: https://www.mdpi.com/journal/entropy/special_issues/causal_inference).

For citation purposes, cite each article independently as indicated on the article page online and as indicated below:

LastName, A.A.; LastName, B.B.; LastName, C.C. Article Title. *Journal Name* **Year**, *Volume Number*, Page Range.

ISBN 978-3-0365-8050-0 (Hbk)
ISBN 978-3-0365-8051-7 (PDF)

Contents

About the Editor

Kateřina Hlaváčková-Schindler

Kateřina Hlaváčková-Schindler is a senior researcher at the Data Mining and Machine Learning research group at the Faculty of Computer Science, University of Vienna, Vienna, Austria. She is engaged with the methods of causal inference and causal discovery.

entropy

MDPI

Editorial

Causal Inference for Heterogeneous Data and Information Theory

Kateřina Hlaváčková-Schindler [1,2]

1 Faculty of Computer Science, University of Vienna, 1090 Vienna, Austria; katerina.schindlerova@univie.ac.at
2 Institute of Computer Science of the Czech Academy of Sciences, 182 00 Prague, Czech Republic

The present Special Issue of Entropy, entitled "Causal Inference for Heterogeneous Data and Information Theory", covers various aspects of causal inference. The issue presents thirteen original contributions that span various topics, namely the role of instrumental variables in causal inference, the estimation of average treatment effects and the temporal causal models. Four papers are devoted to the design of novel causal models using interventions. The contributions use approaches of information theory, probability, algebraic structures, neural networks and with them related machine learning tools. The papers range from the theoretical ones, the paper applying the models, to the papers providing software tools for causal inference. All papers were peer-reviewed and accepted for publication due to their highest quality contribution. Here, we shortly preview the topics of the contributions.

Instrumental variable in causal inference. Papers [1–3] investigate models using instrumental variable in causal inference. Paper [1] deals with the challenge to reconcile the approaches to causal inference based on independence of cause and mechanism, and approaches based on conditional independence. It is shown that methods based on the independence of cause and mechanism indirectly contain traces of the existence of hidden instrumental variables (IV). Paper [2] investigates the problem of selecting instrumental variables relative to a target causal influence $X \to Y$ from observational data generated by linear non-Gaussian acyclic causal models in the presence of unmeasured confounders. A necessary condition for detecting variables that cannot serve as instrumental variables is proposed. Paper [3] used the piecewise linear model to fit the relationship between the continuous instrumental variable and the continuous explanatory variable, as well as the relationship between the continuous explanatory variable and the outcome variable, which generalizes the traditional linear instrumental variable models.

Estimating average treatment effect. Papers [4–7] deal with the estimation of the Average Treatment Effect (ATE). Papers [4,5] approach the estimation of ATE using neural networks. The estimation of ATE as a causal parameter is carried out in two steps [4]. In the first step, the treatment and outcome are modeled to incorporate the potential confounders, and in the second step, the predictions are inserted into the ATE estimators such as the Augmented Inverse Probability Weighting (AIPW) estimator, based on neural networks (NN). Paper [4] proposed the normalization of AIPW (referred to as nAIPW) to overcome the drawbacks of AIPW. Paper [5] builds on [4] and uses architectures with an L_1-regularization on specific NN parameters and investigates how certain hyperparameters should be tuned in the presence of confounders and IVs to achieve a low bias-variance tradeoff for AIPW estimator.

Paper [6] contributes with the novel econometric software to the community dealing with causal inference and heterogeneous treatment effects estimation. The mcf package is an open-source Python package implementing Modified Causal Forest (MCF), a causal machine learner. For all resolutions of treatment effects estimation, which can be identified, the mcf package provides inference and novel insights on causal effect heterogeneity. The mcf constitutes a practical and extensive tool for a modern causal heterogeneous effects analysis.

Citation: Hlaváčková-Schindler, K. Causal Inference for Heterogeneous Data and Information Theory. *Entropy* **2023**, *25*, 910. https://doi.org/10.3390/e25060910

Received: 26 May 2023
Accepted: 6 June 2023
Published: 8 June 2023

Paper [7] investigates causal inference for heterogeneous treatment effects. The estimation of both overall and heterogeneous treatment effects can be hampered when data are structured within groups if one fails to correctly model the dependence between observations. Most machine learning (ML) methods do not readily accommodate such structures. Paper [7] introduces a new algorithm, stan4bart, that combines the flexibility of Bayesian Additive Regression Trees (BART) for fitting nonlinear response surfaces with the computational and statistical efficiencies of using Stan for the parametric components of the model. It is demonstrated how stan4bart can be used to estimate average, subgroup, and individual-level treatment effects with stronger performance than other flexible approaches.

Temporal causal models. Papers [8,9] consider causal models using time. Paper [8] investigates causal discovery in high-dimensional point process networks with hidden nodes. A big challenge in the multivariate causal discovery is the confounding problem. Paper [8] proposes a deconfounding procedure to estimate high-dimensional point process networks with only a subset of the nodes being observed. The method allows flexible connections between the observed and unobserved processes.

Paper [9] deals with the paradox of time in dynamic causal systems. It investigates the role of time in dynamic systems, where causes take continuous values and also continually influence their effects. A question is posed whether interacting with systems that unfold more slowly might reduce the systematic errors that result from these strategies. It is found that slowing the task indeed reduced the frequency of one type of error, albeit at the cost of increasing the overall error rate.

Causal models and modeling under interventions. Paper [10] examines the so-called interventional fairness with indirect knowledge of unobserved protected attributes. Often, the protected attribute is absent from the training dataset for legal reasons. However, datasets still contain proxy attributes that capture protected information and can inject unfairness in the ML model. Paper [10] examines systems flagging individual samples and considers a feedback-based framework where the protected attribute is unavailable and the flagged samples are indirect knowledge. The reported samples are used as guidance to identify the proxy attributes that are causally dependent on the (unknown) protected attribute. The work is done under the causal interventional fairness paradigm. Without requiring the underlying structural causal model a priori, an approach is proposed that performs conditional independence tests on observed data to identify such proxy attributes.

Paper [11] studies causal algebras on Chain Event Graphs (CEG). One popular causal analysis following Pearl [12] and Spirtes et al. [13] to study causal relationships embedded in a system is to use a Bayesian Network (BN). However, certain causal constructions that are particularly pertinent to the study of reliability are difficult to express fully through a BN. The previous work of the authors of [11] demonstrated that an event tree rather than a BN could provide an alternative framework that could capture most of the causal concepts needed within this domain. A causal calculus for a specific type of intervention, called a remedial intervention, was devised on this tree-like graph. Paper [11] builds on their previous work and shows that remedial maintenance interventions but as well as interventions associated with routine maintenance can be well-defined using this alternative class of graphical model.

Universal Causality is a mathematical framework introduced in [14]. This work is based on higher-order category theory, which generalizes previous approaches based on directed graphs and regular categories. The paper presents a hierarchical framework called Universal Causality Layered Architecture (UCLA), where at the top-most level, causal interventions are modeled as a higher-order category over simplicial sets and objects. Causal inference between layers is defined as a lifting problem, a commutative diagram whose objects are categories, and whose morphisms are functors that are characterized as different types of fibrations. UCLA is illustrated using a variety of representations, including causal relational models and other models.

Paper [15] develops a probabilistic theory of causation using measure-theoretical concepts and information-theoretic functionals and suggests practical routines for conducting causal inference. The theory is applicable to both linear and high-dimensional nonlinear models. It is shown that the suggested measure-theoretic approaches do not only lead to better predictive models, but also to more plausible parsimonious descriptions of possible causal flows.

We are convinced that this heterogeneous collection of outstanding papers on causal inference extends the knowledge of the community working in causal inference both in theory and practical applications. We wish the readers a lot of joy by reading.

Funding: This research was supported by the Austrian Science Foundation FWF (Project No. I5113), by the Czech Science Foundation, Project No. GA19-16066S, and by the Czech Academy of Sciences, Praemium Academiae awarded to M. Paluš.

Acknowledgments: I wish to thank all thirty authors for their contributions and for sharing their novel ideas and techniques with this issue. It was a pleasure and honor for me to work with you to create this Special Issue. In addition, I would like to thank and express my appreciation to the reviewers since they spent a considerable amount of time providing accurate and fair manuscript evaluations. I would also like to express my gratitude to the staff of the Editorial Office of *Entropy* for the fruitful and excellent cooperation.

Conflicts of Interest: The author declares no conflict of interest.

References

1. Sokolovska, N.; Wuillemin, P.-H. The role of instrumental variables in causal inference based on independence of cause and mechanism. *Entropy* **2021**, *23*, 928. [CrossRef] [PubMed]
2. Xie, F.; He, Y.; Geng, Z.; Chen, Z.; Hou, R.; Zhang, K. Testability of instrumental variables in linear non-Gaussian acyclic causal models. *Entropy* **2022**, *24*, 512. [CrossRef] [PubMed]
3. Liu, S.S.; Zhu, Y. Simultaneous maximum likelihood estimation for piecewise linear instrumental variable models. *Entropy* **2022**, *24*, 1235. [CrossRef] [PubMed]
4. Rostami, M.; Saarela, O. Normalized augmented inverse probability weighting with neural network predictions. *Entropy* **2022**, *24*, 179. [CrossRef] [PubMed]
5. Rostami, M.; Saarela, O. Targeted L_1-regularization and joint modeling of neural networks for causal inference. *Entropy* **2022**, *24*, 1290. [CrossRef] [PubMed]
6. Bodory, H.; Busshoff, H.; Lechner, M. High resolution treatment effects estimation: Uncovering effect heterogeneities with the modified causal forest. *Entropy* **2022**, *24*, 1039. [CrossRef] [PubMed]
7. Dorie, V.; Perrett, G.; Hill, J.L.; Goodrich, B. Stan and BART for causal inference: Estimating heterogeneous treatment effects using the power of Stan and the flexibility of machine learning. *Entropy* **2022**, *24*, 1782. [CrossRef] [PubMed]
8. Wang, X.; Shojaie, A. Causal discovery in high-dimensional point process networks with hidden nodes. *Entropy* **2021**, *23*, 1622. [CrossRef] [PubMed]
9. Rehder, B.; Davis, Z.J.; Bramley, N. The paradox of time in dynamic causal systems. *Entropy* **2022**, *24*, 863. [CrossRef] [PubMed]
10. Galhotra, S.; Shanmugam, K.; Sattigeri, P.; Varshney, K.R. Interventional fairness with indirect knowledge of unobserved protected attributes. *Entropy* **2021**, *23*, 1571. [CrossRef] [PubMed]
11. Yu, X.; Smith, J.Q. Causal algebras on chain event graphs with informed missingness for system failure. *Entropy* **2021**, *23*, 1308. [CrossRef] [PubMed]
12. Pearl, J. *Causality*; Cambridge University Press: Cambridge, UK, 2009.
13. Spirtes, P.; Glymour, C.N.; Scheines, R. *Causation, Prediction, and Search*; MIT Press: Cambridge, MA, USA, 2000.
14. Mahadevan, S. Universal causality. *Entropy* **2023**, *25*, 574. [CrossRef] [PubMed]
15. Andrée, B.P.J. Conducting causal analysis by means of approximating probabilistic truths. *Entropy* **2022**, *24*, 92. [CrossRef] [PubMed]

entropy

MDPI

Article

The Role of Instrumental Variables in Causal Inference Based on Independence of Cause and Mechanism

Nataliya Sokolovska [1,*] and Pierre-Henri Wuillemin [2]

1 NutriOmics, UMR S 1269, INSERM, Sorbonne University, 91, Boulevard de l'Hôpital, 75013 Paris, France
2 Laboratoire d'Informatique de Paris 6, Sorbonne University, 4 Place Jussieu, 75005 Paris, France; pierre-henri.wuillemin@lip6.fr
* Correspondence: nataliya.sokolovska@sorbonne-universite.fr

Abstract: Causal inference methods based on conditional independence construct Markov equivalent graphs and cannot be applied to bivariate cases. The approaches based on independence of cause and mechanism state, on the contrary, that causal discovery can be inferred for two observations. In our contribution, we pose a challenge to reconcile these two research directions. We study the role of latent variables such as latent instrumental variables and hidden common causes in the causal graphical structures. We show that methods based on the independence of cause and mechanism indirectly contain traces of the existence of the hidden instrumental variables. We derive a novel algorithm to infer causal relationships between two variables, and we validate the proposed method on simulated data and on a benchmark of cause-effect pairs. We illustrate by our experiments that the proposed approach is simple and extremely competitive in terms of empirical accuracy compared to the state-of-the-art methods.

Keywords: common hidden cause; graphical models; probabilistic models

Citation: Sokolovska, N.; Wuillemin, P.-H. The Role of Instrumental Variables in Causal Inference based on Independence of Cause and Mechanism. *Entropy* **2021**, *23*, 928. https://doi.org/10.3390/e23080928

Academic Editor: Kateřina Hlaváčková-Schindler

Received: 1 July 2021
Accepted: 16 July 2021
Published: 21 July 2021

1. Introduction

Causal inference purely from non-temporal observational data is challenging. Instead of learning the causal structure of an entire dataset, some researchers focus on the analysis of causal relations between two variables only. The state-of-the-art conditional independence-based causal discovery methods (see, e.g., [1,2]) construct graphs that are Markov equivalent, but these methods are not applicable in the case of two variables, since $X \to Y$ and $Y \to X$ are Markov equivalent.

The statistical and probabilistic causal inference methods based on assumptions of independence of cause and mechanism (see [3] for a general overview) appeared relatively recently and achieve very reasonable empirical results. The main idea behind these methods is as follows: if a simple function that fits data exists, then it is likely that it also describes a causal relation in the data.

The main goal of our paper is to try to reconcile two modern viewpoints on causal inference: the research direction initiated by [1,2], which is based on the assumption of conditional independencies, and the more recent research avenue where the main claim is that causal inference between two observations only is feasible [4–10], the theory of which relies on the independence of cause and mechanism.

To illustrate the intuition behind our approach, let us consider an example from [3] with altitude and temperature, where A is altitude, T is temperature, $P(A)$ are city locations, and $P(T|A)$ is the physical mechanism of temperature given altitude, and it can be shown that changing the city locations $P(A)$ does not change the conditional probability $P(T|A)$. The postulate of independence of cause and mechanism allows the causal direction $A \to T$ to be inferred. Any latent variables are ignored in this case. However, the city locations depend on a country, since each country has its own urban policy, population density, etc. Thus, in this example, $P(A)$ has at least one latent variable which is county C. However, no matter what country is chosen, the physical mechanism $P(T|A)$ holds, and the true underlying causal structure is $C \to A \to T$. A country defines the distribution of cities. Having two or more countries leads to a family of distributions. This mixture of probability distributions is independent from $P(T|A)$. Thus, this example also explains what is meant under the independence between probability distributions.

To our knowledge, ref. [11] is the most related recent work to our contribution; however, they consider the case of the pseudo-confounders, where all variables, even confounders, are observed. Our contribution is multi-fold:

- Our main theoretical result is an alternative viewpoint on the recently appeared causal inference algorithms that are based on the independence of cause and mechanism. Here, we follow the simplification used by [3]; however, we are aware that the independence of our interest is between the prior of the cause and the mechanism.
- Our main theoretical results are formulated as Theorems 1 and 2.
- Assuming the existence of the hidden instrumental variables, we propose a novel method of causal inference. Since we consider a bivariate causal inference case where only X and Y are observed, we also propose an approach to estimate the latent instrumental variables for cases where the cluster assumption for the observed data holds.
- We propose a simple and original method to identify latent confounders.
- We validate our method on a synthetic dataset on which we perform extensive numerical experiments and on the cause-effect benchmark, which is widely used by the causal inference community.

The paper is organized as follows. Section 2 discusses the state-of-the-art methods of bivariate causal inference. Preliminaries on the instrumental variables are provided in Section 3. We consider the role of the instrumental variables for causal inference, and we introduce our approach in Section 4. In Section 5, we discuss the results of our numerical experiments on synthetic and standard challenges. Concluding remarks and perspectives close the paper.

2. Related Work

In this section, we discuss the state-of-the-art methods of bivariate causal inference and the corresponding assumptions. In the current work, we focus on a family of causal inference methods which are based on a postulate stating that if $X \to Y$, then the marginal distribution $P(X)$ and the conditional distribution $P(Y|X)$ are independent [8,12,13]. These approaches provide causal directions based on the estimated conditional and marginal probability distributions from observed non-temporal data. One of the oldest and most well-studied types of models describing causal relations that is necessary to mention is structural causal models (SCM). An SCM where $X \to Y$ is defined as follows:

$$X = N_X, \quad Y = f_Y(X, N_Y), \tag{1}$$

where N_X and N_Y are independent. Given f_Y and the noise distributions P_{N_Y} and P_{N_X}, we can sample data following an SCM.

A recently proposed but already often used postulate of independence of cause and mechanism is formulated as follows (see, e.g., [8,12,13]). If X causes Y, then $P(X)$ and $P(Y|X)$ estimated from observational data contain no information about each other. Looking for a parallel between the postulate and the SCM, we assume that in an SCM, f_Y and P_{N_Y} contain no information about P_X, and vice versa. The postulate describes the independence of mechanisms and states that a causal direction can be inferred from estimated marginal and conditional probabilities (considered as random variables) from a dataset. In the following, we investigate this research direction.

It is not obvious how to formalise the independence of the marginal and conditional probabilities. A reasonable claim [3] is that an optimal measure of dependence is the algorithmic mutual information that relies on the description length in the sense of Kolmogorov complexity. Since the exact computations are not feasible, there is a need for a practical and reliable approximation. Such an approximation encodes that $P(X)$ and $P(Y|X)$ require more compact models in a causal direction and more complex models in an anticausal direction.

Two families of methods of causal inference dealing with bivariate relations are often discussed. For a more general overview of causal structure learning see [3,14]. Additive noise models (ANM) introduced by [15,16] are an attempt to describe causal relations between two variables. The ANMs assume that if there is a function f and some noise E, such that $Y = f(X) + E$, where E and X are independent, then the direction is inferred to be $X \to Y$. A generalised extension of the ANM, called post-nonlinear models, was introduced by [17]. However, the known drawback of the ANM is that the model is not always suitable for inference on discrete tasks [18].

Another research avenue exploiting the asymmetry between cause and effect is the linear trace (LTr) method [19] and information-geometric causal inference (IGCI) [13]. If the true model is $X \to Y$, and if $P(X)$ is independent from $P(Y|X)$, then the trace condition is fulfilled in the causal direction and violated in the anticausal one. The IGCI method exploits the fact that the density of the cause and the log slope of the function transforming cause to effect are uncorrelated. However, for the opposite direction, the density of the effect and the log slope of the inverse of the function are positively correlated. The trace condition is proved under the assumption that the covariance matrix is drawn from a rotation invariant prior [12]. The method was generalized for non-linear cases [20], and it was shown that the covariance matrix of the mean embedding of the cause in reproducing kernel Hilbert space is free independent with the covariance matrix of the conditional embedding of the effect given cause. The application of the IGCI to high-dimensional variables is considered in [19,21]. Here, the independence between probability distributions is based on the trace condition. The identifiability via the trace condition is proved [3,21] for deterministic relations, and no theory exists for noisy cases, which are much more relevant for real-life applications.

Origo [22] is a causal discovery method based on the Kolmogorov complexity. The minimum description length (MDL) principle can be used to approximate the Kolmogorov complexity for real tasks. Namely, from an algorithmic information viewpoint, if $X \to Y$, then the shortest program that computes Y from X is more compact than the shortest program computing X from Y. The obvious weakness of methods based on the Kolmogorov complexity, and also of Origo, is that the MDL only approximates Kolmogorov complexity and involves unknown metric errors that are difficult to control. The empirical performance is highly dependent on a dataset, and Origo was reported to reach state-of-the-art performance on the multivariate benchmarks (acute inflammation, ICDM abstracts, adult dataset); however, it performs less accurately than the ANM on the bivariate benchmark of cause-effect pairs with known ground truth (the Tübingen data set) [23]. We also use this benchmark for our experiments.

There exist various applications of causal inference. Thus, [24] provides a geometric interpretation of information flow as a causal inference. Speaking of probabilistic causal inference approaches, we would like to mention [25], which is a survey considering probabilistic causal dependencies among variables. Information theory is used in [26] to apply bivariate analysis to discover the causal skeleton for multivariate systems. Note that the method which is proposed in our contribution can also be extended to a multivariate case in a similar way.

The most studied causal inference case is probably the case of time series [27], where the Granger causality can be applied. We would like to underline that we consider the case of observational non-temporal data in the current contribution, and the results on the time series are beyond the scope of our paper.

We would like to underline the differences between [11] and our results. The researchers consider a surrogate variable related to a distribution shift that characterises hidden quantities that imply changes across domains and/or time. It is reported that it is possible to find causal models in each domain or for each time point for non-stationary data, but they propose using the information on the distribution shift to identify one causal model across domains and/or time. This surrogate variable can be seen as a confounder; however, it is assumed that the values of these confounders are fixed and always observed (Assumption 1 and Section 3.2 of [11]). Thus, they are pseudo-confounders. We, on the contrary, assume that the surrogate variable is not observed, and we do not assume that the confounders exist. We pose a challenge to identify their existence and to approximate latent instrumental variables.

3. Independence of Probability Distributions and Instrumental Variables

Let X and Y be two correlated variables. In the settings considered by [3], in order to decide whether $X \to Y$ or $Y \to X$, it is proposed to check if the distributions $P(X)$ and $P(Y|X)$ are independent. As far as we know, this independence between distributions (and not between random variables) does not have any formal definition. However, some useful properties can be derived, and various criteria were constructed for different cases [4–9]. In this paper, we adopt the following definition. Let $P(X,Y)$ be the joint distribution of X,Y in a population $\mathcal{P}$; let $Q(X,Y)$ be the joint distribution of X,Y in another population $\mathcal{Q}$. If X is the cause of Y, the causal mechanism should be the same in the two distributions:

$$P(X,Y) = P(X) \cdot P(Y|X), \tag{2}$$
$$Q(X,Y) = Q(X) \cdot P(Y|X), \tag{3}$$

i.e., $P(Y|X) = Q(Y|X)$, and on the contrary, $P(X|Y) \neq Q(X|Y)$. More generally, for all mixed populations between $\mathcal{P}$ and $\mathcal{Q}$, and for all mixtures $Q_\lambda = \lambda P + (1-\lambda)Q$ with $\lambda \in [0,1]$:

$$\forall\lambda \in [0,1], Q_\lambda(X) \perp\!\!\!\perp Q_\lambda(Y|X) \tag{4}$$
$$\iff Q_\lambda(Y|X) = P(Y|X). \tag{5}$$

Now, we consider λ as a hyper-parameter for a (latent) prior I_X that allows the population $(P(X|I_X = 0) = P(X), P(X|I_X = 1) = Q(X))$ to be selected. In this meta-model, I_X and X are dependent, and X and Y are dependent. However, I_X and Y are independent conditionally to X. On the contrary, if we consider λ as a hyper-parameter for a (latent) prior I_Y, this allows the population $(P(Y|I_Y = 0) = P(Y), P(Y|I_Y = 1) = Q(Y))$ to be selected. In this meta-model, I_Y and Y are dependent, and X and Y are dependent. However, since $P(X|Y) \neq Q(X|Y)$, I_Y and X are not independent, even conditionally to Y.

To provide some intuition behind such a mixture model, let $P(X)$ and $Q(X)$ be the distributions of city locations in two different countries and $P(Y|X)$ be a physical mechanism predicting weather in a given location. Then λ is the hyper-parameter controlling the proportion of observations in each country, and note that λ, $P(X)$, and $Q(X)$ are independent from $P(Y|X)$. Such a representation of the problem as a mixture model with latent priors motivates our proposition to use models with instrumental latent variables.

The aim of models with instrumental variables [28–30] where X, Y, and I_X are observed, and U is an unobserved confounder, is to identify the causal effect of X on Y. Assuming that the relationships are linear, and applying a linear Gaussian structural causal model, one can write

$$X = \alpha_0 + \alpha I_X + \delta U + \epsilon_X, \tag{6}$$
$$Y = \beta_0 + \beta X + \gamma U + \epsilon_Y, \tag{7}$$

where ϵ_X and ϵ_Y are noise terms, independent of each other. It is assumed, without loss of generality, that U, ϵ_X, and ϵ_Y have mean zero. Note that the common cause U can be absent, and we are not going to assume that U exists when modelling dependencies between X and Y. The instrumental variable I_X is uncorrelated with ancestors of X and Y. The instrumental variable is a source of variation for X, and it only influences Y through

X. Studying how X and Y respond to perturbations of I_X can help one deduce how X influences Y. A two-stage least squares [31] can be used to solve the problem.

Probability distributions as random variables

Similar to [3,21], we consider probability distributions as random variables. $P(X)$ is a function of $X \in [0,1]$, and thus, they are random variables distributed in $[0,1]$. Note that a model where a probability is randomly generated is an example of a hierarchical model, or of a model with priors, where some parameters are treated as random variables.

4. Latent Instrumental Variables for Causal Discovery

In this section, we show that the methods based on the independence of cause and mechanism, introduced by [4–9], indirectly contain traces of the existence of the hidden instrumental variable. This can be seen as follows. $P(X)$ generates X in the approaches proposed and investigated by the scientists mentioned above. In our method, we assume that X are generated by I_X. Therefore, there is a strong parallel between $P(X)$ and I_X, which are both priors for the observations. Thus, our method described below also provides some intuition and interpretation of the recently proposed algorithms based on the independence between the "cause and the mechanism". We provide some theoretical results on the independence of the causal mechanisms in terms of probability distributions and information theory. These results allow us to derive a novel algorithm of causal inference which is presented in the section below.

Our observations are X and Y, two one-dimensional vectors of the same length N, and these variables are correlated. Here, we suppose that either causality between these variables exists, and either $X \to Y$, $Y \to X$, or a common latent cause $X \leftarrow U \to Y$ can be identified, where U is a hidden variable that can impact X and/or Y. Let I_X and I_Y denote latent instrumental variables of X and Y, respectively. In the current contribution, we do not observe the instrumental variables; we assume that they exist and can be approximated. We do not assume that the common cause U exists; however, we show how its existence can be deduced, if this is the case.

There are three graphical structures that are of particular interest for us. They are shown on Figure 1: the dark nodes are observed, and the instrumental variables and the common latent cause are not observed from data.

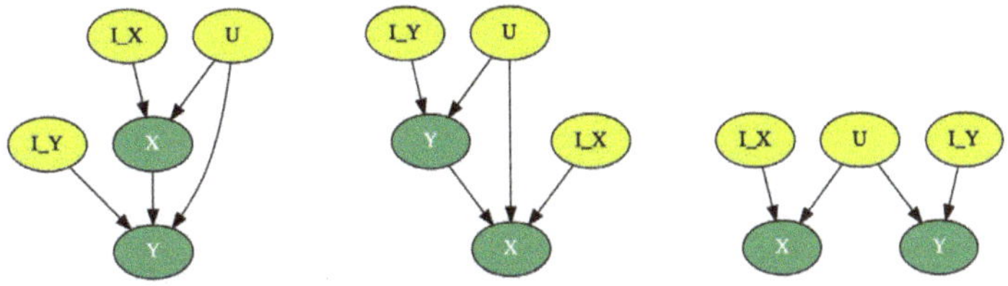

Figure 1. The models of our interest. The dark nodes are observed from data, and the light coloured nodes are latent.

Assumption 1. *In the case of observational non-temporal data, if I_X exists such that $I_X \to X$, and if I_Y exists such that $I_Y \to Y$, and if the random variables X and Y are correlated, then we assume that it is impossible that both $I_X \perp\!\!\!\perp Y|X$ and $I_Y \perp\!\!\!\perp X|Y$ hold.*

Theorem 1. *Let X and Y be two correlated random variables, and they do not have any common cause. We assume that either X causes Y, or vice versa. If there exists a random variable I_X such that $I_X \to X$, and if $I_X \perp\!\!\!\perp Y|X$, then we are able to infer causality and decide that $X \to Y$.*

Proof. Several directed acyclic graphs (DAGs) may be Markov equivalent [1,2]. We assume that once an essential graph is found, the directed arcs of this graph are interpreted causally.

Under the assumption that $I_X \to X$, and if $I_X \perp\!\!\!\perp Y|X$, the only possible directed graph is $I_X \to X \to Y$. In the case where $I_X \not\perp\!\!\!\perp Y|X$, we obtain $I_X \to X \leftarrow Y$. □

Theorem 2. *If the true causal structure is $I_X \to X \to Y$, and X and Y do not have any common cause, then $P(Y|X)$ does not contain any information about $P(X)$, and vice versa; however, $P(X|Y)$ and $P(Y)$ are not independent.*

Proof. Assume that $I_X \perp\!\!\!\perp Y|X$. Let us consider the relation between $P(Y|X)$ and $P(X)$. In the following, we treat $P(Y|X)$, $P(X|Y)$, $P(X)$, and $P(Y)$ as random variables. We can write

$$P(Y|I_X, X) = P(Y|X). \tag{8}$$

Note that we do not have $P(X)$ in Equation (8) when we express $P(Y|X)$ for $I_X \to X \to Y$. Let us consider the relation between $P(X|Y)$ and $P(Y)$ for the same graphical structure. We obtain

$$P(X|Y) = \frac{P(Y|X)P(X|I_X)}{P(Y)}, \tag{9}$$

where the form of the nominator is due to the fixed dependencies $I_X \perp\!\!\!\perp Y|X$. From Equation (9), we clearly see that $P(X|Y)$ is not independent from $P(Y)$ for this graphical structure. □

Table 1 provides the state-of-the-art methods of the bivariate causal inference (left column) and the corresponding equivalent models with the latent instrumental variables I_Y and I_X, if they can be reconstructed (right column).

Table 1. Some state-of-the-art methods for causal discovery for the ground truth $X \to Y$, under the assumption that $I_X \not\perp\!\!\!\perp Y|X$, and the corresponding models with the latent instrumental variables.

The state-of-the-art methods of bivariate causal inference and their main ideas	Existence of hidden instrumental variables, an equivalent model with the latent IV
CURE (unsupervised inverse regression) [8]: It is possible to recover $P(X|Y)$ from $P(Y)$, it is not possible to recover $P(Y|X)$ from $P(X)$	This implies directly that $P(X|I_Y, Y)$, $X \not\perp\!\!\!\perp I_Y|Y$, and therefore, I_Y is needed to recover the conditional probability
Information-geometric approach [13]: $\mathrm{cov}(\log f', P(X)) = 0, \mathrm{cov}(\log f^{-1'}, P(Y)) \geq 0$, f' is log slope of the func. transform. cause to effect	$\mathrm{cov}(P(Y|I_X, X), P(X)) = 0$ $\mathrm{cov}(P(X|I_Y, Y), P(Y)) \geq 0$ $\mathrm{cov}(P(Y|X), P(X)) = 0$ $\mathrm{cov}(P(X|I_Y, Y), P(Y)) \geq 0$
Comparing regression errors [32]: $\mathbb{E}[(Y - \mathbb{E}[Y|X])^2] \leq \mathbb{E}[(X - \mathbb{E}[X|Y])^2]$	$\mathbb{E}[\mathrm{var}(Y|I_X, X)] \leq \mathbb{E}[\mathrm{var}(X|I_Y, Y)]$ $\mathbb{E}[\mathrm{var}(Y|X)] \leq \mathbb{E}[\mathrm{var}(X|I_Y, Y)]$
Using the distance correlation [9]: $\mathcal{D}(P(X), P(Y|X)) \leq \mathcal{D}(P(Y), P(X|Y))$, where $\mathcal{D}$ is distance correlation	$\mathcal{D}(P(X), P(Y|I_X, X)) \leq \mathcal{D}(P(Y), P(X|I_Y, Y))$ $\mathcal{D}(P(X), P(Y|X)) \leq \mathcal{D}(P(Y), P(X|I_Y, Y))$
Via kernel deviance measures [10]: $S_{X \to Y} = \frac{1}{N}\sum_{i=1}^{N}\left(\|\mu_{Y|X=x_i}\|_{\mathcal{H}_y} - \frac{1}{N}\sum_{j=1}^{N}\|\mu_{Y|X=x_j}\|_{\mathcal{H}_y}\right)^2$ $\mathcal{H}_y$ – RKHS, $S_{Y \to X}$ analogously, $S_{X \to Y} \leq S_{Y \to X}$	Compare (μ is cond. mean embedding) $\frac{1}{N}\sum_{i=1}^{N}\left(\|\mu_{Y|I_X, X=x_i}\|_{\mathcal{H}_y} - \frac{1}{N}\sum_{j=1}^{N}\|\mu_{Y|I_X, X=x_j}\|_{\mathcal{H}_y}\right)^2$ vs. $\frac{1}{N}\sum_{i=1}^{N}\left(\|\mu_{X|I_Y, Y=y_i}\|_{\mathcal{H}_x} - \frac{1}{N}\sum_{j=1}^{N}\|\mu_{X|I_Y, Y=y_j}\|_{\mathcal{H}_x}\right)^2$

Construction of the Instrumental Variables

Assumption 2. *(Cluster assumption. [33]) If points are in the same cluster, they are likely to be in the same class.*

In some tasks, the instrumental variables (IV) are observed, and their application is straightforward. In a number of applications, they are not provided. Here, we discuss how the instrumental variables can be approximated, and we draft a procedure to estimate them.

In our experiments, in Section 5, we apply the proposed method for the IV construction. Note that the identification and characterisation of latent variables is a challenge in itself. Our work is slightly similar to [34,35] in that we apply clustering methods to create the latent variables. Taking into account that only X and Y are observed, the instrumental variables can be constructed using either X, Y, or both, and an optimal choice of the variables (X, Y, or both) that are related to the IV is in its turn related to a graphical structure that we try to identify and to orient. Thus, for a structure $I_X \rightarrow X \rightarrow Y$, I_X does not contain information about Y, and I_X has to be constructed from X only. On the contrary, in the case of $X \rightarrow Y \leftarrow I_Y$, I_Y is not independent from X, and I_Y has to contain information about both X and Y.

We rely on clustering methods for the instrumental variables estimation. In our experiments, we apply the k-means clustering; however, other clustering approaches can be used. Algorithm 1 drafts the procedure to approximate the candidates for the IV. We developed a method—Algorithm 2—that makes the decision of whether I_X and I_Y are to be constructed from one or two observed variables. The proposed algorithm constructs the instrumental variables separately from X, Y (I_{X_X}, I_{Y_Y}), and from both ($I_{X_{XY}}$, $I_{Y_{YX}}$), and tests which instrumental variables are more relevant. Algorithm 2 compares the distance (we considered the Euclidean distance in our experiments; however, another measure, e.g., the Kullback–Leibler, can be used) between I_{X_X} and $I_{X_{XY}}$, and between I_{Y_Y} and $I_{Y_{YX}}$. The intuition behind the proposed criterion is as follows. If Y influences clustering of X less than X impacts clustering of Y (the condition $if(\text{dist}(I_{X_X}, I_{X_XY}) < \text{dist}(I_{Y_Y}, I_{Y_YX}))$ in Algorithm 2), then we apply I_X constructed from X only, and I_Y is constructed from X and Y. Furthermore, vice versa. An important remark is that this criterion has a lot in common with the causal discovery methods based on the Kolmogorov complexity and the MDL: to infer causality, our criterion choses a simpler model.

A Symmetric Causal Inference Algorithm

We introduce a simple symmetric algorithm based on the conditional (in)dependence tests to infer causality. It relies on the theoretical foundations provided above. Our algorithm is sketched as a decision tree in Figure 2. It takes I_X, I_Y, X, and Y and returns a causal direction. Precisely, if a conditional independence test states that $Y \perp\!\!\!\perp I_X | X$ is true, then $X \rightarrow Y$ is inferred; otherwise, we test whether $X \perp\!\!\!\perp I_Y | Y$, and if it is true, then Y causes X. The last case where X and Y are correlated but both $Y \perp\!\!\!\perp I_X | X$ and $X \perp\!\!\!\perp I_Y | Y$ are false, let us conclude that there is a common hidden cause U, and $Y \leftarrow U \rightarrow X$.

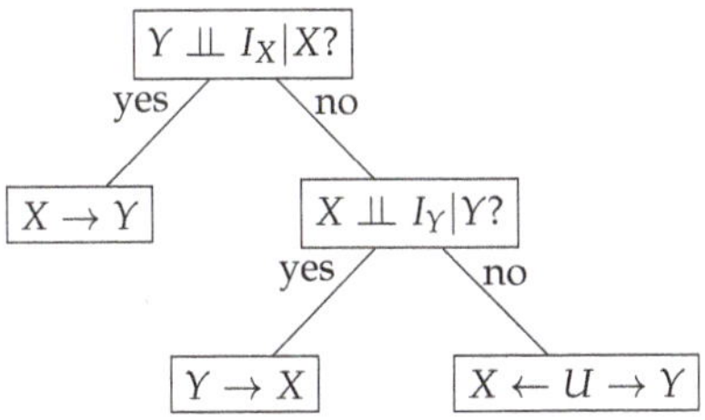

Figure 2. A symmetric causal inference algorithm.

Algorithm 1 Construction of IV Candidates

I_{X_X} (IV variable of X from X)

Fix a number of clusters K
Cluster $\{X_i\}_{i=1}^N$ into K clusters
for $i = 1 : N$ **do**
  I_{i,X_X} is the centre of the cluster where X_i belongs
end for

$I_{X_{XY}}$ (IV variable of X from X and Y)

Fix a number of clusters K
Cluster $\{X_i, Y_i\}_{i=1}^N$ into K clusters
for $i = 1 : N$ **do**
  $I_{i,X_{XY}}$ is the 1st coordinate (corresponding to X) of the clusters centres where (X_i, Y_i) belongs
end for

I_{Y_Y} (IV variable of Y from Y)

is constructed similarly to the IV variable of X from X

$I_{Y_{YX}}$ (IV variable of Y from X and Y)

is constructed similarly to the IV variable of X from (X, Y)
(Take the 2nd coordinate of the clusters centres)

Algorithm 2 Approximation of the Instrumental Variables (IV) I_X and I_Y from X and Y.

Input: Observations X and Y, a clustering algorithm
Output: Instrumental variables I_X and I_Y

// Construct instrumental variables to be tested
Construct IV of X, I_{X_X} using X only
Construct IV of X, $I_{X_{XY}}$ using X and Y
Construct IV of Y, I_{Y_Y} using Y only
Construct IV of Y, $I_{Y_{YX}}$ using X and Y

// Take the decision which IV to use

if $(\text{dist}(I_{X_X}, I_{X_{XY}}) < \text{dist}(I_{Y_Y}, I_{Y_{YX}}))$ **then**
  // the IV of X is constructed from X only
  $I_X = I_{X_X}$
  // the IV of Y is constructed from both X and Y
  $I_Y = I_{Y_{YX}}$
else
  // the IV of Y is constructed from Y
  $I_Y = I_{Y_Y}$
  // the IV of X is constructed from X and Y
  $I_X = I_{X_{XY}}$
end if

5. Experiments

In this section, we illustrate the predictive efficiency of the proposed method on both artificial and real datasets. We run the numerical experiments on a recent MacBook Pro, 2.6GHz 6-core Intel Core i7, 16GB memory. We use the R language and environment for our experiments, in particular the `bnlearn` R package.

Simulated Data

We consider simple discrete and continuous scenarios. In the discrete case, we fix the structures and the probability distributions on the graphs and generate binary variables. In the continuous case, we use a Gaussian distribution. We generate the instrumental variables I_X and I_Y, X and Y, and the hidden variable U. We use the `bnlearn` R package to construct the synthetic datasets, and we also use the conditional independence tests from the same package. For our discrete setting with binary variables, we apply an asymptotic mutual information independence test `ci.test(test='mi')`, and for the continuous setting with Gaussian variables, we apply the exact t-test for Pearson's correlation `ci.test(test='cor')`. Note that the abovementioned conditional independence tests from the `bnlearn` R package return "big" p-values if the variables are conditionally independent, and the p-values are small (with an arbitrary threshold 0.05) for dependent variables.

We consider and simulate discrete and continuous data for two following scenarios: (1) $X \to Y$, and (2) $X \leftarrow U \to Y$. We test a various number of observations, from 10 to 10,000, and we observe that in the discrete case, even for such a simple problem as one with variables taking binary values, a large number of observations is needed to obtain a reasonable performance. Figure 3 illustrates the p-values of the conditional independence tests for the discrete (two plots above) and continuous (two plots below) settings. We show the results for both cases $X \perp\!\!\!\perp I_Y|Y$ and $Y \perp\!\!\!\perp I_X|X$. We observe that for the ground truth $X \to Y$, $X \perp\!\!\!\perp I_Y|Y$ asymptotically converges to small p-values (close to 0), and $Y \perp\!\!\!\perp I_X|X$ returns large p-values, even for a large number of observations.

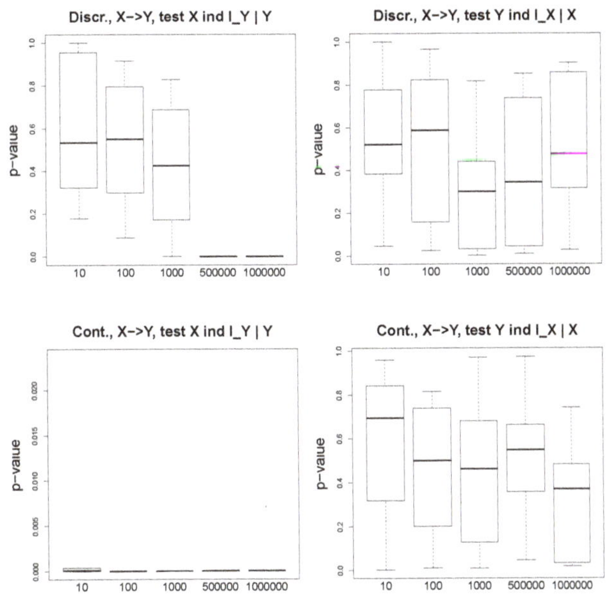

Figure 3. Simulated data. Ground truth: $X \to Y$. Two plots above: discrete data; two plots below: continuous data. The p-values of an asymptotic mutual information test (for the discrete case) and an exact t-test for Pearson's correlation (the continuous case) as a function of the number of observations (x-axis).

Figure 4 shows our results for the scenario $X \leftarrow U \to Y$. For the discrete and continuous experiments, we test whether $Y \perp\!\!\!\perp I_X|X$ and whether $X \perp\!\!\!\perp I_Y|Y$. We see that the variables are not independent. In Figure 5, we demonstrate the p-values of the conditional independence test $Y \perp\!\!\!\perp X|U$, which is a sanity check, and we observe that in this case where the ground truth is $X \leftarrow U \to Y$, the p-values are far from 0 for both continuous and discrete scenarios. In the experiments on the simulated data, our aim is to show that the p-values are reasonable indicators of the conditional independence. We do not report the accuracy values, since it is straightforward according to the proposed algorithm (Figure 2).

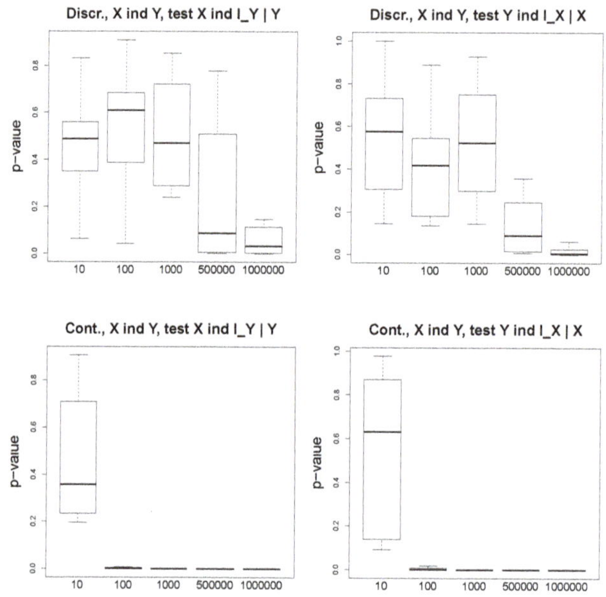

Figure 4. Simulated data. Ground truth: $X \perp\!\!\!\perp Y|U$. Above: two plots for the discrete setting; below: two plots for the continuous setting. The p-values as a function of the number of observations (x-axis).

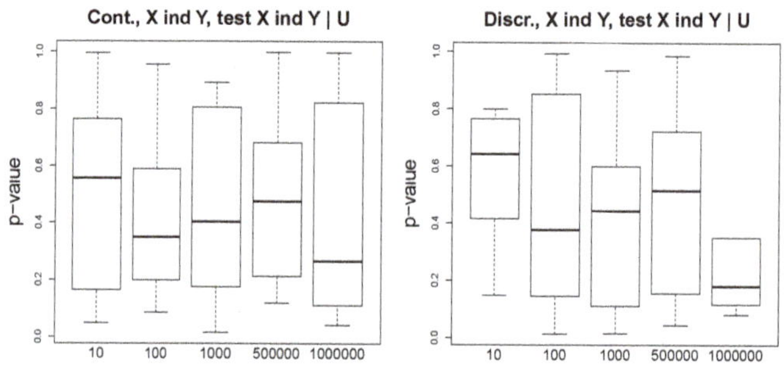

Figure 5. Simulated data. Ground truth: $X \perp\!\!\!\perp Y|U$. The results of the conditional independence tests for $X \perp\!\!\!\perp Y|U$ for continuous (on the left) and discrete (on the right) data. On the x-axis: the number of observations.

Cause-Effect Pairs

We tested the proposed algorithm on the benchmark collection of the cause-effect pairs, obtained from http://webdav.tuebingen.mpg.de/cause-effect (accessed on 15 January 2021), version 1.0. The data set contains 100 pairs from different domains, and the ground truth is provided. The goal is to infer which variable is the cause and which is the effect. The pairs 52–55, 70–71, and 81–83 are excluded from the analysis, since they are multivariate problems. Note that each pair has an associated weight, provided with the data set, since several cause-effect pairs can come from the same scientific problem. In a number of publications reporting results on this dataset, the accuracy is a weighted average. We apply the proposed method, described in Section 4, to infer causality on the cause-effect pairs. In Figure 6, we show the standard (unweighted) accuracy and the weighted accuracy, where the weights for each observation pair are given in the dataset. To increase the stability and also the accuracy, we propose a scenario where we split the data into k-folds, carry out causal inference on each fold separately, and take an ensemble decision on the causal direction. The accuracy for such an ensemble approach is also shown in Figure 6 for both weighted and not weighted performance. The number of folds in our experiments is 10. Speaking of state-of-the-art results on the cause-effect pairs, it was reported that Origo [22] achieves (weighted) accuracy of 58%, and the ANM [16] reaches $72 \pm 6\%$. Figure 6 illustrates that the proposed method outperforms the state-of-the-art algorithms: our weighted accuracy is 83.2%. Note that the ensemble method reduces the variance significantly. We do not provide the results of the extensive numerical comparisons of the state-of-the-art methods on the cause-effect pairs, since these results can be easily found in the original papers (cited in the Related Work section). Moreover, the goal of the current work is not only to achieve state-of-the-art results and to outperform them, which we do, but also to focus on an alternative formulation of the independence of the cause and the causal mechanism, as well as to consider a reasonable method for the identification and construction of the hidden instrumental variables.

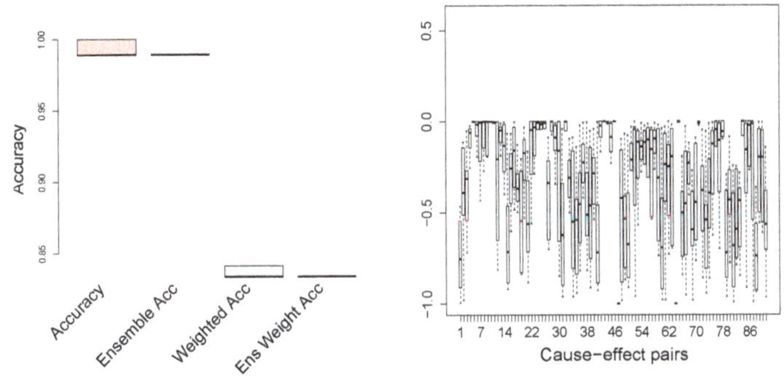

Figure 6. On the **left**: accuracy on the cause-effect benchmark. On the **right**: the difference between the test statistics $X \perp\!\!\!\perp I_Y|Y$ and $Y \perp\!\!\!\perp I_X|X$.

What is central and what is interesting to look at are the p-values of the conditional independence tests (here, the exact t-test for Pearson's correlation from `bnlearn` R package) $X \perp\!\!\!\perp I_Y|Y$ and $Y \perp\!\!\!\perp I_X|X$. In Figure 6 (on the right), we show their difference. If the p-values of the test $X \perp\!\!\!\perp I_Y|Y$ are small (that is, X and I_Y are not independent, given Y) and the results of $Y \perp\!\!\!\perp I_X|X$ are relatively large (or larger than ones of $X \perp\!\!\!\perp I_Y|Y$), stating that Y and I_X are independent, given X, then the plotted difference is negative. This is exactly what is observed for almost all cause-effect pairs.

Figure 6 (on the right) shows our results for the case where the number of clusters, i.e., modalities of the hidden instrumental variables, is set to 15 for both I_X and I_Y. We tested different numbers, K, of clusters for the construction of instrumental variables (see Section 4 for details). For the current task, we did not notice any important impact on the result; however, taking extremely small (2–3) and large (70–100) numbers of clusters degrades the performance. In practical real applications, an optimal K can be fixed using a grid search.

6. Conclusions, Limitations, and Future Research

We posed a challenge to bring together two principle research avenues in causal inference: causal inference using conditional independence and methods based on the postulate of independence of cause and mechanism. We focused on the methods of causal inference based on the independence of cause and mechanism, and we provided some theoretical foundations for this family of algorithms. Our main message is that the role of the hidden instrumental variables cannot be neglected.

The implications of our study are twofold. First, the proposed method will motivate the development of novel theoretical (probabilistic) approaches to recover hidden common causes. Second, our method can already be tested and studied for some real biological and medical applications. However, the application to real problems, especially to medical and biological tasks, should be done in tight collaboration with human experts.

We propose an algorithm to estimate the latent instrumental variables efficiently. We also introduce a simple (and symmetric) algorithm to perform causal inference for the case of two observed variables only, where the corresponding instrumental variables are approximated. Our original approach is simple to implement, since it is based on a clustering algorithm (we used the k-means; however, any other clustering method can be tested) and on conditional independence tests. The introduced approach can be applied to both discrete and continuous data, and we have shown that it is extremely competitive compared to the state-of-the-art methods on a real benchmark, where a cluster assumption holds.

The main limitation of our work is that it is focused on the bivariate case; however, in a number of real applications, there is a need to infer causality between several variables.

Currently, we consider an extension of the proposed algorithm to more complex graphs and potentially huge applications, such as modelling gene interactions. Another avenue of research is novel metrics to measure the conditional independence of variables.

Author Contributions: N.S. and P.-H.W. developed the concept and the algorithm. N.S. implemented the method and ran the numerical experiments. N.S. and P.-H.W. wrote the original manuscript. All authors have read and agreed to the published version of the manuscript.

Funding: This research received no external funding.

Institutional Review Board Statement: Not applicable.

Informed Consent Statement: Not applicable.

Data Availability Statement: The data used in the experiments are publicly available, and can be downloaded from http://webdav.tuebingen.mpg.de/cause-effect.

Acknowledgments: This work was supported by the French National Research Agency (ANR JCJC DiagnoLearn).

Conflicts of Interest: The authors declare no conflict of interest.

References

1. Pearl, J. *Causality: Models, Reasoning and Inference*, 2nd ed.; Cambridge University Press: Cambridge, UK, 2009.
2. Spirtes, P.; Glymour, C.; Scheines, R. *Causation, Prediction, and Search*; MIT Press: Cambridge, MA, USA, 2000.
3. Peters, J.; Janzing, D.; Schölkopf, B. *Elements of Causal Inference*; The MIT Press: Cambridge, MA, USA, 2017.
4. Schölkopf, B.; Janzing, D.; Peters, J.; Sgouritsa, E.; Zhang, K.; Mooij, J. Semi-supervised Learning in Causal and Anticausal Settings. In *Empirical Inference*; Springer: Berlin/Heidelberg, Germany, 2013; pp. 129–141.
5. Parascandolo, G.; Kilbertus, N.; Rojas-Carulla, M.; Schölkopf, B. Learning independent causal mechanisms. In Proceedings of the International Conference on Machine Learning (ICML), Stockholm, Sweden, 10–15 July 2018.
6. Daniusis, P.; Janzing, D.; Mooij, J.; Zscheischler, J.; Steudel, B.; Zhang, K.; Schölkopf, B. Inferring deterministic causal relations. *arXiv* **2010**, arXiv:1203.3475.
7. Schölkopf, B.; Janzing, D.; Peters, J.; Sgouritsa, E.; Zhang, K. On causal and anticausal learning. *arXiv* **2012**, arXiv:1206.6471.
8. Sgouritsa, E.; Janzing, D.; Hennig, P.; Schölkopf, B. Inference of cause and effect with unsupervised inverse regression. In Proceedings of the Eighteenth International Conference on Artificial Intelligence and Statistics, San Diego, CA, USA, 9–12 May 2015.
9. Liu, F.; Chan, L. Causal inference on discrete data via estimating distance correlations. *Neural Comput.* **2016**, *28*, 801–814. [CrossRef] [PubMed]
10. Mitrovic, J.; Sejdinovic, D.D.; Teh, Y.W. Causal inference via Kernel Deviance Measures. *arXiv* **2018**, arXiv:1804.04622.
11. Huang, B.; Zhang, K.; Zhang, J.; Ramsey, J.; Sanchez-Romero, R.; Glymour, C.; Schölkopf, B. Causal discovery from heterogeneous/nonstationary data. *JMLR* **2020**, *21*, 1–53.
12. Janzing, D.; Schölkopf, B. Causal inference using the algorithmic Markov condition. *IEEE Trans. Inf. Theory* **2010**, *56*, 5168–5194. [CrossRef]

13. Janzing, D.; Mooij, J.; Zhang, K.; Lemeire, J.; Zscheischler, J.; Daniusis, P.; Streudel, B.; Schölkopf, B. Information-geometric approach to inferring causal directions. *Artif. Intell.* **2012**, *182*, 1–31. [CrossRef]
14. Heinze-Deml, C.; Maathuis, M.H.; Meinshausen, N. Causal Structure Learning. *arXiv* **2017**, arXiv:1706.09141.
15. Hoyer, P.; Janzing, D.; Mooij, J.; Peters, J.; Schölkopf, B. Nonlinear causal discovery with additive noise models. In Proceedings of the NIPS, Vancouver, BC, Canada, 11 December 2008.
16. Peters, J.; Mooij, J.; Janzing, D.; Schölkopf, B. Causal discovery with continuous additive noise models. *JMLR* **2014**, *1*, 2009–2053.
17. Zhang, K.; Hyvärinen, A. On the identifiability of the post-nonlinear causal models. *arXiv* **2009**, arXiv:1205.2599.
18. Bühlmann, P.; Peters, J.; Ernest, J. Cam: Causal additive models, high-dimensional order search and penalized regression. *Ann. Stat.* **2014**, *42*, 2526–2556. [CrossRef]
19. Zscheischler, J.; Janzing, D.; Zhang, K. Testing whether linear equations are causal: A free probability theory approach. *arXiv* **2011**, arXiv:1202.3779.
20. Liu, F.; Chan, L.W. Causal inference on multidimensional data using free probability theory. *IEEE Trans. Neural Netw. Learn. Syst.* **2017**, *29*, 3188–3198. [CrossRef] [PubMed]
21. Janzing, D.; Hoyer, P.O.; Schölkopf, B. Telling cause from effect based on high-dimensional observations. *arXiv* **2010**, arXiv:0909.4386.
22. Budhathoki, K.; Vreeken, J. Causal inference by compression. In Proceedings of the ICDM, Barcelona, Spain, 12–15 December 2016.
23. Mooij, J.M.; Peters, J.; Janzing, D.; Zscheischler, J.; Schölkopf, B. Distinguishing cause from effect using observational data: methods and benchmarks. *JMLR* **2016**, *17*, 1103–1204.
24. Surasinghe, S.; Bollt, E.M. On Geometry of Information Flow for Causal Inference. *Entropy* **2020**, *22*, 396. [CrossRef]
25. Cox, L.A. Information Structures for Causally Explainable Decisions. *Entropy* **2021**, *23*, 601. [CrossRef]
26. Sigtermans, D. Determining Causal Skeletons with Information Theory. *Entropy* **2021**, *23*, 38. [CrossRef]
27. Liang, X.S. Normalized Multivariate Time Series Causality Analysis and Causal Graph Reconstruction. *Entropy* **2021**, *23*, 679. [CrossRef]
28. Wright, P.G. *The Tariff on Animal and Vegetable Oils*; Investigations in International Commercial Policies; The Macmillan Company: New York, NY, USA, 1928.
29. Heckman, J. Instrumental variables: A study of implicit behavioral assumptions used in making program evaluations. *J. Hum. Resour.* **1997**, *32*, 441–462. [CrossRef]
30. Angrist, J.; Krueger, A. Instrumental Variables and the Search for Identification: From Supply and Demand to Natural Experiments. *J. Econ. Perspect.* **2001**, *15*, 69–85. [CrossRef]
31. Sawa, T. The Exact Sampling Distribution of Ordinary Least Squares and Two-Stage Least Squares Estimators. *J. Am. Stat. Assoc.* **2012**, *64*, 923–937. [CrossRef]
32. Blöbaum, P.; Janzing, D.; Washio, T.; Shimizu, S.; Schölkopf, B. Cause-effect inference by comparing regression errors. In Proceedings of the International Conference on Artificial Intelligence and Statistics (AISTATS), Lanzarote, Spain, 9–11 April 2018.
33. Chapelle, O.; Schölkopf, B.; Zien, A. *Semi-Supervised Learning*; MIT Press: Cambridge, MA, USA, 2006.
34. Janzing, D.; Sgouritsa, E.; Stegle, O.; Peters, J.; Schölkopf, B. Detecting low-complexity unobserved causes. *arXiv* **2011**, arXiv:1202.3737.
35. Sgouritsa, E.; Janzing, D.; Peters, J.; Schölkopf, B. Identifying Finite Mixtures of Nonparametric Product Distributions and Causal Inference of Confounders. *arXiv* **2013**, arXiv:1309.6860.

entropy

MDPI

Article

Testability of Instrumental Variables in Linear Non-Gaussian Acyclic Causal Models

Feng Xie [1,2], Yangbo He [1,*], Zhi Geng [2], Zhengming Chen [3], Ru Hou [1] and Kun Zhang [4,5]

1 School of Mathematical Sciences, Peking University, Beijing 100871, China; xiefeng@math.pku.edu.cn (F.X.); rhou@pku.edu.cn (R.H.)
2 School of Mathematics and Statistics, Beijing Technology and Business University, Beijing 100048, China; zhigeng@btbu.edu.cn
3 School of Computer, Guangdong University of Technology, Guangzhou 510006, China; 2111905124@mail2.gdut.edu.cn
4 Department of Philosophy, Carnegie Mellon University, Pittsburgh, PA 15213, USA; kunz1@cmu.edu
5 Machine Learning Department, Mohamed bin Zayed University of Artificial Intelligence, Abu Dhabi 7909, United Arab Emirates
* Correspondence: heyb@math.pku.edu.cn

Abstract: This paper investigates the problem of selecting instrumental variables relative to a target causal influence $X \to Y$ from observational data generated by linear non-Gaussian acyclic causal models in the presence of unmeasured confounders. We propose a necessary condition for detecting variables that cannot serve as instrumental variables. Unlike many existing conditions for continuous variables, i.e., that at least two or more valid instrumental variables are present in the system, our condition is designed with a single instrumental variable. We then characterize the graphical implications of our condition in linear non-Gaussian acyclic causal models. Given that the existing graphical criteria for the instrument validity are not directly testable given observational data, we further show whether and how such graphical criteria can be checked by exploiting our condition. Finally, we develop a method to select the set of candidate instrumental variables given observational data. Experimental results on both synthetic and real-world data show the effectiveness of the proposed method.

Keywords: instrumental variable; causal graph; non-Gaussianity; causal discovery

Citation: Xie, F.; He, Y.; Geng, Z.; Chen, Z.; Hou, R.; Zhang, K. Testability of Instrumental Variables in Linear Non-Gaussian Acyclic Causal Models. *Entropy* **2022**, *24*, 512. https://doi.org/10.3390/e24040512

Academic Editor: Kateřina Hlaváčková-Schindler

Received: 5 March 2022
Accepted: 3 April 2022
Published: 5 April 2022

1. Introduction

Estimating causal effects from observational data is an important problem, especially in the presence of unmeasured confounding. The instrumental variable (IV or instrument) model is a general approach to estimate causal effect in the presence of unobserved variables [1–4] and is used in a wide range of literature, such as economics [5,6], sociology [4,7], and epidemiology [8,9].

A major challenging problem in an instrumental variable model is how to select a valid IV to infer the causal effect of one variable X on another variable Y. In general, IVs need to be chosen based on domain knowledge or expert experience. However, it is sometimes difficult to select a valid IV without precise prior knowledge of causal structure, and an invalid IV may cause a biased estimation of the effect of X on Y [10]. Therefore, it is desirable to investigate ways of selecting IVs only from observed variables.

Although it is not possible to test whether a variable is a valid IV only from the joint distribution of observed variables, there exist several methods for testing whether a variable of interest is an invalid IV. Pearl [11] provided a necessary condition, called the *instrumental inequality*,for a general instrument model, which can be used to test whether a variable is a candidate IV for discrete variables. Inspired by instrumental inequality, various contributions were made towards discovering the testability of IV validity in different scenarios [12–15]. More recently, Kédagni and Mourifié [16] considered a more general case where treatment is discrete and there are no restrictions on IV and outcome and proposed generalized instrumental inequalities to test the IV independence assumption. However, those approaches fail to work when treatment is a continuous variable. Pearl [11] conjectured that instrument validity cannot be tested in the case where treatment is a continuous variable without any further assumption, which was recently proved by Gunsilius [17].

There exist works in the literature that address the continuous variable setting. Kuroki and Cai [18] utilized vanishing Tetrad conditions [19] and proposed a new necessary condition to solve this problem in the linear structural causal model. However, their method needs at least three valid IVs in the observed variables. Kang et al. [20] proposed the sisVIVE algorithm to estimate the causal effect in the case where more than half of the variables are valid IVs in the observed variables. Later, Silva and Shimizu [21] appear to be the first to exploit the non-Gaussianity property in the linear structural causal model. They utilized the generalized Tetrad conditions (t-separation) [22,23] and designed a IV-TETRAD algorithm to select IVs. Unfortunately, their conditions still require two or more IVs as a prerequisite for instrument testing and may rule out some correct IVs. For instance, consider the causal graph in Figure 1. Assume the causal relationships between variables are linear and that the noise terms follow non-Gaussian distributions. Then, the IV-TETRAD returns an empty set of candidate IVs though Z is a valid IV relative to $X \to Y$.

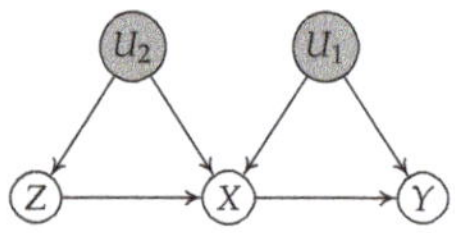

Figure 1. A simple instrumental variable example where X is treatment, Y is outcome, and Z is an IV relative to $X \to Y$.

In this paper, we show that, for continuous data, a single variable Z being a valid IV relative to $X \to Y$ imposes certain constraints in a linear non-Gaussian acyclic causal model. Specifically, we make the following contributions:

1. We propose a necessary condition for detecting variables that cannot serve as (conditional) IVs by the so-called generalized independent noise (GIN) condition [24], which is called instrumental variable generalized independent noise (IV-GIN) condition. We characterize the graphical implications of IV-GIN condition in linear non-Gaussian acyclic causal models.
2. We then further show whether and how the graphical criteria of an instrumental variable can be checked by exploiting the IV-GIN conditions.
3. We develop a method to select the set of candidate IVs for the target causal influence $X \to Y$ from the observational data by IV-GIN conditions.
4. We demonstrate the efficacy of our algorithm on both synthetic and real-word data.

2. Related Work

In this section, we review some of the key works that are most closely related to ours.

2.1. Instrument Variable Models

The instrumental variable (IV) model is a general approach to estimate the causal effect of a treatment X on an outcome Y of interest in presence of unobserved variables [1–3]. That is to say, the IV model is an unbiased estimator of the causal effect of X on Y of interest [4,6]. In practice, one can obtain IVs based on domain knowledge or expert experience. However, it is sometimes difficult to select the valid IV without precise prior knowledge of causal structure, and an invalid IV may cause a biased estimation of the effect of X on Y [10]. In this paper, we investigate data-driven ways of selecting IVs only from observed variables. The current methods for selecting IVs can be roughly divided into the following two settings.

In the literature of the discrete variable setting, Pearl [11] provided a necessary condition, called *instrumental inequality*, which can be used to test whether a variable is an invalid IV. Inspired by instrumental inequality, various contributions were made to discover IV validity's testability in different scenarios. For instance, Manski [12] showed the same instrumental inequality in the missing data model. Palmer et al. [13] and Wang et al. [15] considered useful tests of the instrumental inequality in the binary instrumental variable model. Kitagawa [14] introduced another test of the instrument in the case where the outcome is continuous. More recently, Kédagni and Mourifié [16] proposed generalized instrumental inequalities to test the IV independence assumption in the case where treatment is discrete and there are no restrictions on IV and outcome. Gunsilius [17] recently proved the Pearl's conjecture that instrument validity cannot be tested in the case where treatment is a continuous variable without any further assumption[11].

There exist works in the literature that address the continuous variable setting. For instance, Kuroki and Cai [18] proposed a new necessary condition to resolve this problem in the linear structural causal model using the so-called Tetrad conditions [19]. Later, Kang et al. [20] proposed the sisVIVE algorithm to estimate the causal effect in the case where more than half of the candidate instruments are valid (*majority rule*). Recently, Silva and Shimizu [21] appear to be the first to exploit the non-Gaussianity property in the linear structural causal model. They designed an IV-TETRAD algorithm to select IVs using the generalized Tetrad conditions (t-separation) [22,23]. Unfortunately, the above methods require two or more IVs as a prerequisite for instrument testing, and some methods (e.g., IV-TETRAD approach) may rule out some correct IVs.

Our work focuses on the continuous setting. Unlike the existing works, we show that a single variable Z, being a valid IV relative to $X \rightarrow Y$, imposes certain constraints in a linear non-Gaussian acyclic causal model.

2.2. Causal Graphical Models

Graphical models with latent variables are extensively studied in the literature. Unlike the existing methods of learning the undirected graphical model [25–33], here, we focus only on the most closely related work on causal graphical models, i.e., a directed acyclic graph (DAG) G representing the relations of causation among the variables [4,7]. Within the space of discovering a causal graphical model on observed data, the commonly used strategies are as follows.

One typical strategy for handling this problem is using conditional independence tests to learn the causal graph over the observed variables [4,7]. Well-known algorithms along this line include Fast Causal Inference (FCI) [34], Really Fast Causal Inference (RFCI) [35], and their variants [36]. These methods learn the equivalence class of maximal ancestral graphs (MAGs), as represented by PAG (partial ancestral graph). However, these works focus on estimating the causal structure over only observed variables and can not recover the precise causal graph. In our work, we try to discover the set of candidate IVs from observational variables without prior knowledge of causal graphs.

Another strategy is functional causal model-based approaches. For instance, Hoyer et al. [37] showed that the causal order between any two observed variables is identifiable in the linear non-Gaussian causal model. Later, more efficient methods were proposed to learn the causal graph over observed variables [38,39]. Recently, Salehkaleybar et al. Salehkaleybar et al. [40] showed that the set of all possible causal effects between any two observed variables is identifiable in the same setting. Unfortunately, the size of the equivalence class of the identified causal effects could be very large, and their method requires specifying the number of latent variables a priori [21].

There is also an interesting strategy based on the "Sparse plus Low Rank Matrix Decomposition". Many methods are proposed to address the challenge of learning a latent Gaussian graph model. For instance, Chandrasekaran et al. [26] formulated a convex objective involving nuclear norm penalization maximum likelihood for Gaussian graphical model estimation with a few latent confounders. Zorzi and Sepulchre [28] presented a two-step procedure for estimating autoregressive (AR) latent variable graphical models. Later, Ciccone et al. [41] reformulated this decomposition problem for the setting where only the sample covariance is available, and the difference between the sample covariance and the actual one is non-negligible. Alpago et al. [42] proposed an identification procedure for a sparse graphical model associated with a reciprocal process. However, these methods focus on the undirected graphical model. In the field of a causal graphical model, Frot et al. [43] introduced the LRpSC+GES algorithm to learn the causal structure with some hidden variables. Agrawal et al. [44] proposed a practical algorithm, the DeCAMFounder, to consistently estimate causal relationships in the nonlinear, pervasive confounding setting. Although these methods are used in a range of fields, they usually assume that the underlying graph among the observed variables is sparse, and there are a few hidden variables that have a direct effect on many of the observed variables. The modeling of our paper does not restrict those assumptions and allows arbitrary hidden structures.

In summary, unlike the existing methods of recovering causal graphical models, our goal is to select the set of candidate IVs from observational variables without precise prior knowledge of causal graph.

3. Preliminaries

3.1. Notation and Graph Terminology

We follow the notational conventions used in [7]. Let G be a directed acyclic graph (DAG) with the nodes (or vertex) set $\mathbf{V}$ and the directed edges set $\mathbf{E}$. Here, we use "variable" and "node" interchangeably. A **path** is a sequence of nodes $\{V_1, \ldots, V_r\}$ such that V_i and V_{i+1} are adjacent in G, where $1 \leq i < r$. Furthermore, if the edge between V_i and V_{i+1} has its arrow pointing to V_{i+1} for $i = 1, 2, \ldots, r-1$, we say that the path is **directed** from V_1 to V_r. A **collider** on a path $\{V_1, \ldots, V_p\}$ is a node V_i , $1 < i < p$, such that V_{i-1} and V_{i+1} are parents of V_i. We say a path is **active** if this path can be traced without traversing a collider. A **trek** between V_i and V_j is a path that does not contain any colliders in G. The set of all parents and children of V_i are denoted by $\mathbf{Pa}(V_i)$ and $\mathbf{Ch}(V_i)$, respectively. Besides, for a set $\mathbf{O}$, $|\mathbf{O}|$ denotes the number of elements of set $\mathbf{O}$. Other commonly used concepts in graphical models, such as d-separation, can be found in [4,7].

3.2. Instrumental Variable Model

Here, we follow the notational conventions and definitions used in [45]. Let X be the treatment (exposure), Y be the outcome, and $\mathbf{U}$ be the set of unmeasured confounders between X and Y.

Definition 1 ((Conditional) Instrumental Variable Criteria). *Given the causal graph G, a variable Z is a (conditional) instrumental variable to a target causal effect $X \to Y$ given $\mathbf{W}$, if and only if it satisfies the following conditions:*

1. $\mathbf{W}$ *contains only nondescendants of Y in G;*
2. $\mathbf{W}$ *d-separates Z from Y in the graph obtained by removing the edge $X \to Y$ from G;*
3. $\mathbf{W}$ *does not d-separates Z from X in G.*

For simplicity, we call these three conditions *instrument criteria*.

Definition 2 (IV Estimator). *Suppose variable Z is a (conditional) IV for $X \to Y$ given $\mathbf{W}$, the causal effect of X on Y, denoted by b_{YX}, is identified in a linear model and given by*

$$b_{YX} = \frac{\sigma_{ZY \cdot \mathbf{W}}}{\sigma_{ZX \cdot \mathbf{W}}}, \tag{1}$$

where $\sigma_{ZY \cdot \mathbf{W}}$ denotes the partial covariance between Z and Y given the set $\mathbf{W}$, and $\sigma_{ZX \cdot \mathbf{W}}$ denotes the partial covariance between Z and X given the set $\mathbf{W}$.

Figure 2 illustrates a simple instrumental variable model, where Z is an IV conditioning on $\{W_1, W_2\}$ for the relation $X \to Y$. The causal effect b_{YX} is $\frac{\sigma_{ZY \cdot \{W_1, W_2\}}}{\sigma_{ZX \cdot \{W_1, W_2\}}}$.

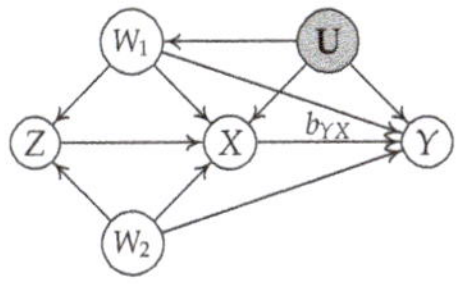

Figure 2. A typical instrumental variable model where X is treatment, Y is outcome, and Z is an IV conditioning on $\{W_1, W_2\}$ relative to $X \to Y$.

3.3. Problem Setup

In this paper, we assume that the system of interest is a linear non-Gaussian acyclic causal model with variables in $\mathbf{V} = \{X, Y\} \cup \mathbf{U} \cup \mathbf{O}$, where X is the treatment, Y is the outcome, $\mathbf{U}$ is the set of unmeasured (latent or hidden) variables, and $\mathbf{O}$ is the set of other measured variables. In particular, without loss of generality, we assume that all variables in $\mathbf{V}$ have a zero mean. Each variable $V_i \in \mathbf{V}$ is generated according to the following linear structural equation model (SEM):

$$V_i = \sum_{V_j \in \mathbf{Pa}(V_i)} b_{ij} V_j + \varepsilon_{V_i} \tag{2}$$

where b_{ij} is the causal strength from V_j to V_i. All noise terms ε_{V_i} are continuous random variables following non-Gaussian distributions with nonzero variances and are independent of each other. We restrict our attention to the recursive model [46]. That is to say, the causal relationships among variables can be represented by a DAG [4,7]. This model is also known as linear, non-Gaussian, acyclic model (LiNGAM) when all variables in $\mathbf{V}$ are observed [47].

Our problem of interest is to study the testability of IV validity for the relation $X \to Y$ in a linear non-Gaussian acyclic causal model. To this end, theoretically, we need to investigate the testability of instrument criteria from observational variables.

4. Necessary Condition for Instrumental Variable

In this section, we first give a simple example to show that a valid IV imposes some constraints with the help of non-Gaussianity. Then, we give our necessary condition for (conditional) IVs by using generalized independent noise (GIN) conditions [24]. Finally, we present the graphical implications of the proposed condition in linear non-Gaussian causal models. To improve readability, we defer all proofs to the Appendix A.

4.1. A Motivating Example

Before showing the theoretical results, let us look at two simple graphs shown in Figure 3. Suppose the generating mechanisms of two subgraphs are as follows:

- Subgraph (a): $U_1 = \varepsilon_{U_1}$, $Z = \varepsilon_Z$, $X = 2Z + 0.5U_1 + \varepsilon_X$, and $Y = 1X + 2U_1 + \varepsilon_Y$;
- Subgraph (b): $U_1 = \varepsilon_{U_1}$, $Z = 1U_1 + \varepsilon_Z$, $X = 2Z + 0.5U_1 + \varepsilon_X$, and $Y = 1X + 2U_1 + \varepsilon_Y$.

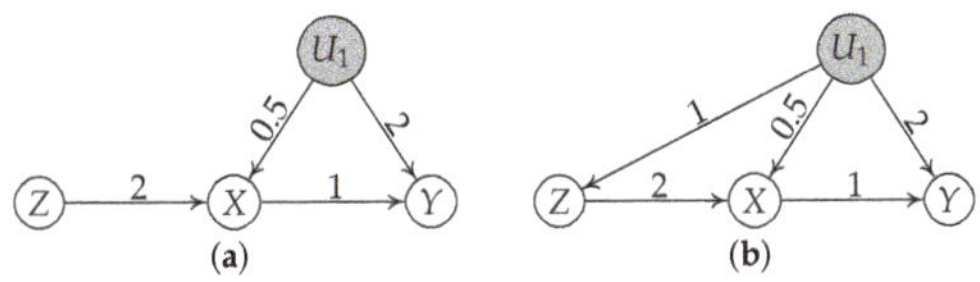

Figure 3. (**a**) Z is a valid IV for the relation $X \to Y$ and (**b**) Z is an invalid IV for the relation $X \to Y$.

Here, we consider two cases, namely Gaussian and uniform cases:

- *Gaussian Case*: All noise terms in subgraphs (a) and (b) are generated from the standard Gaussian distributions.
- *Uniform Case*: All noise terms in subgraphs (a) and (b) are generated from the uniform distributions over the interval $[0, 1]$.

Let $Y - \frac{\sigma_{YZ}}{\sigma_{XZ}}X$ be the surrogate-variable of $\{Y, X\}$ relative to Z. Figure 4 shows the scatter plots of Z and $Y - \frac{\sigma_{YZ}}{\sigma_{XZ}}X$ for two cases. Interestingly, in the Gaussian case, we find that no matter whether Z is an IV or not, Z and $Y - \frac{\sigma_{YZ}}{\sigma_{XZ}}X$ are statistically independent, while in the uniform case, Z and $Y - \frac{\sigma_{YZ}}{\sigma_{XZ}}X$ are statistically dependent if Z is an invalid IV. These observations imply that the non-Gaussianity (as indicated by the uniform distribution) is beneficial to find out whether a continuous variable is a candidate IV relative to $X \to Y$.

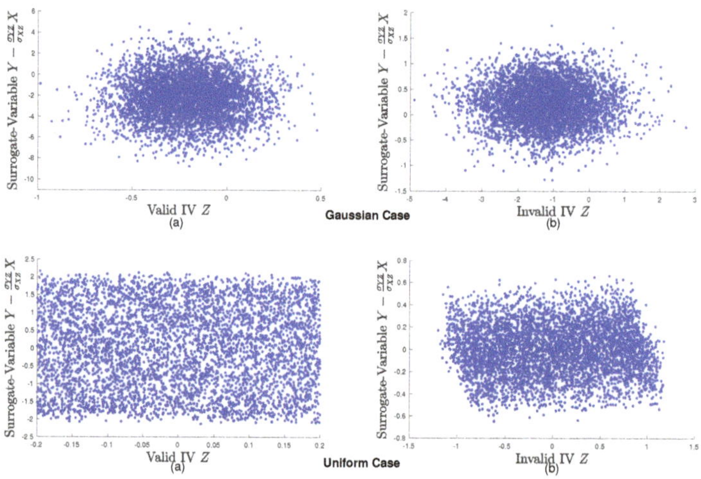

Figure 4. Illustration on the fact that non-Gaussianity leads to dependence between invalid IV Z and surrogate-variable $Y - \frac{\sigma_{YZ}}{\sigma_{XZ}}X$. (**a**) Scatter plot of valid IV Z and surrogate-variable $Y - \frac{\sigma_{YZ}}{\sigma_{XZ}}X$. (**b**) Scatter plot of invalid IV Z and surrogate-variable $Y - \frac{\sigma_{YZ}}{\sigma_{XZ}}X$.

4.2. IV-GIN Condition for Instrumental Variable

Below, we give mathematical characterizations of the above observation by using the GIN condition. Before that, we first review the GIN condition formulated by Xie et al. [24] and the Darmois–Skitovitch theorem that characterizes the independence of two linear statistics given in [48].

Definition 3 (GIN condition). *Let* $\mathbf{P}$ *and* $\mathbf{Q}$ *be two observed random vectors. Suppose the variables follow the linear non-Gaussian acyclic causal model. Define the surrogate-variable of* $\mathbf{P}$ *relative to* $\mathbf{Q}$ *as* $E_{\mathbf{P}||\mathbf{Q}} := \omega^\intercal \mathbf{P}$, *where* ω *satisfies* $\omega^\intercal \mathbb{E}[\mathbf{P}\mathbf{Q}^\intercal] = \mathbf{0}$ *and* $\omega \neq \mathbf{0}$. *We say that* $(\mathbf{Q}, \mathbf{P})$ *follows the GIN condition if and only if* $E_{\mathbf{P}||\mathbf{Q}}$ *is statistically independent from* $\mathbf{Q}$.

Theorem 1 (Darmois–Skitovitch Theorem). *Define two random variables* V_1 *and* V_2 *as linear combinations of independent random variables* $n_1, \ldots, n_p$:

$$V_1 = \sum_{i=1}^{p} \alpha_i n_i, \qquad V_2 = \sum_{i=1}^{q} \beta_i n_i, \tag{3}$$

where the α_i, β_i *are constant coefficients. If* V_1 *and* V_2 *are independent, then the random variables* n_j *for which* $\alpha_j \beta_j \neq 0$ *are Gaussian.*

The above theorem states that if there exists a non-Gaussian n_j for which $\alpha_j\beta_j \neq 0$, V_1 and V_2 are dependent.

We now give the necessary condition of valid IVs by using GIN conditions.

Theorem 2 (Necessary Condition for IV). *Let G be a linear non-Gaussian acyclic causal model. Let treatment X, outcome Y, Z, and* **W** *be correlated random variables in G. Assume faithfulness holds. If Z is a valid IV conditioning on* **W** *relative to* $X \to Y$ *in G, then* $(\{Z, \mathbf{W}\}, \{X, Y, \mathbf{W}\})$ *follows the GIN condition.*

We term this necessary condition the *IV-GIN (instrumental variable-generalized independent noise)* condition. For the rest of the paper, we say that $[Z||\mathbf{W}]$ follows the IV-GIN condition relative to $X \to Y$ if and only if $(\{Z, \mathbf{W}\}, \{X, Y, \mathbf{W}\})$ follows the GIN condition. Theorem 2 indicates that one may test whether a variable Z is an invalid IV conditioning on **W** relative to $X \to Y$ by just testing the IV-GIN condition.

Example 1 (Motivating example, continued). *Let us continue to consider the two causal graphs in Figure 3. Assume that all noise terms follow non-Gaussian distributions. According to the linear generating mechanism and IV-GIN condition, for subgraph (a),*

$$Z = \varepsilon_Z \tag{4}$$

$$E_{\{Y,X\}||Z} = Y - \frac{\sigma_{YZ}}{\sigma_{XZ}} X = 2U_1 + \varepsilon_y. \tag{5}$$

We find that there is no common non-Gaussian independent component shared by $E_{\{Y,X\}||Z}$ *and Z. Thus, we have* $E_{\{Y,X\}||Z}$ *as independent from Z due to the Darmois–Skitovitch Theorem.*

However, for subgraph (b),

$$Z = \varepsilon_{U_1} + \varepsilon_Z \tag{6}$$

$$\begin{aligned} E_{\{Y,X\}||Z} &= Y - \frac{\sigma_{YZ}}{\sigma_{XZ}} X \\ &= (2 - 2.5t)U_1 + \varepsilon_y - 2t\varepsilon_Z - t\varepsilon_X, \end{aligned} \tag{7}$$

where $t = \frac{2\mathrm{Var}(\varepsilon_{U_1})}{2.5\mathrm{Var}(\varepsilon_{U_1}) + 2\mathrm{Var}(\varepsilon_Z)}$. *We find that there is one common, non-Gaussian independent component shared by* $E_{\{Y,X\}||Z}$ *and Z, i.e.,* ε_Z *because* $2t \neq 0$. *Thus, we have* $E_{\{Y,X\}||Z}$ *and Z as dependent due to the Darmois–Skitovitch theorem. These facts theoretically verify the results shown in Figure 4.*

4.3. Graphical Implications of IV-GIN Condition in Linear non-Gaussian causal Models

In this section, we characterize the graphical implications of the IV-GIN condition in linear non-Gaussian causal models. The following theorem shows the connection between IV-GIN condition and the graphical properties of the variables, and an illustrative example is given accordingly.

Theorem 3. *Suppose all variables* **V** *follow the linear non-Gaussian acyclic causal model and that faithfulness holds. Let treatment X, outcome Y, Z, and* **W** *be correlated random variables in* **V**. *Then,* $[Z||\mathbf{W}]$ *follows the IV-GIN condition relative to* $X \to Y$ *and there is no proper subset* $\tilde{\mathbf{W}}$ *of* **W** *such that* $[Z||\tilde{\mathbf{W}}]$ *follows the IV-GIN condition relative to* $X \to Y$ *if and only if the following three conditions hold:*

1. *There exists a node* $C \in \mathbf{V}$, $C \notin \mathbf{W}$, *such that for every trek* π *between a node* $V_p \in \{X, Y, \mathbf{W}\}$ *and a node* $V_q \in \{Z, \mathbf{W}\}$, *(a)* π *goes through at least one node in* $\{C, \mathbf{W}\}$, *denoted by* V_k, *and (b)* V_k *has its arrow pointing to* V_p *in* π. *(In other words,* V_k *is causally earlier (according to the causal order) than* V_p *on* π.*)*
2. *There is at least one directed path between any one node in* $\{C, \mathbf{W}\}$ *and any one node in* $\{X, Y\}$.
3. *There is no proper subset* $\tilde{\mathbf{W}}$ *of* **W** *to satisfy conditions 1 and 2.*

Example 2. *Consider the causal graphs shown in Figure 3 again. For subgraph (a), there exists a node X, and* $\mathbf{W} = \emptyset$ *such that (1) every trek between Z and* $\{X, Y\}$*, e.g.,* $Z \to X \to Y$*, goes through X and that (2) X has its arrow pointing to Y. Besides, there is at least one directed path between X and any one node in* $\{X, Y\}$*. According to Theorem 3, we know that* $[Z||\emptyset]$ *follows the IV-GIN condition relative to* $X \to Y$ *in subgraph (a). However, for subgraph (b), we can not find a node C such that every trek between* $\{Z\}$ *and a node in* $\{X, Y\}$ *goes through C and C is causally earlier than* $\{X, Y\}$*, e.g., treks* $Z \to X$ *and* $Z \leftarrow U_1 \to Y$*. This implies that* $[Z||\emptyset]$ *violates the IV-GIN condition in subgraph (b) according to Theorem 3.*

5. Testability of Instrument Criteria Validity in Terms of IV-GIN Conditions

In this section, we investigate the testability of instrument criteria by exploiting our IV-GIN condition. Note that the last condition of instrument criteria, i.e., that $\mathbf{W}$ does not d-separate Z from X in G, can be easily checked by the d-separation criterion because $\mathbf{W}$, Z, and X are observed variables [4]. Therefore, we focus next on the first two conditions of instrument criteria.

5.1. Condition 1 of Instrument Criteria

Below, we first show that the first condition, i.e., that $\mathbf{W}$ contains only nondescendants of Y in G, is testable by using IV-GIN conditions.

Proposition 1. *Let G be a linear non-Gaussian acyclic causal model. Let treatment X, outcome Y, Z, and* $\mathbf{W}$ *be correlated random variables in G. Assume faithfulness holds, conditions* $2 \sim 3$ *of instrument criteria hold, and there is no proper subset* $\tilde{\mathbf{W}}$ *of* $\mathbf{W}$ *such that* $[Z||\tilde{\mathbf{W}}]$ *follows the IV-GIN condition. If* $\{Z, \mathbf{W}\}$ *contains at least one descendant of Y in G, then* $[Z||\mathbf{W}]$ *must violate the IV-GIN condition.*

Proposition 1 ensures that the IV-GIN condition rules out the invalid IVs that do not satisfy condition 1 of instrument criteria, and an illustrative example is given in Example 3.

Example 3. *Let us consider the causal graph in Figure 5. We find that* $[Z||W_1]$ *follows the IV-GIN condition because Z is a valid IV conditioning on* W_1*. However, we find that* $[Z||W_2]$ *violates the IV-GIN condition because* W_2 *is the descendant of Y.*

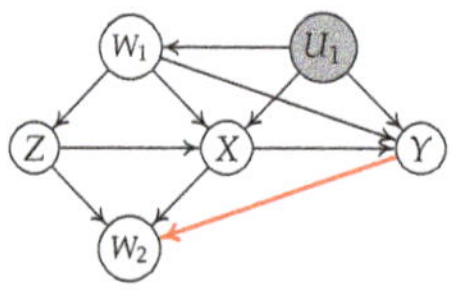

Figure 5. Causal graph where Z is a valid IV conditioning on W_1 relative to $X \to Y$ but an invalid IV conditioning on W_2 relative to $X \to Y$.

5.2. Condition 2 of Instrument Criteria

Now, we study the second condition, i.e., that $\mathbf{W}$ d-separates Z from Y in the graph obtained by removing the edge $X \to Y$ from G. Given the conditional set $\mathbf{W}$, the condition 2 can be phrased as follows:

2a. There is no active nondirected path between Z and Y that does not include X;
2b. There is no active directed path from Z to Y that does not include X.

In the remainder of this subsection, we discuss these two subconditions separately.

5.2.1. Subcondition 2a

It was shown that one can verify the validity of condition 2a in the case where at least two IVs are present in the ground-truth graph [21]. However, their condition is too restricted and rules out some valid IVs. (A similar conclusion is reported in Proposition 17 of [21].) Figure 1 shows an example that their method outputs an empty set of candidate

IVs, though Z is a valid IV. In contrast, our IV-GIN condition is relatively mild and is able to avoid ruling out the valid IVs. Although one might not fully verify the validity of condition 2a using the IV-GIN condition, most invalid IVs that do not satisfy condition 2a are ruled out, as shown in the following theorem.

Proposition 2. *Let G be a linear non-Gaussian acyclic causal model. Let treatment X, outcome Y, Z, and* $\mathbf{W}$ *be correlated random variables in G. Assume faithfulness holds, conditions 1 and 3 of instrument criteria hold, and there is no proper subset* $\tilde{\mathbf{W}}$ *of* $\mathbf{W}$ *such that* $[Z||\tilde{\mathbf{W}}]$ *follows the IV-GIN condition. Furthermore, given* $\mathbf{W}$*, assume there is at least one active nondirected path between Z and Y that does not include X. If given* $\mathbf{W}$*, there is no node* $C \in \mathbf{V}$ *such that all active paths between Z and Y go through C and C has its arrow pointing to Y, then* $[Z||\mathbf{W}]$ *must violate the IV-GIN condition.*

Below, we give an example to illustrate Proposition 2.

Example 4. *Consider the causal diagram shown in Figure 6. Given* W_1*, there is one active nondirected path between Z and Y, i.e.,* $Z \leftarrow U_2 \rightarrow Y$*, and all active paths between Z and Y are* $Z \rightarrow X \rightarrow Y$*, and* $Z \rightarrow U_2 \rightarrow Y$*. Thus, we can not find a node C such that all active paths between Z and Y go through C, and C has its arrow pointing to Y. This fact implies that* $[Z||W_1]$ *violates the IV-GIN condition. That is to say, Z is an invalid IV conditioning on* W_1 *relative to* $X \rightarrow Y$*.*

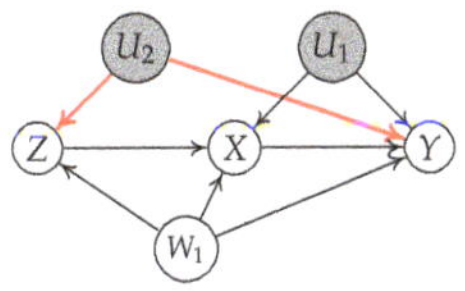

Figure 6. Causal graph where Z is an invalid IV conditioning on W_1 relative to $X \rightarrow Y$ due to the nondirected path $Z \leftarrow U_2 \rightarrow Y$.

Now, we give a simple example to show that though the IV-GIN condition holds, the condition 2a of instrument criteria is violated.

Example 5. *Consider the causal diagram shown in Figure 7. We can find a node* U_2 *such that all active paths between Z and Y go through* U_2 *and* U_2 *has its arrow pointing to Y. This implies that* $[Z||\emptyset]$ *follows the IV-GIN condition according to Proposition 2. This example tells us the IV-GIN condition is necessary, but not sufficient, to test condition 2a.*

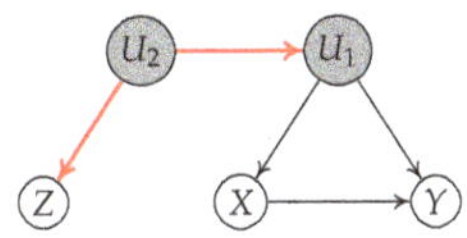

Figure 7. Causal graph where Z is a invalid IV conditioning on an empty set relative to $X \rightarrow Y$ but $(\{Z\}, \{Y, X\})$ follows the GIN condition.

5.2.2. Subcondition 2b

We now show that it is hard to verify the validity of condition 2b, even under the non-Gaussian assumption, through the following simple example.

Let us look at the following graph in Figure 8, where Z is a invalid IV conditioning on an empty set relative to $X \rightarrow Y$.

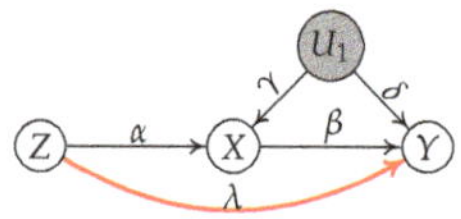

Figure 8. Causal graph where Z is an invalid IV conditioning on an empty set relative to $X \to Y$ due to the directed path $Z \to Y$.

Suppose the generating mechanism of the graph is as follows:

$$U_1 = \varepsilon_{U_1}, Z = \varepsilon_Z, \tag{8}$$
$$X = \alpha Z + \gamma U_1 + \varepsilon_X \tag{9}$$
$$Y = \beta X + \delta U_1 + \lambda Z + \varepsilon_Y \tag{10}$$

According to the definition of GIN condition, we have

$$E_{\{Y,X\}||Z} = Y - \frac{\sigma_{YZ}}{\sigma_{XZ}} X \tag{11}$$
$$= (\delta - \lambda/\alpha)U_1 - (\lambda/\alpha)\varepsilon_x + \varepsilon_Y), \tag{12}$$

Based on the above equation, the component of ε_Z is successfully removed from $E_{\{Y,X\}||Z}$ although Y is generated by $\{Z, X, U_1\}$. This implies that $E_{\{Y,X\}||Z}$ is independent from Z according to the Darmois–Skitovitch theorem. That is to say, $[Z||W_1]$ follows the IV-GIN condition whatever the value of λ (note that there is no directed edge between Z and Y when $\lambda = 0$).

6. Algorithm for Selecting the Candidate IVs

In this section, we leverage the above results and propose a sequential algorithm to select the set of candidate IVs for the target relationship $X \to Y$ without prior knowledge of the causal structure. Notice that the validity of a variable as an IV is dependent on which set $\mathbf{W}$ we condition on. To identify candidate IV efficiently, given an observed variable Z_i, we start with finding IV with an empty conditional set and then increase the number of conditional variables until the IV-GIN condition is satisfied or the length of conditional set equals $|\mathbf{O}| - 1$ (Lines 2∼14 of Algorithm 1). The details of the above process are given in Algorithm 1.

Algorithm 1 IV-GIN

Input: Treatment X, outcome Y, and set of observed variables $\mathbf{O}$.
Output: Set of candidate IVs $\mathbf{C}$ and its corresponding conditional set **Conset**.

1: Initialize the set of candidate IVs: $\mathbf{C} = \emptyset$, the conditional set: **Conset** $= \emptyset$, the length of conditional set: ConsetLen $= 0$, and **Tag** $= \mathbf{O}$;
2: **while** ConsetLen $< |$**Tag**$|$ **do**
3:   **for** each variable $Z_i \in \mathbf{C}$ **do**
4:     **repeat**
5:       Select a subset $\mathbf{W}$ from $\mathbf{O} \setminus Z_i$ such that $\mathbf{W} =$ ConsetLen;
6:       **if** $[Z||\mathbf{W}]$ follows the IV-GIN condition **then**
7:         Add Z_i into $\mathbf{C}$, and delete Z_i from **Tag**;
8:         Set **Conset**$(Z_i) = \mathbf{W}$;
9:         Break the repeat loop of line 4;
10:       **end if**
11:     **until** all subsets with length ConsetLen in $\mathbf{O} \setminus Z_i$ are selected;
12:   **end for**
13:   ConsetLen $=$ ConsetLen $+ 1$;
14: **end while**
15: **Return: C** and **Conset**

In practice, the main issue is how to test IV-GIN conditions, i.e., for any two sets of variables $\mathbf{P}$ and $\mathbf{Q}$, we need to test the independence between $E_{\mathbf{P}||\mathbf{Q}}$ and $\mathbf{Q}$. To do so, we check for pairwise independence with Fisher's method [49] instead of testing for the independence between $E_{\mathbf{P}||\mathbf{Q}}$ and $\mathbf{Q}$ directly. In particular, denote by p_k, with $k = 1, 2, \ldots, |\mathbf{Q}|$, all resulting p-values from pairwise independence between variables use the Hilbert–Schmidt independence criterion (HSIC)-based independence tests [50] due to the non-Gaussianity of the data. We compute the test statistic as $-2\sum_{k=1}^{|\mathbf{Q}|} \log p_k$, which follows the chi-square distribution with $2|\mathbf{Q}|$ degrees of freedom when all the pairs are independent.

Theorem 4 (Completeness of IV-GIN). *Suppose that the data $\mathbf{V} = \{X, Y\} \cup \mathbf{U} \cup \mathbf{O}$ strictly follows the linear non-Gaussian acyclic causal model, that is, all the model assumptions are met, and the sample size is infinite. Furthermore, assume that there exists at least one valid IV Z conditioning on $\mathbf{W}$ for the relation $X \to Y$, where $Z \cup \mathbf{W} \subset \mathbf{V}$. Then, the output $\mathbf{C}$ of IV-GIN method must contain all valid IVs.*

7. Experiments on Synthetic Data

In this section, we evaluate the IV selection performance on synthetic data and demonstrate the correctness of proposed theories.

Comparisons: We make comparisons with two state-of-the-art methods: the sisVIVE algorithm [20] that needs more than half of the variables to be valid IVs, and the IV-TETRAD algorithm [21] that needs two or more variables to be valid IVs. (Here, we adopt the two functions, TestTetrad and TestResiuals, to select IVs in the IV-TETRAD algorithm.) The source codes of sisVIVE and IV-TETRAD are available from https://mirrors.sjtug.sjtu.edu.cn/cran/web/packages/sisVIVE/index.html (accessed on 20 January =2022) and http://www.homepages.ucl.ac.uk/~ucgtrbd/code/iv_discovery/ (accessed on 20 January 2022), respectively.

Scenarios: We designed three scenarios, as shown in Figure 9, where X is treatment, Y is outcome, the variables U_i $(i = 1, 2)$ are unobserved, and Z_j $(j = 1, \ldots, 4)$ are potential IVs. For scenarios S_1 and S_2, nodes Z_2 and Z_3 both are valid IVs conditioning on an empty set relative to $X \to Y$, and node Z_1 is an invalid IV due to the path $Z_1 \leftarrow U_1 \to Y$. The key difference between scenarios S_1 and S_2 is that there is an active nondirected path between Z_3 and X in S_2 while not in S_1. For scenario S_3, Z_1 is a valid IV conditioning on Z_3 relative to $X \to Y$, Z_2 is a valid IV conditioning on an empty set relative to $X \to Y$, Z_3 is an invalid IV due to the paths $Z_3 \to Y$ and $Z_3 \leftarrow U_1 \to Y$, and Z_4 is an invalid IV due to the path $X \to Z_4 \leftarrow Y$.

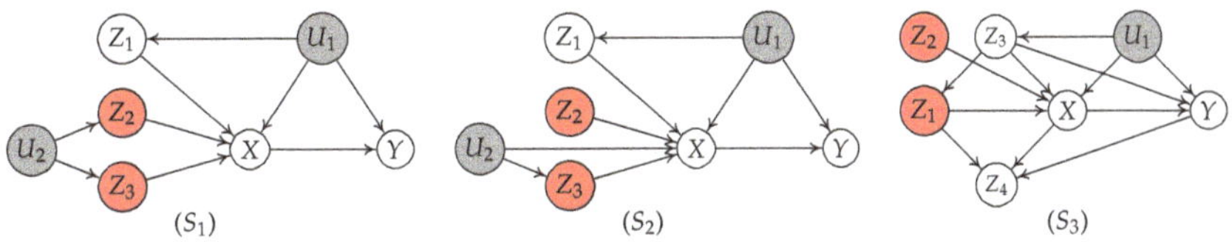

Figure 9. Three different scenarios used in our simulation studies.

Metrics: To evaluate the accuracy of the selected IVs, we used the following two metrics:

- *Correct-selecting rate*: The number of correctly selected valid IVs divided by the total number of valid IVs in the ground-truth graph.
- *Selection commission*: The number of falsely detected IVs divided by the total number of selected IVs in the output $\mathbf{C}$ of the current algorithm.

Experimental setup: We generated data by a linear non-Gaussian causal acyclic model according to the above three scenarios. In detail, the causal strength b_{ij} was generated uniformly in $[-2, -0.5] \cup [0.5, 2]$ and the non-Gaussian noise terms were generated from exponential distributions to the second power. Here, we conducted experiments with the following tasks:

T1. *Sensitivity on the effect of sample size.* We considered different sample sizes $N = 1k, 3k, 5k$, where $k = 1000$.

T2. *Sensitivity on the effect of unmeasured confounders between X and Y.* The coefficients between $\{X, Y\}$ and U_1 are set such that $b_{XU_1} = b_{YU_1} = \lambda$, at two levels, $(0.125, 0.25)$, as that in [21]. The sample size N is 5000.

We used HSIC-based independence tests [50] for the IV-GIN condition due to the non-Gaussianity of the data. Each experiment was repeated 50 times with randomly generated data, and the results were averaged.

Results on Task T1: The experimental results are reported in Table 1. From the table, we can see that our proposed IV-GIN outperforms other methods with both evaluation metrics in all there scenarios and in all sample sizes, indicating that our IV-GIN condition's testability is wider than other algorithms' in the linear non-Gaussian causal models. We found that the IV-TETRAD algorithm does not perform well, especially in scenarios S_2 and S_3, indicating that it is not capable when there is an active nondirected path between valid IV and treatment X (scenario S_2) and a single IV is present (scenario S_3). We further noticed that the sisVIVE algorithm does not perform well in scenario S_3. This is because fewer than half of the variables are valid IV conditioning on the same set in scenario S_3.

Table 1. Performance of IV-GIN, sisVIVE, and IV-TETRAD on selecting valid IVs with different sample sizes.

		Correct-Selecting Rate ↑			**Selection Commission ↓**		
Algorithm		**IV-GIN (Ours)**	**sisVIVE**	**IV-TETRAD**	**IV-GIN (Ours)**	**sisVIVE**	**IV-TETRAD**
Scenario S_1	1k	0.92	0.76	0.84	0.12	0.0	0.16
	3k	0.95	0.81	0.96	0.03	0.0	0.04
	5k	0.97	0.85	0.96	0.0	0.0	0.04
Scenario S_2	1k	0.9	0.92	0.03	0.03	0.08	0.0
	3k	0.95	0.93	0.02	0.0	0.02	0.0
	5k	1.0	0.94	0.0	0.0	0.0	0.0
Scenario S_3	1k	0.75	0.29	0.05	0.1	0.59	0.1
	3k	0.86	0.2	0.02	0.05	0.7	0.05
	5k	0.93	0.24	0.02	0.02	0.63	0.0

Note: ↑ means a higher value is better and ↓ means a lower value is better.

Results on Task T2: The experimental results are reported in Table 2. It is worth noting that stronger confounding makes it more difficult to select valid IVs. From the table, we found IV-GIN gives better performances than other methods with different confounding coefficients in almost all scenarios, indicating that our IV-GIN condition is more efficient than other algorithms. We noticed that although the Correct-selecting rate of sisVIVE is higher than IV-GIN in scenario S_1 when $\lambda = 0.25$, the selection commission of IV-GIN is lower than sisVIVE (lower is better for selection commission).

Table 2. Performance of IV-GIN, sisVIVE, and IV-TETRAD on selecting valid IVs with different effect of unmeasured confounders between treatment and outcome.

		Correct-Selecting Rate ↑			**Selection Commission ↓**		
Algorithm		**IV-GIN (Ours)**	**sisVIVE**	**IV-TETRAD**	**IV-GIN (Ours)**	**sisVIVE**	**IV-TETRAD**
Scenario S_1	$\lambda = 0.125$	0.96	0.83	0.92	0.06	0.01	0.08
	$\lambda = 0.25$	0.85	0.72	0.86	0.01	0.0	0.01
Scenario S_2	$\lambda = 0.125$	0.98	0.93	0.02	0.04	0.06	0.0
	$\lambda = 0.25$	0.92	0.91	0.0	0.08	0.1	0.0
Scenario S_3	$\lambda = 0.125$	0.89	0.22	0.05	0.03	0.58	0.02
	$\lambda = 0.25$	0.85	0.2	0.03	0.07	0.61	0.0

Note: ↑ means a higher value is better and ↓ means a lower value is better.

To conclude, these above findings show a clear advantage of our method over the compared algorithms.

8. Application to Vitamin D Data

In this section, we apply our algorithm to the Vitamin D data set described by Skaaby et al. [51], where the data we analyze are the population-based study Monica10. The data we use are collected from 2571 individuals between 40–71 years, as reported in [52]. In detail, these data contain 5 variables, including treatment *Vitamin D status* (continuous variable), outcome *mortality*, *filaggrin genotype*, *age*, and *time* (follow-up time). As argued by Martinussen et al. [52], unmeasured confounding may arise between *Vitamin D status* and *mortality* due to behavioral and environmental factors. To estimate the causal effect of *Vitamin D status* on *mortality*, one may use the *filaggrin genotype* as instrumental variable, as reported by Martinussen et al. [52]. In our setup, the problem of interest is to verify that *filaggrin genotype* is a valid IV while *age* and *time* are not without the prior knowledge of causal structure.

Here, we also make comparisons with the sisVIVE algorithm and the IV-TETRAD algorithm. In the implementation, the significance level of all methods were set to 0.01. We have the following findings: (1) The output of IV-GIN is that *filaggrin genotype* is a valid IV while *age* and *time* are invalid, which indicates the effectiveness of our method. (2) The output of IV-TETRAD is an empty set. This is because there is only one valid IV, which violates the basic assumption (two or more variables are valid IVs in the system). (3) The output of sisVIVE is that *age* is a valid IV while *filaggrin genotype* and *time* are invalid. This implies that sisVIVE fails to find the valid IV, i.e., *filaggrin genotype*. One reason is that fewer than half of the variables are valid IVs in this dataset. These results again indicate that our algorithm has better performance than the other algorithms for selecting valid IVs.

9. Discussion

The preceding sections presented how to use IV-GIN conditions to select the set of candidate IVs relative a target causal influence $X \to Y$ from observed variables without prior knowledge of causal structure. In this section, we discuss the following two practical questions.

Is it possible to select IVs by learning the whole causal graph? In fact, it is challenging to discover the precise causal graph in the presence of arbitrary hidden variables. To show this fact, we apply the LRpSC+GES algorithm introduced by [43] to learn the diagrams of three scenarios in Section 7, respectively. For simplicity, we set sample size $N = 5k$. We identify the IVs according to the instrument criteria given the learned graph. In detail, if there is a direct edge between candidate variables Z and treatment X and there is no direct edge between candidate variables Z and outcome Y, we think variable Z is a candidate IV. (Note that this selection is relatively loose and not rigorous.) The results are given in the following Table 3. From the table, we can see that the *correct-selecting rate* is close to 0.1, which indicates that almost all valid IVs have been incorrectly removed from the candidate set of IVs. We note that the *selection commissions* are small in the three scenarios. The reason is that in most cases, a valid IV Z has a direct edge to both treatment X and outcome Y in the learned graph by LRpSC+GES algorithm. These findings show that given the learned graph by the LRpSC+GES algorithm, one can not correctly select the set of candidate IVs.

Table 3. Performance of LRpSC+GES on selecting valid IVs with 5k sample sizes.

Metrics	Scenario S_1	Scenario S_2	Scenario S_3
Correct-selecting rate ↑	0.1	0.1	0.09
Selection commission ↓	0.0	0.12	0.3

What happens if we have no background knowledge about $X \to Y$? Theoretically speaking, the IV-GIN algorithm does not need to restrict the relation between X and Y, and the output $\mathbf{C}$ of the IV-GIN algorithm contains all valid IVs for the ground-truth relation, e.g., $X \to Y$ or $Y \to X$. This is because we do not restrict the order of X and Y when we test whether $(\{Z, \mathbf{W}\}, \{X, Y, \mathbf{W}\})$ satisfies the GIN condition in Theorem 2. To show this fact, for the three scenarios in Section 7, we reverse the order of X and Y to make it be

$Y \rightarrow X$ and run our method in these graphs. For simplicity, we set sample size $N = 5k$. The results are shown in Table 4. From this table, we can see that two metrics are almost close to the original graph having the causal influence $X \rightarrow Y$ in Table 1, indicating that our method does not rule out the valid IVs relative to the ground-truth one relationship. It is noteworthy that if one needs to calculate the causal effect between X and Y, the causal order of X and Y must be given in advance. This is because the IV estimator is based on the order of X and Y (see Equation (1)).

Table 4. Performance of IV-GIN on selecting valid IVs with 5k sample sizes where the locations of nodes X and Y are swapped.

Metrics	Scenario S_1	Scenario S_2	Scenario S_3
Correct-selecting rate ↑	0.96	1.0	0.92
Selection commission ↓	0.01	0.0	0.04

10. Conclusions and Further Work

In this paper, we investigated the problem of testability of instrumental variables in linear non-Gaussian acyclic causal models. In particular, we proposed a necessary condition for detecting valid IVs relative to a target causal influence $X \rightarrow Y$, which is called the IV-GIN condition. We then gave the graphical implications of the IV-GIN condition in linear non-Gaussian acyclic causal models. We showed how the conditions of instrument criteria can be checked by exploiting the IV-GIN conditions. Moreover, we proposed a sequential method, which selected the set of candidate IVs for the target causal influence $X \rightarrow Y$ from the observational data without precise prior knowledge of causal structure.

The key difference from the existing research considering the testability of IV in a linear non-Gaussian acyclic causal model, such as IV-TETRAD [21,53], is that: (1) we studied the testability of both conditions 1 and 2 while IV-TETRAD only studies the testability of condition 2 (condition 1 as the prior knowledge), and that (2) we investigated the case where a single IV is present in the ground-truth graph while IV-TETRAD needs at least two IVs present. It is worth noting that one can verify the validity of condition 2a using the IV-GIN method in cases where at least two instruments are present in the ground-truth graph. However, the IV-TETRAD condition is too restrictive and rules out some valid IVs. Table 5 summarizes the testability results using the IV-GIN conditions and IV-TETRAD conditions.

Table 5. Summary of the testability results using the IV-GIN conditions presented in our paper and IV-TETRAD conditions presented in [21].

	Testability of Instrument Criteria		
Method	**Scenario S_1**	**Scenario S_1**	**Scenario S_1**
IV-GIN (ours)	Fully	Partially	None
IV-TETRAD	None	Fully	None

There is another way of estimating the causal effect X on Y in a linear non-Gaussian acyclic causal model. For instance, Refs. [37,40] show that the causal effect between any two observed variables is partially identifiable (output the equivalence class of causal effects) by using overcomplete independent component analysis (O-ICA) [54]. One may naturally have the following question: is it necessary to select the IV for estimating the causal effect X on Y? In fact, as stated in [21], for O-ICA based methods, the size of the equivalence class of the identified causal effects could be very large, and the number of unmeasured confounders between X and Y is not clear. Therefore, it is necessary to select the valid IV relative to a target causal influence $X \rightarrow Y$ when there exist latent confounders between X and Y without prior knowledge of the number of latent confounders.

One direction of future work is to extend the IV-GIN condition to the case of a nonlinear additive noise model, and existing techniques [55–57] may help to address this issue.

Author Contributions: Conceptualization, F.X., Y.H., Z.G. and K.Z.; methodology, F.X., Y.H., Z.G. and K.Z.; experiments, Z.C. and F.X.; validation, F.X., Y.H., Z.G., Z.C. and K.Z.; formal analysis, F.X., Y.H., Z.G. and K.Z.; investigation, F.X., Y.H., Z.G. and K.Z.; writing—original draft preparation, F.X., Y.H., Z.G. and K.Z.; writing—review and editing, F.X., R.H. and K.Z.; visualization, F.X. All authors have read and agreed to the published version of the manuscript.

Funding: This work was supported by the China Postdoctoral Science Foundation (020M680225, BX20200011), the National Natural Science Foundation of China (NSFC 11771028, 12071015, 11971040), and Huawei Technologies. K.Z. would like to acknowledge the support by the National Institutes of Health (NIH) under Contract R01HL159805, by the NSF-Convergence Accelerator Track-D award #2134901, and by the United States Air Force under Contract No. FA8650-17-C7715.

Institutional Review Board Statement: Not applicable.

Informed Consent Statement: Not applicable.

Data Availability Statement: The simulated data can be regenerated using the codes, which can be provided to the interested user via an email request to the correspondence author. The Vitamin D Data used in the experiments come from the ivtools package of CRAN, which can be downloaded from https://mirrors.sjtug.sjtu.edu.cn/cran/web/packages/ivtools/index.html (accessed on 20 January 2022).

Acknowledgments: The authors are grateful to the editors and anonymous reviewers for their insightful comments and suggestions.

Conflicts of Interest: The authors declare no conflict of interest.

Appendix A. Proofs

Before we present the proofs of our results, we need an important theorem, which gives mathematical characterizations of the GIN condition [24]. For simplicity, the notation $\mathbf{P} \perp\!\!\!\perp \mathbf{Q}$ denotes that $\mathbf{P}$ is independent of $\mathbf{Q}$, and the notation $\mathbf{P} \not\perp\!\!\!\perp \mathbf{Q}$ denotes that $\mathbf{P}$ is not independent of $\mathbf{Q}$.

Theorem A1. *Suppose that random vectors* $\mathbf{S}$, $\mathbf{P}$, *and* $\mathbf{Q}$ *are related in the following way:*

$$\mathbf{P} = A\mathbf{S} + \mathbf{E_P}, \tag{A1}$$

$$\mathbf{Q} = B\mathbf{S} + \mathbf{E_Q}. \tag{A2}$$

Denote by l *the dimensionality of* $\mathbf{S}$. *Assume* A *is of full column rank. Then, if (1)* $Dim(\mathbf{P}) > l$, *(2)* $\mathbf{E_P} \perp\!\!\!\perp \mathbf{S}$, *(3)* $\mathbf{E_P} \perp\!\!\!\perp \mathbf{E_Q}$, *and (4) the cross-covariance matrix of* $\mathbf{S}$ *and* $\mathbf{Q}$, $\mathbf{\Sigma}_{LZ} = \mathbb{E}[\mathbf{S}\mathbf{Q}^\intercal]$ *has rank* l, *then* $E_{\mathbf{P}||\mathbf{Q}} \perp\!\!\!\perp \mathbf{Q}$, *i.e.,* $(\mathbf{Q}, \mathbf{P})$ *satisfies the GIN condition.*

Proof. The proof was given by Xie et al. [24]. □

Appendix A.1. Proof of Theorem 3

Proof. The "if" part: First, suppose that there exists a node $C \in \mathbf{V}$, $C \notin \mathbf{W}$, such that for every trek π between a node $V_p \in \{X, Y, \mathbf{W}\}$ and a node $V_q \in \{Z, \mathbf{W}\}$, (a) π goes through at least one node in $\{C, \mathbf{W}\}$, denoted by V_k, and (b) V_k has its arrow pointing to V_p in π. Because of subconditions (a) and (b), and according to the linear acyclic model, each $V_p \in \{X, Y, \mathbf{W}\}$ is a linear function of $\mathbf{Pa}(V_p)$ plus independent noise. We know that V_k can be written as a linear function of $\{C, \mathbf{W}\}$ and independent error ε'_{V_p}, where ε'_{V_p} is independent from $\{C, \mathbf{W}\}$, that is,

$$V_p = A_p \begin{bmatrix} C \\ \mathbf{W} \end{bmatrix} + \varepsilon'_{V_p} \tag{A3}$$

We write $\{X, Y, \mathbf{W}\}$ in a matrix form

$$\begin{bmatrix} X \\ Y \\ \mathbf{W} \end{bmatrix} = A \begin{bmatrix} C \\ \mathbf{W} \end{bmatrix} + \mathbf{E}'_{\mathbf{P}}, \tag{A4}$$

where A is an appropriate linear transformation, $\mathbf{E}'_{\mathbf{P}}$ is independent of $\{C, \mathbf{W}\}$, but its components are not necessarily independent of each other. Note that, in equation (A4), $\{C, \mathbf{W}\}$ and $\mathbf{E}'_{\mathbf{P}}$ are linear combinations of disjoint sets of the noise terms, implied by the directed acyclic structure over all variables.

We now write $\{Z, \mathbf{W}\}$ as linear combinations of the noise terms. Because of subcondition (a), i.e., every trek π between a node $V_q \in \{Z, \mathbf{W}\}$ and a node $V_p \in \{X, Y, \mathbf{W}\}$ goes through at least one node in $\{C, \mathbf{W}\}$, and according to the definition of trek, i.e., every trek does not contain any colliders, we have $\{C, \mathbf{W}\}$ d-separates $\{X, Y, \mathbf{W}\}$ from $\{Z, \mathbf{W}\}$. If any noise term ε_i is present in $\mathbf{E}'_{\mathbf{P}}$, it is not among the noise terms in the expression of $\{Z, \mathbf{W}\}$. Otherwise, if V_j also involves ε_i, then the direct effect of ε_i, among all variables $\mathbf{V}$, is a common cause of Z_j and some component of $\{X, Y, \mathbf{W}\}$. This implies that this path between Z_j and that component of $\{X, Y, \mathbf{W}\}$ cannot be d-separated by $\{C, \mathbf{W}\}$ because no component of $\{C, \mathbf{W}\}$ is on the path, as implied by the fact that when $\{C, \mathbf{W}\}$ is written as a linear combination of the underlying noise terms, ε_i is not among them. Consequently, any noise term in $\mathbf{E}'_{\mathbf{P}}$ does not contribute to $\{C, \mathbf{W}\}$ or $\{Z, \mathbf{W}\}$. Hence, $\{Z, \mathbf{W}\}$ can be expressed as

$$\begin{bmatrix} Z \\ \mathbf{W} \end{bmatrix} = B \begin{bmatrix} C \\ \mathbf{W} \end{bmatrix} + \mathbf{E}'_{\mathbf{Q}}, \tag{A5}$$

where $\mathbf{E}'_{\mathbf{Q}}$, which is determined by $\{C, \mathbf{W}\}$ and $\{Z, \mathbf{W}\}$, is independent of $\mathbf{E}'_{\mathbf{P}}$.

Moreover, because of condition (2), i.e., there is at least one directed path between any one node in $\{C, \mathbf{W}\}$ and any one node in $\{X, Y\}$, we know that the cross-covariance matrix of $\{C, \mathbf{W}\}$ and $\{Z, \mathbf{W}\}$, $\boldsymbol{\Sigma}_{\{C,\mathbf{W}\}\{Z,\mathbf{W}\}} = \mathbb{E}[\{C, \mathbf{W}\}\{Z, \mathbf{W}\}^{\intercal}]$ has rank k, and that A is of full column rank. Based on the above analysis, we immediately know that the four conditions in Theorem A1 are satisfied. This implies that $(\{Z, \mathbf{W}\}, \{X, Y, \mathbf{W}\})$ satisfies the GIN condition, i.e., $[Z||\mathbf{W}]$ follows the IV-GIN condition relative to $X \to Y$.

Now, consider any one subset $\tilde{\mathbf{W}}$ in $\mathbf{W}$. Because of condition 3, i.e., there is no proper subset $\tilde{\mathbf{W}}$ of $\mathbf{W}$ to satisfy condition 2 and 3, we know $(\{Z, \tilde{\mathbf{W}}\}, \{X, Y, \tilde{\mathbf{W}}\})$ violates the GIN condition for any subset $\tilde{\mathbf{W}}$ of $\mathbf{W}$. Therefore, we have that there is no proper subset $\tilde{\mathbf{W}}$ of $\mathbf{W}$ such that $[Z||\tilde{\mathbf{W}}]$ follows the IV-GIN condition relative to $X \to Y$.

The "only-if" part: We suppose $[Z||\mathbf{W}]$ follows the IV-GIN condition relative to $X \to Y$ and there is no proper subset $\tilde{\mathbf{W}}$ of $\mathbf{W}$ such that $[Z||\tilde{\mathbf{W}}]$ follows the IV-GIN condition relative to $X \to Y$. That is to say, $(\{Z, \mathbf{W}\}, \{X, Y, \mathbf{W}\})$ satisfies the GIN condition while there is no proper subset of $\mathbf{W}$ such that $(\{Z, \tilde{\mathbf{W}}\}, \{X, Y, \tilde{\mathbf{W}}\})$ follows the GIN condition. Consider all nodes $C \in \mathbf{V}, C \notin \mathbf{W}$ such that C is causally earlier than $\{X, Y\}$, and we show that at least one of them satisfies conditions (1) and (2).

First, if condition (1) is violated, then there is a trek τ between some leaf node in $\mathbf{Pa}(\{X, Y, \mathbf{W}\})$, denoted by $\mathbf{Pa}(V_z)$ ($V_z \in \{X, Y, \mathbf{W}\}$), and some component of $\{Z, \mathbf{W}\}$, denoted by Z_j, and this trek does not go through any common cause of the variables in $\mathbf{Pa}(\{X, Y, \mathbf{W}\})$. Then, they have some common cause that does not cause any other variable in $\mathbf{Pa}(\{X, Y, \mathbf{W}\})$. Consequently, there exists at least one noise term, denoted by ε_i, that contributes to both $\mathbf{Pa}(V_z)$ (and hence V_z) and Z_j but not any other variables in $\{X, Y, \mathbf{W}\}$. Because of the non-Gaussianity of the noise terms and the Darmois–Skitovitch theorem, if any linear projection of $\{X, Y, \mathbf{W}\}$, $\omega^{\intercal}\{X, Y, \mathbf{W}\}$ is independent of $\{Z, \mathbf{W}\}$, the linear coefficient for V_z must be zero. Hence, $\{(Z, \mathbf{W}\}, \{X, Y, \mathbf{W}\} \setminus \{V_z\})$ satisfies GIN, which contradicts the assumption in the theorem. Therefore, there must exist some $\{C, \mathbf{W}\}$ such that condition (1) holds.

Next, if condition (2) is violated, i.e., there exist one node in $\{C, \mathbf{W}\}$ and one node in $\{X, Y\}$ such that there is no trek between $\{C, \mathbf{W}\}$ and $\{X, Y, \mathbf{W}\}$. This implies that at least one of the following cases holds: (a) the column rank of the covariance matrix of $\{C, \mathbf{W}\}$ and $\{X, Y, \mathbf{W}\}$ is smaller than $|\{C, \mathbf{W}\}|$ and (b) the rank of the covariance matrix of $\{C, \mathbf{W}\}$ and $\{Z, \mathbf{W}\}$ is smaller than $|\{C, \mathbf{W}\}|$. Then, the condition $\omega^{\intercal}\mathbb{E}[\{X, Y, \mathbf{W}\}\{Z, \mathbf{W}\}^{\intercal}] = 0$ does not guarantee that $\omega^{\intercal} A = 0$. Under the faithfulness assumption, we then do not have that $\omega^{\intercal}\{X, Y, \mathbf{W}\}$ is independent of $\{Z, \mathbf{W}\}$. Hence, condition (2) also needs to hold.

Because there is no proper subset $\tilde{\mathbf{W}}$ of $\mathbf{W}$ such that $(\{Z, \tilde{\mathbf{W}}\}, \{X, Y, \tilde{\mathbf{W}}\})$ follows the GIN condition, one can immediately see that condition (3) holds. □

Appendix A.2. Proof of Theorem 2

Proof. We prove this result by Theorem 3. To this end, we need to show that the three conditions of Theorem 3 hold.

Because Z is a valid IV conditioning on $\mathbf{W}$ relative to $X \to Y$, then the instrument criteria hold. Consider the node C in Theorem 3 as X, and we show that for every trek π between a node $V_p \in \{X, Y, \mathbf{W}\}$ and a node $V_q \in \{X, \mathbf{W}\}$ satisfies subconditions (a) and (b). First, because of condition 2 of instrument criteria, i.e., $\mathbf{W}$ d-separates Z from Y in the graph obtained by removing the edge $X \to Y$ from G, we have that π goes through at least one node in $\{X, \mathbf{W}\}$, denoted by V_k. That is to say, subcondition (a) holds. Next, because of condition 1 of instrument criteria, i.e., $\mathbf{W}$ contains only nondescendants of Y in G, we have that V_k is causally earlier than Y on π. Besides, because of $X \to Y$, we further know that V_k is causally earlier than V_p on π, i.e., subcondition (b) holds.

Moreover, because of condition 3 of instrument criteria, i.e., $\mathbf{W}$ does not d-separates Z from X in G, and $X \to Y$, we have that there is at least one directed path between any one node in $\{X, \mathbf{W}\}$ and any one node in $\{X, Y\}$, i.e., condition (2) holds. □

Appendix A.3. Proof of Proposition 1

Proof. Without loss of generality, assume node V_r in $\{Z, \mathbf{W}\}$ is descendant of Y in G and there exists a node $C \in \mathbf{V}$, $C \notin \mathbf{W}$ satisfying conditions in Theorem 3. We show that subcondition (b) in Theorem 3 is violated.

Because of conditions $2 \sim 3$ of instrument criteria, for every trek π between a node $V_p \in \{X, Y, \mathbf{W}\}$ and a node $V_q \in \{Z, \mathbf{W}\}$ goes through at least one node in $\{C, \mathbf{W}\}$, denoted by V_k. Because node V_r is descendant of Y and $V_r \in \{Z, \mathbf{W}\}$, there must exist a trek τ between $\{X, Y, \mathbf{W}\}$ and $\{Z, \mathbf{W}\}$ such that Y has its arrow pointing to V_k, which contradicts the subcondition (b) in Theorem 3 (V_k has its arrow pointing to Y). □

Appendix A.4. Proof of Proposition 2

Proof. Because there is no node $C \in \mathbf{V}$ such that all active paths between Z and Y go through C and C has its arrow pointing to Y, there must exist a trek τ between between Z and Y such that τ does not go through C, or τ goes through C but Y has its arrow pointing to C in τ. This implies that the condition 1 of Theorem 3, i.e., there exists a node $C \in \mathbf{V}$, $C \notin \mathbf{W}$, such that for every trek π between a node $V_p \in \{X, Y, \mathbf{W}\}$ and a node $V_q \in \{Z, \mathbf{W}\}$, (a) π goes through at least one node in $\{C, \mathbf{W}\}$, denoted by V_k, and (b) V_k has its arrow pointing to V_p in π, is violated. Thus, $[Z||\mathbf{W}]$ violates the IV-GIN condition. □

Appendix A.5. Proof of Theorem 4

Proof. The validity of a variable as an IV is dependent on which set $\mathbf{W}$ we condition on. If a node Z_i is a valid IV conditioning on $\mathbf{W}$, it is not necessary to verify whether Z_i is a valid IV conditioning on $\mathbf{W}'$, where $\mathbf{W}'$ contains $\mathbf{W}$. Therefore, given an observed variable Z_i, one needs to find IV with an empty conditional set and then increase the number of conditional variables until the IV-GIN condition is satisfied or the length of the conditional set equals $|\mathbf{O}| - 1$. The process in the Lines $2 \sim 14$ of the IV-GIN algorithm is consistent with the above process. Besides, by Theorem 2, one can not remove the valid IVs, which ensures that the output $\mathbf{C}$ of the IV-GIN method must contain all valid IVs relative to $X \to Y$. □

References

1. Wright, P.G. *Tariff on Animal and Vegetable Oils*; Macmillan Company: New York, NY, USA, 1928.
2. Goldberger, A.S. Structural equation methods in the social sciences. *Econom. J. Econom. Soc.* **1972**, *40*, 979–1001. [CrossRef]
3. Bowden, R.J.; Turkington, D.A. *Instrum. Var.*; Number 8; Cambridge University Press: Cambridge, UK, 1990.
4. Pearl, J. *Causality: Models, Reasoning, and Inference*, 2nd ed.; Cambridge University Press: New York, NY, USA, 2009.
5. Imbens, G.W. Instrumental Variables: An Econometrician's Perspective. *Stat. Sci.* **2014**, *29*, 323–358. [CrossRef]
6. Imbens, G.W.; Rubin, D.B. *Causal Inference for Statistics, Social, and Biomedical Sciences: An Introduction*; Cambridge University Press: Cambridge, UK, 2015.
7. Spirtes, P.; Glymour, C.; Scheines, R. *Causation, Prediction, and Search*; MIT Press: Cambridge, MA, USA, 2000.
8. Hernán, M.A.; Robins, J.M. Instruments for causal inference: an epidemiologist's dream? *Epidemiology* **2006**, *17*, 360–372. [CrossRef] [PubMed]
9. Baiocchi, M.; Cheng, J.; Small, D.S. Instrumental variable methods for causal inference. *Stat. Med.* **2014**, *33*, 2297–2340. [CrossRef] [PubMed]
10. Bound, J.; Jaeger, D.A.; Baker, R.M. Problems with instrumental variables estimation when the correlation between the instruments and the endogenous explanatory variable is weak. *J. Am. Stat. Assoc.* **1995**, *90*, 443–450. [CrossRef]
11. Pearl, J. On the testability of causal models with latent and instrumental variables. In *Proceedings of the Eleventh Conference on Uncertainty in Artificial Intelligence*; Morgan Kaufmann Publishers Inc.: San Francisco, CA, USA, 1995; pp. 435–443.
12. Manski, C.F. *Partial Identification of Probability Distributions*; Springer Science & Business Media: Berlin & Heidelberg, Germany, 2003.
13. Palmer, T.M.; Ramsahai, R.R.; Didelez, V.; Sheehan, N.A. Nonparametric bounds for the causal effect in a binary instrumental-variable model. *Stata J.* **2011**, *11*, 345–367. [CrossRef]
14. Kitagawa, T. A test for instrument validity. *Econometrica* **2015**, *83*, 2043–2063. [CrossRef]
15. Wang, L.; Robins, J.M.; Richardson, T.S. On falsification of the binary instrumental variable model. *Biometrika* **2017**, *104*, 229–236. [CrossRef] [PubMed]
16. Kédagni, D.; Mourifié, I. Generalized instrumental inequalities: Testing the instrumental variable independence assumption. *Biometrika* **2020**, *107*, 661–675. [CrossRef]
17. Gunsilius, F.F. Nontestability of instrument validity under continuous treatments. *Biometrika* **2021**, *108*, 989–995. [CrossRef]
18. Kuroki, M.; Cai, Z. Instrumental variable tests for Directed Acyclic Graph Models. In Proceedings of the International Workshop on Artificial Intelligence and Statistics, Bridgetown, Barbados, 6–8 January 2005; pp. 190–197.
19. Spearman, C. Pearson's contribution to the theory of two factors. *Br. J. Psychol.* **1928**, *19*, 95–101. [CrossRef]
20. Kang, H.; Zhang, A.; Cai, T.T.; Small, D.S. Instrumental variables estimation with some invalid instruments and its application to Mendelian randomization. *J. Am. Stat. Assoc.* **2016**, *111*, 132–144. [CrossRef]
21. Silva, R.; Shimizu, S. Learning instrumental variables with structural and non-gaussianity assumptions. *J. Mach. Learn. Res.* **2017**, *18*, 1–49.
22. Sullivant, S.; Talaska, K.; Draisma, J. Trek separation for Gaussian graphical models. *Ann. Stat.* **2010**, *38*, 1665–1685. [CrossRef]
23. Spirtes, P. Calculation of Entailed Rank Constraints in Partially Non-linear and Cyclic Models. In *Proceedings of the Twenty-Ninth Conference on Uncertainty in Artificial Intelligence*; AUAI Press: Arlington, VA, USA, 2013; pp. 606–615.
24. Xie, F.; Cai, R.; Huang, B.; Glymour, C.; Hao, Z.; Zhang, K. Generalized Independent Noise Conditionfor Estimating Latent Variable Causal Graphs. In Proceedings of the Advances in Neural Information Processing Systems, Virtual, 6–12 December 2020; pp. 14891–14902.
25. Choi, M.J.; Tan, V.Y.; Anandkumar, A.; Willsky, A.S. Learning latent tree graphical models. *J. Mach. Learn. Res.* **2011**, *12*, 1771–1812.
26. Chandrasekaran, V.; Parrilo, P.A.; Willsky, A.S. Latent variable graphical model selection via convex optimization. In Proceedings of the 2010 48th Annual Allerton Conference on Communication, Control, and Computing (Allerton), Monticello, IL, USA, 29 September–1 October 2010; pp. 1935–1967.
27. Meng, Z.; Eriksson, B.; Hero, A. Learning latent variable Gaussian graphical models. In Proceedings of the International Conference on Machine Learning, Beijing, China, 21–26 June 2014; pp. 1269–1277.
28. Zorzi, M.; Sepulchre, R. AR identification of latent-variable graphical models. *IEEE Trans. Autom. Control.* **2015**, *61*, 2327–2340. [CrossRef]
29. Wu, C.; Zhao, H.; Fang, H.; Deng, M. Graphical model selection with latent variables. *Electron. J. Stat.* **2017**, *11*, 3485–3521. [CrossRef]
30. Kumar, S.; Ying, J.; de Miranda Cardoso, J.V.; Palomar, D.P. A Unified Framework for Structured Graph Learning via Spectral Constraints. *J. Mach. Learn. Res.* **2020**, *21*, 1–60.
31. Ciccone, V.; Ferrante, A.; Zorzi, M. Learning latent variable dynamic graphical models by confidence sets selection. *IEEE Trans. Autom. Control.* **2020**, *65*, 5130–5143. [CrossRef]
32. Alpago, D.; Zorzi, M.; Ferrante, A. A scalable strategy for the identification of latent-variable graphical models. *IEEE Trans. Autom. Control.* **2021**. [CrossRef]
33. Bertsimas, D.; Cory-Wright, R.; Johnson, N.A. Sparse Plus Low Rank Matrix Decomposition: A Discrete Optimization Approach. *arXiv* **2021**, arXiv:2109.12701.

34. Spirtes, P.; Meek, C.; Richardson, T. Causal inference in the presence of latent variables and selection bias. In *Proceedings of the Eleventh Conference on Uncertainty in Artificial Intelligence*; Morgan Kaufmann Publishers Inc.: Burlington, MA, USA, 1995; pp. 499–506.
35. Colombo, D.; Maathuis, M.H.; Kalisch, M.; Richardson, T.S. Learning high-dimensional directed acyclic graphs with latent and selection variables. *Ann. Stat.* **2012**, *40*, 294–321. [CrossRef]
36. Kitson, N.K.; Constantinou, A.C.; Guo, Z.; Liu, Y.; Chobtham, K. A survey of Bayesian Network structure learning. *arXiv* **2021**, arXiv:2109.11415.
37. Hoyer, P.O.; Shimizu, S.; Kerminen, A.J.; Palviainen, M. Estimation of causal effects using linear non-Gaussian causal models with hidden variables. *Int. J. Approx. Reason.* **2008**, *49*, 362–378. [CrossRef]
38. Entner, D.; Hoyer, P.O. Discovering unconfounded causal relationships using linear non-gaussian models. In *JSAI International Symposium on Artificial Intelligence*; Springer: Berlin & Heidelberg, Germany, 2010; pp. 181–195.
39. Tashiro, T.; Shimizu, S.; Hyvärinen, A.; Washio, T. ParceLiNGAM: A causal ordering method robust against latent confounders. *Neural Comput.* **2014**, *26*, 57–83. [CrossRef] [PubMed]
40. Salehkaleybar, S.; Ghassami, A.; Kiyavash, N.; Zhang, K. Learning Linear Non-Gaussian Causal Models in the Presence of Latent Variables. *J. Mach. Learn. Res.* **2020**, *21*, 1–24.
41. Ciccone, V.; Ferrante, A.; Zorzi, M. Robust identification of "sparse plus low-rank" graphical models: An optimization approach. In Proceedings of the 2018 IEEE Conference on Decision and Control (CDC), Miami, FL, USA, 17–19 December 2018; pp. 2241–2246.
42. Alpago, D.; Zorzi, M.; Ferrante, A. Identification of sparse reciprocal graphical models. *IEEE Control. Syst. Lett.* **2018**, *2*, 659–664. [CrossRef]
43. Frot, B.; Nandy, P.; Maathuis, M.H. Robust causal structure learning with some hidden variables. *J. R. Stat. Soc. Ser. (Stat. Methodol.)* **2019**, *81*, 459–487. [CrossRef]
44. Agrawal, R.; Squires, C.; Prasad, N.; Uhler, C. The DeCAMFounder: Non-Linear Causal Discovery in the Presence of Hidden Variables. *arXiv* **2021**, arXiv:2102.07921.
45. Brito, C.; Pearl, J. Generalized instrumental variables. In *Proceedings of the Eighteenth Conference on Uncertainty in Artificial Intelligence*; Morgan Kaufmann Publishers Inc.: San Francisco, CA, USA, 2002; pp. 85–93.
46. Bollen, K.A. *Structural Equations with Latent Variable*; John Wiley & Sons: Hoboken, NJ, USA, 1989.
47. Shimizu, S.; Hoyer, P.O.; Hyvärinen, A.; Kerminen, A. A linear non-Gaussian acyclic model for causal discovery. *J. Mach. Learn. Res.* **2006**, *7*, 2003–2030.
48. Kagan, A.M.; Rao, C.R.; Linnik, Y.V. *Characterization Problems in Mathematical Statistics*; John Wiley: New York, NY, USA, 1973.
49. Fisher, R.A. *Statistical Methods for Research Workers*; Springer: Berlin & Heidelberg, Germany, 1950.
50. Zhang, Q.; Filippi, S.; Gretton, A.; Sejdinovic, D. Large-scale kernel methods for independence testing. *Stat. Comput.* **2018**, *28*, 113–130. [CrossRef]
51. Skaaby, T.; Husemoen, L.L.N.; Martinussen, T.; Thyssen, J.P.; Melgaard, M.; Thuesen, B.H.; Pisinger, C.; Jørgensen, T.; Johansen, J.D.; Menné, T.; et al. Vitamin D status, filaggrin genotype, and cardiovascular risk factors: a Mendelian randomization approach. *PLoS ONE* **2013**, *8*, e57647.
52. Martinussen, T.; Nørbo Sørensen, D.; Vansteelandt, S. Instrumental variables estimation under a structural Cox model. *Biostatistics* **2019**, *20*, 65–79. [CrossRef] [PubMed]
53. Silva, R.; Shimizu, S. Learning Instrumental Variables with Non-Gaussianity Assumptions: Theoretical Limitations and Practical Algorithms. *arXiv* **2015**, arXiv:1511.02722.
54. Hyvärinen, A.; Karhunen, J.; Oja, E. *Independent Component Analysis*; John Wiley & Sons: Hoboken, NJ, USA, 2004; Volume 46.
55. Hoyer, P.O.; Janzing, D.; Mooij, J.M.; Peters, J.; Schölkopf, B. Nonlinear causal discovery with additive noise models. In *Advances in Neural Information Processing Systems*; Curran Associates Inc.: Red Hook, NY, USA, 2009; pp. 689–696.
56. Zhang, K.; Hyvärinen, A. On the identifiability of the post-nonlinear causal model. In *Proceedings of the Twenty-Fifth Conference on Uncertainty in Artificial Intelligence*; AUAI Press: Arlington, VA, USA, 2009; pp. 647–655.
57. Peters, J.; Mooij, J.M.; Janzing, D.; Schölkopf, B. Causal Discovery with Continuous Additive Noise Models. *J. Mach. Learn. Res.* **2014**, *15*, 2009–2053.

entropy

MDPI

Article

Simultaneous Maximum Likelihood Estimation for Piecewise Linear Instrumental Variable Models

Shuo Shuo Liu [1,*] and Yeying Zhu [2]

1 Department of Statistics, The Pennsylvania State University, University Park, PA 16801, USA
2 Department of Statistics and Actuarial Science, University of Waterloo, Waterloo, ON N2L 3G1, Canada
* Correspondence: shuoshuo.liu@psu.edu

Abstract: Analysis of instrumental variables is an effective approach to dealing with endogenous variables and unmeasured confounding issue in causal inference. We propose using the piecewise linear model to fit the relationship between the continuous instrumental variable and the continuous explanatory variable, as well as the relationship between the continuous explanatory variable and the outcome variable, which generalizes the traditional linear instrumental variable models. The two-stage least square and limited information maximum likelihood methods are used for the simultaneous estimation of the regression coefficients and the threshold parameters. Furthermore, we study the limiting distribution of the estimators in the correctly specified and misspecified models and provide a robust estimation of the variance-covariance matrix. We illustrate the finite sample properties of the estimation in terms of the Monte Carlo biases, standard errors, and coverage probabilities via the simulated data. Our proposed model is applied to an education-salary data, which investigates the causal effect of children's years of schooling on estimated hourly wage with father's years of schooling as the instrumental variable.

Keywords: causal inference; instrumental variables; piecewise linear; thresholds model

Citation: Liu, S.S.; Zhu, Y. Simultaneous Maximum Likelihood Estimation for Piecewise Linear Instrumental Variable Models. *Entropy* **2022**, *24*, 1235. https://doi.org/10.3390/e24091235

Academic Editor: Kateřina Hlaváčková-Schindler

Received: 26 July 2022
Accepted: 31 August 2022
Published: 2 September 2022

1. Introduction

In observational studies, the measured confounders can be controlled by a variety of methods such as propensity score based matching and regression adjustment. However, when the confounding variable is unmeasured, the traditional causal inference methods usually lead to biased estimators since changes in the unmeasured confounder will lead to changes in the explanatory variable, both of which will result in changes in the response variable. Failing to adjust such a confounder will lead to spurious association between the explanatory variable and the outcome. Analysis of instrumental variables (IV) has gained popularity in causal inference, such as investigating causal graphical structures [1,2] and controlling for unmeasured confounding [3,4]. An instrument is a variable that is correlated with the explanatory variable but not associated with any unmeasured confounders. In addition, the instrumental variable is supposed to have influence on the response variable only through the explanatory variable, i.e., there is no direct effect of this variable on the response. Instrumental variable analysis can be applied to many areas and disciplines, such as economics and epidemiology. For example, causality between the years of schooling and earnings in economics has been studied in the literature [5]. This example exploits the college proximity as the instrumental variable because it is revealed that those living near college or university usually have significantly higher level of education than others. On the other hand, it is believed that college proximity may improve earnings only by increasing the subject's years of schooling. Both indicate that college proximity is a useful instrumental variable. In biomedical and epidemiological research, the main interest is to investigate the causal effect of an exposure variable on a certain disease outcome. A gene can be assumed as a good instrument if it is closely linked to the exposure but has no direct effect on the disease [6]. The study of genetic variants as instrumental variables is known as Mendelian randomization, which is discussed extensively in the literature (e.g., [7,8]). For instance, a set of 32 recently identified genetic variants are used as instrumental variables to study whether child fat mass causally affects academic achievement and blood pressure [9].

1.1. Related Work

Since the development of instrumental variables, a plenty of instrumental variable estimation methods have been proposed for the causal effect estimation. Two-stage least squares (2SLS) [10] is one of the most commonly used methods for the instrumental variable estimation. Theoretical analyses such as consistency and asymptotic normality also exist in the literature. When the response variable is binary, the second stage can be modified with logistic regression in mendelian randomization studies [11]. Another method is the likelihood-based method, particularly the limited information maximum likelihood (LIML) [12]. It is proved that the LIML method is more effective in dealing with the weak instruments [13]. The phenomenon of weak instruments occurs when the correlation between the instrument(s) and the explanatory variable is close to zero. When there are weak instruments, 2SLS is generally unstable and the causal effect estimators are badly biased. The typical rule of thumb to detect weak instruments is the F-statistic, which states that an instrument may be weak if the first-stage F-statistic is less than 10 [14].

Most of the IV approaches impose linear assumptions among the instrument, explanatory and response variables. However, this is not always the case. For example, a subject's years of schooling may only have a positive effect on subsequent earnings if the subject obtained at least a high-school degree. There would be no difference in the earnings if the subject obtained either an elementary or middle school degree. In this hypothetical scenario, a linear regression model between the explanatory and response variables is clearly misspecified. When the null hypothesis of linearity relationship is rejected, one strategy could be to develop piecewise linear models, which is more interpretable compared to the completely nonlinear models.

In this paper, we propose a piecewise linear instrumental variable (PLIV) model for estimating the causal effect via a continuous threshold function. The continuous threshold function assumes that both the explanatory variable and the instrumental variable are continuous. Instrumental variable models with continuous variables have been studied extensively in the literature. For example, continuous instruments have been used in the classical IV models, developed in a structural equation modeling framework [15]. A recent paper proposes semiparametric doubly robust estimators of causal effects with the continuous instruments [16]. Moreover, some discussions about continuous exposure and a continuous response for Mendelian randomization can be found in a review paper [8] .

A threshold in a variable occurs when there is a sudden change in the values of this variable. We call the point where the change happens as a cut-off point or a threshold. The subset causal effect exists when there is a threshold in the explanatory variable. The proposed PLIV model is useful because it can study the subset causal effect when the true model is not linear and it can also degenerate to a linear instrumental variable model when the relationship among the variables is indeed linear. In other words, by using piecewise linear functions, we can quantitatively find the subset effects of the explanatory and the instrumental variables.

We use the Rectified Linear Unit (ReLU) function, mathematically defined in Equation (1), to incorporate the piecewise relationships. Utilization of ReLU function for defining the subset effects have been studied in the literature, such as a regression kink model that tests the presence of the threshold [17] and the segmented and hinge models to study the subset effects in logistic regression [18]. Besides, the continuous threshold models via the ReLU function with two-way interactions is considered in the Cox's proportional hazards model, where the asymptotic normality under mild conditions is established [19]. In this paper, we use a continuous threshold function with multiple thresholds to formulate the piecewise linear instrumental variable models. A similar study of the piecewise linear instrumental variable model through the random slope approach is studied in the literature [20]. It divides the data into a few segments and analyzes the data in each segment individually. However, this method suffers from huge efficiency and accuracy loss.

1.2. Contribution of This Article

In this paper, we consider a piecewise linear model when the linearity assumption of the data is inappropriate and provide a rigorous treatment of the statistical properties of the model. Our contributions can be summarized as follows.

- We simultaneously estimate the coefficients and thresholds of the piecewise linear instrumental variable model by the limited information maximum likelihood (LIML) method, assuming the number of thresholds is known.
- The proposed piecewise linear instrumental variable model will degenerate to the linear instrumental variable model if there are no thresholds. Therefore, it provides a generalization to the linear instrumental variable model. To our best knowledge, this is the first work on the piecewise linear extension to the traditional linear instrumental variable models.
- We also study the theoretical properties of the PLIV model, including the consistency and asymptotic normality of the estimators.

2. Piecewise Linear Instrumental Variable Model

Notations: we denote scalars by unbolded lowercase letters (e.g., sample size n and the i-th observation of outcome variable y_i), random variable by unbolded capital letter (e.g., X), random vectors by boldface lowercase letters (e.g., $\boldsymbol{x}_i$ and $\boldsymbol{\beta}$), and matrices with boldface capital letters (e.g., $\boldsymbol{X}$).

In the ordinary linear regression model $y_i = \boldsymbol{x}_i^\top \boldsymbol{\beta} + \epsilon_i$, there is an assumption that the explanatory variables are uncorrelated with the error term, i.e., cov(x_i,ϵ_i) = 0. However, there are some situations where the covariance between the explanatory variables and error term exists. This leads to inconsistent estimation of ordinary least squares due to the phenomenon of endogeneity in $\boldsymbol{x}$. One way to deal with this issue is to introduce an instrument variable, whose changes are related to changes in the explanatory variable but do not lead to the change in the response variable directly.

Let $(x_i, y_i, z_i), i = 1, \ldots, n$, denotes the observed data for (X, Y, Z), where X is the explanatory variable, Y is the response variable, and Z is the instrumental variable. To estimate the subset causal effect and establish the piecewise linear relationship, for any threshold parameter $t \in \mathbb{R}$, we use a continuous threshold function which is defined as:

$$\varphi(x_i, t) = (x_i - t)I(x_i > t) = (x_i - t)^+, \tag{1}$$

where $I(\cdot)$ is an indicator function. ReLU function, commonly used as an activation function in deep learning, is a special case with $t = 0$ such that $\varphi(x_i,0) = (x_i - 0)I(x_i > 0) = (x_i - 0)^+$.

The proposed model provides sparsity and computational efficiency compared to the smoothing or approximation approach in the literature. The estimation stage involves indicator functions but it does not require an approximation of the indicator function. Let K and J denote the number of thresholds in Z and X, respectively. Denote $\boldsymbol{c} = (c_1, \ldots, c_K)^T$ as the vector of thresholds in Z and denote $\boldsymbol{t} = (t_1, \ldots, t_J)^T$ as the vector of thresholds in X. We propose the following piecewise linear instrumental variable model:

$$x_i = \alpha_0 + \alpha_1\varphi(z_i, c_1) + \cdots + \alpha_K\varphi(z_i, c_K) + \alpha_{K+1}z_i + v_i \tag{2}$$

$$y_i = \beta_0 + \beta_1\varphi(x_i, t_1) + \cdots + \beta_J\varphi(x_i, t_J) + \beta_{J+1}x_i + u_i, \tag{3}$$

where $\boldsymbol{\beta} = (\beta_0, \ldots, \beta_{J+1})^T$ is the vector of coefficients representing the causal effect of X on Y; $\boldsymbol{\alpha} = (\alpha_0, \ldots, \alpha_{K+1})^T$ is the vector of coefficients representing the instrumental effect of Z on X; u_i and v_i are the error terms for the ith observation. In the context of causal inference, we interpret β as the causal effect of x on y. More specifically, for $t_j < x \leq t_{j+1}, 1 \leq j \leq J$ with t_{J+1} denoting the maximum value of x, one unit increase in x leads to $\beta_{J+1} + \sum_{j'=1}^{j} \beta_{j'}$ units change in y. Besides, β_{J+1} represents the change in y that is caused by one unit increase in x for $t_0 < x \leq t_1$ where t_0 is the minimum value of x. To better understand this, in Figure 1, we plot the function $y = \varphi(x,2) + 3 \times \varphi(x,3) + 2x$ where $\beta_1 = 1, \beta_2 = 3, \beta_3 = 2$ as an example. When $2 < x \leq 3$, the slope is $\beta_1 + \beta_3 = 3$. When $3 < x \leq 4$, the slope is $\beta_1 + \beta_2 + \beta_3 = 6$.

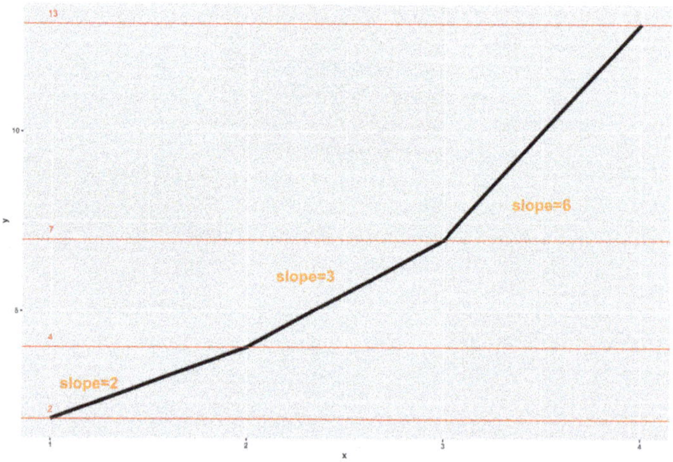

Figure 1. Plot of the function $y = \varphi(x,2) + 3 \times \varphi(x,3) + 2x$.

Here, we assume K and J are prespecified according to some prior knowledge or theoretical justifications. Practically, we may use the Akaike information criterion (AIC) or the Bayesian information criterion (BIC) [21] to select them. A more elegant examination of the condition for the number of thresholds can be found in Newey [22]. In particular, when $\alpha_1 = \cdots = \alpha_K = 0$ and $\beta_1 = \cdots = \beta_J = 0$, our proposed model degenerates to the traditional linear instrumental variable model.

For instrumental variable analysis, an instrumental variable is correlated with the explanatory variable but not correlated with the error term. In our model, $(Z - \boldsymbol{c})^+ = \{(Z - c_1)^+, \cdots, (Z - c_K)^+\}$ is the vector of instrumental variables with the following properties:

- Instrument relevance: $\text{cov}\{(Z - \boldsymbol{c})^+, X\} \neq 0$: $(Z - \boldsymbol{c})^+$ is correlated with the explanatory variable X.
- Instrument exogeneity: $\text{cov}\{(Z - \boldsymbol{c})^+, U\} = 0$: $(Z - \boldsymbol{c})^+$ is uncorrelated with the error term U.

We assume $K \geq J$ for identifiability, i.e., the number of instruments should be larger than or equal to the number of endogenous variables.

Remark 1. *Note that intensive research about nonlinear instrumental variable models has been conducted in the literature, such as the nonparametric instrumental regression [23–25]. We point out that the target of our method is to quantitatively find the thresholds and estimate the subset causal effects. We aim to generalize the traditional linear IV model and fit an interpretable model rather than approximate the data by a nonlinear function.*

To estimate the unknown parameters in (2) and (3), we utilize the two-stage least square (2SLS) method and the limited information maximum likelihood (LIML) method. Details about the proposed estimation methods are discussed below.

3. Simultaneous Maximum Likelihood Estimation

We first introduce how the LIML method is used in our model and initialize the naive estimators by the 2SLS method.

3.1. Limited Information Maximum Likelihood

As discussed in the introduction about the advantages, limited information maximum likelihood is another popular approach for estimation in the instrumental variable models. Here, we assume the error terms (U, V) are jointly normally distributed and correlated to some extent due to the unmeasured confounding effect. Let $\mathbf{0}$ be the zero-mean vector and ρ be the correlation of (U, V). Denote σ_u^2 and σ_v^2 as the variance of the error terms U and V, respectively. Then the probability density function of the bivariate normal (U,V) can be written as:

$$f(U,V) = \frac{1}{2\pi\sigma_u\sigma_v\sqrt{1-\rho^2}} \exp\left[-\frac{1}{2(1-\rho^2)}Q(U,V)\right],$$

where the quadratic form $Q(U,V) = \frac{U^TU}{\sigma_u^2} - \frac{2\rho U^TV}{\sigma_v\sigma_u} + \frac{V^TV}{\sigma_v^2}$. For a single observation, the log-likelihood is

$$\ell(u_i, v_i; \boldsymbol{\theta}) \propto -\log(\sigma_u\sigma_v) - \frac{1}{2}\log(1-\rho^2) - \frac{1}{2(1-\rho^2)}\left(\frac{u_i^2}{\sigma_u^2} - \frac{2\rho u_i v_i}{\sigma_u\sigma_v} + \frac{v_i^2}{\sigma_v^2}\right),$$

where $\boldsymbol{\theta} = (\boldsymbol{\alpha}^T, \boldsymbol{\beta}^T, \boldsymbol{c}^T, \boldsymbol{t}^T, \rho, \sigma_u, \sigma_v)^T$ denote all the model parameters and

$$v_i = x_i - \alpha_0 - \alpha_1\varphi(z_i, c_1) - \cdots - \alpha_K\varphi(z_i, c_K) - \alpha_{K+1}z_i$$

$$u_i = y_i - \beta_0 - \beta_1\varphi(x_i, t_1) - \cdots - \beta_J\varphi(x_i, t_J) - \beta_{J+1}x_i.$$

To simplify notations, we let $\ell(\boldsymbol{\theta}) = \ell(u_i, v_i; \boldsymbol{\theta})$ denote the log-likelihood. The maximum likelihood estimates for $\boldsymbol{\theta}$ is obtained by maximizing the log-likelihood within the compact set $\boldsymbol{\Theta} \subset \mathbb{R}^{D(\boldsymbol{\theta})}$ such that $\hat{\boldsymbol{\theta}}_n = \arg\max_{\boldsymbol{\theta}\in\boldsymbol{\Theta}} \ell_n(\boldsymbol{\theta})$, where $\ell_n(\boldsymbol{\theta}) = 1/n\sum_{i=1}^n \ell(\boldsymbol{\theta})$. However, there is no closed-form solution for $\boldsymbol{\theta}$, so we take the gradient-based algorithm for estimation. This yields approximate M-estimators. To speed up estimation, we use the two-stage least square method to initialize the estimators.

3.2. Initialization: Two-Stage Least Square

The traditional two-stage least squares method regresses the explanatory variable on the instrumental variable and computes the predictions $\hat{x}$ in the first stage. In the second stage, it regresses the response variable on the predictions $\hat{x}$. The causal effect of interest is estimated from the second stage. In our method, we employ 2SLS to obtain the initial values of the parameters of the piecewise linear instrumental variable model. Below we describe the 2SLS procedures for initializations:

Stage 1: First, we regress x on $\{(z-\boldsymbol{c})^+, z\}$ and then obtain the fitted values $\hat{x}$, where $(z-\boldsymbol{c})^+ = \{(z-c_1)^+, \cdots, (z-c_K)^+\}$.

Stage 2: We regress y on $\{(\hat{x}-\boldsymbol{t})^+, \hat{x}\}$, where $(\hat{x}-\boldsymbol{t})^+ = \{(\hat{x}-t_1)^+, \cdots, (\hat{x}-t_J)^+\}$. Thus, in the second stage, we fit the following regression model:

$$y_i = \beta_0 + \beta_1\varphi(\hat{x}_i, t_1) + \cdots + \beta_J\varphi(\hat{x}_i, t_J) + \beta_{J+1}\hat{x}_i + u_i.$$

For each combination of the number of thresholds in X and Z, we could pick $\boldsymbol{c}$, $\boldsymbol{t}$ and the regression coefficients simultaneously through grid search when the sum of squared errors (SSE) of Y is minimized. However, for $J \geq 2$ or $K \geq 2$, it is slightly computationally expensive to conduct grid search. Since we only need 2SLS to provide the initialization of the parameters in our method, we choose $\boldsymbol{c}$ to be a vector of the points that are evenly spaced between the 5% to 95% quantiles of Z. Similarly, we choose $\boldsymbol{t}$ to be a vector of the points that are evenly spaced between the 5% to 95% quantiles of X. We ignore points below and above the 5% to 95% quantiles in order to avoid boundary effects. The regression coefficients are obtained accordingly.

3.3. Theoretical Analysis

Under mild conditions, we study the statistical properties of the proposed model and establish the robust variance-covariance estimators for the estimated parameters under the correctly specified and misspecified models, separately. To investigate the theoretical properties, we consider the following regularity conditions:

- C1. Observations $(X_i, Y_i, Z_i), i = 1, \ldots, n$ are independently and identically distributed on a compact set $\mathcal{X} \otimes \mathcal{Y} \otimes \mathcal{Z} \subset \mathbb{R}^1 \otimes \mathbb{R}^1 \otimes \mathbb{R}^1$. Furthermore, $E(\|X\|^2) < \infty$, $E(\|Y\|^2) < \infty$, and $E(\|Z\|^2) < \infty$.
- C2. The explanatory variable X and the instrumental variable Z are continuous in the parameter space, i.e., they have continuous probability density functions $f_X(\cdot)$ and $f_Z(\cdot)$. The density functions are uniformly bounded, that is, there exist constants $\underline{c}_1$, $\underline{c}_2$, $\bar{c}_1$, and $\bar{c}_2$ such that

$$\underline{c}_1 \le \inf_{Z \in \mathcal{Z}} f_Z(\cdot) \le \sup_{Z \in \mathcal{Z}} f_Z(\cdot) \le \bar{c}_1 \quad \text{and} \quad \underline{c}_2 \le \inf_{X \in \mathcal{X}} f_X(\cdot) \le \sup_{X \in \mathcal{X}} f_X(\cdot) \le \bar{c}_2.$$

  Furthermore, the true value of the coefficients for the threshold effects satisfy $\boldsymbol{\alpha}_0^- \neq \mathbf{0}$ and $\boldsymbol{\beta}_0^- \neq \mathbf{0}$, where $\boldsymbol{\alpha}_0^- = (\alpha_{20}, \ldots, \alpha_{(K-1)0})$ and $\boldsymbol{\beta}_0^- = (\beta_{20}, \ldots, \beta_{(J-1)0})$.
- C3. $\ell(\boldsymbol{\theta})$ is upper-semicontinuous for almost all (X, Y, Z), that is, for every $\boldsymbol{\theta}$,

$$\limsup_{\boldsymbol{\theta}_n \to \boldsymbol{\theta}} \ell(X, Y, Z; \boldsymbol{\theta}_n) \le \ell(X, Y, Z; \boldsymbol{\theta}), \quad \text{a.s.}$$

Remark 2. *Condition C1 is commonly used in regression models. Condition C2 is used for estimating the unknown thresholds and ensures the model is identifiable. The continuity requirements of X and Z are used to estimate the thresholds. Condition C3 is used to establish the consistency and the asymptotic normality of the maximum likelihood estimator.*

In terms of estimation, we take the gradient-based method which depends on the first order derivative $\dot{\ell}(\boldsymbol{\theta}) = \partial \ell(\boldsymbol{\theta}) / \partial \boldsymbol{\theta}$ (details can be found in Appendix A) with the initialized estimators by 2SLS. In this paper, we do not approximate the indicator function by the logistic function as some researchers do (e.g., [18,26,27]). The gradient-based algorithm for the ReLU function has shown success in the context of deep learning and machine learning. Compared to the approximation techniques as discussed in Section 1, model estimation with the ReLU function is computationally cheaper since no approximation of the indicator function is required. In fact, as long as Condition C2 is satisfied which requires variables X and Z to be continuous, the gradients composed of the indicator functions converge to a continuous function of the threshold parameters as $n \to \infty$, for example,

$$\frac{1}{n} \sum_{i=1}^{n} I(z_i > c_k) \xrightarrow{P} E\{I(z_i > c_k)\} = P(z_i > c_k),$$

for $k = 1, \ldots, K$ by the law of large numbers. Therefore, the second order derivative of the ReLU function with respect to the thresholds can be derived based on the resulting continuous probability function. More specifically, the second order derivative with respect to c_k is simply $-f_Z(c_k)$.

To prove the asymptotic normality, we first need to show the consistency of the proposed estimators.

Theorem 1. *Under conditions C1–C4, assume that $\boldsymbol{\Theta}$ is compact and the true parameter vector $\boldsymbol{\theta}_0 = \arg\max_{\boldsymbol{\theta} \in \boldsymbol{\Theta}} E\{\ell(\boldsymbol{\theta})\}$ is unique. Furthermore, for every sufficiently small ball $\mathbb{B} \subset \boldsymbol{\Theta}$, $\sup_{\boldsymbol{\theta} \in \mathbb{B}} \ell(\boldsymbol{\theta})$ is measurable with $E \sup_{\boldsymbol{\theta} \in \mathbb{B}} \ell(\boldsymbol{\theta}) < \infty$, then $\hat{\boldsymbol{\theta}}_n \xrightarrow{P} \boldsymbol{\theta}_0$.*

Proof. The proof follows the Theorem 5.7 of van der Vaart [28]. For completeness, we include it as Theorem A1 in Appendix B. To utilize Theorem 5.7, we need to check the condition that $\ell(\hat{\boldsymbol{\theta}}_n) \geq \ell(\boldsymbol{\theta}_0) - o_P(1)$ for some $\boldsymbol{\theta}_0 \in \boldsymbol{\Theta}_0$. This is true since $\ell_n(\boldsymbol{\theta})$ is continuous in $\boldsymbol{\theta}$, $\ell_n(\boldsymbol{\theta})$ converges to $\ell(\boldsymbol{\theta})$ uniformly, and $\hat{\boldsymbol{\theta}}_n$ (approximately) maximizes $\ell_n(\boldsymbol{\theta})$. Thus, all the conditions are satisfied and the result follows. □

Theorem 2. *Under conditions C1–C4, let $\boldsymbol{\theta}_0$ be the true value of $\boldsymbol{\theta}$. Let $\dot{\ell}(\boldsymbol{\theta})$ be a measurable function with $E\left[\{\dot{\ell}(\boldsymbol{\theta})\dot{\ell}(\boldsymbol{\theta})^T\}_{(i,j)}\right] < \infty$ for $i,j = 1,\ldots,|\boldsymbol{\theta}|_*$, where $|\boldsymbol{\theta}|_*$ denotes the number of elements in $\boldsymbol{\theta}$, then*

$$\sqrt{n}(\hat{\boldsymbol{\theta}}_n - \boldsymbol{\theta}_0) \xrightarrow{d} N\left(\mathbf{0}, V_{\boldsymbol{\theta}_0}^{-1} M_{\boldsymbol{\theta}_0} V_{\boldsymbol{\theta}_0}^{-1}\right),$$

where $M_{\boldsymbol{\theta}_0} = E\{\dot{\ell}(\boldsymbol{\theta}_0)\dot{\ell}(\boldsymbol{\theta}_0)^T\}$ and $\dot{\ell}(\boldsymbol{\theta}_0)$ is the first order derivative of $\ell(\boldsymbol{\theta})$ with respect to $\boldsymbol{\theta}$ evaluated at $\boldsymbol{\theta}_0$ and $V_{\boldsymbol{\theta}_0}$ is the second order derivative of $E\{\ell(\boldsymbol{\theta})\}$ with respect to $\boldsymbol{\theta}$ evaluated at $\boldsymbol{\theta}_0$ (derivations in Appendix A). $V_{\boldsymbol{\theta}}$ has the form

$$V_{\boldsymbol{\theta}} = V_{\boldsymbol{\theta}}^{(1)} + V_{\boldsymbol{\theta}}^{(2)} = V_{\boldsymbol{\theta}}^{(1)} + \begin{pmatrix} 0 & \mathbf{0} & V_{\alpha c}^{(2)} & \mathbf{0} & 0 & 0 & 0 \\ & \mathbf{0} & \mathbf{0} & V_{\beta t}^{(2)} & \mathbf{0} & \mathbf{0} & \mathbf{0} \\ & & V_{cc}^{(2)} & \mathbf{0} & \mathbf{0} & \mathbf{0} & \mathbf{0} \\ & & & V_{tt}^{(2)} & \mathbf{0} & \mathbf{0} & \mathbf{0} \\ & & & & 0 & 0 & 0 \\ & & & & & 0 & 0 \\ sym. & & & & & & 0 \end{pmatrix},$$

where $\mathbf{0}$ denotes a zero vector or a zero matrix and 0 denotes a scalar. Details of $V_{\boldsymbol{\theta}}^{(1)}$ and $V_{\boldsymbol{\theta}}^{(2)}$ are given in the Appendix A.

Proof. First, note that $\ell(\boldsymbol{\theta})$ is Lipschitz continuous in $\boldsymbol{\theta}$. Moreover, the fact that $V_{\boldsymbol{\theta}}$ is continuous in $\boldsymbol{\theta}$ admits the Taylor expansion of $E_{XYZ}\ell(\boldsymbol{\theta})$:

$$E_{(X,Y,Z)}\ell(\boldsymbol{\theta}) = E_{(X,Y,Z)}\ell(\boldsymbol{\theta}_0) + \frac{1}{2}(\boldsymbol{\theta} - \boldsymbol{\theta}_0)V_{\boldsymbol{\theta}_0}(\boldsymbol{\theta} - \boldsymbol{\theta}_0)^T + o_p\left(\|\boldsymbol{\theta} - \boldsymbol{\theta}_0\|^2\right).$$

Since $\hat{\boldsymbol{\theta}}$ is the maximum likelihood estimate of $\boldsymbol{\theta}$, $\frac{1}{n}\sum_{i=1}^n \ell(\hat{\boldsymbol{\theta}}) \geq \sup_{\boldsymbol{\theta}} \frac{1}{n}\sum_{i=1}^n \ell(\boldsymbol{\theta}) - o_P(\frac{1}{n})$. Plus the result from Theorem 1 that $\hat{\boldsymbol{\theta}}_n \xrightarrow{p} \boldsymbol{\theta}_0$, we conclude from Theorem 5.14 of van der Vaart [28] that:

$$\sqrt{n}(\hat{\boldsymbol{\theta}}_n - \boldsymbol{\theta}_0) = -V_{\boldsymbol{\theta}_0}^{-1}\frac{1}{\sqrt{n}}\sum_{i=1}^n \dot{\ell}_i(\boldsymbol{\theta}_0) + o_P(1),$$

which implies an asymptotic normal distribution with mean $\mathbf{0}$ and variance-covariance matrix $V_{\boldsymbol{\theta}_0}^{-1} M_{\boldsymbol{\theta}_0} V_{\boldsymbol{\theta}_0}^{-1}$. □

For completeness, we include Theorem 5.14 of van der Vaart [28] (2000) as Theorem A2 in Appendix B. When the model is correctly specified, $V_{\boldsymbol{\theta}_0} = -M_{\boldsymbol{\theta}_0}$, the asymptotic variance is the inverse of Fisher information. Matrices $V_{\boldsymbol{\theta}_0}$ and $M_{\boldsymbol{\theta}_0}$ are estimated through the replacement of $\boldsymbol{\theta}_0$ by the MLE $\hat{\boldsymbol{\theta}}_n$. Thus, for the correctly specified model, the variance-covariance matrix is estimated by the inverse of $M_{\hat{\boldsymbol{\theta}}_n}$. For the misspecified model, the variance-covariance matrix is estimated by $V_{\hat{\boldsymbol{\theta}}_n}^{-1} M_{\hat{\boldsymbol{\theta}}_n} V_{\hat{\boldsymbol{\theta}}_n}^{-1}$. Let us define V_n as the second derivative of $\ell_n(\boldsymbol{\theta})$ with respect to $\boldsymbol{\theta}$, then we can decompose V_n the same way as $V_{\boldsymbol{\theta}}$ into two matrices $V_n^{(1)}$ and $V_n^{(2)}$. Note that V_n is the empirical process of $V_{\boldsymbol{\theta}}$ and $V_n \xrightarrow{p} V_{\boldsymbol{\theta}}$ by the law of large numbers, so we use the estimated probability densities $\hat{f}_Z(\hat{c}_k)$ and $\hat{f}_X(\hat{t}_j)$ for $f_Z(c_k)$ and $f_X(t_j)$ for $k = 1,\ldots,K$ and $j = 1,\ldots,J$, respectively.

4. Simulation Studies

In this section, we evaluate the performance of the proposed model using simulated datasets. We consider two scenarios with the same sample size $n = 500$. We let error terms U and V be jointly normally distributed with mean $\mathbf{0}$ and correlation $\rho \in \{0.2, 0.5, 0.8\}$. Here, we consider a common standard deviation $\sigma_u = \sigma_v = \sqrt{0.3}$. Besides, we simulate the instrumental variable $Z \sim N(0,1)$. The first scenario has one threshold in X and one threshold in z, and it takes the following form:

$$x_i = -1 + 0.5 \times (z_i - 0.5)^+ + z_i + v_i$$
$$y_i = -0.2 + (x_i - 0)^+ + 0.5 \times x_i + u_i.$$

The true values of the parameters in PLIV models are $\boldsymbol{\alpha} = (-1, 0.5, 1)$, $\boldsymbol{\beta} = (-0.2, 1, 0.5)$, $c = 0.5$, and $t = 0$. The second scenario has two thresholds in x and two thresholds in z, and it takes the following form:

$$x_i = -1 + 0.5 \times (z_i + 1)^+ + (z_i - 1)^+ + z_i + v_i$$
$$y_i = -1 + 1.2 \times (x_i + 1)^+ + (x_i - 2)^+ + 0.5 \times x_i + u_i.$$

The true parameters are $\boldsymbol{\alpha} = (-1, 0.5, 1, 1)$, $\boldsymbol{\beta} = (-1, 1.2, 1, 0.5)$, $\boldsymbol{c} = (-1, 1)$, and $\boldsymbol{t} = (-1, 2)$. We show the simulated piecewise linear instrumental variable models for scenario 1 and scenario 2 in Figure 2. We replicate the simulation 1000 times to evaluate the finite sample properties of the proposed model by the PLIV method.

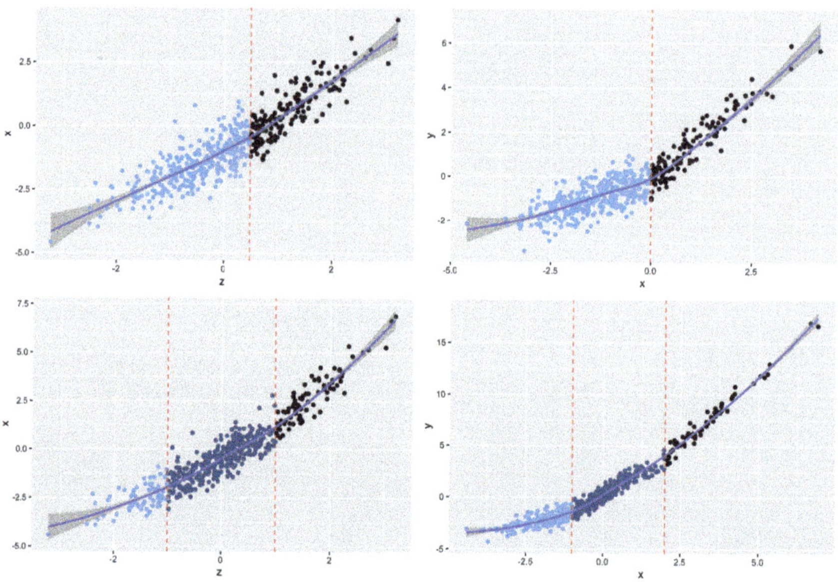

Figure 2. Piecewise linear instrumental variable models with simulated data for scenario 1 and scenario 2. The upper panel plots the simulated X versus Z, Y versus X for scenario 1, respectively. The lower panel plots the simulated X versus Z, Y versus X for scenario 2, respectively.

Table 1 summarizes the biases, standard errors of $\hat{\boldsymbol{\theta}}$ and coverage probabilities of $\boldsymbol{\theta}$ by the proposed PLIV method for scenario 1, where **tse** is the theoretical standard error and **ese** is the empirical standard error. As we can see in the table, all the biases of $\hat{\boldsymbol{\theta}}$ are close to zero. We also find that the theoretical standard error and the empirical standard error are close enough, which confirms the validity of our theoretical results in Section 3. The results show that our model estimation is quite accurate and therefore provides unbiased and consistent estimators. Besides, we notice that the coverage probabilities are around 95% under different values of ρ. Moreover, biases and the standard errors decrease as we increase ρ because the instrumental variables becomes stronger.

Table 1. Empirical biases, theoretical standard errors (tse), and empirical standard errors (ese) of $\hat{\boldsymbol{\theta}}$, as well as 95% coverage probabilities (cp) on $\boldsymbol{\theta}$ for scenario 1.

	$\rho = 0.2$				$\rho = 0.5$				$\rho = 0.8$			
	bias	tse	ese	cp	bias	tse	ese	cp	bias	tse	ese	cp
α_0	−19.25	41.25	45.80	937	−16.43	38.26	41.56	939	−9.10	32.08	33.78	940
α_1	7.65	98.27	102.66	927	6.36	93.13	97.02	924	4.10	77.32	81.80	919
α_2	−16.95	46.20	47.71	931	−14.79	42.82	43.64	933	−8.28	33.52	34.34	943
β_0	−7.86	55.41	54.87	950	−6.88	52.37	52.74	944	−4.28	43.92	44.80	945
β_1	0.48	80.58	77.07	955	−0.35	75.48	74.69	942	−0.58	60.37	62.50	940
β_2	−4.35	34.57	34.06	947	−3.84	32.49	32.60	945	−2.38	26.21	26.57	933
c	−95.15	178.21	247.82	839	−82.89	159.34	224.83	846	−46.25	113.96	165.49	864
t	−14.88	97.77	108.77	922	−12.71	87.80	101.10	908	−6.76	62.69	71.68	908
ρ	2.82	48.99	47.54	951	2.67	37.91	36.81	947	1.62	17.70	17.22	941
σ^2	−2.32	14.00	13.72	954	−1.85	15.65	15.40	953	−1.10	18.12	17.82	956

Note: all numbers are multiplied by 1000. These results are based on 1000 replications.

Table 2 summarizes the biases, standard errors of $\hat{\boldsymbol{\theta}}$ and 95% coverage probabilities of $\boldsymbol{\theta}$ by the PLIV method for scenario 2, where **tse** is the theoretical standard error and **ese** is the empirical standard error. We find the similar patterns as in Table 1 from scenario 1. For instance, all the biases are small. Theoretical standard errors and the empirical standard errors are close to each other. Most coverage probabilities are around 95% when $\rho = 0.2$ and $\rho = 0.5$. We also observe that the coverage probabilities of the thresholds are slightly low when $\rho = 0.8$. The reason might be due to the high correlation between errors. With multiple thresholds and high correlation, it poses challenges to estimate the exact locations.

Table 2. Empirical biases, theoretical standard errors (tse), and empirical standard errors (ese) of $\hat{\boldsymbol{\theta}}$, as well as 95% coverage probabilities (cp) on $\boldsymbol{\theta}$ for scenario 2.

	$\rho = 0.2$				$\rho = 0.5$				$\rho = 0.8$			
	bias	tse	ese	cp	bias	tse	ese	cp	bias	tse	ese	cp
α_0	−51.88	268.22	247.08	946	−38.92	232.37	226.53	939	−20.83	158.06	169.46	921
α_1	29.20	176.58	157.46	966	24.67	157.87	143.26	965	13.44	110.56	107.65	949
α_2	15.11	172.47	166.40	943	11.80	178.03	163.63	949	11.40	146.19	143.76	955
α_3	−26.32	164.95	147.35	945	−19.39	144.98	135.53	931	−9.21	101.13	101.32	934
β_0	−8.36	120.42	116.63	944	−8.23	111.05	108.00	950	−0.84	85.31	82.56	958
β_1	6.61	71.82	71.49	947	6.57	66.84	66.57	948	3.39	52.07	52.12	950
β_2	6.44	115.13	99.07	966	5.38	106.29	90.78	969	3.30	83.05	75.06	962
β_3	−4.14	57.89	56.20	947	−4.33	53.69	52.40	950	−1.10	41.80	40.31	955
c_1	−3.01	253.38	246.83	930	9.41	221.21	257.36	924	6.90	152.06	218.68	898
c_2	2.15	120.17	138.80	913	5.07	139.96	140.17	901	9.10	84.42	134.44	880
t_1	0.79	76.25	79.60	944	1.04	68.31	72.98	939	4.57	48.70	49.52	935
t_2	18.65	168.54	189.81	926	17.60	149.74	174.54	911	16.26	104.90	158.56	922
ρ	2.87	47.44	45.58	950	3.40	36.81	35.35	953	2.14	17.37	16.77	948
σ^2	−3.64	14.00	13.64	939	−2.99	15.55	15.21	946	−1.84	17.99	17.63	955

Note: all numbers are multiplied by 1000. These results are based on 1000 replications.

We include results with a sample size of 1000 in Appendix C, while fixing $\rho = 0.5$. Overall, as n increases, we observe that both biases and standard errors drop.

5. Application

In this section, we revisit the Card's education data [5]. We apply the proposed model to study the causal effect of years of schooling on hourly wage in cents with father's years of schooling as the instrumental variable. The interest here is to find a threshold and study the threshold effect of the years of schooling. It is generally believed that a child's years of schooling has a direct effect on the child's wage and parents' education only affects the child's income by affecting the child's education level. In other words, parents' education level has no direct effect on child's wage. Therefore, the father's years of schooling can be treated as a valid instrumental variable.

In Card's data, we remove the missing values and include a total of $n = 2657$ observations. The explanatory variable X (child's years of education) is between 1 and 18 with median 13, and the instrumental variable Z (father's years of education) has minimum 0, maximum 18, and median 12. Figure 3 indicates that variables X and Y are skewed and have heavy tails so transformations are needed before the analysis. A log transformation is applied to both.

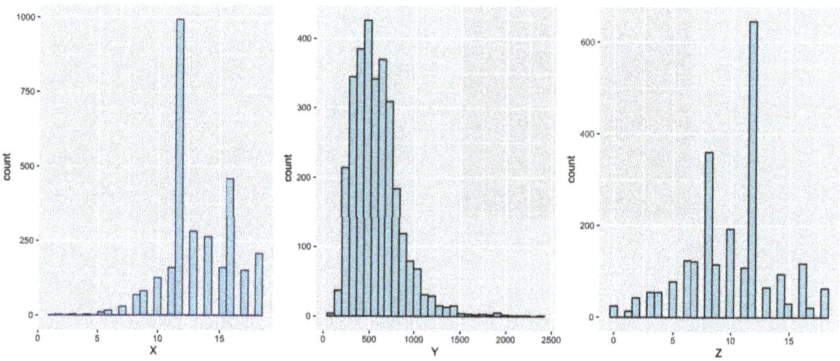

Figure 3. Histogram plots of the raw data X, Y, and Z.

Table 3 shows the point estimate, standard error, and associated 95% confidence interval of $\boldsymbol{\theta}$ by the proposed model with $K = 1$ and $J = 0$, which are selected by BIC. In the table, α_1 and c are the coefficient and threshold for the transformed father's years of schooling, respectively. β_1 is the causal effect of years of schooling on earnings. The estimated causal effect of interest $\hat{\beta}_1$ is 0.87, which results in a difference of $\exp(0.87 \times a)$ units increase in wage if there are a units increase in the log of years of schooling. In economics, $\hat{\beta}_1$ is interpreted as "elasticity". That is, if years of education increases by 1%, the person's income will increase by 0.87% by our estimation. In terms of the instrumental variable, we notice that the threshold c is estimated to be 7.86. The corresponding p-value is not calculated since testing $c = 0$ is meaningless in this context. It shows that there exists a threshold at around 8 in the father's years of schooling. That is, the father's years of schooling only has a positive effect on the child's years of schooling if father receives at least 8 years of education. This information can not be observed if the traditional 2SLS method or nonparametric approaches are applied to analyze the data. The threshold effect as well as the thresholds are all statistically significant since their corresponding p-values are far less than 0.05.

Table 3. Summary table of $\boldsymbol{\theta}$ by the SML-PLIV model.

Parameter	Estimate	Std. Error	z Value	95% C.I.	*p*-Value
α_0: intercept	2.25	0.013	168.8	(2.222, 2.274)	≈0
α_1: $(Z - c)^+$	−0.02	0.003	−4.8	(−0.023, −0.009)	≈0
α_2: Z	0.04	0.003	14.3	(0.033, 0.043)	≈0
β_0: intercept	4.04	0.217	18.6	(3.613, 4.464)	≈0
β_1: $\log X$	0.87	0.084	10.4	(0.705, 1.033)	≈0
c	7.86	0.939	8.4	(6.016, 9.696)	-

6. Discussion, Limitations, and Future Research

In this paper, we propose a simultaneous maximum likelihood estimation for a piecewise linear instrumental variable model. We use the two-stage least square estimators as the initial values and the limited information maximum likelihood methods to estimate the regression coefficients and the threshold parameters simultaneously. We also provide a robust inference of the proposed model. The proposed model with the piecewise linear functions allows us to find the thresholds for both the explanatory and the instrumental variables, which generalizes the traditional linear instrumental variable models. In the simulation study, we evaluate the performance of the proposed model and find that it behaves well in terms of the biases, standard errors, and coverage probabilities in different settings.

In our model, we include a single continuous explanatory variable and a single continuous instrumental variable. We assume the explanatory variable and the instrumental variable are continuous. More complicated cases can be considered. For example, developing a piecewise linear model with count data might be interesting. However, finding the optimal number of thresholds as well as the locations is challenging from the theoretical side. Furthermore, we assume the number of thresholds K and J are prespecified. Treating the numbers of thresholds as random variables, finding the optimal values, and investigating the theoretical properties can be future research.

Author Contributions: Conceptualization, S.S.L. and Y.Z.; methodology, S.S.L. and Y.Z.; experiments and analysis, S.S.L.; original draft writing, S.S.L.; writing review and editing, S.S.L. and Y.Z. All authors have read and agreed to the published version of the manuscript.

Funding: Zhu's research is supported by the National Sciences and Engineering Research Council of Canada (Grant No. RGPIN-2017-04064).

Institutional Review Board Statement: Not applicable.

Informed Consent Statement: Not applicable.

Data Availability Statement: Data used in the application section come from the ivmodel package of CRAN, which can be downloaded from https://github.com/hyunseungkang/ivmodel/tree/master/data (accessed on 31 August 2022). Codes to simulate data, generate tables and plots in Section 4 can be found at https://github.com/shuoshuoliu/PLIV (accessed on 31 August 2022).

Acknowledgments: We thank the editor, the associate editor, and the three reviewers for careful reviews and insightful comments, which have improved this article.

Conflicts of Interest: The authors declare no conflict of interest.

Appendix A. Derivation of the Information and Hessian Matrices

The likelihood to be minimized is

$$\ell_\theta = \frac{1}{n}\sum_{i=1}^{n}\left\{-\log(\sigma_u\sigma_v) - \frac{1}{2}\log(1-\rho^2) - \frac{1}{2(1-\rho^2)}\left(\frac{u_i^2}{\sigma_u^2} - \frac{2\rho u_i v_i}{\sigma_u\sigma_v} + \frac{v_i^2}{\sigma_v^2}\right)\right\}.$$

When the model is specified,

$$E_{XYZ}\ell_\theta = -\log(\sigma_u\sigma_v) - \frac{1}{2}\log(1-\rho^2) - \frac{1}{2(1-\rho^2)}E_{XYZ}\left(\frac{U^TU}{\sigma_u^2} - \frac{2\rho U^TV}{\sigma_v\sigma_u} + \frac{V^TV}{\sigma_v^2}\right).$$

To write out the first order derivative $\dot{\ell}(\boldsymbol{\theta})$ of ℓ_θ with respect to $\boldsymbol{\theta}$, we define the following notations. $\partial\ell_\theta/\partial\boldsymbol{\alpha}\boldsymbol{c}$ is the row concatenation of the first order derivative of ℓ_θ with respect to $\boldsymbol{\alpha}$ and $\boldsymbol{c}$. $\partial\ell_\theta/\partial\boldsymbol{\beta}\boldsymbol{t}$ is the row concatenation of the first order derivative of ℓ_θ with respect to $\boldsymbol{\beta}$ and $\boldsymbol{t}$. For notation simplicity, we drop the subscription i. Let $\boldsymbol{\alpha}I(z > \boldsymbol{c}) =$

$\{\alpha_1 I(z > c_1), \ldots, \alpha_k I(z > c_K)\}$ and $\boldsymbol{\beta} I(x > \boldsymbol{t}) = \{\beta_1 I(x > t_1), \ldots, \beta_j I(x > t_J)\}$. Then we can divide the first order derivative $\dot{\ell}(\boldsymbol{\theta})$ as following

$$
\begin{aligned}
\frac{\partial \ell_{\theta}}{\partial \boldsymbol{\alpha c}} &= \tfrac{1}{n}\textstyle\sum_{i=1}^{n}\left[\{1, (z-\boldsymbol{c})^{+}, z, -\boldsymbol{\alpha} I(z > \boldsymbol{c})\}^{T} \tfrac{1}{(1-\rho^2)}\left(\tfrac{v}{\sigma_v^2} - \tfrac{\rho u}{\sigma_u \sigma_v}\right)\right] \\
\frac{\partial \ell_{\theta}}{\partial \boldsymbol{\beta t}} &= \tfrac{1}{n}\textstyle\sum_{i=1}^{n}\left[\{1, (x-\boldsymbol{t})^{+}, x, -\boldsymbol{\beta} I(x > \boldsymbol{t})\}^{T} \tfrac{1}{(1-\rho^2)}\left(\tfrac{u}{\sigma_u^2} - \tfrac{\rho v}{\sigma_u \sigma_v}\right)\right] \\
\frac{\partial \ell_{\theta}}{\partial \rho} &= \tfrac{1}{n}\textstyle\sum_{i=1}^{n}\left[\tfrac{\rho}{1-\rho^2} - \tfrac{\rho}{(1-\rho^2)^2}\left(\tfrac{u^2}{\sigma_u^2} - \tfrac{2\rho u v}{\sigma_u \sigma_v} + \tfrac{v^2}{\sigma_v^2}\right) + \tfrac{uv}{\sigma_v \sigma_u (1-\rho^2)}\right] \\
\frac{\partial \ell_{\theta}}{\partial \sigma_u} &= \tfrac{u^2}{(1-\rho^2)\sigma_u^3} - \tfrac{\rho u v}{(1-\rho^2)\sigma_v \sigma_u^2} - \tfrac{1}{\sigma_u} \\
\frac{\partial \ell_{\theta}}{\partial \sigma_v} &= \tfrac{v^2}{(1-\rho^2)\sigma_v^3} - \tfrac{\rho u v}{(1-\rho^2)\sigma_u \sigma_v^2} - \tfrac{1}{\sigma_v}
\end{aligned}
\quad . \qquad \text{(A1)}
$$

The interchangeability of expectation and differentiation is satisfied here and it implies $\partial E_{XYZ}\ell(\boldsymbol{\theta})/\partial\boldsymbol{\theta} = E_{XYZ}\{\dot{\ell}(\boldsymbol{\theta})\}$. It is easy to check $\partial E_{XYZ}\ell_{\theta}/\partial\boldsymbol{\theta} = \mathbf{0}$ at $\boldsymbol{\theta}_0$ as it should be. We next derive the second order derivative V_{θ} of $E_{XYZ}\ell_{\theta}$ when the model is specified. We partition the symmetric matrix V_{θ} as two symmetric matrices $V_{1,\theta}$ and $V_{2,\theta}$ such that

$$
V_{\theta} = V_{\theta}^{(1)} + V_{\theta}^{(2)} = V_{\theta}^{(1)} + \begin{pmatrix}
\mathbf{0} & \mathbf{0} & V_{\boldsymbol{\alpha c}}^{(2)} & \mathbf{0} & \mathbf{0} & \mathbf{0} & \mathbf{0} \\
 & \mathbf{0} & \mathbf{0} & V_{\boldsymbol{\beta t}}^{(2)} & \mathbf{0} & \mathbf{0} & \mathbf{0} \\
 & & V_{\boldsymbol{cc}}^{(2)} & \mathbf{0} & \mathbf{0} & \mathbf{0} & \mathbf{0} \\
 & & & V_{\boldsymbol{tt}}^{(2)} & \mathbf{0} & \mathbf{0} & \mathbf{0} \\
 & & & & 0 & 0 & 0 \\
 & & & & & 0 & 0 \\
\text{sym.} & & & & & & 0
\end{pmatrix}.
$$

For the derivation of $V_{\theta}^{(1)}$, let $zc = \{1, (z-\boldsymbol{c})^{+}, z\}$ and $\boldsymbol{xt} = \{1, (x-\boldsymbol{t})^{+}, x\}$. Since the matrix $V_{\theta}^{(1)}$ is symmetric, we only need to derive the upper diagonal elements. The first row of $V_{\theta}^{(1)}$ is is the row concatenation of $\partial^2 E_{XYZ}\ell(\boldsymbol{\theta})/\partial\boldsymbol{\alpha}^2$, $\partial^2 E_{XYZ}\ell(\boldsymbol{\theta})/\partial\boldsymbol{\alpha}\partial\boldsymbol{\beta}$, $\partial^2 E_{XYZ}\ell(\boldsymbol{\theta})/\partial\boldsymbol{\alpha}\partial\boldsymbol{c}$, $\partial^2 E_{XYZ}\ell(\boldsymbol{\theta})/\partial\boldsymbol{\alpha}\partial\boldsymbol{t}$, $\partial^2 E_{XYZ}\ell(\boldsymbol{\theta})/\partial\boldsymbol{\alpha}\partial\rho$, $\partial^2 E_{XYZ}\ell(\boldsymbol{\theta})/\partial\boldsymbol{\alpha}\partial\sigma_u$, and $\partial^2 E_{XYZ}\ell(\boldsymbol{\theta})/\partial\boldsymbol{\alpha}\partial\sigma_v$, such that

$$
V_{1,\theta}^{(1)} = \tfrac{1}{(1-\rho^2)} E_{XYZ}\left[(zc)^{T}\left\{-\tfrac{zc}{\sigma_v^2}, \tfrac{\rho \boldsymbol{xt}}{\sigma_v \sigma_u}, \tfrac{\boldsymbol{\alpha} I(z>\boldsymbol{c})}{\sigma_v^2}, \tfrac{-\rho\boldsymbol{\beta} I(x>\boldsymbol{t})}{\sigma_v \sigma_u}, \tfrac{2\rho v}{\sigma_v^2(1-\rho^2)} - \tfrac{u(1+\rho^2)}{(1-\rho^2)\sigma_v\sigma_u}, \tfrac{\rho u}{\sigma_v \sigma_u^2}, \tfrac{\rho u}{\sigma_v^2 \sigma_u} - \tfrac{2v}{\sigma_v^3}\right\}\right].
$$

The second row of $V_{\theta}^{(1)}$ is the row concatenation of $\partial^2 E_{XYZ}\ell(\boldsymbol{\theta})/\partial\boldsymbol{\beta}^2$, $\partial^2 E_{XYZ}\ell(\boldsymbol{\theta})/\partial\boldsymbol{\beta}\partial\boldsymbol{c}$, $\partial^2 E_{XYZ}\ell(\boldsymbol{\theta})/\partial\boldsymbol{\beta}\partial\boldsymbol{t}$, $\partial^2 E_{XYZ}\ell(\boldsymbol{\theta})/\partial\boldsymbol{\beta}\partial\rho$, $\partial^2 E_{XYZ}\ell(\boldsymbol{\theta})/\partial\boldsymbol{\beta}\partial\sigma_u$, and $\partial^2 E_{XYZ}\ell(\boldsymbol{\theta})/\partial\boldsymbol{\beta}\partial\sigma_v$ such that

$$
V_{2,\theta}^{(1)} = \tfrac{1}{(1-\rho^2)} E_{XYZ}\left[(\boldsymbol{xt})^{T}\left\{-\tfrac{\boldsymbol{xt}}{\sigma_u^2}, -\tfrac{\rho\boldsymbol{\alpha} I(z>\boldsymbol{c})}{\sigma_u \sigma_v}, \tfrac{\boldsymbol{\beta} I(x>\boldsymbol{t})}{\sigma_v^2}, \tfrac{2\rho u}{\sigma_u^2(1-\rho^2)} - \tfrac{v(1+\rho^2)}{(1-\rho^2)\sigma_v\sigma_u}, \tfrac{\rho v}{\sigma_v^3} - \tfrac{2u}{\sigma_u^3}, \tfrac{\rho v}{\sigma_u \sigma_v^2}\right\}\right].
$$

The third row of $V_{\theta}^{(1)}$ is the row concatenation of $\partial^2 E_{XYZ}\ell(\boldsymbol{\theta})/\partial\boldsymbol{c}^2$, $\partial^2 E_{XYZ}\ell(\boldsymbol{\theta})/\partial\boldsymbol{c}\partial\boldsymbol{t}$, $\partial^2 E_{XYZ}\ell(\boldsymbol{\theta})/\partial\boldsymbol{c}\partial\rho$, $\partial^2 E_{XYZ}\ell(\boldsymbol{\theta})/\partial\boldsymbol{c}\partial\sigma_u$, and $\partial^2 E_{XYZ}\ell(\boldsymbol{\theta})/\partial\boldsymbol{c}\partial\sigma_v$ such that

$$
V_{3,\theta}^{(1)} = \tfrac{1}{(1-\rho^2)} E_{XYZ}\left[\{\boldsymbol{\alpha} I(z > \boldsymbol{c})\}^{T}\left\{\tfrac{\boldsymbol{\alpha} I(z>\boldsymbol{c})}{\sigma_v \sigma_u}, \tfrac{\boldsymbol{\beta} I(x>\boldsymbol{t})}{\sigma_u^2}, \tfrac{v(\rho^2+1)}{\sigma_u\sigma_v(1-\rho^2)} - \tfrac{2\rho v}{\sigma_v^2(1-\rho^2)}, -\tfrac{\rho u}{\sigma_v \sigma_u^2}, \tfrac{2v}{\sigma_v^3} - \tfrac{\rho u}{\sigma_u \sigma_v^2}\right\}\right].
$$

The fourth row of $V_{\theta}^{(1)}$ is the row concatenation of $\partial^2 E_{XYZ}\ell(\boldsymbol{\theta})/\partial\boldsymbol{t}^2$, $\partial^2 E_{XYZ}\ell(\boldsymbol{\theta})/\partial\boldsymbol{t}\partial\rho$, $\partial^2 E_{XYZ}\ell(\boldsymbol{\theta})/\partial\boldsymbol{t}\partial\sigma_u$, and $\partial^2 E_{XYZ}\ell(\boldsymbol{\theta})/\partial\boldsymbol{t}\partial\sigma_v$ such that

$$
V_{4,\theta}^{(1)} = \tfrac{1}{(1-\rho^2)} E_{XYZ}\left[\{\boldsymbol{\beta} I(x > \boldsymbol{t})\}^{T}\left\{-\tfrac{\boldsymbol{\beta} I(x>\boldsymbol{t})}{\sigma_v^2}, \tfrac{v(1+\rho^2)}{\sigma_v\sigma_u(1-\rho^2)} - \tfrac{2\rho u}{(1-\rho^2)\sigma_u^2}, \tfrac{2u}{\sigma_v^3} - \tfrac{\rho v}{\sigma_v \sigma_u^2}, -\tfrac{\rho v}{\sigma_u \sigma_v^2}\right\}\right].
$$

The remaining terms in $V_{\theta}^{(1)}$ is given by

$$
\partial^2 E_{XYZ}\ell(\boldsymbol{\theta})/\partial\rho^2 = \frac{1+\rho^2}{(1-\rho^2)^2} - \frac{4uv\rho(\rho^2+1)}{\sigma_u\sigma_v(\rho^2-1)^3} + \frac{2\rho uv}{\sigma_u\sigma_v(\rho^2-1)^2},
$$

$$\partial^2 E_{XYZ}\ell(\boldsymbol{\theta})/\partial\rho\partial\sigma_u = \frac{2\rho u^2}{(1-\rho^2)^2\sigma_u^3} - \frac{2uv\rho^2}{\sigma_u^2\sigma_v(\rho^2-1)^2} - \frac{uv}{\sigma_u^2\sigma_v(1-\rho^2)},$$

$$\partial^2 E_{XYZ}\ell(\boldsymbol{\theta})/\partial\rho\partial\sigma_v = \frac{2\rho v^2}{(1-\rho^2)^2\sigma_v^3} - \frac{2uv\rho^2}{\sigma_u\sigma_v^2(\rho^2-1)^2} - \frac{uv}{\sigma_u\sigma_v^2(1-\rho^2)},$$

$$\partial^2 E_{XYZ}\ell(\boldsymbol{\theta})/\partial\sigma_u^2 = \frac{2\rho uv}{(1-\rho^2)\sigma_v\sigma_u^3} - \frac{3u^2}{\sigma_u^4(1-\rho^2)} + \frac{1}{\sigma_u^2},$$

$$\partial^2 E_{XYZ}\ell(\boldsymbol{\theta})/\partial\sigma_u\sigma_v = \frac{\rho uv}{(1-\rho^2)\sigma_v^2\sigma_u^2},$$

$$\partial^2 E_{XYZ}\ell(\boldsymbol{\theta})/\partial\sigma_v^2 = \frac{2\rho uv}{(1-\rho^2)\sigma_u\sigma_v^3} - \frac{3v^2}{\sigma_v^4(1-\rho^2)} + \frac{1}{\sigma_v^2}.$$

In terms of the matrix $V_\theta^{(2)}$, we decompose the following elements

$$V_{\alpha c}^{(2)} = E_{XYZ}\left[\frac{v}{\sigma_v^2(1-\rho^2)} - \frac{\rho u}{\sigma_u\sigma_v(1-\rho^2)} \times \begin{pmatrix} 0 & \dots & \dots & 0 \\ -I(z>c_1) & 0 & \dots & 0 \\ \vdots & & & \vdots \\ 0 & \dots & \dots & -I(z>c_K) \\ 0 & \dots & \dots & 0 \end{pmatrix}\right],$$

$$V_{\beta t}^{(2)} = E_{XYZ}\left[\frac{u}{\sigma_u^2(1-\rho^2)} - \frac{\rho v}{\sigma_u\sigma_v(1-\rho^2)} \times \begin{pmatrix} 0 & \dots & \dots & 0 \\ -I(x>t_1) & 0 & \dots & 0 \\ \vdots & & & \vdots \\ 0 & \dots & \dots & -I(x>t_J) \\ 0 & \dots & \dots & 0 \end{pmatrix}\right],$$

$$V_{cc}^{(2)} = E_{XYZ}\left[\frac{1}{\sigma_u\sigma_v(1-\rho^2)}\right] \times \begin{pmatrix} -\alpha_1 f_Z(c_1) & 0 & \dots & 0 \\ \vdots & & & \vdots \\ 0 & \dots & \dots & -\alpha_K f_Z(c_K) \end{pmatrix},$$

$$V_{tt}^{(2)} = E_{XYZ}\left[\frac{1}{\sigma_v^2(\rho^2-1)}\right] \times \begin{pmatrix} \beta_1 f_X(t_1) & 0 & \dots & 0 \\ \vdots & & & \vdots \\ 0 & \dots & \dots & \beta_J f_X(t_J) \end{pmatrix}.$$

It is easy to check that when the model is correctly specified, $V_\theta^{(2)} = \mathbf{0}$ and $V_{\boldsymbol{\theta}} = -E_{XYZ}\{\dot{\ell}(\boldsymbol{\theta})\dot{\ell}(\boldsymbol{\theta})^T\}$.

Appendix B. Theorems

Define Pf as the expectation $Ef(X) = \int f dP$ and abbreviate the average $n^{-1}\sum_{i=1}^n f(X_i)$ to $P_n f$, an empirical distribution. Furthermore, we define

$$M_n(\theta) = 1/n\sum_{i=1}^n m_\theta(X_i) = P_n m_\theta \quad \text{and} \quad \Psi_n(\theta) = 1/n\sum_{i=1}^n \psi_\theta(X_i) = P_n\psi_\theta.$$

Theorem A1 (Theorem 5.7 of van der Vaart [28]). *Let M_n be random functions and let M be a fixed function of θ such that for every $\epsilon > 0$*

$$\sup_{\theta\in\Theta}|M_n(\theta) - M(\theta)| \xrightarrow{\text{P}} 0,$$
$$\sup_{\theta:d(\theta,\theta_0)\geq\epsilon} M(\theta) < M(\theta_0).$$

Then every sequence of estimators $\hat{\theta}_n$ *with* $M_n(\hat{\theta}_n) \geq M_n(\theta_0) - o_P(1)$ *converges in probability to* θ_0.

Theorem A2 (Theorem 5.14 of van der Vaart [28]). *For each* θ *in an open subset of Euclidean space, let* $\theta \mapsto \psi_\theta(x)$ *be twice continuously differentiable for every* x. *Suppose that* $P\psi_{\theta_0} = 0$, *that* $P\|\psi_{\theta_0}\|^2 < \infty$ *and that the matrix* $P\dot{\psi}_{\theta_0}$ *exists and is nonsingular. Assume that the second-order partial derivatives are dominated by a fixed integrable function* $\ddot{\psi}(x)$ *for every* θ *in a neighborhood of* θ_0. *Then every consistent estimator sequence* $\hat{\theta}_n$ *such that* $\Psi_n(\hat{\theta}_n) = 0$ *for every* n *satisfies*

$$\sqrt{n}(\hat{\theta}_n - \theta_0) = -\left(P\dot{\psi}_{\theta_0}\right)^{-1} \frac{1}{\sqrt{n}} \sum_{i=1}^{n} \psi_{\theta_0}(X_i) + o_P(1).$$

In particular, the sequence $\sqrt{n}(\hat{\theta}_n - \theta_0)$ *is asymptotically normal with mean zero and covariance matrix* $\left(P\dot{\psi}_{\theta_0}\right)^{-1} P\psi_{\theta_0}\psi_{\theta_0}^T \left(P\dot{\psi}_{\theta_0}\right)^{-1}$.

Appendix C. Additional Simulation Results

Table A1. Empirical biases, theoretical standard errors (tse), and empirical standard errors (ese) of $\hat{\boldsymbol{\theta}}$, as well as 95% coverage probabilities (cp) on $\boldsymbol{\theta}$ for scenario 1 with sample size 1000.

	$\rho = 0.2$				$\rho = 0.5$				$\rho = 0.8$			
	bias	**tse**	**ese**	**cp**	**bias**	**tse**	**ese**	**cp**	**bias**	**tse**	**ese**	**cp**
α_0	−8.30	27.04	29.78	928	−6.48	25.41	27.35	933	−3.28	22.00	22.78	942
α_1	3.08	68.29	70.76	950	2.96	64.99	67.54	932	2.46	53.88	55.17	949
α_2	−7.90	30.92	32.50	936	−6.05	28.90	30.11	938	−2.79	23.05	23.46	955
β_0	−3.61	38.76	39.70	949	−2.80	36.66	37.62	938	−1.77	30.74	31.19	945
β_1	−0.46	55.44	54.45	956	−0.18	52.00	51.80	948	0.65	41.79	42.11	939
β_2	−1.21	24.18	24.78	938	−0.88	22.76	23.35	928	−0.43	18.38	18.42	949
c	−41.08	123.92	167.07	873	−31.07	111.23	148.14	873	−12.70	79.47	98.09	886
t	−7.63	68.18	76.36	919	−4.90	61.13	66.47	920	−1.50	43.69	46.31	935
ρ	1.08	34.23	34.63	948	1.08	26.53	26.77	948	0.72	12.41	12.49	946
σ^2	−0.86	9.82	9.68	949	−0.64	10.96	10.75	949	−0.26	12.68	12.42	946

Note: all numbers are multiplied by 1000. These results are based on 1000 replications.

Table A2. Empirical biases, theoretical standard errors (tse), and empirical standard errors (ese) of $\hat{\boldsymbol{\theta}}$, as well as 95% coverage probabilities (cp) on $\boldsymbol{\theta}$ for scenario 2 with sample size 1000.

	$\rho = 0.2$				$\rho = 0.5$				$\rho = 0.8$			
	bias	**tse**	**ese**	**cp**	**bias**	**tse**	**ese**	**cp**	**bias**	**tse**	**ese**	**cp**
α_0	−25.84	176.86	168.03	943	−15.74	155.65	161.09	929	−7.23	104.42	114.68	927
α_1	8.53	115.79	106.55	956	7.00	103.98	101.28	947	4.01	73.82	75.63	944
α_2	8.49	112.53	105.08	964	5.55	108.98	107.91	958	3.31	98.38	93.69	957
α_3	−11.29	108.14	99.84	951	−5.51	95.98	95.87	934	−1.84	67.37	71.38	935
β_0	−2.87	83.31	84.73	942	−2.03	77.04	78.41	945	−1.09	59.84	62.78	929
β_1	3.86	49.69	50.23	945	2.72	46.32	46.96	942	2.34	36.27	37.33	941
β_2	5.77	72.64	67.82	960	3.88	67.56	63.16	963	2.32	53.65	52.82	939
β_3	−0.69	39.92	40.14	940	-0.48	37.14	37.55	943	−0.11	29.14	31.00	944
c_1	−16.09	171.89	185.99	923	0.96	152.10	212.49	907	2.67	103.26	158.39	891
c_2	−2.69	81.76	95.51	912	4.37	75.10	125.84	903	7.86	56.60	131.88	894
t_1	2.18	53.28	57.74	933	2.08	47.82	52.28	921	2.33	34.17	38.55	921
t_2	20.13	111.57	136.46	925	13.61	99.30	108.45	930	13.30	70.22	85.85	927
ρ	1.21	32.96	33.18	953	1.52	25.63	25.73	950	0.93	12.14	12.31	942
σ^2	−1.41	9.81	9.64	948	−1.17	10.88	10.59	951	−0.58	12.57	12.27	948

Note: all numbers are multiplied by 1000. These results are based on 1000 replications.

References

1. Sokolovska, N.; Wuillemin, P.H. The Role of Instrumental Variables in Causal Inference Based on Independence of Cause and Mechanism. *Entropy* **2021**, *23*, 928. [CrossRef]
2. Zander, B.; Liśkiewicz, M. On searching for generalized instrumental variables. In Proceedings of the Artificial Intelligence and Statistics (PMLR), Cadiz, Spain, 9–11 May 2016; pp. 1214–1222.
3. Angrist, J.D.; Imbens, G.W.; Rubin, D.B. Identification of causal effects using instrumental variables. *J. Am. Stat. Assoc.* **1996**, *91*, 444–455. [CrossRef]
4. Greenland, S. An introduction to instrumental variables for epidemiologists. *Int. J. Epidemiol.* **2000**, *29*, 722–729. [CrossRef] [PubMed]
5. Card, D. *Using Geographic Variation in College Proximity to Estimate the Return to Schooling*; Technical Report; National Bureau of Economic Research: Cambridge, MA, USA, 1993.
6. Didelez, V.; Sheehan, N. Mendelian randomization as an instrumental variable approach to causal inference. *Stat. Methods Med. Res.* **2007**, *16*, 309–330. [CrossRef] [PubMed]
7. Lawlor, D.A.; Harbord, R.M.; Sterne, J.A.; Timpson, N.; Davey Smith, G. Mendelian randomization: using genes as instruments for making causal inferences in epidemiology. *Stat. Med.* **2008**, *27*, 1133–1163. [CrossRef] [PubMed]
8. Burgess, S.; Small, D.S.; Thompson, S.G. A review of instrumental variable estimators for Mendelian randomization. *Stat. Methods Med. Res.* **2017**, *26*, 2333–2355. [CrossRef]
9. von Hinke, S.; Smith, G.D.; Lawlor, D.A.; Propper, C.; Windmeijer, F. Genetic markers as instrumental variables. *J. Health Econ.* **2016**, *45*, 131–148. [CrossRef] [PubMed]
10. Theil, H. *Economic Forecasts and Policy*; 2nd ed.; Palgrave Macmillan: Amsterdam, The Netherlands, 1961.
11. Palmer, T.M.; Holmes, M.V.; Keating, B.J.; Sheehan, N.A. Correcting the Standard Errors of 2-Stage Residual Inclusion Estimators for Mendelian Randomization Studies. *Am. J. Epidemiol.* **2017**, *186*, 1104–1114. [CrossRef]
12. Davidson, R. *Estimation and Inference in Econometrics*; Oxford University Press: New York, NY, USA, 1993.
13. Angrist, J.; Pischke, J. Instrumental Variables in Action: Sometimes You get What You Need. *Most. Harmless Econom. Empiricist's Companion* **2009**, 113–220.
14. Stock, J.; H Wright, J.; Yogo, M. A Survey of Weak Instruments and Weak Identification in Generalized Method Of Moments. *J. Bus. Econ. Stat.* **2002**, *20*, 518–529. [CrossRef]
15. Wooldridge, J.M. *Econometric Analysis of Cross Section and Panel Data*; MIT Press: Cambridge, MA, USA, 2010.
16. Kennedy, E.H.; Lorch, S.; Small, D.S. Robust causal inference with continuous instruments using the local instrumental variable curve. *J. R. Stat. Soc. Ser. B (Stat. Methodol.)* **2019**, *81*, 121–143. [CrossRef]
17. Hansen, B.E. Regression kink with an unknown threshold. *J. Bus. Econ. Stat.* **2017**, *35*, 228–240. [CrossRef]
18. Fong, Y.; Di, C.; Huang, Y.; Gilbert, P.B. Model-robust inference for continuous threshold regression models. *Biometrics* **2017**, *73*, 452–462. [CrossRef] [PubMed]
19. Liu, S.S.; Chen, B.E. Continuous threshold models with two-way interactions in survival analysis. *Can. J. Stat.* **2020**, *48*, 751–772. [CrossRef]
20. Scheines, R.; Cooper, G.; Yoo, C.; Chu, T. Piecewise Linear Instrumental Variable Estimation of Causal Influence. *PMLR* **2001**, 265–271.
21. Schwarz, G. Estimating the dimension of a model. *Ann. Stat.* **1978**, *6*, 461–464. [CrossRef]
22. Newey, W.K. Efficient instrumental variables estimation of nonlinear models. *Econom. J. Econom. Soc.* **1990**, *48*, 809–837. [CrossRef]
23. Darolles, S.; Fan, Y.; Florens, J.P.; Renault, E. Nonparametric instrumental regression. *Econometrica* **2011**, *79*, 1541–1565. [CrossRef]
24. Florens, J.P.; Johannes, J.; Van Bellegem, S. Identification and estimation by penalization in nonparametric instrumental regression. *Econom. Theory* **2011**, *27*, 472–496. [CrossRef]
25. Carroll, R.J.; Ruppert, D.; Crainiceanu, C.M.; Tosteson, T.D.; Karagas, M.R. Nonlinear and nonparametric regression and instrumental variables. *J. Am. Stat. Assoc.* **2004**, *99*, 736–750. [CrossRef]
26. Seo, M.H.; Linton, O. A smoothed least squares estimator for threshold regression models. *J. Econom.* **2007**, *141*, 704–735. [CrossRef]
27. Lin, H.; Zhou, L.; Peng, H.; Zhou, X.H. Selection and combination of biomarkers using ROC method for disease classification and prediction. *Can. J. Stat.* **2011**, *39*, 324–343. [CrossRef]
28. Van der Vaart, A.W. *Asymptotic Statistics*; Cambridge University Press: Cambridge, UK, 2000; Volume 3.

entropy

Article

Normalized Augmented Inverse Probability Weighting with Neural Network Predictions

Mehdi Rostami * and Olli Saarela

Dalla Lana School of Public Health, University of Toronto, 155 College st., Toronto, ON M5T 3M7, Canada; olli.saarela@utoronto.ca
* Correspondence: mehdi.rostamiforooshani@mail.utoronto.ca

Abstract: The estimation of average treatment effect (ATE) as a causal parameter is carried out in two steps, where in the first step, the treatment and outcome are modeled to incorporate the potential confounders, and in the second step, the predictions are inserted into the ATE estimators such as the augmented inverse probability weighting (AIPW) estimator. Due to the concerns regarding the non-linear or unknown relationships between confounders and the treatment and outcome, there has been interest in applying non-parametric methods such as machine learning (ML) algorithms instead. Some of the literature proposes to use two separate neural networks (NNs) where there is no regularization on the network's parameters except the stochastic gradient descent (SGD) in the NN's optimization. Our simulations indicate that the AIPW estimator suffers extensively if no regularization is utilized. We propose the normalization of AIPW (referred to as nAIPW) which can be helpful in some scenarios. nAIPW, provably, has the same properties as AIPW, that is, the double-robustness and orthogonality properties. Further, if the first-step algorithms converge fast enough, under regulatory conditions, nAIPW will be asymptotically normal. We also compare the performance of AIPW and nAIPW in terms of the bias and variance when small to moderate L_1 regularization is imposed on the NNs.

Keywords: causal inference; instrumental variables; neural networks; doubly robust estimation; semi-parametric theory

Citation: Rostami, M.; Saarela, O. Normalized Augmented Inverse Probability Weighting with Neural Network Predictions. *Entropy* **2022**, *24*, 179. https://doi.org/10.3390/e24020179

Academic Editor: Kateřina Hlaváčková-Schindler

Received: 13 November 2021
Accepted: 27 December 2021
Published: 25 January 2022

1. Introduction

Estimation of causal parameters such as the average treatment effect (ATE) in observational data requires confounder adjustment. The estimation and inference are carried out in two steps: In step 1, the treatment and outcome are predicted by a statistical models or machine learning (ML) algorithm, and in the second step the predictions are inserted into the causal effect estimator. If ML algorithms are employed in step 1, the non-linear relationships can potentially be taken into account. The relationship between the confounders and the treatment and outcome can be non-linear which make the application of machine learning (ML) algorithms, which are non-parametric models, appealing. Farrell et al. [1] proposed to use two separate neural networks (double NNs or dNNs) where there is no regularization on the network's parameters except the stochastic gradient descent (SGD) in the NN's optimization [2–5]. They derive the generalization bounds and prove that the NN's algorithms are fast enough so that the asymptotic distribution of causal estimators such as the augmented inverse probability weighting (AIPW) estimator [6–8] will be asymptotically linear, under regulatory conditions and the utilization of cross-fitting [9].

Farrell et al. [1] argue that the fact that SGD-type algorithms control the complexity of the NN algorithm to some extent [2,10] is sufficient for the first step. Our initial simulations and analyses, however, contradict this claim in scenarios where strong confounders and instrumental variables (IVs) exist in the data.

Conditioning on IVs is harmful to the performance of the causal effect estimators such as ATE (Myers et al. [11]) but there may be no prior knowledge about which covariates are IVs, confounders or otherwise. The harm comes from the fact that the complex NNs can provide near-perfect prediction in the treatment model which violates the empirical positivity assumption [12].

The positivity assumption (Section 2) is fundamental to hold to have an identifiable causal parameter in a population. However, in a finite sample, although the parameter is identifiable by making the positivity assumption, the bias and variance of the estimator can be inflated if the estimated propensity scores are close to zero or one bounds (or become zero or one by rounding errors). This is referred to as the empirical positivity assumption which is closely related to the concept of sparsity studied in Chapter 10 of Van der Laan and Rose [8]. The violation of the empirical positivity assumption can cause the inflation of the bias and variance of inverse probability weighting (IPW)-type and AIPW-type estimators.

The inverse probability weighting method dates at least back to Horvitz and Thompson [13] in the literature of sampling with unequal selection probabilities in sub-populations. IPW-type and matching methods have been extensively studied Lunceford and Davidian [7], Rubin [14], Rosenbaum and Rubin [15,16], Busso et al. [17]. IPW is proven to be a consistent estimator of ATE if the propensity scores (that are the conditional probability of treatment assignments) are estimated by a consistent parameter or non-parametric model. The other set of ATE estimators include those involving the modeling of the outcome and inserting the predictions directly into the ATE estimator (Section 2). They are referred to as single robust (SR) estimators as they provide $\sqrt{n}-$consistent estimators for ATE if the outcome model is $\sqrt{n}-$consistent. In this sense, IPW is also single robust as it is consistent if the treatment (or the propensity score) model is $\sqrt{n}-$consistent. The focus of this work is to study the **augmented** IPW-type methods as they involve modeling both treatment and outcome and can be $\sqrt{n}-$consistent estimators of ATE if either of the models is consistent.

We propose and study a simple potential remedy to the empirical positivity violation issue by studying the normalization of the AIPW estimator (similar to the normalization of IPW [7]), here referred to as nAIPW. In fact, both AIPW and nAIPW can be viewed as a more general estimator which is derived via the efficient influence function of ATE [18,19].

A general framework of estimators that includes nAIPW as a special case was proposed by [20]. In their work, the authors did not consider machine learning algorithms for the first-step estimation, but rather assumed parametric statistical models estimated by likelihood-based approaches. They focused on how to consistently estimate ATE within different sub-populations imposed by the covariates. There is a lack of numerical experimentation on these estimators especially when IVs and strong confounders exist in the set of candidate covariates.

To the best of our knowledge, the performance of nAIPW has not been previously studied in the machine learning context, with the assumption that strong confounders and IVs exist in the data. We will prove that this estimator has the doubly robust [6] and the rate doubly robust [19] property, and illustrate that it is robust against extreme propensity score values. Further, nAIPW (similar to AIPW), has the orthogonality property [9] which means that it is robust against small variations in the predictions of the outcome and treatment assignment predictions. One theoretical difference is that AIPW is the most efficient estimator among all the double robust estimators of ATE given both treatment and outcome models are correctly specified [21]. In practice, however, often there is no a priori knowledge about the true outcome and propensity score relationships with the input covariates and thus this feature of AIPW is probably of less practical use.

We argue that for causal parameter estimation, dNN with no regularization may lead to high variance for the causal estimator used in the second step. We compare AIPW and nAIPW through a simulation study where we allow for moderate to strong confounding and instrumental variable effects, that is, we allow for possible violation of the empirical positivity assumption. Further, a comparison between AIPW and nAIPW is made on the Canadian Community Health Survey (CCHS) dataset where the intervention/treatment is the food security vs. food insecurity and the outcome is individuals' body mass index (BMI).

Our contributions include presenting the proof for the orthogonality, doubly robust and rate doubly robust property of nAIPW. Further, it is proven that, under certain assumptions, nAIPW is asymptotically normal and we provide its consistent variance estimator. We analyze the estimation of ATE in the presence of not only confounders, but also IVs, y-predictors and noise variables. We demonstrate that in the presence of strong confounders and IVs, if complex neural networks without L_1 regularizations are used in the step 1 estimation, both AIPW and nAIPW estimators and their asymptotic variances perform poorly, but, relatively speaking, nAIPW performs better. In this paper, the NNs are mostly used as means of estimating the outcome and treatment predictions.

Organization of the article is as follows. In Section 2 we will formally introduce the nAIPW estimator to the readers and state its double robustness property, and in Section 3 we present the first-step prediction model, double neural networks. In Sections 4 and 5 we will present the theoretical aspects of the paper, including the asymptotic normality, doubly robustness and rate doubly robustness orthogonality of the proposed estimator (nAIPW) and the asymptotic normality. We will present the simulation scenarios and results of comparing the nAIPW estimator with other conventional estimators in Section 6. We apply the estimators on a real dataset in Section 7. The article will be concluded with a short discussion on the findings in Section 8. The proofs are straightforward but long and thus are included in Appendix A.

2. Normalized Doubly Robust Estimator

Let data $\mathbf{O} = (O_1, O_2, ..., O_n)$ be generated by a data generating process P, where O_i is a finite dimensional vector $O_i = (Y_i, A_i, W_i)$, with $\mathbf{W}$ being the adjusting factors. P is the true observed data distribution, $\hat{P}_n$ is the distribution of $\mathbf{O}$ such that its marginal distribution with respect to W is its empirical distribution and the expectation of the conditional distribution $Y|A = a, W$, for $a = 0, 1$, can be estimated. We denote the prediction function of the observed outcome given explanatory variables in the treated group $Q^1 := Q(1, W) = \mathbb{E}[Y|A = 1, W]$, and that in the untreated group $Q^0 := Q(0, W) = \mathbb{E}[Y|A = 0, W]$, and the propensity score as $g(W) = \mathbb{E}[A|W]$. Throughout, the expectations $\mathbb{E}$ are with respect to P. The symbol $\hat{}$ on the population-level quantities indicates the corresponding finite sample estimator, and P is replaced by $\hat{P}_n$.

Let the causal parameter of interest be the average treatment effect (ATE)

$$\beta_{ATE} = \mathbb{E}[Y^1 - Y^0] = \mathbb{E}\big[\mathbb{E}[Y^1 - Y^0|W]\big] = \mathbb{E}\big[\mathbb{E}[Y|A = 1, W]\big] - \mathbb{E}\big[\mathbb{E}[Y|A = 0, W]\big], \quad (1)$$

where Y^1 and Y^0 are the potential outcomes of the treatment and controls [6].

For identifiablity of the parameter, the following assumptions must hold true. The first assumption is the conditional independence, or unconfoundedness stating that, given the confounders, the potential outcomes are independent of the treatment assignments ($Y^0, Y^1 \perp A|W$). The second assumption is positivity which entails that the assignment of treatment groups is not deterministic ($0 < Pr(A = 1|W) < 1$). The third assumption is consistency which states that the observed outcomes equal their corresponding potential outcomes ($Y^A = y$). There are other modeling assumptions made such as time order (i.e., the covariates W are measured before the treatment), IID subjects and a linear causal effect.

A list of first candidates to estimate ATE are

$$\begin{aligned}
\text{naive ATE} \quad & \hat{\beta}_{naiveATE} = \frac{1}{n_1}\sum_{i\in A_1}\hat{Q}_i^1 - \frac{1}{n_0}\sum_{i\in A_0}\hat{Q}_i^0, \\
\text{SR} \quad & \hat{\beta}_{SR} = \hat{\mathbb{E}}\Big[\hat{\mathbb{E}}[Y^1 - Y^0|W]\Big] = \frac{1}{n}\sum_{i=1}^{n}\hat{Q}_i^1 - \hat{Q}_i^0, \\
\text{IPW} \quad & \beta_{IPW} = \hat{\mathbb{E}}\Big[\frac{Y^1}{\hat{\mathbb{E}}[A|W]} - \frac{Y^0}{1-\hat{\mathbb{E}}[A|W]}\Big] = \frac{1}{n}\sum_{i=1}^{n}\Big(\frac{A_i y_i}{\hat{g}_i} - \frac{(1-A_i)y_i}{1-\hat{g}_i}\Big), \\
\text{nIPW} \quad & \hat{\beta}_{nIPW} = \sum_{i=1}^{n}\Big(\frac{A_i w_i^{(1)} y_i}{\sum_{j=1}^{n} A_j w_j^{(1)}} - \frac{(1-A_i) w_i^{(0)} y_i}{\sum_{j=1}^{n}(1-A_j) w_j^{(0)}}\Big).
\end{aligned} \tag{2}$$

The naive average treatment effect (naive ATE) is a biased (due to the selection bias) estimator of ATE [22] and is the poorest estimator among all the candidates. The single robust (SR) is not an orthogonal estimator [9] and if ML algorithms which do not belong to the Donsker class ([23], Section 19.2) or have entropy that grows with the sample size are used, this estimator also becomes biased and is not asymptotically normal. The inverse probability weighting (IPW) [13] and its normalization versions adjust (or weight) the observations in the treatment and control groups. IPW and nIPW are also not orthogonal estimators and are similar to SR in this respect. In addition, both $\hat{\beta}_{SR}$ and $\hat{\beta}_{IPW}$ (and $\hat{\beta}_{nIPW}$) are single robust, that is, they are consistent estimators of ATE if the models used are $\sqrt{n}$-consistent [7]. IPW is an unbiased estimator of ATE if g is correctly specified, but nIPW is not unbiased, but is less sensitive to extreme predictions. The augmented inverse probability weighting (AIPW) estimator [21] is an improvement over SR, IPW and nIPW, which involves the predictions for both treatment (the propensity score), and the causal parameter can be expressed as:

$$\beta = \mathbb{E}\Bigg[\Big(\frac{AY - Q(1,W)(A - \mathbb{E}[A|W])}{\mathbb{E}[A|W]}\Big) - \Big(\frac{(1-A)Y + Q(0,W)(A - \mathbb{E}[A|W])}{1 - \mathbb{E}[A|W]}\Big)\Bigg], \tag{3}$$

and the sample version estimator of (3) is

$$\begin{aligned}
\hat{\beta}_{AIPW} = \frac{1}{n}\sum_{i=1}^{n}\Bigg[&\Big(\frac{A_i Y_i - \hat{Q}(1,W_i)(A_i - \hat{\mathbb{E}}[A_i|W_i])}{\hat{\mathbb{E}}[A_i|W_i]}\Big) - \\
&\Big(\frac{(1-A_i)Y_i + \hat{Q}(0,W_i)(A_i - \hat{g}_i)}{1 - \hat{\mathbb{E}}[A_i|W_i]}\Big)\Bigg] = \\
&\frac{1}{n}\sum_{i=1}^{n}\Big(\frac{A_i(y_i - \hat{Q}_i^1)}{\hat{g}_i} - \frac{(1-A_i)(y_i - \hat{Q}_i^0)}{1-\hat{g}_i}\Big) + \hat{\beta}_{SR},
\end{aligned} \tag{4}$$

where $\hat{Q}_i^k = \hat{Q}(k, W_i) = \hat{\mathbb{E}}[Y_i|A_i = k, W_i]$ and $\hat{g}_i = \hat{\mathbb{E}}[A_i|W_i]$.

Among all the doubly robust estimators of ATE, AIPW is the most efficient estimator if both of the propensity score or outcome models are correctly specified, but is not necessarily efficient under incorrect model specification. In fact, this nice feature of AIPW may be less relevant in real-life problems as we might not have a priori knowledge about the predictors of the propensity score and outcome and we cannot correctly model them. Further, in practice, perfect or near-perfect prediction of the treatment assignment can inflate the variance of the AIPW estimator [8]. As a remedy, similar to the normalization of the IPW estimator, we can define a normalized version of the AIPW estimator which is less sensitive to extreme values of the predicted propensity score, referred to as the normalized augmented inverse probability weighting (nAIPW) estimator:

$$\hat{\beta}_{nAIPW} = \sum_{i=1}^{n} \Big(\frac{A_i(y_i - \hat{Q}_i^1) w_i^{(1)}}{\sum_{j=1}^{n} A_j w_j^{(1)}} - \frac{(1-A_i)(y_i - \hat{Q}_i^0) w_i^{(0)}}{\sum_{j=1}^{n} (1-A_j) w_j^{(0)}} \Big) + \hat{\beta}_{SR}, \tag{5}$$

where $w_k^{(1)} = \frac{1}{\hat{g}_k}$ and $w_k^{(0)} = \frac{1}{1-\hat{g}_k}$. Both AIPW and nAIPW estimators add adjustment factors to the SR estimator which involve both models of the treatment and the outcome.

Both AIPW and nAIPW are examples of a class of estimators where

$$\hat{\beta}_{GDR} = \frac{1}{n} \sum_{i=1}^{n} \Big(\frac{A_i(y_i - \hat{Q}_i^1)}{\hat{h}_i^1} - \frac{(1-A_i)(y_i - \hat{Q}_i^0)}{\hat{h}_i^0} \Big) + \hat{\beta}_{SR}, \tag{6}$$

where we refer to this general class as the general doubly robust (GDR) estimator. Letting $\hat{h}^1 = \hat{g}$ and $\hat{h}^0 = 1 - \hat{g}$ gives the AIPW estimators and letting $\hat{h}^1 = \hat{g}\hat{\mathbb{E}}\frac{A}{\hat{g}}$ and $\hat{h}^0 = (1-\hat{g})\hat{\mathbb{E}}\frac{1-A}{1-\hat{g}}$ gives the nAIPW estimator.

The GDR estimator can also be written as

$$\hat{\beta}_{GDR} = \hat{\mathbb{E}}\Big([\frac{A}{\hat{h}^1} - \frac{1-A}{\hat{h}^0}] y - (A - \hat{h}^1)\hat{Q}^1 + (1 - A - \hat{h}^0)\hat{Q}^0 \Big), \tag{7}$$

If h^1 and h^0 are chosen so that

$$\mathbb{E}\big[A - h^1\big] = 0, \ \mathbb{E}\big[1 - A - h^0\big] = 0, \tag{8}$$

by the total law of expectation $\hat{\beta}_{GDR}$ is an unbiased estimator of β.

3. Outcome and Treatment Predictions

The causal estimation and inference when utilizing the AIPW and nAIPW is carried out in two steps. In step 1, the treatment and outcome are predicted by a statistical or machine learning (ML) algorithm, and in the second step the predictions are inserted into the estimator. The ML algorithms in step 1 can capture the linear and non-linear relationships between the confounders and the treatment and the outcome.

Neural networks (NNs) [2–4] are a class of non-linear and non-parametric complex algorithms that can be employed to model the relationship between any set of inputs and some outcome. There has been a tendency to use NNs as they have achieved great success in the most complex artificial intelligence (AI) tasks such as computer vision and natural language understanding [2].

Farrell et al. [1] used two independent NNs for modeling the propensity score model and the outcome with the rectified linear unit (RELU) activation function [2], here referred to as the double NN or dNN:

$$\begin{aligned} \mathbb{E}[Y|A,W] &= \beta_0 + \beta A + \mathbf{W}\alpha + \mathbf{H}\mathbf{\Gamma}_Y \\ \mathbb{E}[A|W] &= \beta_0' + \mathbf{W}'\alpha' + \mathbf{H}'\mathbf{\Gamma}_A, \end{aligned} \tag{9}$$

where two separate neural nets model y and A (no parameter sharing). Farrell et al. [1] proved that dNN algorithms almost attain $n^{\frac{1}{4}}$-rates. By employing the cross-fitting method and theory developed by Chernozhukov et al. [9], an orthogonal causal estimator is asymptotically normal, under some regularity and smoothing conditions, if the dNN is used in the first step (see Theorem 1 in [1]).

These results assume no regularizations imposed on the NNs' weights, and only the stochastic gradient descent (SGD) is used. Farrell et al. claim that the fact that SGD controls the complexity of the NN algorithm to some extent [2,10] is sufficient for the first step. Our initial simulations, however, contradict this claim and we hypothesize that for causal parameter estimation, a dNN with no regularization leads to high variance for the causal estimator used in the second step. Our initial experiments indicate that L_2 regularization and dropout do not perform well in terms of the mean square error (MSE) of AIPW. The loss functions we use contain L_1 regularization (in addition to SGD during the optimization):

$$L_y(\mathcal{P}_y, \beta, \alpha) = \sum_{i=1}^{n} \left[y_i - \alpha' - \beta A_i - \mathbf{W}_i \alpha - H_i^T \mathbf{\Gamma}_Y\right]^2 + C_{L_1} \sum_{\omega \in \mathcal{P}} |\omega|,$$
$$L_A(\mathcal{P}_A, \alpha') = \sum_{i=1}^{n} \left[A_i \log\left(g(H_i^T \mathbf{\Gamma}_A)\right) + (1 - A_i) \log\left(1 - g(H_i^T \mathbf{\Gamma}_A)\right)\right] + \quad (10)$$
$$C'_{L_1} \sum_{\omega \in \mathcal{P}} |\omega|,$$

where C_{L_1}, C'_{L_1} are hyperparameters that can be set before training or be determined by cross-validation, that can cause the training to pay more attention to one part of the output layer. The dNN can have an arbitrary number of hidden layers, or the width of the network ($\mathcal{HL}$) can be another hyperparameter. For a three-layer network, $\mathcal{HL} = [l_1, l_2, ..., l_h]$, where l_j is the number neurons in layer j, $j = 1, 2, ..., h$. $\mathcal{P}_y, \mathcal{P}_A$ are the connection parameters in the non-linear part of the networks, with Ωs being shared for the two outcome and propensity models. Note that the gradient descent-type optimizations in the deep learning platforms (such as pytorch in our case) do not cause the NN parameters to shrink to zero.

4. GDR Estimator Properties

In this section we will see that nAIPW (5) is doubly robust, that is, if either of the outcome or propensity score models are $\sqrt{n}$-consistent, nAIPW will be consistent. Further, nAIPW is orthogonal [9] and is asymptotically linear under certain assumptions and we calculate its asymptotic variance.

4.1. *Consistency and Asymptotic Distribution of nAIPW*

In causal inference, estimating the causal parameter and drawing inference on the parameter are two major tasks. Employing a machine learning algorithm to estimate Q and g in (5) is a means to estimate and draw inference on the causal parameter; the ultimate goal is the relationship between the treatment and the outcome. This allows people to use blackbox ML models with no explanation how these models have learned from the explanatory features. The question is if the consistency and asymptotic normality of the second step causal estimator are preserved if complex ML algorithms are utilized twice for the treatment and outcome models, each with a convergence rate smaller than $\sqrt{n}$, and entropy that grows with n.

Chernozhukov et al. [24] provide numerical experiments illustrating that some estimators are not consistent or asymptotically normal if complex ML models are used that do not belong to the Donsker class and have entropy that grows with n. They further provide a solution by introducing "orthogonal" estimators that, under some regulatory conditions and cross-fitting, are asymptotically normal even if complex ML models can be used as long as their rates of convergence are as small as $n^{\frac{1}{4}}$.

The next two subsections provide an overview of the general theory and prove that nAIPW is asymptotically normal.

4.2. *The Efficient Influence Function*

Hahn [18] derives the efficient influence function (EIF) of $\beta = \beta_1 - \beta_0$ as

$$\phi(O, P) = \left(\frac{A}{g}(Y - Q^1) + Q^1 - \beta_1\right) - \left(\frac{1 - A}{1 - g}(Y - Q^0) + Q^0 - \beta_0\right) \quad (11)$$

To study the asymptotic behaviour of nAIPW, we write the scaled difference

$$\sqrt{n}(\hat{\beta}-\beta) = \frac{1}{\sqrt{n}}\sum_{i=1}^{n}\phi(O_i,P) - \frac{1}{\sqrt{n}}\sum_{i=1}^{n}\phi(O_i,\hat{P}_n) + \sqrt{n}(P_n-P)[\phi(O_i,\hat{P}_n)-\phi(O_i,P)] - \sqrt{n}R(P,\hat{P}_n), \quad (12)$$

where the first term is a normal distribution by the central limit theorem, and the third and fourth terms are controlled if the class of functions are Donsker and standard smoothing conditions are satisfied ([9,23], Theorem 19.26). If the nuisance parameters are not Donsker, data splitting and cross-fitting guarantees plus the regulatory conditions are needed to control these two terms [1,9]. It is unclear, however, how the second term behaves, i.e.,

$$-\frac{1}{\sqrt{n}}\phi(O,\hat{P}_n) = -\frac{1}{\sqrt{n}}\sum_{i=1}^{n}\left[\frac{A_i}{g_i}(Y_i-\hat{Q}_i^1) - \frac{1-A_i}{1-g_i}(Y_i-\hat{Q}_i^0) + \hat{Q}_i^1 - \hat{Q}_i^0\right] - \hat{\beta}, \quad (13)$$

where $\hat{\beta}=\beta(\hat{P}_n)$, as it contains data-adaptive nuisance parameter estimations. There are different tricks to get rid of this term. One method is the one-step method in which we move this term to the left to create a new estimator which is exactly the same as the AIPW estimator with known propensity scores:

$$\sqrt{n}(\hat{\beta}+\frac{1}{n}\phi(O,\hat{P}_n)-\beta) = \sqrt{n}\Big(\frac{1}{n}\sum_{i=1}^{n}\left[\frac{A_i}{g_i}(Y_i-\hat{Q}_i^1) - \frac{1-A_i}{1-g_i}(Y_i-\hat{Q}_i^0) + \hat{Q}_i^1 - \hat{Q}_i^0\right] - \beta\Big). \quad (14)$$

Another trick is to let this term vanish which results in estimating equations whose solution is exactly the same as the one-step estimator. The targetted learning strategy is to manipulate the data generating process which results in a different estimator [8,19] (which we do not study here).

The requirement in the above estimator is that the propensity score is known, which is unrealistic. In reality, this quantity should be estimated using the data. However, replacing g with a data-adaptive estimator changes the remainder term in (12) that needs certain assumptions to achieve asymptotic properties such as consistency. We replace g and $1-g$ in (14) by $\hat{h}^1$ and $\hat{h}^0$, respectively, which provides a more general view of the above one-step estimator.

4.3. Doubly Robustness and Rate Doubly Robustness Properties of GDR

One of the appealing properties of AIPW is its doubly robust property which partially relaxes the restrictions of IPW and SR which require the consistency of the treatment and outcome models, respectively. This property is helpful when the first-step algorithms are $\sqrt{n}$-consistent. The following theorem states that the nAIPW estimator (5) actually possesses the doubly robustness property.

Theorem 1 (nAIPW Double Robustness). *The DR estimator* (5) *is consistent if* $\hat{Q}^k \xrightarrow{p} Q^k$, $k=0,1$ *or* $\hat{g} \xrightarrow{p} g$.

The proof is left to the appendix. Theorem 1 is useful when we *a priori* knowledge about the propensity scores (such as in the experimental studies) or we estimate the propensity scores with $\sqrt{n}$-rate converging algorithms. In practice, however, the correct specification is infeasible in the observational data, but $\sqrt{n}$-rate algorithms such as parametric models, generalized additive models (GAMs) or the models that assume sparsity might be used [25].

This is restrictive and these model assumptions might not hold in practice which is why non-parametric ML algorithms such as NNs are used. As mentioned before, the NN we utilize here does not offer a $\sqrt{n}$-consistent prediction model in the first step of the estimation [1]. This reduces the usefulness of the double robustness property of the GDR estimator when using complex ML algorithms. A more useful property when using complex ML algorithms is the *rate double robustness (RDR)* property [26]. RDR does not require either of the prediction models to be $\sqrt{n}$-consistent; it suffices that they are consistent at any rate but together become $\sqrt{n}$-consistent; that is, if the propensity score and outcome model are consistent at n^{r_A} and n^{r_Y}, respectively ($r_Y, r_A < 0$), we must have $r_A + r_Y = \frac{1}{2}$. To see that the DR has this property (as does DR [25]), note that the remainder (12) can be written as

$$- \sqrt{n}R(P, \hat{P}_n) = \sqrt{n}\mathbb{E}\Big[(\frac{g}{\hat{h}^1} - 1)(Q^1 - \hat{Q}^1)\Big] + \sqrt{n}\mathbb{E}\Big[(\frac{1-g}{\hat{h}^0} - 1)(Q^0 - \hat{Q}^0)\Big], \quad (15)$$

which, by the Hölder inequality, is upper bounded:

$$- \sqrt{n}R(P, \hat{P}_n) \leq \left[\mathbb{E}\Big[\frac{g}{\hat{h}^1} - 1\Big]^2\right]^{\frac{1}{2}} \left[\mathbb{E}\Big[Q^1 - \hat{Q}^1\Big]^2\right]^{\frac{1}{2}} + \left[\mathbb{E}\Big[\frac{1-g}{\hat{h}^0} - 1\Big]^2\right]^{\frac{1}{2}} \left[\mathbb{E}\Big[Q^0 - \hat{Q}^0\Big]^2\right]^{\frac{1}{2}} \quad (16)$$

Making the standard assumptions that

$$\begin{aligned} &\left[\mathbb{E}\Big[g - \hat{h}^k\Big]^2\right]^{\frac{1}{2}} \left[\mathbb{E}\Big[Q^k - \hat{Q}^k\Big]^2\right]^{\frac{1}{2}} = o(n^{-\frac{1}{2}}), \quad k = 0, 1, \\ &\mathbb{E}\Big[g - \hat{h}^k\Big]^2 = o(1), \quad \mathbb{E}\Big[Q^k - \hat{Q}^k\Big]^2 = o(1), \quad k = 0, 1, \\ &\text{Empirical Positivity} \quad c_1 < \hat{h}^k < 1 - c_2, \text{ for some } c_1, c_2 > 0, \end{aligned} \quad (17)$$

implies

$$- \sqrt{n}R(P, \hat{P}_n) = o(n^{-\frac{1}{2}}), \quad (18)$$

that is, the GDR has the rate double robustness property.

The assumptions in (17) are less restrictive than needing at least one of the prediction models to be $\sqrt{n}$-consistent for the double robust property [19,25]. This means that the outcome and propensity score models can be at least as fast as $o(n^{-\frac{1}{4}})$ (which is an attainable generalization bound for many complex machine learning algorithms [9]), and the GDR estimator is still consistent. Farrell et al. [1] proves that two neural networks without regularization (except the one imposed by the stochastic gradient descent optimization) satisfy such bounds and can provide a convenient first-step prediction algorithm (when they utilize the AIPW estimator and the cross-fitting strategy proposed by Chernozhukov et al. [9]).

In order for a special case of GDR estimator to outperform the AIPW estimator, we must have $Ah^1 \geq Ag$ and $(1-A)h^0 \geq (1-A)(1-g)$, in addition to conditions in (17). Note that these two conditions are satisfied for nAIPW; replacing h^1 and h^0 with $\hat{g}\hat{\mathbb{E}}\frac{A}{\hat{g}}$ and $(1-\hat{g})\hat{\mathbb{E}}\frac{1-A}{1-\hat{g}}$ can help stabilize the bias and variance magnitude and help shrink the remainder (15) to zero. The scenario analysis performed in Section 4.4 provides an insight about the reduction in the sensitivity to the violation of the empirical positivity assumption.

4.4. Robustness of nAIPW against Extreme Propensity Scores

There are two scenarios in which the empirical positivity is violated, where the probability of receiving the treatment for the people who are treated is 1, that is, $A_k = 1$ and $P(A_k = 1|W) = 1$ (or vice versa for the untreated group $A_k = 0$ and $P(A_k = 0|W) = 0$), and where there are a handful of treated subjects whose probability of receiving the treatment is 0, that is, $A_k = 1$ and $P(A_k = 1|W) = 0$ (and vice versa for the untreated group, that is, $A_k = 0$ and $P(A_k = 0|W) = 1$). Although the identifiability assumptions guarantee that such scenarios do not occur, in practice, extremely small or large probabilities similar to the second scenario above, that is, where there exists a treated individual who has a near-zero probability of receiving the treatment, can impact the performance of the estimators that involve propensity score weighting. For example, replacing h^1 with $\hat{g}$ and h^0 with $1-\hat{g}$ in practice can increase both the bias and variance of AIPW [8]. This can be seen by viewing the bias and variance of these weighting terms. As noted before, the AIPW and nAIPW add adjustments to the single robust estimator $\mathbb{E}Q^1 - Q^0$. The adjustments involve weightings $\frac{A}{g}$ or $\frac{A}{g\mathbb{E}\frac{A}{g}}$ to the residuals of Y and $Q^k, k = 0,1$. Under a correct specification of the propensity score g, these weights have the same expectations. The difference is in their variances:

$$\begin{aligned} Var(\frac{A}{g}) &= \frac{1}{g} - 1, \\ Var\Big(\frac{A}{g\mathbb{E}\frac{A}{g}}\Big) &= \frac{1}{\mathbb{E}^2\frac{A}{g}}(\frac{1}{g} - 1), \end{aligned} \tag{19}$$

under the correct specification of the propensity score g. By letting g tend to zero in violation of the empirical positivity assumption, it can be seen that the nAIPW is less volatile than the AIPW estimator. That is, the weights in AIPW might have a larger variance than those in nAIPW.

4.5. Scenario Analysis

A scenario analysis is performed to see how nAIPW stabilizes the estimator: Assume that the empirical positivity is violated, that is, there is at least an observation k where $A_k = 1$ where $\hat{g}_k$ is extremely close to zero, such as $\hat{g}_k = 10^{-s}$ for $s \gg 0$. AIPW will blow up in this case:

$$\begin{aligned} \beta_{1,AIPW} &= \frac{1}{n}\Big(10^s(Y_k^1 - Q_k^1) + \sum_{i\in I_{-k}^1} \frac{Y_i^1 - Q_i^1}{g_i}\Big) + \frac{1}{n}\sum_{i=1}^{n} Q_i^1, \\ \beta_{0,AIPW} &= \frac{1}{n}\Big(\sum_{i\in I^0} \frac{Y_i^0 - Q_i^0}{1-g_i}\Big) + \frac{1}{n}\sum_{i=1}^{n} Q_i^0, \end{aligned} \tag{20}$$

where $I^a = \{j : A_j = a\}$, $I_{-k}^a = \{j : A_j = a\}$, and subscripts $a = 1$ and $a = 0$ refer to the estimators of the first and the second components in ATE (1). However, nAIPW is robust against this empirical positivity violation:

$$\beta_{1,nAIPW} = \Big(\frac{Y_k^1 - Q_k^1}{10^{-s}(10^s + \sum_{j\neq k}\frac{A_j}{g_j})} + \sum_{i\in I_{-k}^1} \frac{Y_i^1 - Q_i^1}{g_i(10^s + \sum_{j\neq k}\frac{A_j}{g_j})}\Big) + \frac{1}{n}\sum_{i=1}^{n} Q_i^1, \tag{21}$$

and

$$\beta_{0,nAIPW} = \Big(\frac{0\times(Y_k^1 - Q_k^0)}{\star} + \sum_{i\in I_{-k}^0} \frac{Y_i^0 - Q_i^0}{(1-g_i)(\sum_{j=1}^{n}\frac{1-A_j}{1-g_j})}\Big) + \frac{1}{n}\sum_{i=1}^{n} Q_i^0. \tag{22}$$

Thus

$$\beta_{1,nAIPW} \approx \Big(\frac{Y_k^1 - Q_k^1}{1 + 10^{-s}(n-1)} + \sum_{i \in I_{-k}^1} \frac{Y_i^1 - Q_i^1}{g_i 10^s + g_i(n-1)} \Big) + \frac{1}{n} \sum_{i=1}^{n} Q_i^1, \tag{23}$$

The factor 10^s in (20) can blow up the AIPW if $10^s \gg n$ (and the outcome estimation is not close enough to the observer outcome), but this factor does not appear in the numerator of the nAIPW estimator. For such large factors, (23) can be simplified to

$$\beta_{1,nAIPW} \approx Y_k^1 - Q_k^1 + \frac{1}{n} \sum_{i=1}^{n} Q_i^1. \tag{24}$$

Thus, the extreme probability does not make $\beta_{1,nAIPW}$ blow up, but the adjustment to the $\beta_{1,SR}$ that accounts for confounding effects. The second factor $\beta_{0,nAIPW}$ is not impacted in this scenario.

Considering a scenario that there is another treated individual with extremely small probability, such as $\hat{g}_l = 10^{-t}$, such that, without loss of generality, $t > s \gg 0$, we will have:

$$\beta_{1,nAIPW} \approx \frac{Y_k^1 - Q_k^1}{1 + 10^{t-s} + 10^{-s}(n-2)} + \frac{Y_l^1 - Q_l^1}{1 + 10^{s-t} + 10^{-t}(n-2)} + \frac{1}{n} \sum_{i=1}^{n} Q_i^1. \tag{25}$$

Depending on the values s and t, one of the first two terms in (25) might vanish, but the estimator does not blow up. There is at most only a handful of treated individuals with extremely small probabilities and, based on the above observation, the nAIPW estimator does not blow up. That said, nAIPW might not sufficiently correct the β_{SR} for the confounding effects, although confounders have been taken into account in the calculation of β_{SR} to some extent.

The same observation can be made in the asymptotic variance of these estimators. This shows how extremely small probabilities for treated individuals (or extremely large probabilities for untreated individuals) can result in a biased and unstable estimator, while neither of the bias or variance of nAIPW suffer as much. Although not performed, the same observation can be made for the untreated individuals with extremely large probabilities.

The above scenario analysis indicates the bias and variance of nAIPW might go up in cases of the violation of empirical positivity, but it still is less biased and more stable than AIPW. The remainder term (15) is also more likely to be $o(n^{-\frac{1}{2}})$ in nAIPW versus AIPW as it contains k's where $A_k = 1$, $g_k \mathbb{E}_n \frac{A_k}{g_k} \geq g_k$.

5. Asymptotic Sampling Distribution of nAIPW

Replacing g in the denominator of the von Mises expansion (12) with the normalizing terms is enough to achieve the asymptotic distribution of the nAIPW and its asymptotic standard error. However, we can see that nAIPW is also the solution to (extended) estimating equations. The solution to the estimating equations is important as van der Vaart (Chapters 19 and 25) proves that under certain regulatory conditions, if the prediction models belong to the Donsker class, the solutions to Z-estimators are consistent and asymptotically normal ([23], Theorem 19.26). Thus, nAIPW that is the solution to a Z-estimator (also referred to an M-estimator) will inherit the consistency and asymptotic normality, assuming certain regulatory conditions and that the first-step prediction models belong to the Donsker class:

$$\mathbb{E}\left[\frac{A(Y^1 - Q^1)}{\gamma g} - \frac{(1-A)(Y^0 - Q^0)}{\lambda(1-g)} + (Q^1 - Q^0 - \beta)\right] = 0,$$
$$\mathbb{E}\left[\frac{A}{g} - \gamma\right] = 0, \quad (26)$$
$$\mathbb{E}\left[\frac{1-A}{1-g} - \lambda\right] = 0.$$

The Donsker class assumption prevents too complex algorithms in the first step, algorithms such as tree-based models, NNs, cross-hybrid algorithms or their aggregations [19,27]. The Donsker class assumption can be relaxed if sample splitting (or cross-fitting) is utilized and the target parameter is orthogonal [9]. In the next section we see that nAIPW is orthogonal and, thus, theoretically, we can relax the Donsker class assumption under certain smoothing regulatory conditions. Before seeing the orthogonality property of nAIPW, let us review the smoothing regularity conditions necessary for asymptotic normality. Let β be the causal parameter, $\eta \in T$ be the infinite dimensional nuisance parameters where T is a convex set with a norm. Additionally, let the score function $\phi : \mathbb{O} \times \mathcal{B} \times T \to \mathbb{R}$ be a measurable function, $\mathbb{O}$ be the measurable space of all random variables O with probability distribution $P \in \mathcal{P}_n$ and $\mathcal{B}$ be an open subset of $\mathbb{R}$ containing the true causal parameter. Let the sample $O = (O_1, O_2, ..., O_n)$ be observed and the set of probability measures $\mathcal{P}_n$ expand with sample size n. In addition, let $\beta \in \mathcal{B}$ be the solution to the estimating equation $\mathbb{E}\phi(\mathbb{O}, \beta, \eta) = 0$. The assumptions that guarantee that the second-step orthogonal estimator $\hat{\beta}$ is asymptotically normal are [9]: (1) β does not fall on the boundary of $\mathcal{B}$; (2) the map $(\beta, \eta) \to \mathbb{E}_P\phi(\mathbf{O}, \beta, \eta)$ is twice Gateauax differentiable (this holds by the positivity assumption). β is identifiable; (3) $\mathbb{E}_P\phi(\mathbf{O}, \beta, \eta)$ is smooth enough; (4) $\hat{\eta} \in \mathcal{T}$ with high probability and $\eta \in \mathcal{T}$. $\hat{\eta}$ converges to η_0 at least as fast as $n^{-\frac{1}{4}}$ (similar but slightly stronger than first two assumptions in (17)); (5) score function(s) $\phi(., \beta, \eta)$ has finite second moment for all $\beta \in \mathcal{B}$ and all nuisance parameters $\eta \in \mathcal{T}$; (6) the score function(s) $\phi(., \beta, \eta)$ is measurable; (7) the number of folds increases by sample size.

5.1. Orthogonality and the Regulatory Conditions

The orthogonality condition [9] is a property related to the estimating equations

$$\mathbb{E}\phi(\mathbf{O}, \beta, \eta) = 0. \quad (27)$$

We refer to an estimator drawn from the estimating Equation (27) as an orthogonal estimator.

Let $\eta \in T$, where T is a convex set with a norm. Additionally, let the score functions $\phi : \mathbb{O} \times \mathcal{B} \times T \to \mathbb{R}$ be a measurable function, $\mathbb{O}$ is measurable space of all random variables O with probability distribution $P \in \mathcal{P}_n$ and $\mathcal{B}$ is an open subset of $\mathbb{R}$ containing the true causal parameter. Let the sample $O = (O_1, O_2, ..., O_n)$ be observed and the set of probability measures $\mathcal{P}_n$ can expand with sample size n. The score function ϕ follows the Neyman orthogonality condition with respect to $\mathcal{T} \subseteq T$, if the Gateauax derivative operator exists for all $\epsilon \in [0, 1)$:

$$\partial_{\tilde{\eta}}\mathbb{E}_P\phi(\mathbf{O}, \beta_0, \tilde{\eta})\Big|_{\tilde{\eta}=\eta}[\tilde{\eta} - \eta] := \partial_\epsilon \mathbb{E}_P\phi(\mathbf{O}, \beta_0, \eta + \epsilon(\tilde{\eta} - \eta))\Big|_{\epsilon=0} = 0. \quad (28)$$

Chernozhukov et al. [24] presents a few examples of orthogonal estimating equations including the AIPW estimator (4). Utilizing cross-fitting, under standard regulatory conditions, the asymptotic normality of estimators with orthogonal estimating equations is guaranteed even if the nuisance parameters are estimated by ML algorithms not belonging to the Donsker class and without finite entropy conditions [24]. The regulatory conditions to be satisfied are (1) β does not fall on the boundary of $\mathcal{B}$; (2) the map $(\beta, \eta) \to \mathbb{E}_P\phi(\mathbf{O}, \beta, \eta)$

is twice Gateauax differentiable. β is identifiable; (3) $\mathbb{E}_P\phi(\mathbf{O},\beta,\eta)$ is smooth enough; (4) $\hat{\eta} \in \mathcal{T}$ with high probability and $\eta \in \mathcal{T}$. $\hat{\eta}$ converges to η_0 at least as fast as $n^{-\frac{1}{4}}$; (5) score function(s) $\phi(.,\beta,\eta)$ has finite second moment for all $\beta \in \mathcal{B}$ and all nuisance parameters $\eta \in \mathcal{T}$; (6) the score function(s) $\phi(.,\beta,\eta)$ is measurable; (7) the number of folds increases by sample size.

By replacing λ and γ in the first line of (26) with their solutions in the second and third equations:

$$\mathbb{E}_P\phi(\mathbf{O},\beta,Q^1,Q^0,g) = \mathbb{E}\left[\frac{A(Y^1-Q^1)}{g\mathbb{E}\frac{A}{g}} - \frac{(1-A)(Y^0-Q^0)}{(1-g)\mathbb{E}\frac{1-A}{1-g}} + (Q^1-Q^0-\beta)\right] = 0, \quad (29)$$

Implementing the orthogonality condition (28), it can be verified that nAIPW (5) is also an example of an orthogonal estimator. To see this, we apply the definition of orthogonality [9]:

$$\begin{aligned}
&\partial_\eta \mathbb{E}_P\phi(\mathbf{O},\beta,\eta)\Big|_{\eta=\eta_0}[\eta-\eta_0] = \\
&\partial_\eta \mathbb{E}_P\Big(Q^1 + \frac{A(Y^1-Q^1)}{g\mathbb{E}\frac{A}{g}} - Q^0 - \frac{(1-A)(Y^0-Q^0)}{(1-g)\mathbb{E}\frac{1-A}{1-g}} - \beta\Big)|_{\eta=\eta_0}[\eta-\eta_0] \\
&\propto \partial_\epsilon \mathbb{E}_P\Big(Q^1_\epsilon + \frac{A(Y^1-Q^1_\epsilon)}{g_\epsilon\mathbb{E}\frac{A}{g_\epsilon}} - Q^0_\epsilon - \frac{(1-A)(Y^0-Q^0_\epsilon)}{(1-g_\epsilon)\mathbb{E}\frac{1-A}{1-g_\epsilon}} - \beta\Big)|_{\epsilon=0} = \\
&\mathbb{E}\Big((\tilde{Q}^1-Q^1) + \frac{A}{g\mathbb{E}\frac{A}{g}}\big(-(\tilde{Q}^1-Q^1)\big) + A(Y-Q^1)a(g,\tilde{g}-g)\Big) - \\
&\mathbb{E}\Big((\tilde{Q}^0-Q^0) + \frac{1-A}{(1-g)\mathbb{E}\frac{1-A}{1-g}}\big(-(\tilde{Q}^0-Q^0)\big) + \\
&(1-A)(Y-Q^0)b(g,\tilde{g}-g)\Big) = 0, \quad (30)
\end{aligned}$$

where $Q^k_\epsilon = \epsilon\tilde{Q}^k + (1-\epsilon)Q^k$, $k=0,1$, and $g_\epsilon = \epsilon\tilde{g} + (1-\epsilon)g$, and for some functions a and b. The last equality is because $\mathbb{E}A(Y-Q^1)=0$, $\mathbb{E}(1-A)(Y-Q^0)=0$, $\mathbb{E}\frac{A}{g\mathbb{E}\frac{A}{g}}=1$ and $\mathbb{E}\frac{1-A}{(1-g)\mathbb{E}\frac{1-A}{1-g}}=1$, under correct specification of the propensity score g.

Thus, nAIPW is orthogonal, and by utilizing cross-fitting for the estimation, nAIPW is consistent and asymptotically normal, under certain regulatory conditions.

5.2. Asymptotic Variance of nAIPW

To evaluate the asymptotic variance of nAIPW, we employ the M-estimation theory [23,28]. For causal inference for M-estimators, the bootstrap for the estimation of causal estimator variance is not generally valid even if the nuisance parameter estimators are $\sqrt{n}$-convergent. However, sub-sampling m out of n observations [29] can be shown to be universally valid, provided $m \to \infty$ and $\frac{m}{n} \to 0$. In practice, however, we can face computational issues since nuisance parameters must be separately estimated (possibly with ML models) for each subsample/bootstrap sample.

The variance estimator of AIPW (4) is [7]

$$\begin{aligned}
&\hat{\sigma}^2_{AIPW} = \\
&\frac{1}{n^2}\sum_{i=1}^{n}\Big(\frac{A_iY_i - \hat{Q}^1_i(A_i-\hat{g}_i)}{\hat{g}_i} - \frac{(1-A_i)Y_i + \hat{Q}^0_i(A_i-\hat{g}_i)}{1-\hat{g}_i} - \hat{\beta}_{AIPW}\Big)^2 = \\
&\frac{1}{n^2}\sum_{i=1}^{n}\Big(\frac{A_i(y_i-\hat{Q}^1_i)}{\hat{g}_i} - \frac{(1-A_i)(y_i-\hat{Q}^0_i)}{1-\hat{g}_i} + \hat{\beta}_{SR} - \hat{\beta}_{AIPW}\Big)^2. \quad (31)
\end{aligned}$$

The theorem below states that the variance estimator of AIPW (31) can intuitively extend to calculate the variance estimator of nAIPW (5) by moving the denominator n^2 to the square term in the summation and replacing it with $\hat{g}\hat{\mathbb{E}}(\frac{A}{\hat{g}})$ or $(1-\hat{g})\hat{\mathbb{E}}(\frac{1-A}{1-\hat{g}})$ in the terms containing g and $1-g$ in the denominator, respectively.

Theorem 2. *The asymptotic variance of the nAIPW (5) is*

$$\hat{\sigma}^2_{nAIPW} = \sum_{i=1}^{n}\Big(\frac{A_i(y_i-\hat{Q}_i^1)w_i^{(1)}}{\sum_{j=1}^{n}A_jw_j^{(1)}} - \frac{(1-A_i)(y_i-\hat{Q}_i^0)w_i^{(0)}}{\sum_{j=1}^{n}(1-A_j)w_j^{(0)}} + \frac{1}{n}(\hat{\beta}_{SR}-\hat{\beta}_{nAIPW})\Big)^2, \quad (32)$$

where $\hat{Q}_i^k = \hat{Q}(k, W_i)$ *and* $\hat{g}_i = \hat{\mathbb{E}}[A_i|W_i]$.

The proof utilizing the estimating equation technique is straightforward and is left to Appendix A. The same result can be seen when deriving the estimator in the one-step method (see (12) and (14)). Since nAIPW is orthogonal, $\hat{\sigma}^2_{nAIPW}$ is consistent by applying the theories of [1,9], if the assumptions are met, cross-fitting is used, and the step 1 ML algorithms have the required convergence rates.

The above theorem states that the variance estimator of AIPW (31) can intuitively extend to calculate the variance estimator of nAIPW (5) by moving the denominator n^2 to the square term in the summation and replacing it with $\hat{g}\hat{\mathbb{E}}(\frac{A}{\hat{g}})$ or $(1-\hat{g})\hat{\mathbb{E}}(\frac{1-A}{1-\hat{g}})$ in the terms containing g and $1-g$ in the denominator, respectively. This is intuitive because, by the law of total probability, $\mathbb{E}$ the first two terms is n.

6. Monte Carlo Experiments

A Monte Carlo simulation study (with 100 iterations) was performed to compare AIPW and nAIPW estimators, where the dNN is used for the first-step prediction. There are a total of 2 case scenarios according to the size of the data. We fixed the sample sizes to be $n = 750$ and $n = 7500$, with the number of covariates being $p = 32$ and $p = 300$, respectively. The predictors include four types of covariates: The confounders, X_c, instrumental variables, X_{iv}, the outcome predictors, X_y, and the noise or irrelevant covariates, X_{irr}. Their sizes for the scenarios are $\#X_c = \#X_{iv} = \#X_y = \#X_{irr} = 8, 75$ and they are independent from each other and drawn from the multivariate normal (MVN) distribution as $X \sim \mathcal{N}(\mathbf{0}, \Sigma)$, with $\Sigma_{kj} = \rho^{j-k}$ and $\rho = 0.5$. The models to generate the treatment assignment and outcome were specified as

$$\begin{aligned} &A \sim Ber(\frac{1}{1+e^{-\eta}}), \text{with } \eta = f_a(X_c)\gamma_c + g_a(X_{iv})\gamma_{iv}, \\ &y = 3 + A + f_y(X_c)\gamma_c' + g_y(X_y)\gamma_y + \epsilon, \end{aligned} \quad (33)$$

and $\beta = 1$. The functions f_a, g_a, f_y, g_y select 20% of the columns and apply interactions and non-linear functions listed below (35). The strength of the instrumental variable and confounding effects were chosen as $\gamma_c, \gamma_c', \gamma_y \sim Unif(r_1, r_2)$ where $(r_1 = r_2 = 0.25)$, and $\gamma_{iv} \sim Unif(r_3, r_4)$ where $(r_3 = r_4 = 0.25)$.

The non-linearities are randomly selected from among the following functions:

$$\begin{aligned} l(x_1, x_2) &= e^{\frac{x_1 x_2}{2}} \\ l(x_1, x_2) &= \frac{x_1}{1+e^{x_2}} \\ l(x_1, x_2) &= (\frac{x_1 x_2}{10} + 2)^3 \\ l(x_1, x_2) &= (x_1 + x_2 + 3)^2 \\ l(x_1, x_2) &= g(x_1) \times h(x_2) \end{aligned} \quad (34)$$

where $g(x) = -2I(x \leq -1) - I(-1 \leq x \leq 0) + I(0 \leq x \leq 2) + 3I(x \geq 2)$, and $h(x) = -5I(x \leq 0) - 2I(0 \leq x \leq 1) + 3I(x \geq 1)$, or $g(x) = I(x \geq 0)$ and $h(x) = I(x \geq 1)$.

The networks' activation function is rectified linear unit (ReLU), with 3 hidden layers as large as the input size (p), with L_1 regularization and batch size equal to $3 * p$ and 200 epochs. The adaptive moment estimation (Adam) optimizer [30] with learning rate 0.01 and momentum 0.95 was used to estimate the network's parameters, including the causal parameter (ATE).

Simulation Results

The oracle estimations are plotted in all the graphs to compare the real-life situations with the truth. In almost all the scenarios we cannot obtain perfect causal effect estimation and inference.

Figure 1 shows the distribution of AIPW and nAIPW for different hyperparameter settings of NNs. The nAIPW estimator outperforms AIPW in almost all the scenarios. As the AIPW gives huge values in some simulation iterations, the log of the estimation is taken in Figure 1.

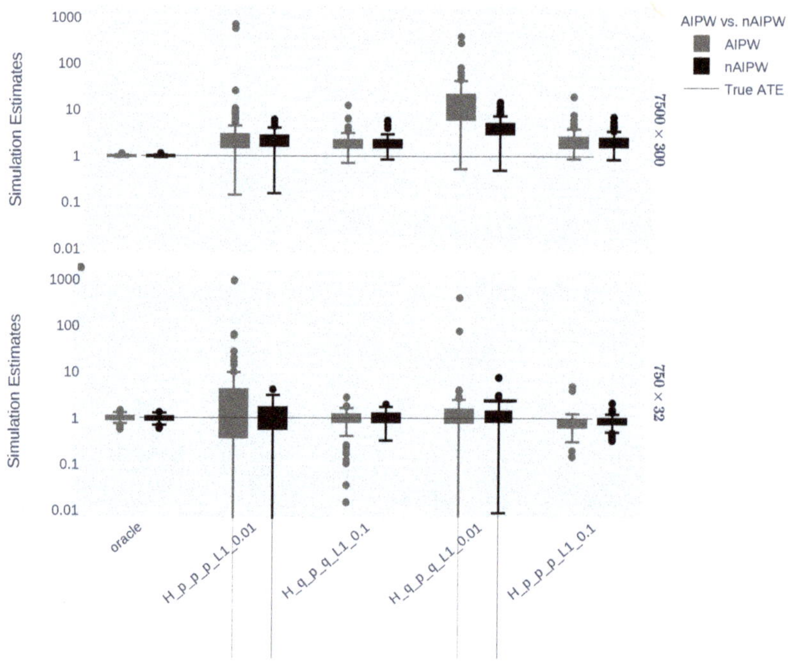

Figure 1. The distribution of log of the estimated AIPW and nAIPW in the 100 simulated iterations. The performance of nAIPW is clearly superior to the performance of AIPW as it is less dispersed and is more stable in terms of different hyperparameter settings. p is either 32 or 300 for the small or large datasets and $q \approx \frac{p}{10}$, that is, 3 or 30.

We also compare the estimators in different scenarios with bias, variance and their tradeoff measures:

$$\begin{aligned}
&\text{Bias} \quad \hat{\delta} = \beta - \frac{1}{m}\sum_{j=1}^{m}\hat{\beta}_j \\
&\text{MC std} \quad \hat{\sigma}_{MC} = \sqrt{\frac{1}{m}\sum_{j=1}^{m}(\hat{\beta}_j - \hat{\mu})^2} \\
&\text{MC RMSE} \quad RMSE = \sqrt{\hat{\sigma}_{MC}^2 + \hat{\delta}^2} \\
&\text{Asymptotic StdErr} \quad \hat{\sigma}_{SE} = \frac{1}{m}\sum_{j=1}^{m}\hat{\sigma}_j,
\end{aligned} \tag{35}$$

where $\beta = 1$, with $\hat{\beta}_j$s being the AIPW or nAIPW estimations in the jth simulation round, $\hat{\mu} = \frac{1}{m}\sum_{j=1}^{m}\hat{\beta}_j$ and $m = 100$ being the number of simulation rounds and $\hat{\sigma}$ being the square root of (31) or (32).

Figure 2 demonstrates the bias, MC standard deviation (MC std) and the root mean square error (RMSE) of AIPW and nAIPW estimators for the scenarios where $n = 750$ and $n = 7500$, and for four hyperparameter sets (L_1 regularization and width of the dNN). In general, in each figure of the panel, the hyperparameter scenarios in the left imply a more complex model (with less regularization or a narrower network). In these graphs, the lower the values, the better the estimator. For the smaller data size $n = 750$ in the left three panels, the worst results are attributed to AIPW when there is the least regularization and the hidden layers are as wide as the number of inputs. To have more clear plots for comparison, we skipped plotting the upper bounds as they were large numbers; the lower bounds are enough to show the significance of the results. In the scenarios where there are smaller numbers of hidden neurons with 0.01 L_1 regularization, the bias, variance and their tradeoff (here measured by RMSE) are more stable. By increasing the L_1 regularization, these measures go down which indicates the usefulness of regularization and AIPW normalization for causal estimation and inference. Almost the same pattern is seen for the larger size ($n = 7500$) scenario, except for the bump in all the three measures in the hyperparameter scenario where regularization remains the same ($L_1 = 0.01$) and the numbers of neurons in the first and last hidden layers are small too. In all three measures of bias, standard deviation and RMSE, nAIPW is superior to AIPW, or at least there is no statistically significant difference between AIPW and nAIPW.

We have noted that the results of the step 1 NN architecture without L_1 regularization are too unstable and cannot be visually presented in the graphs. To avoid that, we have allowed a span of values for the L_1 regularization strengths: $L_1 = 0.01$ and $L_1 = 0.1$. The former case is close to no regularization. So, if the results of the latter are better than the former's, this is evidence that enough L_1 must be imposed.

Figure 3 illustrates how the theoretical standard error formulas perform in MC experiments, and how accurately they estimate the MC standard deviations. In these two graphs, smaller does not necessarily imply superiority. In fact, the best results will be achieved as long as the confidence intervals of asymptotic SEs and MC SDs intersect. In the left two scenarios where the NN's complexity is high, the MC std and SE are far from each other. Additionally, in the hyperparameter scenarios where both the width of the NNs is small and regularization is higher, the MC std and SE are well separated. The scenario with largest regularization and wide NN architecture seems to the best scenario. That said, none of the scenarios confirm the consistency of SEs, which would likely also result in low coverage probability of the resulting confidence intervals.

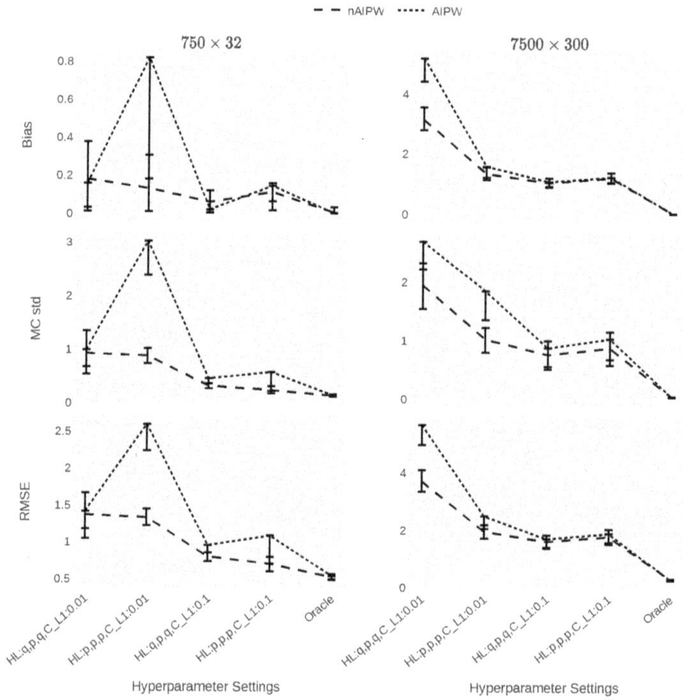

Figure 2. The bias, MC standard error and the root mean square error of the AIPW and nAIPW estimators for different data sizes and NN hyperparameters (L_1 regularization and width of the network). p is either 32 or 300 for the small or large datasets and $q \approx \frac{p}{10}$, that is, 3 or 30. The estimates are capped at -10 and 10.

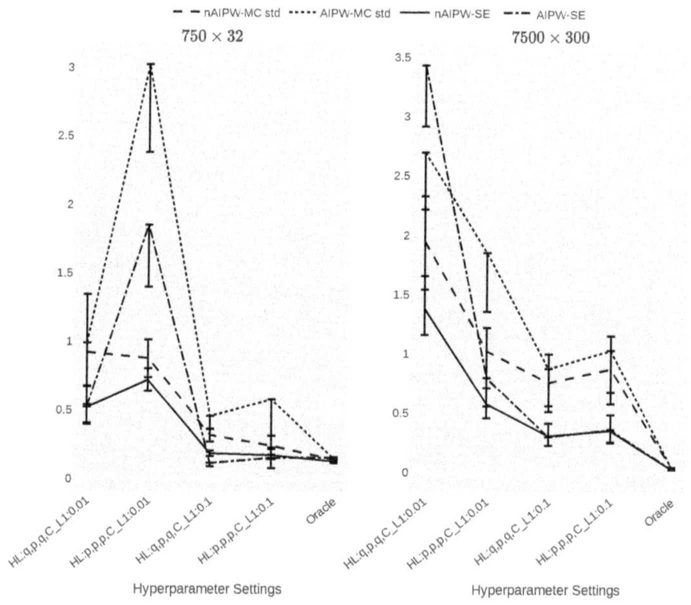

Figure 3. The MC standard deviation and the standard error of the AIPW and nAIPW estimators for different data sizes and NN hyperparameters (L_1 regularization and width of the network).

7. Application: Food Insecurity and BMI

The Canadian Community Health Survey (CCHS) is a cross-sectional survey that collects data related to health status, health care utilization and health determinants for the Canadian population in multiple cycles. The 2021 CCHS covers the population 12 years of age and over living in the ten provinces and the three territorial capitals. Excluded from the survey's coverage are: Persons living on reserves and other Aboriginal settlements in the provinces and some other sub-populations that altogether represent less than 3% of the Canadian population aged 12 and over. Examples of modules asked in most cycles are: General health, chronic conditions, smoking and alcohol use. For the 2021 cycle, thematic content on food security, home care, sedentary behavior and depression, among many others, was included. In addition to the health component of the survey are questions about respondent characteristics such as labor market activities, income and socio-demographics.

In this article, we use the CCHS dataset to investigate the causal relationship of food insecurity and body mass index (BMI). Other gathered information in the CCHS is used which might contain potential confounders, y-predictors and instrumental variables. The data are from a survey and need special methods such as the resampling or bootstrap methods to estimate the standard errors. However, here, we use the data to illustrate the utilization of a dNN on the causal parameters in the case of empirical positivity violation. In order to reduce the amount of variability in the data, we have focused on the sub-population 18–65 years of age.

Figure 4 shows the ATE estimates and their 95% asymptotic confidence intervals with nIPW, DR and nDR methods, with four different neural networks which vary in terms of width and strength of L_1 regularization. The scenario that results in the largest R^2 (as a measure of outcome prediction performance) outperforms the other scenarios. The scenario that results in the largest AUC (as a measure of treatment model performance) results in the largest confidence intervals. This is because of more extreme propensity scores in this scenario. It is worth noting that the normalized IPW has smaller confidence intervals as compared to AIPW. However, as we do not know the truth about the ATE in this dataset, we can never know which estimator outperforms the other. To gain insight about this using the input matrix of this data, we simulated multiple treatments and outcomes with small to strong confounders and IVs and compared AIPW and nAIPW. In virtually all of them, the nAIPW is the best one. We do not present these results in this paper, but they can be provided to readers upon request.

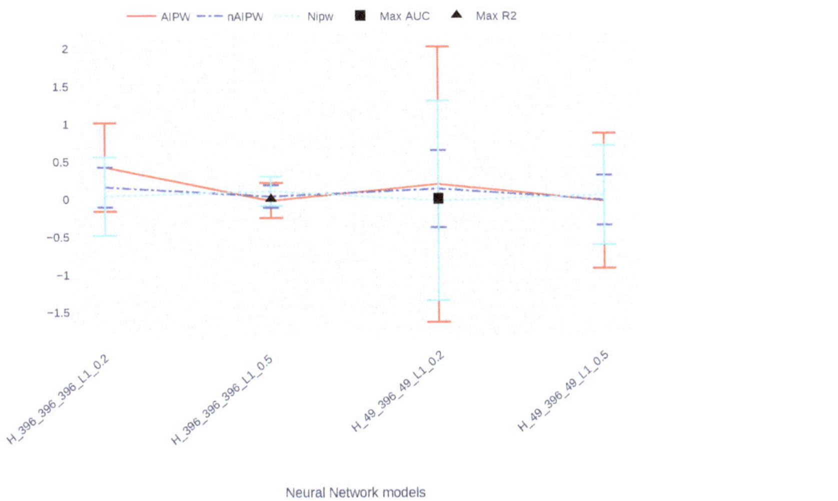

Figure 4. The ATE estimates and their asymptotically calculated 95% confidence intervals with NIPW, AIPW and nAIPW methods.

8. Discussion

Utilizing machine learning algorithms such as NNs in the first-step estimation process is comforting as the concerns with regard to the non-linear relationships between the confounders and the treatment and outcome are addressed. However, there is no free lunch, and using NNs has its own caveats including theoretical as well as numerical challenges. Farrell et al. [1] addressed the theoretical concerns where they calculated the generalization bounds when two separate NNs are used to model the treatment and the outcome. However, they did not use or take into account regularization techniques such as L_1 or L_2 regularization. As NNs are complex algorithms, they provide perfect prediction for the treatment when the predictors are strong enough (or might overfit). Through Monte Carlo (MC) simulations, we illustrated that causal estimation and inference with double NNs can fail without the usage of regularization techniques such as L_1 and/or extreme propensity scores are not taken care of. If L_1 regularization is not used, the normalization of the AIPW estimator (i.e., nAIPW) is advised to be employed as it dilutes the extreme predictions of the propensity score model and provides better bias, variance and RMSE. Our scenario analysis also showed that in the case of violation of the empirical positivity assumption in AIPW, normalization helps avoid blowing up the estimator (and standard error), but might be ineffective in taking into account confounding effects for some observations.

We note that the nAIPW estimator cannot perform better when the empirical positivity is violated as compared to when it is not. However, when the empirical positivity is violated, nAIPW can perform better than AIPW. If the empirical positivity is not violated, our results indicated that AIPW outperforms nAIPW.

An alternative estimator might be trimming the propensity scores to avoid extreme values. However, the causal effect estimator will no longer be consistent and there is no determined method for where to trim. We hypothesize that $\hat{h}^1 = \hat{g}\hat{\mathbb{E}}\frac{A}{\hat{g}} \times I(\hat{g} \in (0,\epsilon)) + \hat{g} \times I(\hat{g} \in (\epsilon,1))$ and $\hat{h}^0 = (1-\hat{g})\hat{\mathbb{E}}\frac{1-A}{1-\hat{g}} \times I(\hat{g} \in (1-\epsilon,1)) + (1-\hat{g}) \times I(\hat{g} \in (0,1-\epsilon))$ where $\epsilon = \frac{1}{n}$ will result in a consistent estimator, making the right assumptions, and will outperform both AIPW and nAIPW in the case of the empirical positivity violation. We will study this hypothesis in a future article.

Another reason why NNs without regularization fail in the causal estimation and inference is that the networks are not targeted, and are not directly designed for these tasks. NNs are complex algorithms with strong predictive powers. This does not accurately serve the purpose of causal parameter estimation, where the empirical positivity assumption can be violated if strong confounders and/or instrumental variables [22] exist in the data. Ideally, the network should target the confounders and should be able to automatically limit the strength of predictors so that the propensity scores are not extremely close to 1 or 0. This was not investigated in this article and a solution to this problem is postponed to another study.

In Section 7, we applied the asymptotic standard errors of both AIPW and nAIPW, where the latter achieves smaller standard errors. That said, we acknowledge the fact that the asymptotic standard errors when using complex ML are not reliable and, in fact, they underestimate the calculated MC standard deviations, as illustrated in the simulations Section 6. This is partly because of the usage of complex algorithms such as NNs for estimation of the nuisance parameters in the first step. Further, the asymptotic distributions of the estimators are not symmetric (and thus are not normal). However, nAIPW is more symmetric than AIPW, according to the simulations, while both estimators suffer from outliers. We will investigate the reasons and possible remedies for both the asymptotic distribution and standard errors of the estimators in a future paper. The consistency of the variance of nAIPW (and AIPW) relies on meeting the assumptions. More investigations are needed on how to achieve consistent and asymptotically normal estimators for ATE with a consistent variance estimator. Potential avenues can include proposing alternative estimators or improving the step 1 ML algorithms.

Author Contributions: Data curation, M.R.; Formal analysis, M.R.; Investigation, M.R.; Methodology, M.R. and O.S.; Project administration, M.R. and O.S.; Resources, M.R.; Software, M.R.; Supervision, O.S.; Validation, M.R. and O.S.; Visualization, M.R.; Writing—original draft, M.R.; Writing—review & editing, O.S. All authors have read and agreed to the published version of the manuscript.

Funding: The work of Olli Saarela was supported by a Discovery Grant from the Natural Sciences and Engineering Research Council of Canada.

Data Availability Statement: The simulated data can be regenerated using the codes, which can be provided to the interested user via an email request to the correspondence author. The CCHS data is not publicly available and only the authorized people can access and perform analyses on it.

Conflicts of Interest: The authors declare no conflict of interest.

Appendix A

First, let us review the proof sketch of the AIPW double robustness:
(3) can be consistently estimated by

$$\hat{\beta}_{AIPW} = \frac{1}{n}\sum_{i=1}^{n}\Bigg[\Big(\frac{A_iY_i - \hat{Q}(1,W_i)(A_i - \hat{\mathbb{E}}[A_i|W_i])}{\hat{\mathbb{E}}[A_i|W_i]}\Big) - \Big(\frac{(1-A_i)Y_i + \hat{Q}(0,W_i)(A_i - \hat{g}_i)}{1-\hat{\mathbb{E}}[A_i|W_i]}\Big)\Bigg] = \frac{1}{n}\sum_{i=1}^{n}\Bigg([\frac{A_i}{\hat{g}_i} - \frac{1-A_i}{1-\hat{g}_i}]y_i - \frac{A_i - \hat{g}_i}{\hat{g}_i(1-\hat{g}_i)}[(1-\hat{g}_i)\hat{Q}_i^1 + \hat{g}_i\hat{Q}_i^0]\Bigg) = \frac{1}{n}\sum_{i=1}^{n}\Big(\frac{A_i(y_i - \hat{Q}_i^1)}{\hat{g}_i} - \frac{(1-A_i)(y_i - \hat{Q}_i^0)}{1-\hat{g}_i}\Big) + \frac{1}{n}\sum_{i=1}^{n}(\hat{Q}_i^1 - \hat{Q}_i^0) \quad \text{(A1)}$$

The second formula guarantees the consistency of AIPW if $\hat{g}$ is consistent, and the third expression shows that the consistency of $\hat{Q}_i^0$ and $\hat{Q}_i^1$ is consistent.

Theorem A1 (nAIPW double robustness). *Let the nAIPW estimator of risk difference be*

$$\hat{\beta}_{nAIPW} = \hat{\mathbb{E}}(\hat{Q}^1 - \hat{Q}^0) + \hat{\mathbb{E}}\Big(\frac{A(Y - \hat{Q}^1)}{\hat{g}\hat{\mathbb{E}}[\frac{A}{\hat{g}}]} - \frac{(1-A)(Y-\hat{Q}^0)}{(1-\hat{g})\hat{\mathbb{E}}[\frac{1-A}{1-\hat{g}}]}\Big). \quad \text{(A2)}$$

Then, $\hat{\beta}_{nAIPW}$ is a consistent estimator of β if $\hat{g} \xrightarrow{p} g$ or $\hat{Q}^k \xrightarrow{p} Q^k$, $k = 0, 1$.

Proof. From (A2), $\hat{\beta}_{nAIPW}$ is a consistent estimator of β if $\hat{Q}_i^0$ and $\hat{Q}_i^1$ are consistent. This is because the first term $\hat{\mathbb{E}}(\hat{Q}^1 - \hat{Q}^0)$ converges to β, while the second term tends to zero.

By re-expressing (A2), the other argument is clear. Letting $\hat{w}^1 = \hat{\mathbb{E}}[\frac{A}{\hat{g}}]$ and $\hat{w}^0 = \hat{\mathbb{E}}[\frac{1-A}{1-\hat{g}}]$, we have:

$$\hat{\beta}_{nAIPW} = \frac{1}{n}\sum_{i=1}^{n}\Bigg([\frac{A_i}{\hat{g}_i\hat{w}_i^1} - \frac{1-A_i}{(1-\hat{g}_i)\hat{w}_i^0}]y_i\Bigg) + \hat{\mathbb{E}}\Big(\hat{Q}^1 - \hat{Q}^0 - \frac{A_i\hat{Q}^1}{\hat{g}\hat{w}^1} + \frac{(1-A_i)\hat{Q}^0}{(1-\hat{g})\hat{w}^0}\Big) = \frac{1}{n}\sum_{i=1}^{n}\Bigg([\frac{A_i}{\hat{g}_i\hat{w}_i^1} - \frac{1-A_i}{(1-\hat{g}_i)\hat{w}_i^0}]y_i - \hat{Q}_i^1(A_i - \hat{g}_i\hat{w}_i^1) + \hat{Q}_i^0(1 - A_i - (1-\hat{g}_i)\hat{w}_i^0)\Bigg) \quad \text{(A3)}$$

The first expression in (A3) is the same as the nIPW estimator which is a consistent estimator of β [7]. Now, under the consistency of $\hat{g}$, the second term tends to zero, as $\hat{w}_1 \xrightarrow{p} 1$ and $\hat{w}_0 \xrightarrow{p} 1$.

In the theorem below, it is shown that there is an M-estimation equivalent to β_{nAIPW} and w^1 and w^0. This, plus the continuous mapping theorem, proves that $\sum_{i=1}^{n} \frac{A_i}{\hat{g}_i}$ converges in probability to n if $\hat{g} \xrightarrow{p} g$.

□

Theorem A2. *The asymptotic variance of the nAIPW (5) is*

$$\hat{\sigma}^2_{nAIPW} = \sum_{i=1}^{n}\Big(\frac{A_i(y_i - \hat{Q}_i^1)w_i^{(1)}}{\sum_{j=1}^{n} A_j w_j^{(1)}} - \frac{(1-A_i)(y_i - \hat{Q}_i^0)w_i^{(0)}}{\sum_{j=1}^{n}(1-A_j)w_j^{(0)}} + \frac{1}{n}(\hat{\beta}_{SR} - \hat{\beta}_{nAIPW})\Big)^2, \quad \text{(A4)}$$

where $\hat{Q}_i^k = \hat{Q}(k, W_i)$ *and* $\hat{g}_i = \hat{\mathbb{E}}[A_i|W_i]$.

Proof. Let us define a few notations first:

$$\begin{aligned} q &= Q^1 - Q^0, \\ g &= \mathbb{E}[A|W], \\ f &= y - Q^1, \\ h &= y - Q^0, \\ v &= \frac{A}{g}, \\ u &= \frac{1-A}{1-g}. \end{aligned} \quad \text{(A5)}$$

With this set of notations, the *nAIPW* estimator (5) can be written as

$$\hat{\beta}_{nAIPW} = \sum_{i=1}^{n}\Big(\frac{v_i f_i}{\sum_{j=1}^{n} v_j} - \frac{u_i h_i}{\sum_{j=1}^{n} u_j} + \frac{q_i}{n}\Big), \quad \text{(A6)}$$

Following the methods in [28], to find an estimating equation whose solution is $\hat{\beta}_{nAIPW}$, we introduce two more estimating equations. Employing the M-estimation theory, we will prove that nAIPW is asymptotically normal, and we will calculate its standard error.

It can be seen that (A6) is not a solution to an M-estimator directly. However, by defining two more parameters and concatenating their estimating equations, we obtain 3-dim multivariate estimating equations:

$$\begin{aligned} \sum_{i=1}^{n}\Big(\frac{v_i f_i}{\gamma} - \frac{u_i h_i}{\lambda} + \frac{1}{n}(q_i - \beta)\Big) &= 0, \\ \sum_{i=1}^{n}\Big(v_i - \frac{\gamma}{n}\Big) &= 0, \\ \sum_{i=1}^{n}\Big(u_i - \frac{\lambda}{n}\Big) &= 0. \end{aligned} \quad \text{(A7)}$$

To ease the calculations, we modify the first estimating equation with an equivalent one, but the results will not differ:

$$\sum_{i=1}^{n} \lambda v_i f_i - \gamma u_i h_i + \frac{\gamma\lambda}{n}(q_i - \beta) = 0,$$
$$\sum_{i=1}^{n} v_i - \frac{\gamma}{n} = 0, \tag{A8}$$
$$\sum_{i=1}^{n} u_i - \frac{\lambda}{n} = 0.$$

By defining the following notations,

$$\psi = \begin{pmatrix} \phi \\ \eta \\ \Omega \end{pmatrix} = \begin{pmatrix} \lambda v f - \gamma u h + \frac{\gamma\lambda}{n}(q - \beta) \\ v - \frac{\gamma}{n} \\ u - \frac{\lambda}{n} \end{pmatrix},$$

we have $\sum_{i=1}^{n} \psi_i = 0$, or

$$\sum_{i=1}^{n} \phi_i, = 0,$$
$$\sum_{i=1}^{n} \eta_i = 0, \tag{A9}$$
$$\sum_{i=1}^{n} \Omega_i = 0.$$

The M-estimation theory implies that under regulatory conditions, the solutions to these estimating equations converge in distribution to a multivariate normal distribution:

$$\sqrt{n}\begin{pmatrix} \hat{\beta}_{nAIPW} \\ \hat{\gamma} \\ \hat{\lambda} \end{pmatrix} \sim MVN(\theta\,, \mathbf{I}^{-1}(\theta)\mathbf{B}(\theta)\mathbf{I}^{-1}(\theta)^T)$$

where

$$\theta = \begin{pmatrix} \beta \\ \gamma \\ \lambda \end{pmatrix},$$

$$\mathbf{I}(\theta) = -\mathbb{E}\frac{\partial\psi}{\partial\theta^T} = \frac{1}{n}\begin{pmatrix} \frac{\lambda\gamma}{n} & \mathbb{E}(uh - \frac{\lambda}{n}(q-\beta)) & -\mathbb{E}(vf + \frac{\gamma}{n}(q-\beta)) \\ 0 & \frac{1}{n} & 0 \\ 0 & 0 & \frac{1}{n} \end{pmatrix}, \tag{A10}$$

whose inverse is

$$\mathbf{I}^{-1}(\theta) = \frac{n}{\gamma\lambda}\begin{pmatrix} 1 & -n\mathbb{E}(uh - \lambda(q-\beta)) & n\mathbb{E}(vf + \frac{\gamma}{n}(q-\beta)) \\ 0 & \gamma\lambda & 0 \\ 0 & 0 & \gamma\lambda \end{pmatrix}, \tag{A11}$$

and,

$$\mathbf{B}(\theta) = \mathbb{E}\psi\psi^T = \begin{pmatrix} \mathbb{E}\phi^2 & \mathbb{E}\phi\eta & \mathbb{E}\phi\Omega \\ \mathbb{E}\phi\eta & \mathbb{E}\eta^2 & \mathbb{E}\eta\Omega \\ \mathbb{E}\phi\Omega & \mathbb{E}\eta\Omega & \mathbb{E}\Omega^2 \end{pmatrix}. \tag{A12}$$

In order to estimate the variance of $\hat{\beta}_{nAIPW}$, we do not need to calculate all entries of the variance–covariance matrix, only the first entry:

$$\frac{1}{n}(\frac{n^2}{(\gamma\lambda)^2})\begin{pmatrix}\mathbb{E}\phi^2+\epsilon & \star & \star\\ \star & \star & \star\\ \star & \star & \star\end{pmatrix}. \tag{A13}$$

The $\star$ entries are irrelevant to the calculation of variance of nAIPW and the term ϵ is a very long expression which involves terms converging to zero faster than the actual estimating Equation (A9) [19] (also verified by simulations):

$$\begin{aligned}\epsilon = &-\mathbb{E}\phi\eta(n\mathbb{E}uh+\lambda(\beta-q))+\mathbb{E}\phi\Omega(n\mathbb{E}vf-\gamma(\beta-q))-\\ &(n\mathbb{E}uh+\lambda(\beta-q))(-\mathbb{E}\eta^2(n\mathbb{E}uh+\lambda(\beta-q))+\mathbb{E}\eta\Omega(n\mathbb{E}vf-\gamma(\beta-q))+\\ &\mathbb{E}\phi\eta)+(n\mathbb{E}vf-\gamma(\beta-q))(-\mathbb{E}\eta\Omega(n\mathbb{E}uh+\lambda(\beta-q))+\\ &\mathbb{E}\Omega^2(n\mathbb{E}vf-\gamma(\beta-q))+\mathbb{E}\phi\Omega).\end{aligned} \tag{A14}$$

Further,

$$\sqrt{n}\begin{pmatrix}\hat{\beta}_{nAIPW}\\ \hat{\gamma}\\ \hat{\Omega}\end{pmatrix} \sim MVN(\theta\,,\,\hat{\mathbf{I}}^{-1}(\hat{\theta})\hat{\mathbf{B}}(\hat{\theta})\hat{\mathbf{I}}^{-1}(\hat{\theta})^T) \tag{A15}$$

where we replace $\mathbb{E}$ with sample averages in Expressions (A10)–(A12) and θ with their corresponding solutions to Equation (A8). Following this recipe, we obtain

$$\hat{\sigma}^2_{nAIPW} = \frac{1}{n}(\frac{n^2}{(\gamma\lambda)^2})\hat{\mathbb{E}}\phi^2+\hat{\epsilon} \approx \sum_{i=1}^{n}\Big(\frac{v_i f_i}{\hat{\gamma}}-\frac{u_i h_i}{\hat{\lambda}}+\frac{1}{n}q_i-\hat{\beta}_{nAIPW})\Big)^2, \tag{A16}$$

which is the same as (A4).

□

References

1. Farrell, M.H.; Liang, T.; Misra, S. Deep neural networks for estimation and inference: Application to causal effects and other semiparametric estimands. *arXiv* **2018**, arXiv:1809.09953.
2. Goodfellow, I.; Bengio, Y.; Courville, A.; Bengio, Y. *Deep Learning*; MIT Press: Cambridge, UK, 2016; Volume 1.
3. Cheng, X.; Khomtchouk, B.; Matloff, N.; Mohanty, P. Polynomial regression as an alternative to neural nets. *arXiv* **2018**, arXiv:1806.06850.
4. Xu, B.; Wang, N.; Chen, T.; Li, M. Empirical evaluation of rectified activations in convolutional network. *arXiv* **2015**, arXiv:1505.00853.
5. Yan, S.; Nguang, S.K.; Gu, Z. H_infinity Weighted Integral Event-Triggered Synchronization of Neural Networks With Mixed Delays. *IEEE Trans. Ind. Inform.* **2020**, *17*, 2365–2375. [CrossRef]
6. Robins, J.M.; Rotnitzky, A.; Zhao, L.P. Estimation of regression coefficients when some regressors are not always observed. *J. Am. Stat. Assoc.* **1994**, *89*, 846–866. [CrossRef]
7. Lunceford, J.K.; Davidian, M. Stratification and weighting via the propensity score in estimation of causal treatment effects: A comparative study. *Stat. Med.* **2004**, *23*, 2937–2960. [CrossRef]
8. Van der Laan, M.J.; Rose, S. *Targeted Learning: Causal Inference for Observational and Experimental Data*; Springer Science & Business Media: Cham, Switzerland, 2011.
9. Chernozhukov, V.; Chetverikov, D.; Demirer, M.; Duflo, E.; Hansen, C.; Newey, W.; Robins, J. Double/debiased machine learning for treatment and structural parameters. *Econom. J.* **2018**, *21*, C1–C68. [CrossRef]
10. Zhang, C.; Bengio, S.; Hardt, M.; Recht, B.; Vinyals, O. Understanding deep learning (still) requires rethinking generalization. *Commun. ACM* **2021**, *64*, 107–115. [CrossRef]
11. Myers, J.A.; Rassen, J.A.; Gagne, J.J.; Huybrechts, K.F.; Schneeweiss, S.; Rothman, K.J.; Joffe, M.M.; Glynn, R.J. Effects of adjusting for instrumental variables on bias and precision of effect estimates. *Am. J. Epidemiol.* **2011**, *174*, 1213–1222. [CrossRef]
12. Díaz, I. Doubly robust estimators for the average treatment effect under positivity violations: Introducing the *e*-score. *arXiv* **2018**, arXiv:1807.09148.
13. Horvitz, D.G.; Thompson, D.J. A generalization of sampling without replacement from a finite universe. *J. Am. Stat. Assoc.* **1952**, *47*, 663–685. [CrossRef]

14. Rubin, D.B. Using multivariate matched sampling and regression adjustment to control bias in observational studies. *J. Am. Stat. Assoc.* **1979**, *74*, 318–328.
15. Rosenbaum, P.R.; Rubin, D.B. The central role of the propensity score in observational studies for causal effects. *Biometrika* **1983**, *70*, 41–55. [CrossRef]
16. Rosenbaum, P.R.; Rubin, D.B. Constructing a control group using multivariate matched sampling methods that incorporate the propensity score. *Am. Stat.* **1985**, *39*, 33–38.
17. Busso, M.; DiNardo, J.; McCrary, J. New evidence on the finite sample properties of propensity score reweighting and matching estimators. *Rev. Econ. Stat.* **2014**, *96*, 885–897. [CrossRef]
18. Hahn, J. On the role of the propensity score in efficient semiparametric estimation of average treatment effects. *Econometrica* **1998**, *66*, 315–331. [CrossRef]
19. Hines, O.; Dukes, O.; Diaz-Ordaz, K.; Vansteelandt, S. Demystifying statistical learning based on efficient influence functions. *arXiv* **2021**, arXiv:2107.00681.
20. Słoczyński, T.; Wooldridge, J.M. A general double robustness result for estimating average treatment effects. *Econom. Theory* **2018**, *34*, 112–133. [CrossRef]
21. Scharfstein, D.O.; Rotnitzky, A.; Robins, J.M. Adjusting for nonignorable drop-out using semiparametric nonresponse models. *J. Am. Stat. Assoc.* **1999**, *94*, 1096–1120. [CrossRef]
22. Angrist, J.D.; Pischke, J.S. *Mostly Harmless Econometrics: An Empiricist's Companion*; Princeton University Press: Princeton, NJ, USA, 2008.
23. Van der Vaart, A.W. *Asymptotic Statistics*; Cambridge University Press: Cambridge, UK, 2000; Volume 3.
24. Chernozhukov, V.; Chetverikov, D.; Demirer, M.; Duflo, E.; Hansen, C.; Newey, W.K. *Double Machine Learning for Treatment and Causal Parameters*; Technical Report, Cemmap Working Paper; 2016. Available online: https://ifs.org.uk/uploads/cemmap/wps/cwp491616.pdf (accessed on 12 November 2021).
25. Farrell, M.H. Robust inference on average treatment effects with possibly more covariates than observations. *J. Econom.* **2015**, *189*, 1–23. [CrossRef]
26. Smucler, E.; Rotnitzky, A.; Robins, J.M. A unifying approach for doubly-robust l1 regularized estimation of causal contrasts. *arXiv* **2019**, arXiv:1904.03737.
27. Friedman, J.; Hastie, T.; Tibshirani, R. *The Elements of Statistical Learning*; Springer Series in Statistics; Springer: New York, NY, USA, 2001; Volume 1.
28. Stefanski, L.A.; Boos, D.D. The calculus of M-estimation. *Am. Stat.* **2002**, *56*, 29–38. [CrossRef]
29. Politis, D.N.; Romano, J.P. The stationary bootstrap. *J. Am. Stat. Assoc.* **1994**, *89*, 1303–1313. [CrossRef]
30. Kingma, D.P.; Ba, J. Adam: A method for stochastic optimization. *arXiv* **2014**, arXiv:1412.6980.

entropy

Article

Targeted L_1-Regularization and Joint Modeling of Neural Networks for Causal Inference

Mehdi Rostami * and Olli Saarela

Dalla Lana School of Public Health, University of Toronto, Toronto, ON M5T 3M7, Canada
* Correspondence: mehdi.rostamiforooshani@mail.utoronto.ca

Abstract: The calculation of the Augmented Inverse Probability Weighting (AIPW) estimator of the Average Treatment Effect (ATE) is carried out in two steps, where in the first step, the treatment and outcome are modeled, and in the second step, the predictions are inserted into the AIPW estimator. The model misspecification in the first step has led researchers to utilize Machine Learning algorithms instead of parametric algorithms. However, the existence of strong confounders and/or Instrumental Variables (IVs) can lead the complex ML algorithms to provide perfect predictions for the treatment model which can violate the positivity assumption and elevate the variance of AIPW estimators. Thus the complexity of ML algorithms must be controlled to avoid perfect predictions for the treatment model while still learning the relationship between the confounders and the treatment and outcome. We use two NN architectures with an L_1-regularization on specific NN parameters and investigate how their certain hyperparameters should be tuned in the presence of confounders and IVs to achieve a low bias-variance tradeoff for ATE estimators such as AIPW estimator. Through simulation results, we will provide recommendations as to how NNs can be employed for ATE estimation.

Keywords: causal Inference; instrumental variables; neural networks; doubly robust estimation; regularization

Citation: Rostami, M.; Saarela, O. Targeted L_1-Regularization and Joint Modeling of Neural Networks for Causal Inference. *Entropy* **2022**, *24*, 1290. https://doi.org/10.3390/e24091290

Academic Editor: Kateřina Hlaváčková-Schindler

Received: 2 August 2022
Accepted: 8 September 2022
Published: 13 September 2022

1. Introduction

There are generally two approaches to address causal inference in observational studies. The first one is to draw population-level causal inference which goes back at least to the 1970s [1]. The second is to draw conditional causal inference which has received attention more recently [2,3]. An example of a population-level causal parameter the average treatment effect (ATE),

$$\beta_{ATE} = \mathbb{E}[Y^1 - Y^0] = \mathbb{E}\big[\mathbb{E}[Y^1 - Y^0|W]\big]. \tag{1}$$

The quantity $\mathbb{E}[Y^1 - Y^0|W]$ is referred to as the conditional average treatment effect (CATE) [4–10]. CATE is NOT an individual-level causal parameter. The latter is impossible to estimate accurately unless both potential outcomes are observed for each individual (under parallel worlds!), or W contains all the varying factors that make the causal relationship deterministic, which are unlikely to hold in practice. That said, under certain assumptions, the counterfactual loss, the loss due to the absence of counterfactual outcome, can be upper bounded [11]. The present article focuses on the estimation of ATE which does not require those assumptions.

Through a number of attempts, researchers have utilized ML models for the causal parameter estimation [12–17]. While the ultimate goal of a ML algorithm is to predict the outcome of interest as accurately as possible, it does not optimally serve the main purpose of the causal parameter estimation. In fact, ML algorithms minimize some prediction loss containing the treatment or the observed outcome (and not counterfactual outcome) and without targeting any relevant predictor(s) such as confounding variables [18].

Including confounders for the estimation of ATE in observational studies avoids potential selection bias [19], however, in practice, we do not have a priori knowledge about the confounders and the ML algorithm minimizes the loss function without discriminating between the input covariates. In fact, the ML algorithm can successfully learn the linear and non-linear relationships between the confounders and the treatment and outcome, but at the same time, might learn from potential Instrumental Variables (IVs) present in the data as well (the variables that predict the treatment, but not the outcome). If there are strong confounders or IVs among the covariates, the predictions of treatments (i.e., the propensity scores) can become extreme (near zero or one) which in turn can make the estimates unstable. While possibly reducing the bias, the variance gets elevated at the same time. Less complex models, on the other hand, may suffer from large bias (underfitting) but can obtain more stable causal parameter estimation. This conflict between the necessary complexity in the model(s) and the bias-variance tradeoff motivates to develop ML algorithms for step 1 that provide a compromise between learning from confounders and IVs to entail a balance between the bias and variance of the causal parameter in step 2. In addition to a low bias-variance tradeoff, the asymptotic normality of the causal effect estimator is wanted for inferential statistics.

Chernozhukov et al. [16] investigated the asymptotic normality of orthogonal estimators of ATE (including Augmented Inverse Probability Weighting (AIPW)) when two separate ML algorithms model the treatment and outcome, referred to as the Double Machine Learning (DML). With the same objective, Farrell et al. [17] utilized two separate neural networks (we refer to as the double NN or dNN), without the usage of any regularization other than using the Stochastic Gradient Descent (SGD) for model optimization. SGD does impose some regularization but is insufficient to control the complexity of NN algorithms where strong predictors exist in the data [20]. Rostami and Saarela [20] experimentally showed that when AIPW is utilized, dNN performs poorly. The normalization of AIPW helps control both the bias and variance of the estimator. Further, they illustrated that imposing the L_1 regularization on all of the parameters (without targeting a specific set of input features) helps reduce the bias, variance, and Mean Square Error (MSE) of the ATE estimators up to some extent. Simulations indicated that when dNN is used, with or without regularization, the normalized AIPW (nAIPW) outperforms AIPW. For a comprehensive literature review on the doubly robust estimators (including AIPW) see Moosavi et al. [21].

The strategy of targeting a specific type of features can be designed in NN architectures along with the necessary optimization and regularization techniques. Flexible NN structures, optimizations and regularization techniques are easily programmed in deep learning platforms such as pytorch.

Shi et al. [22] proposes a neural network architecture, referred to as the DragonNet, that jointly models the treatment and outcome, in which a multi-tasking optimization technique is employed. In the DragonNet architecture, the interaction of the treatment and non-linear transformations of the input variables are considered. Chernozhukov et al. [23] uses the Riesz Representer [16] as the minimizer of a stochastic loss, which provides an alternative for the propensity score estimation, and aims to prevent the empirical consistency assumption violation issue [20]. Chernozhukov et al. [23] also use the joint modeling of the Riesz Representer and the outcome through multi-tasking, and they call their method auto Double Machine Learning (Auto-DML). Chernozhukov et al. [24] optimized an L_1 regularized loss function to estimate weights rather than estimating propensity scores and plugging them into the AIPW estimator. Chernozhukov et al. [25] proposed optimizing a minimax loss function for the same purpose. In this body of work, it is still unclear how to hyperparameter tune the chosen NN architecture for causal inference, especially for the ATE estimation.

Other techniques of feature selection before propensity score estimation have been proposed in the literature [26]. However, hard thresholding might ignore important information hidden in the features.

The objective of this research is to experimentally investigate how NN-type methods can be utilized for ATE estimation, and how the hyperparameters can be tuned to achieve the best bias-variance tradeoff for the ATE estimators. This is done in the presence of strong IVs and confounders. The papers cited above do not consider this general scenario.

In this research our goal is not any of the following: 1. We do not aim to compare NNs with other ML algorithms to see which ones outperform the others. By the no-free-lunch theorem, [27], there is no specific algorithm that can learn all relationships sufficiently well. Thus, it is expected that some ML algorithms are better in some scenarios and other algorithms in other scenarios. 2. We do not aim to study different types of causal parameters. 3. We do not aim to study different estimators of the Average Treatment Effect. 4. We do not aim to study feature selection or other types of methods that can prevent IVs to feed into the model of the treatment in the first step inference.

Throughout this research, we utilize nAIPW as it outperforms AIPW estimator in the presence of strong confounders and IVs [20]. To target the relevant inputs, we propose two methods. First, employing a type of L_1 regularization on top of the common L_1 regularization on all the network parameters. Second, we propose a joint model of the treatment and outcome in a Neural Network (jNN) architecture where we place both the treatment and outcome on the output layer of a multi-layer perceptron [28]. This NN architecture is appealing as it models the treatment and outcome simultaneously which can potentially target the relevant covariates that are predictive of both treatment and outcome (or confounder) and can mitigate or ignore the IVs' effects on the predictions. We will investigate if both or either of these ideas improves the bias-variance tradeoff of the causal effect estimator as compared to a dNN model.

In this research, the NN architecture that jointly models the treatment and outcome here referred to as jNN. The parameters or weights are estimated by minimizing a regularized multi-task loss which is the summation of the Cross-Entropy (for modeling the binary treatment) and MSE loss (for modeling the continuous outcome) [29]. Multi-task learning can help target the predictors of both treatment and outcome that are placed in the output layer, and also it helps to resist against over-fitting in case of many irrelevant inputs [30]. Other benefits of multi-task learning are listed in Section 2.2. Also, two types of L_1 regularization terms are used in order to dampen the instrumental variables and strong confounders.

To show the effectiveness of jNN and dNN, a thorough simulation study is performed and these methods are compared in terms of the number of confounders and IVs that are captured in each scenario, the prediction measures, and the bias and variance of causal estimators. To investigate whether our network targets confounders rather than IVs and also dampens the impact of strong confounders on the propensity scores, we calculate the bias-variance tradeoff of causal estimators (i.e., minimal MSE) utilizing the NN predictions; Low bias means the model has mildly learned from confounders and other types of covariates for the outcome, and low variance means the model has ignored IVs and has dampened strong confounders in the treatment model. Further, a comparison between the methods is made on the Canadian Community Health Survey (CCHS) dataset where the intervention/treatment is food security versus food insecurity and the outcome is individuals' body mass index (BMI).

The organization of this paper is as follows. In Section 1.2 we define the problem setting and the causal parameter to be estimated. In Section 2 we introduce the NN-type methods, their loss functions, and hyperparameters. Section 3 provides a quick review of the ATE estimators. In Section 4 our simulation scenarios are stated along with their results in Section 4.2. The results of the application of our methods on a real dataset are presented in Section 5. We conclude the paper in Section 6 with some discussion on the results and future work.

1.1. Notation

Let data $\mathbf{O} = (O_1, O_2, ..., O_n)$ be generated by a data generating process F, where O_i is a finite dimensional vector $O_i = (Y_i, A_i, W_i)$, with Y as the outcome, A as the treatment and $\mathbf{W} = (X_c, X_y, X_{iv}, X_{irr})$, where we assumes $A = f_1(X_c, X_{iv}) + \epsilon_1$, and $Y = f_2(A, X_c, X_y) + \epsilon_2$, for some functions f_1, f_2. X_c is the set of confounders, X_{iv} is the set of instrumental variables, X_y is the set of y-predictors (independent of the treatment), and X_{irr} is a set of given noise or irrelevant inputs (Figure 1). P is the true observed data distribution, $\hat{P}_n$ is the distribution of **O** such that its marginal distribution with respect to W is its empirical distribution, and the expectation of the conditional distribution $Y|A = a, W$, for $a = 0, 1$, can be estimated. We denote the prediction function of observed outcome given covariates in the treated group $q^1 := q(1, W) = \mathbb{E}[Y|A = 1, W]$, and that in the untreated group $q^0 := q(0, W) = \mathbb{E}[Y|A = 0, W]$, and the propensity score as $g(W) = \mathbb{E}[A|W]$. Throughout, the expectations $\mathbb{E}$ are with respect to P. The symbol ^ on the population-level quantities indicates the corresponding finite sample estimator, and P is replaced by $\hat{P}_n$.

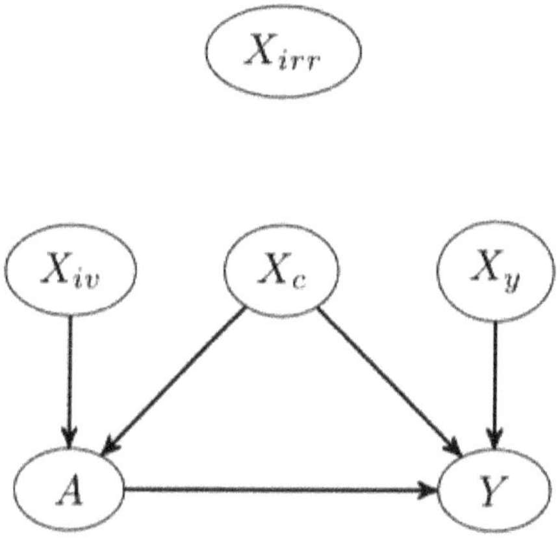

Figure 1. The causal relationship between A and y in the presence of other factors in an observational setting.

1.2. Problem Setup and Assumptions

The fundamental problem of causal inference states that individual-level causality cannot be exactly determined since each person can experience only one value of A. Thus, it is customary to only estimate a population-level causal parameter, in this research Average Treatment Effect (ATE) (1).

For identifiablity of the parameter, the following assumptions must hold true. The first assumption is the Conditional Independence, Ignorability or Unconfoundedness stating that, given the confoudners, the potential outcomes are independent of the treatment assignments ($Y^0, Y^1 \perp A|W$). The second assumption is Positivity which entails that the assignment of treatment groups is not deterministic ($0 < Pr(A = 1|W) < 1$) ([18], page 344). The third assumption is Consistency which states that the observed outcomes equal their corresponding potential outcomes ($Y^A = y$). There are other modeling assumptions made such as time order (i.e., the covariates W are measured before the treatment), IID subjects, and a linear causal effect.

2. Prediction Models

Neural Networks (NNs) are complex nonparametric models that approximate the underlying relationship between inputs and the outcome. The objective in causal inference, however, is not necessarily to leverage the maximum prediction strength of NNs and in fact, the NN architecture should be designed and tuned so that it pays more attention to the confounders.

The most important requirement of ML models such as NNs in causal inference is that although the outcome prediction model should minimize the corresponding loss (fit to get the best outcome prediction possible), given all of the covariates, the loss function associated with the propensity score model should not necessarily be minimized. Ideally, the instrumental variables or strong confounders which can give extreme fitted probability values (near zero or one) should be controlled when minimizing the loss. This can help prevent the elevation of the variance of the causal estimator (i.e., prevent the violation/near violation of the positivity assumption [18,31]). In summary, the prediction models should be strong enough to learn the linear and non-linear relationships between the confounders and treatment, but should not provide perfect predictions. We hypothesize that the employed NNs methods with the regularization techniques have the property of ignoring or damping strong confouders and/or instrumental variables.

2.1. Joint Neural Network

The joint Neural Network (jNN) architecture is a combination of multiple ideas (see Sections 2.2–2.4) for causal parameter estimation purposes mentioned above.

The jNN models are:

$$\begin{bmatrix} \mathbb{E}[Y|A,W] \\ \mathbb{E}[A|W] \end{bmatrix} = \begin{bmatrix} \alpha_0 + \beta A + \mathbf{W}\alpha + \mathbf{H}\boldsymbol{\Gamma}_Y \\ g(\gamma_0 + \mathbf{W}\gamma + \mathbf{H}\boldsymbol{\Gamma}_A) \end{bmatrix} \tag{2}$$

where $\mathbf{H} = f(f(...(f(\mathbf{W}\boldsymbol{\Omega}_1)\boldsymbol{\Omega}_2)...)\boldsymbol{\Omega}_L)$ is the last hidden layer matrix which is a non-linear representation of the inputs (L is the number of hidden layers), g is the logistic link function, and $\boldsymbol{\Gamma}_A$ and $\boldsymbol{\Gamma}_Y$ are the parameters that regress $\mathbf{H}$ to the log-odds of the treatment assignment or to the outcome in the output layer. The large square brackets around the equations above is meant to emphasize that both treatment and outcome models are trained jointly. The non-linear relationships between the inputs and the treatment and outcome can have arbitrary forms (which might not be the same for the treatment and outcome). The NNs can approximate such non-linear relationships even though one activation function is used. In fact, this property of NNs frees us from pre-specifying basis functions [26] as they can be estimated automatically.

The jNN architecture minimizes a multi-task loss Section 2.2 to estimate the networks parameters:

$$\begin{aligned} L(\mathcal{P},\beta,\alpha) = a\sum_{i=1}^{n}\Big[Y_i - \alpha' - \beta A_i - \mathbf{W}_i\alpha - H_i^T\boldsymbol{\Gamma}_Y\Big]^2 + \\ b\sum_{i=1}^{n}\Big[A_i \log\Big(g(H_i^T\boldsymbol{\Gamma}_A)\Big) + (1-A_i)\log\Big(1 - g(H_i^T\boldsymbol{\Gamma}_A)\Big)\Big] + \\ C_{L_1}\sum_{\omega\in\mathcal{P}}|\omega| + C_{L_{1TG}}\Big(\sum_{\omega\in\boldsymbol{\Gamma}_A}|\omega| + \sum_{\omega\in\boldsymbol{\Omega}_1}|\omega|\Big), \end{aligned} \tag{3}$$

where $a, b, C_{L_1}, C_{L_{1TG}}$ are hyperparameters, that can be set before training or be determined by Cross-Validation, that can convey the training to pay more attention to one part of the output layer.

The jNN can have an arbitrary number of hidden layers, or the width of the network ($\mathcal{H}$) is another hyperparameter. For a 3-layer network, $\mathcal{H} = [l_1, l_2, ..., l_h]$, where l_j is the number neurons in layer j, $j = 1, 2, ..., h$. $\mathcal{P} = \{\omega \in \Omega_1 \cup \Omega_2 \cup \Omega_3 \cup \Gamma_Y \cup \Gamma_A\}$, are the connection parameters in the nonlinear part of the network, with Ω's being shared for the two outcome and propensity models. Noted that the number of parameters with L_1 regularization (third term on (3)) is $|\mathcal{P}| = (p+1) \times l_1 + (l_1+1) \times l_2 + ... + (l_{h-1}+1) \times l_h + (l_h+1) \times 2$, including the intercepts in each layer.

The following subsections list the potential benefits and the rationale behind the proposed network (Equations (2) and (3)).

2.2. Bivariate Prediction, Parameters Sharing, and Multi-Task Learning

One of the main components of the jNN architecture is that both treatment and outcome are placed and modeled in the output layer simultaneously. The hypothesis here is that the network learns to get information from the inputs that predict both treatment and outcome, i.e., the confounders. This bivariate structure is intertwined with a multi-task learning or optimization. Ruder [30] reviews the multi-tasking in machine learning and lists its benefits such as implicit data augmentation, regularization, attention focusing, Eavesdropping and Representation bias. Caruana [32] showed that overfitting declines by adding more nodes to the output layer as compared to modeling each output separately Baxter [33]. The multi-task is used when more than one output is used. Multi-task learning is common in the field of Artificial Intelligence and Computer Vision, for example, for the object detection task where the neural network predicts the coordinates of the box around objects and also classifies the object(s) inside the box (see for example [34]). Multi-task learning is used in jNN in order to investigate if the model pays more attention to the confounders than other types of inputs.

2.3. Regularization

The jNN will be resistant to overfitting by adding regularization to the network. Preliminary simulations revealed that L_2, and the Dropout Goodfellow et al. [35] regularization techniques do not result in satisfactory causal effect estimation, and the inherent regularization in the Stochastic Gradient Descent Goodfellow et al. [35] is also insufficient, while L_1 regularization is effective. We did not use the early-stopping as a regularization technique.

The L_1 regularization, third summation in (3), shrinks the magnitude of the parameter estimates of the non-linear part of the architecture which, in effect, limits the influence of X_{irr} and X_{iv}, X_y, and X_c on both treatment and the outcome. The motivation behind the L_1 regularization is to avoid overfitting for better generalization.

The ideal situation for causal parameter estimation is to damp the instrumental variables and learn from confounders and y-predictors only. Henceforth another version of the L_1 regularization is introduced here, referred to as the targeted L_1 regularization, or L_{1TG}, to potentially reduce the impact of instrumental variables on the outcome and more importantly on the propensity scores. The motivation is that by introducing shrinkage on the connections between the last hidden layer and the treatment, the neural network is trained to learn more about confounders than IVs in the last hidden layer as the outcome model is free to learn as much as possible from confounders. The caveat here might be that if the last hidden layer is large enough, some of the neurons can learn confounders while other learn from IVs, thus motivating to consider limiting the number of neurons in the last hidden layer. These hypotheses and ideas are considered in the simulation studies.

2.4. Linear Effects and Skip Connections

The terms $\beta A + \mathbf{W}\alpha$ and $\mathbf{W}\gamma$ in (2) are responsible for potential linear effects. Theoretically, the non-linear parts of the NNs can estimate linear effects, but it is preferable to use linear terms if the relationship between the some of the inputs and the outcome/treatment are linear for more accurate linear effect estimation. The benefit of including linear terms in the equations has been verified in our preliminary simulation studies.

These linear terms are referred to the skip-connections in ML literature He et al. [36] which connect some layers to two or more layers forward. In ML literature, they are primarily used in very deep neural networks to facilitate optimizations. But they are used in jNN to model the linear effects directly. More specifically, skip connections connect the covariates to both treatment and outcome in the output layers and connect the treatment in the input layer to the outcome in the output layer. The latter skip connection is shown in Figure 2. It should be noted that this skip connection in particular is independent of the treatment in the output layer to avoid perfect prediction of the propensity scores.

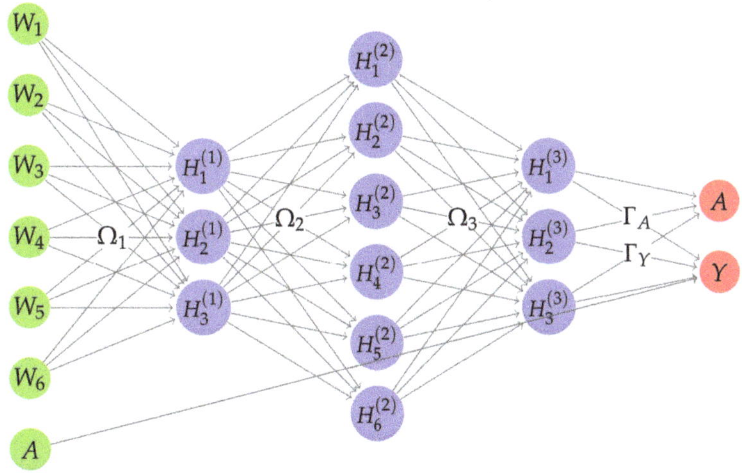

Figure 2. A Joint Neural Network architecture that incorporates linear effect of the treatment on the outcome, and the nonlinear relationship between the covariates and the treatment assignment and the outcome, all three tasks at the same time.

2.5. Double Neural Networks

In order to study the significance of the proposed method through simulations, we compare jNN with the double Neural Networks (dNN) Chernozhukov et al. [37] method. dNN is generally referred to the strategy of modeling the treatment and outcome separately utilizing two different models:

$$\begin{aligned} \mathbb{E}[Y|A,W] &= \beta_0 + \beta A + \mathbf{W}\alpha + \mathbf{H}\mathbf{\Gamma}_Y \\ \mathbb{E}[A|W] &= \alpha_0 + \mathbf{U}\alpha + \mathbf{K}\mathbf{\Gamma}_A, \end{aligned} \tag{4}$$

where two separate neural nets model y and A (no parameter sharing). In this paper, the dNN algorithm refers to two neural networks to model the treatment and outcome separately. To make the two jNN and dNN models comparable, we let the NN architectures to be as similar as possible in terms of skip connections and regularization techniques. The loss functions in dNN to be optimized are:

$$\begin{aligned} &L_y(\mathcal{P}_y,\beta,\alpha) = \sum_{i=1}^{n}\Big[Y_i - \alpha' - \beta a_i - \mathbf{W}_i\alpha - \mathbf{H}_i^T\mathbf{\Gamma}_Y\Big]^2 + C'_{L_1}\sum_{\omega\in\mathcal{P}}|\omega|, \\ &L_A(\mathcal{P}_A) = \sum_{i=1}^{n}\Big[a_i\log\Big(g(\mathbf{K}_i^T\mathbf{\Gamma}_A)\Big) + (1-a_i)\log\Big(1-g(\mathbf{K}_i^T\mathbf{\Gamma}_A)\Big)\Big] + C''_{L_1}\sum_{\omega\in\mathcal{P}}|\omega| + \\ &C_{L_1TG}\Big(\sum_{\omega\in\mathbf{\Gamma}_A}|\omega| + \sum_{\omega\in\mathbf{\Omega}_1}|\omega|\Big), \end{aligned} \tag{5}$$

3. ATE Estimation

The Causal Parameter Estimation algorithm is a two stage process. The regression functions $\mathbb{E}[A|W]$, $\mathbb{E}[Y|A=1,W])$, $\mathbb{E}[Y|A=0,W]$ are estimated using the ML algorithms such as jNN or dNN in step 1. And in step 2, the predictions are inserted into the causal estimators such as (6), below.

ATE Estimators

There is a wealth of literature on how to estimate the ATE and there are various versions of estimators including the Augmented Inverse Probability Weighting (AIPW), Normalized Augmented Inverse Probability Weighting (nAIPW):

$$\begin{aligned}\hat{\beta}_{AIPW} &= \frac{1}{n}\sum_{i=1}^{n}\Big(\frac{A_i(Y_i-\hat{q}_i^1)}{\hat{g}_i} - \frac{(1-A_i)(Y_i-\hat{q}_i^0)}{1-\hat{g}_i}\Big) + \frac{1}{n}\sum_{i=1}^{n}\hat{q}_i^1 - \hat{q}_i^0, \\ \hat{\beta}_{nAIPW} &= \sum_{i=1}^{n}\Big(\frac{A_i(Y_i-\hat{q}_i^1)w_i^{(1)}}{\sum_{j=1}^{n}A_j w_j^{(1)}} - \frac{(1-A_i)(Y_i-\hat{q}_i^0)w_i^{(0)}}{\sum_{j=1}^{n}(1-A_j)w_j^{(0)}}\Big) + \frac{1}{n}\sum_{i=1}^{n}\hat{q}_i^1 - \hat{q}_i^0.\end{aligned} \tag{6}$$

where $\hat{q}_i^k = \hat{q}(k, W_i) = \hat{\mathbb{E}}[Y_i|A_i = k, W_i]$ and $\hat{g}_i = \hat{\mathbb{E}}[A_i|W_i]$, and A_1 is the treatment group with size n_1 and A_0 is the treatment group with size n_1.

In the second step of estimation procedure, the predictions of the treatment (i.e., propensity score, PS) and/or the outcome $\hat{\mathbb{E}}[Y_i|A_i = k, W_i]$, $k = 0, 1$, can be inserted in these estimators (6). Generalized Linear Models (GLM), any relevant Machine Learning algorithm such as tree-based algorithms and their ensemble Friedman et al. [28], SuperLearner Van der Laan et al. [38], or Neural Network-based models (such as ours) can be applied as prediction models for the first step prediction task. We will use jNN and dNN in this article.

4. Simulations

A simulation study (with 100 iterations) was performed to compare the prediction methods jNN, and dNN by inserting their predictions in the nAIPW (causal) estimators (6). There are a total of 8 scenarios according to the size of the data (i.e., the number of subjects and number of covariates), and the confounding and instrumental variables strengths. We fixed the sample sizes to be $n = 750$ and $n = 7500$, with the number of covariates $p = 32$ and $p = 300$, respectively. The four sets of covariates had the same sizes $\#X_c = \#X_{iv} = \#X_y = \#X_{irr} = 8.75$ and independent from each other were drawn from the Multivariate Normal (MVN) Distribution as $X \sim \mathcal{N}(\mathbf{0}, \Sigma)$, with $\Sigma_{kj} = \rho^{j-k}$ and $\rho = 0.5$. Let $\beta = 1$. The models to generate the treatment assignment and outcome were specified as

$$\begin{aligned} &A \sim Ber\Big(\frac{1}{1+e^{-\eta}}\Big), \text{with } \eta = f_a(X_c)\gamma_c + g_a(X_{iv})\gamma_{iv}, \\ &Y = 3 + A + f_y(X_c)\gamma_c' + g_y(X_y)\gamma_y + \epsilon, \end{aligned} \tag{7}$$

The functions f_a, g_a, f_y, g_y select 30% of the columns and apply interactions and non-linear functions listed below (8). The strength of instrumental variable and confounding effects were chosen as $\gamma_c, \gamma_c', \gamma_y \sim Unif(r_1, r_2)$ where $(r_1 = r_2 = 0.1)$ or $(r_1 = 0.1, r_2 = 1)$, and $\gamma_{iv} \sim Unif(r_3, r_4)$ where $(r_3 = r_4 = 0.1)$ or $(r_3 = 0.1, r_4 = 1)$.

The non-linearities for each pair of covariates are randomly selected among the following functions:

$$\begin{aligned} l(x_1, x_2) &= e^{\frac{x_1 x_2}{2}} \\ l(x_1, x_2) &= \frac{x_1}{1+e^{x_2}} \\ l(x_1, x_2) &= (\frac{x_1 x_2}{10} + 2)^3 \\ l(x_1, x_2) &= (x_1 + x_2 + 3)^2 \\ l(x_1, x_2) &= g(x_1) \times h(x_2) \end{aligned} \tag{8}$$

where $g(x) = -2I(x \leq -1) - I(-1 \leq x \leq 0) + I(0 \leq x \leq 2) + 3I(x \geq 2)$, and $h(x) = -5I(x \leq 0) - 2I(0 \leq x \leq 1) + 3I(x \geq 1)$, or $g(x) = I(x \geq 0)$, and $h(x) = I(x \geq 1)$.

In order to find the best set of hyperparameter values for the NN architectures, we ran an initial series of simulations to find the best set of hyperparameters for all scenarios, presented here. The networks' activation function is Rectified Linear Unit (ReLU), with 3 hidden layers as large as the input size (p), with L_1 regularization and batch size equal to $3 * p$ and 200 epochs. The Adaptive Moment Estimation (Adam) optimizer Kingma and Ba [39] with learning rate 0.01 and momentum 0.95 were used to estimate the network's parameters, including the causal parameter (ATE).

As in practice the RMSE and covariate types are unknown, prediction measures of the outcome and treatment should be used to choose the best model in a K-fold cross-validation. R^2 and AUC each provide insight about the outcome and treatment models, respectively, but in our framework, both models should be satisfactory. To measure the goodness of the prediction models (jNN and dNN) for causal inference purposes, we define and utilize a statistic which is a compromise (geometric average) between R^2 and AUC, here referred to as *geo*,

$$geo(R, D) = \sqrt[3]{R^2 \times D \times (1 - D)}, \tag{9}$$

where $D = 2(AUC - 0.5)$, the Somers' D index. This measure was not utilized in the optimization process (i.e., training the neural networks), and is rather introduced here to observe if the compromise between R^2 and AUC agrees with the models that capture more confounders than IVs. We will refer to $geo(R, D)$ simply as *geo*.

4.1. Selected Covariate Types

In order to identify which types of covariates (confounders, IVs, y-predictors, and irrelevant covariates) the prediction methods have learned from, we calculate the association between the inputs and the predicted values ($\hat{\mathbb{E}}[Y|A, W]$ and $\hat{\mathbb{E}}[A|W]$), and after sorting the inputs (from large to small values) based on the association values, we count the number of different types of covariates within top 15 inputs. The association between two variables here is estimated using the distance correlation statistic [40] whose zero values entail independence and non-zero values entail statistical dependence between the two variables.

4.2. Results

Figures 3–8 present the overall comparison of different hyperparameter settings of jNN and dNN architectures in terms of five different measures, respectively: (1) The average number of captured confounders/IVs/y-predictors, (2) Average Root Mean Square Error (RMSE) of causal estimators, (3) Average R^2, AUC and their mixture measure *geo* (9), (4) Bias, (5) MC standard deviation of nAIPW. The bootstrap confidence intervals for the bias, standard deviation and RMSE are calculated to capture significant differences between the simulation scenarios. The x-axis includes 16 hyperparameter settings, and as a general rule here, models in the left are most complex (less regularization and wider neural nets) and in the right are least complex. Noted that L_{1TG} regularization is only targeted at the treatment model.

The Figures 3 and 4 show how the complexity of both dNN and jNN (x-axis) impact the number of captured covariate types (i.e., confounders/IVs/y-predictors) (top graph), RMSE (middle graph) and prediction measures (bottom graph). In almost all the hyperparameter settings, especially when $C_{L_{1TG}}$ is non zero, the number of captured confounders is larger and the number of captured IVs is smaller in jNN as compared to dNN. This shows the joint modeling has a benefit of focusing on the confounders, rather than IVs, especially in the large data scenario.

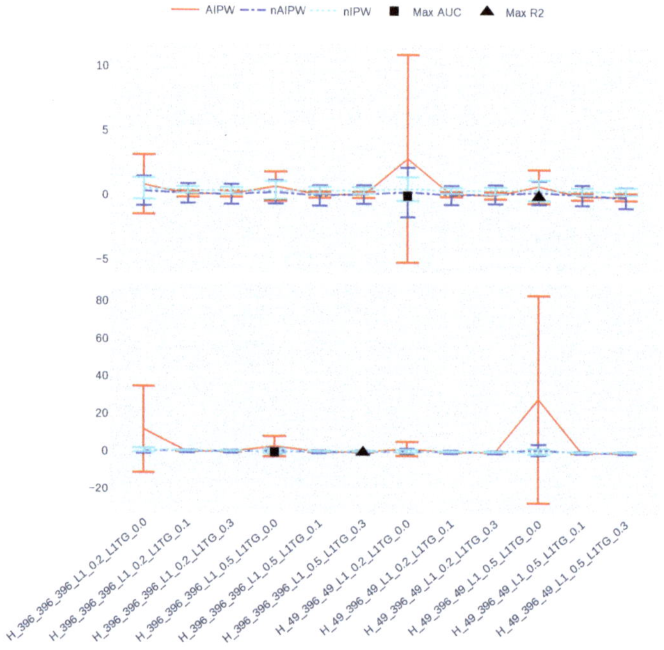

Figure 3. The ATE estimates and their asymptotically calculated 95% confidence intervals with nIPW, AIPW, and nAIPW methods.

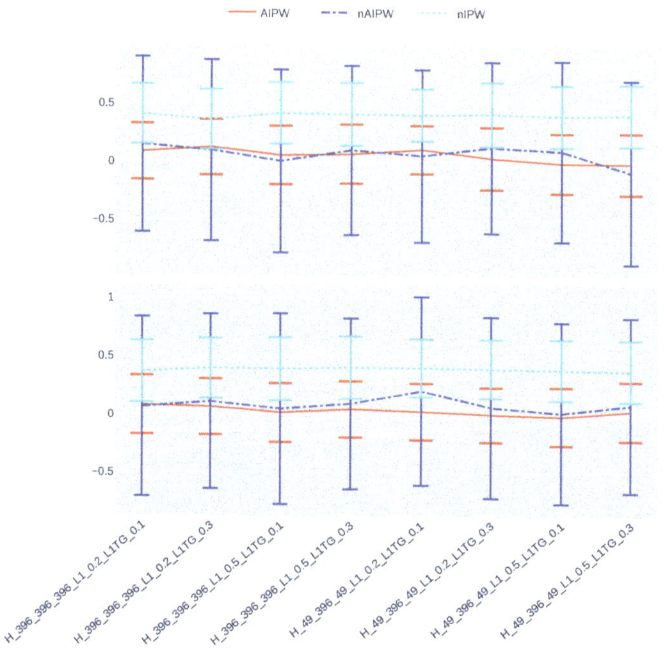

Figure 4. The ATE estimates and their asymptotically calculated 95% confidence intervals with nIPW, AIPW, and nAIPW methods.

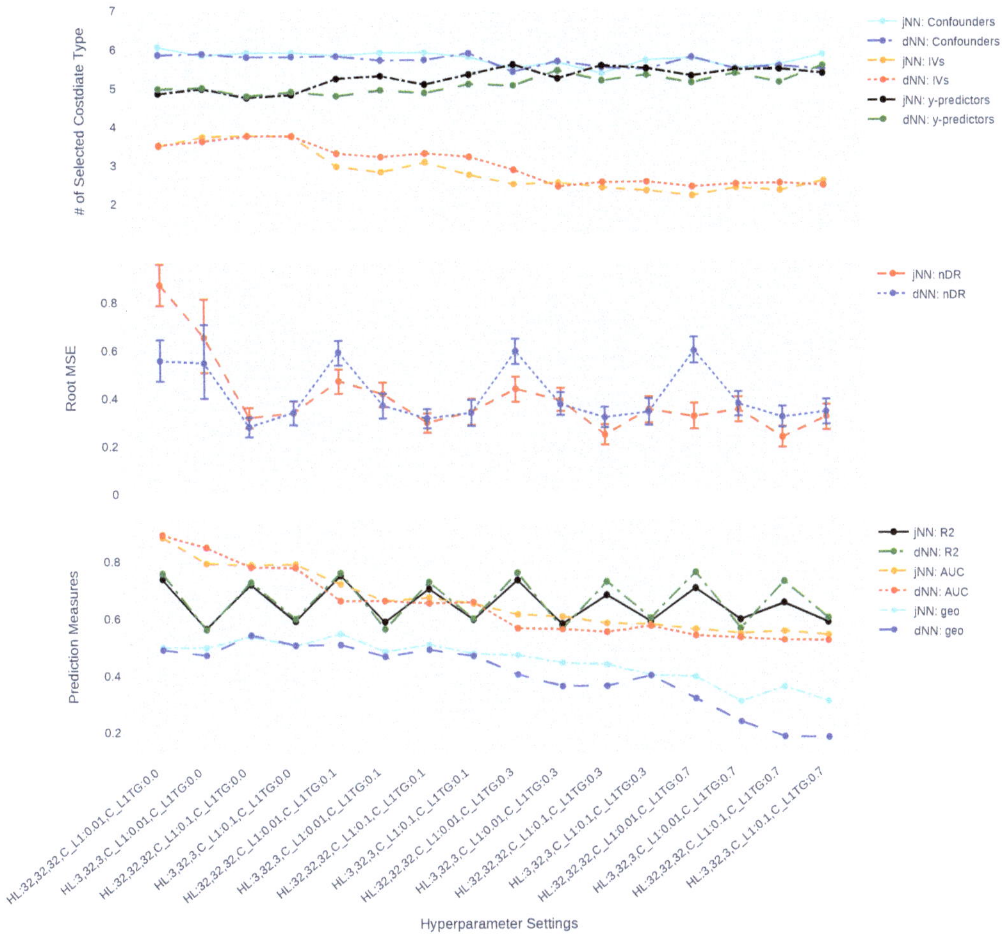

Figure 5. The comparison of captured number of confounders, IVs and y-predictors, RMSE of nAIPW and its bootstrap 95% confidence interval, and prediction measures R^2, AUC and geo (geometric mean of R^2, AUC) for different hyperparameter settings and where the predictions come from jNN or dNN models. (n = 750, p = 32).

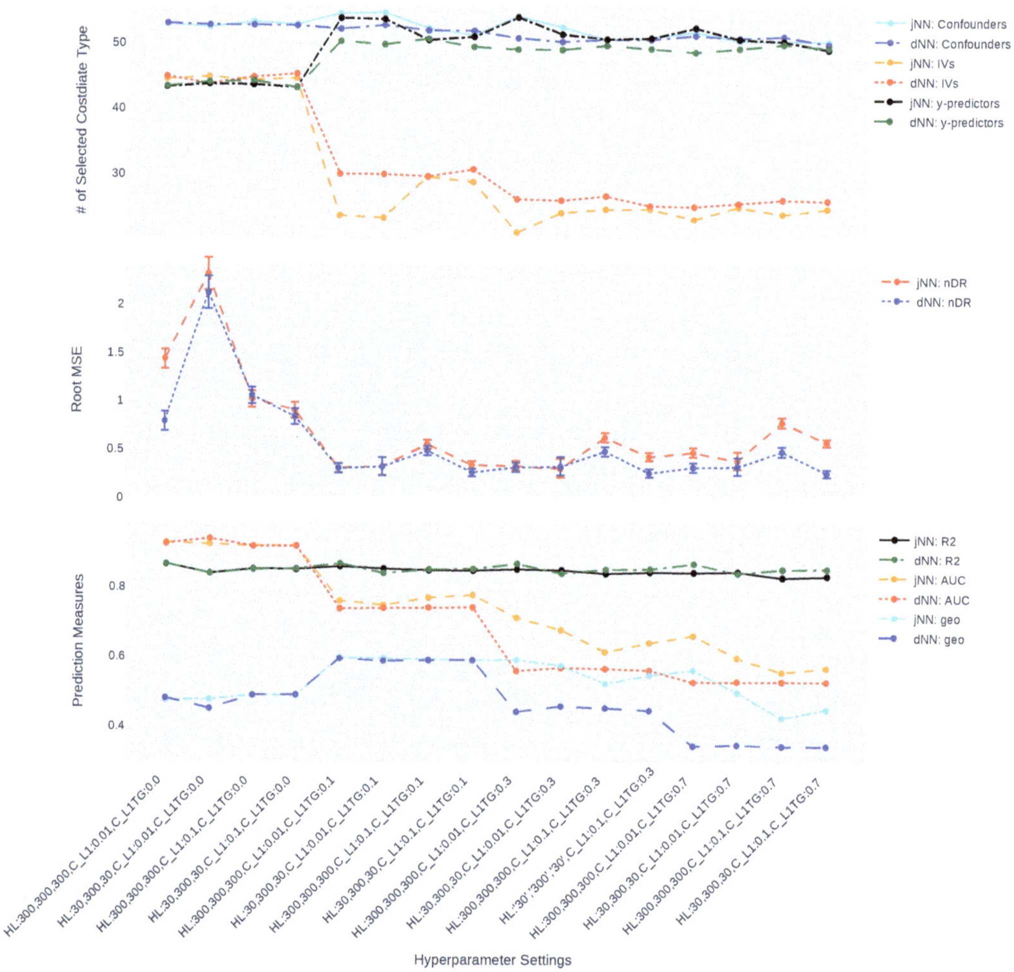

Figure 6. The comparison of captured number of confounders, IVs and y-predictors, RMSE of nAIPW and its bootstrap 95% confidence interval, and prediction measures R^2, AUC and geo (geometric mean of R^2, AUC) for different hyperparameter settings and where the predictions come from jNN or dNN models. (n = 7500, p = 300).

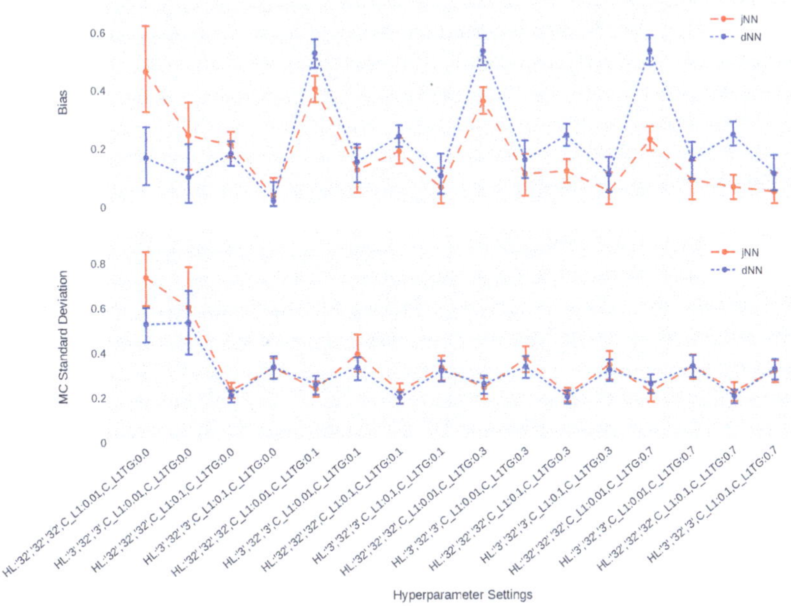

Figure 7. The bias and standard deviation of nAIPW and their bootstrap 95% confidence intervals for different hyperparameter settings where the predictions come from jNN or dNN models. (n = 750, p = 32).

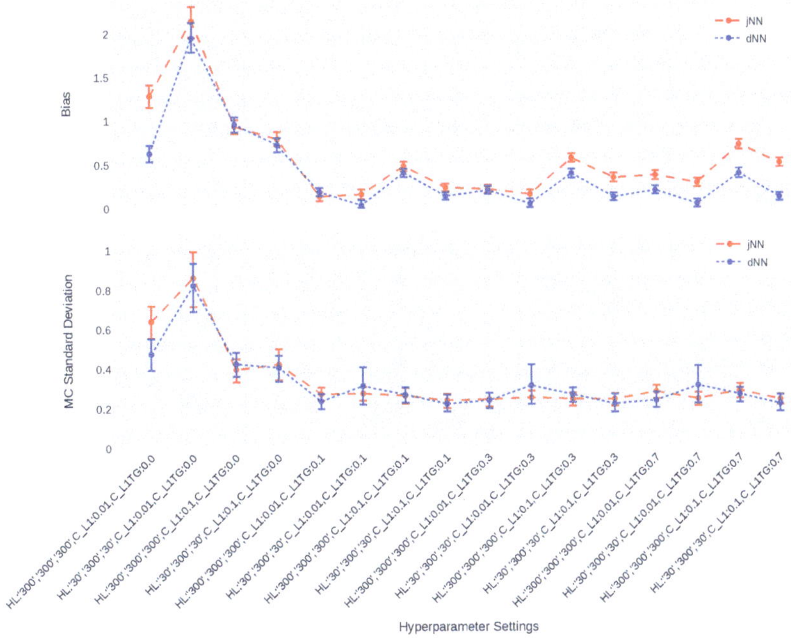

Figure 8. The comparison of bias, Monte Carlo standard deviation and their bootstrap 95% confidence intervals of nAIPW, for different hyperparameter settings and the predictions come from jNN or dNN models. (n = 7500, p = 300).

The RMSE of jNN is larger than that of dNN for models with zero targetted regularization (the scenarios in the left). With decreasing the complexity of the treatment model, the RMSE of both jNN and dNN decline. The jNN outperforms dNN in almost all of the hyperparameter settings in case of $n = 750$, but does not show a clear pattern in case of $n = 7500$. Further, the impact of the width of architectures (H) changes based on C_{L_1} regularization: wider architectures ($H = [p, p, p]$, p: number of covariates) with large C_{L_1} outperform other combinations of these two hyperparameters. This observation is more clear for smaller sized data, and for dNN model. In the small size scenarios, when the width is small ($H = [3, 32, 3]$), the outcome model is affected and has a smaller R^2. This means there are not enough neurons (on the first or last layer) to provide more accurate outcome predictions. In the best scenarios, the RMSE confidence intervals of jNN model are below those of dNN, illustrating a small preference of jNN over dNN in terms of RMSE. Comparing the three hyperparameters, $C_{L_{1TG}}$ is most effective, and zero values of this hyperparameter results in very large RMSEs for both dNN and jNN.

From Figures 3 and 4, it is observed that both jNN and dNN models have roughly the same values for the R^2 (outcome model performance) across hyperparameter settings and for both data sizes ($n = 7500$, and $n = 750$). That is, the targeted regularization in jNN does not impact the performance of the outcome model. The AUC, on the other hand, declines with higher values of $C_{L_{1TG}}$, and is almost always smaller or equal in dNN as compared to jNN. Further, larger values of geo in the small size data correspond to smaller RMSE, but no such pattern can be seen in the large data scenario.

Overall, the trends favor the idea that more complex treatment models capture larger number of IVs, have larger AUC (smaller geo.), and have larger RMSE. That is, more complex models are less favorable.

Figures 7 and 8 illustrate the bias and standard deviation of the causal estimators. As expected and mentioned in the Section 1, the models that do not dampen IVs suffer from large bias and standard deviation. The bias and standard deviation have opposite behavior in different settings, such that settings that produce larger standard deviation, results in small bias, and vice versa, except for the one setting that produces both largest bias and standard deviation. The fluctuations of the bias-variance across hyperparameter settings are larger in $n = 750$ case than in $n = 7500$ case. For small sample $n = 750$, the best scenario for jNN is $H = [32, 32, 32], C_{L_1} = 0.1, C_{L_{1TG}} = 0.7$ where both bias and standard deviation of jNN are small in the same direction. For the large sample $n = 7500$, however, the best scenario for jNN is $H = [30, 300, 30], C_{L_1} = 0.01, C_{L_{1TG}} = 0.7$ with a similar behavior. The best scenarios for dNN are slightly different. For small sample $H = [32, 32, 32], C_{L_1} = 0.1, C_{L_{1TG}} = 0.7$ and for the large sample H = [30,300,30], C_{L_1} = 0.01, $C_{L_{1TG}}$ = 0.7 are most favorable.

5. Application: Food Insecurity and BMI

The Canadian Community Health Survey (CCHS) is a cross-sectional survey that collects data related to health status, health care utilization and health determinants for the Canadian population in multiple cycles. The 2021 CCHS covers the population 12 years of age and over living in the ten provinces and the three territorial capitals. Excluded from the survey's coverage are: Persons living on reserves and other Aboriginal settlements in the provinces and some other sub-populations that altogether represent less than 3% of the Canadian population aged 12 and over. Examples of modules asked in most cycles are: General health, chronic conditions, smoking and alcohol use. For the 2021 cycle, thematic content on food security, home care, sedentary behavior and depression, among many others, was included. In addition to the health component of the survey are questions about respondent characteristics such as labor market activities, income and socio-demographics.

In this article, we use the CCHS dataset to investigate the causal relationship of food insecurity and body mass index (BMI). Other gathered information in the CCHS is used which might contain potential confounders, y-predictors and instrumental variables. The data are from a survey and need special methods such as the resampling or bootstrap methods to estimate the standard errors. However, here, we use the data to illustrate the utilization of jNN and dNN with different hyperparameters choices in the presence of possible empirical positivity violations. In order to reduce the amount of variability in the data, we have focused on the sub-population 18–65 years of age.

Figures 5 and 6 present the ATE estimates and their 95% asymptotic confidence intervals with nIPW, AIPW and nAIPW methods. Figure 5 contains hyperparameter settings where there is no targeted regularization and it shows how important this regularization technique is, especially for the AIPW estimator that has no normalization. We have removed these scenarios in Figure 6 for a more clear comparison between the remaining scenarios. The estimates and 95% CIs seem similar across the hyperparameter settings, but there is a clear difference between those of AIPW and nAIPW. This means that for this dataset, normalization might not be needed as the propensity scores do not behave extremely and AIPW does not blow up.

6. Discussion

In this paper, we have studied how hyperparameters of the Neural Network predictions in the first step can affect the Average Treatment Effect (ATE) estimator. We have considered a general Data Generating Process (DGP) that four types of covariates that exist in the dataset, confounders, IVs, y-predictors, and irrelevant covariates. Two general NN architectures have been studied, jNN and dNN where in the former both the outcome and treatment are modeled jointly (with an appropriate loss function) and in the latter, they are modeled separately. We have observed that L_1 regularization especially the ones that targets the treatment model (L_{1TG}) is an effective hyperparameter for achieving a better bias-variance trade-off for the normalized Augmented Inverse Probability Weighting (nAIPW) estimator. And, the number of neurons in the first and last layer of the network becomes irrelevant as long as the value of L_{1TG} is sufficient. Further, we have observed that in the hyperparameter settings where the IV effects are controlled, the estimation is less biased and more stable. Thus the targeted regularization is successful in dampening the IVs and preventing perfect prediction in the treatment model. Figures 3–8 illustrate that jNN is overall more stable and has a smaller RMSE in the small sample dataset scenario as compared to dNN. We utilized nAIPW in our simulations as they outperform or at least do not underperform AIPW and other estimators such as IPW, nIPW, AIPW, and SR. The nAIPW estimator has a normalization factor in the denumerator which can dilute the impact of extreme predictions of the propensity score model and protect the estimator against the positivity assumption violation Van der Laan and Rose [18].

We utilized a geometric-type average of the R^2 and AUC to choose among the first step models. As the objective of optimization in the first step is increasing prediction performance which is not necessarily the same as the causal inference objectives, the usage of either R^2, AUC or their geometric average is sub-optimal. In a future study alternative approaches will be explored and compared with the said prediction measure.

A real strength of NNs would be to uncover hidden information (and thus confounder effects) in unstructured data such as text or image data. However, in this article, we have not studied the presence of unstructured data and it is left for future research.

There are limitations due to the assumptions and simulation scenarios and, thus, some questions are left to future studies to be explored. For example, the outcome here was assumed to be continuous, and the treatment to be binary. We also did not cover heavy tail outcomes or rare treatment scenarios. Also, the ratio of dimension to the size of the data was considered to be fairly small ($p \ll n$), and we have not studied the case where $n < p$. Furthermore, we did not study the asymptotic behavior of nAIPW when jNN or dNN predictions are used.

A limitation of jNN as compared to dNN is that if one needs to shrink the final hidden layer to control the complexity of the treatment model, by structure, we are limiting the complexity of the outcome model which might not be necessary. This might be resolved by another architectural design, which is left to future studies on the subject.

The usage of another regularization technique that controls the extremeness of propensity score values is a plausible approach. For example, a data-dependent term can be added to the loss function $\sum_{i=1}^{n} \frac{1}{g_i} + \frac{1}{1-g_i}$. Such a term discourages the network to obtain values extremely close to zero or one, as opposed to the negative log-likelihood term that encourages such tendencies. This approach might also focus less on the inputs that cause extreme values such as strong confounders or IVs. Examination of this approach is left to future studies.

In the design of the optimization, we did not consider a formal early stopping as a regularization technique. However, in the preliminary exploration, our simulations performed better with fewer iterations (in fact epochs). In modern NNs, researchers usually run the NN algorithms in many iterations, but that is partly due to the dropout regularization technique. We did not use drop-out (and L2) regularization in the final simulations, as the preliminary results did not confirm dropout as promising as L_1 regularization.

Further, we utilized NNs to learn the underlying relationships between the covariates and the outcome and treatment by targeting the relevant features through regularization and joint modeling of the treatment and outcome. NNs with other structures that might target confounders have not been explored, nor have other Machine Learning algorithms such as tree-based models. The Gradient Boosting Machines (GBM) algorithm Friedman [41] can be alternatively used to learn these non-linear relationships while targeting the right set of features. This is postponed to a future article.

Author Contributions: Data curation, M.R.; Formal analysis, M.R.; Investigation, M.R.; Methodology, M.R. and O.S.; Project administration, M.R. and O.S.; Resources, M.R.; Software, M.R.; Supervision, O.S.; Validation, M.R. and O.S.; Visualization, M.R.; Writing—original draft, M.R.; Writing—review & editing, O.S. All authors have read and agreed to the published version of the manuscript.

Funding: The work of Olli Saarela was supported by a Discovery Grant from the Natural Sciences and Engineering Research Council of Canada as well as a New Researcher Award from the Connaught Fund.

Data Availability Statement: The simulated data can be regenerated using the codes, which can be provided to the interested user via an email request to the correspondence author. The CCHS data is not publicly available and only the authorized people can access and perform analyses on it.

Conflicts of Interest: The authors declare no conflict of interest.

References

1. Rubin, D.B. Multivariate matching methods that are equal percent bias reducing, I: Some examples. *Biometrics* **1976**, *32*, 109–120. [CrossRef]
2. van der Laan, M.J.; Petersen, M.L. Causal effect models for realistic individualized treatment and intention to treat rules. *Int. J. Biostat.* **2007**, *3*. [CrossRef]
3. Johansson, F.; Shalit, U.; Sontag, D. Learning representations for counterfactual inference. In Proceedings of the International Conference on Machine Learning, New York, NY, USA, 19–24 June 2016; pp. 3020–3029.
4. Foster, J.C.; Taylor, J.M.; Ruberg, S.J. Subgroup identification from randomized clinical trial data. *Stat. Med.* **2011**, *30*, 2867–2880. [CrossRef]
5. Taddy, M.; Gardner, M.; Chen, L.; Draper, D. A nonparametric bayesian analysis of heterogenous treatment effects in digital experimentation. *J. Bus. Econ. Stat.* **2016**, *34*, 661–672. [CrossRef]
6. Athey, S.; Imbens, G. Recursive partitioning for heterogeneous causal effects. *Proc. Natl. Acad. Sci. USA* **2016**, *113*, 7353–7360. [CrossRef]
7. Li, J.; Ma, S.; Le, T.; Liu, L.; Liu, J. Causal decision trees. *IEEE Trans. Knowl. Data Eng.* **2017**, *29*, 257–271. [CrossRef]
8. Wager, S.; Athey, S. Estimation and inference of heterogeneous treatment effects using random forests. *J. Am. Stat. Assoc.* **2018**, *113*, 1228–1242. [CrossRef]
9. Lu, M.; Sadiq, S.; Feaster, D.J.; Ishwaran, H. Estimating individual treatment effect in observational data using random forest methods. *J. Comput. Graph. Stat.* **2018**, *27*, 209–219. [CrossRef]
10. Imai, K.; Ratkovic, M. Estimating treatment effect heterogeneity in randomized program evaluation. *Ann. Appl. Stat.* **2013**, *7*, 443–470. [CrossRef]
11. Shalit, U.; Johansson, F.D.; Sontag, D. Estimating individual treatment effect: Generalization bounds and algorithms. In Proceedings of the 34th International Conference on Machine Learning, Sydney, NSW, Australia, 6–11 August 2017; Volume 70, pp. 3076–3085.

12. Van Der Laan, M.J.; Rubin, D. Targeted Maximum Likelihood Learning. *Int. J. Biostat.* **2006**, *2*. [CrossRef]
13. Belloni, A.; Chen, D.; Chernozhukov, V.; Hansen, C. Sparse models and methods for optimal instruments with an application to eminent domain. *Econometrica* **2012**, *80*, 2369–2429.
14. Belloni, A.; Chernozhukov, V.; Hansen, C. Inference on treatment effects after selection among high-dimensional controls. *Rev. Econ. Stud.* **2014**, *81*, 608–650. [CrossRef]
15. Alaa, A.M.; Weisz, M.; Van Der Schaar, M. Deep counterfactual networks with propensity-dropout. *arXiv* **2017**, arXiv:1706.05966.
16. Chernozhukov, V.; Chetverikov, D.; Demirer, M.; Duflo, E.; Hansen, C.; Newey, W.; Robins, J. Double/debiased machine learning for treatment and structural parameters. *Econom. J.* **2018**, *21*, C1–C68. [CrossRef]
17. Farrell, M.H.; Liang, T.; Misra, S. Deep neural networks for estimation and inference: Application to causal effects and other semiparametric estimands. *arXiv* **2018**, arXiv:1809.09953.
18. Van der Laan, M.J.; Rose, S. *Targeted Learning: Causal Inference for Observational and Experimental Data*; Springer Science & Business Media: Berlin, Germany, 2011.
19. Angrist, J.D.; Pischke, J.S. *Mostly Harmless Econometrics: An Empiricist's Companion*; Princeton University Press: Princeton, NJ, USA, 2008.
20. Rostami, M.; Saarela, O. Normalized Augmented Inverse Probability Weighting with Neural Network Predictions. *Entropy* **2022**, *24*, 179. [CrossRef]
21. Moosavi, N.; Häggström, J.; de Luna, X. The costs and benefits of uniformly valid causal inference with high-dimensional nuisance parameters. *arXiv* **2021**, arXiv:2105.02071.
22. Shi, C.; Blei, D.M.; Veitch, V. Adapting Neural Networks for the Estimation of Treatment Effects. *arXiv* **2019**, arXiv:1906.02120.
23. Chernozhukov, V.; Newey, W.; Quintas-Martıénez, V.M.; Syrgkanis, V. RieszNet and ForestRiesz: Automatic Debiased Machine Learning with Neural Nets and Random Forests. In Proceedings of the International Conference on Machine Learning, PMLR, Baltimore, MD, USA, 17–23 July 2022; pp. 3901–3914.
24. Chernozhukov, V.; Newey, W.K.; Singh, R. Automatic debiased machine learning of causal and structural effects. *Econometrica* **2022**, *90*, 967–1027. [CrossRef]
25. Chernozhukov, V.; Newey, W.; Singh, R.; Syrgkanis, V. Adversarial estimation of riesz representers. *arXiv* **2020**, arXiv:2101.00009.
26. Farrell, M.H. Robust inference on average treatment effects with possibly more covariates than observations. *J. Econom.* **2015**, *189*, 1–23. [CrossRef]
27. Shalev-Shwartz, S.; Ben-David, S. *Understanding Machine Learning: From Theory to Algorithms*; Cambridge University Press: Cambridge, UK, 2014.
28. Friedman, J.; Hastie, T.; Tibshirani, R. *The Elements of Statistical Learning*; Springer series in statistics New York; Springer: New York, NY, USA, 2001; Volume 1.
29. Bishop, C.M. *Pattern Recognition and Machine Learning*; Springer: Berlin, Germnay, 2006.
30. Ruder, S. An overview of multi-task learning in deep neural networks. *arXiv* **2017**, arXiv:1706.05098.
31. Petersen, M.L.; Porter, K.E.; Gruber, S.; Wang, Y.; Van Der Laan, M.J. Diagnosing and responding to violations in the positivity assumption. *Stat. Methods Med. Res.* **2012**, *21*, 31–54. [CrossRef] [PubMed]
32. Caruana, R. Learning many related tasks at the same time with backpropagation. *Adv. Neural Inf. Process. Syst.* **1995**, 657–664.
33. Baxter, J. A Bayesian/information theoretic model of learning to learn via multiple task sampling. *Mach. Learn.* **1997**, *28*, 7–39. [CrossRef]
34. Redmon, J.; Divvala, S.; Girshick, R.; Farhadi, A. You only look once: Unified, real-time object detection. In Proceedings of the IEEE Conference on Computer Vision and Pattern Recognition, Las Vegas, NV, USA, 27–30 June 2016; pp. 779–788.
35. Goodfellow, I.; Bengio, Y.; Courville, A.; Bengio, Y. *Deep Learning*; MIT Press Cambridge: Cambridge, MA, USA, 2016; Volume 1.
36. He, K.; Zhang, X.; Ren, S.; Sun, J. Deep residual learning for image recognition. In Proceedings of the IEEE Conference on Computer Vision and Pattern Recognition, Las Vegas, NV, USA, 27–30 June 2016; pp. 770–778.
37. Chernozhukov, V.; Chetverikov, D.; Demirer, M.; Duflo, E.; Hansen, C.; Newey, W.K. *Double Machine Learning for Treatment and Causal Parameters*; Technical Report, Cemmap Working Paper; Centre for Microdata Methods and Practice (cemmap): London, UK, 2016.
38. Van der Laan, M.J.; Polley, E.C.; Hubbard, A.E. Super learner. *Stat. Appl. Genet. Mol. Biol.* **2007**, *6*. [CrossRef]
39. Kingma, D.P.; Ba, J. Adam: A method for stochastic optimization. *arXiv* **2014**, arXiv:1412.6980.
40. Székely, G.J.; Rizzo, M.L.; Bakirov, N.K. Measuring and testing dependence by correlation of distances. *Ann. Stat.* **2007**, *35*, 2769–2794. [CrossRef]
41. Friedman, J.H. Greedy function approximation: A gradient boosting machine. *Ann. Stat.* **2001**, *29*, 1189–1232. [CrossRef]

entropy

Article

High Resolution Treatment Effects Estimation: Uncovering Effect Heterogeneities with the Modified Causal Forest

Hugo Bodory [1,†], Hannah Busshoff [2,*,†] and Michael Lechner [2,†]

1 Vice-President's Board (Research & Faculty), University of St. Gallen, Dufourstrasse 50, 9000 St. Gallen, Switzerland; hugo.bodory@unisg.ch
2 Swiss Institute for Empirical Research, University of St. Gallen, Varnbüelstrasse 14, 9000 St. Gallen, Switzerland; michael.lechner@unisg.ch
* Correspondence: hannah.busshoff@unisg.ch
† These authors contributed equally to this work.

Abstract: There is great demand for inferring causal effect heterogeneity and for open-source statistical software, which is readily available for practitioners. The mcf package is an open-source Python package that implements Modified Causal Forest (mcf), a causal machine learner. We replicate three well-known studies in the fields of epidemiology, medicine, and labor economics to demonstrate that our mcf package produces aggregate treatment effects, which align with previous results, and in addition, provides novel insights on causal effect heterogeneity. For all resolutions of treatment effects estimation, which can be identified, the mcf package provides inference. We conclude that the mcf constitutes a practical and extensive tool for a modern causal heterogeneous effects analysis.

Keywords: econometrics software; causal machine learning; statistical learning; conditional average treatment effects; individualized treatment effects; multiple treatments; selection-on-observables

JEL Classification: C21; C870; J68

Citation: Bodory, H.; Busshoff, H.; Lechner, M. High Resolution Treatment Effects Estimation: Uncovering Effect Heterogeneities with the Modified Causal Forest. *Entropy* **2022**, *24*, 1039. https://doi.org/10.3390/e24081039

Academic Editor: Kateřina Hlaváčková-Schindler

Received: 15 June 2022
Accepted: 23 July 2022
Published: 28 July 2022

1. Introduction

Supervised machine learning algorithms, which learn a model by minimizing prediction errors, do not generalize per se to evaluate treatment effects due to the missing data problem. For each unit of observation, only one potential outcome is observed; hence, the individualized treatment effect (ITE) remains unknown. This disallows to train a model by minimizing the prediction error of the ITE. With the onset of causal machine learning in recent years, flexible methods have been developed, which integrate supervised machine learners into the classical analysis of causality. The causality literature defines the set of conditions required to identify the causal parameters of interest and deals with the missing data by imputing counterfactuals for adequate subpopulations [1], while the machine learning (ML) literature provides methods to flexibly estimate treatment effects and deal with a potentially large number of features. The causal machine learning literature has also opened the door to systematic heterogeneous treatment effects estimation. There is considerable interest in understanding heterogeneous treatment effects in various scientific fields, including business, economics, epidemiology, marketing, and medicine (as discussed in, e.g., [2]). The underlying premise is that treatment responses vary for subpopulations. Uncovering this variation informs our understanding of the distributional implications of a treatment and the underlying causal mechanisms, and potentially hints at more efficient targeting rules.

Ref. [3] structure the rich universe of causal machine learners. They distinguish between generic causal machine learners, which integrate a variety of off-the-shelf machine learning estimators, e.g., [4], and estimator-specific approaches, where a specific machine learner is adapted to the causal question, e.g., the tree-based methods [5–8].

The causal forest by [7] is most related to the mcf estimator [9]. In each tree in the causal forest, the feature space is recursively split to maximize the implied effect heterogeneity greedily. The authors of [7] showed that this is equivalent to minimizing the mean squared prediction error of treatment effects. Treatment effects are obtained as leaf-specific average differences averaged over all trees in the forest. Ref. [9] innovated the causal forest estimator [5,7] in two dimensions. First, the splitting criterion in the tree growing step is adapted to account for covariance structures in estimation errors of mean conditional outcomes and selection bias. Ref. [9] demonstrated in extensive simulations that the bias adjustment results in considerable performance improvements. Second, ref. [9] stipulated a computationally efficient outcome-weight-based approach, which facilitates an approximate inference of causal effects at all levels of resolution from estimating the modified causal forest once.

Since June 2021, an open-source Python implementation of the estimator has been made available on the Python Package Index (PyPI). The Python package provides an off-the-shelf tool for practitioners to analyze effect heterogeneity for multiple treatment models in a selection-on-observables setting. Related statistical software includes the Python package EconML [10] and the R package grf [11]. Both implement forest-based causal machine learners (orthogonal random forest, forest double machine learning estimator, forest doubly robust estimator, the generalized random forest). However, in contrast to the mcf, the cited packages do not infer causal effects at all levels of resolution in one estimation round.

We present the package and demonstrate its core functionality—inference of heterogeneous causal effects at different levels of resolution—in the replication of three well-published studies in the realm of epidemiology, medicine, and labor economics. Code and data can be accessed on GitHub [12]. We found that the mcf matches results on aggregate treatment effects estimation and provides additional insights on underlying effect heterogeneity as measured by the individualized and group average treatment effects.

We contribute to the literature in five dimensions: First, we present the open-source Python package that implements the mcf. Second, we provide novel results on causal effect heterogeneity for benchmark studies in epidemiology, medicine, and labor economics. In that scope, we demonstrate that the mcf matches previous results on aggregate treatment effects and effectively deals with binary and multi-valued treatments and arbitrary outcome and feature distributions. Third, for all resolutions of causal effect heterogeneity, which can be statistically identified, we provide inference. Fourth, we uncover relevant effect heterogeneity, which is potentially instructive for tailoring treatment assignments in constrained settings. Fifth, we provide data, data documentation, and code to replicate our results.

The remainder of this paper proceeds as follows. In Section 2, we delineate identification, the estimands of interest, estimation, and the package's infrastructure. For a detailed discussion of the methodology, refer to [9]. Section 3 presents the results of our replications. Finally, Section 4 concludes.

2. Framework

The mcf is a tree-based causal machine learner that produces valid causal estimates in the selection-on-observables setting. To set the scene, we detail the identification setting, define the causal parameters of interest at different levels of resolution, and outline the core ideas of the mcf and the package's infrastructure. For details of the algorithmic implementation, we refer the reader to the official documentation [9,13].

The necessary assumptions to identify causal effects in the selection-on-observables setting are the conditional independence assumption (CIA), exogeneity of the confounders, common support, and stable unit treatment value assumption (SUTVA). The CIA stipulates that treatment selection conditional on the set of so-called confounders is as good as random. By the exogeneity assumption, confounders need to be invariant to treatment assignment. The common support assumption demands that the probability of receiving a particular treatment is strictly bounded away from zero. Finally, SUTVA dictates that the observed outcome equals potential outcomes for the observed treatment state, ruling out interference between observational units or multiple versions of a treatment.

The causal parameters of interest comprise the individualized treatment effect (IATE), the group average treatment effect (GATE), and the average treatment effect (ATE). The IATE captures the expected causal impact of some treatment over another for a subpopulation, which is defined by a particular realization of confounders and further variables that are relevant for the heterogeneity analysis. To clarify, the number of comparisons that we take interest in in the multi-treatment setting with k treatments, which includes the control state, is $k(k-1)/2$. The GATE aggregates the IATEs to more coarse subpopulations, and the variables in the conditioning set are referred to as policy features. The conditioning feature(s) are (is) a low-dimensional subset of the set of confounders. Finally, the ATE is the expected causal impact for the entire population and hence obtained as a weighted average of the IATEs. For all parameters defined above, the conditioning set can be extended to include treatment group memberships. The causal parameters are then referred to as average treatment effect of the treated (ATET) and group average treatment effect of the treated (GATET), respectively.

The mcf is an instantiation of a causal forest, where splits in the tree growing process minimize the estimation error of the IATEs greedily. Ref. [9] showed that the expected mean-squared error (MSE) of the IATE can be decomposed into three parts: the two MSEs of estimating the conditional mean responses of the two treatments, which are causally compared, and the covariance of these two estimation errors (MCE). The estimates of the MSEs and the MCE are obtained as sample analogues. If no exact matches are found in all treatment leaves, the mcf uses the closest neighbor instead to compute the MCE. To guard against selection issues in finite samples, the mcf splitting rule seeks to assign individuals with different propensities of receiving a treatment to different partitions in the tree and hence prefers splits with high propensity score homogeneity. Estimates are then obtained as mean differences in the appropriate leaves. The mcf also builds upon the honesty principle, e.g., [8].

In the multiple treatment setting, one can grow the forests separately for each of the treatment comparisons or jointly for all unique treatment comparisons. For the latter case, the splits are chosen to minimize the sum of the estimated mean squared errors of the IATEs and the penalized propensity score heterogeneity. For inference, the mcf exploits that every causal forest can be written as a weighted sum of outcomes. Maintaining that observations are independent and identically distributed, ref. [9] derived an expression for the variance, which admits a utilization of standard non-parametric machine learners. The default method is k-Nearest Neighbor (k-NN) regression, but Nadaraya–Watson kernel estimation is also supported.

The *modified_causal_forest()* function in the mcf Python package implements the mcf. The user specifies treatment, outcome, confounders, policy variables, and the relevant resolutions of causal effect heterogeneity. Optionally, the user may override the defaults in the implementation—such as the grids for the parameter tuning in the forest growing process and the mode of parallelization. A detailed exposition of the functional inputs is given in the official documentation [13]. Whenever relevant, the documentation flags input arguments as critical for runtime management.

3. Empirical Studies

In this section, we demonstrate the functionality of the mcf. For three distinct research settings, we inquire to which extent the mcf matches previous estimation results on average treatment effects and provides novel insights on underlying effect heterogeneity.

3.1. Maternal Smoking during Pregnancy

Infants born at low birth weight (LBW) are more likely to experience health and development issues. Studies have found lower educational attainment, a poorer self-reported health status, and reduced employment and earnings for LBW infants, e.g., [14]. Study [15] is a well-known study that examines the impact of maternal smoking during pregnancy on birth weight, amongst other health outcomes. Adjusting for potential confounding factors, the authors of [15] estimated a negative impact of maternal smoking on birth weight. Later, ref. [16] deployed the [15] database to study multi-valued treatment effects. Ref. [16] found evidence for both (i) treatment heterogeneities and (ii) non-linearities in the effect sizes. We aimed to estimate the dose responses and to analyze IATEs along with GATEs to inform about effect heterogeneities.

We used the linked birth–infant death data in [15], which was made available to us by the author of [16]. The database compiles information for 511,940 births in Pennsylvania for the years 1989 to 1991—including details on birth weight, pregnancy, and parental characteristics. Smoking doses are defined as in [16]. We mapped the number of daily smoked cigarettes to a multivalued treatment variable, T, which takes on 6 distinct values: $T \in \{0, 1, 2, 3, 4, 5\}$ for the cigarette-bin-categories $\{0, 1-5, 6-10, 11-15, 16-20, 21+\}$. The bins were chosen to capture the mass points in the distribution, which occur roughly every five cigarettes (a quarter of a US cigarette pack).

For identification, we stipulated the prototypical selection-on-observables setting. We note that this is not an innocuous assumption as, for example, [17] convincingly discussed. We informed our choice of confounders by [15,16]. We included parental socio-demographics (age, education, and race), pregnancy-related information (number of prenatal visits, adequacy of care, indicator if alcohol was consumed during the pregnancy, number of months elapsed since last pregnancy), birth-related information (month of birth, county of birth), and mother-related information (number of previous pregnancies, number of children born dead, indicator if born abroad). A detailed summary is given in Table S14 in the Supplementary Materials file.

We explored treatment response heterogeneities for different values of (i) maternal age, (ii) race, and (iii) number of care visits. The motivation for maternal age stems from the consideration that oocytes (eggs) and embryos from older mothers tend to be more susceptible to harmful environmental conditions such as smoking, e.g., [18]. Previous empirical studies have informed the other grouping features, including [19] and [20], respectively.

We took a random draw from the largest treatment group in the training data to speed up computations. The decrease in memory requirements and increase in computational speed was achieved at relatively low cost in terms of statistical precision.

Overall, our estimation results are consistent with [15,16]. We found that smoking tends to reduce birth weight and that dose matters. Smoking more cigarettes is more detrimental in terms of birth weights (compare Table 1). The ATE for smoking one to five cigarettes over no cigarette consumption decreases from -136 to -252 for smoking 16 to 20 cigarettes over no cigarette consumption. The more detrimental effect of higher cigarette dosages is also suggested by the shifted distribution of the IATEs in Figure 1. However, none of the IATEs is significantly different from the corresponding ATEs.

We found statistically significant GATEs for race, age, and number of prenatal visits (compare Tables S1, S3, and S5 in the Supplementary Materials file). Figure 2 illustrates the estimated GATEs for the different races. The effect is significantly different from zero for races Other, Hispanic, and White, but not so for Black. The estimated GATEs for race, age class, and number of prenatal visits are all not statistically significantly different from the ATE (compare Tables S2, S4, and S6 in the Supplementary Materials file). We conclude that the mcf does not indicate statistically significant effect heterogeneity.

Table 1. ATEs in the maternal smoking during pregnancy study.

TC	[16]	mcf
T1-T0	−146 *	−136 *
T2-T0	−217 *	−213 *
T3-T0	−254 *	−228 *
T4-T0	−255 *	−252 *
T5-T0	−252 *	−250 *
T2-T1	−71 *	−77 *
T3-T1	−108 *	−92 *
T4-T1	−109 *	−115 *
T5-T1	−106 *	−114
T3-T2	−37	−15
T4-T2	−38 *	−38
T5-T2	−35 *	−37
T4-T3	−1	−23
T5-T3	2	−22
T5-T4	3	1

Notes: TC denotes treatment comparison; estimates from [16] are printed in column two, estimates from the mcf in column three. * denotes significance at the 5% level.

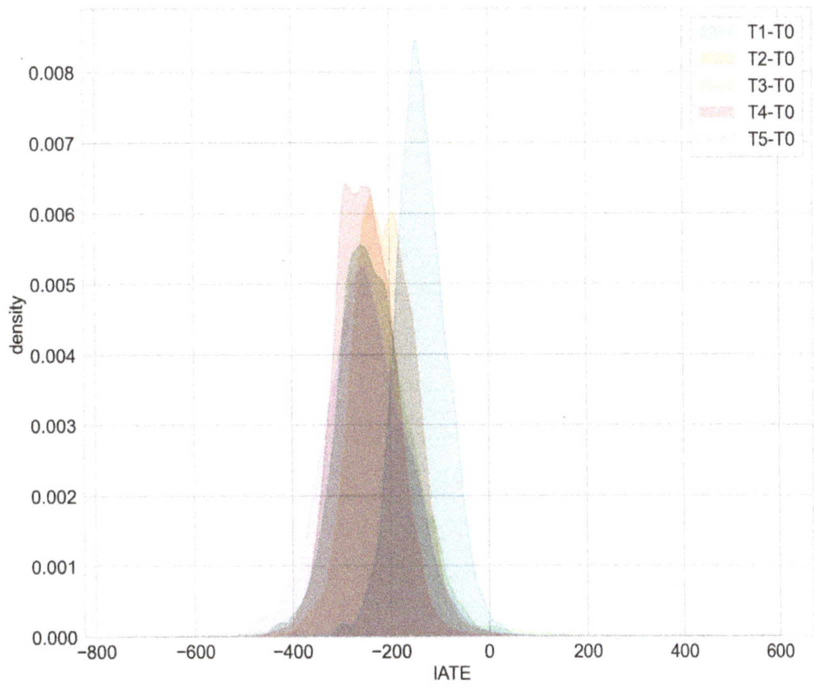

Notes: Reference treatment is no smoking during pregnancy.

Figure 1. Distribution of IATEs in the maternal smoking during pregnancy study.

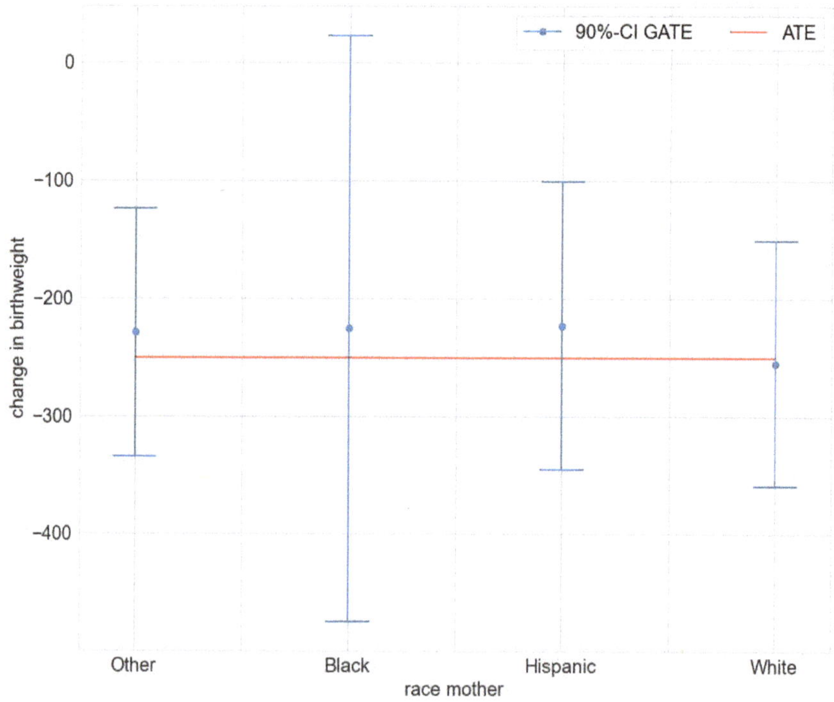

Notes: Treatment comparison is T5 versus T0.

Figure 2. GATEs for maternal race in the maternal smoking during pregnancy study.

3.2. Right Heart Catheterization

Right Heart Catheterization (RHC) is a surgical intervention widely used to monitor critically ill patients. In a seminal contribution, ref. [21] investigated the efficacy of this treatment measured by different outcomes (subsequent survival, length of stay, intensity of care, cost of care). Deploying propensity score matching, [21] found that RHC is positively associated with mortality, costs, and length of stay. The authors of [22–24] used alternative estimators and confirmed the findings in [21]. We matched previous results on the average effects of RHC on survival. Extending previous work, we added insights on effect heterogeneity, which the average treatment effect potentially masks.

The data we used are the same as in [21–24] and come from the SUPPORT prospective cohort study [25]. The data were made available by [24] (among others) and comprise information on 5735 critically ill and hospitalized adult patients between 1989 and 1994 in five medical centers spread throughout the US. Out of the 5735 patients, 2184 individuals received an RHC. In our analysis, we focused on survival within six months after treatment. As before, identification was achieved by stipulating unconfoundedness. In total, we included 55 features. For details refer to Table S15 in the Supplementary Materials file.

In the analysis of effect heterogeneity, we informed our choice of policy features by expert opinions who classified eight features as high-priority factors [22]. The high-priority factors include the nine primary disease categories, the estimated probability of surviving two months, the acute physiology and chronic health evaluation score, the Glasgow coma score indicator, age, an index of activities of daily living two weeks prior to admission, mean blood pressure, and an indicator for resuscitate status on the first day.

Table 2 juxtaposes results on the estimated average effects of RHC on mortality after six months from [22] and the mcf. Findings for the ATE and ATET are congruent in terms of effect size and statistical significance and confirm that, on average, the RHC intervention decreases survival chances. Interestingly, as displayed in Figure 3, the distribution of the IATEs shows that there is a non-negligible mass left to zero. Abstracting from estimation uncertainty, some parts of the populations are estimated to benefit from the RHC intervention. An analysis of the difference of IATEs against the ATE confirms that subpopulations, which have IATEs at the tails of the distribution in Figure 4, have treatment effects that are statistically different from the ATE.

Table 2. ATEs and ATETs in the RHC study.

Method	Estimand	Point Estimate	p-Value
ps match	ATET	0.063	0.005
gm match	ATET	0.046	0.037
mcf	ATE	0.048	0.013
mcf	ATET	0.065	0.001

Notes: ps match and gm match refer to propensity score and genetic matching applied in [22], respectively. ATE stands for the average treatment effect, ATET denotes the average treatment effect on the treated.

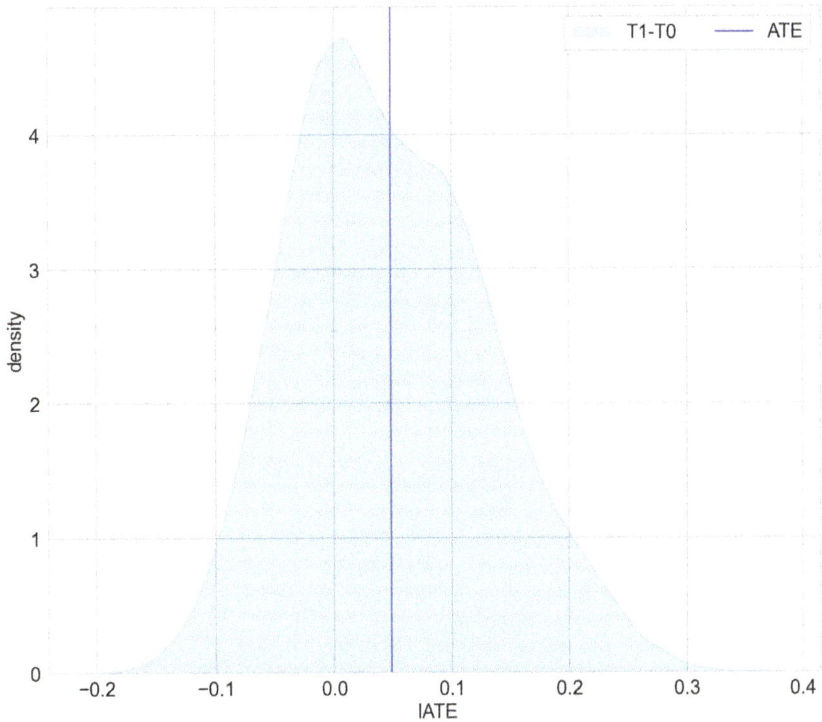

Notes: Treatment comparison is T1 versus T0.

Figure 3. Distribution of IATEs in the RHC study.

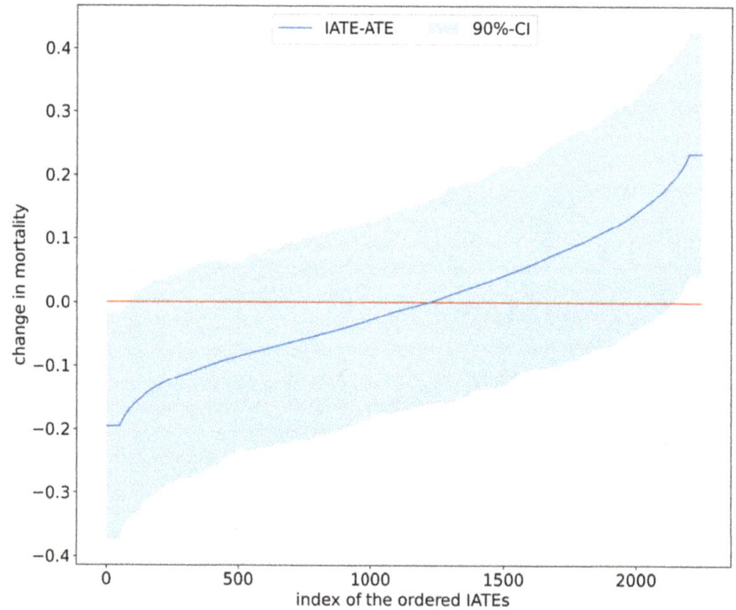

Figure 4. Sorted IATEs versus ATE in the RHC study.

The mcf uncovered group effect heterogeneity, as Table 3 shows. Six out of eight policy features exhibit significant differences of the GATEs from the ATEs, pointing to effect heterogeneity in these policy features. Four policy features exhibit statistically significant GATEs.

Exemplarily, Figure 5 summarizes the deviation of GATEs from the ATE for the policy feature blood pressure. The corresponding data for Figure 5 are included in Table S7 in the Supplementary Materials file. Figure 5 shows a significantly higher death risk for patients with extremely low diastolic blood pressure from 35 to 57 and lower death risk for a blood pressure from 106 to 145. Note that a diastolic blood pressure of zero may occur in cases of severe hypotension, stiff arteries in the elderly, diabetes, arteriovenous malformation, aortic dissection, or due to monitoring malfunction [26]. In the Supplementary Materials file we provide further results on effect heterogeneity in Tables S8 and S9. Patients with APACHE III scores ranging from 21 to 45 experience, on average, a significant increase in survival. Those with scores ranging from 55 to 66 have a significantly lower survival probability. For the policy feature summarizing the patient's primary disease, Table S9 displays a significantly higher death risk than the average for patients with non-traumatic coma.

Table 3. GATE results for the RHC study.

Feature	Evaluation Points	Number of Significant GATEs	Number of Significant GATEs-ATEs
adld3pc	27	0	0
age	50	3	9
aps1	49	15	26
cat1	9	0	1
dnr1	2	0	0
meanbp1	49	15	32
scoma1	11	0	2
surv2md1	50	1	1

Notes: The significance level was set to 10%; adld3pc is the index of activities of daily living two weeks prior to admission; aps1 is the acute physiology and chronic health evaluation score; cat1 are the nine primary disease classes; dnr1 is an indicator for resuscitate status on the first day; meanbp1 is the mean blood pressure; scoma1 is the Glasgow coma score; surv2md1 is the probability of surviving two months based on support model estimation.

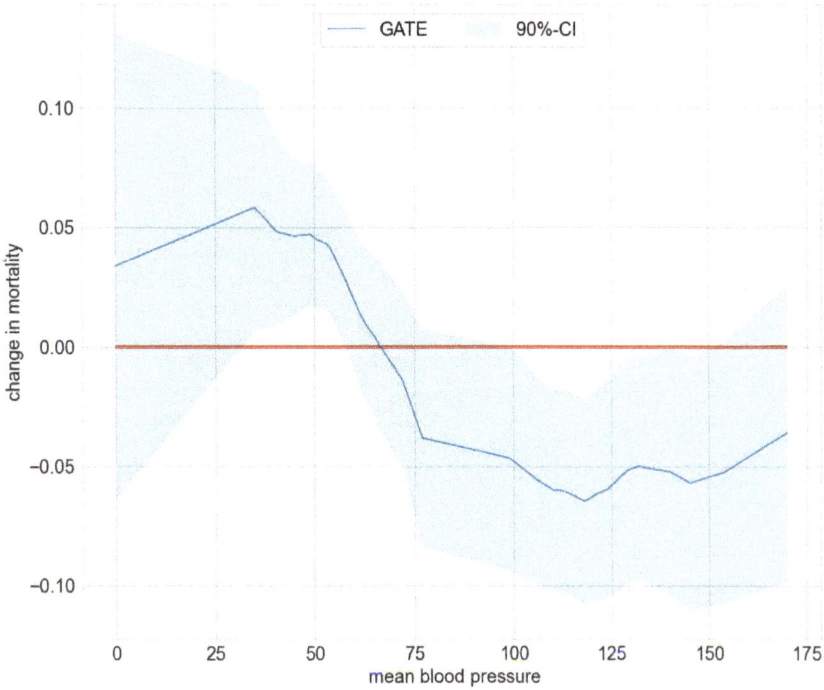

Figure 5. GATEs —ATE for mean blood pressure in the RHC study.

3.3. *The Workforce Investment Act Programs*

The Workforce Investment Act of 1998 (WIA) is the central federal workforce development legislation in the United States, which succeeded the Job Training Partnership Act (JTPA) and became operational from 1999 to 2000. The WIA programs provide services for education and training to increase the labor market prospects of adults, displaced workers, and youth. Participation in WIA services often starts in so-called one-stop centers, which are spread out over the US. In total, there are 3000 one-stop centers. More details on the WIA are summarized in [27]. Individuals participate in WIA-funded services voluntarily. The services for adults and dislocated workers fall into four categories: self-service core services, staff-assisted core services, intensive services, and training services. There are no eligibility criteria for the core services [28]. Individuals usually set up an individual training account to participate in a training service and select training and provider. Caseworkers may encourage or discourage participation in specific programs. Unlike in some European countries, caseworkers cannot sanction the clients [28,29]. The WIA was replaced by the Workforce Innovation and Opportunity Act (WIOA) in 2013. Neither the basic set of services nor eligibility were much affected by the new legislation [28,30].

Previous studies found a positive impact of receivers of training over the core and/or intensive services for WIA participants [28], and for WIA participants over Employment Service (ES) participants [31] or unemployment insurance claimants and ES participants. The authors of [30] found relevant heterogeneity in levels of program participation for the examined WIA population. For identification, refs. [28,31] relied upon a selection-on-observables framework and [30] on the invariance of conditional distributions. The authors of [28] added an analysis where selection is on unobservables but maintained bias stability across time and found similar results.

We used the database from [30]. The database synthesizes information on 85,440 individuals served by WIA and WIOA programs in California between 2012 and 2016. Treatment takes four values, $T \in \{1, 2, 3, 4\}$, where 1 indicates core services, 2 intensive service, 3 basic/general training, and 4 occupational training service. Following [30], we defined the outcome as the differences in average earnings four quarters after exiting the program and three quarters before entering it. As before, identification was achieved by stipulating conditional independence of treatment assignment and potential outcomes controlling for all observables. In total, we included 24 features. For details refer to Table S16.

Table 4 juxtaposes results on the estimated average effects from [30]—columns two to four—and the mcf—columns five to seven. Point estimates for the two estimators are aligned. The effects range from $317 to $1957 for the mcf and from $99 to $1739 for the doubly robust GMM estimation method based on inverse probability weighting applied in [30]. We observed the largest effect for the treatment pair occupational training service (T4) and core services (T1). Participating in occupational training compared to core services increased earnings on average by $1957 ([30] estimated $1739). Note that the estimated weights-based standard errors of the mcf are larger than the bootstrapped standard errors of [30], which were based on resampling estimates of the influence function.

The superiority of occupational training over core services is also reflected in Figure 6. Ignoring estimation uncertainty, the estimated IATEs for comparing occupational training (T4) versus core services (T1) are prevailingly positive.

Table 4. ATEs in the WIA programs study.

		[30]			mcf	
TC	**ATE**	**SE**	***p*-Value**	**ATE**	**SE**	***p*-Value**
T2-T1	99	41	0.02	335	63	0.00
T3-T1	1273	56	0.00	1640	87	0.00
T4-T1	1739	85	0.00	1957	126	0.00
T3-T2	1174	53	0.00	1305	81	0.00
T4-T2	1640	82	0.00	1622	122	0.00
T4-T3	466	89	0.00	317	136	0.02

Notes: TC stands for treatment comparison, ATE for average treatment effects, SE for standard errors.

Our group heterogeneity analysis focused on two policy features—claim to unemployment compensation and age. The authors of [30] showed that unemployment compensation status is an important confounding feature and hence may give rise to effect heterogeneity. Indeed, the GATE deviates statistically significantly from the ATE for the policy feature unemployment compensation. The deviations are negative for subjects with a claim to unemployment for T3 versus T1, T3 versus T2, and positive for T4 versus T3. Contrariwise, the deviations are positive for subjects without a claim to unemployment for T3 versus T1, T3 versus T2, and negative for T4 versus T2. The results also hint at meaningful effect heterogeneity for the policy feature age as measured by a significant deviation of the GATE from the ATE. For example, when comparing treatment groups T3 versus T1, the GATE deviates positively from the ATE for ages 21 to 33 and negatively for ages 45 to 67 (compare Figure 7). This hints at an optimal assignment rule that should target clients of different ages and unemployment compensation statuses differently when resource or capacity constraints are binding. Detailed results on the GATEs and GATEs minus the ATEs for both policy features age and claim to unemployment compensation are included in Tables S10–S13 in the Supplementary Materials file.

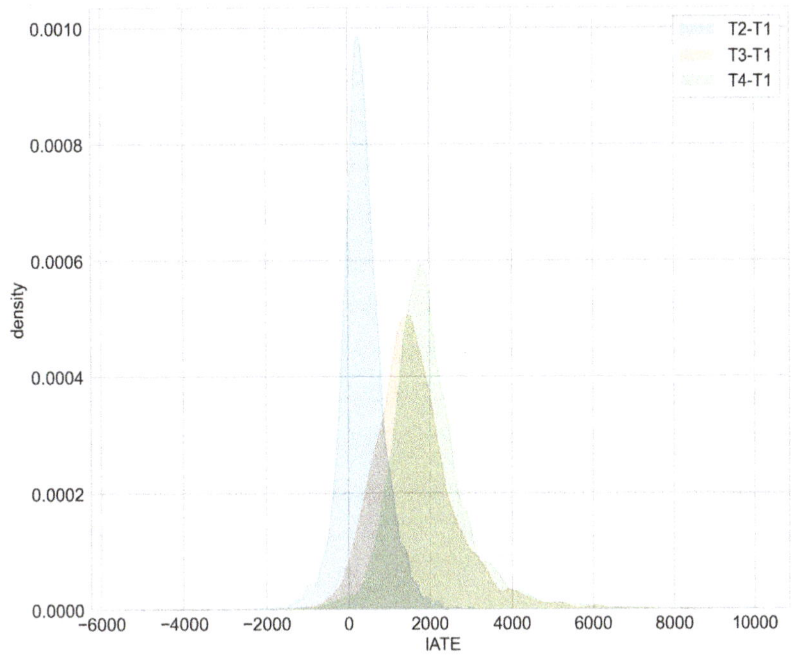

Notes: Reference treatment is treatment 1.

Figure 6. Distribution of IATEs in the WIA programs study.

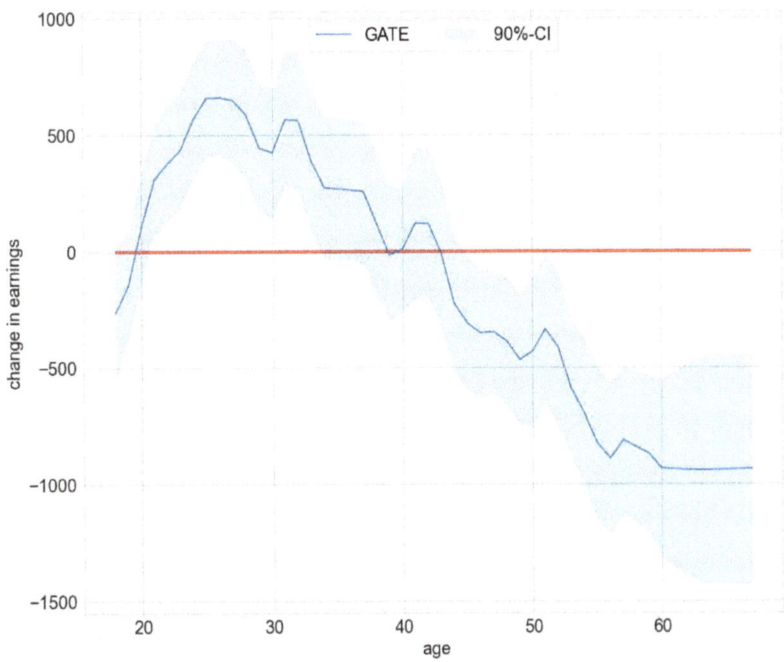

Notes: Treatment comparison is T3 versus T1.

Figure 7. GATEs —ATE by age in the WIA programs study.

4. Discussion

The modified causal forest (mcf) matched results on aggregate treatment effects estimation and provided novel insights on underlying effect heterogeneity. The distilled effect heterogeneity exhibited meaningful patterns for the RHC and WIA studies in that some populations benefited more or less than the average from the treatment intervention. The generated insights hint at more efficient targeting rules when resource or capacity constraints are binding. Mirroring the burgeoning literature in optimal policy learning, since version 0.1.0 the mcf includes a functionality to learn minimax regret optimal treatment assignments when the policy class is restricted to decision trees.

The mcf is under ongoing development to incorporate new functionalities. Since version 0.2.0, the mcf accommodates continuous treatment effects estimation as an experimental feature. In addition, the mcf provides statistics on balancing and common support to evaluate the quality of the obtained causal parameters. There is ongoing research to formalize the underlying statistics and provide critical values for practitioners.

Supplementary Materials: The supporting information can be downloaded at https://www.mdpi.com/article/10.3390/e24081039/s1. Tables S1–S13 compile results from the group average treatment affects (GATEs) analysis. Tables S14–S16 provide an exhaustive variable description of the three data sets used in the empirical analysis.

Author Contributions: All authors contributed to conceptualization, data curation, formal analysis, software, visualization, and writing (original draft, review, and editing). All authors have read and agreed to the published version of the manuscript.

Funding: Hannah Busshoff and Michael Lechner gratefully acknowledge financial support from the Swiss National Science Foundation (SNSF) (grant number SNSF 407740_187301).

Data Availability Statement: All data are made available on GitHub [12].

Conflicts of Interest: The authors declare no conflict of interest.

References

1. Imbens, G.; Wooldridge, J. Recent Developments in the Econometrics of Program Evaluation. *J. Econ. Lit.* **2009**, *47*, 5–86. [CrossRef]
2. Athey, S.; Imbens, G. The State of Applied Econometrics: Causality and Policy Evaluation. *J. Ocf Eonomic Perspect.* **2017**, *31*, 3–32. [CrossRef]
3. Knaus, M.C.; Lechner, M.; Strittmatter, A. Machine Learning Estimation of Heterogeneous Causal Effects: Empirical Monte Carlo Evidence. *Econom. J.* **2021**, *24*, 134–161. [CrossRef]
4. Chernozhukov, V.; Demirer, M.; Duflo, E.; Fernandez-Val, I. Generic Machine Learning Inference on Heterogeneous Treatment Effects in Randomized Experiments, with an Application to Immunization in India. Technical Report, National Bureau of Economic Research. 2018. Available online: https://econpapers.repec.org/paper/arxpapers/1712.04802.htm (accessed on 22 July 2022).
5. Athey, S.; Tibshirani, J.; Wager, S. Generalized Random Forests. *Ann. Stat.* **2019**, *47*, 1148–1178. [CrossRef]
6. Su, X.; Tsai, C.; Wang, H.; Nickerson, D.; Li, B. Subgroup Analysis via Recursive Partitioning. *J. Mach. Learn. Res.* **2009**, *10*, 141–158. [CrossRef]
7. Wager, S.; Athey, S. Estimation and Inference of Heterogeneous Treatment Effects using Random Forests. *J. Am. Stat. Assoc.* **2018**, *113*, 1228–1242. [CrossRef]
8. Athey, S.; Imbens, G. Recursive Partitioning for Heterogeneous Causal Effects. *Proc. Natl. Acad. Sci. USA* **2016**, *113*, 7353–7360. [CrossRef]
9. Lechner, M. Modified Causal Forests for Estimating Heterogeneous Causal Effects. *arXiv* **2019**, arXiv:1812.09487v2.
10. Available online: https://github.com/microsoft/EconML (accessed on 22 July 2022).
11. Available online: https://github.com/grf-labs/grf/ (accessed on 22 July 2022).
12. Available online: https://github.com/MCFpy/replication-BBL_2022 (accessed on 22 July 2022).
13. Available online: https://mcfpy.github.io/mcf/ (accessed on 22 July 2022).
14. Almond, D.; Currie, J.; Duque, V. Childhood Circumstances and Adult Outcomes: Act II. *J. Econ. Lit.* **2018**, *56*, 1360–1446. Available online: https://www.aeaweb.org/articles?id=10.1257/jel.20171164 (accessed on 22 July 2022). [CrossRef]
15. Almond, D.; Chay, K.; Lee, D. The Costs of Low Birth Weight. *Q. J. Econ.* **2005**, *120*, 1031–1083. Available online: https://www.princeton.edu/~davidlee/wp/birthweight.pdf (accessed on 22 July 2022).

16. Cattaneo, M. Efficient Semiparametric Estimation of Multi-Valued Treatment Effects under Ignorability. *J. Econom.* **2010**, *150*, 138–154. [CrossRef]
17. Caetano, C. A test of exogeneity without instrumental variables in models with bunching. *Econometrica* **2015**, *83*, 1581–1600. Available online: https://onlinelibrary.wiley.com/doi/abs/10.3982/ECTA11231 (accessed on 22 July 2022). [CrossRef]
18. Catt, J.; Henman, M. Toxic Effects of Oxygen on Human Embryo Development. *Hum. Reprod.* **2000**, *15*, 199–206. [CrossRef]
19. Zimmert, M.; Lechner, M. Nonparametric Estimation of Causal Heterogeneity under High-Dimensional Confounding. *arXiv* **2019**, arXiv:1908.08779v1.
20. Heiler, P.; Knaus, M. Effect or Treatment Heterogeneity? Policy Evaluation with Aggregated and Disaggregated Treatments. *arXiv* **2021**, arXiv:2110.01427.
21. Connors, A., Jr.; Speroff, T.; Thomas, C.; Dawson, N.; Harrell, F., Jr.; Wagner, D.; Desbiens, N.; Goldman, L.; Wu, A.; Califf, R.; et al. The Effectiveness of Right Heart Catheterization in the Initial Care of Critically Ill Patients. *J. Am. Med. Assoc.* **1996**, *276*, 889–897. Available online: https://pubmed.ncbi.nlm.nih.gov/8782638/ (accessed on 22 July 2022). [CrossRef]
22. Ramsahai, R.; Grieve, R.; Sekhon, J. Extending iterative matching methods: An approach to improving covariate balance that allows prioritisation. *Health Serv. Outcomes Res. Methodol.* **2011**, *11*, 95–114. [CrossRef]
23. Keele, L.; Small, D. Pre-analysis Plan for a Comparison of Matching and Black Box-based Covariate Adjustment. *Obs. Stud.* **2018**, *4*, 97–110. [CrossRef]
24. Keele, L.; Small, D. Comparing Covariate Prioritization via Matching to Machine Learning Methods for Causal Inference Using Five Empirical Applications. *Am. Stat.* **2021**, *75*, 355–363. [CrossRef]
25. Knaus, W.; Harrell, F.; Lynn, J.; Goldman, C.; Phillips, R.; Connors, A.; Dawson, N.; Fulkerson, W.; Califf, R.; Desbiens, N.; et al. The SUPPORT Prognostic Model: Objective Estimates of Survival for Seriously Ill Hospitalized Adults. *Ann. Intern. Med.* **1995**, *122*, 191–203. [CrossRef]
26. Choudhary, D.; Suthar, O.; Bhatia, P.; Biyani, G. 'Zero' diastolic blood pressure. *Indian Anaesth. Forum* **2016**, *17*, 32–33. [CrossRef]
27. Bradley, D.H. The Workforce Investment Act and the One-Stop Delivery System. *Congr. Res. Serv. Rep.* **2013**, *7*, 1–47. Available online: https://sgp.fas.org/crs/misc/R41135.pd (accessed on 22 July 2022).
28. Andersson, F.; Holzer, H.; Lane, J.; Rosenblum, D.; Smith, J. Does Federally-Funded Job Training Work? Nonexperimental Estimates of WIA Training Impacts Using Longitudinal Data on Workers and Firms. Technical report, National Bureau of Economic Research. 2013. Available online: https://www.nber.org/papers/w19446 (accessed on 22 July 2022).
29. Social Policy Research Associates with contributions by TATC Consulting. The Workforce Investment Act after Five Years: Results from the National Evaluation of the Implementation of WIA. 2004. Available online: https://www.dol.gov/sites/dolgov/files/ETA/reports/pdfs/SPR-WIA_Final_Report.pdf (accessed on 22 July 2022).
30. Ao, W.; Calonico, S.; Lee, Y. Multivalued Treatments and Decomposition Analysis: An Application to the WIA Program. University of Miami Business School Research Paper No. 18-16. 2019. Available online: https://ssrn.com/abstract=3276370 (accessed on 22 July 2022). [CrossRef]
31. Hollenbeck, K.; King, C.; Huang, W.; Schroeder, D. Net impact estimates for services provided through the Workforce Investment Act. 2005. Available online: https://purl.fdlp.gov/GPO/gpo21781 (accessed on 22 July 2022).

entropy

Article

Stan and BART for Causal Inference: Estimating Heterogeneous Treatment Effects Using the Power of Stan and the Flexibility of Machine Learning

Vincent Dorie [1], George Perrett [2], Jennifer L. Hill [2,*] and Benjamin Goodrich [3]

1 Code for America, San Francisco, CA 94103, USA
2 Department of Applied Statistics, Social Science, and the Humanities, New York University, New York, NY 10003, USA
3 Department of Political Science, Columbia University, New York, NY 10025, USA
* Correspondence: jennifer.hill@nyu.edu

Abstract: A wide range of machine-learning-based approaches have been developed in the past decade, increasing our ability to accurately model nonlinear and nonadditive response surfaces. This has improved performance for inferential tasks such as estimating average treatment effects in situations where standard parametric models may not fit the data well. These methods have also shown promise for the related task of identifying heterogeneous treatment effects. However, the estimation of both overall and heterogeneous treatment effects can be hampered when data are structured within groups if we fail to correctly model the dependence between observations. Most machine learning methods do not readily accommodate such structure. This paper introduces a new algorithm, `stan4bart`, that combines the flexibility of Bayesian Additive Regression Trees (BART) for fitting nonlinear response surfaces with the computational and statistical efficiencies of using Stan for the parametric components of the model. We demonstrate how `stan4bart` can be used to estimate average, subgroup, and individual-level treatment effects with stronger performance than other flexible approaches that ignore the multilevel structure of the data as well as multilevel approaches that have strict parametric forms.

Keywords: BART; Stan; causal inference; machine learning; heterogeneous treatment effects; multilevel data; grouped data

Citation: Dorie, V. ; Perrett, G.; Hill, J.L.; Goodrich, B. Stan and BART for Causal Inference: Estimating Heterogeneous Treatment Effects Using the Power of Stan and the Flexibility of Machine Learning. *Entropy* **2022**, *24*, 1782. https://doi.org/10.3390/e24121782

Academic Editor: Kateřina Hlaváčková-Schindler

Received: 15 August 2022
Accepted: 6 November 2022
Published: 6 December 2022

1. Introduction

Causal effects represent comparisons between outcomes in factual and counterfactual worlds. That is, for each observation in a study, we need to be able to not only measure the outcome the subjects experienced under the treatment regime they were exposed to, we also have to predict what their outcome *would have been* in a counterfactual world where they were exposed to a different treatment. Since we have no data from the counterfactual world, estimation in causal inference requires solving a difficult missing data problem. In the absence of a randomized experiment, this is often approached by conditioning treatment effect estimates on many pretreatment covariates in an attempt to ensure that estimates have adjusted for any relevant differences across groups. An increasing number of causal inference strategies approach this missing data problem (implicitly or explicitly) by predicting these missing outcomes using flexible machine learning algorithms (for example, [1–7]).

In many causal inference settings, we additionally expect that data will have a grouped structure. For instance, we might have measurements of students within schools, patients within hospitals, or individuals incarcerated within institutions. In such settings, observations may have correlated error structures within these groups. We may also have reason to believe that the impact of the treatment exposure will vary across these groups. Most current machine-learning-based causal inference strategies either ignore such error structure or assume that errors are independently and identically distributed. Moreover, while these approaches may allow for estimation of treatment effect heterogeneity across groups they typically do so inefficiently and fail to capitalize on a potential distribution for these varying effects. In essence, typically these algorithms can at best accommodate a fixed effects approach to groups rather than a random effects approach.

On the other hand, multilevel models, in various forms, have been used for decades to accommodate grouped error structures and to efficiently estimate varying treatment effects [8–10]. This approach has been particularly successful in the context of randomized experiments where the concern about appropriately incorporating covariates is minimized for two key reasons. The most primal reason is that in a completely randomized experiments, we do not need to condition on covariates at all to obtain unbiased estimates of treatment effects. However, even if we do fit a model conditional on covariates to experimental data (for example, to achieve greater efficiency), treatment effects estimates should be relatively robust to model misspecification due to the fact that common support across treatment groups is ensured in expectation [9,11].

This paper introduces a multilevel machine-learning-based approach to causal effect estimation that combines the strengths of these two existing modeling frameworks. It builds on an established machine learning algorithm, Bayesian Additive Regression Trees (BART; [12,13]), that provides a flexible fit to the relationship between the outcome and the covariates. The traditional form of the model is extended, however, to include a parametric component that allows for covariates to be included with explicit parametric forms and additionally allows group-level deviations from the common parameters to be modeled with a hierarchical structure. The Markov chain Monte Carlo algorithm in Stan is used to draw the unknowns in the parametric component and the hierarchical structure, given the trees, and the BART algorithm is used to draw the trees, given the parametric and hierarchical components. This Gibbs sampling algorithm is, to our knowledge, the first to combine BART and Stan updates.

2. Background and Context

This section provides some background and a summary of the building blocks of our new algorithm, `stan4bart`. It also discusses other approaches to causal inference for heterogeneous treatment effect estimation in settings with grouped data.

2.1. BART

Bayesian Additive Regression Trees (BART; [12,13]) is a Bayesian machine learning algorithm that can provide a flexible fit for a wide variety of conditional expectations of the general form $\mathrm{E}[Y \mid X]$, where Y denotes the outcome of interest and X represents a vector of covariates or predictors. The standard BART algorithm has been implemented in several packages including `BayesTree`, `bartMachine`, and `BART`. We focus on the `dbarts` [14] software package because it has an efficient implementation of the base BART algorithm and was explicitly designed to incorporate model extensions of the kind described in this paper.

While the standard BART implementation assumes a continuous response and normal, independent, and identically distributed errors, many extensions have been proposed. One of the original BART papers describes a variation for a binary response based on a probit link [13]. Extensions of this implementation capitalize on better priors or the use of cross-validation to choose hyperparameters for the default priors resulting in better performance (for example see [15]). Subsequent work has extended BART for a wide variety of different regression models for categorical, count, zero-inflated, multivariate, and right-censored survival responses [16–20].

2.2. BART for Causal Inference

BART has been proposed as a strategy for estimating causal effects [1]. The basic idea is to use the algorithm to fit $\mathrm{E}[Y \mid X, Z]$ in a way that minimizes assumptions about the parametric relationships between the outcome, Y, and the covariates, X, while allowing that relationship to vary across treatment groups defined by Z. This provides a flexible approach to making predictions about missing counterfactual values (for example, the outcome a participant would be predicted to experience under a different treatment regime) based on the observed covariates. Moreover, this approach allows for the estimation of posterior predictive distributions for each potential outcome, which enables the formation of coherent uncertainty intervals both for potential outcomes and causal effects. The use of BART for causal inference is explained in more detail later in the paper.

BART has been shown to have strong performance relative to standard parametric models as well as a variety of machine learning approaches to regression [1,12,15,21–25]. Functions to facilitate the use of BART for causal inference have been implemented in the `bartCause` function (with `dbarts` at its foundation), which is described in more detail in Section 5.1.

2.3. Causal Inference with Multilevel Data

The standard BART model assumes that error terms are independently, identically, and normally distributed, which limits its applicability. Extensions have been proposed to accommodate heteroskedasticity in error terms and non-Gaussian response variables [17,20,26]. However, none of these approaches allow for a dependence between error terms. Bisbee [27] used BART in an explicitly multilevel setting, however, groups were only incorporated as fixed effects, and thus no direct correlations were modeled. Zeld et al. [6] fit a semiparametric model with an arbitrary linear term, but no multilevel component. Moreover, Hahn et al. [7] proposed an extension of BART for causal inference, Bayesian causal forests (BCF), which has advantages for estimating heterogeneous treatment effects. In the standard implementation, however, the errors were assumed to be independent. Multilevel extensions to BCF (random intercepts and varying slopes on treatment assignment) have been used in applied work [28–30] but no software has been made available.

Suk and Kang [31] fit models that are in some ways conceptually similar to those in `stan4bart`, with arbitrarily complex, machine learning components as well as parametric, linear ones. However, their primary aim was to produce consistent estimates in the presence of unmeasured, group-level confounders and as such, their approach addressed a different issue. Another related BART extension was described in Spanbauer and Sparapani [32]. This approach incorporated random effects for longitudinal repeated measures into the BART model as well as subject clustering within groups.

As a precursor to `stan4bart`, BART with varying intercepts was implemented as `rbart_vi` in the `dbarts` package. It was also independently developed in [33]. `stan4bart` allows for more general multilevel structures. This paper compares the performance of traditional BART with `rbart_vi` and `stan4bart`, as well as several other options.

3. Notation, Estimands, and Assumptions

We formalize our model and assumptions relying on the Rubin–Neyman causal model [34,35]. For simplicity, we focus on situations with a binary treatment variable, Z. Exposure to Z_i for observation i allows the potential outcome under treatment, $Y_i(Z_i = 1) \equiv Y_i(1)$, to manifest. A lack of exposure (or possibly exposure to a different treatment modality) leads to the expression of the other potential outcome $Y_i(Z_i = 0) \equiv Y_i(0)$. The observed outcome $Y_i = Y_i(0) \times (1 - Z_i) + Y_i(1) \times Z_i$ is thus a function of the potential outcomes and the treatment assignment. Even though we focus on group-structured data, this article only considers situations where treatment assignment occurs at the individual level.

3.1. Estimands

In our framework, several estimands are of interest. In this section, we index observations by i and refrain from further indexing by groups as this is unnecessary for our purposes and merely clutters the notation. We start by defining an individual-level causal effect on unit i as $\tau_i = Y_i(1) - Y_i(0)$. The estimand is rarely an inferential goal because it is not identifiable without extremely strong assumptions [36]. However, the individual-level causal effect is a building block for many common causal estimands, which can be expressed as averages of this estimand over different subsamples.

Consider, for instance, the sample average treatment effect (SATE) which takes an average of these individual effects over the entire sample, SATE $= \frac{1}{N}\sum_i^N \tau_i$, where N denotes the size of our analytic sample. In observational studies we often care more about estimating the average treatment effect for those who we observe to self-select into a treatment or program, or conversely on those who have not yet had access to a treatment or program. These concepts map more closely to estimands referred to as the effect of the treatment on the treated or the effect of the treatment on the controls. This paper focuses on the former quantity measured for our sample. This estimand, the sample average treatment effect on the treated (SATT), can be formalized as SATT $= \frac{1}{N_t}\sum_i^N \tau_i \mathrm{I}(Z_i = 1)$, where $N_t = \sum_i^N Z_i$ is the number of people in the treatment group. It is worth noting, however, that BART and `stan4bart` can be used to estimate population and conditional versions of these estimates as well [1].

Researchers with access to observational multilevel data might also be curious to explore whether treatment effects vary over the groups that define the multilevel data structure. Thus, we also explore the performance of our estimation strategy with regard to group-level causal estimands that can capture the heterogeneity in average treatment effects across groups (such as hospitals, schools, or counties). If we use $g[i]$ to denote the group membership of person i, we can define a group-level sample average treatment effect for group g as GSATE(g) $= \frac{1}{n_g}\sum_i^N \tau_i \mathrm{I}(g[i] = g)$, where $n_g = |\{i : g[i] = g\}|$ denotes the sample size in group g. A group-level analog to the SATT is thus the group-level sample average treatment for group g among the treated, GSATT(g) $= \frac{1}{n_g^1}\sum_i^N \tau_i \mathrm{I}(g[i] = g)\mathrm{I}(Z_i = 1)$. Here, n_g^1 denotes the number of treated observations in group g such that $n_g^1 = |\{i : g[i] = g, Z_i = 1\}|$.

To understand the treatment effect heterogeneity at a more fine-grained level it would help to be able to estimate individual-level causal effects directly. Since τ_i is generally not identifiable without extreme assumptions, researchers increasingly focus instead on the conditional average treatment effect function, CATE(x) $= \mathrm{E}[\tau_i | X_i = x_i]$. An important property of the CATE is that the estimator with the smallest mean squared error (MSE) for CATE will also have the smallest MSE for the individual causal effect, τ_i [4]. If we can obtain accurate estimates of the CATE across the instantiations of the covariate values defined in our sample, it will allow us to explore the treatment effect heterogeneity more flexibly (see, for instance, [37]). Henceforth, we refer to each CATE that reflects the covariate values specific to an individual in our sample as an iCATE; the collection of these for our sample is referred to as the iCATEs for our sample.

3.2. Assumptions

The BART and stan4bart approaches to causal inference yield unbiased estimates only if several assumptions are satisfied. The first assumption requires that we have measured all confounders for the effect of Z on Y. This so-called unconfoundedness, or ignorability, assumption can be formalized as $Y(0), Y(1) \perp Z \mid X$ [34], where X denotes all measured pretreatment covariates in our analysis, both at the individual and group level (we drop the subscripts here for convenience). The intuition behind this assumption is that it allows us to use information from observations in one treatment condition to help make predictions about the other counterfactual outcome of a similar observation in a different treatment condition. Here, similarity is defined by the covariates. This is generally considered to be a strong assumption and it is untestable. For strategies to address potential violations of this assumption see, for instance, Dorie et al. [23], Carnegie et al. [38].

If for a given individual no similar observations exist that received a different treatment, it may be challenging to make a prediction for that individual's potential outcome under that different treatment. Therefore, we additionally make an assumption that all neighborhoods of the covariate space with observations have a nonzero probability of having both treated and control observations. This is often referred to as an overlap or common support assumption and can be formalized as $0 < \Pr(Z = z \mid X) < 1$. If this assumption fails to hold, a general strategy is to identify which observations lack empirical counterfactuals. Several BART-based strategies have been developed to identify and discard these observations [22] and there is evidence that these perform better than traditional propensity score strategies.

Our definition of potential outcomes above implicitly assumed that the only treatment assignment that is necessary to define the potential outcomes for observation k is the treatment received by that observation, Z_k. Moreover, for a treatment effect estimand to have meaning, we must assume that the treatment assigned to each of the different observations and referred to as Z takes only one form. As a crude example, it would not make sense to define an estimand with weight loss intervention, Z, if Z_a refers to a drug and Z_b refers to an exercise regime. These assumptions are often jointly referred to as the stable unit treatment value assumption (SUTVA) [39]. While studies can be designed to increase the plausibility of SUTVA, researchers often have access to data where they do not have this type of control over the study design and rather hope that it holds approximately. To decrease the complexity of the issues addressed in this paper, we assume that SUTVA holds.

When these structural assumptions hold, then $E[Y(0) \mid X] = E[Y \mid Z = 0, X]$ and $E[Y(1) \mid X] = E[Y \mid Z = 1, X]$. That means that our task as data analysts can be reduced to a modeling task. Our goal then is to reduce the parametric assumptions required to estimate these conditional expectations and appropriately reflect our uncertainty about these estimates. The proposed algorithm is intended to provide robust inference in this setting.

4. Combining Stan and BART: `stan4bart`

This section describes how Stan [40] and BART are integrated to form a new modeling strategy. Since this section focuses on modeling strategies for observed data, we now use lower-case letters for observed covariates, x, and treatment assignment, z, when we condition on these in our model. When it is desired to extrapolate the following results to population level quantities, X can once more be treated as a random variable.

4.1. Stan and Variations on the No-U-Turn Sampler

One of the original motivations [41] for developing the MCMC algorithm in Stan was to draw from the posterior distribution of multilevel models more efficiently than the pure Metropolis–Hastings and Gibbs sampling algorithms that preceded it. Pure Metropolis–Hastings algorithms often have an optimal acceptance probability below 0.25, implying that only about one in four MCMC iterations move from the previous state and that the mixing is slow. Gibbs samplers draw a unique value of each parameter (block) from its full-conditional distributions, but when the variance of the full-conditional distribution is small, they do not move very far from the previous state.

Stan has not relied on the algorithm described in [41] since the release of version 2.10 in 2016, but its current performance is at least as good [42]. Hamiltonian MCMC algorithms, like the one in Stan, work by analogy to Hamiltonian physics [41,43]. The vector of unknown *location* parameters is augmented with a vector of *momentum* parameters of the same size. These momentum parameters are assumed to be independent, and each has a Gaussian prior with mean zero and a standard deviation that is tuned during the warm-up phase of the algorithm. Since the momentum parameters do not enter the likelihood function, their posterior distribution is the same as their prior distribution. However, the realizations of the momentum parameters serve as a catalyst to provide an initial push to the location parameters that moves them through a parameter space whose topology is defined by the log-likelihood function with the logarithm of the probability density functions (PDFs) specified for the prior on the location parameters. The location parameters continue to evolve forward (that is, with the momentum realization) and backward (that is, opposite the momentum realization) in time until the Euclidean distance between the forward-moving and backward-moving location parameters starts to shrink, at which point a *U-turn* is declared and a realization of the location parameters is taken from the footprints they made along their journey via multinomial sampling with products of Metropolis-like acceptance probabilities. However, unlike pure Metropolis–Hasting algorithms, the algorithm in Stan yields an acceptance probability that is usually very close to 1. The realized parameter vector is then used as the starting point for the next iteration when a new realization of the momentum parameters is obtained.

As a result—and unlike both Gibbs sampling and pure Metropolis–Hastings algorithms—the first-order autocorrelation between consecutive realizations of a parameter tends to be negative with Stan and the autocorrelations at higher lags tend to dissipate quickly. The formula for effective sample size used by Stan is $\frac{S}{1+\sum_{j=1}^{\infty}\rho_j}$, where S is the nominal number of MCMC draws and ρ_j is the j-th order autocorrelation between draws that are separated by j steps. If the first-order autocorrelation is sufficiently negative, then the denominator is less than 1, and the estimator of the mean is better than would be obtained from independent draws even if it were possible to obtain independent draws.

4.2. *Stan for Multilevel Models*

Our work seeks to augment the BART model with a grouped error structure such as those found in more traditional multilevel models. We review that framework first.

A general, linear, multilevel model for one observation can be written as

$$\begin{aligned} Y \mid \vec{\beta}, \vec{\lambda}, \epsilon &= x^{\beta}\vec{\beta} + w\vec{\lambda} + \epsilon, \\ \vec{\lambda} \mid \Sigma_{\lambda} &\sim \mathrm{N}(0, \Sigma_{\lambda}), \\ \epsilon \mid \sigma &\sim \mathrm{N}(0, \sigma^2). \end{aligned} \tag{1}$$

Here, $\vec{\beta}$ is a traditional linear, parametric vector of coefficients and x^{β} is a standard linear model design vector. The first element of x^{β} is often the constant "1", so that the first element of $\vec{\beta}$ enters the model as an offset or baseline. $\vec{\lambda}$ is the vector of all parametric random intercepts and slopes and w is a sparse vector which serves to select out and weight the appropriate random values, essentially containing group-level dummy variables and interactions between the group-level dummy variables and other predictors in x^{β}. To imply the correct covariance structure, Σ_{λ} consists of block-diagonal repetitions of the covariance matrices of the values for one or more grouping factors. For an explanation of the design of $\vec{\lambda}$, w, and Σ_{λ}, see [44]. Finally, the errors (ϵ) are independent of the group variation and normally distributed with an expectation of zero and a variance of σ^2. All inference is conditional on both the x^{β} and w vectors.

The Bayesian version of such a model fit by Stan—and extended by `stan4bart`— includes prior distributions for $\vec{\beta}$, Σ_{λ}, and σ (or σ^2). The prior distribution on the covariance matrix, Σ_{λ}, can be rather consequential but rarely do researchers have strong beliefs about it. It is now commonplace when using Stan to decompose covariance matrix as $\Sigma = DCD$, where D is a diagonal matrix of standard deviations and C is a correlation matrix. The prior on the standard deviations is fairly easy to specify, as any proper distribution for positive random variables would do and even improper ones often work fine. By default, the prior on the standard deviations is an exponential prior, which has maximum entropy among positive random variables with a given expectation. The prior on the correlation matrix—if it has more than one row and column—is jointly uniform by default over all symmetric, positive definite matrices that have ones along their diagonal. This LKJ prior for correlation matrices is used the vast majority of the time in Stan programs, but a shape hyperparameter can be specified to a value greater than 1 to concentrate on the identity matrix [45]. A shape hyperparameter value between zero and one is mathematically possible, which would make sense if the identity matrix were thought to be the least likely correlation matrix rather than the prior mode.

Unlike frequentist estimators of multilevel models [44] that integrate $\vec{\lambda}$ out of the original likelihood function to form a new likelihood function that can be maximized with respect to $\vec{\beta}$ and the group-level (co-)variances only, the Bayesian approach can—and in our case, does—condition on the group-level structure defined by w and draws posterior realizations of $\vec{\lambda}$ jointly along with the other parameters. In our experience, maximizing the integrated likelihood function often yields an optimum on the boundary of the parameter space where some diagonal element of the error covariance matrix is zero or the covariance matrix is otherwise numerically singular. Bates et al. [46] report a similar experience with such models in the field of psychological linguistics but recommends eliminating variance components until numerical maximization is reliable and substantively useful. This problem is avoided automatically with MCMC and proper priors that constrain all the draws to be on the interior of the parameter space to yield good estimates of posterior means, medians, and quantiles, even if the posterior mode might be on the boundary of the parameter space.

4.3. Bayesian Additive Regression Trees

The BART algorithm consists of two pieces: a sum-of-trees model and a regularization prior. We describe the algorithm in a slightly extended way as compared to the original paper [12] to distinguish between the treatment variable, z, and the rest of the predictors, x. For a response variable Y ranging continuously between -0.5 and 0.5, a treatment variable z, and predictors x, we describe the sum-of-trees model by $Y = f(x, z; \vec{T}, \vec{M}) + \epsilon$, where $\epsilon \sim N(0, \sigma^2)$ and $f(x, z; \vec{T}, \vec{M}) = g(x, z; T_1, M_1) + g(x, z; T_2, M_2) + \cdots + g(x, z; T_m, M_m)$. (T_j, M_j) defines a single regression tree submodel where T_j is the tree topology and branching rules, M_j are constants associated with each leaf node, and $g(x, z; T_j, M_j)$ is a function that uses T_j to map (x, z) to a value in M_j. The number of trees is typically allowed to be large (Chipman et al. [12,13] originally suggested 200, though some recent work suggests that 50 may be sufficient [47], and in practice this number should not exceed the number of observations in the sample). As is the case with related sum-of-trees strategies (such as boosting), the algorithm requires a strategy to avoid overfitting. With BART this is achieved through a regularization prior that allows each (T_j, M_j) tree to contribute only a small part to the overall fit. BART fits the sum-of-trees model using an MCMC algorithm that cycles between draws of (T_j, M_j) conditional on σ and draws of σ conditional on all of the (T_j, M_j). Convergence can be monitored by plotting the residual standard deviation σ over time, though in general it makes sense to choose a statistic more relevant to one's inferential goals.

The BART prior works to avoid overfitting by specifying distributions that help control the size of each tree, the shrinkage applied to the fit from each tree, and the uncertainty associated with the residual standard error. Interested readers can find more information on the model, prior, and fitting algorithms in Chipman et al. [12,13]. The key point is that BART can be used to flexibly fit even highly nonlinear response surfaces, which is consistent with our goal to fit $E[Y(1) \mid x] - E[Y(0) \mid x]$ without making undue parametric assumptions.

Finally, we note that binary outcomes can be modeled by fixing σ to 1 and treating Y as a latent variable where $Y' = \mathrm{I}\{Y > 0\}$ is observed.

4.4. `stan4bart`

For an arbitrary continuous response variable, `stan4bart` augments the multilevel model above by fitting the following, conditioned on covariates:

$$\begin{aligned} Y \mid \vec{\beta}, \vec{\lambda}, \epsilon, \vec{M}, \vec{T} &= x^{\beta}\vec{\beta} + f(x, z; \vec{M}, \vec{T}) + w\vec{\lambda} + \epsilon, \\ \vec{\lambda} \mid \Sigma_{\lambda} &\sim \mathrm{N}(0, \Sigma_{\lambda}), \\ \epsilon \mid \sigma &\sim \mathrm{N}(0, \sigma^2). \end{aligned} \tag{2}$$

This model differs from that of Equation (1) in the inclusion of $f(x; \vec{M}, \vec{T})$, a nonparametric sum-of-trees fit by BART (note that this component may or may not include z, we keep the term in the model for generality). The same latent variable formulation that allows BART to fit binary outcomes applies here.

The two sets of covariates, x and x^{β}, are integrated into a single model by first eliminating the global intercept term from x^{β}. Instead, for continuous outcomes the prior over the mean is explicitly set to the midpoint of the range of the response, and for binary outcomes it is set to 0.5. Shrinkage to different values in the binary case is supported by manually supplying a constant on the probit scale, as in [13]. In addition, having two design vectors raises the practical question when specifying a model of choosing which variables are included in each set. We discuss this at greater length below in Section 4.5; however, at this point it is sufficient to say that x and x^{β} can share components without restriction.

At a high level, the model is implemented as a Gibbs sampler [48]. The parametric components given the nonparametric one are jointly sampled using a Hamiltonian Monte Carlo, no-U-turn sampler with a diagonal Euclidean adaptation matrix [41,42] and the converse is sampled sequentially through trees using the original BART's *Bayesian backfitting* approach [12]. As discussed above, $\vec{\beta}$, σ, and Σ_{λ} are all given priors and are included in the parametric sampling step.

In practical terms, this is accomplished by modifying and compiling into C++ a parametric Stan model that fits the above equation, with $f(x, z; \vec{M}, \vec{T})$ treated as a generic linear *offset*, that is, a fixed value that shifts the mean of the response. The model itself is adapted from those used in the `rstanarm` package, a collection of model fitting functions implemented in Stan for the `R` programming language [49]. This C++ code is encapsulated in a custom mutable Stan sampler object which is coupled with a BART sampler set to have a fixed variance parameter and an offset term of its own. Using a "$\text{vec}_i \cdot$" operator to denote a vector that comprises $i = 1, \ldots, N$ scalar values to run the Stan sampler collects the current draws of the BART sum-of-trees predictions for all observations into $\text{vec}_i f(x_i, z_i; \vec{M}, \vec{T})$. It uses these to produce a draw of $\vec{\beta}, \vec{\lambda}, \sigma, \Sigma_{\lambda} \mid \vec{Y}, \text{vec}_i f(x_i, z_i; \vec{M}, \vec{T})$. From this, σ and $\text{vec}_i \left[x_i^{\beta} \vec{\beta} + w_i \vec{\lambda} \right]$ are passed to BART. Then, the BART sampler produces a draw of each tree, $M_j, T_j \mid \vec{Y}, \text{vec}_i \left[x_i^{\beta} \vec{\beta} + w_i \vec{\lambda} \right], \sigma, M_{-j}, T_{-j}$. $\text{vec}_i f(x_i, z_i; \vec{M}, \vec{T})$ is passed back to Stan, completing the cycle. This proceeds from starting points sampled from the prior distribution over BART trees with the offset and variance estimated from a linear or binary, multilevel model maximum likelihood fit, repeats through a warm-up phase during which the Stan sampler performs adaptation of its proposal distribution, and finally iterates through the set of samples from the posterior that are intended for inference. While this strategy is similar to a similar proposal [50], our approach allows the same covariates in the parametric and nonparametric components and has a shareable software implementation.

4.5. `stan4bart` *Model Specification*

Individual level covariates can enter a `stan4bart` model in the parametric mean component, the nonparametric mean component, or both. Parametric terms for covariates that are not included in the nonparametric component of the model have the benefit of being interpretable as Bayesian multilevel regression coefficients with the downside of potentially requiring nonlinearities and interactions to be explicitly specified. On the other hand, exclusively nonparametric terms are more flexible, but suffer from reduced explicability [51].

The pros and cons of including covariates in both components of the model are not clear-cut, however, we can consider some use cases. For instance, suppose we know that some of the covariates are particularly important for predicting the outcome, but we are unsure that the relationship will be easily captured by a parametric model. We may also believe that the stronger a continuous covariate's association with the outcome, the harder it is to accurately approximate its true relationship to the outcome with step functions and regression trees. In that case, including such a covariate in both model components may have computational benefits because it may simplify the nonparametric model, which now just has to account for the part of the response surface that *is not* linear. This specification might lead to faster convergence and, potentially, more precise estimates.

On the other hand, what if we are fairly confident in our specification of a parametric model for some covariates? In that case, one might wonder what could be gained from additionally including one or more of the covariates from that parametric model in the nonparametric component. However, in this setting, including a covariate in both components is an example of *parameter expansion*, a technique often employed in Gibbs samplers to reduce dependence between parameters and increase the efficiency of the sampler [52–54]. In such a case, neither the parametric nor the nonparametric components would be directly identifiable but crucially their sum would still be. Thus, while we might not strive to overparametrize, we are hopeful it need not be problematic if we do. More research will need to be performed to confirm this.

Consequently, we offer the following practical guidance on how to include predictors in `stan4bart` models:

- If a parameter *must* be interpreted as a regression coefficient or if the functional form of its relationship to the response is known, include it only in the parametric component.
- Otherwise, include all individual predictors in the nonparametric component.
- Consider including strong predictors or ones that are substantively associated with the outcome in both components, but be mindful that in doing so, the *linear model coefficients are not directly interpretable*.
- Users who are comfortable with the above caveat can center their model on a simple linear regression, so that BART effectively handles only the non-linearities in the residuals of that fit.

4.6. *stan4bart Software*

The `stan4bart` package in R, available on the Comprehensive R Archive Network (CRAN), provides a user-friendly, multithreaded implementation of the algorithm above. Models are specified by using the following language constructs, chosen to be familiar to users of other R software packages:

- The R standard left-hand-side–tilde–right-hand-side formula construct gives the base of a parametric linear model, for example, `response ~ covariate_a + covariate_b + covariate_a:covariate_b`.
- Multilevel structure is included by adding to the formula, terms of the form `(1 + covariate_c | grouping_factor)`, where the left-hand side of the vertical bar gives intercepts and slopes, while the right-hand side specifies the variable across which those values should vary. The full set of syntax implemented is described in Bates et al. [44].
- The BART component is specified by adding to the formula, a term of the form `bart(covariate_d + covariate_e)`. In this case, the "+" symbol is symbolic, indicating the inclusion of additional variables among those eligible for tree splits.

As a convenience, a "`.`" can be used to specify all available variables, and subtraction ("`-`") can be used to remove variables from that set. A typical shorthand for fitting a causal model with varying intercepts and slope for treatment would be specified similar to the formula `response ~ treatment + bart(. - group) + (1 + treatment | group)`.

5. BART and stan4bart for Causal Inference

It is straightforward to use BART and `stan4bart` to estimate any of a variety of average treatment effects under the assumptions above. We first describe the standard BART implementation and then discuss the additional modeling choices that arise when using `stan4bart`.

5.1. *BART for Causal Inference*

When using BART for causal inference the first step is to fit BART to the observed data, that is, the outcome given the treatment indicator and covariates. Based on evidence from simulations and previous data analysis challenges, we recommend running 8 to 10 chains for each BART fit [55] and checking convergence using a statistic that is meaningful for the desired estimand (such as the SATT estimate [37]).

The model fit can be used to make predictions for two counterfactual datasets [1]. The covariates are kept intact for both; however, in one, all treatment values are set to 0, and in the other they are all set to 1. This allows BART or `stan4bart` to draw from the posterior distribution for $\mathrm{E}[Y(0) \mid X = x]$ and $\mathrm{E}[Y(1) \mid X = x]$ for each person, meaning that we can also obtain draws from $\mathrm{E}[Y(1) - Y(0) \mid X = x]$, the iCATE for each person. Various combinations of these posterior distributions and the observed data can then be used to obtain posterior distributions of average treatment effects either for the full dataset or any subset thereof, and for sample, condition, and population quantities.

For example, consider the SATT estimand. Our best guess of $Y_i(1)$ for anyone in the treatment group is simply their observed outcome, Y_i. Our estimate of $Y_j(0)$, however, is the mean (or median) draw from the posterior predictive distribution for the counterfactual outcome for individual i in group j, $\tilde{Y}_i(0)$. We can thus define a new quantity $\tilde{\tau}_i$ to be the draw of the individual treatment effect for individual i from its posterior predictive distribution. Averages of these draws can be used to estimate the SATT. More specific subsets of this summation can be used to estimate any subgroup estimand of interest including the SGATE, SGATT, and iCATEs defined above.

The R package `bartCause` (available on CRAN) provides a handy wrapper function for the `dbarts` implementation of BART and `stan4bart` that simplifies the process of using BART for causal inference by implementing the fitting and prediction steps described above and by setting the defaults for the prior specification and model fitting (number of chains, iterations per chain, etc.) to values found to be useful in practice. It is straightforward to make inferences about any of the estimands described in this article either as estimates and confidence intervals or draws from the (Monte Carlo approximation to the) relevant posterior or posterior predictive distribution.

5.2. *stan4bart for Causal Inference*

To use `stan4bart` for causal inference, we can also use the algorithm directly. The key is to specify the model so that it is possible to extract information about the appropriate estimands. There are now two additional parametric pieces of the model to specify, however, $x^{\beta}\vec{\beta}$ and $w\vec{\lambda}$. As described above, we advise parsimony when specifying $x^{\beta}\vec{\beta}$. It should be used for predictors that have special significance (for instance, the treatment variable in a causal analysis), predictors (or transformations thereof) suspected to have a linear relationship with the outcome, or suspected moderators. $w\vec{\lambda}$ captures intercepts and slopes that vary across groups.

Suppose you wanted to fit a model for causal inference, assuming that the response variable, y, treatment variable, z, and a grouping variable, g, are in a data frame `data` together with any additional confounders The following code demonstrates how to specify the `stan4bart` function to estimate treatment effects in a setting where you suspect that observations are correlated within groups (operationalized as g).

```
# varying intercepts
# we will train the model on the observed data in "data"
# but we also need to construct a dataset, "data.test",
# we use data.test to obtain counterfactual predictions
data.test <- data
data.test$z <- 1 - data.test$z
fit <- stan4bart(
# this next line only includes varying intercepts
y ~ z + bart(. - g) + (1 | g),
train = data,
test = data.test
)
```

To fit a `stan4bart` model that additionally accommodates varying slopes, the group structure term can be altered as follows to account for varying slopes across groups:

```
# varying intercepts and slopes
# this code is similar to above in creating training and
```

```
# test datasets
data.test <- data
data.test$z <- 1 - data.test$z
fit <- stan4bart(
# this next line includes the varying slopes for z
y ~ z + bart(. - g) + (1 + z | g),
train = data,
test = data.test
)
```

stan4bart has been integrated into the bartCause package for ease of use producing estimates of a variety of causal estimands. However, they can be manually extracted in the following manner:

```
## CATE
# Each draw is from the posterior of the expected value
# of the response under the observed and counterfactual
# treatment conditions.

# Matrices of size: n.observations x n.samples
mu.obs.samples <- extract(fit, sample = "train")
mu.cf.samples  <- extract(fit, sample = "test")

z <- data$z
mu.1.samples <- z * mu.obs.samples + (1 - z) * mu.cf.samples
mu.0.samples <- (1 - z) * mu.obs.samples + z * mu.cf.samples

icate.samples <- mu.1.samples - mu.0.samples
cate.samples <- rowMeans(icate.samples)

# Estimands
cate <- mean(cate.samples)
cate.lb <- cate - 1.96 * sd(cate.samples)
cate.ub <- cate + 1.96 * sd(cate.samples)

## SATE
# Draw from the posterior predictive distribution.
y.obs <- data$y
y.cf.samples <- extract(fit, sample = "test", value = "ppd")

y.1.samples <- z * y + (1 - z) * y.cf.samples
y.0.samples <- (1 - z) * y + z * y.cf.samples

ite.samples <- y.1.samples - y.0.samples
sate.samples <- rowMeans(ite.samples)

sate <- mean(sate.samples)
sate.lb <- sate - 1.96 * sd(sate.samples)
sate.ub <- sate + 1.96 * sd(sate.samples)
```

To obtain intervals and estimates for effects on the treated population, subset the individual effect matrices prior to averaging across rows.

5.3. Fixed vs. Random Effects

It is worth noting that we assume that our causal assumptions have not changed from above. That is, the grouping variables are not acting as confounders, they impact only the error structure of the data generating process (henceforth, DGP). Of course, in practice, in any given setting, it is always possible that ignorability would not be satisfied solely given the other covariates but would be satisfied when conditioning on the grouping variable as well. In that case it might be helpful to include the grouping variable as a fixed effect as well, since the random effects assumption would not be expected to hold, and conditioning on group level fixed effects allows one to control for any unmeasured group level confounders. In the most likely scenario that ignorability is not satisfied even conditional on the grouping variable—that is, there are unmeasured individual level confounders—a random effects specification tends to be a reasonable compromise between ignoring the group level structure entirely and using fixed effects, as fixed effects can act as bias-amplifying covariates [56,57].

6. Simulation Design

We designed a set of simulations to better understand the properties of `stan4bart` relative to close alternatives that either (1) have parametric assumptions or (2) cannot explicitly accommodate more general error structures. This section outlines our simulation design which has the general goal of trying to mimic a realistic data structure.

6.1. Original IHDP Simulation

The basic structure of our simulation mimics the simulation structure developed by Hill [1] in the paper that first introduced machine learning for causal inference. This simulation used data from a randomized experiment called the Infant Health and Development Program (IHDP; [58,59]) conducted in the 1980s to understand whether intensive childcare in the first few years of life could have a positive impact on the development of children who were born low-birth-weight and premature.

This study randomized roughly one third of the 985 participating families to participate in the IHDP intervention. Participants were eligible for intensive, high-quality child care and home visits from a trained provider during the first three years of infancy. A subset of the covariates collected during the baseline phase of that study and used frequently in subsequent evaluations of the IHDP program were included as the covariates for that simulation. Thus, the simulation reflected the actual distributions for and associations among covariates found naturally in existing data. The simulation covariates comprised six continuous, nine binary, and two unordered categorical variables reflecting child measurements at birth, the mother's sociodemographic characteristics at the time of birth, behaviors engaged in during pregnancy, and indicators for the study site.

To construct an observational study for the simulation, a hypothetical treatment assignment was induced by removing a nonrandom portion of the originally randomized treatment group, those children born to nonwhite mothers. This destroyed the independence between the originally randomized treatment assignment and the covariates but maintained the common support for the new treatment group. By simulating outcomes for the remaining sample with a mean structure that was a function solely of the treatment and covariates, ignorability was satisfied by construction.

To explore the ability of BART to flexibility fit nonlinear response surfaces, three different DGPs were used to generate potential outcomes. Response surface A was linear for both $\mathrm{E}[Y(0) \mid X = x]$ and $\mathrm{E}[Y(1) \mid X = x]$ and had a constant treatment effect. Response surface B created heterogeneous treatment effects by keeping the model for $E[Y(0) \mid X = x]$ linear but allowing the model for $\mathrm{E}[Y(1) \mid X = x]$ to be nonlinear by exponentiating a linear combination of the covariates. Response surface C created heterogeneous treatment effects by including a variety of squared terms and interactions.

In the original paper [1], this simulation was used to demonstrate the superior performance of BART for causal inference relative to linear regression and a generic implementation of propensity score methods. Since Hill [1] was published, testing grounds have been developed that allow for comparisons between BART and propensity score methods, in which the propensity score methods were able to be more carefully curated by methodologists who were experts in that field. These have also shown superior performance of BART [15]. While that paper also explored performance in settings where the common support assumption was violated, the current study restricted attention to scenarios where common support was satisfied to allow space for exploring features of the data specific to multilevel settings.

6.2. *Extensions to the Original IHDP Simulation*

This section details how we extended the original IHDP simulation to allow for a group structure and explore other features of the DGP.

6.2.1. Adding Group Structure to the Response Surfaces

We wanted to create a grouped structure that would mimic those features of a grouped data structure that exist naturally. Therefore, we repurposed two variables that were used as covariates in the original IHDP simulation and treated them as grouping variables in the current simulation. The first of these was the collection of eight indicators for the study site (a blocking variable in the original IHDP experiment). The other was a variable representing the mothers' age at birth (treated as continuous in the original simulation) which had 26 levels.

These groups were incorporated into the response surface in two different ways. The **varying intercepts** setting generated data from the respective response surface

$$\begin{aligned} Y_i(0) \mid \lambda^{\text{int}}_{g[i]}, \epsilon^0_i &= h^z(x_i) + \lambda^{\text{int}}_{g[i]} + \epsilon^0_i, \\ Y_i(1) \mid \lambda^{\text{int}}_{g[i]}, \epsilon^1_i &= h^z(x_i) + \lambda^{\text{int}}_{g[i]} + \tau^* + \epsilon^1_i, \\ \lambda^{\text{int}}_g &\sim \text{N}(0, \sigma_{\lambda^{\text{int}}}), \\ \epsilon^0_i &\sim \text{N}(0, \sigma_0), \\ \epsilon^1_i &\sim \text{N}(0, \sigma_1), \end{aligned}$$

where $h^z(x_i)$ reflects the function of the covariates specific to the given potential outcome and either response surface A, B, or C. τ^* only appears in the model for $Y(1)$ and represents the constant treatment effect when $h^0(x_i) = h^1(x_i)$ in response surface A. In response surface B and C, these are not equal an thus heterogenous treatment effects that vary with levels of the covariates are induced. The asterisk is meant to remind the reader that τ^* should not necessarily be interpreted as a constant or average treatment effect. λ^{int}_g is the varying intercept that corresponds to the grouping variable in question.

In contrast, the **varying intercepts and slopes** setting generated data from an augmented version of the above

$$\begin{aligned} Y_i(0) \mid \lambda^{\text{int}}_{g[i]}, \epsilon^0_i &= h^z(x_i) + \lambda^{\text{int}}_{g[i]} + \epsilon^0_i, \\ Y_i(1) \mid \lambda^{\text{int}}_{g[i]}, \lambda^{\text{slo}}_{g[i]}, \epsilon^1_i &= h^z(x_i) + \lambda^{\text{int}}_{g[i]} + \lambda^{\text{slo}}_{g[i]} + \epsilon^1_i, \\ \lambda^{\text{int}}_g &\sim \text{N}(0, \sigma_{\lambda^{\text{int}}}), \\ \lambda^{\text{slo}}_g &\sim \text{N}(0, \sigma_{\lambda^{\text{slo}}}), \\ \epsilon^0_i &\sim \text{N}(0, \sigma_0), \\ \epsilon^1_i &\sim \text{N}(0, \sigma_1). \end{aligned}$$

This specification allowed the model for $Y(1)$ to include the term $\lambda^{\text{slo}}_{g[i]}$ rather than the τ^* in the varying intercepts specification so that treatment effects could vary explicitly by group according to a distribution of varying slopes.

The choice of grouping variable and whether or not the varying slopes were included in the DGP represented two distinct simulation knobs, each with two levels. Combined with the three response surfaces discussed above, this created 12 different settings within which to evaluate performance.

6.2.2. Additional Simulation Knobs Explored

We also explored the variation in performance across two settings that are not represented in the results in the next section for the sake of parsimonious exposition. First, we assessed the variation in performance based on the size of the treatment effect. Expressed in units standardized by the standard deviation of the outcome, these effect sizes we examined were 0, 0.2, 0.5, and 0.8. We found no difference in results across these choices. We also tested the differences in performance based on intraclass correlation values of 0.2, 0.333 and 0.5. We also found no difference in results across these choices.

6.3. *Methods Compared*

We compared the performance of a variety of methods in an attempt to understand the advantages of combining flexible modeling with the ability to explicitly incorporate more complicated grouped error structures.

6.3.1. Linear Models

We fit several linear models to the data. **Linear full pool** is a linear regression where the groups are ignored entirely. **Linear f.e.** is a linear regression with fixed effects included for the grouping variables; this represents our no pooling option. **Linear v.i.** is a linear regression with varying intercepts. **Linear v.i.s** is a linear regression with varying intercepts and varying slopes, where the slopes in question are the coefficients on the treatment variable. Each of the last two were fit using the `stan_lmer` function in `rstanarm`.

Given that the group-level estimands were one of our areas of focus it seemed unfair to not include versions of the above that more explicitly targeted these estimands. We included two additional models with this in mind. **LinearX f.e.** is a standard linear regression that includes both fixed effects and interactions between the fixed effects and the treatment variable. **LinearX v.i.s.** is an implementation of the `stan_lmer` function that allows for both varying intercepts and varying treatment effects.

6.3.2. BART-Based Models

We also fit several different versions of BART models. **vanilla BART** uses a traditional BART specification similar to that used in Hill [1] but specifically omitting the grouping variables and including the propensity score as a covariate. **BART f.e.** extends this basic implementation by adding fixed effects for the grouping variables. **BART v.i.** is a BART implementation that allows for varying intercepts through the `rbart_vi` function in `dbarts`. All BART implementations included a propensity score as suggested by Hahn et al. [7]. The propensity score was estimated using BART using a hyperprior on the end-node variance, making it extremely unlikely to take on small values and thus overfit, essentially guarding against the problems induced by the originally proposed implementation [37]. Finally, we also implemented Bayesian causal forests, which we denote **vanilla BCF** and **BCF f.e.**

6.3.3. `stan4bart` Implementations

We implemented two different versions of `stan4bart`. The simpler version, **stan4bart v.i.**, allows for varying intercepts. The slightly more complicated version, **stan4bart v.i.s.**, allows for varying intercepts and slopes.

To fit **stan4bart v.i.**, models with varying intercepts were specified as:

```
fit <- stan4bart(
y ~ bart(. - g) + (1 | g),
train = data,
test = data.test
)
```

Fitting **stan4bart v.i.s.** allowed for a variation in both intercepts and slopes and was specified as:

```
fit <- stan4bart(
y ~  bart(. - g) + (1 + z | g),
train = data,
test = data.test
)
```

7. Simulation Results

We compared methods based on performance with respect to several criteria for each of our targeted estimands. We present the results for each estimand in turn.

7.1. SATT

We evaluated the performance with respect to SATT for each of our methods across the six different settings by focusing on the root-mean-square error (RMSE), average interval length, and coverage. The RMSE and interval length were standardized by the standard deviation of the outcome variable so that the absolute size of each measure was more meaningful.

Figure 1 displays the results of our simulations for each method with respect to SATT as measured by RMSE (y-axis) and the average interval length using six plots. Rows correspond to response surfaces (A, B, or C) and columns to the metric displayed (RMSE or interval length). The results specific to the choice of grouping variable (group 1 or group 2) are displayed on each plot with different shapes (triangle or circle, respectively). The grouping structure is represented by whether the plotted shape is hollow (varying intercept) or filled (varying intercept and slope).

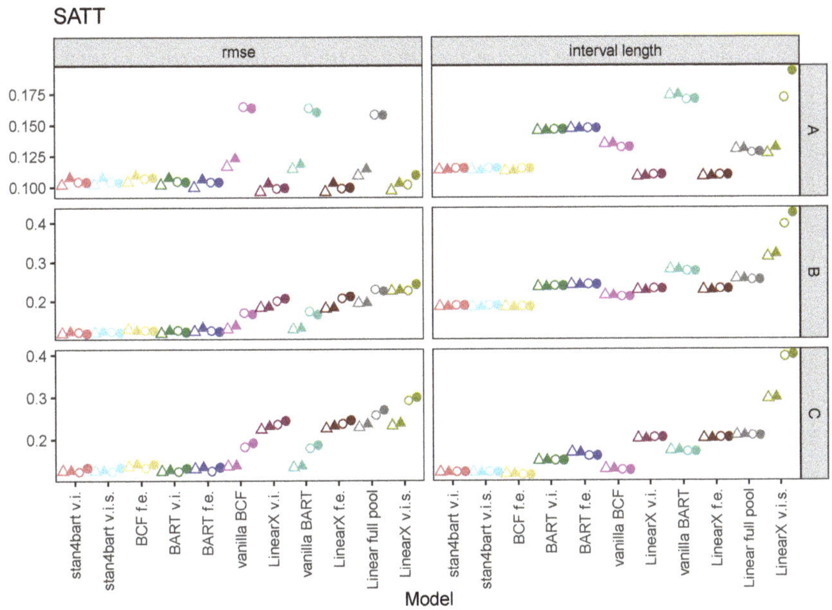

Figure 1. Results of our simulations for each method with respect to SATT as measured by RMSE (**left** panel) and average interval length (**right** panel). Each row corresponds to one of the three response surfaces (A, B, or C). Shapes are used to represent one of two grouping structures, triangles are for results from grouping structure 1, and circles for results from grouping structure 2. Hollow shapes represent results from DGPs with random intercepts and solid shapes represent results from DGPs with random intercepts and random slopes.

The results for the linear response surface (A) demonstrate strong performance overall from all methods with regard to RMSE with the possible exceptions of the vanilla BART and

BCF implementations and the pooled linear regressions in the group 2 version of the DGPs. Given the simplicity of the response surface, these results are not surprising—the only complexity is the grouping structure. The differences across methods are more apparent in the average interval lengths. Here, the linear models that allow for variation (either intercept or slope) have the shortest intervals followed by the BCF and `stan4bart` methods. These are followed by BCF with fixed effects and linear regression, and then the BART methods with fixed effects and varying effects. The BART implementations that completely ignore the grouped variables not surprisingly performs the worst overall on this metric. One odd result is the linear model with varying slopes, which performs reasonably well with regard to the interval length for the first grouping variable but much worse for the second. We suspect that this has to do with the fact that while the group 1 version has more levels, the correlation structure of group 2 is more complex. The effect of different correlation on the performance of different methods is beyond the scope of this paper but is an issue that could be explored in future simulation studies.

The ordering with regard to performance changes for some methods once we move to the results for the nonlinear response surfaces in the second and third rows. These are more challenging for all of the methods (note the change in the y-axis) but particularly for those that have strict linear parametric requirements. The strongest consistent performers with regard to RMSE are the `stan4bart` methods, **BCF f.e.**, **BART v.i.**, and **BART f.e.**. The versions of BCF and BART that ignore the group structure perform fine in the setting with the first grouping variable (triangles) but less well with the second (circles). The linear models perform the worst. The best performers with regard to the average interval length are again the flexible fitters with an edge once again for the `stan4bart` and BCF methods.

The performance with regard to the interval length for response surfaces B and C highlights the differences between the `stan4bart` methods and **BCF f.e.** relative to vanilla BCF (with just slightly longer intervals) and the BART methods with grouping structure. The linear methods trail with **LinearX v.i.s.**, demonstrating by far the longest intervals. Vanilla BART has longer intervals than the best linear models for response surface B and slightly longer ones for response surface C.

A shorter interval length is only an asset, however, if nominal coverage is achieved. Figure 2 displays the coverage results for the top contenders across our 12 settings. In addition, the plots include the average interval length across grouping settings for each response surface as part of the method label on the x-axis. These plots indicate that the `stan4bart` methods seem to strike the best balance between having a low RMSE and shorter intervals while still maintaining nominal coverage. The BCF methods which performed similarly to the `stan4bart` methods with regard to the RMSE and interval length struggled a bit more to achieve nominal coverage, particularly for response surface B.

7.2. GSATT

The results for the group-level ATTs are more complicated because we have many more estimands to consider (one for each group). Thus, we organized the plots to display the RMSE and interval length results on separate plots. Since there was virtually no distinction in the results between the two grouping settings—varying intercept versus varying intercept and slope—we elected to collapse those results. Instead, we broke out our group 1 and group 2 results into separate sets of plots (top and bottom panels).

Figure 3 displays the RMSE for each method (x-axis) and group-level estimand across the six settings defined by the response surface (columns) and grouping variable (rows). The performance for each method is displayed in its own column with separate points for each estimand (group-level ATT). The average RMSE across estimands for each method is displayed next to the label for its name for each response surface (collapsed across settings defined by grouping variable). Across all of the response surfaces, the `stan4bart` methods perform the best followed very closely by **BCF f.e.** and then the other BART-based methods. The linear methods perform noticeably worse in all settings but in particular when the response surface is nonlinear (B) and additionally when the treatment effects are heterogeneous by covariate values (C).

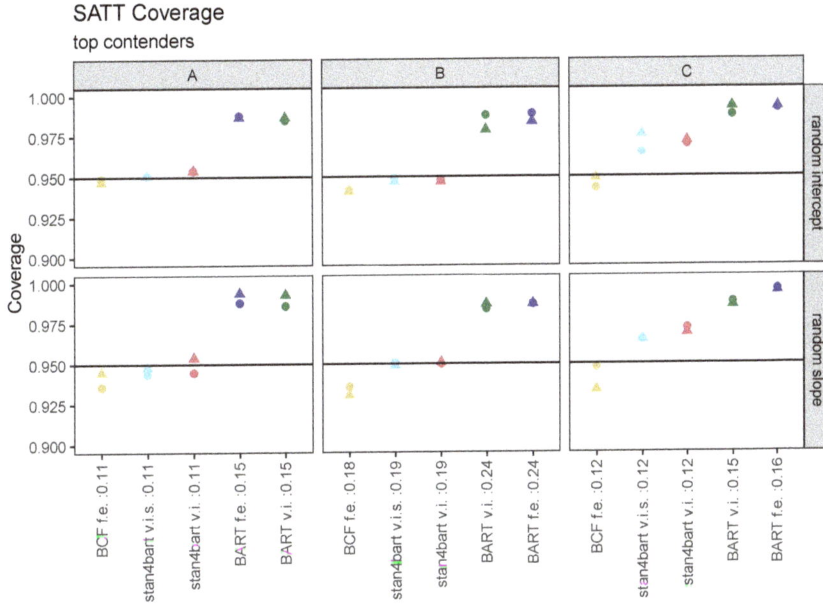

Figure 2. Percentage of 95% intervals that covered the true SATT for each of the top-performing methods. Results are presented separately by settings defined by response surface (columns A, B, C) and multilevel structure (rows: varying intercepts or varying intercepts and slopes). Results from settings defined by grouping variable are displayed on the same plot with different symbols. Labels on the x-axis additionally provide the average interval length (across both grouping settings).

Figure 4 displays the average interval length for each method (x-axis) across the six settings defined by the response surface (columns) and grouping variables (rows). The performance for each method is displayed in its own column with separate points for each estimand (group-level ATT). The results that achieved nominal coverage for a given estimand are displayed with solid rather than open circles for each group-level estimand.

The average coverage for each method and response surface combination (collapsed across other sources of variability) is displayed next to the name of each method. For response surface A, the linear methods with varying intercepts and slopes have the shortest intervals; however, the coverage with respect to the group estimands is quite poor, averaging 41% and 44%. The interval length for these methods increases with the more complicated response surfaces and in the scenarios with the first group variable is more variable across group estimands. **LinearX f.e.** performs the worst in terms of interval length but has better coverage properties across the board.

The other methods perform reasonably similarly with regard to the distribution of interval lengths across group-level estimands; however, the `stan4bart` implementations and **BCF f.e.** are also able to maintain the best coverage. **stan4bart v.i.s** is the only method that achieves nominal average coverage across all three response surfaces and **vanilla BCF** performs the worst in this regard with an average coverage dipping to 80% for response surface B.

Figure 5 displays the coverage percentages separately for each combination of method, grouping variable, and estimand and is thus capable of revealing greater distinctions across methods that looked similar in the previous plot. With one exception, the `stan4bart` demonstrate the least variability in coverage rates across groups. **vanilla BCF** has the greatest variability in coverage among the flexible models. **LinearX t.e.** is unable to provide reasonable coverage in the setting with the second grouping variable; however, it performs far better with respect to the covariate of group-level estimands than the other linear methods for the setting defined by the first grouping variable.

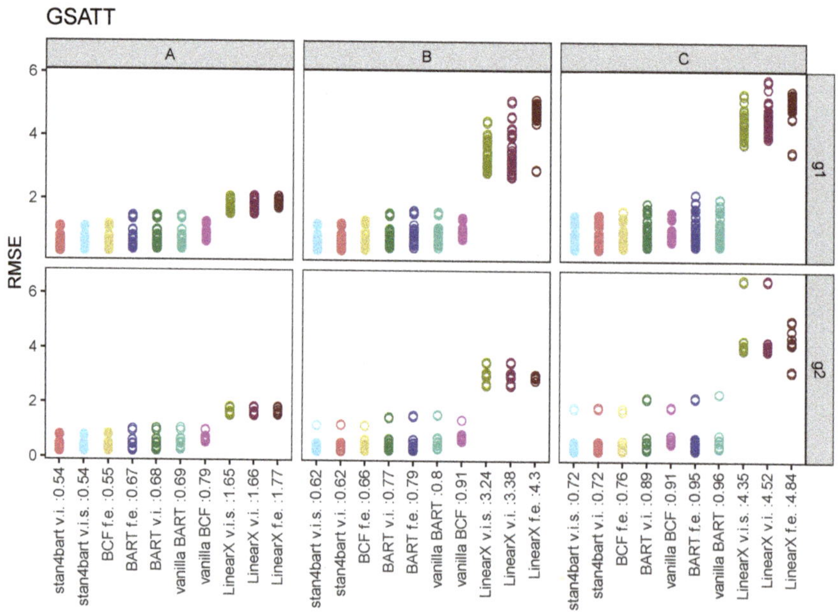

Figure 3. RMSE results for the group-level estimands across methods. Each plot corresponds to a setting defined by grouping variable (row) and response surface (column). Results are collapsed across the settings defined by varying intercepts versus varying intercepts and slopes. Average RMSE across these settings and across estimands are displayed numerically next to the name of each method, separately for each response surface. Estimands that were covered by a 95% interval produced by the method were filled in rather than left hollow.

7.3. *iCATEs*

We evaluated the ability of each method to estimate the CATE for each combination of covariate values that manifested in each sample as the iCATEs. To compare performance, we used the metric proposed in Hill [1], the precision in estimation of heterogeneous effects measure, or PEHE. This was calculated within each dataset for a given method as the square root of the average of the squared differences between the estimate of the iCATE and the true iCATE for each person.

Figure 6 displays the PEHE results for each of the methods across the six settings defined by response surface and multilevel setting (varying intercepts versus varying intercepts and slopes). Results are collapsed across the DGPs defined by the grouping variable.

For the linear response surface A, which has a constant treatment effect, all of the methods perform similarly which is not surprising given the ease of the task. The only method that noticeably performs a bit worse is the linear model with fixed effects interacted with the treatment, likely because it is overfitting. The landscape changes for the nonlinear response surfaces where the top performing methods are the flexible models with the strongest performance demonstrated by the `stan4bart` methods, BCF with fixed effects, and BART with varying intercepts.

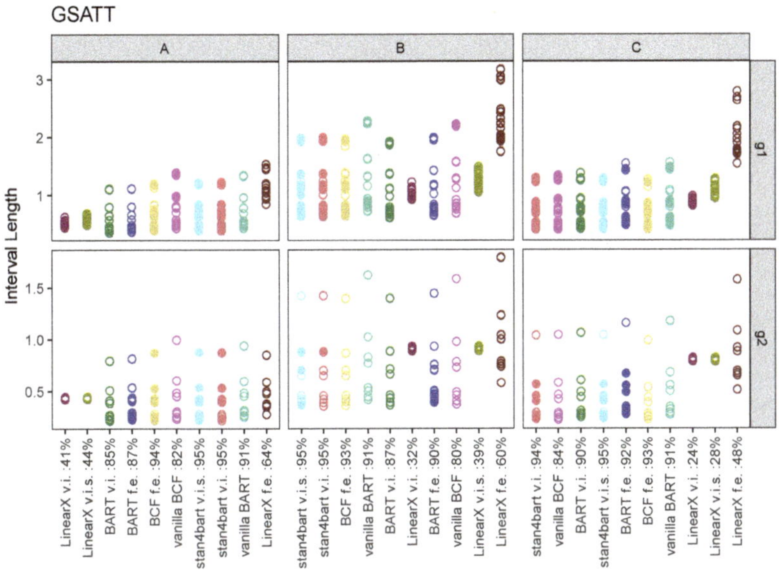

Figure 4. Interval length results for the group-level estimands across methods. Each plot corresponds to a setting defined by grouping variable (row) and response surface (column). Results are collapsed across the settings defined by varying intercepts versus varying intercepts and slopes. Average coverage across these settings and across estimands are displayed numerically next to the name of each method, separately for each response surface. Within each vertical panel the methods are ordered by average interval length across both grouping variable settings and estimands. Estimands that were covered by a 95% interval produced by the method were filled in rather than left hollow.

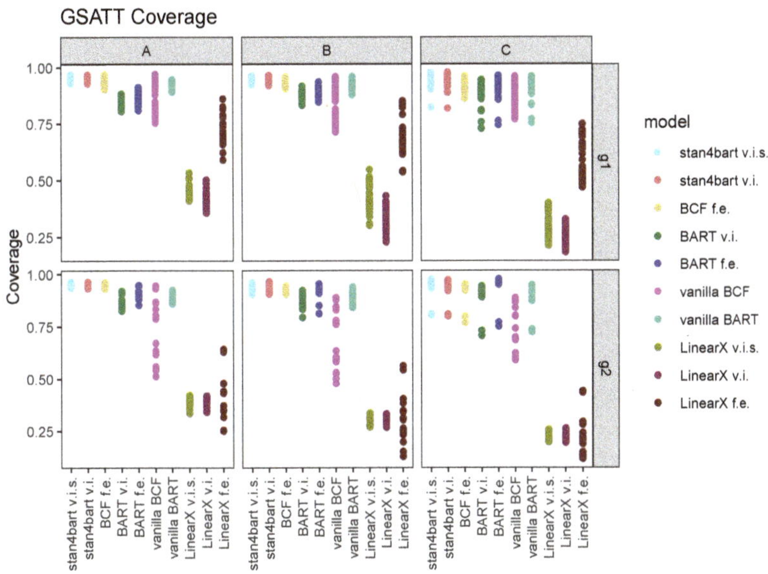

Figure 5. Coverage rates for each method with respect to each of the group-level estimands. Plots vary by settings defined by grouping variable (rows) and response surface (columns A, B, and C) and are collapsed across grouping scenarios (varying intercept versus varying intercept and slope).

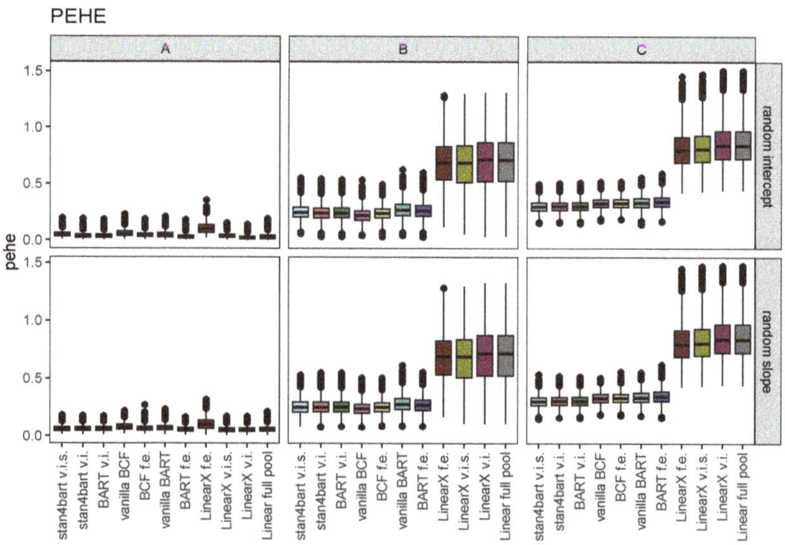

Figure 6. PEHE results for each of the methods across the six settings defined by response surface (columns A, B, and C) and multilevel setting (rows corresponding to varying intercepts versus varying intercepts and slopes). Results are collapsed across the DGPs defined by the grouping variable.

8. Discussion

The goal of this work was to develop a method that could extend the BART framework for the flexible fitting of response surfaces to accommodate more complex error structures. We evaluated the utility of this approach by assessing performance in a causal inference context that allowed for varying intercepts or varying intercepts and slopes. For one of our three response surfaces, this heterogeneity was in addition to the heterogeneity in treatment effects that was a systematic (nonrandom) function of observed confounders.

Our results indicated that the `stan4bart` models provided superior performance when compared against both methods with flexible fit that did not allow for a more complicated error structure as well as methods that explicitly accommodated a grouped error structure but assumed a linear parametric mean structure. Throughout, BCF was a strong competitor on all performance measures even though it did not explicitly accommodate the error structure.

We evaluated `stan4bart` in a causal setting, which is generally more challenging than standard prediction settings. Given its strong performance in this challenging setting, we recommend the use of `stan4bart` both in causal and noncausal settings. More broadly, we hope that `stan4bart` will be a jumping-off point for the further development of methods that aim to marry flexible mean structures with parametric approaches to either the mean structure or the grouped error structure.

Author Contributions: Conceptualization, J.L.H., V.D. and B.G.; methodology, V.D.; software, V.D. and G.P.; validation, V.D. and G.P.; formal analysis of properties of estimators, G.P.; investigation, G.P.; resources, J.L.H. and B.G.; data curation, G.P.; writing—original draft preparation, J.L.H., V.D., B.G. and G.P.; writing—review and editing, J.L.H., V.D., B.G. and G.P.; visualization, G.P.; supervision, J.L.H.; project administration, J.L.H. and G.P.; funding acquisition, J.L.H. and B.G. All authors have read and agreed to the published version of the manuscript.

Funding: This research was funded by the Office of Naval Research grant number N00014-17-1-2141, the Institute of Education Sciences grant number R305D200019, and the National Science Foundation grant numbers 2051246 and 2153019.

Institutional Review Board Statement: Not applicable.

Data Availability Statement: This data can be found here: https://github.com/gperrett/stan4bart-study (accessed on 14 August 2022).

Conflicts of Interest: The authors declare no conflict of interest.

References

1. Hill, J. Bayesian nonparametric modeling for causal inference. *J. Comput. Graph. Stat.* **2011**, *20*, 217–240. [CrossRef]
2. LeDell, E. *h2oEnsemble: H2O Ensemble Learning*. R Package Version 0.1.8. 2016.
3. Wager, S.; Athey, S. Estimation and Inference of Heterogeneous Treatment Effects using Random Forests. *J. Am. Stat. Assoc.* **2018**, *113*, 1228–1242. [CrossRef]
4. Künzel, S.R.; Sekhon, J.S.; Bickel, P.J.; Yu, B. Metalearners for estimating heterogeneous treatment effects using machine learning. *Proc. Natl. Acad. Sci. USA* **2019**, *116*, 4156–4165. [CrossRef] [PubMed]
5. Ju, C.; Gruber, S.; Lendle, S.D.; Chambaz, A.; Franklin, J.M.; Wyss, R.; Schneeweiss, S.; van der Laan, M.J. Scalable collaborative targeted learning for high-dimensional data. *Stat. Methods Med. Res.* **2019**, *28*, 532–554. [CrossRef] [PubMed]
6. Zeldow, B.; Lo Re, V.R.; Roy, J. A Semiparametric Modeling Approach Using Bayesian Additive Regression Trees with an Application to Evaluate Heterogeneous Treatment Effects. *Ann. Appl. Stat.* **2019**, *13*, 1989–2010. [CrossRef]
7. Hahn, P.R.; Murray, J.S.; Carvalho, C.M. Bayesian Regression Tree Models for Causal Inference: Regularization, Confounding, and Heterogeneous Effects (with Discussion). *Bayesian Anal.* **2020**, *15*, 965–2020. [CrossRef]
8. Dehejia, R.H. Was There a Riverside Miracle? A Hierarchical Framework for Evaluating Programs With Grouped Data. *J. Bus. Econ. Stat.* **2003**, *21*, 1–11. [CrossRef]
9. Gelman, A.; Hill, J. *Data Analysis Using Regression and Multilevel/Hierarchical Models*; Cambridge University Press: New York, NY, USA, 2007.
10. Hill, J. *The SAGE Handbook of Multilevel Modeling*; Chapter Multilevel Models and Causal Inference; SAGE: London, UK, 2013; pp. 1248–1318.
11. Lin, W. Agnostic notes on regression adjustments to experimental data: Reexamining Freedman's critique. *Ann. Appl. Stat.* **2013**, *7*, 295–318. [CrossRef]
12. Chipman, H.; George, E.; McCulloch, R. Bayesian Ensemble Learning. In *Advances in Neural Information Processing Systems 19*; Schölkopf, B., Platt, J., Hoffman, T., Eds.; MIT Press: Cambridge, MA, USA, 2007.
13. Chipman, H.A.; George, E.I.; McCulloch, R.E. BART: Bayesian Additive Regression Trees. *Ann. Appl. Stat.* **2010**, *4*, 266–298. [CrossRef]
14. Dorie, V. *dbarts: Discrete Bayesian Additive Regression Trees Sampler*. R Package Version 0.9-22. 2022.
15. Dorie, V.; Hill, J.; Shalit, U.; Scott, M.; Cervone, D. Automated versus do-it-yourself methods for causal inference: Lessons learned from a data analysis competition. *Stat. Sci.* **2019**, *34*, 43–68. [CrossRef]
16. Bonato, V.; Baladandayuthapani, V.; Broom, B.M.; Sulman, E.P.; Aldape, K.D.; Do, K.A. Bayesian ensemble methods for survival prediction in gene expression data. *Bioinformatics* **2010**, *27*, 359–367. [CrossRef] [PubMed]
17. Pratola, M.; Chipman, H.; George, E.; McCulloch, R. Heteroscedastic BART using multiplicative regression trees. *J. Comput. Graph. Stat.* **2020**, *29*, 405–417. [CrossRef]
18. Linero, A.R.; Sinha, D.; Lipsitz, S.R. Semiparametric mixed-scale models using shared Bayesian forests. *Biometrics* **2020**, *76*, 131–144. [CrossRef]
19. George, E.; Laud, P.; Logan, B.; McCulloch, R.; Sparapani, R. Fully nonparametric Bayesian additive regression trees. In *Topics in Identification, Limited Dependent Variables, Partial Observability, Experimentation, and Flexible Modeling: Part B*; Emerald Publishing Limited: Bingley, UK, 2019; Volume 40, pp. 89–110.
20. Murray, J.S. Log-Linear Bayesian Additive Regression Trees for Multinomial Logistic and Count Regression Models. *J. Am. Stat. Assoc.* **2021**, *116*, 756–769. [CrossRef]
21. Hill, J.L.; Weiss, C.; Zhai, F. Challenges With Propensity Score Strategies in a High-Dimensional Setting and a Potential Alternative. *Multivar. Behav. Res.* **2011**, *46*, 477–513. [CrossRef] [PubMed]
22. Hill, J.; Su, Y.S. Assessing lack of common support in causal inference using Bayesian nonparametrics: Implications for evaluating the effect of breastfeeding on children's cognitive outcomes. *Ann. Appl. Stat.* **2013**, *7*, 1386–1420. [CrossRef]
23. Dorie, V.; Carnegie, N.B.; Harada, M.; Hill, J. A flexible, interpretable framework for assessing sensitivity to unmeasured confounding. *Stat. Med.* **2016**, *35*, 3453–3470. [CrossRef]
24. Kern, H.L.; Stuart, E.A.; Hill, J.L.; Green, D.P. Assessing methods for generalizing experimental impact estimates to target samples. *J. Res. Educ. Eff.* **2016**, *9*, 103–127.
25. Wendling, T.; Jung, K.; Callahan, A.; Schuler, A.; Shah, N.; Gallego, B. Comparing methods for estimation of heterogeneous treatment effects using observational data from health care databases. *Stat. Med.* **2018**, *37*, 3309–3324. [CrossRef]
26. Sparapani, R.; Spanbauer, C.; McCulloch, R. Nonparametric Machine Learning and Efficient Computation with Bayesian Additive Regression Trees: The BART R Package. *J. Stat. Softw.* **2021**, *97*, 1–66. [CrossRef]
27. Bisbee, J. BARP: Improving Mister P Using Bayesian Additive Regression Trees. *Am. Political Sci. Rev.* **2019**, *113*, 1060–1065. [CrossRef]
28. Yeager, D.S.; Hanselman, P.; Walton, G.M.; Murray, J.S.; Crosnoe, R.; Muller, C.; Tipton, E.; Schneider, B.; Hulleman, C.S.; Hinojosa, C.P.; et al. A national experiment reveals where a growth mindset improves achievement. *Nature* **2019**, *573*, 364–369. [CrossRef]

29. Yeager, D.; Bryan, C.; Gross, J.; Murray, J.S.; Cobb, D.K.; Santos, P.H.F.; Gravelding, H.; Johnson, M.; Jamieson, J.P. A synergistic mindsets intervention protects adolescents from stress. *Nature* **2022**, *607*, 512–520. [CrossRef] [PubMed]
30. Yeager, D.S.; Carroll, J.M.; Buontempo, J.; Cimpian, A.; Woody, S.; Crosnoe, R.; Muller, C.; Murray, J.; Mhatre, P.; Kersting, N.; et al. Teacher Mindsets Help Explain Where a Growth-Mindset Intervention Does and Doesn't Work. *Psychol. Sci.* **2022**, *33*, 18–32. [CrossRef] [PubMed]
31. Suk, Y.; Kang, H. Robust Machine Learning for Treatment Effects in Multilevel Observational Studies Under Cluster-level Unmeasured Confounding. *Psychometrika* **2022**, *87*, 310–343. [CrossRef] [PubMed]
32. Spanbauer, C.; Sparapani, R. Nonparametric machine learning for precision medicine with longitudinal clinical trials and Bayesian additive regression trees with mixed models. *Stat. Med.* **2021**, *40*, 2665–2691. [CrossRef] [PubMed]
33. Tan, Y.V.; Flannagan, C.A.C.; Elliott, M.R. Predicting human-driving behavior to help driverless vehicles drive: random intercept Bayesian additive regression trees. *Stat. Its Interface* **2018**, *11*, 557–572. [CrossRef]
34. Rubin, D.B. Using Multivariate Matched Sampling and Regression Adjustment to Control Bias in Observational Studies. *J. Am. Stat. Assoc.* **1979**, *74*, 318–328.
35. Holland, P. Statistics and Causal Inference. *J. Am. Stat. Assoc.* **1986**, *81*, 945–970. [CrossRef]
36. Vegetabile, B.G. On the Distinction Between "Conditional Average Treatment Effects" (CATE) and "Individual Treatment Effects" (ITE) Under Ignorability Assumptions. *arXiv* **2021**, arXiv:2108.04939.
37. Carnegie, N.; Dorie, V.; Hill, J. Examining treatment effect heterogeneity using BART. *Obs. Stud.* **2019**, *76*, 491–511. [CrossRef]
38. Carnegie, N.B.; Harada, M.; Hill, J. Assessing sensitivity to unmeasured confounding using a simulated potential confounder. *J. Res. Educ. Eff.* **2016**, *9*, 395–420. [CrossRef]
39. Rubin, D.B. Bayesian Inference for Causal Effects: The role of randomization. *Ann. Stat.* **1978**, *6*, 34–58. [CrossRef]
40. Team, S.D. *Stan Modeling Language Users Guide and Reference Manual*; Version 2.29; 2022. Available online: https://mc-stan.org/docs/2_29/stan-users-guide/ (accessed on 14 August 2022)
41. Hoffman, M.D.; Gelman, A. The No-U-Turn Sampler: Adaptively Setting Path Lengths in Hamiltonian Monte Carlo. *J. Mach. Learn. Res.* **2014**, *15*, 1593–1623.
42. Betancourt, M. A conceptual introduction to Hamiltonian Monte Carlo. *arXiv* **2017**, arXiv:1701.02434.
43. Neal, R.M. MCMC using Hamiltonian dynamics. *Handb. Markov Chain. Monte Carlo* **2011**, *2*, 2.
44. Bates, D.; Mächler, M.; Bolker, B.; Walker, S. Fitting Linear Mixed-Effects Models Using lme4. *J. Stat. Softw.* **2015**, *67*, 1–48. [CrossRef]
45. Lewandowski, D.; Kurowicka, D.; Joe, H. Generating random correlation matrices based on vines and extended onion method. *J. Multivar. Anal.* **2009**, *100*, 1989–2001. [CrossRef]
46. Bates, D.; Kliegl, R.; Vasishth, S.; Baayen, H. Parsimonious Mixed Models. *arXiv* **2015**, arXiv:1506.04967.
47. Bleich, J.; Kapelner, A.; George, E.I.; Jensen, S.T. Variable selection for BART: An application to gene regulation. *Ann. Appl. Stat.* **2014**, *8*, 1750–1781. [CrossRef]
48. Casella, G.; George, E.I. Explaining the Gibbs Sampler. *Am. Stat.* **1992**, *46*, 167–174.
49. Stan Development Team. *RStan: The R Interface to Stan*. R Package Version 2.21.5. 2022.
50. Tan, Y.V.; Roy, J. Bayesian additive regression trees and the General BART model. *Stat. Med.* **2019**, *38*, 5048–5069. [CrossRef] [PubMed]
51. Guidotti, R.; Monreale, A.; Ruggieri, S.; Turini, F.; Giannotti, F.; Pedreschi, D. A Survey of Methods for Explaining Black Box Models. *ACM Comput. Surv.* **2018**, *51*, 1–41. [CrossRef]
52. Liu, J.S.; Wu, Y.N. Parameter Expansion for Data Augmentation. *J. Am. Stat. Assoc.* **1999**, *94*, 1264–1274. [CrossRef]
53. Meng, X.L.; van Dyk, D. Seeking efficient data augmentation schemes via conditional and marginal augmentation. *Biometrika* **1999**, *86*, 301–320. [CrossRef]
54. Gelman, A.; van Dyk, D.A.; Huang, Z.; Boscardin, J.W. Using Redundant Parameterizations to Fit Hierarchical Models. *J. Comput. Graph. Stat.* **2008**, *17*, 95–122. [CrossRef]
55. Carnegie, N. Contributions of Model Features to BART Causal Inference Performance Using ACIC 2016 Competition Data. *Stat. Sci.* **2019**, *34*, 90–93. [CrossRef]
56. Middleton, J.; Scott, M.; Diakow, R.; Hill, J. Bias Amplification and Bias Unmasking. *Political Anal.* **2016**, *24*, 307—323. [CrossRef]
57. Scott, M.; Diakow, R.; Hill, J.; Middleton, J. Potential for Bias Inflation with Grouped Data: A Comparison of Estimators and a Sensitivity Analysis Strategy. *Obs. Stud.* **2018**, *4*, 111–149. [CrossRef]
58. Infant Health and Development Program. Enhancing the outcomes of low-birth-weight, premature infants. *J. Am. Med Assoc.* **1990**, *22*, 3035–3042.
59. Brooks-Gunn, J.; Liaw, F.R.; Klebanov, P.K. Effects of early intervention on cognitive function of low birth weight preterm infants. *J. Pediatr.* **1991**, *120*, 350–359. [CrossRef] [PubMed]

entropy

Article

Causal Discovery in High-Dimensional Point Process Networks with Hidden Nodes

Xu Wang and Ali Shojaie *

Department of Biostatistics, University of Washington, Seattle, WA 98195, USA; wangxu85@uw.edu
* Correspondence: ashojaie@uw.edu

Abstract: Thanks to technological advances leading to near-continuous time observations, emerging multivariate point process data offer new opportunities for causal discovery. However, a key obstacle in achieving this goal is that many relevant processes may not be observed in practice. Naïve estimation approaches that ignore these hidden variables can generate misleading results because of the unadjusted confounding. To plug this gap, we propose a deconfounding procedure to estimate high-dimensional point process networks with only a subset of the nodes being observed. Our method allows flexible connections between the observed and unobserved processes. It also allows the number of unobserved processes to be unknown and potentially larger than the number of observed nodes. Theoretical analyses and numerical studies highlight the advantages of the proposed method in identifying causal interactions among the observed processes.

Keywords: causal discovery; Hawkes process; high-dimensional statistics; hidden confounder

Citation: Wang, X.; Shojaie, A. Causal Discovery in High-Dimensional Point Process Networks with Hidden Nodes. *Entropy* **2021**, *23*, 1622. https://doi.org/10.3390/e23121622

Academic Editor: Kateřina Hlaváčková-Schindler

Received: 22 September 2021
Accepted: 27 November 2021
Published: 1 December 2021

1. Introduction

Learning causal interactions from observational multivariate time series is generally impossible [1,2]. Among many challenges, two of the most important ones are that (i) the data acquisition rate may be much slower than the underlying rate of changes; and (ii) there may be unmeasured confounders [1,3]. First, due to the cost or technological constraints, the data acquisition rate may be much slower than the underlying rate of changes. In such settings, the most commonly used procedure for inferring interactions among time series, Granger causality, may both miss true interactions and identify spurious ones [4–6]. Second, the available data may only include a small fraction of potentially relevant variables, leading to unmeasured confounders. Naïve connectivity estimators that ignore these confounding effects can produce highly biased results [7]. Therefore, reliably distinguishing causal connections between pairs of observed processes from correlations induced by common inputs from unobserved confounders remains a key challenge.

Learning causal interactions between neurons is critical to understanding the neural basis of cognitive functions [8,9]. Many existing neuroscience data, such as data collected using functional magnetic resonance imaging (fMRI), have relatively low temporal resolutions, and are thus of limited utility for causal discovery [10]. This is because many important neuronal processes and interactions happen at finer time scales [11]. New technologies, such as calcium florescent imaging that generate spike train data, make it possible to collect 'live' data at high temporal resolutions [12]. The spike train data, which are multivariate point processes containing spiking times of a collection of neurons, are increasingly used to learn the latent brain connectivity networks and to glean insight into how neurons respond to external stimuli [13]. For example, Bolding and Franks [14] collected spike train data on neurons in mouse olfactory bulb region at 30 kHz under multiple laser intensity levels to study the odor identification mechanism. Despite progress in recording the activity of massive populations of neurons [15], simultaneously monitoring a complete network of spiking neurons at high temporal resolutions is still beyond the reach of the current technology. In fact, most experiments only collect data on a small fraction of neurons, leaving many unobserved neurons [16–18]. These hidden neurons may potentially interact with the neurons inside the observed set and cannot be ignored. Nevertheless, given its high temporal resolution, spike train data provide an opportunity for causal discovery if we can account for the unmeasured confounders.

When unobserved confounders are a concern, causal effects among the observed variables can be learned using causal structural learning approaches, such as the Fast Causal Inference (FCI) algorithm and its variants [1,19]. However, these algorithms may not identify all causal edges. Specifically, instead of learning the directed acyclic graph (DAG) of causal interactions, FCI learns the maximally ancestral graph (MAG). This graph includes causal interactions between variables that are connected by directed edges, but also bi-directed edges among some other variables, leaving the corresponding causal relationships undetermined. As a result, causality discovery using these algorithms is not always satisfactory. For example, Malinsky and Spirtes [20] recently applied FCI to infer causal network of time series and found a low recall for identifying the true casual relationships. Additionally, despite recent efforts [21], causal structure learning remains computationally intensive, because the space of candidate causal graphs grows super-exponentially with the number of network nodes [22].

The Hawkes process [23] is a popular model for analyzing multivariate point process data. In this model, the probability of future events for each component can depend on the entire history of events of other components. Under straightforward conditions, the multivariate Hawkes process reveals Granger causal interactions among multivariate point processes [24]. Moreover, assuming that all relevant processes are observed in a linear Hawkes process, causal interactions among components can also be inferred [25]. The Hawkes process thus provides a flexible and interpretable framework for investigating the latent network of point processes and is widely used in neuroscience applications [26–32].

In modern applications, it is common for the number of measured components, e.g., the number of neurons, to be large compared to the observed period, e.g., the duration of neuroscience experiments. The high-dimensional nature of data in such applications poses challenges to learning the connectivity network of a multivariate Hawkes process. To address this challenge, Hansen et al. [33] and Chen et al. [34] proposed ℓ_1-regularized estimation procedures and Wang et al. [35] recently developed a high-dimensional inference procedure to characterize the uncertainty of these regularized estimators. However, due to the confounding from unobserved neurons in practice, existing estimation and inference procedures assuming complete observation from all components, may not provide reliable estimates.

Accounting for unobserved confounders in high-dimensional regression has been the subject of recent research. Two such examples are HIVE [36] and trim regression [37], which facilitate causal discovery using high-dimensional regression with unobserved confounders. However, these methods are designed for linear regression with independent observations and do not apply to the long-history temporal dependency setting of Hawkes processes. Moreover, they rely on specific assumptions on observed and unobsvered causal effects, which are not clear to hold in neuronal network settings.

In this paper, we consider learning causal interactions among high-dimensional point processes with (potentially many) hidden confounders. Considering the generalization of the above two approaches to the setting of Hawkes processes, we show that the assumption required by trim regression is more likely to hold in a stable point process network, especially when the confounders affect many observed nodes. Motivated by this finding, we propose a generalization of the trim regression, termed *hp-trim*, for causal discovery from high-dimensional point processes in the presence of (potentially many) hidden confounders. We establish a non-asymptotic convergence rate in estimating the network edges using this procedure. Unlike the previous result for independent data [37], our result considers both the temporal dependence of the Hawkes processes as well as the network sparsity. Using simulated and real data, we also show that *hp-trim* has superior finite-sample performance compared to the corresponding generalization of HIVE for point processes and/or the naïve approach that ignores the unobserved confounders.

2. The Hawkes Processes with Unobserved Components

2.1. The Hawkes Process

Let $\{t_k\}_{k\in\mathbb{Z}}$ be a sequence of real-valued random variables, taking values in $[0,T]$, with $t_{k+1} > t_k$ and $t_1 \geq 0$ almost surely. Here, time $t = 0$ is a reference point in time, e.g., the start of an experiment, and T is the duration of the experiment. A simple point process N on $\mathbb{R}$ is defined as a family $\{N(A)\}_{A\in\mathcal{B}(\mathbb{R})}$, where $\mathcal{B}(\mathbb{R})$ denotes the Borel σ-field of the real line and $N(A) = \sum_k \mathbf{1}_{\{t_k\in A\}}$. The process N is essentially a simple counting process with isolated jumps of unit height that occur at $\{t_k\}_{k\in\mathbb{Z}}$. We write $N([t,t+dt))$ as $dN(t)$, where dt denotes an arbitrarily small increment of t.

Let $\mathbf{N}$ be a p-variate counting process $\mathbf{N} \equiv \{N_i\}_{i\in\{1,\dots,p\}}$, where, as above, N_i satisfies $N_i(A) = \sum_k \mathbf{1}_{\{t_{ik}\in A\}}$ for $A \in \mathcal{B}(\mathbb{R})$ with $\{t_{i1}, t_{i2}, \dots\}$ denoting the event times of N_i. Let $\mathcal{H}_t$ be the history of $\mathbf{N}$ prior to time t. The intensity process $\{\lambda_1(t), \dots, \lambda_p(t)\}$ is a p-variate $\mathcal{H}_t$-predictable process, defined as

$$\lambda_i(t)dt = \mathbb{P}(dN_i(t) = 1 \mid \mathcal{H}_t). \quad (1)$$

Hawkes [23] proposed a class of point process models in which past events can affect the probability of future events. The process $\mathbf{N}$ is a *linear Hawkes process* if the intensity function for each unit $i \in \{1,\dots,p\}$ takes the form

$$\lambda_i(t) = \mu_i + \sum_{j=1}^{p} (\omega_{ij} * dN_j)(t), \quad (2)$$

where

$$(\omega_{ij} * dN_j)(t) = \int_0^{t-} \omega_{ij}(t-s)dN_j(s) = \sum_{k:t_{jk}<t} \omega_{ij}(t-t_{jk}). \quad (3)$$

Here, μ_i is the background intensity of unit i and $\omega_{ij}(\cdot) : \mathbb{R}^+ \to \mathbb{R}$ is the *transfer function*. In particular, $\omega_{ij}(t - t_{jk})$ represents the influence from the kth event of unit j on the intensity of unit i at time t.

Motivated by neuroscience applications [38,39], we consider a parametric transfer function $\omega_{ij}(\cdot)$ of the form

$$\omega_{ij}(t) = \beta_{ij}\kappa_j(t) \quad (4)$$

with a *transition kernel* $\kappa_j(\cdot) : \mathbb{R}^+ \to \mathbb{R}$ that captures the decay of the dependence on past events. This leads to $(\omega_{ij} * dN_j)(t) = \beta_{ij}x_j(t)$, where the *integrated stochastic process*

$$x_j(t) = \int_0^{t-} \kappa_j(t-s)dN_j(s) \quad (5)$$

summarizes the entire history of unit j of the multivariate Hawkes processes. A commonly used example is the exponential transition kernel, $\kappa_j(t) = e^{-t}$ [40].

Assuming that the model holds and all relevant processes are observed, it follows from [40] that the *connectivity coefficient* β_{ij} represents the strength of the *causal* dependence of unit i's intensity on unit j's past events. A positive β_{ij} implies that past events of unit j *excite* future events of unit i and is often considered in the literature (see, e.g., [40,41]). However, we might also wish to allow for negative β_{ij} values to represent *inhibitory* effects [34,42], which are expected in neuroscience applications [43].

Denoting $\boldsymbol{x}(t) = (x_1(t), \dots, x_p(t))^\top \in \mathbb{R}^p$ and $\boldsymbol{\beta}_i = (\beta_{i1}, \dots, \beta_{ip})^\top \in \mathbb{R}^p$, we can write

$$\lambda_i(t) = \mu_i + \boldsymbol{x}^\top(t)\boldsymbol{\beta}_i. \quad (6)$$

Furthermore, let $Y_i(t) = dN_i(t)/dt$ and $\epsilon_i(t) = Y_i(t) - \lambda_i(t)$. Then the linear Hawkes process can be written compactly as

$$Y_i(t) = \mu_i + \boldsymbol{x}^\top(t)\boldsymbol{\beta}_i + \epsilon_i(t). \tag{7}$$

2.2. *The Confounded Hawkes Process*

Because of technology constraints, neuroscience experiments usually collect data from only a small portion of neurons. As a result, many other neurons that potentially interact with the observed neurons will be unobserved. Consider a network of $p+q$ counting processes, where we only observe the first p components. The number of unobserved neurons, q, is usually unknown and likely much greater than p. Extending (7) to include the unobserved components, we obtain the *confounded Hawkes model*,

$$Y_i(t) = \mu_i + \boldsymbol{x}^\top(t)\boldsymbol{\beta}_i + \boldsymbol{z}^\top(t)\delta_i + \epsilon_i(t), \tag{8}$$

in which $\boldsymbol{z}(t) = (x_{p+1}(t), \ldots, x_{p+q}(t))^\top \in \mathbb{R}^q$ denotes the integrated processes of the hidden components, and $\delta_i \in \mathbb{R}^q$ denotes the connectivity coefficients from the unobserved components to unit i.

Unless the observed and unobserved processes are independent, the naïve estimator that ignores the unobserved components will produce misleading conclusion about the causal relationship among the observed components. This is illustrated in the simple linear vector autoregressive process of Figure 1. This example includes three continuous random variables generated according to the following set of equations

$$\begin{aligned}
Y_1(t) &= Y_1(t-1) + Y_2(t-1) + \epsilon_1(t-1) \\
Y_2(t) &= Y_3(t-1) + \epsilon_2(t-1) \\
Y_3(t) &= Y_3(t-1) + \epsilon_2(t-1),
\end{aligned}$$

where ϵ_i are mean zero innovation or error terms. The Granger causal network corresponding to the above process is shown in Figure 1A. Figure 1B shows that if Y_3 is not observed, the conditional means of the observed variables Y_1 and Y_2, namely,

$$\begin{aligned}
\mathbb{E}\{Y_1(t) \mid Y_1(t-1), Y_2(t-1)\} &= Y_1(t-1) + Y_2(t-1) \\
\mathbb{E}\{Y_2(t) \mid Y_1(t-1), Y_2(t-1)\} &= Y_2(t-1),
\end{aligned}$$

leads to incorrect Granger causal conclusions—in this case, a spurious autoregressive effect from the past values of Y_2. The same phenomenon occurs in Hawkes processes with unobserved components.

Throughout this paper, we assume that the confounded linear Hawkes model in (8) is *stationary*, meaning that for all units $i = 1, \ldots, p$, the spontaneous rates μ_i and strengths of transition $(\boldsymbol{\beta}_i, \delta_i)$ are constant over the time range $[0, T]$ [44,45].

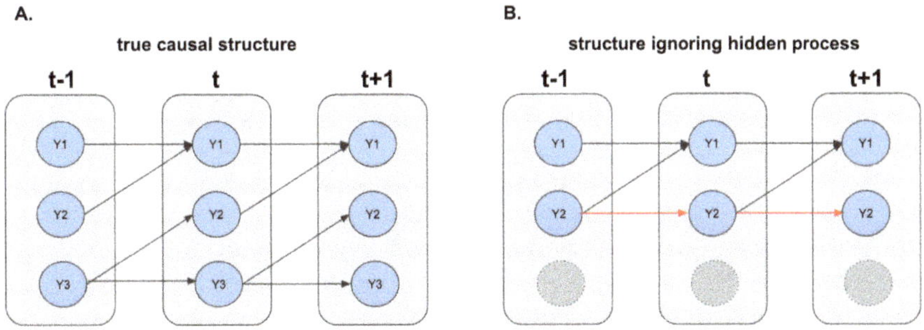

Figure 1. Illustration of the effect of hidden confounders on inferred causal interactions among the observed variables. (**A**) The true causal diagram for the complete processes. (**B**) The causal structure of the observed process when the hidden component, Y_3, is ignored, including a spurious autoregressive effect of Y_2 on its future values.

3. Estimating Causal Effects in Confounded Hawkes Processes

3.1. Extending Trim Regression to Hawkes Processes

Let $\boldsymbol{b}_i \in \mathbb{R}^p$ be the projection coefficient of $\boldsymbol{z}^\top(t)\boldsymbol{\delta}_i$ onto $\boldsymbol{x}(t)$ such that

$$\mathrm{Cov}\Big(\boldsymbol{x}(t), \boldsymbol{z}^\top(t)\boldsymbol{\delta}_i - \boldsymbol{x}^\top(t)\boldsymbol{b}_i\Big) = 0. \tag{9}$$

We can write the confounded linear Hawkes model in (8) in the form of the *perturbed linear model* [37]:

$$Y_i(t) = \mu_i + \boldsymbol{x}^\top(t)(\boldsymbol{\beta}_i + \boldsymbol{b}_i) + \nu_i(t), \tag{10}$$

where $\nu_i(t) = \big(\boldsymbol{z}^\top(t)\boldsymbol{\delta}_i - \boldsymbol{x}^\top(t)\boldsymbol{b}_i\big) + \epsilon_i(t)$. By the construction of $\boldsymbol{b}_i$, $\nu(t)$ is uncorrelated with the observed processes $\boldsymbol{x}(t)$ and $\boldsymbol{b}_i$ represents the bias, or the perturbation, due to the confounding from $\boldsymbol{z}^\top(t)\boldsymbol{\delta}_i$. In general, $\boldsymbol{b}_i \neq 0$ unless $\mathrm{Cov}(\boldsymbol{x}(t), \boldsymbol{z}(t)) = 0$.

The perturbed model in (10) is generally unidentifiable because we can only estimate $\boldsymbol{\beta}_i + \boldsymbol{b}_i$ from the observed data, e.g., by regressing $Y_i(t)$ on $\boldsymbol{x}(t)$. The *trim regression* [37] is a two-step deconfounding procedure to estimate $\boldsymbol{\beta}_i$ for independent and Gaussian-distributed data. The method first applies a simple spectral transformation, called trim transformation (described below), to the observed data. It then estimates $\boldsymbol{\beta}_i$, using penalized regression. When $\boldsymbol{b}_i$ is sufficiently small, the method consistently estimates $\boldsymbol{\beta}_i$. Although this condition is generally not valid for Gaussian-distributed data, previous work on Hawkes processes [34] implies that the confounding magnitude cannot be large when the underlying network is stable, particularly when the confounders affect many observed components (see the discussion following Corollary 1 in Section 4). This allows us to generalize the trim regression to learn the network of multivariate Hawkes processes.

Assume, without loss of generality, that the first p components are observed at times indexed from 1 to T. Let $X \in \mathbb{R}^{T\times p}$ be the design matrix of the observed integrated process and $Y_i = (Y_i(1), \ldots, Y_i(T))^\top \in \mathbb{R}^T$ be the vector of observed outcomes. Further, let $X = UDV^\top$ be the singular value decomposition on X, where $U \in \mathbb{R}^{T\times r}$, $D \in \mathbb{R}^{r\times r}$ and $V \in \mathbb{R}^{p\times r}$; here, $r = \min(T, p)$ is the rank of X. Denoting the non-zero diagonal entries of D by $d_1, \ldots, d_r$, the *spectral transformation* $F : \mathbb{R}^{T\times p} \to \mathbb{R}^{T\times p}$ is given by

$$F = U\begin{pmatrix} \tilde{d}_1/d_1 & 0 & \ldots & 0 \\ 0 & \tilde{d}_2/d_2 & \ldots & 0 \\ \vdots & \vdots & \ddots & \vdots \\ 0 & 0 & \ldots & \tilde{d}_r/d_r \end{pmatrix} U^\top. \tag{11}$$

Denoting by $\widetilde{D}$ a diagonal matrix with entries $\tilde{d}_1, \ldots, \tilde{d}_r$, the first step of *hp-trim* involves applying the spectral transformation to the observed data to obtain

$$\widetilde{X} = FX = U\widetilde{D}V^\top, \tag{12}$$

$$\widetilde{Y} = FY. \tag{13}$$

The spectral transformation is designed to reduce the magnitude of confounding. In particular, when $\boldsymbol{b}_i$ aligns with the top eigen-vectors of X, for an appropriate F, e.g., $\tilde{d}_k = \min(\tau, d_k)$ as used in previous work [37], the magnitude of $\widetilde{X}\boldsymbol{b}_i$ is small compared with $X\boldsymbol{b}_i$. Here, τ is a threshold parameter and the trim transformation is a special case of the spectral transformation when $\tau = \text{median}(d_1, \ldots, d_r)$. See Ćevid et al. [37] for additional details.

In the second step, we then estimate the network connectivities using the transformed data by solving the following optimization problem

$$\arg \min_{\substack{\mu_i \in \mathbb{R}, \boldsymbol{\beta}_i \in \mathbb{R}^p \\ 1 \le i \le p}} \sum_{i=1}^{p} \left\{ \frac{1}{T} \left\| \widetilde{Y}_i - \mu_i - \widetilde{X}\boldsymbol{\beta}_i \right\|_2^2 + \lambda \|\boldsymbol{\beta}_i\|_1 \right\}, \tag{14}$$

which is an instance of lasso regression [46] and can be solved separately for each $i \in \{1, \ldots, p\}$.

3.2. An Alternative Approach

HIdden Variable adjustment Estimation (HIVE) [36] is an alternative method for estimating coefficients of a linear model with independent and Gaussian-distributed data in the presence of latent variables. Adapted to the network of multivariate point processes, HIVE first estimates the latent column space of the unobserved connectivity matrix, $\Delta = \begin{pmatrix} \delta_1 & \ldots & \delta_p \end{pmatrix}^\top \in \mathbf{R}^{p \times q}$, with δ_i defined in (8). It then projects the outcome vector, $Y(t) = \left(Y_1(t), \ldots, Y_p(t)\right)^\top$, onto the space orthogonal to the column space of Δ. Assuming that the column space of the observed connectivity matrix, $\Theta = \begin{pmatrix} \boldsymbol{\beta}_1 & \ldots & \boldsymbol{\beta}_p \end{pmatrix}^\top \in \mathbf{R}^{p \times p}$ is orthogonal to that of Δ, HIVE consistently estimates Θ using the transformed data. While the orthogonality assumption might be satisfied when the hidden processes are external, such as experimental perturbations in genetic studies [47], it might be too stringent in a network setting. However, when the orthogonality assumption fails, HIVE may lead to poor edge selection performance, and potentially worse than the naïve method that ignores the hidden processes. HIVE also requires the number of hidden variables to be known. Although methods in selecting the number of hidden variables have been proposed, the resulting theoretical guarantees would only be asymptotic. An over- or under-estimated number can either miss the true edges or generate false ones. Given these limitations, we outline the extension of HIVE for Hawkes processes in Appendix A and refer the interested reader to Bing et al. [36] for details.

4. Theoretical Properties

In this section we establish the recovery of the network connectivity in the presence of hidden processes. Technical proofs for the results in this section are given in Appendix B.

We start by stating our assumptions. For a square matrix A, let $\Lambda_{\max}(A)$ and $\Lambda_{\min}(A)$ be its maximum and minimum eigenvalues, respectively.

Assumption 1. *Let* $\Omega = \{\Omega_{ij}\}_{1 \le i,j \le p+q} \in \mathbb{R}^{(p+q)\times(p+q)}$ *with entries* $\Omega_{ij} = \int_0^\infty |\omega_{ij}(\Delta)| d\Delta$. *There exists a constant* γ_Ω *such that* $\Lambda_{\max}(\Omega^T\Omega) \le \gamma_\Omega^2 < 1$.

Assumption 1 is necessary for stationarity of a Hawkes process [34]. The constant γ_Ω does not depend on the dimension $p + q$. For any fixed dimension, Brémaud and Massoulié [44] show that given this assumption the intensity process of the form (6) is stable in distribution and, thus, a stationary process exists. Since our connectivity coefficients of interest are ill-defined without stationarity, this assumption provides the necessary context for our estimation framework.

Assumption 2. *There exists* $\lambda_{\min}$ *and* $\lambda_{\max}$ *such that*

$$0 < \lambda_{\min} \leq \lambda_i(t) \leq \lambda_{\max} < \infty, \quad t \in [0, T]$$

for all $i = 1, \ldots, p + q$.

Assumption 2 requires that the intensity rate is strictly bounded, which prevents degenerate processes for all components of the multivariate Hawkes processes. This assumption has been considered in the previous analysis of Hawkes processes [33–35,42,48].

Assumption 3. *The transition kernel* $\kappa_j(t)$ *is bounded and integrable over* $[0, T]$, *for* $1 \leq j \leq p + q$.

Assumption 4. *There exists constants* $\rho_r \in (0, 1)$ *and* $0 < \rho_c < \infty$ *such that*

$$\max_{1 \leq i \leq p+q} \sum_{j=1}^{p+q} \Omega_{ij} \leq \rho_r \qquad \text{and} \qquad \max_{1 \leq j \leq p+q} \sum_{i=1}^{p+q} \Omega_{ij} \leq \rho_c.$$

Assumption 3 implies that the integrated process $x_j(t)$ in (5) is bounded. Assumption 4 requires maximum in- and out- intensity flows to be bounded, which provides a sufficient condition for bounding the eigenvalues of the cross-covariance of $\boldsymbol{x}(t)$ [35]. A similar assumption is considered by Basu and Michailidis [49] in the context of VAR models. Together, Assumptions 3 and 4 imply that the model parameters are bounded, which is often required in time-series analysis [50]. Specifically, these assumptions restrict the influence of the hidden processes from being too large.

Define the set of active indices among the observed components, $S_i = \{j : \beta_{ij} \neq 0, 1 \leq j \leq p\}$, and $s_i = |S_i|$ and $s^* \equiv \max_{1 \leq i \leq p} s_i$. Let $Q = \frac{1}{T}\sum_{t=1}^{T} \begin{pmatrix} 1 \\ \boldsymbol{x}(t) \end{pmatrix} (1 \quad \boldsymbol{x}^\top(t))$, and $\gamma_{\min} \equiv \Lambda_{\min}(Q)$ and $\gamma_{\max} \equiv \Lambda_{\max}(Q)$. Our first result provides a fixed sample bound on the error of estimating the connectivity coefficients.

Theorem 1. *Suppose each of the p-variate Hawkes processes with intensity function defined in* (8) *satisfies Assumptions 1–4. Assume* $(\log p) \vee (s^*)^{1/2} = o(T^{1/5})$. *Then, taking* $\lambda = O(\Lambda_{\max}^2(F) T^{-2/5})$,

$$\left\| \boldsymbol{\beta}_i - \widehat{\boldsymbol{\beta}}_i \right\|_1 \leq C_1 \Lambda_{\max}^2(F) \frac{s^*}{\gamma_{\min}^2} T^{-2/5} + C_2 \Lambda_{\max}^{-2}(F) T^{-3/5} \left\| \widetilde{X} \boldsymbol{b}_i \right\|_2^2, \quad 1 \leq i \leq p,$$

with probability at least $1 - c_1 p^2 T \exp(-c_2 T^{1/5})$, *where* $C_1, C_2, c_1, c_2 > 0$ *depend on the model parameters and the transition kernel.*

Compared to the case with independent and Gaussian-distributed data ([37], Theorem 2), we obtain a slower convergence rate because of the complex dependency of the Hawkes processes. Our rate takes into account the network sparsity among the observed components. It also does not depend on the size of unobserved components, q, which is critical in neuroscience experiments because q is often unknown and potentially very large.

The result in Theorem 1 is different from the corresponding result obtained when all processes are observed ([35], Lemma 10). More specifically, our result includes an extra error term, $\|\widetilde{X}\boldsymbol{b}_i\|_2^2$, which captures the effect of unobserved processes. Next, we show that when $\|\boldsymbol{b}_i\|_2^2$ is sufficiently small, we obtain a similar rate of convergence as the one obtained when all processes are observed.

Corollary 1. *Under the same assumptions in Theorem 1, suppose, in addition,* $\|\boldsymbol{b}_i\|_2^2 = O\left(\frac{s^*}{\gamma_{\min}^2 \gamma_{\max}} T^{-4/5} \Lambda_{\max}^2(F)\right)$,

$$\left\|\boldsymbol{\beta}_i - \widehat{\boldsymbol{\beta}}_i\right\|_1 = O\left(\frac{s^*}{\gamma_{\min}^2} \Lambda_{\max}^2(F) T^{-2/5}\right), \quad 1 \leq i \leq p,$$

with probability at least $1 - c_1 p^2 T \exp(-c_2 T^{1/5})$*, where* $c_1, c_2 > 0$ *depending on the model parameters and the transition kernel.*

The spectral transformation empirically reduces the magnitude of $\frac{1}{T}\|\widetilde{X}\boldsymbol{b}_i\|_2^2$, especially when the confounding vector, $\boldsymbol{b}_i$, stays in the sub-space spanned by top right singular vectors of X; however, this is not guaranteed to hold for arbitrary $\boldsymbol{b}_i$. Corollary 1 specifies a condition on $\boldsymbol{b}_i$ that leads to consistent estimation of $\boldsymbol{\beta}_i$, regardless of the empirical performance of the spectral transformation. While the condition does not always hold for arbitrary stochastic process, it is satisfied for a stable network of high-dimensional multivariate Hawkes processes when the confounding is dense. Specifically, by the construction of $\boldsymbol{b}_i$ in (9), Assumption 4 implies that $\|\boldsymbol{b}_i\|_1 = O(\|\boldsymbol{\delta}_i\|_1) = O(1)$. When the confounding effects are relatively dense—i.e., $\|\boldsymbol{b}_i\|_0 = O(p)$, meaning that there are large number of interactions from unobserved nodes to the observed ones—we obtain $\|\boldsymbol{b}_i\|_2^2 = O(1/p)$. Therefore, the constraint on $\|\boldsymbol{b}_i\|_2^2$ is likely satisfied under a high-dimensional network, when $p \gg T$. The high-dimensional network setting is common in modern neuroscience experiments where the number of neurons is often large compared to the duration of experiments.

Next we introduce an additional assumption to establish the edge selection consistency. To this end, we consider the *thresholded connectivity estimator*,

$$\widetilde{\beta}_{ij} = \widehat{\beta}_{ij} \mathbf{1}\left(\left|\widehat{\beta}_{ij}\right| > \tau\right), \quad 1 \leq i, j \leq p.$$

Thresholded estimators are used for variable selections in high-dimensional network estimation [51] as they alleviate the need for restrictive irrepresentability assumptions [52].

Assumption 5. *There exists* $\tau > 0$ *such that*

$$\min_{1 \leq i,j \leq p} \beta_{ij} \geq \beta_{min} > 2\tau.$$

Assumption 5 is called the β-min condition [53] and requires sufficient signal strength for the true edges in order to distinguish them from 0. Let the estimated edge set $\widehat{S} = \left\{(i,j) : \widetilde{\beta}_{ij} \neq 0, 1 \leq i,j \leq p\right\}$ and the true edge set $S = \{(i,j) : \beta_{ij} \neq 0, 1 \leq i,j \leq p\}$. The next result shows that the estimated edge set consistently recovers the true edge set.

Theorem 2. *Under the same conditions in Theorem 1, assume Assumption 5 is satisfied with* $\tau = O\left(\frac{s^*}{\gamma_{\min}^2} \Lambda_{\max}^2(F) T^{-2/5}\right)$*. Then,*

$$\mathbb{P}\left(\widehat{S} = S\right) \geq 1 - c_1 p^2 T \exp\left(-c_2 T^{1/5}\right),$$

where $c_1, c_2 > 0$ *depending on the model parameters and the transition kernel.*

Theorem 2 guarantees the recovery of causal interactions among the observed components. As before, the result is valid irrespective of the number of unobserved components, which is important in neuroscience applications.

5. Simulation Studies

We compare our proposed method, *hp-trim*, with two alternatives, HIVE and the naïve approach that ignores the unobserved nodes. To this end, we compare the methods in terms of their abilities to identify the correct causal interactions among the observed components.

We consider a point process network consisting of 200 nodes with half of the nodes being observed; that is $p = q = 100$. The observed nodes are connected in blocks of five nodes, and half of the blocks are connected with the unobserved nodes (see Figure 2a). This setting exemplifies neuroscience applications, where the orthogonality assumption of HIVE is violated. As a sensitivity analysis, we also consider a second setting similar to the first, in which we remove the connections of the blocks that are not connected with the unobserved nodes This setting, shown in Figure 3a, satisfies HIVE's orthogonality assumption.

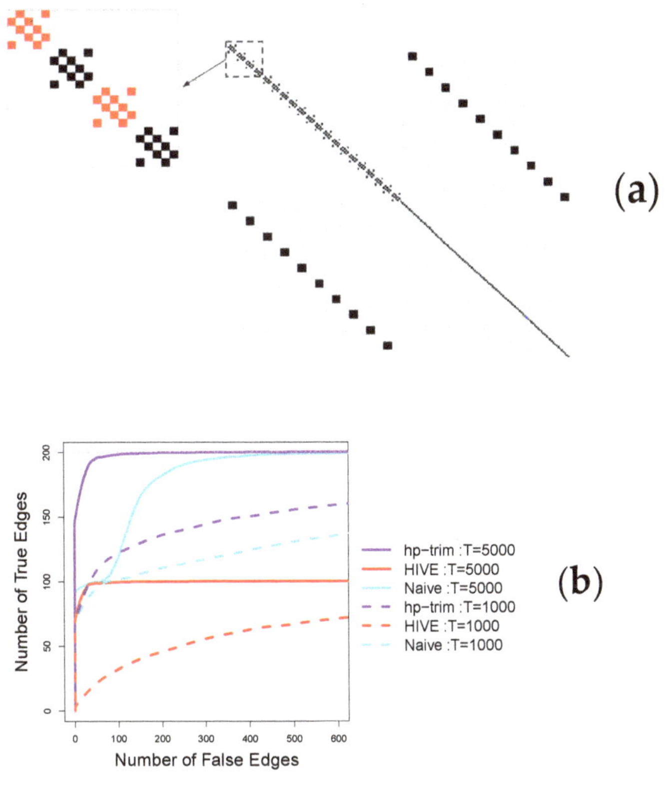

Figure 2. Edge selection performance of the proposed *hp-trim* approach compared with estimators based on HIVE (run with the known (oracle) number of latent features) and the naïve approach. Here, $p = q = 100$. (**a**) Visualization of the connectivity matrix, with unobserved connecitivies colored in gray and entries corresponding to edges shown in black. This setting violates the orthogonality condition of HIVE because of the connections between the observed and the hidden nodes (represented by the non-zero coefficients colored in red). (**b**) Average number of true positive and false positive edges detected using each method over 100 simulation runs.

To generate point process data, we consider $\beta_{ij} = 0.12$ and $\delta_{ij} = 0.10$ in the setting of Figure 2a, and $\beta_{ij} = 0.2$ and $\delta_{ij} = 0.18$ in the setting of Figure 3b. The background intensity, μ_i, is set to 0.05 in both settings. The transfer kernel function is chosen to be $\exp(-t)$. These settings satisfy the assumptions of stationary Hawkes processes. In both settings, we set the length of the time series to $T \in \{1000, 5000\}$.

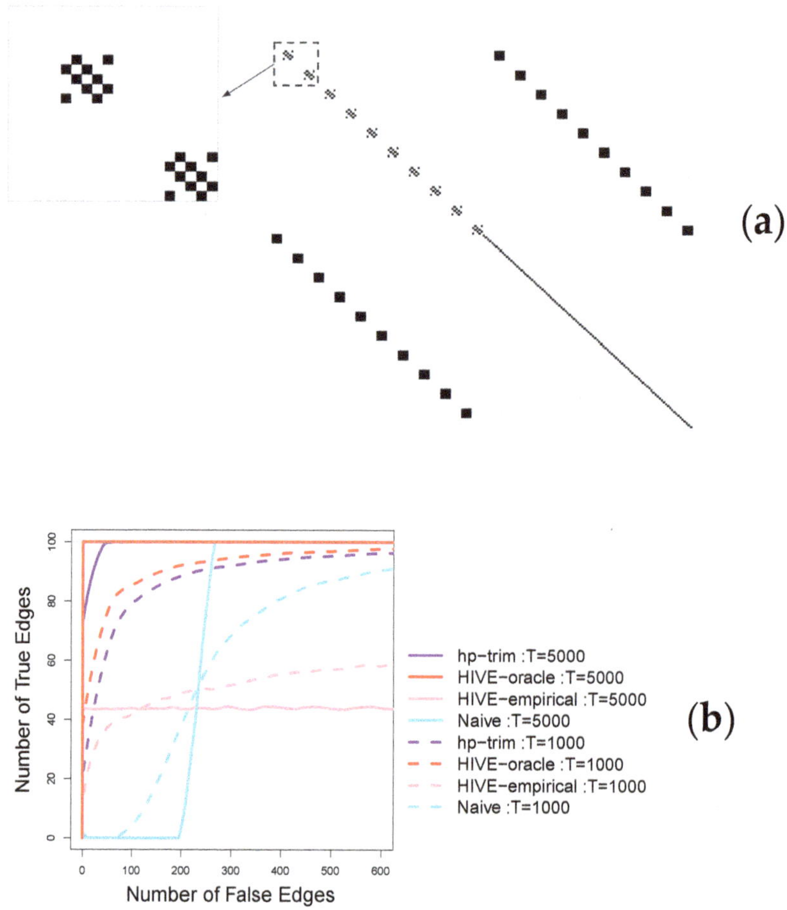

Figure 3. Edge selection performance of the proposed *hp-trim* approach compared with estimators based on HIVE and the naïve approach. Here, $p = q = 100$. (**a**) Visualization of the connectivity matrix, with unobserved connecitivies colored in gray and entries corresponding to edges shown in black. This setting satisfies the orthogonality condition of HIVE, which is run both with and without assuming known number of latent features. These two versions are denoted HIVE-oracle and HIVE-empirical, respectively. In HIVE-empirical the number of latent factors is estimated based on the estimate with highest frequency over the 100 simulation runs (estimated $\hat{q} = 79$). (**b**) Average number of true positive and false positive edges detected using each method over 100 simulation runs.

The results in Figure 2b shown that *hp-trim* offers superior performance for both small and large sample sizes in the first setting. For example, with large sample size, $T = 5000$, *hp-trim* is able to detect almost all 200 true edges at the expense of about 50 falsely detected edges; this is almost twice as large as the number of true edges detected by HIVE and the naïve method, which only detect half of the true edges at the same level of falsely detected edges. The naïve method eventually detects all true edges but at much bigger cost of about 400 falsely detected edges. In this case, HIVE performs poorly and detects at most half of the true edges, no matter the tolerance level of the number of falsely detected edges. The poor performance of HIVE is because its stringent orthogonality condition is violated in this simulation setting. When the orthogonality condition is satisfied (Figure 3a), HIVE shows the best performance. Specifically, with large sample size, $T = 5000$, HIVE detects all true edges almost without identifying any falsely detected edges (the red solid line in

Figure 3b). However, this advantage requires knowledge of the correct number of latent features. When the number of latent features is unknown and estimated from data, HIVE's performance deteriorates, especially with an insufficient sample size. For example, HIVE with empirically estimated number of latent features only detect about 40 true edges (out of a total of 100) at the expense of 100 falsely detected edges (pink lines in Figure 3b). In contrast, *hp-trim*'s performance with both moderate and large sample sizes is close to the oracle version of HIVE (HIVE-oracle). Specifically, with a large sample size, $T = 5000$, *hp-trim* captures all 100 true edges at the expense of 50 falsely detected edges, again than twice as many true edges as HIVE-empirical.

Although our main focus is on the edge selection relevant for causal discovery, in Appendix C we also examine the estimation performance of our algorithm on the connectivity coefficients associated with the observed processes. Not surprisingly, the results indicate that *hp-trim* can also offer advantages in estimating the parameters, especially in settings where it offers improved edge selection.

6. Analysis of Mouse Spike Train Data

We consider the task of learning causal interactions among the observed population of neurons, using the spike train data from Bolding and Franks [14]. In this experiment, spike times are recorded at 30 kHz on a region of the mice olfactory bulb (OB), while a laser pulse is applied directly on the OB cells of the subject mouse. The laser pulse has been applied at increasing intensities from 0 to 50 (mW/mm^2). The laser pulse at each intensity level lasts 10 seconds and is repeated 10 times on the same set of neuron cells of the subject mouse.

The experiment consists of spike train data multiple mice and we consider data from the subject mouse with the most detected neurons (25) under laser (20 mW/mm^2) and no laser conditions. In particular, we use the spike train data from one laser pulse at each intensity level. Since one laser pulse spans 10 seconds and the spike train data is recorded at 30 kHz, there are 300,000 time points per experimental replicate.

The population of observed neurons is a small subset of all the neurons in mouse's brain. Therefore, to discover causal interactions among the $p = 25$ observed neurons, we apply our estimation procedure, *hp-trim*, along with HIVE and naïve approaches, separately for each intensity level, and obtain the estimated connectivity coefficients for the observed neurons. For ease of comparison, the tuning parameters for both methods are chosen to have about 30 estimated edges; moreover, for HIVE, q is estimated following the procedure in Bing et al. [36], which is based on the maximum decrease in eigenvalue of the covariance matrix of the errors, $\widetilde{E}(t)$ in (A1).

Figure 4 shows the estimated connectivity coefficients specific to each laser condition in a graph representation. In this representation, each node represents a neuron, and a directed edge indicates a non-zero estimated connectivity coefficient. We see different network connectivity structures when laser stimulus is applied, which agrees with the observation by neuroscientists that the OB response is sensitive to the external stimuli [14].

Compared to our proposed method, the naïve approach generates a more similar network than HIVE under both laser and no-laser conditions, which is likely an indication that the naïve estimate is incorrect in this application.

As discussed in Section 4, our inference procedure is asymptotically valid. In other words, with large enough sample size, if the other assumptions in Section 4 are satisfied, the estimated edges should represent the true edges. Assessing the validity of the assumptions and selecting the true edges in real data applications is challenging. However, we can assess the sample size requirement and the validity of assumptions by estimating the edges over a subset of neurons as if the other removed neurons are unobserved. If the sample size is sufficient and the other assumptions are satisfied, we should obtain similar connectivities among the observed subset of neurons, even when some neurons are hidden. Figure 5 shows the result of such a stability analysis for the laser condition using *hp-trim*. Comparing the connectivities in this graph with those in Figure 4 indicates that the estimated edges using the subsets of neurons are all consistent with those estimated using all neurons. Thus, the assumptions are likely satisfied in this application.

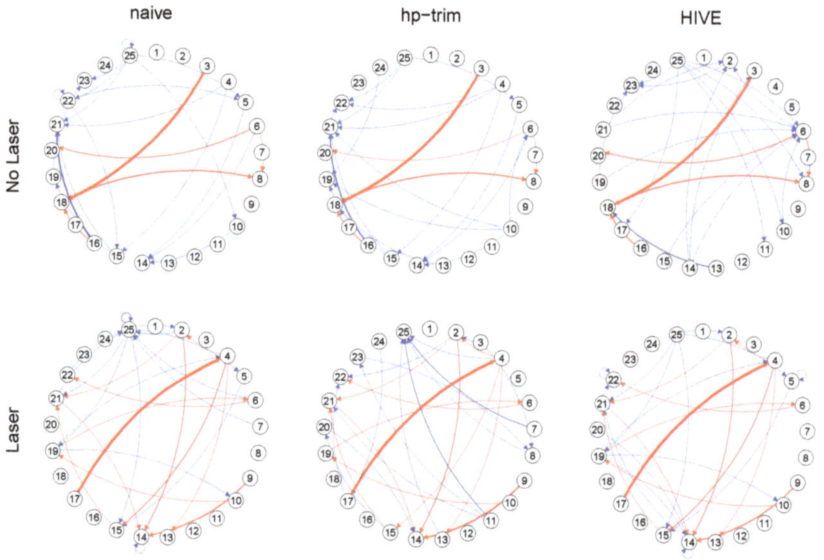

Figure 4. Estimated functional connectivities among neurons using mouse spike train data from laser and no-laser conditions [14]. Common edges estimated by the three methods are in red and the method-specific edges are in blue. Thicker edges indicate estimated connectivity coefficients of larger magnitudes.

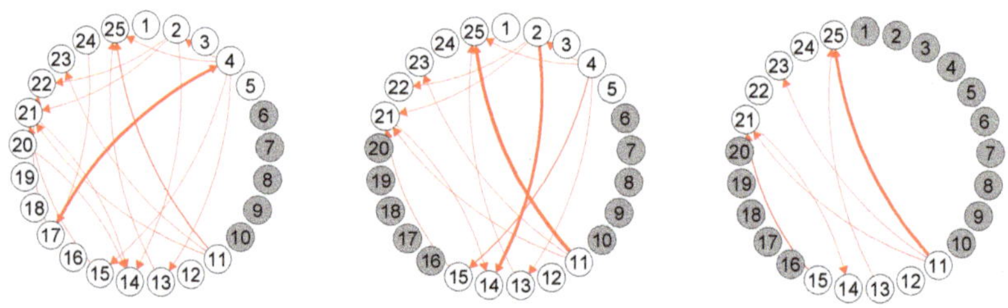

(a) (b) (c)

Figure 5. Estimated functional connectivities using *hp-trim* among multiple subset of neurons. Here, data is the same as that used in Figure 4 under the laser condition, except that 5, 10 and 15 neurons (shown in gray) are considered hidden. Thicker edges indicate estimated connectivity coefficients of larger magnitudes. All estimated edges using the subsets of neurons are also found in the estimated network using all neurons (**a**–**c**).

7. Conclusions and Future Work

We proposed a causal-estimation procedure with theoretical guarantees for high-dimensional network of multivariate Hawkes processes in the presence of hidden confounders. Our method extends the trim regression [37] to the setting of point process data. The choice of trim regression as the starting point was motivated by the fact that its assumptions are less stringent than conditions required for the alternative HIVE procedure, especially for a stable point process network with dense confounding effects. Empirically, our procedure, *hp-trim*, shows superior performance in identifying edges in the causal network compared with HIVE and a naïve method that ignores the unobserved nodes.

Causal discovery from observational time series is a challenging problem and the success of our method is not without limitations. First, the theoretical guarantees for *hp-trim* require the magnitude of the hidden confounding to be bounded. As we discussed in the paper, this condition is likely met for a stable network of high-dimensional multivariate Hawkes processes when the confounding is dense. Nonetheless a careful examination of this condition is required when applying the method in other settings. When certain structure exists between the observed and hidden network connectivities, more structure-specific methods, such as HIVE, may be able to better utilize the structural property of the network for improved performance in identifying the causal effects. Second, our estimates assume a linear Hawkes process with a particular parametric form of the transition function. We also assume the underlying Hawkes process is stationary, where certain structural requirements of the process (specified as assumptions in Section 4) must be satisfied. The proposed method is guaranteed to identify causal effects only if these modeling assumptions are valid. When the modeling assumptions are violated, the estimated effects may not be causal. In other words, the method is primarily designed to generate causal hypotheses—or facilitate *causal discovery*—and the results should be interpreted with caution. Extending the proposed approach to model the transition function nonparametrically, learning its form adaptively from data and capturing time-varying processes would be important future research directions. Finally, given that non-linear link functions are often used when analyzing spike train data [54,55], it would also be of interest to develop causal-estimation procedure for non-linear Hawkes processes.

Author Contributions: Conceptualization, X.W. and A.S.; methodology, X.W. and A.S.; formal analysis, X.W.; writing—original draft preparation, X.W.; writing—review and editing, A.S. All authors have read and agreed to the published version of the manuscript.

Funding: The authors gratefully acknowledge the support from the U.S. National Science Foundation (grant DMS-1722246) and U.S. National Institutes of Health (grant R01GM133848).

Institutional Review Board Statement: Not applicable.

Informed Consent Statement: Not applicable.

Data Availability Statement: Data collected by [14] have been deposited at the CRCNS (https://crcns.org, accessed on 25 November 2021) and can be accessed at https://doi.org/10.6080/K00C4SZB, accessed on 25 November 2021.

Conflicts of Interest: The authors declare no conflict of interest.

Appendix A. Additional Details on HIVE

We introduce additional notations before illustrating the method.

Let $Y(t) = \left(Y_1(t), \ldots, Y_p(t)\right)^\top$, $X(t) = \left(x_1(t), \ldots, x_p(t)\right)^\top$, $Z(t) = \left(z_1(t), \ldots, z_q(t)\right)^\top$ and $E(t) = \left(\epsilon_1(t), \ldots, \epsilon_p(t)\right)^\top$. Then, we rewrite (8) simultaneously for all components:

$$Y(t) = \boldsymbol{\mu} + \Theta X(t) + \Delta Z(t) + E(t), \tag{A1}$$

where $\Theta = \begin{pmatrix} \beta_1^\top \\ \cdots \\ \beta_p^\top \end{pmatrix} \in \mathbf{R}^{p\times p}$ and $\Delta = \begin{pmatrix} \delta_1^\top \\ \cdots \\ \delta_p^\top \end{pmatrix} \in \mathbf{R}^{p\times q}$ are connectivity matrix between the observed and unobserved components, respectively. $\boldsymbol{\mu} = \left(\mu_1, \ldots, \mu_p\right)^\top \in \mathbf{R}^p$ is the vector of spontaneous rate.

To illustrate the confounding induced by the hidden process, we project $Z(t)$ onto the space spanned by $X(t)$ as

$$Z(t) = \nu + AX(t) + W(t), \tag{A2}$$

where A is the projection matrix, representing the cross-sectional correlation between Z and X. Then, (A1) becomes

$$Y(t) = \widetilde{\mu} + \widetilde{\Theta}X(t) + \widetilde{E}(t), \quad \text{(A3)}$$

where

$$\begin{aligned} \widetilde{\mu} &= \mu + \Delta\nu, \\ \widetilde{\Theta} &= \Theta + \Delta A, \\ \widetilde{E}(t) &= E(t) + \Delta W(t). \end{aligned}$$

From the above, it is easy to see that the correlations between the observed and unobserved processes determine the strength the confounding. Specifically, unless $A = 0$—i.e., when the observed and unobserved processes are independent, directly regressing $Y(t)$ on $X(t)$ produces biased estimates on Θ. Under the condition that $\Theta \perp \Delta$—i.e., the column space of Θ is orthogonal to the column space of Δ, HIVE gets around this issue by finding a projection matrix, $P_{\Delta^\perp}$, that projects Δ onto its orthogonal space—i.e., $P_{\Delta^\perp}\Delta = 0$. Moreover, because of the orthogonality assumption, $P_{\Delta^\perp}\Theta = \Theta$. Therefore, when multiplying both sides in (A1) by $P_{\Delta^\perp}$, the unobserved term disappears. Specifically, letting $\widetilde{Y}(t) = P_{\Delta^\perp}Y(t)$, (A1) becomes

$$\widetilde{Y}(t) = P_{\Delta^\perp}\mu + \Theta X(t) + P_{\Delta^\perp}E(t). \quad \text{(A4)}$$

Consequently, regressing $\widetilde{Y}(t)$ on $X(t)$ produces unbiased estimates on Θ (using penalized regression with ℓ_1-penalty on Θ under the high-dimensional setting when p is allowed to grow with the sample size T). In order to obtain $P_{\Delta^\perp}$, HIVE first calculates $\widetilde{E}(t)$ in (A3) and then implement *heteroPCA* algorithm [56] to estimate the latent column space of Δ thus to obtain P_Δ. Then, the method obtains the corresponding orthogonal project as $P_{\Delta^\perp} = I - P_\Delta$. We refer the interested readers to Bing et al. [36] for details about the method.

Appendix B. Proof of Main Results

Since our focus is on the estimation error for β_i, we consider the perturbation model in (10) in the following.

Let $\theta_i = \begin{pmatrix}\mu_i & \beta_i\end{pmatrix}^\top$ be the true model parameter and $\widehat{\theta}_i = \begin{pmatrix}\widehat{\mu}_i & \widehat{\beta}_i\end{pmatrix}^\top$ be the optimizer for (14). Recall that the set of active indices, $S_i = \{j : \beta_{ij} \neq 0, 1 \leq j \leq p\}$, and $s_i = |S_i|$ and $s^* \equiv \max_{1 \leq i \leq p} s_i$. Because optimization problem (14) can be solved separately for each component process, in the follows we focus on the estimation consistency for one component process. For ease of notation, we drop the subscript i; that is, we use $\boldsymbol{x}(t)$ for $\boldsymbol{x}_i(t)$, θ for θ_i, $dN(t)$ for $dN_i(t)$, $\lambda(t)$ for $\lambda_i(t)$, $\boldsymbol{b}$ for $\boldsymbol{b}_i$, S for S_i and $\widetilde{S}$ for $\widetilde{S}_i$.

Next, we state two lemmas that will be used in the proof of main results.

Lemma A1 (van de Geer [57]). *Suppose there exists $\lambda_{\max}$ such that $\lambda(t) \leq \lambda_{\max}$ where $\lambda(t)$ is the intensity function of Hawkes process defined in (2). Let $H(t)$ be a bounded function that is $\mathcal{H}_t$-predictable. Then, for any $\epsilon > 0$,*

$$\frac{1}{T}\int_0^T H(t)\Big\{\lambda(t)dt - dN(t)\Big\} \leq 4\bigg\{\frac{\lambda_{\max}}{2T}\int_0^T H^2(t)dt\bigg\}^{1/2}\epsilon^{1/2},$$

with probability at least $1 - C\exp(-\epsilon T)$, for some constant C.

Lemma A2 (Wang et al. [35]). *Suppose the Hawkes process defined in (2) satisfies Assumptions 1–4. Let $Q = \frac{1}{T}\int_0^T \begin{pmatrix} 1 \\ \boldsymbol{x}(t) \end{pmatrix} (1 \quad \boldsymbol{x}^\top(t))dt$, where $\boldsymbol{x}(t)$ is defined in (5). Then, there exists $\gamma_{\max} \geq \gamma_{\min} > 0$ such that*

$$\gamma_{\max} \geq \Lambda_{\max}(Q) \geq \Lambda_{\min}(Q) \geq \gamma_{\min} > 0,$$

with probability at least $1 - c_1 p^2 T \exp(-c_2 T^{1/5})$, where constants c_1, c_2 depending on the model parameters and the transition kernel.

Proof of Theorem 1. While the skeleton of the proof follows from (Ćevid et al. [37], Theorem 2), the following two conditions are needed because of the Hawkes process data's unique dependency structure. □

Condition 1. *There exist constants $\gamma_{\min}, c, C > 0$ such that*

$$\mathbb{P}\left(\min_{\Delta \in \mathcal{C}(L,S)} \frac{1}{T} \left\| \widetilde{X}\Delta \right\|_2^2 \geq \gamma_{\min} \|\Delta\|_2^2 \right) \geq 1 - cp^2 T \exp(-CT^{1/5}),$$

where $\mathcal{C}(L,S) = \{\boldsymbol{\alpha} : \|\boldsymbol{\alpha}_{S^c}\|_1 \leq L \|\boldsymbol{\alpha}_S\|_1\}$.

Condition 1 is referred as the restrict strong convexity (RSC) [58]. Lemma A2 by Wang et al. [35] has shown Condition 1 holds when $\widetilde{X} = X$ under Assumptions 1–4. Since the min eigenvalue of $\widetilde{X}$ stays the same with our choice of F, Condition 1 holds for $\widetilde{X} = FX$.

Condition 2. *There exist $c, C > 0$ such that*

$$\mathbb{P}\left(\frac{1}{T} \left\| \widetilde{X} \nu \right\|_\infty \leq C \Lambda_{\max}^2(F) T^{-2/5} \right) \geq 1 - cp \exp(-T^{1/5}),$$

where ν is defined in (10).

Condition 2 holds as a result of Lemma A1 by van de Geer [57].
Under the two conditions, we achieve the conclusion as follows.
Because $\widehat{\boldsymbol{\theta}}$ is the optimizer for (14),

$$\frac{1}{T}\|\widetilde{Y} - \widetilde{X}\widehat{\boldsymbol{\theta}}\|_2^2 + \lambda\|\widehat{\boldsymbol{\beta}}\|_1 \leq \frac{1}{T}\|\widetilde{Y} - \widetilde{X}\boldsymbol{\theta}\|_2^2 + \lambda\|\boldsymbol{\beta}\|_1$$

$$\frac{1}{T}\left\|\widetilde{X}\left(\widehat{\boldsymbol{\theta}} - \boldsymbol{\theta} - \boldsymbol{b}\right)\right\|_2^2 + \lambda\|\widehat{\boldsymbol{\beta}}\|_1 \leq \frac{2}{T}\int_{t=0}^T \nu(t)\widetilde{X}(t)\left(\widehat{\boldsymbol{\theta}} - \boldsymbol{\theta}\right) + \frac{1}{T}\|\widetilde{X}\boldsymbol{b}\|_2^2 + \lambda\|\boldsymbol{\beta}\|_1$$

Under Condition 2,

$$\frac{2}{T}\int_{t=0}^T \nu(t)\widetilde{X}(t)\left(\widehat{\boldsymbol{\theta}} - \boldsymbol{\theta}\right) \leq \frac{2}{T}\left\|\int_{t=0}^T \nu(t)\widetilde{X}(t)\right\|_\infty \left\|\widehat{\boldsymbol{\theta}} - \boldsymbol{\theta}\right\|_1 \leq \psi\left\|\widehat{\boldsymbol{\theta}} - \boldsymbol{\theta}\right\|_1,$$

with probability at least $1 - c_1 p \exp(-T^{1/5})$, where $\psi = C_1\Lambda_{\max}^2(F)T^{-2/5}$.
Letting $\boldsymbol{\theta}_S = (u \quad \boldsymbol{\beta}_S)^\top$ and $\boldsymbol{\theta}_{S^c} = (u \quad \boldsymbol{\beta}_{S^c})^\top$,

$$\frac{1}{T}\left\|\widetilde{X}\left(\widehat{\boldsymbol{\theta}} - \boldsymbol{\theta} - \boldsymbol{b}\right)\right\|_2^2 + \lambda\|\widehat{\boldsymbol{\beta}}\|_1 \leq \psi\left\|\widehat{\boldsymbol{\theta}} - \boldsymbol{\theta}\right\|_1 + \frac{1}{T}\|\widetilde{X}\boldsymbol{b}\|_2^2 + \lambda\|\boldsymbol{\beta}\|_1$$

$$\frac{1}{T}\left\|\widetilde{X}\left(\widehat{\boldsymbol{\theta}} - \boldsymbol{\theta} - \boldsymbol{b}\right)\right\|_2^2 + (\lambda - \psi)\|\widehat{\boldsymbol{\theta}}_{S^c} - \boldsymbol{\theta}_{S^c}\|_1 \leq (\lambda + \psi)\left\|\widehat{\boldsymbol{\theta}}_S - \boldsymbol{\theta}_S\right\|_1 + \frac{1}{T}\|\widetilde{X}\boldsymbol{b}\|_2^2$$

Next, we discuss in two conditions: i) $\frac{1}{T}\|\widetilde{X}\boldsymbol{b}\|_2^2 \leq \lambda\left\|\widehat{\boldsymbol{\theta}}_S - \boldsymbol{\theta}_S\right\|_1$ and ii) $\frac{1}{T}\|\widetilde{X}\boldsymbol{b}\|_2^2 \geq \lambda\left\|\widehat{\boldsymbol{\theta}}_S - \boldsymbol{\theta}_S\right\|_1$.

First, when $\frac{1}{T}\|\widetilde{X}\boldsymbol{b}\|_2^2 \leq \lambda\left\|\widehat{\boldsymbol{\theta}}_S - \boldsymbol{\theta}_S\right\|_1$,

$$\frac{1}{T}\left\|\widetilde{X}\left(\widehat{\boldsymbol{\theta}} - \boldsymbol{\theta} - \boldsymbol{b}\right)\right\|_2^2 + (\lambda - \psi)\|\widehat{\boldsymbol{\theta}}_{S^c} - \boldsymbol{\theta}_{S^c}\|_1 \leq (2\lambda + \psi)\left\|\widehat{\boldsymbol{\theta}}_S - \boldsymbol{\theta}_S\right\|_1.$$

The above implies

$$(\lambda - \psi)\|\widehat{\boldsymbol{\theta}}_{S^c} - \boldsymbol{\theta}_{S^c}\|_1 \leq (2\lambda + \psi)\left\|\widehat{\boldsymbol{\theta}}_S - \boldsymbol{\theta}_S\right\|_1,$$

which means $\widehat{\boldsymbol{\alpha}}_{S^c} - \boldsymbol{\alpha}_{S^c} \in \mathcal{C}(L, S) = \{\boldsymbol{\alpha} : \|\boldsymbol{\alpha}_{S^c}\|_1 \leq L\|\boldsymbol{\alpha}_S\|_1\}$ for $L = \frac{2\lambda+\psi}{\lambda-\psi}$.

Taking $\lambda = 2\psi$,

$$\begin{aligned}
&\frac{1}{T}\left\|\widetilde{X}\left(\widehat{\boldsymbol{\theta}} - \boldsymbol{\theta} - \boldsymbol{b}\right)\right\|_2^2 + (\lambda - \psi)\left\|\widehat{\boldsymbol{\theta}} - \boldsymbol{\theta}\right\|_1 \\
\leq& 3\lambda\sqrt{s^*}\|\widehat{\boldsymbol{\theta}}_S - \boldsymbol{\theta}_S\|_2 \\
\leq& 3\lambda\sqrt{s^*}\frac{1}{\gamma_{\min}\sqrt{T}}\left\|\widetilde{X}\left(\widehat{\boldsymbol{\theta}} - \boldsymbol{\theta}\right)\right\|_2 \\
\leq& 3\lambda\sqrt{s^*}\frac{1}{\gamma_{\min}\sqrt{T}}\left\{\left\|\widetilde{X}\left(\widehat{\boldsymbol{\theta}} - \boldsymbol{\theta} - \boldsymbol{b}\right)\right\|_2 + \left\|\widetilde{X}\boldsymbol{b}\right\|_2\right\} \\
\leq& 3\lambda\sqrt{s^*}\frac{1}{\gamma_{\min}\sqrt{T}}\left\|\widetilde{X}\left(\widehat{\boldsymbol{\theta}} - \boldsymbol{\theta} - \boldsymbol{b}\right)\right\|_2 + 3\lambda\sqrt{s^*}\frac{1}{\gamma_{\min}\sqrt{T}}\left\|\widetilde{X}\boldsymbol{b}\right\|_2 \\
\leq& \frac{9}{2}\lambda^2 s^*\frac{1}{\gamma_{\min}^2} + \frac{1}{T}\left\|\widetilde{X}\left(\widehat{\boldsymbol{\theta}} - \boldsymbol{\theta} - \boldsymbol{b}\right)\right\|_2^2 + \frac{1}{T}\left\|\widetilde{X}\boldsymbol{b}\right\|_2^2,
\end{aligned}$$

where the second inequality is by Condition 1 and the last step is by using $xy \leq \frac{1}{4}x^2 + y^2$ twice. Therefore, we get

$$(\lambda - \psi)\left\|\widehat{\boldsymbol{\theta}} - \boldsymbol{\theta}\right\|_1 \leq \frac{9}{2}\lambda^2 s^*\frac{1}{\gamma_{\min}^2} + \frac{1}{T}\left\|\widetilde{X}\boldsymbol{b}\right\|_2^2.$$

When $\frac{1}{T}\|\widetilde{X}\boldsymbol{b}\|_2^2 \geq \lambda\left\|\widehat{\boldsymbol{\theta}}_S - \boldsymbol{\theta}_S\right\|_1$,

$$\frac{1}{T}\left\|\widetilde{X}\left(\widehat{\boldsymbol{\theta}} - \boldsymbol{\theta} - \boldsymbol{b}\right)\right\|_2^2 + (\lambda - \psi)\left\|\widehat{\boldsymbol{\theta}} - \boldsymbol{\theta}\right\|_1 \leq \frac{3}{T}\left\|\widetilde{X}\boldsymbol{b}\right\|_2^2.$$

Combining the two cases, we always have

$$(\lambda - \psi)\left\|\widehat{\boldsymbol{\theta}} - \boldsymbol{\theta}\right\|_1 \leq \frac{9}{2}\lambda^2 s^*\frac{1}{\gamma_{\min}^2} + \frac{3}{T}\left\|\widetilde{X}\boldsymbol{b}\right\|_2^2.$$

Thus, taking $\lambda = 2\psi = O(\Lambda_{\max}^2(F)T^{-2/5})$ and dividing both sides by $\frac{1}{2}\lambda$, we achieve the conclusion that

$$\left\|\widehat{\boldsymbol{\theta}} - \boldsymbol{\theta}\right\|_1 \leq C_1\Lambda_{\max}^2(F)\frac{s^*}{\gamma_{\min}^2}T^{-2/5} + C_2T^{-3/5}\Lambda_{\max}^{-2}(F)\left\|\widetilde{X}\boldsymbol{b}\right\|_2^2.$$

Proof of Corollary 1. Notice that

$$\frac{1}{T}\|\widetilde{X}b\|_2^2 \leq \Lambda_{\max}^2(F)\frac{1}{T}\|Xb\|_2^2 \leq \Lambda_{\max}^2(F)\gamma_{\max}\|b\|_2^2,$$

with probability at least $1 - c_1p^2T\exp(-c_2T^{1/5})$, where the second inequality is by Lemma A2.

Then, Corollary 1 is a direct result from Theorem 1 by plugging in $\|b\|_2^2$. □

Proof of Theorem 2. Recall $S = \{\beta_{ij} : \beta_{ij} \neq 0, 1 \leq i,j \leq p\}$ and $S_C = \{\beta_{ij} : \beta_{ij} = 0, 1 \leq i,j \leq p\}$. To establish selection consistency, we need two parts. First, we show that our estimates on the true zero and non-zero coefficients can be separated with high probability; that is, there exists some constant $\Delta > 0$ such that for $\beta_S \in S$ and $\beta_{S_C} \in S_C$, $|\widehat{\beta}_S - \widehat{\beta}_{S_C}| \geq \Delta$ with high probability. By the β-min condition specified in Assumption 5, we have $\beta_{ij} \in S \geq 2\tau$. Theorem 1 shows that for $1 \leq i,j \leq p$, $|\widehat{\beta}_{ij} - \beta_{ij}| \leq \tau$ with probability at least $1 - c_1 p^2 T \exp(-c_2 T^{1/5})$. Then, for any $\beta_S \in S$ and $\beta_{S_C} \in S_C$,

$$\begin{aligned}|\widehat{\beta}_S - \widehat{\beta}_{S_C}| &= |\widehat{\beta}_S - \beta_S - (\widehat{\beta}_{S_C} - \beta_{S_C}) + \beta_S - \beta_{S_C}| \\ &\geq |\beta_S - \beta_{S_C}| - |\widehat{\beta}_S - \beta_S| - |\widehat{\beta}_{S_C} - \beta_{S_C}| \\ &\geq \beta_{min} - 2\tau.\end{aligned}$$

This means the estimates on zero and non-zero coefficients can be separated with high probability.

Next, we show there exists a post-selection threshold that allows to correctly identify S and S_C based on the estimates. In fact, the post-selection estimator is

$$\widetilde{\beta} = \widehat{\beta}\mathbf{1}(|\widehat{\beta}| > \tau).$$

By Theorem 1, we have $|\widehat{\beta}_{S_C}| \leq \tau$, with probability $1 - c_1 p^2 T \exp(-c_2 T^{1/5})$. Then,

$$\widetilde{\beta}_{S_C} = \widehat{\beta}_{S_C}\mathbf{1}(\widehat{\beta}_{S_C} > \tau_S) = 0,$$

which means $\widetilde{\beta}$ selects β_{S_C} into S_C with high probability. In addition, since $|\widehat{\beta}_S - \beta_S| \leq \tau$,

$$|\widehat{\beta}_S| \geq |\beta_S| - \tau \geq \beta_{min} - \tau > \tau > 0.$$

Therefore,

$$\widetilde{\beta}_S = \widehat{\beta}_S\mathbf{1}(|\widehat{\beta}_S| > \tau) = \widehat{\beta}_S \neq 0,$$

which means $\widetilde{\beta}_S$ selects β_S into S with high probability.

Combining the two sides, the post-selection estimator $\widetilde{\beta}$ identifies S and S_C with high probability. □

Appendix C. Parameter Estimation Performance

In this section we examine estimation performance of our algorithm on the connectivity coefficients associated with the observed processes. To this end, we compare the optimal root-mean squared error (RMSE) of the various methods (*hp-trim*, HIVE and Naïve) over all connectivity coefficients for the observed processes. Here, the optimal RMSE is the minimum RMSE for each estimation method over the range of tuning parameters in each simulation run.

We find that in the case when *hp-trim* performs the best in terms of edge selection (i.e., under the setting by Figure 2a), the method also gives the lowest RMSE (see Unorthogonal ($T = 5000$ and $T = 1000$) in Figure A1). In contrast, when the orthogonality condition is met for HIVE (i.e., under the setting by Figure 3a), HIVE-oracle gives the best RMSE (see Orthogonal ($T = 5000$ and $T = 1000$) in Figure A1). However, HIVE-oracle is not available in practice, and even when the orthogonality assumption is satisfied, the empirical version of HIVE (HIVE-empirical) performs worse than *hp-trim*.

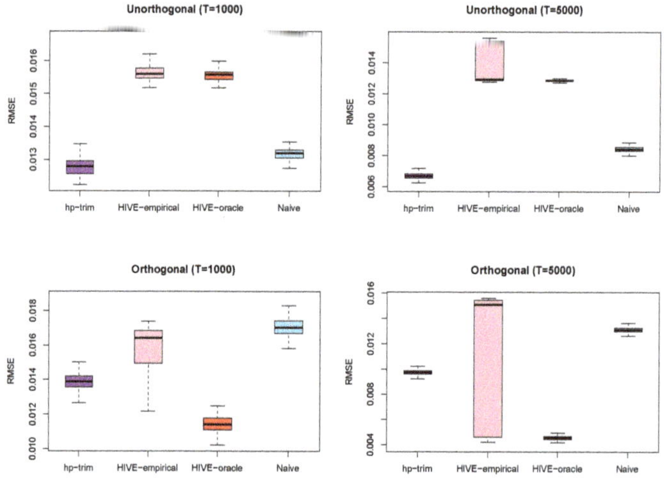

Figure A1. Boxplot of optimal RMSE over all connectivity coefficients for *hp-trim*, HIVE and Naïve. Unorthogonal ($T = 5000$ and $T = 1000$) conditions refer to the setting in Figure 2a in the main text; Orthogonal ($T = 5000$ and $T = 1000$) conditions refer to the setting in Figure 3a in the main text. RMSE over all connectivity coefficients is calculated as $\sqrt{\frac{1}{p^2}\sum_{1\leq i,j,\leq p}(\hat{\beta}_{ij}^{(k)} - \beta_{ij})^2}$, where $\hat{\beta}_{ij}^{(k)}$ is the estimate of the true parameter value, β_{ij}, from the kth simulation run ($k = 1, \ldots, 100$) and $p = 100$ observed processes are considered as in the simulation study in the main text.

References

1. Glymour, C.; Zhang, K.; Spirtes, P. Review of causal discovery methods based on graphical models. *Front. Genet.* **2019**, *10*, 524. [CrossRef] [PubMed]
2. Shojaie, A.; Fox, E.B. Granger causality: A review and recent advances. *arXiv* **2021**, arXiv:2105.02675.
3. Reid, A.T.; Headley, D.B.; Mill, R.D.; Sanchez-Romero, R.; Uddin, L.Q.; Marinazzo, D.; Lurie, D.J.; Valdés-Sosa, P.A.; Hanson, S.J.; Biswal, B.B.; et al. Advancing functional connectivity research from association to causation. *Nat. Neurosci.* **2019**, *22*, 1751–1760. [CrossRef]
4. Breitung, J.; Swanson, N.R. Temporal aggregation and spurious instantaneous causality in multiple time series models. *J. Time Ser. Anal.* **2002**, *23*, 651–665. [CrossRef]
5. Silvestrini, A.; Veredas, D. Temporal aggregation of univariate and multivaraite time series models: A survey. *J. Econ. Surv.* **2008**, *22*, 458–497. [CrossRef]
6. Tank, A.; Fox, E.B.; Shojaie, A. Identifiability and estimation of structural vector autoregressive models for subsampled and mixed-frequency time series. *Biometrika* **2019**, *106*, 433–452. [CrossRef]
7. Soudry, D.; Keshri, S.; Stinson, P.; hwan Oh, M.; Iyengar, G.; Paninski, L. A shotgun sampling solution for the common input problem in neural connectivity inference. *arXiv* **2014**, arXiv:1309.3724.
8. Yang, Y.; Qiao, S.; Sani, O.G.; Sedillo, J.I.; Ferrentino, B.; Pesaran, B.; Shanechi, M.M. Modelling and prediction of the dynamic responses of large-scale brain networks during direct electrical stimulation. *Nat. Biomed. Eng.* **2021**, *5*, 324–345. [CrossRef] [PubMed]
9. Bloch, J.; Greaves-Tunnell, A.; Shea-Brown, E.; Harchaoui, Z.; Shojaie, A.; Yazdan-Shahmorad, A. Cortical network structure mediates response to stimulation: An optogenetic study in non-human primates. *bioRxiv* **2021**. [CrossRef]
10. Lin, F.H.; Ahveninen, J.; Raij, T.; Witzel, T.; Chu, Y.H.; Jääskeläinen, I.P.; Tsai, K.W.K.; Kuo, W.J.; Belliveau, J.W. Increasing fMRI sampling rate improves Granger causality estimates. *PLoS ONE* **2014**, *9*, e100319. [CrossRef] [PubMed]
11. Zhou, D.; Zhang, Y.; Xiao, Y.; Cai, D. Analysis of sampling artifacts on the Granger causality analysis for topology extraction of neuronal dynamics. *Front. Comput. Neurosci.* **2014**, *8*, 75. [CrossRef] [PubMed]
12. Prevedel, R.; Yoon, Y.G.; Hoffmann, M.; Pak, N.; Wetzstein, G.; Kato, S.; Schrödel, T.; Raskar, R.; Zimmer, M.; Boyden, E.S.; et al. Simultaneous whole-animal 3D imaging of neuronal activity using light-field microscopy. *Nat. Methods* **2014**, *11*, 727–730. [CrossRef] [PubMed]
13. Okatan, M.; Wilson, M.A.; Brown, E.N. Analyzing functional connectivity using a network likelihood model of ensemble neural spiking activity. *Neural Comput.* **2005**, *17*, 1927–1961. [CrossRef] [PubMed]

14. Bolding, K.A.; Franks, K.M. Recurrent cortical circuits implement concentration-invariant odor coding. *Science* **2018**, *361*, 6407. [CrossRef] [PubMed]
15. Berényi, A.; Somogyvári, Z.; Nagy, A.J.; Roux, L.; Long, J.D.; Fujisawa, S.; Stark, E.; Leonardo, A.; Harris, T.D.; Buzsáki, G. Large-scale, high-density (up to 512 channels) recording of local circuits in behaving animals. *J. Neurophysiol.* **2014**, *111*, 1132–1149. [CrossRef] [PubMed]
16. Trong, P.K.; Rieke, F. Origin of correlated activity between parasol retinal ganglion cells. *Nat. Neurosci.* **2008**, *11*, 1343–1351. [CrossRef]
17. Tchumatchenko, T.; Geisel, T.; Volgushev, M.; Wolf, F. Spike correlations—What can they tell about synchrony? *Front. Neurosci.* **2011**, *5*, 68. [CrossRef]
18. Huang, H. Effects of hidden nodes on network structure inference. *J. Phys. A Math. Theor.* **2015**, *48*, 355002. [CrossRef]
19. Spirtes, P.; Glymour, C.; Scheines, R. *Causation, Prediction, and Search*, 2nd ed.; MIT Press: Cambridge, MA, USA, 2000.
20. Malinsky, D.; Spirtes, P. Causal structure learning from multivariate time series in settings with unmeasured confounding. In Proceedings of 2018 ACM SIGKDD Workshop on Causal Disocvery, London, UK, 20 August 2018; Le, T.D., Zhang, K., Kıcıman, E., Hyvärinen, A., Liu, L., Eds.; PMLR: London, UK, 2018; Volume 92, pp. 23–47.
21. Chen, W.; Drton, M.; Shojaie, A. Causal structural learning via local graphs. *arXiv* **2021**, arXiv:2107.03597.
22. Shojaie, A.; Michailidis, G. Penalized likelihood methods for estimation of sparse high-dimensional directed acyclic graphs. *Biometrika* **2010**, *97*, 519–538. [CrossRef]
23. Hawkes, A.G. Spectra of some self-exciting and mutually exciting point processes. *Biometrika* **1971**, *58*, 83–90. [CrossRef]
24. Eichler, M.; Dahlhaus, R.; Dueck, J. Graphical modeling for multivariate Hawkes processes with nonparametric link functions. *J. Time Ser. Anal.* **2017**, *38*, 225–242. [CrossRef]
25. Bacry, E.; Muzy, J. First- and second-order statistics characterization of Hawkes processes and non-parametric estimation. *IEEE Trans. Inf. Theory* **2016**, *62*, 2184–2202. [CrossRef]
26. Brillinger, D.R. Maximum likelihood analysis of spike trains of interacting nerve cells. *Biol. Cybern.* **1988**, *59*, 189–200. [CrossRef] [PubMed]
27. Johnson, D.H. Point process models of single-neuron discharges. *J. Comput. Neurosci.* **1996**, *3*, 275–299. [CrossRef]
28. Krumin, M.; Reutsky, I.; Shoham, S. Correlation-based analysis and generation of multiple spike trains using Hawkes models with an exogenous input. *Front. Comput. Neurosci.* **2010**, *4*, 147. [CrossRef] [PubMed]
29. Pernice, V.; Staude, B.; Cardanobile, S.; Rotter, S. How structure determines correlations in neuronal networks. *PLoS Comput. Biol.* **2011**, *7*, e1002059. [CrossRef] [PubMed]
30. Reynaud-Bouret, P.; Rivoirard, V.; Tuleau-Malot, C. Inference of functional connectivity in neurosciences via Hawkes processes. In Proceedings of the 2013 IEEE Global Conference on Signal and Information Processing, Austin, TX, USA, 3–5 December 2013; pp. 317–320.
31. Truccolo, W. From point process observations to collective neural dynamics: Nonlinear Hawkes process GLMs, low-dimensional dynamics and coarse graining. *J. Physiol.-Paris* **2016**, *110*, 336–347. [CrossRef]
32. Lambert, R.C.; Tuleau-Malot, C.; Bessaih, T.; Rivoirard, V.; Bouret, Y.; Leresche, N.; Reynaud-Bouret, P. Reconstructing the functional connectivity of multiple spike trains using Hawkes models. *J. Neurosci. Methods* **2018**, *297*, 9–21. [CrossRef]
33. Hansen, N.R.; Reynaud-Bouret, P.; Rivoirard, V. Lasso and probabilistic inequalities for multivariate point processes. *Bernoulli* **2015**, *21*, 83–143. [CrossRef]
34. Chen, S.; Shojaie, A.; Shea-Brown, E.; Witten, D. The multivariate Hawkes process in high dimensions: Beyond mutual excitation. *arXiv* **2019**, arXiv:1707.04928.
35. Wang, X.; Kolar, M.; Shojaie, A. Statistical inference for networks of high-dimensional point processes. *arXiv* **2020**, arXiv:2007.07448.
36. Bing, X.; Ning, Y.; Xu, Y. Adaptive estimation of multivariate regression with hidden variables. *arXiv* **2020**, arXiv:2003.13844.
37. Ćevid, D.; Bühlmann, P.; Meinshausen, N. Spectral deconfounding via perturbed sparse linear models. *arXiv* **2020**, arXiv:1811.05352.
38. Linderman, S.; Adams, R. Discovering latent network structure in point process data. In *International Conference on Machine Learning*; PMLR: Beijing, China, 2014; Volume 32.
39. De Abril, I.M.; Yoshimoto, J.; Doya, K. Connectivity inference from neural recording data: Challenges, mathematical bases and research directions. *Neural Netw.* **2018**, *102*, 120–137.
40. Bacry, E.; Mastromatteo, I.; Muzy, J. Hawkes processes in finance. *Mark. Microstruct. Liq.* **2015**, *1*, 1550005. [CrossRef]
41. Etesami, J.; Kiyavash, N.; Zhang, K.; Singhal, K. Learning network of multivariate Hawkes processes: A time series approach. *arXiv* **2016**, arXiv:1603.04319.
42. Costa, M.; Graham, C.; Marsalle, L.; Tran, V.C. Renewal in Hawkes processes with self-excitation and inhibition. *arXiv* **2018**, arXiv:1801.04645.
43. Babington, P. *Neuroscience*, 2nd ed.; Sinauer Associates: Sunderland, MA, USA, 2001.
44. Brémaud, P.; Massoulié, L. Stability of nonlinear Hawkes processes. *Ann. Probab.* **1996**, *24*, 1563–1588. [CrossRef]
45. Daley, D.J.; Vere-Jones, D. *An Introduction to the Theory of Point Processes: Volume I: Elementary Theory and Methods*; Probability and its Applications; Springer: New York, NY, USA, 2003.
46. Tibshirani, R. Regression shrinkage and selection via the Lasso. *J. R. Stat. So. Ser. B (Methodol.)* **1996**, *58*, 267–288. [CrossRef]

47. Lee, S.; Sun, W.; Wright, F.A.; Zou, F. An improved and explicit surrogate variable analysis procedure by coefficient adjustment. *Biometrika* **2017**, *104*, 303–316. [CrossRef]
48. Cai, B.; Zhang, J.; Guan, Y. Latent network structure learning from high dimensional multivariate point processes. *arXiv* **2020**, arXiv:2004.03569.
49. Basu, S.; Michailidis, G. Regularized estimation in sparse high-dimensional time series models. *Ann. Stat.* **2015**, *43*, 1535–1567. [CrossRef]
50. Safikhani, A.; Shojaie, A. Joint structural break detection and parameter estimation in high-dimensional nonstationary VAR models. *J. Am. Stat. Assoc.* **2020**, 1–14. [CrossRef]
51. Shojaie, A.; Basu, S.; Michailidis, G. Adaptive thresholding for reconstructing regulatory networks from time-course gene expression data. *Stat. Biosci.* **2012**, *4*, 66–83. [CrossRef]
52. Van de Geer, S.; Bühlmann, P.; Zhou, S. The adaptive and the thresholded Lasso for potentially misspecified models (and a lower bound for the Lasso). *Electron. J. Stat.* **2011**, *5*, 688 – 749. [CrossRef]
53. Buhlmann, P. Statistical significance in high-dimensional linear models. *Bernoulli* **2013**, *19*, 1212–1242. [CrossRef]
54. Paninski, L.; Pillow, J.; Lewi, J. Statistical models for neural encoding, decoding, and optimal stimulus design. In *Computational Neuroscience: Theoretical Insights into Brain Function*; Elsevier: Amsterdam, The Netherlands, 2007; Volume 165, pp. 493–507.
55. Pillow, J.; Shlens, J.; Paninski, L.; Sher, A.; Litke, A.; Chichilnisky, E.; Simoncelli, E. Spatio-temporal correlations and visual signaling in a complete neuronal population. *Nature* **2008**, *454*, 995–999. [CrossRef]
56. Zhang, A.; Cai, T.T.; Wu, Y. Heteroskedastic PCA: Algorithm, optimality, and applications. *arXiv* **2019**, arXiv:1810.08316.
57. van de Geer, S. Exponential inequalities for martingales, with application to maximum likelihood estimation for counting processes. *Ann. Stat.* **1995**, *23*, 1779–1801. [CrossRef]
58. Negahban, S.; Wainwright, M. Restricted strong convexity and weighted matrix completion: Optimal bounds with noise. *J. Mach. Learn. Res.* **2010**, *13*, 1665–1697.

entropy

MDPI

Article

The Paradox of Time in Dynamic Causal Systems

Bob Rehder [1,*], Zachary J. Davis [1] and Neil Bramley [2]

[1] Department of Psychology, New York University, 6 Washington Place, New York, NY 10003, USA; zachdavis99@gmail.com
[2] Psychology Department, The University of Edinburgh, Edinburgh EH8 9JZ, UK; neil.bramley@ed.ac.uk
* Correspondence: bob.rehder@nyu.edu

Abstract: Recent work has shown that people use temporal information including order, delay, and variability to infer causality between events. In this study, we build on this work by investigating the role of time in dynamic systems, where causes take continuous values and also continually influence their effects. Recent studies of learning in these systems explored short interactions in a setting with rapidly evolving dynamics and modeled people as relying on simpler, resource-limited strategies to grapple with the stream of information. A natural question that arises from such an account is whether interacting with systems that unfold more slowly might reduce the systematic errors that result from these strategies. Paradoxically, we find that slowing the task indeed reduced the frequency of one type of error, albeit at the cost of increasing the overall error rate. To explain these results we posit that human learners analyze continuous dynamics into discrete events and use the observed relationships between events to draw conclusions about causal structure. We formalize this intuition in terms of a novel *Causal Event Abstraction* model and show that this model indeed captures the observed pattern of errors. We comment on the implications these results have for causal cognition.

Keywords: causal inference; causal graphs; dynamic systems; causal learning; time; continuous; event cognition; interventions

Citation: Rehder, B.; Davis, Z.J.; Bramley, N. The Paradox of Time in Dynamic Causal Systems. *Entropy* **2022**, *24*, 863. https://doi.org/10.3390/e24070863

Academic Editor: Kateřina Hlaváčková-Schindler

Received: 3 April 2022
Accepted: 16 June 2022
Published: 23 June 2022

1. Introduction

Learning about causal structure is central to higher level cognition because it allows people to predict the future, select beneficial actions, and make sense of the past. The study of how people learn causal structure has historically focused on simple scenarios involving the presence or absence of binary variables (e.g., did a patient take a drug, and did they feel better?). This has taught us much about how people use causal structure for a host of decisions (e.g., [2–5]). However, this focus on simple stimuli obscures other important questions, such as how we incorporate continuous covariation and temporal information into our causal judgments.

Time is central to our notions of causality [6], making it unsurprising that temporal contiguity is one of the strongest psychological cues to causality [7]. Sophisticated expectations about delays between events shape causal judgments [8,9], interventions [10], and goal directed actions [11]. People also judge that highly variable delays are less causal [12] and use variability as a cue for structure in the absence of order or covariational cues [10].

Prior work on the role of time in causality has focused on delay distributions, i.e., the time that it takes for one event to influence another, where events are largely treated as punctate rather than extended in time. In this project we instead study a fully continuous setting in which continuous valued causes continually affect *rates of change* of their effects, introducing a different set of representational challenges. Rather than reasoning directly about rates of occurrence of events or delay distributions between events, people must reason from unfolding timeseries data.

How might varying the speed at which a continuous system evolves affect what people learn about it? Extrapolating from the literature on events cited above, one might expect that a more slowly evolving system would make learners less likely to infer the presence of causal linkages between variables. Yet a system that unfolds more slowly may have advantages as well. In the setting originally explored by [1], people were well described with a *Local Computations* (LC) model, which characterized them as focusing on establishing the relationship between pairs of variables independently, that is, rather than controlling for other variables, as one would if one considered the full space of possible structural models. The key support for the LC model came from a particular characteristic error. Participants frequently inferred direct connections between variables that were indirectly related (e.g., in the network $X \rightarrow Y \rightarrow Z$ concluding incorrectly that additionally $X \rightarrow Z$). This error was first observed in studies with binary variables observed at discrete time points [13,14]. One potential explanation of these errors in [1] is that participants failed to notice the relative time delays among the variables. In network $X \rightarrow Y \rightarrow Z$, the mediated influence of X on Z will be delayed in time compared to the direct influences of X on Y and of Y on Z. A learner who fails to notice these temporal differences will incorrectly conclude that $X \rightarrow Z$. This hypothesis predicts that increasing the saliency of these time delay differences by slowing the system will reduce instances of these errors.

We also aim to understand how people learn causal structure from a continuous flow of information by comparing different formal accounts of how people represent continuous information and use it to infer causal relationships. Firstly, we follow [1] in describing people as computing likelihoods on the basis of the continuous dynamics directly—either considering all hypotheses in parallel (normative model), or focusing separately on individual edges (Local Computations variant). Secondly, we introduce a new account of how people might handle continuous information in time—the *Causal Event Abstraction* (CEA) model—that characterizes people as segmenting the continuous stream into discrete events, and using those to infer causal structure.

In summary, we ask two questions. Firstly, does slowing the dynamics of the system reduce the systematic errors that have been previously observed? We do find the expected reduction in those errors but at the cost of accuracy on other types of causal links. Secondly, how do people represent continuous information in dynamic systems? We find that a model describing people as segmenting continuous information into discrete events captures people's behavior across conditions.

1.1. Ornstein–Uhlenbeck Networks

The stimuli in our task were generated using a new approach for simulating continuous causal systems first proposed in [15]. See [1] for a full explication of the generative process, but briefly Ornstein–Uhlenbeck (OU) networks represent causality with autoregressive processes that move towards a basin point as a function of time [16]. Importantly, however, when one variable is causally influenced by another (as defined by the causal structure of the OU network), this is modelled by making the effect's basin point nonstationary, following some function of the state of its cause(s). Specifically, we stipulate that the basin point is the sum of the causal influences exerted by each of the effect's causal parents. Formally, the change in a variable v_i following time t, Δv_i^t, is given by

$$P(\Delta v_i^t | v^t, \omega, \sigma, \theta_{\bullet i}) = \omega \Big[[\sum_j \theta_{ji} \cdot v_j^t] - v_i^t \Big] + N(0, \sigma) \quad (1)$$

where v_i^t is the value of variable i at time t, θ_{ji} is the causal influence of variable j on variable i, $\sum_j \theta_{ji} v_j^t$ (the sum of v_i's causal parents, each multiplied by its corresponding θ_{ji}) is the basin to which v_i is attracted, and σ is the endogenous noise of each variable. ω (also known as the "spring rigidity" of the system) is the rate at which v_i reverts to its basin. For example, $\omega = 0.10$ means that the variable's expected value will move 10% of the way toward the basin.

We now consider a number of alternative hypotheses regarding how OU networks are learned.

1.2. An Optimal Learner

The normative account of learning of a causal graph in an OU networks involves inverting the above generative model. (Note that although we specify normative learning in light of observed data and the interventions on the causal system made by a learner, we do not specify what interventions a learner should perform to maximize learning). Assuming an initially-uniform prior, the inferred causal structure is the one most likely to produce the changes in all variables at all time points, taking into account the learner's interventions. Consider a hypothesis space G in which a learner's task to estimate the likelihood of discrete causal hypotheses, ones where the θ associated with every potential causal relationship has been trichotomized into one of three states: positive, inverse (negative), or zero. For a system with three variables, G would contain 729 distinct causal hypotheses. (In this work, we exclude the possibility of self-cycles in which a variable is causally influenced by itself. That is, $\theta_{ii} = 0$ for all i).

The likelihood of observing the change in variable v_i at t given graph g is therefore,

$$P(\Delta v_i^t | g, \omega, \sigma, \iota_i^t) = \int_{\theta_{\bullet i}} P(\Delta v_i^t | v^t, \omega, \sigma, \theta_{\bullet i}, \iota_i^t) P(\theta_{\bullet i} | g) P(g) d\theta_{\bullet i} \tag{2}$$

where $\int_{\theta_{\bullet i}}$ is a multiple integral over each of v_i's incoming causal strengths, $\theta_{\bullet i}$. $P(\theta_{\bullet i}|g)$ represents the priors over $\theta_{\bullet i}$ corresponding to hypothesis g. For example, for a graph g that includes a positive $X \rightarrow Y$ causal relationship, $P(\theta_{XY}|g) = 0$ for all $\theta_{XY} \leq 0$ but otherwise represents the learner's priors over the strength of a positive causal relationship when $\theta_{XY} > 0$.

ι_i^t is an indicator variable that is true if v_i is intervened on at t and false otherwise. We accommodate interventions by the standard notion of graph surgery [17]. Thus, if v_i is manipulated at time t, the likelihood of the observed Δv_i^t is 1 (i.e., is independent of v_i's current value or the value of its causes). Otherwise, it is given by Equation (1). That is,

$$P(\Delta v_i^t | v^t, \omega, \sigma, \theta_{\bullet i}, \iota_i^t) = \begin{cases} 1 & \iota_i^t \text{ True} \\ N(\omega(\sum_j \theta_{ji} v_j^t - v_i^t), \sigma) & \iota_i^t \text{ False} \end{cases} \tag{3}$$

The likelihood of all observed variables at all time points, taking into account potential uncertainty regarding ω and σ, is,

$$P(v|g, \iota) = \prod_{i=1}^{N} \prod_{t=1}^{T-1} \int_{\omega} \int_{\sigma} P(\Delta v_i^t | v^t, g, \omega, \sigma, \iota_i^t) P(\omega) P(\sigma) d\omega d\sigma \tag{4}$$

$P(\omega)$ and $P(\sigma)$ represent the learner's priors over ω and σ. See [1] for additional details and explanation.

Simulations of an Optimal Learner

We now present simulations of an optimal learner to identify some key factors that determine its success at learning a causal network. Several assumptions were made to make these simulations relevant to the experiment that appears at the end of this paper. In that experiment, the variables of the OU system are presented as sliders that take on a value between −100 and 100 (see Figure 1 for an example). Human learners are asked to identify the causal structure that relates these variables.

First, because learners will be allowed to manipulate the variables of the OU network, our theoretical analysis will assume the presence of manipulations qualitatively similar to those observed in [1]. In particular, we assume that each variable is manipulated by first setting it to one extreme value (100) and then the other (–100) during each learning trial. Figure 2 shows examples of the variable manipulations that were presented to the optimal learner.

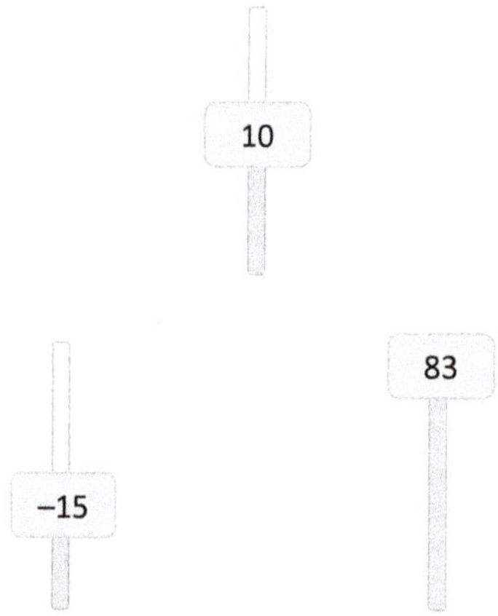

Figure 1. An OU system with three variables displayed as "sliders" on a computer screen. The values of the sliders take on values from −100 to 100 and are updated continuously as a function of the input they receive from their causal parents and system noise σ.

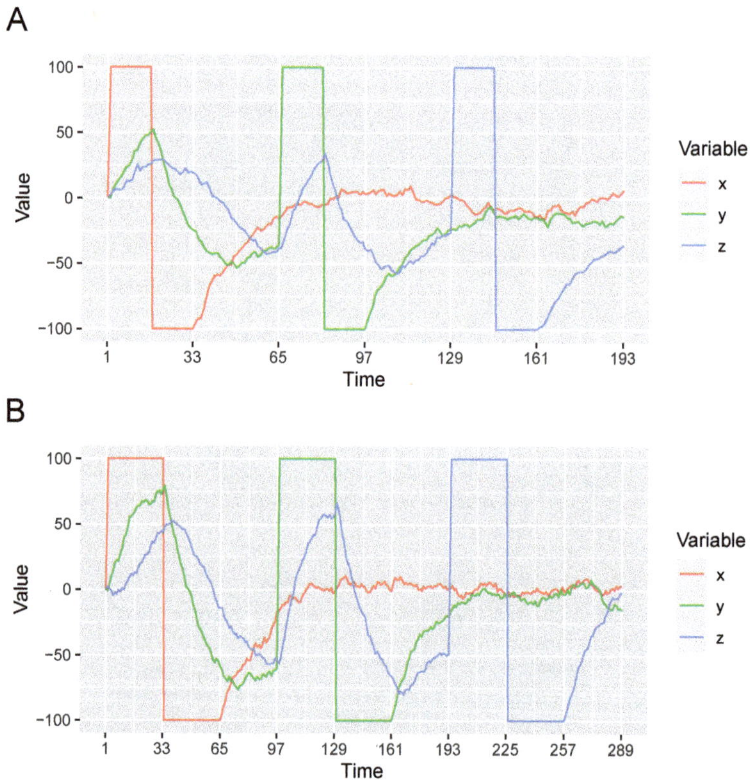

Figure 2. Examples of manipulating an OU network with three variables that form a causal chain $X \rightarrow Y \rightarrow Z$. In each panel X is first manipulated, followed by Y and then Z. Each manipulation consists holding the variable at 100 and then -100. Panels (**A**,**B**) present manipulations that last 32 and 64 time units, respectively. Interventions were separated by 32 time units, allowing the variables to return to a baseline value near 0. The resulting changes in in X, Y, and Z reflect the $X \rightarrow Y \rightarrow Z$ causal relationships. $\theta_{XY} = \theta_{YZ} = 1$, $\omega = 0.05$, and $\sigma = 2$.

Second, the upcoming experiment will present subjects with four instructional videos. These will present examples of OU systems with values of ω and σ, and possible values of θ (-1, 0, or 1), that are the same as those of OU systems they are subsequently asked to learn. Thus, for simplicity the simulations were derived assuming that learners extract from the videos those values of ω and σ and the possible values of the θs.

Third, without modification the normative model is powerful enough to almost perfectly identify the correct hypothesis given the amount of time subjects are allowed to examine how the OU network evolves over time. We think that such extreme performance is psychologically unrealistic because human learners presumably experience simple resource limitations (e.g., lapses of attention). Thus, in presenting the simulation results we will pass the normative model's posterior probabilities through a softmax function.

$$P(g|v,\iota) = \frac{P(v|g,\iota)^{-\tau}}{\sum_k P(v|g,\iota)^{-\tau}} \tag{5}$$

Values of $\tau < 1$ yield a posterior distribution over G that is less "sharp", that is, one that favors the true hypothesis less decisively than it would otherwise. In the simulations below $\tau = 40$.

Note that it is straightforward to go from a posterior distribution over G to the posterior probability of a positive, negative, or zero causal relationship from one variable to another via Bayesian model averaging. Define G_l as the subset of graphs that includes a particular causal link l (e.g., a positive $X \rightarrow Y$ causal relationship). Then, the posterior probability of l is simply,

$$P(l|v,\iota) = \sum_{g \in G_l} P(g|v,\iota) \tag{6}$$

Our simulations focus on the chain network $X \rightarrow Y \rightarrow Z$ because it is an example of a causal system that is susceptible to the local computations error described earlier (i.e., incorrectly inferring that X and Z are directly rather than indirectly causally related). The normative model's ability to learn $X \rightarrow Y \rightarrow Z$ is examined as a function two properties, properties that turn out to discriminate an optimal learner from the two alternative models described later. The first is the OU network's spring rigidity ω. The second is a property of the variable manipulations that we refer to as *intervention duration*. Intervention duration is the amount of time that a variable is manipulated to both extreme values (100 or –100). Whereas in Figure 2A the manipulation of each variable lasts 32 time steps, in Figure 2B they last 64 time steps.

Figure 3 presents learning accuracy on the $X \rightarrow Y \rightarrow Z$ causal network as a function of ω and intervention duration. Direct links (left panel of Figure 3) refers to the average accuracy on the causal links that make up the causal chain, namely, $X \rightarrow Y$ and $Y \rightarrow Z$. Accuracy on these links consists of correctly identifying the presence of a link between these pairs of variables. The indirect link (middle panel) refers to a potential $X \rightarrow Z$ link. Because there is no such link in the $X \rightarrow Y \rightarrow Z$ causal chain, accuracy consists of correctly identifying the *absence* of such a causal relationship. Other links (right panel) refers to other potential causal relations between the variables (i.e., $Y \rightarrow X$, $Z \rightarrow Y$, $Z \rightarrow X$), and again accuracy consists of correctly identifying the absence of those relations.

Figure 3 confirms that an important factor determining the learnability of an OU network's causal relations is its rigidity ω: Causal links are more easily identified when an effect variable exhibits a larger change in value (due to a larger ω) in response to a change in value of its cause. This is so because a large change is less likely to be due to system noise. Of course, this result generalizes findings reviewed above that temporal contiguity between events promotes the identification of causal relations to continuous variables that react more quickly to causal interventions.

Figure 3 also reveals that longer interventions also aid learning. This is so for a reason that is analogous to the effect of rigidity: A longer intervention allows more time for a change to become apparent against a background of system noise.

Note that another important factor that influences learning in OU systems (one not shown in Figure 3) is the *range* of the intervention, that is, the absolute magnitude of the change that the manipulated variable undergoes. Whereas in Figure 3 the variables are manipulated to their extreme values of 100 and −100, less extreme manipulations will result in degraded learning. In our Supplementary Materials (https://osf.io/rfx2q) we present simulations that vary intervention range while holding intervention duration constant that show results analogous to those in Figures 3–5. We will also evaluate the effect of both intervention duration and range when presenting the results of the upcoming experiment.

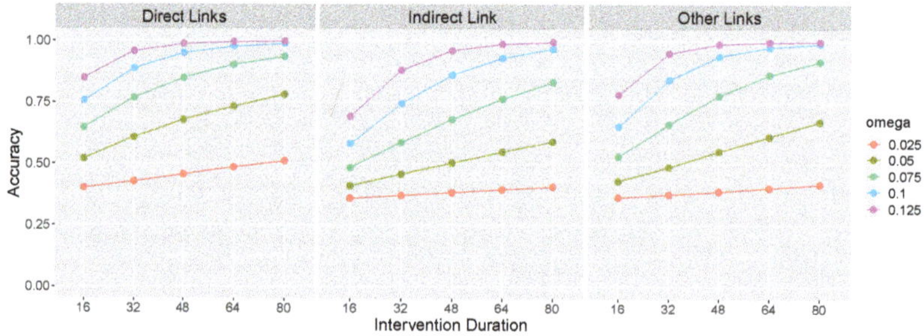

Figure 3. Accuracy for an optimal learner learning the causal graph $X \rightarrow Y \rightarrow Z$ as a function of ω and intervention duration. The first panel presents accuracy at correctly identifying the presence of the $X \rightarrow Y$ and $Y \rightarrow Z$ causal relationships. The second panel presents accuracy at correctly identifying the absence of an $X \rightarrow Z$ causal relationship. The third panel presents accuracy at correctly identifying the absence of the remaining potential causal relationships ($Y \rightarrow X$, $Z \rightarrow Y$, $Z \rightarrow X$). $\theta_{XY} = \theta_{YZ} = 1$, $\sigma = 5$ and $\tau = 40$. Results are averaged over 1000 simulations of each parameter combination.

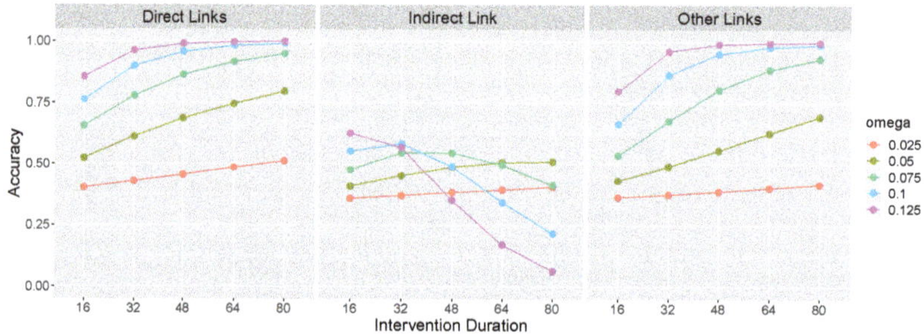

Figure 4. Accuracy of the Local Computations (LC) model under the same parameterization as Figure 3. Results are averaged over 1000 simulations of each parameter combination.

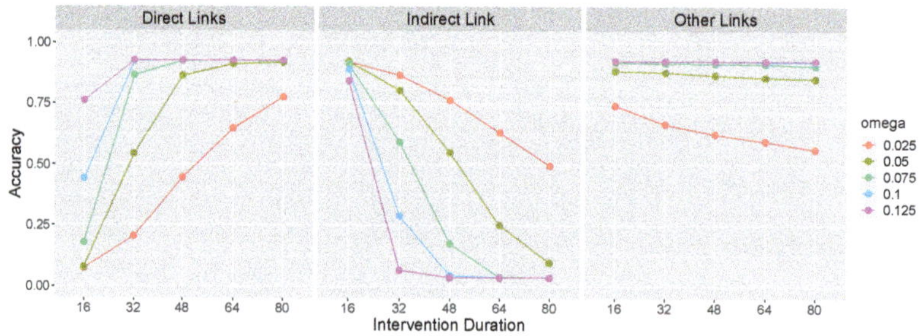

Figure 5. Accuracy of the Causal Event Abstraction (CEA) model under the same parameterization as Figures 3 and 4. CEA's threshold parameter was 50 and its guessing parameter was 0.10. Results are averaged over 1000 simulations of each parameter combination.

1.3. The Local Computations Model

We compare an optimal learner to the Local Computations (LC) model. As mentioned, LC has been advocated as a general-purpose account of causal learning behavior [13,18]. Applied to an OU network, the LC model entails deciding, for each potential causal relationship considered in isolation, whether the observed values of those two variables implies a positive, inverted (negative), or zero causal relation.

LC can be formalized by rewriting Equation (3) in the case that ι_i^t is false with,

$$P(\Delta v_i^t | v^t, \omega, \sigma, \theta_{\bullet i}) = \sum_{j, j \neq i}^{N} N(\omega(\theta_{ji} v_j^t - v_i^t), \sigma) \tag{7}$$

Whereas Equation (3) computes the probability of observing Δv_i^t by considering the simultaneous influences of all of v_i's causal parents, Equation (7) does so by considering each parent in isolation, failing to control for the fact that Δv_i^t might partly be due to one of the other causal parents. For example, given an OU network with three variables X, Y, and Z, the likelihood of a change in, say, Z, Δv_Z^t, is computed by computing the likelihood of the Δv_Z^t given X ignoring Y, the likelihood of the Δv_Z^t given Y ignoring X, and summing the two. LC-based models have been proposed as accounts of how people build causal models in a resource-efficient way [13,19].

Simulations of an LC Learner

Figure 4 shows the performance of the LC model on the causal graph $X \to Y \to Z$ as a function of the same parameters as in Figure 3. Like the normative model, LC's performance generally improves as the rigidity ω and intervention duration increase. However, the middle panel reveals that these same factors result in LC becomes increasingly vulnerable to committing local computation errors (i.e., incorrectly inferring $X \to Z$). Indeed, a rigid OU system with ω = 0.125 and interventions of length 80 will almost certainly be perceived as including a $X \to Z$ causal relationship in addition to $X \to Y$ and $Y \to Z$. This is so because a long intervention on X combined with a large ω results in a large and rapid change to Z, which is easily mistaken as evidence for $X \to Z$.

1.4. The Causal Event Abstraction Model

Whereas the normative learning model and the LC model both compute likelihoods associated with the observed data, the *Causal Event Abstraction* (CEA) model posits that people use a simple heuristic to identify causal relations. In particular, it assumes that, while one variable of an OU system is being manipulated, people track the changes that occur to the system's other variables. Should a change to a variable during that intervention be sufficiently large, it is recorded as a change 'event' providing evidence for a causal relationship from the manipulated variable to the changed one.

CEA's main parameter is the *threshold* value that the absolute value of the purported effect variable must exceed during an intervention to be classified as undergoing a change. In the simulations below, the threshold is 50 and so a change event is recorded if the variable goes above 50 or below −50. For example, Figure 6 shows variable Z changing in response to a manipulation on X. Because Z exceeds the threshold (dashed line in Figure 6) a change event would be recorded as evidence for a causal relation between X and Z (To only register events when a threshold is *crossed*, CEA excludes all cases where a potential end variable is above threshold before the intervention begins). For all timepoints during the intervention that the variable exceeds the threshold, CEA compares the signs of it and the manipulated variable and records evidence for a regular (positive) causal link if on average the signs match and an inverse (negative) one otherwise. For example, after Z exceeds the threshold in Figure 6, the sign of both it and X are positive so the change event would be recorded as evidence for a positive $X \to Z$ relationship. For variables that did not change during the intervention, no evidence of a causal link between it and the manipulated variable is recorded.

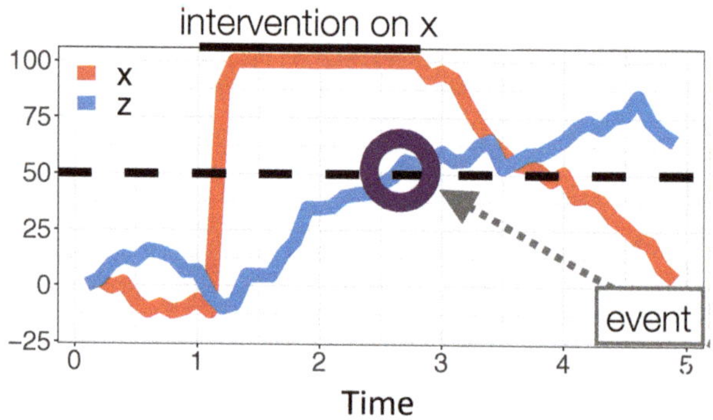

Figure 6. Illustration of the CEA model. During the learner's manipulation of X, which takes place during seconds 1–3, Z crosses threshold (here shown as 50).

The probability of a causal relationship (say, a positive $X \rightarrow Z$ relationship) is then computed by CEA by dividing the number of positive changes to Z induced by the manipulation of X divided by the number of times that X was manipulated. This calculation is also moderated by a guessing parameter (0.10 in the simulations) that corresponded to the probability of responding counter to the predictions of the events model. Note that the CEA model is insensitive to temporal delays in that it only depends on whether a variable exceeds the threshold, not how quickly. It only infers a causal relationship from a variable if that variable has been manipulated at least once.

Simulations of a CEA Learner

Figure 5 show the performance of the CEA model on the causal graph $X \rightarrow Y \rightarrow Z$ as a function of both spring rigidity (ω) and intervention duration. As in the previous models, CEA's success at identifying the $X \rightarrow Y$ and $Y \rightarrow Z$ causal relations (left side of Figure 5) generally increases as ω increases. Unlike the previous models however, accuracy on the relations also increases sharply as the duration of the interventions increase. This is so because short interventions will not allow sufficient time for the effect variables to cross the threshold.

In addition, the middle panel of Figure 5 reveals that CEA is also vulnerable to committing local computation errors (incorrectly inferring $X \rightarrow Z$), just as LC is. This panel reveals that both increasing ω and intervention duration result greater local computation errors. This is so because both of these factors increase the probability that Z will cross the threshold in response to a manipulation of X.

1.5. Summary of Learning Models

The following experiment tests these model predictions by explicitly manipulating the rigidity parameter ω, varying it between the values of 0.05, representing a more flexible system that responds more slowly to changes in inputs, and 0.10, representing a more rigid system that responds more quickly. We also analyze how learning success varies with the duration and range of the interventions that learners choose to make.

Figure 7 summarizes the predictions shown in Figures 3–5 for ω values of 0.05 and 0.10 and an intervention duration of 64. Figure 7 reveals that the LC and CEA models capture what we have referred to as the paradox of time in learning causal systems. Generally, these models predict that the correct identification of both the presence and absence of causal relationships is promoted when a learner's interventions result in a system undergoing more rapid changes due to a larger ω. However, more rapid changes also makes it more likely that these models will incorrectly conclude that two variables that are indirectly causally related (X and Z in $X \rightarrow Y \rightarrow Z$) have a direct causal relation between them. We ask whether human learners also exhibit this pattern. We also predict that longer and more extreme interventions will have an effect that is analogous to rigidity, namely, better performance overall but more local computation errors. Finally, we fit all three models to the learning results to determine which model provides the best quantitative account of the data.

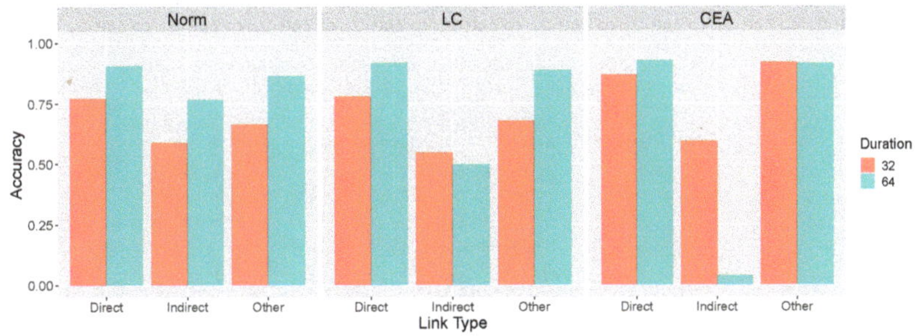

Figure 7. Predictions of the three models for three causal link types for intervention duration of 64.

2. Materials and Methods

2.1. Participants

107 participants were recruited from Amazon Mechanical Turk using psiTurk [20]. They were paid a base payment of \$3 plus performance related bonuses (M = \$0.97, SD = \$0.46) and the task took 32.6 minutes (SD = 18.3). Participants were randomly assigned to either the rigid or the flexible condition. Those who made a causal judgment before intervening on any slider on over 90% of trials were excluded, leaving 87 participants (29 female, 58 male; age M = 37.6, SD = 11.8). The results presented below are based on 42 and 45 participants in the flexible and rigid conditions, respectively.

2.2. Materials

Participants interacted with a number of causal devices represented by three vertical sliders that moved on their own according to the hidden causal structure and OU process, but could also be intervened on, by clicking and dragging to set their levels, overriding their normal causes (see Figure 8A) (See zach-davis.github.io for a demo). The sliders were constrained to be between −100 and 100, and the buttons on the slider presented a rounded integer value in addition to moving up and down. A timer at the top of the page counted down from 45 s at 1 s increments, and at the bottom of the page were six additional sliders (one for each potential causal relation). Responses could be one of three options: 'Inverted', 'None', or 'Regular', corresponding to $\theta < 0$, no relationship ($\theta = 0$), and $\theta > 0$, respectively. Participants were pretrained on these terms in the instructions.

2.3. Stimuli and Design

Participants were tested on 25 causal graphs (see Figure 8B) that were roughly balanced across a number of factors, such as the number of inverted and regular links and the number of links between each variable. The graphs were presented in random order for a total of 25 trials. The OU parameters used during training and the test were $\sigma = 5$ and $\theta = [1, 0, -1]$ for regular, none, or inverse connections, respectively. The sliders were updated with the OU system's next set of variable values every 100 ms.

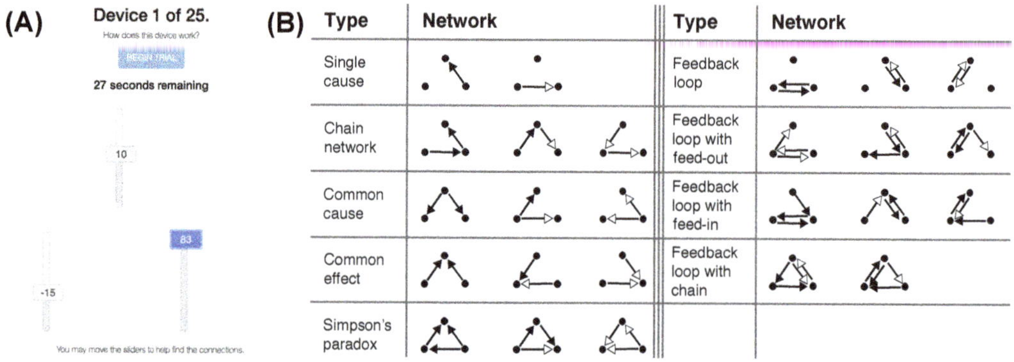

Figure 8. Stimuli. (**A**) Task environment. Sliders turn blue when intervened on. (**B**) All tested causal graphs, presented in random order. Black arrowheads denote regular connections, white arrowheads denote inverse connections.

Participants were randomly assigned to one of two conditions in which the rigidity ω parameter was either 0.05 ("flexible") or 0.10 ("rigid" condition). Recall that ω sets the rate at which the process asymptotes: When $\omega = 0.05$ (0.10) a variables move 5% (10%) of the way toward its current basin (see Figure 9).

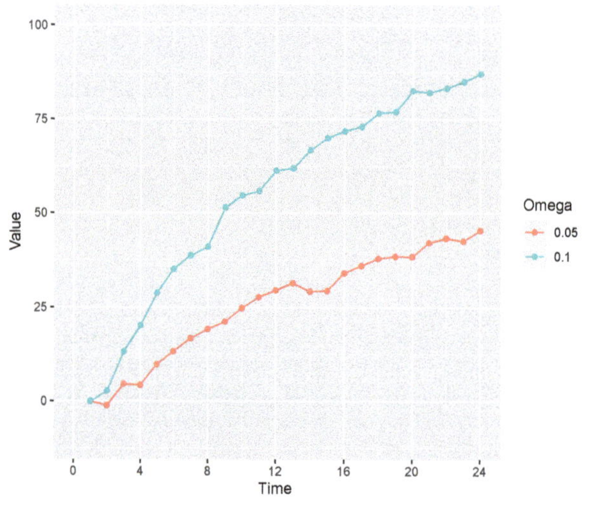

Figure 9. An OU variable's rate of change toward a basin of 100 for two values of ω. Stimuli were generated with a small amount of noise ($\sigma = 2$).

2.4. Procedure

Participants first completed an interactive instruction section that used a sequence of videos to explain the nature and goals of the task, how to intervene, as well as the trial duration. They were instructed that, for a randomly selected trial, they would receive a bonus of $0.25 for each correct causal link judgment (out of 'no link', 'regular' and 'inverse' for each of the 6 directed links). Importantly, this bonus scheme was demonstrated with a hypothetical participant who observed a chain network and correctly identified the two existing causal links but incorrectly added an additional direct link between the indirect effects. Participants were told that this participant received a reward of $1.25 for the correct responses but missed out on an additional $0.25 for marking the direct connection between indirect effects. Participants could not proceed to the task until they correctly answered five comprehension check questions probing if they knew the duration of each trial, the difference between a regular and inverted connection, that there can be more than one connection per network, and that they would have to provide a response for all six possible connections on each trial.

In the main task, participants completed 25 trials lasting 45 s each. A trial was initiated by pressing the "Start" button at the top of the page, whereupon the sliders began updating according to the OU process every 100 ms. Participants were free to click, drag, or hold any slider to any value for any amount of time, overriding its normal causal input, if any. After releasing a slider, it continued to move according to the OU process.

Participants could make (and revise) their causal judgments at any point during the trial, but could not proceed to the next trial until they had entered a judgment for all six potential causal relations. No feedback was provided. After completing the 25 trials, participants were informed of their bonus and completed a brief post-test questionnaire.

3. Results

Across all conditions, participants were above chance (0.33) in identifying causal links (M = 0.763, SD = 0.203), $t(86) = 19.80, p < 0.0001$. They were slightly more likely to correctly identify regular (0.869) than inverse (0.837) causal links, $t(86) = 3.14, p = 0.002$. Participants were also more likely to correctly classify causal links as the experiment progressed, as confirmed by a regression with subject-level intercept and slope for trial number (mean $\beta = 0.004$), $t(86) = 5.24, p < 0.001$. Accuracy was 0.789, 0.788, 0.753, and 0.642 for OU networks with 1, 2, 3, and 4 causal links, respectively, $F(3, 258) = 23.3, p < 0.0001$, indicating that learning difficulty increased with the complexity of the network.

3.1. Effect of Rigidity on Accuracy

Consistent with the theoretical analyses presented earlier, overall accuracy increased as the rigidity of the system increased, from 0.731 in the flexible (ω = 0.05) to 0.800 in the rigid (ω = 0.10) condition, an effect that was marginally significant $t(86) = 1.50, p = 0.137$. However, the key theoretical question is how accuracy varied with type of causal link across rigidity conditions, as shown in Figure 10. In the rigid condition, accuracy was generally good, except for the very poor (indeed, below chance) performance on the indirect links. This result reflects learners' tendency to mistakenly infer a direct causal relationship between two variables that are only indirectly related (e.g., X and Z in $X \rightarrow Y \rightarrow Z$) and replicates past findings [1]. The important result is that this pattern of errors interacted with the manipulation of ω: When the system was more flexible, accuracy decreased on the direct and other links but, paradoxically, improved on the indirect links.

These findings were supported by statistical analysis. A two-way mixed ANOVA with repeated measures on the link type factor revealed a main effect of link type $F(2, 170) = 204.1$, $p < 0.0001$, no main effect of rigidity $F < 1$, but an interaction, $F(2, 170) = 12.7, p < 0.0001$. Accuracy on indirect links decreased as system rigidity increased, $t(85) = 3.17, p = 0.002$. In contrast, accuracy on other links increased, $t(85) = 2.20, p = 0.030$. Accuracy on the direct links also increased, although not significantly so, $t < 1$. Note that the total number of causal links inferred per causal network in the flexible (3.51) and rigid (3.19) conditions were not significantly different, $t(85) = 1.50, p = 0.137$.

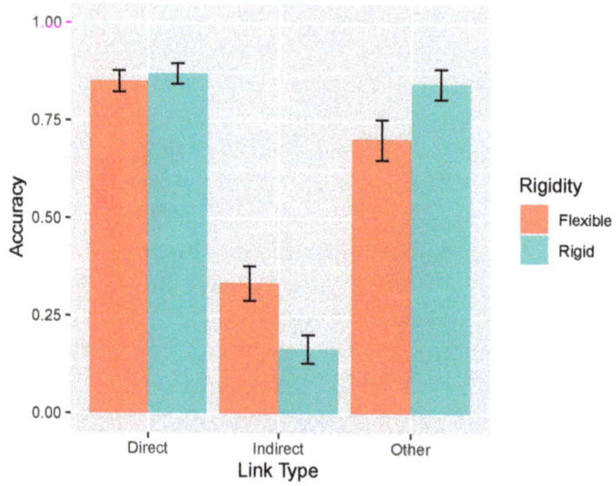

Figure 10. Accuracy identifying causal links by rigidity condition (ω = 0.05 or 0.10) and type of causal link. Causal links are categorized in the same manner as Figures 3–6, namely, as direct, indirect, and other. For example, in a $X \rightarrow Y \rightarrow Z$ network the direct links are $X \rightarrow Y$ and $Y \rightarrow Z$, the indirect link is $X \rightarrow Z$, and the other links are $Y \rightarrow X$, $Z \rightarrow Y$, $Z \rightarrow X$. Accuracy on direct links means correctly identifying the presence of a causal link (and its sign) and accuracy on the remaining links means correctly identifying their absence. Error bars are standard errors of the mean.

3.2. *Effect of Interventions on Accuracy*

As mentioned, successful learning relies on effective interventions, that is, ones that are extended in time and involve large swings of each variable's value. The average intervention duration did not differ between the flexible (3.86 s) and rigid (3.79 s) conditions, $t < 1$. To assess how the duration of participants' intervention affected their learning, we repeated the 2×3 analysis corresponding to Figure 10 with intervention duration added as a per-participant covariate. This analysis yielded an effect of intervention duration, $F(1, 83) = 8.08, p = 0.006$, indicating that longer interventions were associated with greater accuracy, but also an interaction between duration and causal link type, $F(2, 166) = 20.18, p < 0.0001$. This interaction is depicted in Figure 11A in which interventions have been dichotimized via a median split into those that are short and long. Although overall accuracy improved as the duration of interventions increased, accuracy on the indirect links was lower when interventions were longer. The explanation for this result is straightforward. For example, in the network $X \rightarrow Y \rightarrow Z$, longer interventions allow time for the value of variable Z to change in response to an intervention on X, allowing the learner to incorrectly infer the existence of a direct $X \rightarrow Z$ relationship. Separate analyses of each link type revealed that longer interventions resulted in significantly higher accuracy on direct and other links (both $ps < 0.0001$) and marginally lower accuracy on the indirect links, $t(85) = 1.59, p = 0.121$. Note that the two-way interaction depicted in Figure 11A did not itself significantly interact with rigidity condition, $F(2, 166) = 2.01, p = 0.138$.

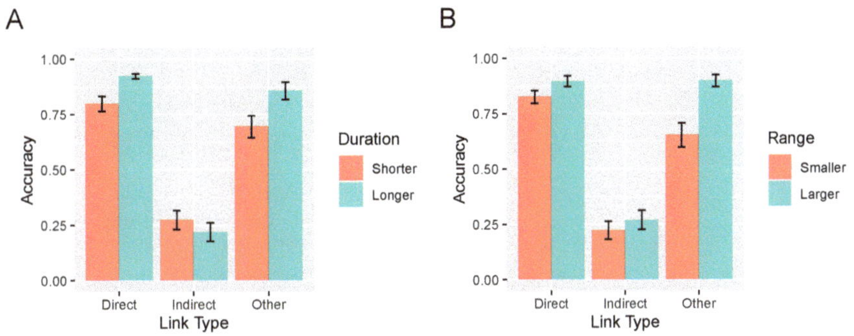

Figure 11. (**A**) Accuracy identifying causal links by intervention duration and type of causal link. (**B**) Accuracy identifying causal links by intervention range and type of causal link. Error bars are standard errors of the mean.

The average range of interventions—defined as the minimum slider value subtracted from the maximum value during an intervention bout—was 141.4 in the rigid condition as compared to 126.5 in the flexible condition, a difference that arose because rigid condition participants were more likely to swing the variable between extremes (e.g., from 100 to −100). This difference did not reach statistical significance however, $t(85) = 1.59, p = 0.115$. To assess how intervention range affected learning, we again repeated the 2 (rigidity condition) × 3 (link type) analysis now with intervention range as a per-participant covariate. This analysis yielded an effect of range, $F(1, 83) = 28.1, p < 0.0001$, indicating that interventions of a larger magnitude were associated with greater accuracy, but also an interaction between range and causal link type, $F(2, 166) = 5.19, p = 0.007$. This interaction is depicted in Figure 11B in which intervention range has been dichotimized via a median split into smaller and larger. The interaction reflects the fact that the increase in accuracy brought about by increased range was lower for indirect links than the other link types. Again, this result is explicable under the assumption that larger interventions increase the likelihood that indirect causal links will be mistaken for direct ones. Separate analyses of each link type revealed that more extreme interventions resulted in significantly higher accuracy on direct and other links (both $ps < 0.0001$). In contrast, accuracy on the indirect links did not vary with range, $t(85) = 1.09, p = 0.279$. The two way interaction in Figure 11B between range and link type did not itself interact with rigidity condition, $F < 1$.

3.3. Modeling

To better understand participants' judgments, we compared them to the causal structure learning models presented above. For each participant and model, the model received as input the slider values and the participant's interventions and yielded a posterior distribution over the 729 causal graphs. As mentioned, the normative model inverts the generative model to optimally infer the structure most likely to have produced the evidence. We assumed a uniform prior over the hypothesis space. We also assumed priors over the parameters ω, θ, and σ. Because they observed four instructional videos of OU networks with those parameter values, we assume that subjects induced the true values of those parameters albeit with some uncertainty. (See our Supplementary Materials at https://osf.io/rfx2q for details). A softmax function was applied to the posterior over graphs, with a separate temperature parameter τ fit for each participant.

The Local Computations (LC) model focuses on pairs of variables rather than evaluating the evidence with respect to the full space of possible causal models (Equation (7)). In other respects the LC model is identical to the normative model. Note that [1] showed that the LC model best fit participants in a very similar task to this study's rigid condition. Here we test the extent to which these results generalize to different time characteristics.

The Causal Event Abstraction (CEA) model describes people as abstracting continuous variables into events and using those events as cues for causality. To account for uncertainty in participant judgments, we fit not only a per participant threshold parameter but also a guessing parameter that corresponded to the probability of responding counter to the predictions of the events model.

Finally, we compare the models above to a baseline model that assumes participants have an equal probability of responding for any graph. It has no fitted parameters.

3.4. Modeling Results

For the normative model, the median fitted values of the softmax τ parameter was 6.15 and 6.35 in the flexible and rigid conditions, respectively, whereas for the LC model they were 5.98 and 6.81. For the CEA model, the median fitted values of the threshold and guessing parameter were 53.1 and 0.284, respectively, in the flexible condition and 64.3 and 0.107 in the rigid condition.

The left panel of Figure 12 shows the relative performance of the models as measured by mean Bayesian Information Criterion (BIC) per participant. Overall, CEA is the best-fitting model. This greater performance of CEA is also reflected in the number of participants best fit by each model (right panel of Figure 12). Although the CEA model fits the majority of participants in both conditions, its advantage over the other models was slightly greater in the rigid as compared to the flexible condition.

Note that the CEA models also explains one way that learners' interventions varied across experimental conditions. For example, a good intervention for the CEA model involves holding an intervened-on variable at or near a particular value for an extended period (providing the time needed for an effect variable to cross its threshold so that an event is recorded). Although the duration and range of interventions did not vary significantly with rigidity, our Supplementary Materials (https://osf.io/rfx2q) presents the proportion of interventions that are held *at one value* over time in each experimental condition. In fact, as the time increased for a variable to cross some threshold because of lower rigidity, learners were more likely to hold the intervened-on variable at one value, a behavior consistent with a CEA learner.

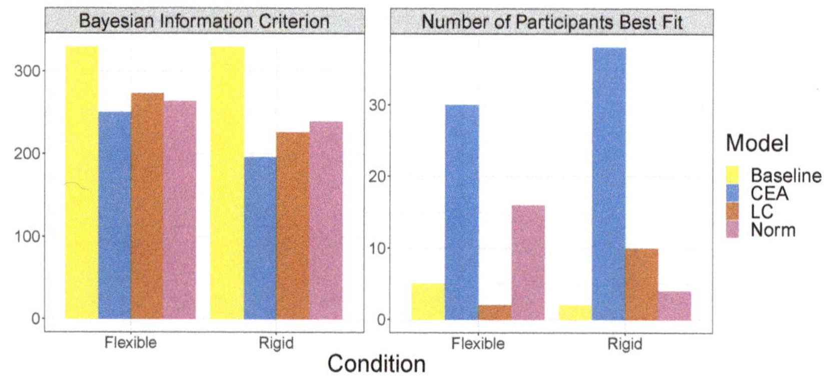

Figure 12. Evaluation measures for the theoretical models. Left panel: Mean BIC per participant. Right panel: Number of participants best fit by each model as measured by BIC. The normative and LC models were fit with a softmax temperature parameter per participant. The CEA model was fit with a threshold and guessing parameter per participant.

3.5. Replication Experiment

We augment these results by reporting in our Supplementary Materials (https://osf.io/rfx2q) the results of a replication experiment that was identical except that the rate at which the computer screen was updated to include the next OU system state (100 ms in the current experiment) was set to 300 ms instead. The results were qualitatively identical, including the interactions shown in Figures 10 and 11 and the general superiority of the CEA model.

4. Discussion

This paper investigated the impact of timing on causal learning in continuous dynamic systems. Specifically, by manipulating an OU system's rigidity we varied the rate at which causes influence their effects. We hypothesized doing so would moderate a particular type of error previously captured by the Local Computations model—given $X \rightarrow Y \rightarrow Z$, incorrectly inferring a direct relationship between X and Z—because in a less rigid system learners would be more likely to note that the influence of X on Z was time delayed, making the possibility that this relationship was mediated by Y more salient. Yet, we also noted that people are generally less likely to infer a causal relationship the greater the time delay between cause and effect. In fact, we found just this paradoxical effect of time on learning: While slowing the dynamics resulted in increased accuracy for indirect effects, it also resulted in reduced accuracy on other types of causal links. That is, rather than having a uniformly positive or negative effect, changes in system timing led to a trade-off between different types of errors.

Although we could not manipulate the interventions that learners chose to make, we also predicted that both the duration and range of those interventions would have effects that were analogous to those of rigidity. In fact, we found that longer interventions were associated with better learning performance overall but at the cost of increasing the prevalence of local computation errors. Interventions of a greater range (i.e., achieved by setting intervened-on variables to more extreme values) were also associated with better overall performance. Although greater range did not numerically increase local computation errors, it did not improve performance on the indirect links as it did on the other link types. Note that the interactions between the pattern of errors and system rigidity, intervention duration, and intervention range were not predicted by the optimal learning model.

To make sense of this pattern of results, we drew on a foundational principle in cognitive psychology: that a major part of what brains do is abstract and discretize continuous inputs into quantities and concepts amenable to structured symbolic processing [21,22]. Along these lines, we explored the idea that people form a greatly simplified representation of the causal dynamics they are observing, viewing them as constituted by causal events triggered by interventions, and using this representation to drive their structure inferences.

We introduced this principle in the form of the Causal Event Abstraction (CEA) model, finding that it better captured the majority of our participants. The success of this model fits nicely with work suggesting that people naturally abstract continuous streams of information into discrete events (for review, see, [22]). That said, the CEA model in its current form is highly exploratory with plenty of room for improvement and further testing. First, CES's current notion of a threshold is absolute in that it is defined relative to 0. This was perhaps a reasonable simplifying assumption for the OU networks tested here in which variables tended to revert to a basin of 0 in the absence of interventions. In other setting, a more realistic model would consider the change in a variable relative to its starting value. Second, CEA's threshold is also binary: An effect variable either crosses it or not. In reality, evidence for a causal relation in human learners may be more graded in that it depends on the distance from the threshold. (We thank an anonymous reviewer for mentioning this possibility). Third, in its current form CEA only infers a direct connection between an intervened-on root variable and end variable that registers an effect, whereas people have been shown to infer structure by linking sequences of events [10]. Fourth, future studies could apply the event abstraction principle as an account of observational causal inference as well as interventional learning. Fifth, given the importance of interventions to produce events for the CEA to learn from, a future direction would be modeling the CEA's prescriptions for how one should intervene to maximize learning. It seems probable that the a goal of producing causally-indicative event sequences would predict markedly different behaviours than the goal of generating the most normatively "invertable" continuous dynamics. Finally, the real-time setting explored here also has rich implications for issues of bounded rationality in active learning. For instance, given the potentially overwhelming complexity of real time dynamics, learners might choose interventions that generate evidence that is informative but not so complex that it cannot be used (cf. [23–25]).

While we manipulated the "speed" of the system dynamics here, even our supposedly slow (i.e., flexible) condition reflects what we believe is the fast end of the spectrum of the dynamics people reckon with in daily life. From economic conditions to climate patterns, many decision-relevant causal dynamics unfold orders of magnitude slower that those we probed in this experiment. It is an open question what relationship such radical clock-time shift has on the interactions between human cognition, intervention choice, event abstraction and causal learning. Recent work examining causal inference from observations spanning hours [26] and days [27] suggests people have at least as much difficulty identifying relationships and dealing with confounds and dependencies. In such settings it seems likely that processing bottlenecks are caused as much by the structure and limits of long term memory and retrieval as by limited online processing bandwidth.

Learning the relationships between continually shifting variables in real-time is as challenging as it is common. In this paper, we identified factors that modulate performance in continuous dynamic environments, and proposed a new model for causal learning inspired by people's ability to abstract and discretize their experiences. We find support for the idea that, in these informationally rich settings, people use events triggered by their actions to infer causal structure.

Supplementary Materials: The following supporting information can be downloaded at: https://osf.io/rfx2q, accessed on 2 April 2022.

Author Contributions: Investigation and data curation, Z.J.D.; formal analysis, resources, software, visualization, and writing—original draft preparation, B.R. and Z.J.D.; conceptualization, methodology, validation, writing—review and editing, B.R., Z.J.D. and N.B. All authors have read and agreed to the published version of the manuscript.

Funding: This research received no external funding.

Institutional Review Board Statement: The study was conducted according to the guidelines of the Declaration of Helsinki, and approved by the Institutional Review Board of New York University (protocol IRB-FY2020-3963, 25 November 2019).

Informed Consent Statement: Informed consent was obtained from all subjects involved in the study.

Data Availability Statement: Empirical data for this experiment can be accessed at Supplementary Materials (https://osf.io/rfx2q).

Conflicts of Interest: The authors declare no conflict of interest.

References

1. Davis, Z.J.; Bramley, N.R.; Rehder, B. Causal structure learning in continuous systems. *Front. Psychol.* **2020**, *11*, 244. [CrossRef] [PubMed]
2. Ali, N.; Chater, N.; Oaksford, M. The mental representation of causal conditional reasoning: Mental models or causal models. *Cognition* **2011**, *119*, 403–418. [CrossRef] [PubMed]
3. Fernbach, P.M.; Erb, C.D. A quantitative causal model theory of conditional reasoning. *J. Exp. Psychol. Learn. Mem. Cogn.* **2013**, *39*, 1327. [CrossRef] [PubMed]
4. Hayes, B.K.; Hawkins, G.E.; Newell, B.R.; Pasqualino, M.; Rehder, B. The role of causal models in multiple judgments under uncertainty. *Cognition* **2014**, *133*, 611–620. [CrossRef] [PubMed]
5. Sloman, S.A. *Causal Models: How People Think about the World and Its Alternatives*; Oxford University Press: Oxford, UK, 2005.
6. Hume, D. An enquiry concerning human understanding. In *Seven Masterpieces of Philosophy*; Routledge: New York, NY, USA, 1740; pp. 191–284.
7. Lagnado, D.A.; Sloman, S.A. Time as a guide to cause. *J. Exp. Psychol. Learn. Mem. Cogn.* **2006**, *32*, 451. [CrossRef] [PubMed]
8. Hagmayer, Y.; Waldmann, M.R. How temporal assumptions influence causal judgments. *Mem. Cogn.* **2002**, *30*, 1128–1137. [CrossRef] [PubMed]
9. Pacer, M.D.; Griffiths, T.L. Elements of a rational framework for continuous-time causal induction. In Proceedings of the Annual Meeting of the Cognitive Science Society, Sapporo, Japan, 1–4 August 2012; Volume 34.

10. Bramley, N.R.; Gerstenberg, T.; Mayrhofer, R.; Lagnado, D.A. Time in causal structure learning. *J. Exp. Psychol. Learn. Mem. Cogn.* **2018**, *44*, 1880. [CrossRef] [PubMed]
11. Buehner, M.J.; May, J. Rethinking temporal contiguity and the judgement of causality: Effects of prior knowledge, experience, and reinforcement procedure. *Q. J. Exp. Psychol. Sect. A* **2003**, *56*, 865–890. [CrossRef] [PubMed]
12. Greville, W.J.; Buehner, M.J. Temporal predictability facilitates causal learning. *J. Exp. Psychol. Gen.* **2010**, *139*, 756. [CrossRef]
13. Fernbach, P.M.; Sloman, S.A. Causal learning with local computations. *J. Exp. Psychol. Learn. Mem. Cogn.* **2009**, *35*, 678. [CrossRef]
14. Rottman, B.M.; Keil, F.C. Causal structure learning over time: Observations and interventions. *Cogn. Psychol.* **2012**, *64*, 93–125. [CrossRef] [PubMed]
15. Davis, Z.J.; Bramley, N.R.; Rehder, B. Causal structure learning with continuous variables in continuous time. In Proceedings of the 40th Annual Conference of the Cognitive Science Society, Madison, WI, USA, 25–28 July 2018.
16. Uhlenbeck, G.E.; Ornstein, L.S. On the theory of the Brownian motion. *Phys. Rev.* **1930**, *36*, 823. [CrossRef]
17. Pearl, J. *Causality*; Cambridge University Press: Cambridge, UK, 2009.
18. Bramley, N.R.; Lagnado, D.A.; Speekenbrink, M. Conservative forgetful scholars: How people learn causal structure through interventions. *J. Exp. Psychol. Learn. Mem. Cogn.* **2015**, *41*, 708–731. [CrossRef] [PubMed]
19. Bramley, N.R.; Dayan, P.; Griffiths, T.L.; Lagnado, D.A. Formalizing Neurath's ship: Approximate algorithms for online causal learning. *Psychol. Rev.* **2017**, *124*, 301. [CrossRef]
20. Gureckis, T.M.; Martin, J.; McDonnell, J.; Rich, A.S.; Markant, D.; Coenen, A.; Halpern, D.; Hamrick, J.B.; Chan, P. psiTurk: An open-source framework for conducting replicable behavioral experiments online. *Behav. Res. Methods* **2016**, *48*, 829–842. [CrossRef] [PubMed]
21. Cohen, B.; Murphy, G.L. Models of concepts. *Cogn. Sci.* **1984**, *8*, 27–58. [CrossRef]
22. Zacks, J.M. Event perception and memory. *Annu. Rev. Psychol.* **2020**, *71*, 165–191. [CrossRef] [PubMed]
23. Gong, T.; Gerstenberg, T.; Mayrhofer, R.; Bramley, N.R. Active Causal Structure Learning in Continuous Time. *Cogn. Psych.* 2022, *submitted*.
24. Kidd, C.; Piantadosi, S.T.; Aslin, R.N. The Goldilocks effect: Human infants allocate attention to visual sequences that are neither too simple nor too complex. *PLoS ONE* **2012**, *7*, e36399. [CrossRef] [PubMed]
25. Christiansen, M.H.; Chater, N. The now-or-never bottleneck: A fundamental constraint on language. *Behav. Brain Sci.* **2016**, *39*, e62. [CrossRef] [PubMed]
26. Zhang, Y. Causal Learning with Delays Up to 21 Hours. Ph.D. Thesis, University of Pittsburgh, Pittsburgh, PA, USA, 2022.
27. Willett, C.L.; Rottman, B.M. The accuracy of causal learning over long timeframes: An ecological momentary experiment approach. *Cogn. Sci.* **2021**, *45*, e12985. [CrossRef] [PubMed]

entropy

MDPI

Article

Interventional Fairness with Indirect Knowledge of Unobserved Protected Attributes

Sainyam Galhotra [1,*], Karthikeyan Shanmugam [2], Prasanna Sattigeri [2] and Kush R. Varshney [2]

1 Department of Computer Science, University of Chicago, Chicago, IL 60637, USA
2 IBM Research, Yorktown Heights, NY 10598, USA; karthikeyan.shanmugam2@ibm.com (K.S.); psattig@us.ibm.com (P.S.); krvarshn@us.ibm.com (K.R.V.)
* Correspondence: sainyam@uchicago.edu

Abstract: The deployment of machine learning (ML) systems in applications with societal impact has motivated the study of fairness for marginalized groups. Often, the protected attribute is absent from the training dataset for legal reasons. However, datasets still contain proxy attributes that capture protected information and can inject unfairness in the ML model. Some deployed systems allow auditors, decision makers, or affected users to report issues or seek recourse by flagging individual samples. In this work, we examine such systems and consider a feedback-based framework where the protected attribute is unavailable and the flagged samples are indirect knowledge. The reported samples are used as guidance to identify the proxy attributes that are causally dependent on the (unknown) protected attribute. We work under the causal interventional fairness paradigm. Without requiring the underlying structural causal model a priori, we propose an approach that performs conditional independence tests on observed data to identify such proxy attributes. We theoretically prove the optimality of our algorithm, bound its complexity, and complement it with an empirical evaluation demonstrating its efficacy on various real-world and synthetic datasets.

Keywords: causal fairness; responsible data science

Citation: Galhotra, S.; Shanmugam, K.; Sattigeri, P.; Varshney K.R. Interventional Fairness with Indirect Knowledge of Unobserved Protected Attributes. *Entropy* **2021**, *23*, 1571. https://doi.org/10.3390/e23121571

Academic Editors: Kateřina Hlaváčková-Schindler and Sotiris Kotsiantis

Received: 22 September 2021
Accepted: 22 November 2021
Published: 25 November 2021

Publisher's Note: MDPI stays neutral with regard to jurisdictional claims in published maps and institutional affiliations.

1. Introduction

Due to the societal impact of automated systems, fairness in supervised learning has been a topic of prime importance. There have been numerous advances in defining fairness in terms of associational and causal effects of protected attributes on the prediction attribute [1–4], thereby mitigating unwanted bias. The majority of these algorithms assume that the protected attribute is accurately specified for the training dataset, which is then used to mitigate unwanted biases by processing the input dataset or modifying the training algorithm (in-processing) or post-processing the output of the prediction algorithm. However, the protected attribute is often unavailable or anonymized for legal reasons [5–7].

The absence of protected attributes from the training dataset does not guarantee fairness of the prediction algorithm. One of the primary reasons for this is the presence of proxy attributes that are causally dependent on the protected attributes. In such settings, a key challenge to ensure fairness is to identify these proxy attributes that may percolate bias into the prediction algorithm and then develop ways to mitigate such biases. Even if the dataset lacks any information about these attributes, software testing by legal auditors, recourse analysis of certain samples [8], or complaints from customers often uncover the presence of bias. In this work, we formalize a framework that leverages such indirect knowledge to identify proxy attributes, which can then help to improve fairness. We motivate this setting with the following example.

Example 1. *Imagine that you are a manager examining a machine learning-powered resume screening app that your software company is starting to use internally [9]. You notice that a candidate named Latanya Sweeney—with an S.M. degree in electrical engineering and computer*

science from MIT and professional experience in minimizing privacy risk—has not been prioritized for your requisition for a staff software engineer to work on a HIPAA-compliant cloud infrastructure project. Suspecting algorithmic bias, you flag Latanya's resume as feedback to the resume app.

In this example of possible unfairness, neither the app nor the manager had access to any protected attributes such as race and gender for legal reasons [5,6]. The missingness of the protected attribute, however, did not prevent the manager from mentally using proxies for race and gender to flag the prediction. In this case, the name Latanya Sweeney is correlated with black women. If the machine learning model behind the app did have unwanted bias providing systematic disadvantage to black people and/or women, the algorithm must have used proxy attributes (like zip code, projects, or writing style) to reconstruct the information in the protected attributes. However, it is difficult to know what those proxy attributes were; it is usually not as simple as just the name of the individual or their zip code.

In this paper, we study fairness in terms of the causal effect of protected attributes on the prediction output/outcome attribute [1–4] and sought to identify the proxy attributes that are causally dependent on the protected attributes (that we do not know and do not have). A variable X is said to be causally dependent on another attribute X' if $X' \to X$ in the causal graph, i.e., X is functionally dependent on X' and any manipulation of X' would impact X. However, we needed some extra information to help us on this quest. The information we utilized is precisely the indirect knowledge that we can glean from the flagging of possibly unfair decisions that the manager in our example submitted as feedback. We do not assume that the causal graph is known a priori.

We formalized the feedback-based framework to identify proxy attributes that are causally dependent on the unknown protected attribute. In terms of the causal graph, a proxy attribute is defined as the child of a protected attribute. We proposed efficient polynomial time algorithms that identify various connectivity properties of the causal graph that differ in the input dataset and the samples that are flagged by an auditor (indirect knowledge). It then uses these properties to identify constraints over pairs of input attributes, which are then used to formulate a constraint satisfaction problem (CSP). The solution of the CSP returns the set of proxy attributes.

Contributions. Our primary contributions are as follows.

1. We formalized a novel problem of using indirect signals to identify proxy attributes that are causally dependent on the protected attribute.
2. We identified unique connectivity properties of the causal graph, which are leveraged to develop a suite of efficient polynomial time algorithms that do not require the causal graph as an input. Our proposed techniques use off-the-shelf conditional independence tests to identify these attributes.
3. We proved theoretical guarantees that our algorithm accurately identifies the proxy attributes and runs in polynomial time. We showed that the complexity of our algorithm is linear in the number of attributes for sparse graphs.
4. We performed an end-to-end evaluation of our proposed techniques on various real-world and synthetic datasets. In real-world datasets, we showed that the classifier trained using our methods is fair and maintains high accuracy. On synthetic datasets, we validated the correctness of our algorithm by comparing with the ground truth.

2. Problem Setup

We denote random variables (also known as dataset attributes or features) by uppercase letters like X, S, A and their corresponding sample values in lowercase like x, s, a. Table 1 summarizes the notation.

Table 1. Notation Table.

Symbol	Meaning
S	Unobserved protected attribute
$\mathcal{V}$	Set of attributes (also known as variables of the causal graph)
D	Input dataset containing $\mathcal{V}$ attributes
Y	Prediction attribute
Y'	Classifier output
F	Feedback attribute
D'	Feedback set
$\mathcal{V}' \subseteq \mathcal{V}$	Proxy attributes
$\mathcal{V}_F \subseteq \mathcal{V}$	Parents of F in the causal graph

Causal DAG and interventions A *causal* directed acyclic graph (DAG), G over a set of attributes $\mathcal{V}$ is a DAG that models the functional dependence between attributes in $\mathcal{V}$. Each node X represents an attribute in $\mathcal{V}$ that is functionally determined by its parents $Pa(X)$ in the DAG and some unobserved variables. An intervention to a causal graph is where an attribute X is set to some specific value, say x, and its effect on the distribution of the learned target attribute Y is observed. The do-operator allows this effect to be computed on a causal DAG, denoted $P(Y|\mathtt{do}(X = x))$. To compute this value, we assumed that X is determined by a constant $X = x$. This assumption is equivalent to a modified graph with all incoming edges into X removed, and the value of X was set to x.

We assumed that the causal graph G on $\mathcal{V}$ is faithful to the observational distribution on $\mathcal{V}$. This means that if two nodes A and B are connected by an edge in the causal graph, the data cannot result in any incorrect conditional independence of the form $A \perp B \mid C$ for any subset $C \subset \mathcal{V} \setminus \{A, B\}$. It is one of the most common assumptions in the causal discovery literature [1,3,10–19]. We use $\perp$ to denote independence. We denote the edges of the causal graph E as a list of pairs (X_1, X_2) such that either X_1 causes X_2 or vice versa.

Unobserved Protected Attribute Consider a dataset D consisting of attributes $\mathcal{V} = \{X_1, \ldots, X_n\}$ along with a target attribute Y. Let S denote the protected attribute that is not available in the dataset D. S is considered as the common confounder for the set of attributes $\mathcal{V}' \subseteq \mathcal{V}$. This is generally the case in settings where the protected attribute is the root node (has no parent) of the causal graph [3].

Interventional Fairness In this work, we consider the causal interventional fairness [3] paradigm that does not allow the protected attributes to affect the classifier output Y' through any attribute that is not admissible ($\mathcal{A}$). Intuitively, an admissible attribute is the one that is allowed to percolate bias into the training algorithm. In Example 1, attributes like race and gender are considered protected attributes, and user preferences like type of job and expected salary are admissible.

Definition 1 (Causal Interventional Fairness). *For a given set of admissible attributes $\mathcal{A}$, a classifier is considered fair if for any collection of values a of $\mathcal{A}$ and output Y', the following holds: $Pr(Y' = y|\,do(\mathcal{S}) = s, do(\mathcal{A} = a)) = Pr(Y' = y|\,do(\mathcal{S}) = s', do(\mathcal{A} = a))$ for all values of $\mathcal{A}$, $\mathcal{S}$ and Y'.*

Intuitively, this definition means that the probability distribution of the classifier output Y' is independent of the protected attributes when we intervene on the admissible attributes. In terms of the causal graph, this holds when all paths from the protected attribute to Y' are blocked by the admissible attributes. For more details about this definition, please refer to [3]. As discussed in the example, the current classifier output Y' does not satisfy this fairness criterion, and we wanted to identify the proxy attributes in order to train a fair classifier.

Feedback Attribute In this problem setup, we assume that a biased classifier outputs Y' are available and that an auditor inspects a subset of these records to identify biased outcomes. These flagged records are denoted with an extra attribute F, where $F = 1$ denotes an example that was flagged by the auditor. As discussed in Example 1, the auditor processes a subset of the features, say, $\mathcal{V}' \subseteq \mathcal{V}$, to flag a data point. Therefore, F is a function of a subset $\mathcal{V}' \subseteq \mathcal{V}$ and the learned target Y' such that $F = 1$ refers to a biased prediction. In terms of the causal graph, the attributes that were used as a signal to flag the classifier output are parents of F.

Complaint set. In order to define the complaint set, we assume a subset of the records from marginalized groups are discriminated, and a small subset of these discriminated records are reported as complaints. Therefore, all individuals in the complaint set are assumed to correspond to a specific subset of the marginalized group. The set of complaints are denoted by D', comprising attributes $\mathcal{V}$ for a small subset where $F = 1$. (Note that the complaints D' does not contain all samples that suffer from biased prediction but only the ones that have been flagged.) Therefore, any conditional independence test of the form $A \perp_{D'} B|C$ on the sample D' is equivalent to conditioning on the attribute F along with C, denoted by $(A \perp_D B|C, F)$. Whenever it is clear from context, we ignore the subscript D from the expressions. Unless specified, we always write the expression in terms of $\perp_D$. The operator $\perp_{D'}$ is equivalent to $\perp_D$ with a conditioning on F. Since the feedback $F = 1$ refers to a sample of biased predictions, we assumed that the majority of the samples with $F = 1$ correspond to the members of marginalized or otherwise unprivileged communities.

Assumption 1. *Considering the set of complaints (dataset D' where $F = 1$), the protected attribute $S = s$ is fixed for some records in the marginalized group $S = s$ that have been flagged.*

This assumption is crucial to ensure that the feedback set D' contains indirect information about the marginalized group of individuals. Without this assumption, the set D' cannot be used to relate the complaints with the marginalized group. Note that the set D' does not contain all datapoints that have $S = s$. Therefore, adding a new column that treats all records in feedback set as $S = s$ and all others as $S = s'$ cannot be used as the protected attribute of individuals. Let $\mathcal{V}_F \subseteq \mathcal{V}$ denote the set of attributes that are used by the auditor to flag the datapoint. In terms of the causal graph, F is functionally dependent on F. Since F is a common descendant of all these attributes, any pair of attributes $X_1, X_2 \in \mathcal{V}_F$ cannot be d-separated over D' i.e., $(X_1 \not\perp_{D'} X_2|A) \equiv (X_1 \not\perp_D X_2|A, F), \forall A \subseteq \mathcal{V} \setminus \{X_1, X_2\}$.

Proxy variables. We defined the proxy variables as the non-admissible set of attributes that are functionally dependent on the unobserved protected attribute and that, therefore, have the maximum causal impact of the protected attribute. Due to the absence of the protected attribute, considering the proxy attributes as protected while employing any prior fairness-aware learning algorithm would guarantee a causally fair classifier. More formally, we claim the following.

Lemma 1. *Consider a causal graph G over a set of attributes $\mathcal{V}$, with unobserved protected attribute S. Let Children of the protected attribute S be denoted by $Ch(S)$. If*

$$Pr(Y'|do(Ch(S) \setminus \mathcal{A}) = c, do(\mathcal{A}) = a) = P(Y'|do(Ch(S) \setminus \mathcal{A}) = c', do(\mathcal{A}) = a)$$

then Y' is causally fair, i.e., $P(Y'|do(\mathcal{A}) = a, do(S) = s) = P(Y'|do(\mathcal{A}) = a, do(S) = s')$

Proof. Let $\mathcal{T}$ denote the children of S in the causal graph. If $Pr(Y'|\mathrm{do}(\mathcal{T}) = c, do(\mathcal{A}) = a) = P(Y'|\mathrm{do}(\mathcal{T}) = c', do(\mathcal{A}) = a)$, then all paths from the attributes $\mathcal{T}$ to Y' are blocked when incoming edges of $\mathcal{T}$ and $\mathcal{A}$ are removed from G. In order to show that a classifier that obeys the condition of causal fairness with respect to S, we need to prove the following. After removing all incoming edges of S and $\mathcal{A}$, there should be no directed paths from S

to Y' without a collider (Y' should not be a descendant of S). Since all incoming edges of S have been removed, all directed paths from S to Y' pass through the children $\mathcal{T}$. These paths $S \rightarrow X \rightarrow \ldots \rightarrow Y'$ where $X \in \mathcal{T}$: these paths that contain outgoing edges from $\mathcal{T}$ are all blocked because $Pr(Y'|\mathtt{do}(\mathcal{T}) = c, do(\mathcal{A}) = a) = P(Y'|\mathtt{do}(\mathcal{T}) = c', (\mathcal{A}) = a)$. This shows that whenever the proxy variables are considered as protected while training a fair classifier, causal fairness of the outcome is guaranteed. □

Note that any superset of the children of S (multi-hop descendants) is a valid set of proxy variables as they may be causally dependent on S. However, $Children(S)$ is the smallest set of attributes that need to be accounted for fair classification. Considering more variables as proxies could affect the overall classification accuracy.

3. Problem Statement and Solution Approach

In this section, we first define the problem statement and give high-level observations about the connectivity properties of the causal graph. We then use these properties to design a simple algorithm, which is then improved by formulating a constraint satisfaction problem. We then improve the efficiency of the algorithm by leveraging the sparsity properties of causal graphs.

Based on the notation we defined in the previous section, we can state the problem of identifying proxy-protected attributes as follows.

Problem 1. *Given a dataset D comprising attributes $\mathcal{V}$ with a classifier output Y' and a biased feedback set D', identify the smallest subset $\mathcal{V}' \subseteq \mathcal{V}$ such that the hidden protected attribute S is a common confounder for the attributes in $\mathcal{V}'$.*

Now let us work towards a solution. Let us first identify the condition under which proxies for the protected attribute can be identified from observational data and develop efficient techniques for the same. Consider a simple toy causal graph example, shown in Figure 1, where only the protected attribute is unobserved. We made a simplistic assumption that only the protected attribute is unobserved for this example. Our technique and theoretical analysis extends to the general case where many other attributes may be unobserved. Note that we have access to the training dataset D containing $\mathcal{V} = \{X_1, X_2, X_3\}$ and a small feedback dataset D', which is equivalent to conditioning $F = 1$. The subset of the data that has $F = 1$ may not overlap with the training data. In this example, the attributes that impact F are $\mathcal{V}_F = \{X_1, X_3\}$, and the proxy attributes are $\mathcal{V}' = \{X_1, X_2\}$. We can see that identifying proxy attributes is an easy task if the causal graph is known. Now, let us look at some of the properties of D and D' that can help in the absence of the causal graph.

1. Consider the attributes X_1 and X_2, which are confounded by the protected attribute S and $(X_1, X_2) \notin E$. Since S is unobserved in the dataset D, X_1 and X_2 cannot be d-separated, i.e., $X_1 \not\perp_D X_2 | A, \forall A \subseteq \mathcal{V} \setminus \{X_1, X_2\}$. However, the feedback F is equivalent to considering a smaller sub-population (conditioning on S), which breaks the confounding relation between X_1 and X_2. Therefore, $X_1 \perp_D X_2 | F \equiv X_1 \perp_{D'} X_2$. This equation can be easily tested by performing a CI test on the flagged samples.
2. Consider the attributes X_1 and X_3, which are not confounded by the protected attribute S. For such attributes, there exists a subset $A \subseteq \mathcal{V} \setminus \{X_1, X_3\}$ such that $X_1 \perp X_3 | A$. In Figure 1, $A = \phi$. However, $X_1, X_3 \in \mathcal{V}_F$ means that the collider path $X_1 \rightarrow Y' \leftarrow X_3$ gets unblocked given F, implying $X_1 \not\perp_D X_3 | A, F \equiv X_1 \not\perp_{D'} X_3 | A$, $\forall A \subseteq \mathcal{V} \setminus \{X_1, X_3\}$. Therefore, X_1 and X_3 can never be d-separated in the feedback dataset D'.

These observations show that different attributes in the causal graph satisfy different properties based on their membership. We formalize these intuitions for general graphs and prove the following properties for any pair of attributes. Lemma 2 proves the condition in which X_1 and X_2 can be d-separated with respect to D and D', if X_1, X_2 are proxy attributes.

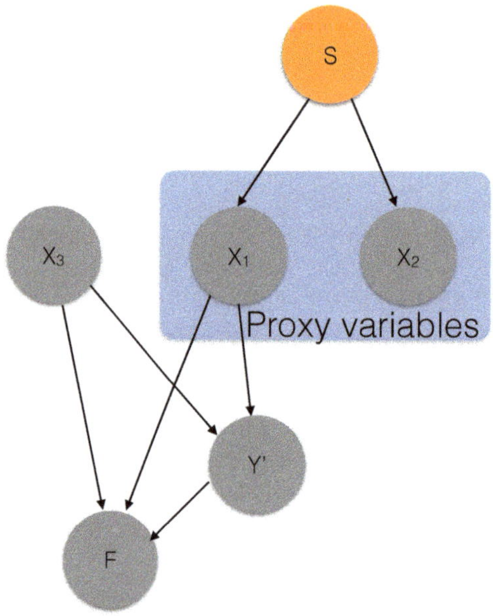

Figure 1. Example dataset where the protected attribute S and the causal graph are unobserved. The attribute Y' denotes the learned target attribute; F is the feedback attribute, which refers to the selection variable for the complaints flagged by an auditor; and X_1 and X_2 are proxy attributes.

Lemma 2. *Consider a pair of attributes X_1 and $X_2 \in \mathcal{V}$ with $(X_1, X_2) \notin E$. $X_1, X_2 \in \mathcal{V}'$, and at least one of X_1 and X_2 does not belong to $\mathcal{V}_F$ iff*

1. $X_1 \not\perp X_2|A$ *for all* $A \subseteq \mathcal{V} \setminus \{X_1, X_2\}$ *and*
2. $X_1 \perp X_2|A, F$ *for some* $A \subseteq \mathcal{V} \setminus \{X_1, X_2\}$

Proof. We consider the two sides of the lemma separately. First, let us assume that $(X_1, X_2) \notin E$, $X_1, X_2 \in \mathcal{V}'$ and at least one of X_1 and X_2 do not belong to $\mathcal{V}_F$. This implies the following conditions.

- If $X_1, X_2 \in \mathcal{V}'$, then S is a common confounder for both X_1 and X_2. Therefore, X_1 and X_2 can not be d-separated, implying $(X_1 \not\perp X_2|A)\ \forall A \subseteq \mathcal{V} \setminus \{X_1, X_2\}$ because S is not observed.
- If at least one of X_1 and X_2 do not belong to $\mathcal{V}_F$ and $(X_1, X_2) \notin E$, then there exists some A such that X_1 and X_2 are d-separated given A, F. This is because conditioning on the feedback F implies $S = 1$ (conditioning on S), which breaks the confounding relationship between X_1 and X_2.

  For the other direction,
- If $X_1 \perp X_2|A, F$ for some $A \subseteq \mathcal{V} \setminus \{X_1, X_2\}$, then both X_1 and X_2 cannot be in V_F and $(X_1, X_2) \notin E$. This is because if $X_1, X_2 \in \mathcal{V}_F$, then $X_1 \not\perp X_2|A, F$ for any A (by definition of $\mathcal{V}_F$).
- If $X_1 \not\perp X_2|A$ for all A but $\exists A' \mid X_1 \perp X_2|A', F$ (we also know that $(X_1, X_2) \notin E$.). Suppose X_1, X_2 are not confounded by S. Conditioning on F and A' blocks all paths from X_1 to X_2. Since conditioning on F does not open any new paths between X_1 and X_2, there will exist A' such that $X_1 \perp X_2|A'$ if X_1 and X_2 are not confounded by S. This is a contradiction, implying X_1 and X_2 are confounded by S.

□

Lemma 3 proves the properties for X_1 and X_2, whenever both of these attributes are considered by the auditor to flag the datapoint.

Lemma 3. *For a pair of attributes X_1 and $X_2 \in \mathcal{V}$ with $(X_1, X_2) \notin E$, $X_1, X_2 \in \mathcal{V}_F$, and at least one of X_1 and X_2 does not belong to $\mathcal{V}'$ iff*

1. $X_1 \perp X_2 | A$ *for some* $A \subseteq \mathcal{V} \setminus \{X_1, X_2\}$
2. $X_1 \not\perp X_2 | A, F$ *for all* $A \subseteq \mathcal{V} \setminus \{X_1, X_2\}$

Proof. First, let us assume that $(X_1, X_2) \notin E$, $X_1, X_2 \in \mathcal{V}_F$, and at least one of X_1 and X_2 do not belong to $\mathcal{V}'$.

- If at least one of X_1 and X_2 do not belong to $\mathcal{V}'$ and $(X_1, X_2) \notin E$, then there exists some $A \subseteq \mathcal{V} \setminus \{X_1, X_2\}$ such that X_1 and X_2 are d-separated given A.
- If $X_1, X_2 \in \mathcal{V}_F$, then $X_1 \rightarrow F \leftarrow X_2$ forms a collider path, which is unblocked given F. Therefore, $(X_1 \not\perp X_2 | A, F)$ $\forall A \subseteq \mathcal{V} \setminus \{X_1, X_2\}$

  For the other direction,
- If $X_1 \perp X_2 | A$ for some $A \subseteq \mathcal{V} \setminus \{X_1, X_2\}$, then both X_1 and X_2 cannot be in $\mathcal{V}'$ and $(X_1, X_2) \notin E$. This is because if $X_1, X_2 \in \mathcal{V}'$, then $X_1 \not\perp X_2 | A$, $\forall A \subseteq \mathcal{V}$ because of an unblocked path $X_1 \leftarrow S \rightarrow X_2$
- If $X_1 \not\perp X_2 | A, F$ for all A but $\exists A$ such that $X_1 \perp X_2 | A$. We also know that $(X_1, X_2) \notin E$. Consider the A for which $X_1 \perp X_2 | A$. In this causal graph, all paths from X_1 to X_2 are blocked but on conditioning F along with A, some path gets unblocked. Since X_1 and X_2 cannot be d-separated when we condition on F, $X_1, X_2 \in \mathcal{V}_F$.

□

For simplicity, we proved these properties for two cases. These properties can be extended for any combination of attributes based on their occurrence in $\mathcal{V}'$ and $\mathcal{V}_F$. Table 2 lists these conditional independence/dependence behavior of all possible combination of attributes X_1 and X_2. For example, the first row shows that if X_1 and $X_2 \in \mathcal{V}_F \cap \mathcal{V}'$, then $X_1 \not\perp X_2 | A$ for all $A \subseteq \mathcal{V} \setminus \{X_1, X_2\}$.

3.1. Simple Algorithm

Using the properties listed in Table 2, Algorithm 1 presents the pseudocode of a simple algorithm that identifies proxy-protected attributes. It iterates over all pair of attributes and performs two types of conditional independence tests (one with conditioning on $A \subseteq \mathcal{V} \setminus \{X_1, X_2\}$ and the other with conditioning on A and F, i.e., with respect to D'). Following Lemma 2, if $\exists A$ such that $X_1 \perp X_2 | F, A$ and $X_1 \not\perp X_2 | A, \forall A$, then X_1 and X_2 are both added to the set $\mathcal{V}'$. Lemma 4 analyzes the conditions when an attribute $X_1 \in \mathcal{V}'$ is correctly identified by Algorithm 1.

Table 2. Conditional independence properties for a pair of attributes $X_1, X_2 \in \mathcal{V}$ such that $(X_1, X_2) \notin E$ where the output of conditional independence tests varies based on the set that X_1, X_2 belong to and vice versa. For example, $X_1, X_2 \in \mathcal{V}' \cap \mathcal{V}_F$ iff $X_1 \not\perp X_2 | A$ and $X_1 \not\perp X_2 | A, F$ for all $A \subseteq \mathcal{V} \setminus \{X_1, X_2\}$.

Conditions on X_1, X_2	Conditioning on D	Conditioning on D'
$X_1, X_2 \in \mathcal{V}' \cap \mathcal{V}_F$	$X_1 \not\perp X_2 \| A$ for all $A \subseteq \mathcal{V} \setminus \{X_1, X_2\}$	$X_1 \not\perp X_2 \| A, F$ for all $A \subseteq \mathcal{V} \setminus \{X_1, X_2\}$
$X_1, X_2 \in \mathcal{V}_F$ and ($X_1 \notin \mathcal{V}'$ and/or $X_2 \notin \mathcal{V}'$) (Lemma 3) and	$X_1 \perp X_2 \| A$ for some $A \subseteq \mathcal{V} \setminus \{X_1, X_2\}$	$X_1 \not\perp X_2 \| A, F$ for all $A \subseteq \mathcal{V} \setminus \{X_1, X_2\}$
$X_1, X_2 \in \mathcal{V}'$ and ($X_1 \notin \mathcal{V}_F$ and/or $X_2 \notin \mathcal{V}_F$) (Lemma 2)	$X_1 \not\perp X_2 \| A$ for all $A \subseteq \mathcal{V} \setminus \{X_1, X_2\}$	$X_1 \perp X_2 \| A, F$ for some $A \subseteq \mathcal{V} \setminus \{X_1, X_2\}$
$X_1 \in \mathcal{V}' \setminus \mathcal{V}_F$ and $X_2 \in \mathcal{V}_F \setminus \mathcal{V}'$	$X_1 \perp X_2 \| A$ for some $A \subseteq \mathcal{V} \setminus \{X_1, X_2\}$	$(X_1 \perp X_2 \| A, F)$ for some $A \subseteq \mathcal{V} \setminus \{X_1, X_2\}$
$X_1 \notin \mathcal{V}' \cup \mathcal{V}_F$	$X_1 \perp X_2 \| A$ for some $A \subseteq \mathcal{V} \setminus \{X_1, X_2\}$	$(X_1 \perp X_2 \| A, F)$ for some $A \subseteq \mathcal{V} \setminus \{X_1, X_2\}$

Algorithm 1 Proxy identification.

Input: attributes $\mathcal{V}, F$
$\mathcal{V}' \leftarrow \phi$
for $X_1 \in \mathcal{V} \setminus \mathcal{V}'$ **do**
    for $X_2 \in \mathcal{V}$ **do**
        if $\exists A \subseteq \mathcal{V} \setminus \{X_1, X_2\} \mid (X_1 \perp X_2 | F, A)$ **then**
            if $\forall A \subseteq \mathcal{V} \setminus \{X_1, X_2\} \mid (X_1 \not\perp X_2 | A)$ **then**
                $\mathcal{V}' \leftarrow \mathcal{V}' \cup \{X_1, X_2\}$
return $\mathcal{V}'$

Lemma 4. *An attribute $X \in \mathcal{V}'$ is correctly identified to belong to $\mathcal{V}'$ if $\exists X' \in \mathcal{V}'$ such that $(X, X') \notin E$ and $|\mathcal{V}_F \cap \{X, X'\}| \leq 1$.*

Proof. Consider an attribute $X \in \mathcal{V}'$, and let $X' \in \mathcal{V}'$ such that $\mathcal{V}_F \cap \{X, X'\} \leq 1$. Therefore, one of X and $X' \notin \mathcal{V}_F$. Using Lemma 2, $X \not\perp X' | A, \forall A \subseteq \mathcal{V} \setminus \{X_1, X_2\}$, and $\exists A \subseteq \mathcal{V} \setminus \{X_1, X_2\}$ such that $X \perp X' | A, F$ holds. Therefore, Algorithm 1 correctly identifies X and $X' \in \mathcal{V}'$. □

However, Algorithm 1 has two main drawbacks:

1. In dense graphs, there may exist an attribute $X \in \mathcal{V}'$ such that $\nexists X' \in \mathcal{V}'$ where $(X, X') \notin E$. Such attributes may not be identified by Algorithm 1.
2. The conditional independence test of the form $X_1 \not\perp X_2 | A, \forall A \subseteq \mathcal{V} \setminus \{X_1, X_2\}$ requires us to test the conditional dependence for every subset $A \subseteq \mathcal{V} \setminus \{X_1, X_2\}$. This condition requires an exponential number of conditional independence tests.

We now present a constraint satisfaction problem-based formulation that overcomes the first limitation (Section 3.2) and an efficient mechanism to optimize the total number of required conditional independence tests (Section 3.3).

3.2. Constraint Satisfaction Formulation

In this section, we leverage the properties of Table 2 to formulate a constraint satisfaction problem (CSP), which is then solved to identify the membership of the attributes. Let us first define the set of variables for this CSP. For each attribute $X \in \mathcal{V}$, define two binary variables X^F and $X^S \in \{0, 1\}$ such that $X^F = 1$ if $X \in \mathcal{V}_F$ and 0 otherwise. Similarly, $X^S = 1$ if $X \in \mathcal{V}'$ and 0 otherwise. Given a pair of attributes X_1 and X_2, we can perform conditional independence tests as described in Table 2 and introduce one of the following constraints based on their output.

- If $X_1 \not\perp X_2 | A, \forall A \subseteq \mathcal{V} \setminus \{X_1, X_2\}$ and $\exists A \subseteq \mathcal{V} \setminus \{X_1, X_2\}$ such that $X_1 \perp X_2 | A, F$, then both X_1 and $X_2 \in \mathcal{V}'$ and at least one of the two attributes does not belong to $\mathcal{V}_F$ (Using Lemma 2). Therefore, $X_1^S = X_2^S = 1$ and $X_1^F + X_2^F \leq 1$.
- If $\exists A \subseteq \mathcal{V} \setminus \{X_1, X_2\}$ such that $X_1 \perp X_2 | A$ and $X_1 \not\perp X_2 | A, F\ \forall A \subseteq \mathcal{V} \setminus \{X_1, X_2\}$, then both attributes X_1 and X_2 belong to $\mathcal{V}_F$, and at least one of the attributes does not belong to $\mathcal{V}'$ (Using Lemma 3). Therefore, $X_1^F = X_2^F = 1$ and $X_1^S + X_2^S \leq 1$
- If $\exists A \subseteq \mathcal{V} \setminus \{X_1, X_2\}$ such that $X_1 \perp X_2 | A$ and $\exists A' \subseteq \mathcal{V} \setminus \{X_1, X_2\}$ such that $X_1 \perp X_2 | A', F$, then X_1 and $X_2 \notin \mathcal{V}' \cap \mathcal{V}_F$. Therefore, $X_1^F + X_1^S + X_2^F + X_2^S \leq 2$.

Using this strategy, we introduce constraints for every pair of attributes $X_1, X_2 \in \mathcal{V}$. The membership of all attributes can be identified by solving this constraint satisfaction problem. To solve this constraint satisfaction problem (containing at most $O(\binom{n}{2})$ constraints), we can use any standard CSP solver [20]. Note that most of the presented constraints are binary, and we can easily implement a polynomial time solver to calculate their membership. An efficient implementation of this instance would be to construct a complete graph over the attributes $\mathcal{V}$ with constraints on nodes and edges. For example, the constraint of the form $X_1^S + X_1^F \leq 1$ is a constraint on the node (as these constraints involve a single attribute), and the ones of the form $X_1^F + X_2^F \leq 1$ refer to edge constraints.

To identify a feasible solution, we iteratively remove the constraints by processing node constraints that fix the values of variables and then propagating their effect on the edge constraints. In this constraint satisfaction formulation, membership of all variables that have a unique value are correctly identified. All other variables that do not have a unique value cannot be classified correctly and are considered as proxy attributes. However, we next show that membership of all attributes are correctly identified for realistic settings (sparse graphs). The membership may not be identified in case a number of attributes have a very high degree (see Lemma 4). As an extreme case, membership of an attribute that is functionally dependent on all other attributes would not be identified by the CSP. However, it is impossible to identify its membership as all attributes are dependent on this high-degree attribute.

The main advantage of this algorithm over Algorithm 1 is that we leveraged properties from Table 2 to identify the membership of an attribute X. If an attribute X is attached to every other attribute $X' \in \mathcal{V}$, then our techniques would not be able to pin-point whether X is a proxy attribute or not. In such cases, it returns three sets of attributes (a) proxy attributes having $X^S = 1$, (b) non-proxy attributes ($X^S = 0$), and (c) undecided attributes (high-degree nodes for which X^S is not uniquely determined). If all the proxy and undecided attributes are not used, the trained classifier is guaranteed to be fair.

3.3. *Efficient Implementation*

Algorithm 1 and the constraint satisfaction problem rely on conditional independence tests that consider all possible subsets $A \subseteq \mathcal{V} \setminus \{X_1, X_2\}$. Therefore, a naive implementation of Algorithm 1 requires $O(2^{|\mathcal{V}|})$ tests. This may not be feasible for large values of $|\mathcal{V}|$, especially when it has to be performed for all pairs of attributes.

In order to improve the overall complexity, we made the following observation for sparse causal graphs. If there exist two attributes X_1 and $X_2 \notin \mathcal{V}'$ where $(X_1, X_2) \notin E$, then they are not connected to any length-2 collider path (paths of the form $X_1 \rightarrow X' \leftarrow X_2$ for some $X' \in \mathcal{V}$) iff $X_1 \perp X_2 | \mathcal{V} \setminus \{X_1, X_2\}$. This holds because when we condition on all attributes except X_1 and X_2, all paths from X_1 and X_2 are blocked except length-2 collider paths of the form $X_1 \rightarrow X_3 \leftarrow X_2$. Since there are no such paths, it means that the test $X_1 \not\perp X_2 | A, \forall A \subseteq \mathcal{V} \setminus \{X_1, X_2\}$ is equivalent to testing for $X_1 \not\perp X_2 | \mathcal{V} \setminus \{X_1, X_2\}$ for such pairs of attributes. Lemma 5 extends this observation to general scenarios where the number of such length-2 collider paths between a pair of attributes is bounded.

Lemma 5. *Consider a pair X_1 and X_2 such that $(X_1, X_2) \notin E$ and at least one of the two attributes does not belong to $\mathcal{V}'$. The following conditions hold:*

1. *X_1 and X_2 are independent when conditioned on all other attributes ($X_1 \perp X_2 | \mathcal{V} \setminus \{X_1, X_2\}$) iff there does not exist $X' \in \mathcal{V}$ such that $X_1 \rightarrow X' \leftarrow X_2$ form a collider path.*
2. *$\exists \mathcal{V}_1$ such that $X_1 \perp X_2 | \mathcal{V}_1$ where $|\mathcal{V}_1| \geq n - t$ iff the number of attributes in set $\mathcal{V}'$ is less than t, where $\mathcal{V}'$ contains all attributes $X \in \mathcal{V}$ that form a length-2 collider path $X_1 \rightarrow X \leftarrow X_2$ or X is a descendant of some attribute $X' \in \mathcal{V}'$, where X' forms a length-2 collider path.*

Proof of Lemma 5. Consider a pair of attributes X_1 and X_2 such that $(X_1, X_2) \notin E$ and at least one of $X_1, X_2 \notin \mathcal{V}'$. If X_1 and X_2 do not have any length-2 collider path, conditioning on all attributes d-separates X_1 and X_2. This holds because for any collider path of length more than 2 (say $X_1 \rightarrow X_i \ldots \leftarrow X_j \leftarrow X_2$), then both X_i or X_j are conditioned. Similarly for any path with incoming edges into X_1 or X_2 (backdoor paths), the parents of both attributes are also conditioned on. Therefore, $X_1 \perp X_2 | \mathcal{V} \setminus \{X_1, X_2\}$.

If a set of attributes $\mathcal{X}', |\mathcal{X}'| \leq t$ where $\mathcal{X}'$ contains all X such that attributes forming length-2 collider of the form $X_1 \rightarrow X \leftarrow X_2$ or X is a descendant of an attribute $X' \in \mathcal{X}'$. In this case, X_1 and X_2 can be d-separated by conditioning on all attributes except $\mathcal{X}'$ because conditioning on any ancestor of X_1 and X_2 does not open new paths. Similarly, if the collider path has a length greater than 2, then the path is blocked by conditioning on all attributes that are not in $\mathcal{X}'$. For example, if the collider path is length 3, $X_1 \rightarrow X_3 \rightarrow X_4 \leftarrow X_2$, then conditioning on X_3 and X_4 does not open this collider path.

More formally, consider any collider path of length greater than 2, say $X_1 \rightarrow X_i \ldots X_j \leftarrow X_2$. If $X_i, X_j \in \mathcal{X}'$, then all descendants of X_i and X_j also belong to $\mathcal{X}'$. Therefore, this path is blocked. If $X_i \notin \mathcal{X}'$, this path is blocked by conditioning on X_i, and conditioning on X_i does not open any length-2 collider paths because $X_i \notin \mathcal{X}'$. Any > 2 length collider path that is unblocked by conditioning on X_i get blocked by another $X_{j'}$, which is a child of X_1 or X_2 in that path. Therefore, conditioning on $\mathcal{V} \setminus \mathcal{X}'$ does not open any path from X_1 to X_2. □

Algorithm 2 uses this property to optimize the number of conditional independence tests required to calculate the membership of each attribute. It initializes with $t = |\mathcal{V}|$ (line 3) and iteratively decreases t to consider attributes with at most $|\mathcal{V}| - t$ length-2 collider paths. For an iteration t, it considers all subsets of $\mathcal{V}$ of size $n - t$ (denoted by $\mathcal{T}$) as the conditioning set (line 6). Using this conditioning set, it evaluates conditional independence constraints for every pair of attributes $X_1, X_2 \in \mathcal{V}$ (Algorithm 3). These constraints are the same as the ones discussed in Section 3.2. The `SolveCSP` subroutine then solves the CSP with new constraints and removes the attributes from U for which X^S has been uniquely determined (line 9). The procedure stops as soon as the X^S values of all attributes $X \in \mathcal{V}$ have been uniquely identified ($U = \phi$) and returns the subset for which $X^S = \{1\}$.

Algorithm 2 Proxy identification.

1: **Input:** attributes $\mathcal{V}, F$
2: $U \leftarrow \mathcal{V}, C \leftarrow \phi$
3: $X^S, X^F \leftarrow \{0,1\}, \forall X \in \mathcal{V}$
4: $t \leftarrow |\mathcal{V}|$
5: **while** $t \geq 0$ and $U \neq \phi$ **do**
6: $\quad \mathcal{T} \leftarrow$ IDENTIFYSUBSET$(\mathcal{V}, t)$
7: $\quad C \leftarrow C \cup$ `PairwiseConstraints`$(\mathcal{V}, \mathcal{T})$
8: $\quad$ `SolveCSP`$(\mathcal{V}, C)$
9: $\quad U \leftarrow \{X : 0,1 \in X^S, X \in \mathcal{V}\}$
10: $\quad t \leftarrow t - 1$
11: $\mathcal{V}' \leftarrow \{X : X^S = \{1\}\}$
12: **return** $\mathcal{V}'$

Algorithm 3 `Pairwise constraints`.

Input: Attributes $\mathcal{V}, F, \mathcal{T}$
$C \leftarrow \phi$
for $(X_1, X_2) \in \mathcal{V} \times \mathcal{V}$ **do**
$\quad$ **if** $\exists T \in \mathcal{T} \mid X_1 \perp X_2 | T \setminus \{X_1, X_2\}$ and $X_1 \not\perp X_2 | T \setminus \{X_1, X_2\}, F\ \forall T \in \mathcal{T}$ **then**
$\quad\quad C \leftarrow C \cup \{X_1^F, X_2^F \leftarrow 1\}$
$\quad\quad C \leftarrow C \cup \{X_1^S + X_2^S \leq 1\}$
$\quad$ **if** $X_1 \not\perp X_2 \mid T \setminus \{X_1, X_2\}$ and $X_1 \perp X_2 \mid T \setminus \{X_1, X_2\}, F$ **then**
$\quad\quad C \leftarrow C \cup \{X_1^S, X_2^S \leftarrow 1\}$
$\quad\quad C \leftarrow C \cup \{X_1^F + X_2^F \leq 1\}$
$\quad$ **if** $X_1 \perp X_2 \mid T \setminus \{X_1, X_2\}$ and $X_1 \perp X_2 \mid T \setminus \{X_1, X_2\}, F$ **then**
$\quad\quad C \leftarrow C \cup \{X_1^S + X_1^F + X_2^S + X_2^F \leq 2\}$
return C

`PairwiseConstraints`. Algorithm 3 presents the pseudocode for this subroutine. It iterates over pairs of attributes and performs CI tests to identify the corresponding constraint, guided by Table 2.

In order to prove the correctness of Algorithm 2, we argue that it does not introduce any spurious constraints in the CSP optimization. Lemma 6 shows that if a pair X_1 and X_2 have more than α length-2 collider paths, then X_1 and X_2 cannot be d-separated by conditioning on any subset of size more than $n-\alpha$. Since each new constraint introduced by Algorithm 3 requires conditional independence of X_1 and X_2 with respect to some subset on D or D', it does not identify incorrect constraints. We now prove Lemma 6.

Lemma 6. *Consider a pair of attributes X_1 and X_2 such that the total number of length-2 collider paths ($X_1 \rightarrow X \leftarrow X_2$ where $X \in \mathcal{V}'$) is at least α. Any CI test between X_1 and X_2 conditioning on A where $|A| > n-\alpha$ returns $X_1 \not\perp X_2|A$.*

Proof. If a pair of attributes X_1 and X_2 have more than α length-2 collider paths, then conditioning on any subset of size more than $n-\alpha$ implies conditioning on at least one of the collider nodes. Therefore, $X_1 \not\perp X_2|A$ whenever $|A| > n-\alpha$. □

3.4. Time Complexity

We now analyze the running time of Algorithm 2 for commonly studied causal graph models. Theorem 1 bounds the total number of CI tests required for a degree-bounded graph, and then we extend our analysis to Erdős-Renyi graphs.

Theorem 1. *For a causal graph where each node $X \in \mathcal{V}$ has a degree less than α and $|\mathcal{V}' \setminus \mathcal{V}_F| > \alpha^2$, Algorithm 2 requires $O(n^2)$ CI tests to identify all proxy attributes.*

Proof. For a node X with degree $< \alpha$, the maximum number of 2-hop neighbors of X is $\leq (\alpha-1)^2$. This analysis considers all edges as undirected and can be tightened by considering directions and splitting α into incoming and outgoing degrees of each node. Therefore, X can have at most $(\alpha-1)^2$ length-2 collider paths. This means that if $\mathcal{V}' \setminus \mathcal{V}_F$ contains more than $(\alpha-1)^2$ two-hop and $\alpha-1$ one-hop attributes, then $\exists X' \in \mathcal{V}'$ such that X' is at least 2-hops away from X. Since $\alpha^2 > (\alpha-1)^2 + (\alpha-1)$, $\exists X' \in \mathcal{V}'$ that satisfies this condition. Such attributes are identified in the CI test $X \perp X'|F, \mathcal{V} \setminus \{X, X'\}$. Therefore, all attributes are correctly identified in 1 test for every pair of attributes. □

Erdős-Renyi Graphs. We consider a randomized generative model for the causal graph construction where each pair of attributes are causally related independently with a probability p. We show that whenever $p < 1/\sqrt{n}$, Algorithm 2 identifies all proxy attributes in $O(n^2)$ running time. Such connectivity models for causal graphs have been widely studied [21]. Lemma 7 bounds the expected number of length-2 collider paths between a pair of attributes X_1 and X_2.

Lemma 7. *Consider a pair of attributes X_1 and X_2 such that $(X_1, X_2) \notin E$. The probability that X_1 and X_2 have a length-2 collider path between them is less than $p^2(n-2)$.*

Proof. Let X_v denote a binary random variable such that $X_v = 1$ if $X_1 \rightarrow X \leftarrow X_2$ forms a collider path for $X \in \mathcal{V}$. The probability that $(X_1, X) \in E$ and $(X, X_2) \in E$ is $p \times p = p^2$. Therefore, $Pr[X_v = 1] = p^2$. □

Using this result, we prove the following complexity of our algorithm.

Theorem 2. *Algorithm 2 identifies the proxy attributes in less than $O(n^2)$ CI tests if $p = o(\sqrt{1/n})$*

Proof. Given a pair of attributes X_1 and X_2, the probability that X_1 and X_2 are within 2-hops from each other is $p^2(n-2) = o(1)$ if $p = o(\sqrt{1/n})$. Therefore, $\forall X \in \mathcal{V}'$, there will exist $X' \in \mathcal{V}'$ such that $(X, X') \notin E$ and the two attributes are more than 2-hops away. Therefore, $X \not\perp X'|A \forall A \subseteq \mathcal{V} \setminus \{X, X'\}$ and $X \perp X'|A, F$ for some $A \subseteq \mathcal{V} \setminus \{X, X'\}$.

This means that all attributes in $\mathcal{V}'$ have been recovered in the first iteration of Algorithm 2. □

3.5. Graphical Lasso-Based Algorithm

In this section, we study a specific class of causal graphs where the structural equations are Gaussian. In this setting, we show that Algorithm 2 can be implemented efficiently using the graphical lasso algorithm.

Graphical lasso [22] is one of the widely studied methods to infer the precision matrix of the underlying causal model in settings where the structural equations are Gaussian. (The precision matrix is the inverse of the covariance matrix; its non-zero values encode the edges in the graph.) Following the properties of Lemma 2, we know that $X_1 \not\perp X_2|A$, $\forall A \subseteq \mathcal{V} \setminus \{X_1, X_2\}$ if $X_1, X_2 \in \mathcal{V}'$. Therefore the precision matrix identified over D would contain (X_1, X_2) as an edge. Similarly, Lemma 2 also shows that $\exists A \subseteq \mathcal{V} \setminus \{X_1, X_2\}$ such that $X_1 \perp X_2|A, F$ iff $X_1, X_2 \in \mathcal{V}'$. This means that the entry corresponding (X_1, X_2) in the precision matrix will be 0. Using this property, a simple algorithm to identify the proxy attributes is as follows. (a) Step 1: Run graphical lasso on the original dataset D. Let P denote the returned precision matrix. (b) Step 2: Run graphical lass on the dataset D'. Let P' denote the returned precision matrix. (c) Step 3: Calculate the set difference $P \setminus P'$. All attributes with degree more than 0 in $P \setminus P'$ are the proxy attributes. One of the advantages of this technique is that the graphical lasso algorithm is highly efficient, but it is restricted to multivariate Gaussian causal models and does not generalize to general datasets.

4. Experiments

In this section, we evaluate the effectiveness of our techniques to identify proxy attributes that capture protected information such that removing these attributes improves classifier fairness. The protected attributes are hidden from the dataset and are used only to evaluate the fairness of the learned classifier.

4.1. Setup

4.1.1. Datasets

We consider the following real-world datasets.

- *Medical Expenditure* (MEPS) [23]: This dataset is used to predict the total number of hospital visits from patient medical information. Healthcare utilization is sometimes used as a proxy for allocating preventative care management. We consider "arthritis diagnosis" as admissible. Race is considered protected and is hidden for experimentation. The dataset contains 7915 training and 3100 test records.
- *German Credit* [24] dataset contains attributes of various applicants, and the goal was to classify them based on credit risk. The account status is taken as admissible, and whether the person is below the mean age is considered protected. The dataset contains 800 training and 200 test records.
- *Adult* dataset [25] contains demographic information of individuals along with their information on their level of education, occupation, working hours, etc. The task was to predict whether or not the annual income of an individual exceeds 50K. Race was treated as the protected attribute, and education was treated as admissible. The dataset contains around 32K training and 16K test records.

4.1.2. Baselines

Our experimental setup is similar to that of [3], where the input dataset contains admissible attributes (denoted by $\mathcal{A}$), referring to the set of attributes that are allowed to inject bias into the trained classifier. In the implementation of our algorithm, we identified all proxy attributes and trained a new classifier after removing them from the dataset. Due to the small size of $\mathcal{A}$, classifiers trained on $\mathcal{A}$ tend to predict a single class if the training data are not balanced. Therefore, we compare the performance of the trained classifier on both original and balanced data. All algorithms were implemented in Python, and we use Scikit-Learn's logistic regression classifier with default parameters.

Since causal fairness cannot be tested on real datasets, we evaluate the fairness of the classifier in terms of absolute odds difference (AOD) as a proxy. AOD is calculated as the difference in the false-positive rate and the true-positive rate between the privileged and unprivileged/marginalized groups. The set of privileged and unprivileged/marginalized groups are identified according to the sensitive attribute. For example, white individuals are considered privileged in MEPS dataset. The feedback sample is constructed randomly by considering a small sample of unprivileged records that received negative outcomes (less than 100 data points). We used the RCIT package [26] for CI testing, and the Glass package [27] for graphical lasso. These packages are in R. Unless specified, we used Algorithm 2 for our experiments. We considered the following baselines. (i) A uses the attributes in the admissible set. (ii) ALL uses all attributes present in the dataset.

4.2. Solution Quality

Table 3 compares the accuracy and average precision of the trained classifier along with absolute odds difference to measure fairness. Among all datasets, the accuracy of our approach is similar to All, and the fairness is similar to that of A. This experiment validates that the removal of proxy attributes from the dataset does not worsen the overall accuracy but helps to improve fairness of the trained classifier. Low average precision (less than 0.60) for A shows that it does not learn the target attributes Y and predicts the same label for each datapoint. On the other hand, All has high accuracy but is highly unfair. As an example, it has an odds difference of 0.38 on the Adult and 0.27 on the MEPS dataset.

Table 3. Comparison of accuracy (Acc), average precision (AvgP), and absolute odds difference (AOD).

Dataset	OurApproach			All			$\mathcal{A}$		
	Acc	AvgP	OD	Acc	AvgP	OD	Acc	AvgP	OD
Adult	0.79	0.78	0.025	0.80	0.75	0.06	0.75	0.47	0.03
Adult-balanced	0.78	0.71	0.068	0.65	0.59	0.38	0.63	0.59	0.40
MEPS	0.85	0.75	0.09	0.86	0.77	0.15	0.83	0.41	0
MEPS-balanced	0.77	0.67	0.25	0.77	0.67	0.27	0.76	0.59	0.05
German	0.74	0.7	0.075	0.79	0.71	0.12	0.72	0.44	0.003
German-balanced	0.70	0.66	0.06	0.72	0.67	0.13	0.6	0.53	0.05

On training a balanced classifier for the Adult dataset, our algorithm achieved higher accuracy than All and almost a 0 odds difference. On investigating this dataset, we noticed that the identified proxy attributes did not help with prediction, and ignoring those attributes helped with both accuracy and fairness. Some of the attributes used by our technique for classifier training after removing the proxy attributes were education and capital in Adult and purpose and age in German. In MEPS, our approach used diagnostic features like cancer diagnosis and blood pressure for prediction. We observed similar results on changing the training algorithm to random forest and AdaBoost classifier.

In addition to comparing the odds difference, we considered the causal graph for Adult and German from the prior literature [2] and used it as a ground truth to test the correctness of our algorithm. Overall, Algorithm 2 identified 95% of the proxy attributes for these datasets. In terms of running time, our presented technique was completed in less than 10 min on all datasets.

4.3. Synthetic Dataset

In this experiment, we considered different synthetic datasets and calculated the fraction of proxy attributes identified by Algorithm 2. Since the causal graph was used to generate data, we can verify the correctness of identified proxy attributes for these datasets.

The first experiment considered causal graphs corresponding to `Adult` and `German` where the structural equations of the causal graph followed a multivariate Gaussian distribution. We used the graphical lasso variant of our algorithm for these datasets. Our algorithm identified all proxy attributes on both datasets, and none of the non-proxy attributes were labeled incorrectly.

The second experiment considered random causal graphs containing 20, 40, 60, 80, and 100 attributes consisting of 5 proxy-protected attributes, generated according to the Erdős-Renyi model where every pair of attributes was connected with probability $p = 0.2$. In this case, Algorithm 2 achieved 100% accuracy to identify proxy attributes. To further study the effect of probability p, we considered higher values of $p = 0.5$ and 0.75. In such cases, Algorithm 2 identified 83% of the proxy attributes correctly where the high degree nodes were not identified. These attributes were neither labeled as proxy nor non-proxy.

Complexity Figure 2a shows the effect of an increase in the number of proxy attributes $\mathcal{V}'$ on the number of required conditional independence tests by Algorithms 1 and 2. In this experiment, we considered a causal graph of 50 attributes and varied the number of proxy attributes from 5 to 30. The complexity of both techniques increased linearly with an increase in $|\mathcal{V}'|$, and Algorithm 2 is orders of magnitude better than Algorithm 1. In Figure 2b, we varied the edge formation probability p of the generative model while keeping the size of $\mathcal{V}'$ constant. In this experiment, the total number of tests required increased with increasing p, but Algorithm 1 required much more tests as compared to Algorithm 2. This experiment validated the effectiveness of Algorithm 2 to reduce the number of CI tests required to identify proxy attributes.

In terms of running time, Algorithm 2 ran within 10 minutes for all real-world datasets. In Figure 2, its running time increased proportionally to the increase in the number of CI tests.

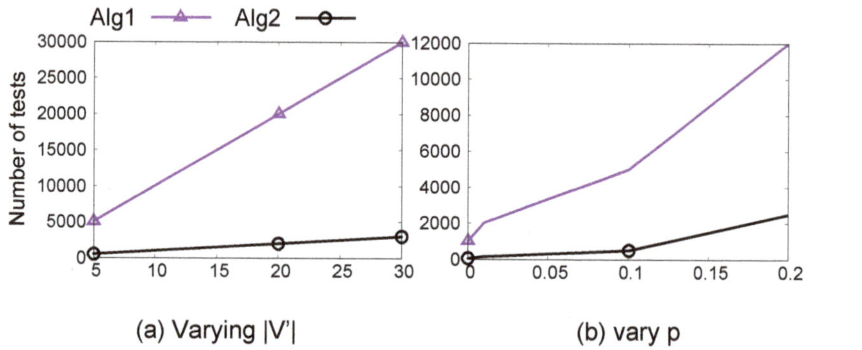

Figure 2. Complexity comparison of our techniques for varying dataset sizes.

Effect of feedback set size As an additional experiment, we varied the feedback set size and evaluated the difference in results for real datasets. We observed that our approach ensures fairness whenever the feedback set contains more than 25 samples. An increase in feedback ensures that our technique is stable and ensures fairness across different runs. Whenever the number of samples is small, the behavior of our approach varies. This varied behavior is because our algorithm uses RCIT as a black-box algorithm to test conditional independence, and it returns spurious answers for small sizes of the feedback set.

Overall, this experiment validates that our technique is effective in identifying proxy attributes and mitigating unwanted biases.

5. Related Work

There has been very little work to consider fairness in the absence of protected attributes. Refs. [28,29] consider adversarial reweighting and empirical risk minimization techniques to learn a fair classifier in the absence of demographic information. These techniques do not assume knowledge of protected attributes, but do not study the causal impact of the unobserved features on the target attribute. Ref. [7] tackles the absence of protected attributes using transfer learning from a different dataset that does have protected attributes. Ref. [30] studies fair class balancing techniques in the absence of protected attributes. There has been some recent interest in studying the effect of noisy attributes on the fairness of classification. Ref. [31] studied the problem of training a fair classifier in the presence of noisy protected attributes. This work does not consider the causal fairness paradigm and does not directly extend to settings where the protected attribute is unobserved. Ref. [32] considered fairness in the presence of noise in the target attribute. These techniques are not directly applicable to our problem setting.

The literature on mitigating unwanted biases considers two types of fairness measures: associational and causal. Associational methods [33–38] have been shown to fail in distinguishing spurious correlations and causal dependence between attributes [3]. Identifying proxy attributes for these techniques is outside the scope of this work. There has been much recent interest in studying causal fairness frameworks [1,10–15,17–19,39] to achieve fairness. Ref. [2] studies the effect of different causal paths from the protected attributes on the target attribute assuming knowledge of the protected attribute and the underlying causal graph. Ref. [3] studies the problem of changing input data distribution in order to ensure interventional fairness. All these techniques require accurate characterization of the protected attribute for all data points. Extending these techniques [2,3] to leverage the information about proxy attributes in the absence of protected attributes is orthogonal to this work and an interesting question for future work.

6. Conclusions

In this work, we formalized a feedback based framework for interventional fairness in settings where the protected attribute is unobserved. Specifically, we examined systems where the auditors, decision makers, or affected individuals report issues in the deployed classifier. These flagged samples that suffered from biased prediction are considered indirect knowledge about the unobserved protected attributes. In this setting, we developed efficient techniques that use conditional independence (CI) testing over the observational data to formulate a constraint satisfaction problem, which identifies the proxy variables. Our techniques partition the variables into different categories based on the output of the performed CI tests. We theoretically proved the correctness of our algorithm, bound its complexity for popular causal graph models, and demonstrated its efficacy on real-world and synthetic datasets.

Author Contributions: Conceptualization, S.G., K.S., P.S. and K.R.V.; methodology, S.G., K.S., P.S. and K.R.V.; experiments, S.G..; validation, S.G., K.S., P.S. and K.R.V.; formal analysis, S.G., K.S., P.S. and K.R.V.; investigation, S.G., K.S., P.S. and K.R.V.; writing—original draft preparation, S.G., K.S., P.S. and K.R.V.; writing—review and editing, S.G., K.S., P.S. and K.R.V.; visualization, S.G. All authors have read and agreed to this version of the manuscript.

Funding: This research did not receive any external funding.

Institutional Review Board Statement: Not applicable.

Informed Consent Statement: Not applicable.

Data Availability Statement: The datasets used in the study are openly available, and we provide the relevant citations.

Conflicts of Interest: Galhotra has worked at the University of Massachusetts, Amherst, and the University of Chicago in the last two years. Shanmugam, Sattigeri, and Varshney have worked at IBM Research in the last two years.

entropy

Article

Causal Algebras on Chain Event Graphs with Informed Missingness for System Failure

Xuewen Yu [1,*] and Jim Q. Smith [1,2]

1 Statistics Department, University of Warwick, Coventry CV4 7AL, UK; j.q.smith@warwick.ac.uk
2 The Alan Turing Institute, London NW1 2DB, UK
* Correspondence: xuewen.yu@warwick.ac.uk

Abstract: Graph-based causal inference has recently been successfully applied to explore system reliability and to predict failures in order to improve systems. One popular causal analysis following Pearl and Spirtes et al. to study causal relationships embedded in a system is to use a Bayesian network (BN). However, certain causal constructions that are particularly pertinent to the study of reliability are difficult to express fully through a BN. Our recent work demonstrated the flexibility of using a Chain Event Graph (CEG) instead to capture causal reasoning embedded within engineers' reports. We demonstrated that an event tree rather than a BN could provide an alternative framework that could capture most of the causal concepts needed within this domain. In particular, a causal calculus for a specific type of intervention, called a remedial intervention, was devised on this tree-like graph. In this paper, we extend the use of this framework to show that not only remedial maintenance interventions but also interventions associated with routine maintenance can be well-defined using this alternative class of graphical model. We also show that the complexity in making inference about the potential relationships between causes and failures in a missing data situation in the domain of system reliability can be elegantly addressed using this new methodology. Causal modelling using a CEG is illustrated through examples drawn from the study of reliability of an energy distribution network.

Keywords: Chain Event Graphs; interventions; causal calculus

Citation: Yu, X.; Smith, J.Q. Causal Algebras on Chain Event Graphs with Informed Missingness for System Failure. *Entropy* **2021**, *23*, 1308. https://doi.org/10.3390/e23101308

Academic Editor: Kateřina Hlaváčková-Schindler

Received: 10 September 2021
Accepted: 2 October 2021
Published: 6 October 2021

1. Introduction

The use of Bayesian Networks (BN) for the study of reliability has been widely advocated in the literature [1]. However, the asymmetric processes that are common in system reliability can hardly be fully captured by the framework of a BN.

Fortunately, it has been shown that any discrete BN can be embellished into a tree-based graph called a Chain Event Graph (CEG) [2,3]. The CEG is a graphical model that is a function of an underlying event tree and certain context specific conditional independence statements. In particular, the CEG can model and depict the types of structural asymmetries that the BN framework struggles to embody [4]. This can then provide a framework for studying the causal mechanisms behind the failures of a given system. For example, Cowell and Smith [2] developed a dynamic programming algorithm for maximum a posterior (MAP) structural learning for causal discovery within a restricted class of CEGs called stratified CEGs.

Conventional causal algebras have been adapted from Pearl's *do*-calculus for BNs [5] to the singular manipulation on a CEG, and the *back-door* theorem has been generalised to estimate the effect of this manipulation by previous research [6,7]. In a different strand of research, Barclay, Hutton, and Smith [8] developed a class of CEGs suited for incorporating various missing data structures directly through its topology. Unlike BNs, conjugate inference is still well supported by the structure of CEGs even in the presence of missingness [2].

In Section 2, we adapt the MAP structural learning algorithm [2] to search for the best scoring structure of a CEG when some data is informedly missing. The selected model provides the best explanation of the observed data that has been informedly censored. By assuming that each candidate CEG is causal in the sense formally defined in [6,7], the best scoring CEG is of a CEG in idle mode, and then causal deductions can be made from it.

In our recent work [9], we demonstrated how to embed the causal reasoning underlying engineering reports for CEGs designed specifically for applications in system reliability. The causal calculus we developed there only provided a framework to study and analyse the impact of *remedial interventions*, i.e., interventions designed to rectify the root cause after a failure had been observed.

In Section 3, we extend the use of the CEG causal framework with missingness to express and analyse a different kind of intervention called a *routine intervention*. This new class of intervention is necessary when we are evaluating the impact of interventions within scheduled maintenance regimes. These regimes are prepared in advance and are used to inspect machines with the objective of preventing future failures that might be about to happen. In this context, although the data may be informedly missing, we can still develop algorithms that, under certain stated hypotheses, produce formulae to give quantitative estimates of the impacts of various candidate routine interventions of this type.

In this paper, we can, therefore, show how we can use the underlying CEG model to predict the effect of various types of such interventions. In particular we report a new back-door criterion—an analogue of Pearl's back-door criterion for BNs [5]. This gives a quick sufficient condition as to whether the effect of such an intervention is identifiable when data is censored in a way that induces informed missingness. This criterion significantly increases the scope of the original causal calculus using CEGs designed for the singular manipulation [6] and the stochastic manipulation established for BNs [5]. It, thus, enables us to transfer causal technologies so that they apply to this graphical family.

In Section 4, we demonstrate how to interpret the causal structures of a best scoring CEG by a simple example of a conservator system. Furthermore, comparative experiments are designed to show that the proposed new causal algebras can embellish the current structural learning algorithm to capture the causal effects of a routine intervention.

The contributions of this paper are threefold. First, we formally derive a method for selecting a CEG providing the framework of a probability model of maintenance regimes, which acknowledges the presence of informed missingness within the fitted data endemic in these applications. Second, we devise new causal algebras for the routine intervention and prove the identifiability of its causal effects in presence of the types of missing data that we might expect from this application. Third, we demonstrate how important this new intervention calculus can be in making valid inferences and how naive inferences that treat the system as uncontrolled and ignore the underlying causal structure within this application can severely mislead the analyst.

2. Causal Identifiability on Chain Event Graphs with Informed Missingness

We begin this section by briefly reviewing and then extending the definition of a CEG [2,3,6–8] before providing a systematic approach to embedding information about the context-specific missingness into a CEG customised for the domain of reliability [9,10].

Suppose we have a vector of variables $\boldsymbol{X} = (X_1, X_2 ..., X_n)$ taking values in a state space $\mathbb{X} = \mathbb{X}_1 \times \cdots \times \mathbb{X}_n$, among which we explore various putative causal hypotheses. An *event tree* $\mathcal{T}(\boldsymbol{X}) = (V_{\mathcal{T}}, E_{\mathcal{T}})$ can be constructed to represent relationships embedded in $\boldsymbol{X}$, where $V_{\mathcal{T}}$ denotes the vertex set and $E_{\mathcal{T}}$ denotes the edge set of $\mathcal{T}(\boldsymbol{X})$. Each non-leaf node is also called a *situation*. Let $S_{\mathcal{T}}$ denote the set of non-leaf nodes. The *floret* of a situation $v \in S_{\mathcal{T}}$ is a subtree of $\mathcal{T}(\boldsymbol{X})$, denoted by $\mathcal{F}(v) = (V_{\mathcal{F}(v)}, E_{\mathcal{F}(v)})$. The vertex set of $\mathcal{F}(v)$ consists of v and the vertices in $S_{\mathcal{T}}$ connected from v by a directed edge in $E_{\mathcal{T}}$: $V_{\mathcal{F}(v)} = \{v\} \cup \{v' \in V_{\mathcal{T}} | e_{v,v'} \in E_{\mathcal{T}}\}$. The edge set of $\mathcal{F}(v)$ is a subset of $E_{\mathcal{T}}$ satisfying $E_{\mathcal{F}(v)} = \{e_{v,v'} : v' \in V_{\mathcal{T}}, e_{v,v'} \in E_{\mathcal{T}}\}$.

Let $\mathcal{F}_{\mathcal{T}} = \{\mathcal{F}(v)\}_{v \in S_{\mathcal{T}}}$ denote the collection of all florets on the tree $\mathcal{T}$. Let $\mu(v_0, v)$ denote a subpath from the root node v_0 to a node $v \in V_{\mathcal{T}}$ on the event tree. Every floret $\mathcal{F}(v)$ represents a random variable conditional on $\mu(v_0, v)$. We denote this conditional random variable by $X(v) = X|\mu(v_0, v)$ for $X \in \mathbf{X}$. Each emanating edge $e_{v,v'}$ of v is labelled by a value $x \in \mathbb{X}(v)$. Thus, every conditional variable X_i, $i \in \{1, ..., n\}$, is represented on a set of florets on the event tree, denoted by $\mathcal{F}(v(X_i))$. Previous research [3,4,6,7] has demonstrated the capability of a tree-like structure to encode the asymmetric information. The corresponding event tree $\mathcal{T}$ associated with this description can be asymmetric and non-stratified [2,4] so that the florets representing the same variable can have different distances from the root node v_0.

Figure 1 depicts an event tree for a conservator system. Its variables are $\mathbf{X} = (X_{cause}, X_{leak}, X_{alarm}, X_{s/b}, X_{fail})$. The categorical variable X_{cause} represents causes of defects and has three levels {temperature, seal/pipe, and breathing system}; X_{leak} is the oil leak indicator; X_{alarm} is the alarm indicator; $X_{s/b}$ is an indicator of whether there is a sight glass defect or a buchholz defect; and X_{fail} is a failure indicator. This tree is constructed under the assumption that the fault caused by low temperature is irrelevant to the sight glass or buchholz defect, labelled as s/b on the tree. The situations of the tree are annotated as $\{v_0, \cdots, v_{37}\}$, and the leaves are the unlabelled vertices. Since the last variable modelled on this tree is X_{fail}, the leaves represent the status of the conservator being failed or operational.

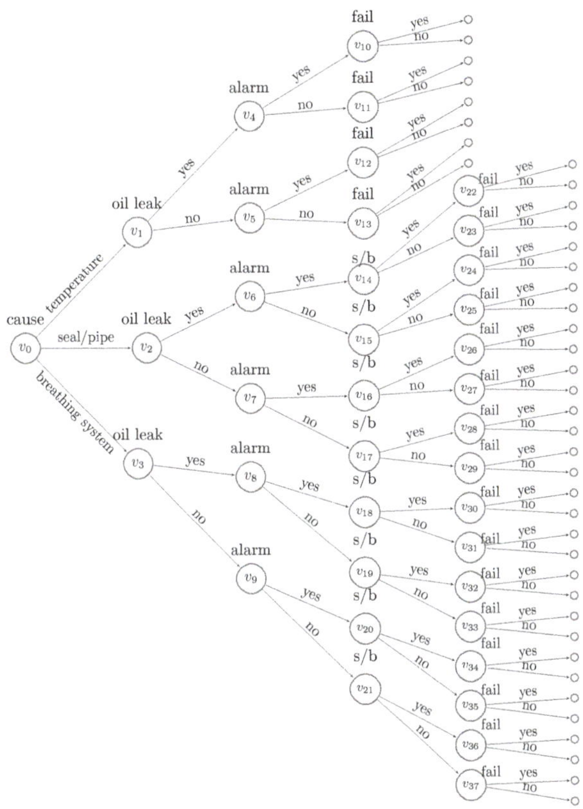

Figure 1. An event tree constructed for the conservator system of a transformer.

Let $\Lambda_{\mathcal{T}}$ denote the set of all root-to-leaf paths on the tree and $\lambda(v, v') \in \Lambda_{\mathcal{T}}$ denote the root-to-leaf paths passing through vertices $v, v' \in V_{\mathcal{T}}$. The vector $\boldsymbol{\theta}_v = \mathbb{P}(X(v)) = \mathbb{P}(X|\mu(v_0, v))$ is called the vector of primitive probabilities. Let $\boldsymbol{\theta}_{\mathcal{T}} = (\boldsymbol{\theta}_v)_{v \in V_{\mathcal{T}}}$, which satisfies $\sum_{v' \in ch(v)} \theta_{v,v'} = 1$ and $\theta_{v,v'} \in (0, 1)$ for all $v \in V_{\mathcal{T}}$, where $ch(v) = \{v' \in V_{\mathcal{T}} | e_{v,v'} \in E_{\mathcal{T}}\}$. Then, the pair $(\mathcal{T}(\mathbf{X}), \boldsymbol{\theta}_{\mathcal{T}})$ indexes the *probability tree* [2,3] defined over $\mathbf{X}$.

The BN is capable of handling the missing data whenever this applies to all values of a pre-assigned set of variables by assigning a missingness indicator to each unobservable variable within that set. It is, therefore, possible to use the BN as a framework for identifying when causal hypotheses are identifiable in this rather restricted setting. The associated analyses use various graphically stated criteria—such as the front-door and the back-door criteria—see e.g., [11–13]. However, unfortunately, the types of missingness that routinely occur in reliability—and, in particular, those associated with the data we collect when performing routine maintenance—are rarely missing across the original random vector associated with the system in this sort of symmetric way. This is because we only learn about those parts of a system that we have chosen to inspect.

In contrast, the probability tree provides a natural and more flexible way to visualise and model the context-specific missingness, where the unobservability of the variable partially depends on which path it lies on the tree. Here, we import the informed missingness into the event tree by defining the *floret-dependent missingness* [14]. Thus, consider a floret $\mathcal{F}(v)$, if the value of the corresponding variable $X(v)$ is unobservable, then we classify this floret into $\mathcal{F}(v) \in \mathcal{F}^M$.

On the other hand, if conditioned on $\mu(v_0, v)$, the value of the variable $X(v)$ is always observed, and then the corresponding floret is classified into $\mathcal{F}(v) \in \mathcal{F}^O$. Accordingly, we have two subsets of florets, $\mathcal{F}^M$ and $\mathcal{F}^O$, representing unobservable florets and fully observed florets, respectively. Then, $\mathcal{F}^M \cap \mathcal{F}^O = \emptyset$ and $\mathcal{F}^M \cup \mathcal{F}^O = \mathcal{F}_\mathcal{T}$. For every unobservable floret $\mathcal{F}(v_j) \in \mathcal{F}^M$, we define a *missing floret indicator* as:

$$B_{\mathcal{F}(v_j)} = \begin{cases} 1 & \text{if } x(v_j) \text{ is missing,} \\ 0 & \text{otherwise.} \end{cases} \tag{1}$$

Then, $B_{\mathcal{F}(v_j)}$ represents the conditional missingness and

$$\mathbb{P}(B_{\mathcal{F}(v_j)} = 1) = \mathbb{P}(X(v_j) \text{ missing} | \mu(v_0, v_j)). \tag{2}$$

When $\mathbb{P}(B_{\mathcal{F}(v_j)} = 1) \in (0,1)$, we construct a floret representing this indicator, denote this by $\mathcal{F}(v(B_{\mathcal{F}(v_j)}))$, and call it a *missing indicator floret*. We then reconstruct an event tree by importing the missing indicator florets on to $\mathcal{T}$. We call this a *missingness event tree* (m-tree). Here, we assume that $B_{\mathcal{F}(v_j)}$ precedes $X(v_j)$, denoted by $B_{\mathcal{F}(v_j)} \prec X(v_j)$. In particular $\mathcal{F}(v_j)$ is appended to the edge emanating from $v(B_{\mathcal{F}(v_j)})$ labelled by $B_{\mathcal{F}(v_j)} = 0$. This artificially introduced ordering has already been shown to be useful for interpreting an event tree constructed with informed missingness [8]. The m-tree then has a new class of florets $\mathcal{F}^{MI} = \mathcal{F}(v(\boldsymbol{B}))$ for $\boldsymbol{B} = \{B_\mathcal{F}\}_{\mathcal{F} \in \mathcal{F}^M}$, which is the set of missing indicator florets. The variables associated to the m-tree are expanded to $(\boldsymbol{X}, \boldsymbol{B})$. We denote the topology of the m-tree by $\mathcal{T}(\boldsymbol{X}, \boldsymbol{B})$. An example of the missingness event tree is shown in Figure 2.

Having a missingness event tree, we further elicit a *missingness staged tree* from $\mathcal{T}(\boldsymbol{X}, \boldsymbol{B})$. For two situations v and w, if $\mathcal{F}(v)$ and $\mathcal{F}(w)$ represent the same variable, then these two situations are in the same stage whenever $\boldsymbol{\theta}_v = \boldsymbol{\theta}_w$ [3], and the emanating edge $e_{v,v'}$ is labelled the same value of X as $e_{w,w'}$ when $\theta_{v,v'} = \theta_{w,w'}$. Here, we relax the restrictions for a *stratified staged tree* where two situations in the same stage have the same distance from the root node [2,4]. For example, v_{18} can be in the same stage as v_{38} in the missingness event tree in Figure 2, similar example see [8].

Here, we assume that situations along the same root-to-leaf path cannot be in the same stage. This is the *square-free* condition defined by Collazo et al. [3]. Vertices in the same stage are assigned a unique colour, and the edges emanating from the same stage with the same label are assigned the same colour. Such a coloured tree that embeds context-specific conditional independence relations is a missingness staged tree. Let $U = \{u_1, .., u_l\}$ denote the set of stages in the m-tree. Let $u(X_i)$ represent the set of stages associated with variable X_i and $U(\boldsymbol{X}) = \{u(X_1), \cdots, u(X_n)\}$. Let $U(\boldsymbol{B}) = U/U(\boldsymbol{X})$ denote the set of stages associated to the missing floret indicators. An example of a missingness staged tree of the m-tree in Figure 2 is depicted in Figure 3.

Two situations $v_j, v_k \in u_i \in U$ in the same stage are in the same *position* w if the rooted subtrees $\mathcal{T}_{v_j}(\boldsymbol{X}, \boldsymbol{B})$ and $\mathcal{T}_{v_k}(\boldsymbol{X}, \boldsymbol{B})$ are isomorphic. This clustering gives a finer partition of vertices than U, denoted by $W = \{w_1, ..., w_m\}$. A *missingness chain event graph* (MCEG) $\mathcal{C}(\boldsymbol{X}, \boldsymbol{B}) = (V_\mathcal{C}, E_\mathcal{C})$ can be constructed from a missingness staged tree as follows. A sink node w_∞ is created by merging all the leaves of $\mathcal{T}(\boldsymbol{X}, \boldsymbol{B})$. Then, the vertex set is $V_\mathcal{C} = W \bigcup w_\infty$.

For any two $w, w' \in V_\mathcal{C}$, we create an edge for every $v \in w$ and the child node $v' \in ch(v) \in V_\mathcal{T}$, which belongs to the position w', where the annotating edge probability is the same as that of $e_{v,v'} \in E_\mathcal{T}$ and is inherited from the original tree. The colours of the vertices and edges of the MCEG are the same as the corresponding stages and edges in the missingness staged tree [15].

Note that the events on the event tree are chronologically ordered. By definition, a cause comes before its effects. We can be reasonably confident in providing $\boldsymbol{X}$ with a plausible order. For example, the trajectory of the events that lead to a machine's failure always starts with a cause, followed by symptoms, and terminates with a failure. Therefore, we can construct event trees for analysing system failures following this order. In this case, having failed or not is always modelled on the leaves of the tree. Examples are shown in Figures 1 and 2.

It follows that, for this special application of CEGs in system reliability, it is convenient to adapt the semantics and to replace the sink node w_∞ defined above by w_∞^f and w_∞^n. In this way, w_∞^f is the receiving node of the edges labelled by a failure, while w_∞^n is the receiving node of the edges labelled by an operational condition.

Thus, we can classify the root-to-sink paths into two categories: failure paths and deteriorating paths. The former terminate in w_∞^f, while the latter terminate in w_∞^n. Figure 4 gives an example of such a MCEG derived from Figure 3.

It is possible to perform conjugate inference on an idle MCEG even when the data is informed censored [8,16]. This enables us to greatly speed up the search for good explanatory models. The simplest prior to set up in this context assumes each stage vector $\boldsymbol{\theta}_u = (\theta_{u_1}, ..., \theta_{u_l})$ is independently Dirichlet with parameters $(\alpha_{u1}, ..., \alpha_{um_u})$ [3,8]. This is identical to the case when there are no missingness indicators:

$$f(\boldsymbol{\theta}|\mathcal{C}(\boldsymbol{X}, \boldsymbol{B})) = \prod_{u \in U} \frac{\Gamma(\sum_{j=1}^{m_u} \alpha_{uj})}{\prod_{j=1}^{m_u} \Gamma(\alpha_{uj})} \prod_{j=1}^{m_u} \theta_{uj}^{\alpha_{uj}}. \tag{3}$$

Let $\alpha_u = \sum_{j=1}^{m_u} \alpha_{uj}$ so that, in particular, the equivalent sample size is $\alpha = \sum_{u \in U} \sum_{j=1}^{m_u} \alpha_{uj}$.

Then, given a set of observations D, the posterior can be computed in a closed form due to Dirichlet-multinomial conjugacy. Thus,

$$\begin{aligned} f(\boldsymbol{\theta}|D, \mathcal{C}(\boldsymbol{X}, \boldsymbol{B})) &= \prod_{u \in U} f(\boldsymbol{\theta}_u|D, \mathcal{C}(\boldsymbol{X}, \boldsymbol{B})) \\ &= \prod_{u \in U} \frac{\Gamma(\sum_{j=1}^{m_u} \alpha_{uj+})}{\prod_{j=1}^{m_u} \Gamma(\alpha_{uj+})} \prod_{j=1}^{m_u} \theta_{uj}^{\alpha_{uj+}}, \end{aligned} \tag{4}$$

where $\alpha_{uj+} = \alpha_{uj} + n_{uj}$, and $\boldsymbol{\alpha}_{u+} = \boldsymbol{\alpha}_u + \boldsymbol{n}_u$ is the updated parameter vector.

The log-likelihood score for a MCEG $\mathcal{C}(\boldsymbol{X}, \boldsymbol{B})$ can be decomposed into local scores associated with the variables $\boldsymbol{X}$ and the missingness indicators $\boldsymbol{B}$.

$$\log Q(\mathcal{C}(\boldsymbol{X}, \boldsymbol{B})) = \log f_{\mathcal{C}(\boldsymbol{X}, \boldsymbol{B})}(D) = \sum_{i=1}^{n} \log Q_{u(X_i)}(\mathcal{C}(\boldsymbol{X}, \boldsymbol{B})) + \sum_{u \in U(\boldsymbol{B})} \log Q_u(\mathcal{C}(\boldsymbol{X}, \boldsymbol{B})) \tag{5}$$

We can explicitly compute the log-likelihood in a closed form:

$$\log Q(\mathcal{C}(\boldsymbol{X},\boldsymbol{B})) = \sum_{u \in U} (\log\Gamma(\alpha_u) - \log\Gamma(\alpha_{u+}) - \sum_{j=1}^{m_u} (\log\Gamma(\alpha_{uj}) - \log\Gamma(\alpha_{uj+}))). \quad (6)$$

To elicit a best scoring CEG from an event tree, it is necessary to search over all possible orderings over the variables modelled by the tree when the total order over the variables is unknown. The event tree is defined to be built with respect to $\boldsymbol{X}$, and the associated missingness event tree is built as a function of $\mathcal{T}(\boldsymbol{X})$ with appropriate hypotheses of missingness. Therefore, even when the dataset has missing values, we still only search over permutations over $\boldsymbol{X}$ to find an appropriate ordering that best explains the observed process.

Let Π denote an ordering of $\boldsymbol{X}$. This could be a set of partial orderings. All variables represented on the m-tree can automatically be ordered given Π. We denote the m-tree with a specified ordering Π by $\mathcal{T}(\boldsymbol{X}(\Pi),\boldsymbol{B}) = (V_{\mathcal{T}}, E_{\mathcal{T}})$.

It is non-trivial to identify causal structure from a finite observational dataset. However, the idle model first needs to be estimated before any causal relations can be explored. Many advances have been made in casting the causal discovery as a Bayesian model selection problem [2,17,18]. The MAP structural learning algorithm is a popular and well-developed tool for selecting a best topology of CEGs that best explains the data.

Under the hypothesis that there are no unobserved confounders [2], we render the best scoring structure selected by the MAP algorithm causal and assume it is the model of the idle system when there is no intervention imported. This enables us to further perform causal analysis. Given such a causal graph, we can derive causal hypotheses from the structure and estimate causal effects under different hypothesised underlying causal mechanisms.

Sometimes there is only a putative partial order rather than total order on the variables $\boldsymbol{X}$ whose causal relationship needs to be explored. However, in this setting we can still perform the search over candidate CEGs for the best fitting model, providing that the missing variables only extend to later nodes of the tree.

Cowell and Smith [2] and Collazo et al. [3] presented a recursive algorithm to find the best sink variable for every subset of $\boldsymbol{X}$ ordered by increasing size. This algorithm can be simply adapted for the tree built for the informedly missing data. Let $\boldsymbol{X}_j \subseteq \boldsymbol{X}$ denote the subset of variables whose ordering is needed to be learned and $\Pi_{\boldsymbol{X}_j}$ denote the best partial ordering over $\boldsymbol{X}_j$.

Then, through applying the algorithm designed by [2,3] on every $\boldsymbol{X}_j$, we can find the best ordering over the variables defined on the tree, where $\Pi = \{\Pi_{\boldsymbol{X}_j}\}_j$. Here, we search over subspaces $\mathbb{X}_{j_1} \times \cdots \times \mathbb{X}_{j_k}$ for $X_{j_1}, ..., X_{j_k} \in \boldsymbol{X}_j$ and compute the local scores with respect to the corresponding $\boldsymbol{Y}$. In particular, for every $\boldsymbol{X}_j^{(l)} = \{X_{j_1}, ..., X_{j_l}\}$, where $l \in \{1, ..., k-1\}$, we find a best sink variable $X' \in \boldsymbol{X}_j^{(l)}$ for every $\boldsymbol{X}_j^{(k-1)} \subseteq \boldsymbol{X}_j^{(k)}$ that has been ordered appropriately. The best sink variable X' is found by computing the local score of the best subtree spanned by $\boldsymbol{X}_j^{(k-1)} \cup \{X_s\}$ for every $X_s \in \boldsymbol{X}_j^{(k)}$ together with the corresponding missingness indicators.

The MAP score can be evaluated directly from the local scores that have been computed because the total score is the sum of local scores as shown in Equation (5). Two MCEGs $\mathcal{C}_1$ and $\mathcal{C}_2$ with respect to the same data set can be compared by the log-posterior Bayes factor. Suppose both trees have Dirichlet priors whose hyperparameters are $\boldsymbol{\alpha}_1$ and $\boldsymbol{\alpha}_2$. The Bayes factor, then, has a closed form [3]:

$$lpBF(\mathcal{C}_1, \mathcal{C}_2) = \log q(\mathcal{C}_1) - \log q(\mathcal{C}_2) + \log Q(\mathcal{C}_1) - \log Q(\mathcal{C}_2), \quad (7)$$

where $\log q(\mathcal{C}_i)$ denotes the log prior. Different priors over models can be chosen given expert judgement on different missingness mechanisms and conditional dependencies.

When using a uniform prior, $\log q(\mathcal{C}_1) - \log q(\mathcal{C}_2) = \frac{1}{N_C} - \frac{1}{N_C} = 0$, where N_C denotes the total number of models.

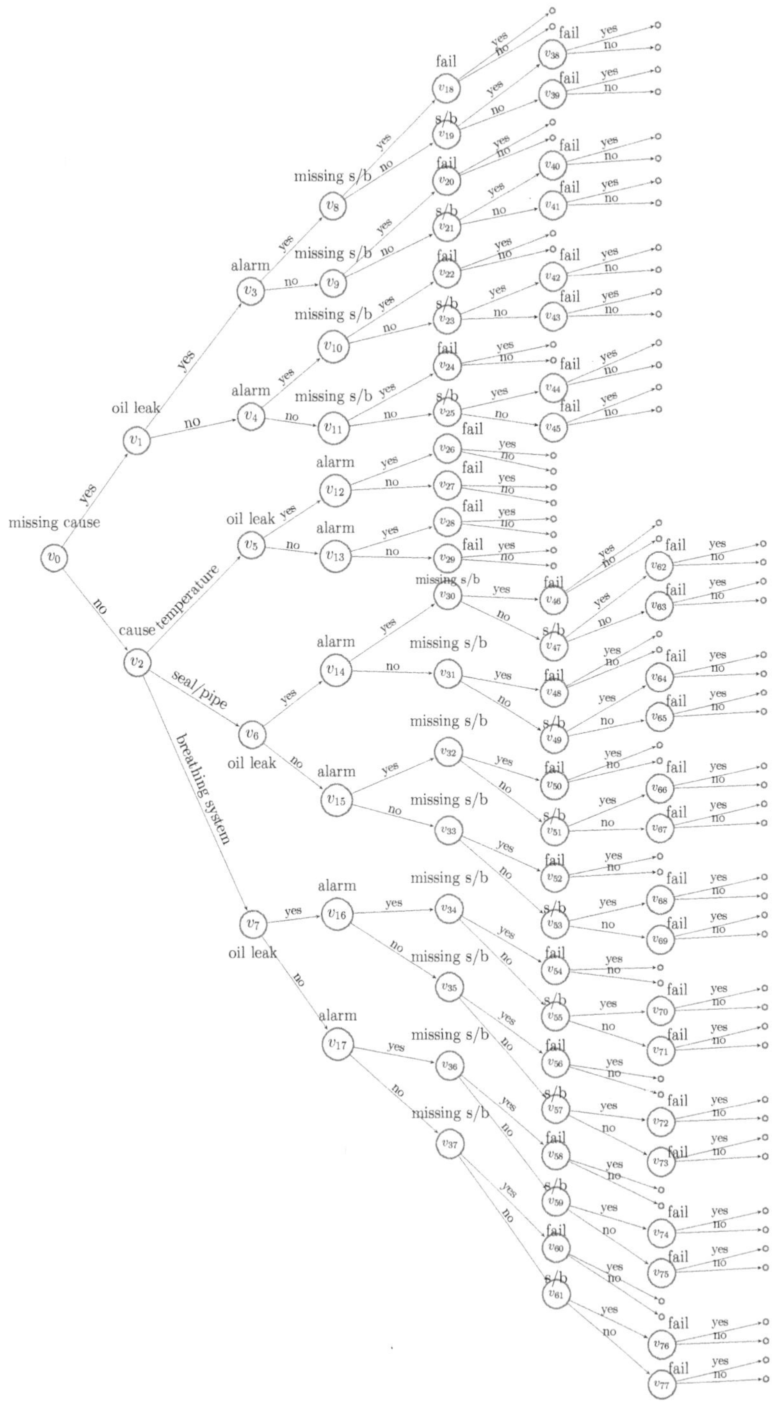

Figure 2. A missingness event tree constructed from Figure 1.

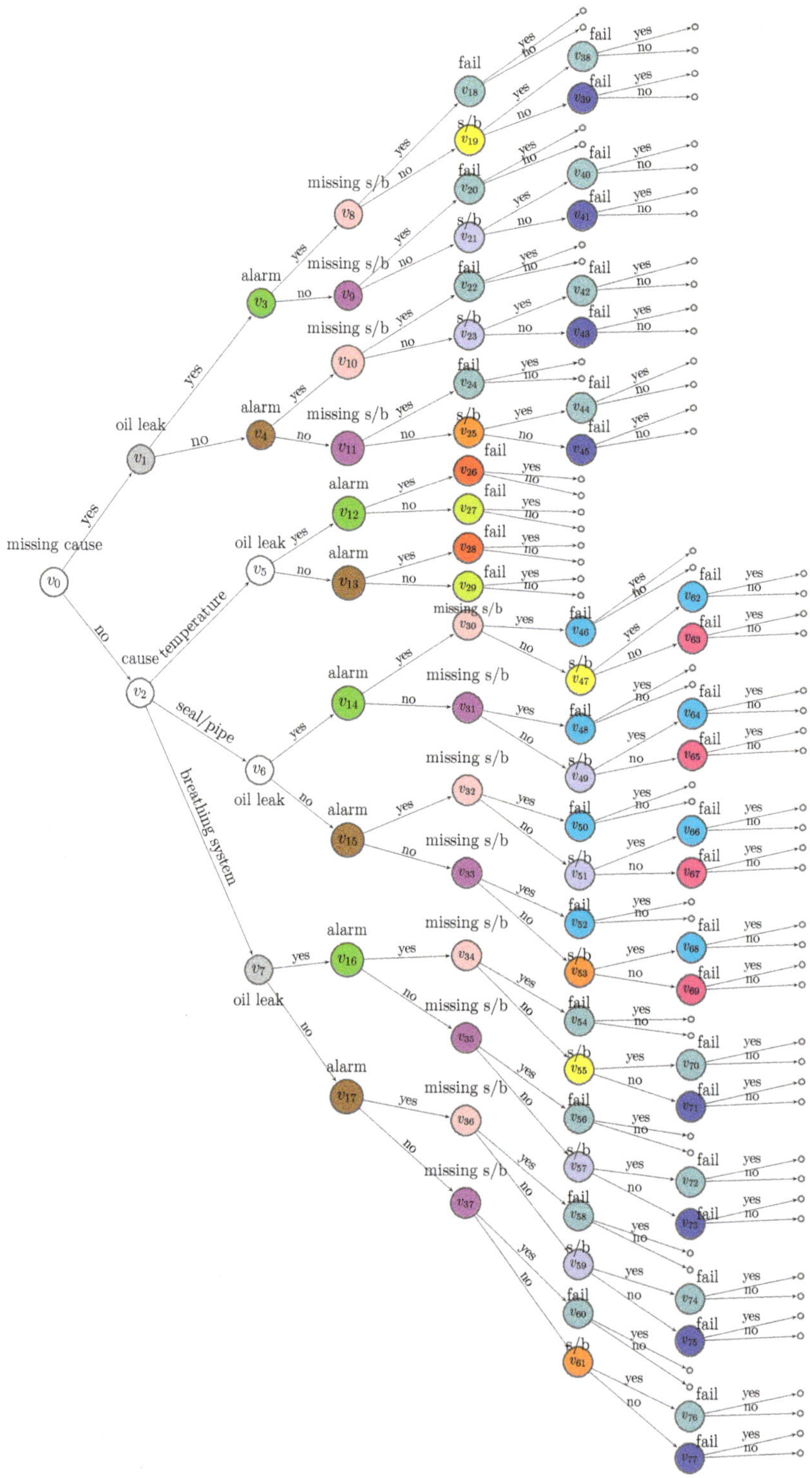

Figure 3. A missingness staged tree of the m-tree in Figure 2.

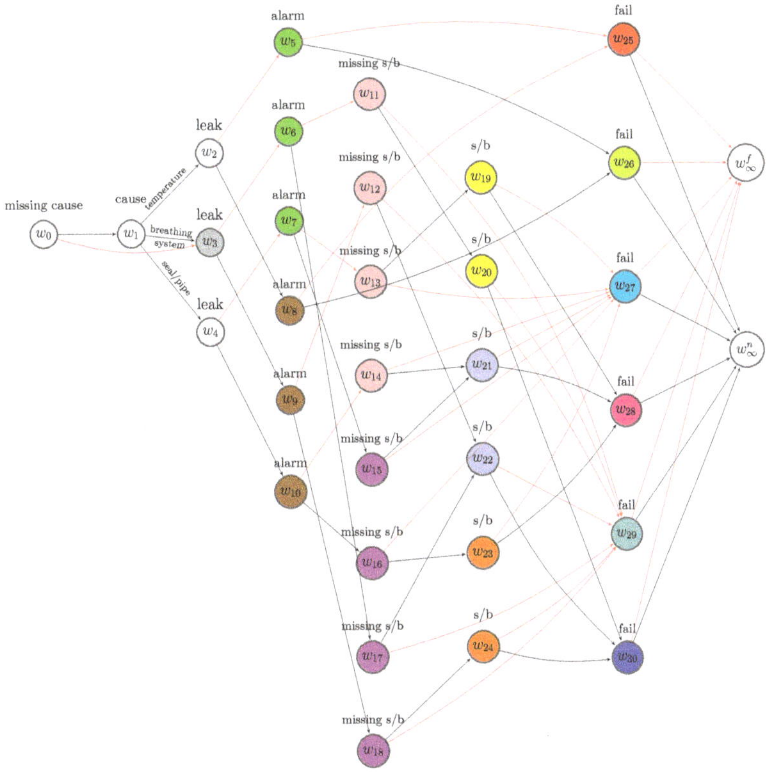

Figure 4. A MCEG derived from Figure 3. For simplicity, the edges labelled "no" are coloured in red.

3. Causal Algebras for Routine Maintenance

By assuming the best scoring CEG causal and treating it as the idle system, one can always design experiments to collect data under the influence of interventions, and thus we can estimate the causal effects from the partially observed system. By controlling certain events on the tree, the semantics of a causal CEG allow us to explore its effect on the events that lie downstream of the controlled events along the root-to-sink paths. For a reliability analysis, it is extremely useful to trace and discover the potential causes of abnormal conditions or failures. By designing causal algebras for different interventions, we can make predictive inferences about the effects of a variety of types of maintenance and thus improve the prediction of system failures.

Having defined the remedial intervention on the CEG for the reliability system in [9], here, we investigate a new class of intervention regime. In the reliability literature, there are two main categories of maintenance: *corrective maintenance* (CM) and *preventive maintenance* (PM) [19]. CM takes place after a failure, while PM often refers to a scheduled maintenance that helps to identify and prevent problems during inspections before a failure occurs [20]. In this section, we carefully customise causal algebras for the intervention in light of the latter case, calling this a *routine intervention*. A routine intervention not only has an impact on the lifetime of the maintained equipment but also affects the likelihood of different defects that may occur in the equipment.

3.1. Effects on Lifetime

In the context of reliability, the interventions largely consist of replacing failed components of the system. This type of intervention—unusual in most causal analyses—requires special attention, especially as there are some very well-known effects of such interventions that need to be incorporated before it is possible to realistically model the effects of interventions. In particular, when describing the failure of equipment, the bathtub effect [20] is widely applicable. This divides the lifetime of an equipment into three periods: the early life of a new component has a decreasing failure rate; this is followed by a period with a constant failure rate; the failure rate rises during the wear-out period [21]. A Weibull distribution whose density is given by

$$f(t) = \frac{\beta}{\eta}(\frac{t}{\eta})^{\beta-1}e^{-(\frac{t}{\eta})^{\beta}} \tag{8}$$

is often used by reliability engineers to model this varying hazard [20], where the scale parameter is $\eta > 0$, and the shape parameter is $\beta > 0$. The survival function takes the form:

$$1 - F(t) = e^{-(\frac{t}{\eta})^{\beta}}. \tag{9}$$

Let $\Lambda_{\mathcal{C}}$ denote the set of all root-to-sink paths on the MCEG $\mathcal{C}(\boldsymbol{X}(\Pi), \boldsymbol{B})$. Then, the lifetime of the repaired equipment can be modelled on the associated root-to-sink paths, denoted by $\tilde{\Lambda} \subseteq \Lambda_{\mathcal{C}}$. For $\lambda \in \tilde{\Lambda}$, let $T(\lambda)$ represent the total lifetime of the equipment when the failure trajectory is modelled on the path λ.

For a repairable system, the PM prolongs the life of the component [22–24]. By adopting the Arithmetic Reduction of Age (ARA) model, which assumes the life of the equipment is shortened up to proportionality [23], we now establish methods to evaluate the effect of the scheduled PM on the equipment's lifetime.

Let Z_s^{λ} represent the failure time of an equipment with observed age s given a failure process that is modelled on the path λ. Then, the survival function is

$$\mathbb{P}(Z_s^{\lambda} > t) = \frac{1 - F_{\lambda}(s+t)}{1 - F_{\lambda}(s)} = e^{-(\frac{s+t}{\eta_{\lambda}})^{\beta_{\lambda}} + (\frac{s}{\eta_{\lambda}})^{\beta_{\lambda}}}, \tag{10}$$

where $F_{\lambda}(\cdot)$ denotes the reliability distribution for failure trajectory λ.

In an idle system, for $\lambda \in \tilde{\Lambda}$, $T(\lambda)$ has the same distribution as Z_0^{λ}, i.e., $T(\lambda) \stackrel{d}{=} Z_0^{\lambda}$. Thus,

$$\mathbb{P}(T(\lambda) > t) = \mathbb{P}(Z_0^{\lambda} > t) = 1 - F_{\lambda}(t). \tag{11}$$

Preventive maintenance can be scheduled periodically. However, for simplicity, we only demonstrate the effect of a single time routine maintenance in this paper. We suppose that an equipment is diagnosed during a routine maintenance and is repaired at age τ. Kijima [24] and Guessoum and Aupiedy [23] introduced a parameter representing the degree of repair, denoted by $A \in [0,1]$. When $A = 0$, the repair is *perfect* and restores the maintained part to *as good as new* (AGAN). On the other hand, $A = 1$ corresponds to a *minimal repair*, after which the maintained part is functioning as it was just prior to the repair.

Since the repaired equipment is rejuvenated, the virtual age [23,24] after maintenance is then $A\tau$. Let $T^*(\lambda)$ denote the post-intervention time to failure. Then, after a routine intervention, the residual lifetime of the maintained equipment has the same distribution as $Z_{A\tau}^{\lambda}$. Therefore,

$$\mathbb{P}(T^*(\lambda) > t) = \mathbb{P}(Z_{A\tau}^{\lambda} > t) = \frac{1 - F_{\lambda}(t + A\tau)}{1 - F_{\lambda}(A\tau)}. \tag{12}$$

3.2. Manipulations on the MCEG

If $X_i \in \boldsymbol{X}$ takes value x_{ij}, let $e(x_{ij}) \in E_{\mathcal{C}}$ denote the edges labelled by this value that emanate from $w(X_i)$. The set of vertices receiving $e(x_{ij})$ are represented by $w(x_{ij})$. The path related probability, denoted by $\pi(\lambda)$ for $\lambda \in \Lambda_{\mathcal{C}}$, can then be factorised as:

$$\pi(\lambda) = \prod_{e \in E_\lambda} \theta_e, \tag{13}$$

where E_λ represents a collection of edges lying along the path λ.

When there is a routine intervention, we are only interested in the process portrayed by the deteriorating paths. We denote this set of paths by $\Lambda_{x_{fail,0}} = \Lambda(e(x_{fail,0}))$, where $x_{fail,0}$ represents $X_{fail} = 0$. Whatever this preventive action is, an analogue of the *do*-operation $do(X_{fail} = 0)$ is imported into the idle MCEG. Thus, we force $e(x_{fail,0})$ to have probability 1 and $e(x_{fail,1})$ to have probability 0, or, equivalently, we manipulate $\Lambda_{x_{fail,0}}$. Therefore, we always have the post-intervened path probability:

$$\hat{\pi}^{\Lambda_{x_{fail,0}}}(\lambda) = \begin{cases} \frac{\prod_{e \in E_\lambda} \theta_e}{\theta_{e(x_{fail,0})}} & \text{if } \lambda \in \Lambda_{x_{fail,0}}; \\ 0 & \text{otherwise,} \end{cases} \tag{14}$$

This is a singular manipulation on the MCEG and yields a manipulated MCEG with respect to $\Lambda_{x_{fail,0}}$. We denote this by $\hat{\mathcal{C}}^{\Lambda_{x_{fail,0}}}$.

Depending on the preventive action taken, other manipulations can also be imported into the MCEG in addition to the singular manipulation on $\Lambda_{x_{fail,0}}$. We next demonstrate two scenarios of composite manipulations.

3.2.1. Composite Singular Manipulations under Routine Intervention

In this section, we discuss the situation where the preventive maintenance perfectly repaired a problem, and, as a consequence of this repair, an event x_r is forced to occur. The event x_r is labelled on a set of edges $e(x_r)$ whose receiving nodes are $w(x_r)$ and emanating nodes are $pa(w(x_r))$. In this case, the unit will be forced to pass through every edge $e \in e(x_r)$ with probability 1. We, therefore, have a composition of singular manipulations, and the manipulated events are $\boldsymbol{x} = \{x_{fail,0}, x_r\}$. On an MCEG, the controlled event is represented by

$$\Lambda_{\boldsymbol{x}} = \Lambda(e(\boldsymbol{x})) = \Lambda(e(x_{fail,0})) \cap \Lambda(e(x_r)). \tag{15}$$

Let $\mathcal{F}(e(\boldsymbol{x}))$ denote the set of florets that the edges $e(\boldsymbol{x})$ lie in.

If we are interested in the effect of the routine maintenance on event y, then, on the MCEG, we represent it by $\Lambda_y = \Lambda(e(y))$. The set of florets that $e(y)$ lies in is denoted by $\mathcal{F}(e(y))$.

Given a CEG, let $\pi(\Lambda_y || \Lambda_{\boldsymbol{x}})$ denote the probability of observing event y given a manipulation that forces the events $\boldsymbol{x}$ to occur. We aim to estimate this probability from the observed data and to demonstrate that the effects of a routine intervention are identifiable. We have shown in [9] that causal effects from a singular manipulation are estimable, also called *recoverable*, by adapting the back-door theorem [5]. Here, we simply extend our previous results [9] so that it now also applies to the types of composite manipulations that we discuss here.

The MCEG provides flexible choices of events $\boldsymbol{z}$ to be the back-door partition so that $\Lambda_{\boldsymbol{z}}$ partitions $\Lambda_{\mathcal{C}}$ [6,7]. We first impose a constraint on $\boldsymbol{z}$ that $\mathcal{F}(e(\boldsymbol{z})) \nsubseteq \mathcal{F}^{MI}$, i.e., that cannot be a missingness indicator. This is to ensure that $\pi(\Lambda_y || \Lambda_{\boldsymbol{x}})$ can be estimated from the partially observed data [9]. Note that any of $\mathcal{F}(e(\boldsymbol{x})), \mathcal{F}(e(y)), \mathcal{F}(e(\boldsymbol{z}))$ might be unobservable. Let

$$\mathcal{F}_{\boldsymbol{x} \cup y \cup \boldsymbol{z}} = \{\mathcal{F} : \mathcal{F} \in \mathcal{F}(e(\boldsymbol{x})) \cup \mathcal{F}(e(y)) \cup \mathcal{F}(e(\boldsymbol{z})) \text{ and } \mathcal{F} \notin \mathcal{F}^{MI}\}. \tag{16}$$

We define the *manifest paths* to be the largest set of root-to-sink paths on the MCEG passing along edges labelled by x, y and z. We let $\boldsymbol{b}_{\mathcal{F}(e(\boldsymbol{x})),0} = \{b_{\mathcal{F},0}\}_{\mathcal{F}\in\mathcal{F}(e(\boldsymbol{x}))}$ denote the set of missingness indicators of florets $\mathcal{F}(e(\boldsymbol{x}))$ taking value 0, i.e., values of the corresponding floret variables are observed. Then, the manifest paths are

$$\Lambda(w(\boldsymbol{b}_{\mathcal{F}_{\boldsymbol{x}\cup y\cup \boldsymbol{z},0}})) = \Lambda(w(\boldsymbol{b}_{\mathcal{F}(e(\boldsymbol{x})),0})) \cap \Lambda(w(\boldsymbol{b}_{\mathcal{F}(e(y)),0})) \cap \Lambda(w(\boldsymbol{b}_{\mathcal{F}(e(\boldsymbol{z})),0})). \tag{17}$$

We can construct a sub-MCEG $\mathcal{C}^M$ using the manifest paths. Let the collection of the root-to-sink paths of this subgraph be $\Lambda_{\mathcal{C}^M} = \Lambda(w(\boldsymbol{b}_{\mathcal{F}_{\boldsymbol{x}\cup y\cup \boldsymbol{z},0}}))$. We call this sub-MCEG the *manifest MCEG*. This construction ensures that there is no edge in the manifest MCEG associated with a controlled event, effect, or partition event being missing.

We next reconstruct $\pi(\Lambda_y||\Lambda_{\boldsymbol{x}})$ from the manifest MCEG. Let $\pi^{\Lambda_{\mathcal{C}^M}}(\Lambda_y||\Lambda_{\boldsymbol{x}})$ denote the probability of observing an event y given a manipulation forcing $\boldsymbol{x}$ to happen within the manifest MCEG. Note that the manipulated MCEG is a subgraph of the manifest MCEG. For a singular manipulation on $\Lambda_{\boldsymbol{x}}$, the manipulated paths on the manifest MCEG are

$$\Lambda_* = \Lambda(w(\boldsymbol{b}_{\mathcal{F}_{\boldsymbol{x}\cup y\cup \boldsymbol{z},0}})) \cap \Lambda_{\boldsymbol{x}}. \tag{18}$$

The manipulated MCEG with respect to Λ_* is then denoted by $\hat{\mathcal{C}}^{\Lambda_*}$ and satisfies $\Lambda_{\hat{\mathcal{C}}^{\Lambda_*}} = \Lambda_*$.

Theorem 1 (The m-back-door criterion for composite singular manipulations). *When a dataset has missing values, the effect of a singular manipulation on $\boldsymbol{x}$ on y is identifiable on the MCEG if we can find a partition $\Lambda_{\boldsymbol{z}}$ of $\Lambda_{\mathcal{C}^M}$ such that*

$$\pi^{\Lambda_{\mathcal{C}^M}}(\Lambda_y||\Lambda_{\boldsymbol{x}}) = \sum_z \pi(\Lambda_y|\Lambda_{\boldsymbol{x}}, \Lambda_z, \Lambda(w(\boldsymbol{b}_{\mathcal{F}_{\boldsymbol{x}\cup y\cup \boldsymbol{z},0}})))\pi(\Lambda_z|\Lambda(w(\boldsymbol{b}_{\mathcal{F}_{\boldsymbol{x}\cup y\cup \boldsymbol{z},0}}))). \tag{19}$$

For the proof of this theorem, see [9,14].

Example 1. *Given the causal MCEG in Figure 4 of a conservator system, we demonstrate how the formulae defined above works for a specific routine maintenance that successfully prevents an oil leak. This is equivalent to importing a combination of $do(X_{fail} = 0)$ and $do(X_{leak} = 0)$ operations to the idle MCEG. The controlled events are $\boldsymbol{x} = \{x_{fail,0}, x_{leak,0}\}$. From Figure 4, we next identify the associated root-to-sink paths. In particular,*

$$\Lambda_{x_{fail,0}} = \bigcup_{w\in\{w_{25},\cdots,w_{30}\}} \Lambda(e_{w,w^n_\infty}), \tag{20}$$

$$\Lambda_{x_{leak,0}} = \Lambda(e_{w_2,w_8}) \cup \Lambda(e_{w_3,w_9}) \cup \Lambda(e_{w_4,w_{10}}), \tag{21}$$

and $\Lambda_{x_{fail,0},x_{leak,0}} = \Lambda_{x_{fail,0}} \cap \Lambda_{x_{leak,0}}$.

To next focus on alarm, the effect event is $x_{alarm,1}$. The associated set of paths is $\Lambda_{x_{alarm,1}} = \Lambda(e_{w_5,w_{25}}) \cup \Lambda(e_{w_6,w_{11}}) \cup \Lambda(e_{w_7,w_{13}}) \cup \Lambda(e_{w_8,w_{25}}) \cup \Lambda(e_{w_9,w_{12}}) \cup \Lambda(e_{w_{10},w_{14}})$. The causal query with respect to $\boldsymbol{x}$ is identifiable whenever $\pi(\Lambda_{x_{alarm,1}}||\Lambda_{x_{fail,0},x_{leak,0}})$ can be recovered from the MCEG by estimating it from the dataset with missing entries. There are a variety of possible choices for the partition events $\boldsymbol{z}$. Here, we simply let $\boldsymbol{z}$ be X_{cause} whose corresponding positions lie upstream of the controlled events $x_{leak,0}$ on the tree. The corresponding floret is, then, $\mathcal{F}(e(\boldsymbol{z}))$ $= \mathcal{F}(w_1)$.

We now construct the manifest MCEG and the manipulated MCEG in order to identify the effects of the intervention. Notice that the controlled events and the effect events are always observable in our example. Thus,

$$\Lambda(w(b_{\mathcal{F}(e(\boldsymbol{x})),0})) = (\bigcup_{w\in\{w_{25},\cdots,w_{30}\}} \Lambda(w)) \cap (\bigcup_{w\in\{w_2,w_3,w_4\}} \Lambda(w)) = \Lambda_{\mathcal{C}}, \tag{22}$$

$$\Lambda(w(b_{\mathcal{F}(e(\boldsymbol{y})),0})) = \bigcup_{w\in\{w_5,\cdots,w_{10}\}} = \Lambda_{\mathcal{C}}, \tag{23}$$

However, the back-door partition events might be missing. The collection of paths along which $\mathbf{z}$ *are observed is*

$$\Lambda(w(b_{\mathcal{F}(e(\mathbf{z})),0})) = \Lambda(w_1). \tag{24}$$

Following Equation (17), the manifest paths are $\Lambda(w(\boldsymbol{b}_{\mathcal{F}_{\mathbf{x}\cup\mathbf{y}\cup\mathbf{z},0}})) = \Lambda_{\mathcal{C}} \cap \Lambda(w_1) = \Lambda(w_1)$*. Thus, to investigate this, we construct the manifest MCEG with respect to* $\Lambda(w_1)$*. This is a subgraph of the idle MCEG in Figure 4 obtained by simply removing the edge* e_{w_0,w_3}*, which represents the causes that are missing. We further elicit the manipulated MCEG from the manifest MCEG. By the definition of the manipulated paths given in Equation (18), we select the manipulated paths from the manifest paths:* $\Lambda_* = \Lambda(w_1) \cap \Lambda_{x_{fail,0}, x_{leak,0}}$*. Since the intervention forces* $x_{fail,0}$ *and* $x_{leak,0}$ *to happen, the events* $x_{fail,1}$ *and* $x_{leak,1}$ *should never be observed. Thus, the probability of a manipulated path passing along the edges* $e(x_{fail,1})$ *and* $e(x_{leak,1})$ *is 0.*

Equivalently, the positions $w(x_{fail,1}) = w_\infty^f$ *and* $w(e(x_{leak,1})) = \{w_5, w_6, w_7\}$ *should never be passed through by any path in the manipulated graph. Then, by removing the nodes and edges that are not traversed by the manipulated paths in the manifest MCEG, we can derive the manipulated MCEG with respect to* Λ_**, see Figure 5. We can then estimate the causal effects on alarm using the formula given in the m-back-door theorem defined above. The conditional path probabilities in Equation (19) can simply be evaluated using the factorisation of the corresponding primitive probabilities in the manipulated MCEG.*

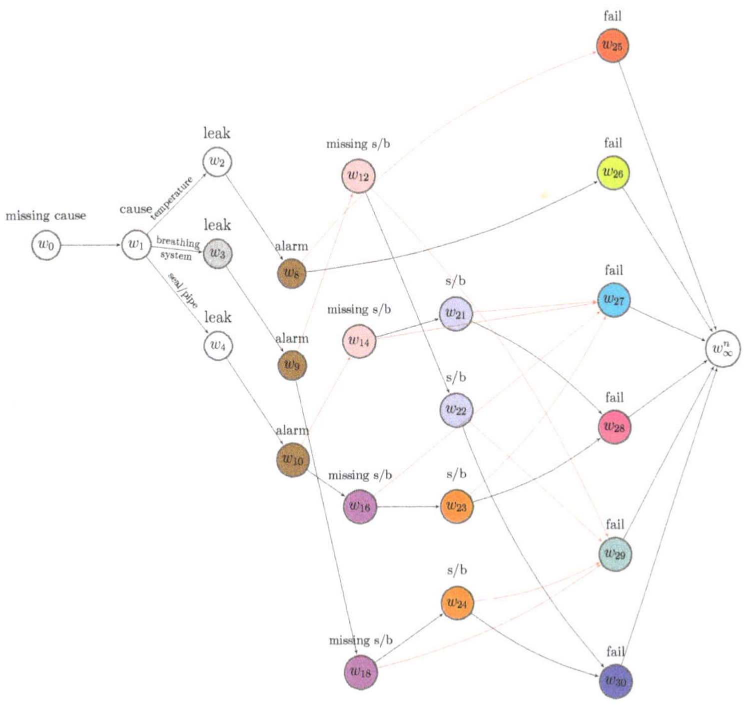

Figure 5. The manipulated MCEG when controlling $x_{leak,0}$ and $x_{fail,0}$

3.2.2. Composite Singular and Stochastic Manipulations under Routine Intervention

During routine inspections, the field engineers may clean the components, check the oil level and leakage, replace some units, and so on [25]. Since there are different types of repair and because the degree of this repair varies, the manipulations enacted by the routine intervention could be more complicated than forcing a specific event to happen. In fact, repairing or replacing an equipment could affect multiple units or multiple defects of a unit.

Therefore, depending on the repaired subcomponent and the degree of repair, multiple florets can be influenced separately and simultaneously. Thus, a routine intervention could introduce more uncertainty to the probability distributions over these relevant florets. Therefore, the distributions of some of the primitive probabilities may need to be reassigned. This manipulation is then called a stochastic manipulation on the MCEG.

Unlike a remedial intervention [9], a stochastic manipulation induced by a routine intervention is not restricted to root causes. Consider a floret $\mathcal{F}$ whose distribution is manipulated by a routine intervention. The events represented by this floret could be defects or symptoms of the maintained equipment.

Let $\boldsymbol{x}_r$ denote the controlled events of a routine intervention. Suppose we can find the edges labelled by these events, denoted by $e(\boldsymbol{x}_r)$, then $\mathcal{F}(e(\boldsymbol{x}_r))$ is the set of florets whose distribution are manipulated under the routine intervention. Let $\boldsymbol{w}^* = pa(w(\boldsymbol{x}_r))$ denote the set of emanating nodes of edges $e(\boldsymbol{x}_r)$. We can then conclude that $\mathcal{F}(\boldsymbol{w}^*) = \mathcal{F}(e(\boldsymbol{x}_r))$.

For $w \in \boldsymbol{w}^*$, we update the probability distribution after a routine intervention via the transformation:

$$\hat{q}(\boldsymbol{\theta}_w) = G[q(\boldsymbol{\theta}_w)] \tag{25}$$

where $\hat{q}(\cdot)$ represents the post-intervened distribution. The transformation G preserves the properties of the transition probabilities so that $\sum_{e \in E(w)} \theta_e = 1$ and $\theta_e > 0$.

Motivated by the steady model [26,27], one straightforward option is to map distributions to distributions through non-linear state space models. A possible transformation to increase uncertainty in a distribution is the *power steady transformation* [26,28], which can be characterised by information loss after the intervention takes.

$$\hat{q}(\boldsymbol{\theta}_w) \propto q(\boldsymbol{\theta}_w)^{\phi}, \tag{26}$$

where $\phi \in (0,1]$. Assume that the value of ϕ can be assessed and informed by the domain experts. Then, a power steady evolution assumes that such information loss is linear and proportional to ϕ so that:

$$\mathbb{E}[\log \hat{q}(\boldsymbol{\theta}_w)] = \phi \mathbb{E}[\log q(\boldsymbol{\theta}_w)] + c, \tag{27}$$

for some constant c.

For a Dirichlet prior $\boldsymbol{\theta}_w \sim Dirichlet(\boldsymbol{\alpha}_w)$ with concentration parameters $\boldsymbol{\alpha}_w = (\alpha_{w1}, \cdots, \alpha_{wm_w})$, following [29], we can transform it to $Dirichlet(\hat{\boldsymbol{\alpha}}_w)$, where $\hat{\boldsymbol{\alpha}}_w = (\hat{\alpha}_{w1}, \cdots, \hat{\alpha}_{wm_w})$ and $\hat{\alpha}_{wj} - 1 = \phi(\alpha_{wj} - 1)$, for $j \in \{1, \cdots, m_w\}$. By this transformation, the mode remains the same. We can consider such manipulations when searching for the best scoring MCEG for causal discovery. This is explained in Section 4.

Having updated the transition probabilities, the path probabilities under the stochastic manipulation given a routine intervention can be re-evaluated. Let $\Lambda(\boldsymbol{w}^*)$ denote the set of root-to-sink paths on the MCEG passing through any position $w \in \boldsymbol{w}^*$. Let $\overline{\Lambda}(\boldsymbol{w}^*) = \Lambda_C / \Lambda(\boldsymbol{w}^*)$. Then, the probabilities of paths in $\Lambda_{x_{fail,0}} \cap \Lambda(\boldsymbol{w}^*)$ are affected by both the singular manipulation on $x_{fail,0}$ and the stochastic manipulation on $\mathcal{F}(\boldsymbol{w}^*)$. The probabilities of paths in $\Lambda_{x_{fail,0}} \cap \overline{\Lambda}(\boldsymbol{w}^*)$ are affected by the singluar manipulation on $x_{fail,0}$. Therefore, the post-intervened path probabilities on the MCEG are:

$$\hat{\pi}(\lambda) = \begin{cases} \frac{\prod_{e \in E_\lambda} \theta_e}{\theta_{e(x_{fail,0})} \prod_{e' \in E(\boldsymbol{w}^*) \cap E_\lambda} \theta_{e'}} \times \prod_{e' \in E(\boldsymbol{w}^*) \cap E_\lambda} \hat{\theta}_{e'} & \text{if } \lambda \in \Lambda_{x_{fail,0}} \cap \Lambda(\boldsymbol{w}^*), \\ \frac{\prod_{e \in E_\lambda} \theta_e}{\theta_{e(x_{f,0})}} & \text{if } \lambda \in \Lambda_{x_{fail,0}} \cap \overline{\Lambda}(\boldsymbol{w}^*), \\ 0 & \text{otherwise.} \end{cases} \tag{28}$$

Let $\boldsymbol{x}^*$ denote the set of all events represented on $\mathcal{F}(\boldsymbol{w}^*)$ and let $\boldsymbol{x} = x_{fail,0} \cap \boldsymbol{x}^*$ denote the set of events that are manipulated. Then, the set of florets associated with the manipulated events, the effect event and the partition events is

$$\mathcal{F}_{\boldsymbol{x}\cup y\cup \boldsymbol{z}} = \{\mathcal{F} : \mathcal{F} \in \mathcal{F}(e(x_{fail,0})) \cup \mathcal{F}(\boldsymbol{w}^*) \cup \mathcal{F}(e(y)) \cup \mathcal{F}(e(\boldsymbol{z})) \text{ and } \mathcal{F} \notin \mathcal{F}^{MI}\}. \quad (29)$$

The manifest paths are defined analogously to Equation (17) so that no event of interest, i.e., $\boldsymbol{x}, y,$ and $\boldsymbol{z}$, is missing in this restricted class of paths.

$$\Lambda(w(\boldsymbol{b}_{\mathcal{F}_{\boldsymbol{x}\cup y\cup \boldsymbol{z}},0})) = \Lambda(w(b_{\mathcal{F}(e(x_{fail,0})),0})) \cap \Lambda(\boldsymbol{w}^*) \cap \Lambda(w(b_{\mathcal{F}(e(y)),0})) \cap \Lambda(w(b_{\mathcal{F}(e(\boldsymbol{z})),0})). \quad (30)$$

We next show the identifiability of the effects by adapting the back-door criterion for stochastic manipulation [9]. More specifically, this is possible whenever we need to identify a $\Lambda_{\boldsymbol{z}}$ that partitions the root-to-sink paths of the manifest MCEG $\mathcal{C}^M$ so that

$$\begin{aligned}\pi^{\Lambda_{\mathcal{C}^M}}(\Lambda_y||\Lambda_{x_{fail,0}}, \hat{\boldsymbol{\theta}}_{w^*}) = \sum_{x\in \boldsymbol{x}}\sum_{z} &\pi(\Lambda_y|\Lambda_x, \Lambda_z, \Lambda(w(\boldsymbol{b}_{F_{\boldsymbol{x}\cup y\cup \boldsymbol{z}},0})))\pi(\Lambda_z|\Lambda_x, \Lambda(w(\boldsymbol{b}_{F_{\boldsymbol{x}\cup y\cup \boldsymbol{z}},0}))) \\ &\times \hat{\pi}(\Lambda_x|\Lambda(w(\boldsymbol{b}_{F_{\boldsymbol{x}\cup y\cup \boldsymbol{z}},0}))),\end{aligned} \quad (31)$$

where

$$\hat{\pi}(\Lambda_x|\Lambda(w(\boldsymbol{b}_{F_{\boldsymbol{x}\cup y\cup \boldsymbol{z}},0}))) = \frac{\hat{\pi}(\Lambda_x, \Lambda(w(\boldsymbol{b}_{F_{\boldsymbol{x}\cup y\cup \boldsymbol{z}}})))}{\hat{\pi}(\Lambda(w(\boldsymbol{b}_{F_{\boldsymbol{x}\cup y\cup \boldsymbol{z}},0})))}. \quad (32)$$

The numerator and denominator are the post-intervened path probabilities. Note that these can be computed using Equation (28). Assuming that a stochastic manipulation on $\hat{\boldsymbol{\theta}}_{w^*}$ is equivalent to forcing each x with probability $\pi(\Lambda_x||\hat{\boldsymbol{\theta}}_{w^*})$ for every $x \in x^*$ [5], we can obtain Equation (31) by expressing the causal query as

$$\pi^{\Lambda_{\mathcal{C}^M}}(\Lambda_y||\Lambda_{x_{fail,0}}, \hat{\boldsymbol{\theta}}_{w^*}) = \sum_{x\in \boldsymbol{x}^*} \pi^{\Lambda_{\mathcal{C}^M}}(\Lambda_y||\Lambda_{x_{fail,0},x})\pi^{\Lambda_{\mathcal{C}^M}}(\Lambda_x|\Lambda_{x_{fail,0}}, \hat{\boldsymbol{\theta}}_{w^*}). \quad (33)$$

The first component on the right hand side of the equation can be evaluated by applying the results in Equation (19), and the second component can be simplified to Equation (32). By doing this, we have the expression in Equation (31).

Example 2. *Given the idle system in Figure 4, suppose routine maintenance involved in checking the oil level, cleaning the leakage, and topping up the oil, but this did not fully prevent the oil leak. The manipulations imported to the idle system under this intervention are then different from the one we discussed in Example 1. Suppose florets* $\mathcal{F}(w_2), \mathcal{F}(w_3), \mathcal{F}(w_4)$ *are directly affected in response to the maintenance. Then, these florets are stochastically manipulated, and* $\boldsymbol{w}^* = \{w_2, w_3, w_4\}$. *This gives the same* $\Lambda(w(b_{\mathcal{F}(e(\boldsymbol{x})),0}))$ *as in Example 1. If we are interested in how the sight glass or buchholz defect is affected by this intervention, then the effect event is* $x_{s/b,1}$. *Note that this event is unobservable and* $\Lambda(w(b_{\mathcal{F}(e(x_{s/b,1})),0})) = \bigcup_{w\in\{w_{19},\cdots,w_{24}\}} \Lambda(w)$.

Here, we can choose X_{alarm} *as the partition events* $\boldsymbol{z}$, *and these are always observable. Next the manifest MCEG is constructed from the idle MCEG by removing the paths that do not traverse any position in* $\{w_{19}, \cdots, w_{24}\}$. *The manipulated MCEG is obtained by further deleting the paths that terminate in* w_∞^f *from the manifest MCEG, see Figure 6. If the post-intervention probabilities* $\hat{\boldsymbol{\theta}}_{w^*}$ *are known, then we can evaluate the path probabilities in the manipulated MCEG following the factorisations we specified in Equation (28). Then, conditional on the manifest paths, each probability in Equation (31) can be computed to estimate the effects of the observed maintenance on the sight glass or the buchholz.*

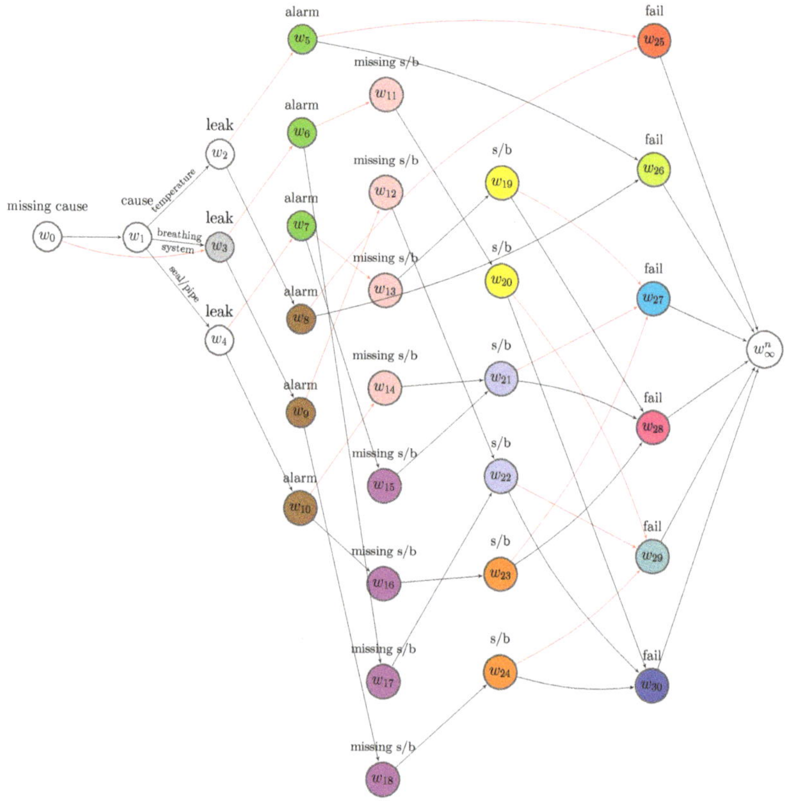

Figure 6. The manipulated MCEG for Example 2.

4. Experiments

Due to commercial sensitivity, we cannot disclose the real maintenance data from the energy distribution company and examine our methodology on it. Here, we show experimentally, using synthetic data, how the structural learning algorithm over a class of MCEGs can be used to provide useful causal inferences. We, then, perform a comparative study to demonstrate how the predictions are improved when incorporating the causal algebras we specified in previous section into the algorithm for the synthetic experimental data.

4.1. Causal Discovery with the Structural Learning Algorithm

Assume a ground truth missingness staged tree in Figure 3 and a corresponding MCEG in Figure 4 are valid. Assume the causal ordering here is $\Pi_1 = X_{cause} \prec X_{leak} \prec X_{alarm} \prec X_{s/b} \prec X_{fail}$. The oil leak, alarm, and sight glass or buchholz defect are faults that may appear before a failure or routine maintenance. Thus, the oil leak could be a potential cause of alarm and the defect in buchholz or sight glass. We assume that, for any floret, the parameters of primitive probability vector are independent, and the vectors of primitive probabilities associated with each stage are mutually independent.

This ensures a model search based on product of independent Dirichlet priors over the model parameters and a closed-form conjugate analysis [30]. Based on these assumptions, we now generate observation data D_1 of size 5000 from the ground truth MCEG with the corresponding hypothesized transition probabilities. This emulates the dataset in a situation when there has been no intervention to the system.

To begin to learn a best model for D_1 given the event tree in Figure 2, we specify the Dirichlet hyperparameters. We use established methods and treat each α_{uj} as the number of phantom units [3], which is believed to arrive at j^{th} child of stage u. We let the total phantom units entering the root vertex v_0 be 1 and denote this by $\alpha = 1$.

By performing the MAP algorithm, the best scoring MCEG is shown in Figure 7. In this MCEG, denoted by $\mathcal{C}(\boldsymbol{X}(\Pi_1), \boldsymbol{B})$, the positions representing the same variable $X_i \in \boldsymbol{X}$ are vertically aligned in descending order with respect to $\mathbb{P}(X_i(w) = 1 | D_1, \mu(w_0, w))$. For transparency, the edges that are supposed to have a label "yes" have been coloured red for clarity.

The posterior means for each stage are summarised in Table 1. The score of this selected model is −20,389.83. The stages for X_{leak}, X_{alarm} and the missing indicator of s/b defect in this tree are accurately learned by the algorithm when these are compared with the stages in the ground truth MCEG. In terms of the stages for $X_{s/b}$, the stage assigned to v_{23} is wrong. There are 15 misclassifications appearing for X_{fail}. One possible reason is that the dataset is not sufficiently large to provide sufficient information on the last event modelled on the tree.

The best scoring MCEG in Figure 7 has a complex topology because many stages for the last variable modelled on the tree are misspecified. However, we can still summarise some causal explanations from it when assuming it is causal. We read the causal relationships from the semantics of a causal CEG in an analogous way to a causal BN [3,6]. For example, from Figure 7, we see that all the edges representing oil leak point to the stage $u' = \{w_6, \cdots, w_9\}$, which is coloured in green, while the edges representing no leak point to the stage $u'' = \{w_{10}, \cdots, w_{13}\}$, which is coloured in brown. The stage u' is located above u'' on the tree, meaning the mean posterior probability of alarm at this stage is higher than that at u''.

Therefore, the oil leak gives rise to the likelihood of alarm. Root causes also lie upstream of alarm on the tree and can affect the possibility of alarm. However, from Figure 7, whether the cause is missing and which cause is observed appear to have no influence on alarm given an oil leak. Thus, given the oil leak, the alarm is independent of the root causes we specified for this model. We could say that the oil leak is the main cause of alarm given the hypothesised causal ordering Π_1. One causal implication of this discovery is that we could prevent an alarm by fixing or preventing the oil leak. For positions associated with failure indicators, w_{37} is aligned at the lowest position. This means that the probability $\mathbb{P}(X_{fail} = 1 | \mu(w_0, w_{37}), D_1)$ is the lowest compared with the probability of failure conditional on the position w_{34} or w_{35} or w_{36}. There are eight edges pointing to w_{37} labelled by no s/b defect and only one edge pointing to it labelled by a s/b defect. Thus, to increase the reliability of the machine, we can schedule the preventive maintenance for the sight glass or the buchholz.

4.2. A Comparison Study

Now, we assume the routine intervention described in Example 2 has occurred, and Figure 4 portrays the real causal structure. We, then, simulate synthetic data D_2 of size 5000 from this intervened model to emulate an experimental dataset by the following setups. First, we assume the 5000 pieces of equipment here have been intervened in the same way by the same routine maintenance. Second, a complete and unique root-to-sink path on the tree can be identified for each case in D_2. Third, assume we have the estimated posteriors from the past failure data before conduction of routine maintenance, and these are now used as priors to generate the data that would be observed after the routine maintenance.

Here, the prior independence assumptions are still assumed to be valid so that conjugate sampling can be characterised. To simulate from the intervened system instead of the idle system, the florets $\mathcal{F}(w_2), \mathcal{F}(w_3), \mathcal{F}(w_4)$ are stochastically manipulated in response to the routine maintenance, and we adjust the corresponding Dirichlet hyperparameters as described in the previous section.

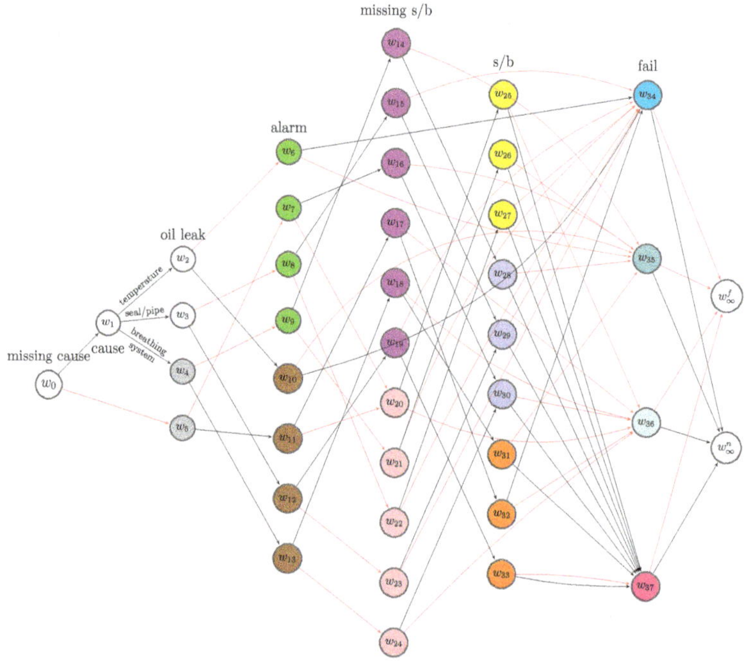

Figure 7. The best scoring MCEG selected for D_1 with hypothesised causal ordering Π_1.

Table 1. Mean posterior probabilities $\mathbb{P}(X = 1|stage, D_1)$.

	$X_{leak} = 1$			$X_{alarm} = 1$		$B_{s/b} = 1$		$X_{s/b} = 1$			$X_{fail} = 1$			
stage	w_2	w_3	w_4, w_5	$w_6, \cdots, w_9$	$w_{10}, \cdots, w_{13}$	$w_{14}, \cdots, w_{19}$	$w_{20}, \cdots, w_{24}$	w_{25}, w_{26}, w_{27}	w_{28}, w_{29}, w_{30}	w_{31}, w_{32}, w_{33}	w_{34}	w_{35}	w_{36}	w_{37}
estimate	0.77	0.69	0.50	0.69	0.49	0.51	0.29	0.80	0.67	0.51	0.78	0.70	0.59	0.45

It is possible to embody the effects of this intervention when learning the causal structure by incorporating the stochastic manipulations we developed in the previous section into the MAP algorithm. We can check whether this improves the causal structure learning and parameter estimations. On the corresponding missingness event tree, see Figure 2, we accordingly revise the Dirichlet hyperparameters of florets $\mathcal{F}(v_1), \mathcal{F}(v_5), \mathcal{F}(v_6)$ and $\mathcal{F}(v_7)$ using the method we proposed in Section 3.2.2.

We defined ϕ in Equation (27) to add uncertainties to the intervened floret distributions. In this study, we aim to compare the estimates learned from the best scoring model selected by the algorithm when no distributions are manipulated, i.e., $\phi = 1$, with the estimates learned from the best scoring model selected by the algorithm when inputting $\phi < 1$. In particular, we consider six different cases here: $\phi = 0.1, \phi = 0.3, \phi = 0.5, \phi = 0.7, \phi = 0.9$, and $\phi = 1$.

Now, we run the algorithm for $\alpha = 0.001, \alpha = 0.01, \alpha = 0.1, \alpha = 1, \alpha = 3, \alpha = 5$, where α is the prior parameter representing the number of phantom units entering the root node. We assess the resulted models in terms of situational errors [31] and MAP scores. The situational error (The total situational error of a tree is evaluated as $\gamma(\mathcal{T}) = \sum_{v \in V_{\mathcal{T}}} ||\boldsymbol{\theta}_v^* - \tilde{\boldsymbol{\theta}}_v||_2$) for a situation v measures the Euclidean distance between the true conditional probabilities $\boldsymbol{\theta}_v^*$ and the mean posterior probabilities $\tilde{\boldsymbol{\theta}}_v$ estimated on the best scoring model.

The results are shown in Figure 8. The upper panel of each plot displays the total situational errors, while the lower panel displays the MAP scores for the best scoring models for different values of ϕ. For any prior parameter α we choose, we observe that the best scoring model is selected from the algorithm by setting $\phi = 0.1$, which gives the smallest situational error and the highest MAP score. In particular, the situational error rises when ϕ increases towards 1. Thus, the posterior parameters are better estimated by incorporating the manipulations into the learning algorithm when modelling the experimental data for an intervened system.

When $\phi = 1$ (i.e., the distributions are not manipulated), the MAP score in each plot of Figure 8 is much lower than that for $\phi = 0.1$. This means the best structure selected with $\phi = 0.1$ is more consistent with the dataset D_2 than the best model selected by the algorithm without importing stochastic manipulations.

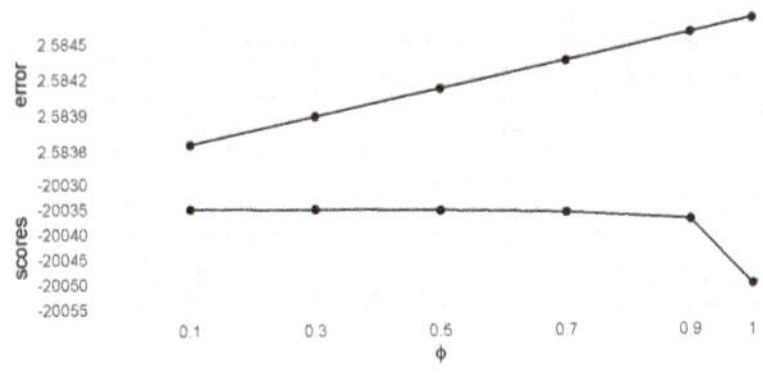

(a) $\alpha = 0.001$

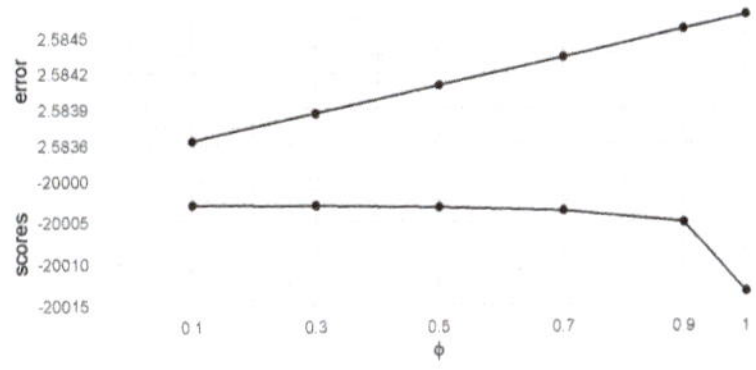

(b) $\alpha = 0.01$

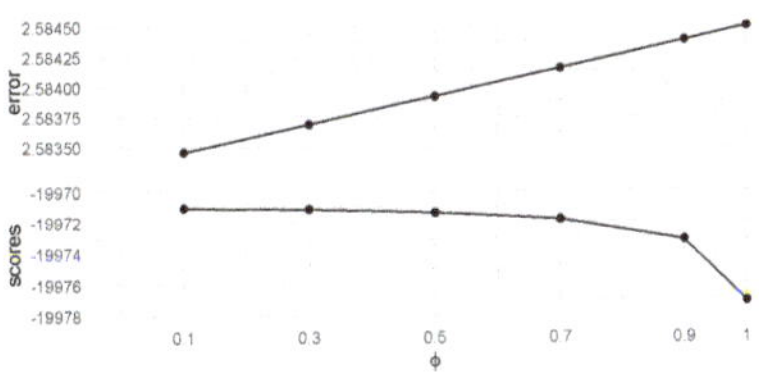

(c) $\alpha = 0.1$

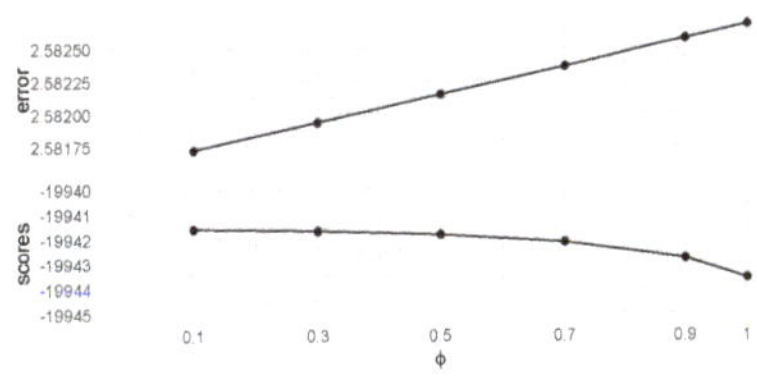

(d) $\alpha = 1$

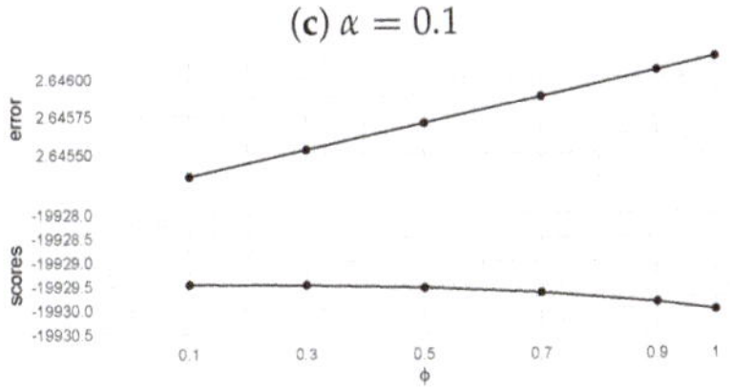

(e) $\alpha = 3$

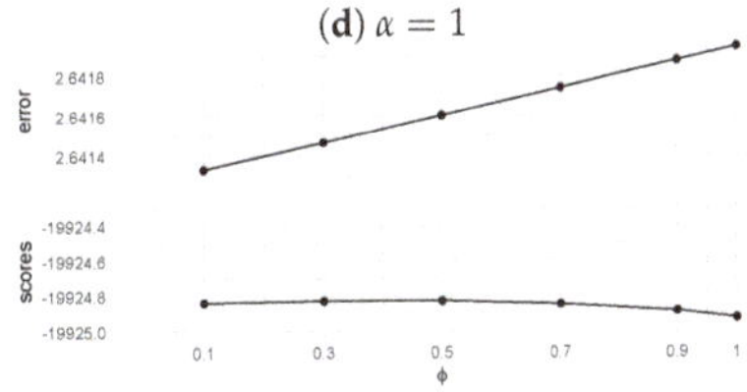

(f) $\alpha = 5$

Figure 8. Comparing situational errors and MAP scores for the best scoring models selected to fit D_2. The x-axis of each plot is labelled by different values of ϕ, where $\phi = 1$ refers to the case when no manipulation is imported to the prior. Each plot displays results for a specified total phantom number α.

5. Discussion

Thus far, we demonstrated how the context-specific CEG is a compelling graphical tool for analysing system failure data. This happens not only because of its ability to represent structural asymmetries but also its flexibility in being able to perform the necessary analyses in a straightforward way even in the presence of censored data that are informedly missing; causal analyses can be performed through simple MAP structural learning algorithms. We developed bespoke causal algebras for the routine intervention and extended the back-door theorems for identifying its causal effects on the MCEG. The results from our designed experiments confirm the usefulness of these bespoke causal algebras in structural learning to improve the predictions needed for system reliability.

One concern of the study is that the model classes containing the best explanation can become huge when the systems are very large. However, the established methodology allows us to scale up the search space for more complex models with up to 20 variables [32]. Furthermore, these challenges associated with scalability are generic ones and are currently being actively researched. Each new development can be simply translated into causal analyses of reliability systems using the technologies we described above.

Author Contributions: Development of the methodology behind the use of CEGs for modeling routine maintenance regimes was led by X.Y. with contributions by J.Q.S.; software and data analysis, X.Y.; presentation of the material led by X.Y. with contributions from J.Q.S. Both authors have read and agreed to the published version of the manuscript.

Funding: This research was funded by Engineering and Physical Sciences Research Council (EPSRC) with grant number EP/L016710/1 and the statistics department of the University of Warwick. Professor Jim Q. Smith is supported by the Alan Turing Institute and EPSRC with grant number EP/K039628/1.

Data Availability Statement: The data used to support the findings of this study are available from the corresponding author upon request.

Conflicts of Interest: The authors declare no conflict of interest.

References

1. Langseth, H.; Portinale, L. Bayesian networks in reliability. *Reliab. Eng. Syst. Saf.* **2007**, *92*, 92–108. [CrossRef]
2. Cowell, R.G.; Smith, J.Q. Causal discovery through MAP selection of stratified chain event graphs. *Electron. J. Stat.* **2014**, *8*, 965–997. [CrossRef]
3. Collazo, R.A.; Görgen, C.; Smith, J.Q. *Chain Event Graphs*; CRC Press: Boca Raton, FL, USA, 2018.
4. Görgen, C.; Smith, J.Q. A differential approach to causality in staged trees. In Proceedings of the Conference on Probabilistic Graphical Models, Lugano, Switzerland, 6–9 September 2016.
5. Pearl, J. *Causality: Models, Reasoning and Inference*; MIT press: Cambridge, MA, USA, 2000; Volume 29.
6. Thwaites, P.; Smith, J.Q.; Riccomagno, E. Causal analysis with chain event graphs. *Artif. Intell.* **2010**, *174*, 889–909. [CrossRef]
7. Thwaites, P. Causal identifiability via chain event graphs. *Artif. Intell.* **2013**, *195*, 291–315. [CrossRef]
8. Barclay, L.M.; Hutton, J.L.; Smith, J.Q. Chain event graphs for informed missingness. *Bayesian Anal.* **2014**, *9*, 53–76. [CrossRef]
9. Yu, X.; Smith, J.Q. Hierarchical Causal Analysis of Natural Languages on a Chain Event Graph. *arXiv* **2021**, arXiv:2110.01129.
10. Yu X; Smith, J.Q.; Nichols, L. Bayesian Learning of Causal Relationships for System Reliability. In Proceedings of the 7th International Symposium on Reliability Engineering and Risk Management, Beijing, China, 12–14 November 2020.
11. Mohan, K.; Pearl, J. Graphical models for recovering probabilistic and causal queries from missing data. *Adv. Neural Inf. Process. Syst.* **2014**, *27*, 1520–1528.
12. Mohan, K.; Pearl, J. Graphical models for processing missing data. *arXiv* **2018**, arXiv:1801.03583.
13. Saadati, M.; Tian, J. Adjustment criteria for recovering causal effects from missing data. In Proceedings of the Joint European Conference on Machine Learning and Knowledge Discovery in Databases, Würzburg, Germany, 16–20 September 2019; pp. 561–577.
14. Yu, X. Hierarchical Causal Analysis on Chain Event Graphs. Ph.D. Thesis, University of Warwick, Coventry, UK, Unpublished.
15. Barclay, L.M.; Collazo, R.A.; Smith, J.Q.; Thwaites, P.A.; Nicholson, A.E. The dynamic chain event graph. *Electron. J. Stat.* **2015**, *9*, 2130–2169. [CrossRef]
16. Freeman, G.; Smith, J.Q. Dynamic staged trees for discrete multivariate time series: Forecasting, model selection and causal analysis. *Bayesian Anal.* **2011**, *6*, 279–305. [CrossRef]
17. Pensar, J.; Talvitie, T.; Hyttinen, A.; Koivisto, M. A Bayesian approach for estimating causal effects from observational data. In Proceedings of the AAAI Conference on Artificial Intelligence, New York, NY, USA, 7–12 February 2020; pp. 5395-5402.
18. Cooper, G.F.; Yoo, C. Causal discovery from a mixture of experimental and observational data. *arXiv* **2013**, arXiv:1301.6686.
19. 9 types of Maintenance: From Preventive Maintenance to Corrective Maintenance and Everything in Between. Available online: https://www.roadtoreliability.com/types-of-maintenance/ (accessed on 19 February 2021).
20. Bedford, T.; Cooke, R. *Probabilistic Risk Analysis: Foundations and Methods*; Cambridge University Press: Cambridge UK, 2001.
21. Lienig, J.; Bruemmer, H. Reliability Analysis. In *Fundamentals of Electronic Systems Design*; Springer: Cham, Switzerland, 2017; pp. 45–73.
22. Bicen, Y. Monitoring of critical substation equipment. In Proceedings of the 3rd International Istanbul Smart Grid Congress and Fair (ICSG), Istanbul, Turkey, 29–30 April 2015; pp. 1–4.
23. Guessoum, Y.; Aupiedy J. Modeling the impact of preventive maintenance over the lifetime of equipments. In Proceedings of the International Conference on Electricity Distribution, Lyon, France, 7–8 June 2010.
24. Kijima, M. Some results for repairable systems with general repair. *J. Appl. Probab.* **1989**, *26*, 89–102. [CrossRef]
25. Preventive Maintenance Checklist for Transformer. *Learn Electrician*. Available online: https://learnelectrician.com/preventive-maintenance-checklist-for-transformer/(accessed on 1 June 2021).
26. Smith, J.Q. Non-linear state space models with partially specified distributions on states. *J. Forecast.* **1990**,*9*, 137–149. [CrossRef]
27. Smith, J.Q. A comparison of the characteristics of some Bayesian forecasting models. *Int. Stat. Rev. Int. Stat.* **1992**, *60*, 75–87. [CrossRef]
28. Smith, J.Q. The multiparameter steady model. *J. R. Stat. Soc. Ser. (Methodological)* **1981**, *43*, 256–260. [CrossRef]

29. Smith, J.Q. A generalization of the Bayesian steady forecasting model. *J. R. Stat. Soc. Ser. (Methodological)* **1979**, *41*, 375–387. [CrossRef]
30. Freeman, G.; Smith, J.Q. Bayesian MAP model selection of chain event graphs. *J. Multivar. Anal.* **2011**, *102*, 1152–1165. [CrossRef]
31. Collazo, R.A.; Smith, J.Q. A new family of non-local priors for chain event graph model selection. *Bayesian Anal.* **2016**, *11*, 1165–1201. [CrossRef]
32. Carli, F.; Leonelli, M.; Riccomagno, E.; Varando, G. The R package stagedtrees for structural learning of stratified staged trees. *arXiv* **2020**, arXiv:2004.06459.

entropy

MDPI

Article

Universal Causality

Sridhar Mahadevan

Adobe Research, 345 Park Avenue, San Jose, CA 95110, USA; smahadev@adobe.com

Abstract: Universal Causality is a mathematical framework based on higher-order category theory, which generalizes previous approaches based on directed graphs and regular categories. We present a hierarchical framework called UCLA (Universal Causality Layered Architecture), where at the top-most level, causal interventions are modeled as a higher-order category over simplicial sets and objects. Simplicial sets are contravariant functors from the category of ordinal numbers Δ into sets, and whose morphisms are order-preserving injections and surjections over finite ordered sets. Non-random interventions on causal structures are modeled as face operators that map n-simplices into lower-level simplices. At the second layer, causal models are defined as a category, for example defining the schema of a relational causal model or a symmetric monoidal category representation of DAG models. The third layer corresponds to the data layer in causal inference, where each causal object is mapped functorially into a set of instances using the category of sets and functions between sets. The fourth homotopy layer defines ways of abstractly characterizing causal models in terms of homotopy colimits, defined in terms of the nerve of a category, a functor that converts a causal (category) model into a simplicial object. Each functor between layers is characterized by a universal arrow, which define universal elements and representations through the Yoneda Lemma, and induces a Grothendieck category of elements that enables combining formal causal models with data instances, and is related to the notion of *ground graphs* in relational causal models. Causal inference between layers is defined as a lifting problem, a commutative diagram whose objects are categories, and whose morphisms are functors that are characterized as different types of fibrations. We illustrate UCLA using a variety of representations, including causal relational models, symmetric monoidal categorical variants of DAG models, and non-graphical representations, such as integer-valued multisets and separoids, and measure-theoretic and topological models.

Keywords: artificial intelligence; higher-order category theory; causality; machine learning; statistics

Citation: Mahadevan, S. Universal Causality. *Entropy* **2023**, *25*, 574. https://doi.org/10.3390/e25040574

Academic Editor: Kateřina Hlaváčková-Schindler

Received: 5 January 2023
Revised: 11 March 2023
Accepted: 22 March 2023
Published: 27 March 2023

1. Introduction

Applied category theory [1] has been used to design algorithms for dimensionality reduction and data visualization [2], resolve impossibility theorems in data clustering [3] and propose schemes for knowledge representation [4]. Universal Causality (UC) is a mathematical framework based on applied higher-order category theory, which applies to graph-based [5] and non-graphical representations [6–8], and statistical [9] and non-statistical frameworks [10,11] (see Table 1 and Figure 1). Ordinary categories are defined as a collection of *objects* that interact pairwise through a collection of *morphisms*. Higher-order categories, such as simplicial sets [12], quasicategories [13] and ∞-categories [14], model higher-order interactions among groups of objects, and generalize both directed graphs and ordinary categories. Our approach builds extensively on categories over *functors*. Causal interventions are defined over the functor category of simplicial objects, mapping ordinal numbers into sets or category objects. Causal inference is defined over the functor category of presheafs $\mathbf{Hom}_{\mathcal{C}}(-, c)$, mapping an object c in category $\mathcal{C}$ into the set of morphisms into it. *Adjoint functors* define a pair of opposing functors between categories. Causal models are often characterized in terms of their underlying conditional independence structures. We model this relationship by adjoint functors between the category of conditional independence structures [15], based on algebraic representations such as *separoids* [10], and the category of causal models, defined by graphical approaches [16] or non-graphical approaches, such as integer-valued multisets [8] or measure-theoretic information fields [6,7]. We build extensively on *universal constructions*, such as colimits and limits, defined through *lifting diagrams* [17].

Table 1. Category theory provides a unifying mathematical framework for relating the diverse formalisms used to study causal inference.

Representation	Objects	Morphisms	Citation
Rank-ordered statistics	Plants	Total ordering	Darwin [18]
Structural equation models	Variables	Algebraic equations	Wright [19]
Potential outcomes	Humans	Drug effects	Imbens and Rubin [9]
Directed Acyclic Graphs	Vertices	Paths	Pearl [5]
Distributive lattices	Subsets	Joins/Meets	Beerenwinkel et al. [20]
Relational causal models	Database schemas	Database relations	Maier et al. [21]
Information fields	Measurable Spaces	Measurable functions	Witsenhausen [6]
Resource Models	Monoidal resources	Profunctors	Fong and Spivak [1]
Universal Decision Models	UDM States	UDM morphisms	Mahadevan [22]
Counterfactual logic	Propositions	Proofs	Lewis [11]
Variational inequalities	Consumers/Producers	Trade	Nagurney [23]
Discourse sheaves	Users	Communication	Hansen and Ghrist [24]
String diagram surgery	Tensored objects	Tensored morphisms	Jacobs et al. [25]
Mean embeddings	RKHS embeddings	Mean maps	Muandet et al. [26]

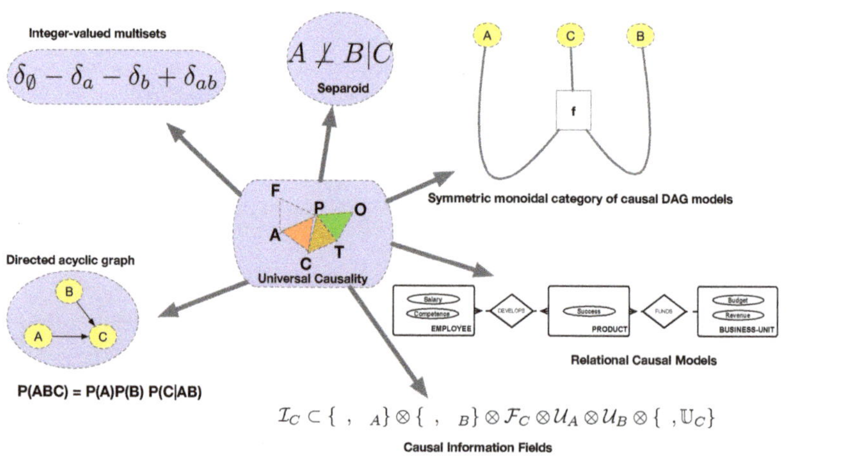

Figure 1. UC is a *representation-independent* framework that can be applied to many causal representations.

Over the past 150 years, causality has been studied using diverse formalisms (Table 1). While causal effects are inherently *directional*, differing from symmetric statistical models of correlation and invertible Bayesian inference, many causal discovery methods rely on querying a (symmetric) conditional independence oracle on submodels resulting from interventions on arbitrary subsets of variables (such as a *separating set* [27,28]). Abstractly, we can classify the causal representations in Table 1 using category theory in terms of their underlying *objects* and their associated *morphisms*. Causal morphisms can be algebraic, graph-based, logical, measure-theoretical, probabilistic or topological. For example, counterfactual mean embeddings [26] generalizes Rubin's potential outcome model to reproducing kernel Hilbert spaces (RKHS), where the kernel mean map is used to embed a distribution in an RKHS, and the average treatment effect (ATE) is computed using mean maps. As Figure 1 emphasizes, UC is representation agnostic, and while it is related to category-theoretic approaches of causal DAG models that use symmetric monoidal categories [25,29,30], it differs substantially in many ways. UC introduces many novel ideas into the study of causal inference, including higher-order categorical structures based on simplicial sets and objects [12–14,31], adjoint functors mapping categories based on algebraic models of conditional independence [10] into actual causal models, lifting diagrams [17], and Grothendieck's category of elements that generalizes the notion of *ground graphs* in relational causal models [32]. As we show later, any category, including symmetric monoidal categories, can be converted into simplicial objects by using the nerve functor, but its left adjoint that maps a simplicial set into a category is lossy, and preserves structure only up to $n \leq 2$-simplices. Higher-order category structures can be useful in modeing causal inference under interference [33], where the traditional stable unit treatment value assumption (SUTVA) is violated. Higher-order categories can also help model hierarchical interventions over groups of objects.

As Studeny [8] points out, Bayesian DAG models capture only a small percentage of all conditional independence structures. In particular, the space of DAG models grows exponentially in the number of variables, whereas the number of conditional independence structures grows super-exponentially proportional to the number of Boolean functions. Consequently, UC is intended to be a general framework that applies to representations that are more expressive than DAG models. In particular, UC can be used to analyze recent work on relational causal models [21,32]. The notion of a *ground graph* in relational causal models is a special case of the Grothendieck category of elements that plays a key role in the UCLA architecture. UC applies equally well to non-graphical algebraic representations that are much more expressive than DAG models, including integer-valued multisets [8], separoids [10], as well as measure-theoretic representations, such as causal information fields [6,7], that have been shown to generalize Pearl's d-separation calculus [5].

Specifically, taking the simple example of a collider in Figure 1, in the Bayesian DAG parameterization, a well-established theoretical framework [34] specifies how to decompose the overall probability distribution into a product of local distributions. In contrast, in causal information fields [6,7], each variable is defined as a measurable space over a discrete or continuous set, and each local function is defined as a measurable function over its information field. For example, the information field $\mathcal{I}_C$ for variable C is defined to be some measurable subset over a product σ-algebra that includes the σ-algebras $\mathcal{U}_A$ and $\mathcal{U}_B$ over its parents A and B, but the information field of C cannot depend on its own values, hence its local σ-algebra is defined as $\{\emptyset, \mathbb{U}_C\}$, where $\mathbb{U}_C$ is the space of possible values of C. A full discussion of causal information fields is given in [7], who show it generalizes d-separation to models that include cycles and other more complex structures. Similarly, Studeny [8] proposed an algebraic framework called integer-valued multisets (imsets) for representing conditional independence structures far more expressive than DAG models. For the specific case of a DAG model $G = (V, E)$, an imset in standard form [8] is defined as

$$u_G = \delta_V - \delta_\emptyset + \sum_{i \in V} (\delta_{\mathbf{Pa}_i} - \delta_{i \cup \mathbf{Pa}_i})$$

where each δ_V term is the characteristic function associated with a set of variables V. Finally, separoids [10] is an algebraic framework for characterizing conditional independence as an abstract property, defined by a join semi-lattice equipped with a partial ordering $\leq$, and a ternary property $\perp\!\!\!\perp$ over triples of elements such that $X \perp\!\!\!\perp Y | Z$ defines the property that X is conditionally independent of Y given Z. It is worth pointing out that separoids are more general than the graphoid axiomatization [16] that underpins causal DAG models, since as Studeny [8] shows, graphoids are defined in terms of disjoint subsets of variables, which seriously limits their expressiveness. All these non-graphical representations can be naturally modeled within the UC framework. One of the unique aspects of UC is that causal interventions are themselves modeled as a (higher-order) category. Many approaches to causal discovery use a sequence of interventions, which naturally compose and form a category. To achieve representation independence, we model interventions as a higher-order category defined by simplicial sets and objects [12]. One strength of the simplicial objects framework for modeling causal interventions is that it enables modeling hierarchical interventions over groups of objects.

UC builds on the concept of *universal arrows* [35] to illuminate in a representation-independent manner the central abstractions employed in causal inference. Figure 2 explains this concept with an example, which also illustrates the connection between categories and graphs. For every (directed) graph G, there is a universal arrow from G to the "forgetful" functor U mapping the category **Cat** of all categories to **Graph**, the category of all (directed) graphs, where for any category C, its associated graph is defined by $U(C)$. Intuitively, this forgetful functor "throws" away all categorical information, obliterating for example the distinction between the primitive morphisms f and g vs. their compositions $g \circ f$, both of which are simply viewed as edges in the graph $U(C)$. To understand this functor, consider a directed graph $U(C)$ defined from a category C, forgetting the rule for composition. That is, from the category C, which associates to each pair of composable arrows f and g, the composed arrow $g \circ f$, we derive the underlying graph $U(C)$ simply by forgetting which edges correspond to elementary arrows, such as f or g, and which are composites. For example, consider a partial order as the category $\mathcal{C}$, and then define $U(\mathcal{C})$ as the directed graph that results from the transitive closure of the partial ordering.

The universal arrow from a graph G to the forgetful functor U is defined as a pair $\langle C, u : G \to U(C) \rangle$, where u is a "universal" graph homomorphism. This arrow possesses the following *universal property*: for every other pair $\langle D, v : G \to H \rangle$, where D is a category, and v is an arbitrary graph homomorphism, there is a functor $f' : C \to D$, which is an arrow in the category **Cat** of all categories, such that *every* graph homomorphism $\phi : G \to H$ uniquely factors through the universal graph homomorphism $u : G \to U(C)$ as the solution to the equation $\phi = U(f') \circ u$, where $U(f') : U(C) \to H$ (that is, $H = U(D)$). Namely, the dotted arrow defines a graph homomorphism $U(f')$ that makes the triangle diagram "commute", and the associated "extension" problem of finding this new graph homomorphism $U(f')$ is solved by "lifting" the associated category arrow $f' : C \to D$. This property of universal arrows, as we show in the paper, provide the conceptual underpinnings of universal causality in the UCLA architecture, leading to the defining property of a universal causal representation through the Yoneda Lemma [35]. Recent work on causal discovery of DAG models [27,28] can be seen as restricted ways of defining adjoint functors between causal categories of DAG models and their underlying graphs, assuming access to a conditional independence oracle that can be queried on causal sub-models resulting from interventions on arbitrary subsets of variables.

Universal causal models are defined in terms of universal constructions, such as the pullback, pushforward, (co)equalizer, and (co)limits. Figure 3 illustrates how universal causal models are functors that map from some indexing category of abstract diagrams into an actual causal model. For instance, **COVID-19 Lockdown** caused a reduction in **Traffic** and **Agricultural Fires**, which in turn caused a significant reduction in **Pollution**. In UC, we are interested in a deeper question, namely whether the pullback of **Traffic** and **Agricultural Fires** could have been some other common cause that mediated between **COVID-19 Lockdown** and its effects. If such a common cause exists, it will be viewed as a limit of an abstract causal diagram, a functor that maps from the indexing category of all diagrams to the actual causal model shown.

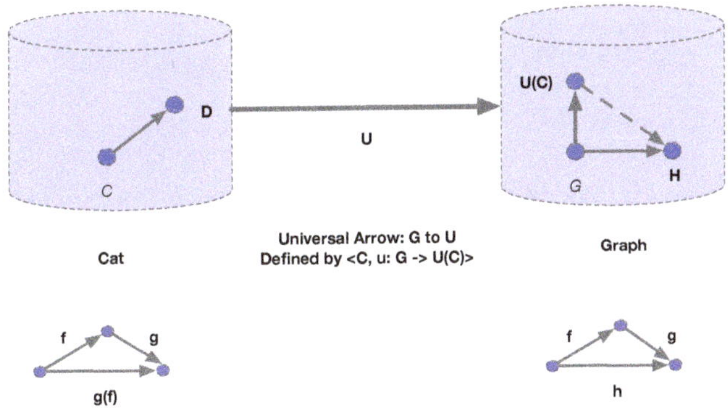

Figure 2. Universal arrows play a central role in the UCLA framework. In this example, the forgetful functor U between **Cat**, the category of all categories, and **Graph**, the category of all (directed) graphs, maps any category into its underlying graph, forgetting which arrows are primitive and which are compositional. The universal arrow from a graph G to the forgetful functor U is defined as a pair $\langle C, u : G \to U(C) \rangle$, where u is a "universal" graph homomorphism. The universal arrow property asserts that every graph homomorphism $\phi : G \to H$ uniquely factors through the universal graph homomorphism $u : G \to U(C)$, where $U(C)$ is the graph induced by category C defining the universal arrow property. In other words, the associated *extension* problem of "completing" the triangle of graph homomorphisms in the category of **Graph** can be uniquely solved by "lifting" the associated category arrow $h : C \to D$.

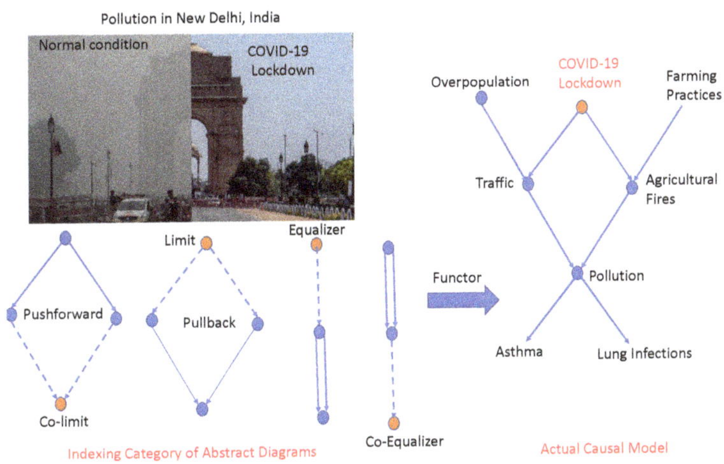

Figure 3. A causal model of climate change and COVID-19 lockdown. Universal causality defines causal models as functors mapping from an indexing category of abstract diagrams to the actual causal model.

Figure 4 illustrates the concept of causal simplicial structures. Here, X denotes a causal structure represented as a category. $X[0]$ represents the "objects" of the causal structure, defined formally as the contravariant functor $X[0] : [0] \to X$ from the simplicial category Δ to the causal category X. The arrows representing causal effects are defined as $X[1] : [1] \to X$. Note that since $[1] = \{0, 1\}$ is a category by itself, it has one (non-identity) arrow $0 \to 1$ (as well as two identity arrows). The mapping of this arrow onto X defines the "edges" of the causal model. Similarly, X_2 represents oriented "triangles" of three objects. Note that there is one edge from X_0 to X_1, labeled by s_0. This is a co-degeneracy operator from the simplicial layer that maps each object A into an identity edge $\mathbf{1}_A$. Similarly, there are two edges marked d_0 and d_1 from X_1 to X_0. These are co-face operators that map an edge to its source and target vertices correspondingly. Notice also that there are three edges from X_2 to X_1, marked d_0, d_1, and d_2. These are the "faces" of each 2-simplex as shown. Consider the fragment of the causal DAG model from Figure 3 shown on the right in Figure 4. The *order complex* of a DAG forms a simplicial object as shown, where the simplices are represented by the nonempty chains. In particular, each path of length n defines a simplex of size n. For example, the path from O (representing **Overpopulation**) to T (representing **Traffic**) to P (representing **Pollution**) defines a simplex of size 2, shown as the green shaded triangle. Note the simplices are *oriented*, which is not shown for simplicity in Figure 4. Thus, the 2-simplex formed from the chain from **O** to **T** to **P** is oriented such that **O** "points to" **T**, which in turn "points to" **P**. This mapping from chains over DAGs to simplicial objects is a special case of a more general construction discussed later in the paper, based on constructing the *nerve* of a category that provides a faithful functor embedding any (causal) category as a simplicial object. For example, the symmetric monoidal category representations of causal DAG models [25,29,30] can be faithfully embedded as simplicial objects by constructing their nerve.

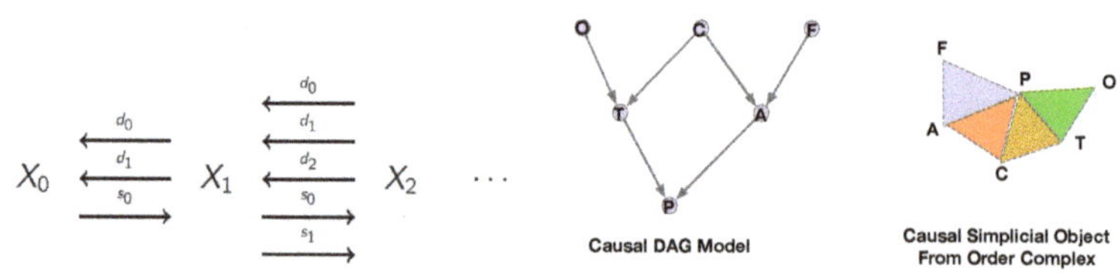

Figure 4. (**Left**) generic structure of a simplicial set. (**Right**) an oriented simplicial complex formed from the order complex of nonempty chains of the DAG model from Figure 3.

2. A Layered Architecture for Universal Causality

In this paper, we propose a layered architecture that defines the framework called UCLA (Universal Causality Layered Architecture). This architecture is illustrated in Figure 5. Table 2 describes the composition of each layer. Many variants are possible, as we will discuss in the paper. As functors compose with each other, it is also possible to consider "collapsed" versions of the UCLA hierarchy.

The UCLA architecture is built on the theoretical foundation of ordinary category theory [35–38] and higher-order category theory, including quasicategories [13], and ∞-categories [14]. As Figure 5 illustrates, at the top layer of UCLA, we model causal interventions itself as a higher-order category defined over simplicial sets and objects [12]. Causal discovery often involves a sequence of interventions, which naturally compose to form a category. Simplicial sets and simplicial objects [12] have long been a foundational framework in algebraic topology [39]. Modeling interventions using simplicial sets permits a *hierarchical* language for expressing interventions, as (co)face operators in simplicial sets and objects operate over groups of objects of arbitrary sizes. This category-theoretic approach of formalizing causal interventions gives an algebraic formalism that are related to topological notions used in causal discovery methods, such as *separating sets* [27,28] that can be defined in terms of lifting diagrams [17]. Although we will not delve into this elaboration in this paper, it is possible to define causal inference over "fuzzy" simplicial sets as well [2], which associate a real number $p \in I = (0,1]$ with each simplicial object that denotes the uncertainty associated with a causal object or morphism. In this case, we define a fuzzy simplicial object as the functor $\Delta^{op} \times I \to C$. Fuzzy simplicial sets have been recently used in data visualization [2].

Table 2. Each layer of UCLA represents a categorical abstraction of causal inference.

Layer	Objects	Morphisms	Description
Simplicial	$[n] = \{0, 1, \ldots, n\}$	$f = [m] \to [n]$	Category of interventions
Relational	Vertices V, Edges E	$s, t : E \to V$	Causal Model Category
Tabular	Sets	Functions on sets $f : S \to T$	Category of instances
Homotopy	Topological Spaces	Causal equivalence	Causal homotopy

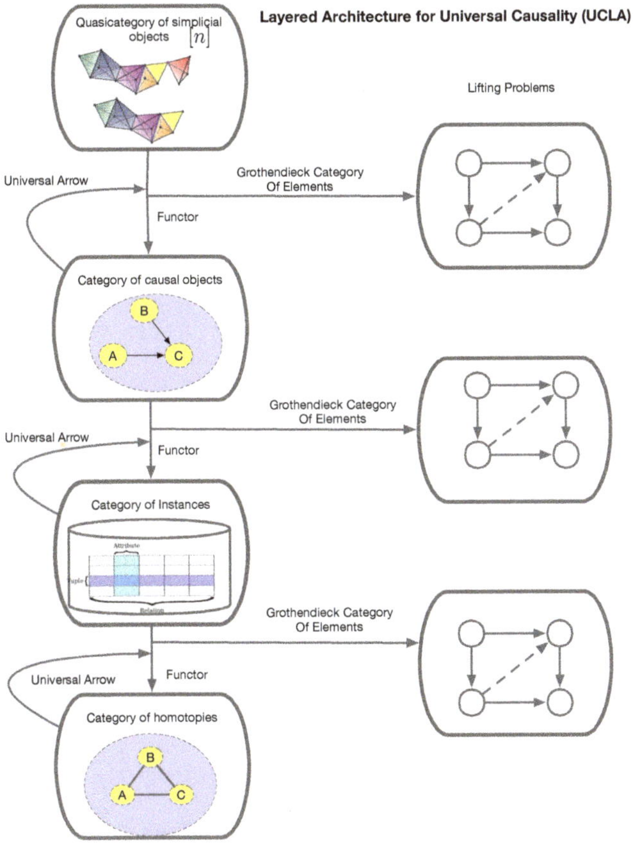

Figure 5. UCLA is a layered architecture that defines Universal Causality.

The second layer of the model represents the causal category itself, which could be a causal DAG [5], a symmetric monoidal category defining a causal DAG [25], a semi-join lattice defining a conditional independence structure, such as an integer-valued multiset [8], a relational database defining a relational causal model [21], or a causal information field [6,7], which uses a measure-theoretic notion of causality. At the third layer, we model the actual data defining a causal model by a category of instances. Finally, at the bottom-most layer, we use a homotopy category to define equivalences among causal models.

The *Grothendieck Category of Elements* (GCE) is a type of universal construction [35,37,40] that plays a central role in the UCLA architecture. It is remarkably similar to other representations widely used in database theory, and specifically in the context of causal inference, it is related to the *ground graph* used in relational causal models [21,32]. However, GCE is far more general than the ground graph construction in that it can be used to embed any object or indeed any category in **Cat**, the category of all categories.

We use *lifting diagrams* [17] to formalize causal inference at each layer of the hierarchy. A lifting problem in a category $\mathcal{C}$ is a morphism $h : B \to X$ in $\mathcal{C}$ satisfying $p \circ h = \nu$ and $h \circ f = \mu$ as indicated in the commutative diagram below.

$$\begin{array}{ccc} A & \xrightarrow{\mu} & X \\ {\scriptstyle f}\downarrow & \overset{h}{\nearrow} & \downarrow{\scriptstyle p} \\ B & \xrightarrow{\nu} & Y \end{array}$$

Lifting diagrams were shown to be capable of expressing SQL queries in relational databases [4]. Here, we extend this approach to model causal inference under non-random interventions, exploiting the capability of the simplicial layer to impose non-random "surgical" operations on a causal category.

Finally, to explain the bottom-most layer in UCLA of homotopy categories, it is well known that causal models are not identifiable from observations alone [5]. For example, the three distinct causal DAG models over three variables $A \leftarrow B \to C$, $A \to B \to C$ and $A \leftarrow B \leftarrow C$ have the same conditional independence structure, and are equivalent given a dataset of values of the variables. To model the non-distinguishability of causal models under observation, we introduce the concept of homotopic equivalence comes from topology, and is intended to reflect equivalence under some invertible mappings. A *homotopy* from a morphism $f : X \to Y$ to another morphism $g : X \to Y$ is a continuous function $h : X \times [0,1] \to Y$ satisfying $h(0,x) = f(x)$ and $h(x,1) = g(x)$. In the category **Top** of topological spaces, homotopy defines an equivalence class on morphisms. In the application to causal inference, we can define causal homotopy [41] as finding the "quotient space" of the category of all causal models under a given set of invertible morphisms mapping one causal model into another equivalent model.

3. Categories, Functors, and Universal Arrows

We introduce the basic theory underlying UC in more depth now, building on relationship between categories and graphs illustrated in Figure 2. Given a graph, we can define the "free" category associated with it where we consider all possible paths between pairs of vertices (including self-loops) as the set of morphisms between them. In the reverse direction, given a category, we can define a "forgetful" functor that extracts the underlying graph from the category, forgetting the composition rule.

Definition 1. *A* **graph** $\mathcal{G}$ *(sometimes referred to as a quiver) is a labeled directed multi-graph defined by a set O of* objects, *a set A of* arrows, *along with two morphisms $s : A \to O$ and $t : A \to O$ that specify the domain and co-domain of each arrow. In this graph, we define the set of composable pairs of arrows by the set*

$$A \times_O A = \{\langle g, f \rangle \mid g, f \in A, \;\; s(g) = t(f)\}$$

A **category** $\mathcal{C}$ *is a graph $\mathcal{G}$ with two additional functions:* $\mathbf{id} : O \to A$, *mapping each object $c \in C$ to an arrow $\mathbf{id}_c$ and $\circ : A \times_O A \to A$, mapping each pair of composable morphisms $\langle f, g \rangle$ to their composition $g \circ f$.*

It is worth emphasizing that no assumption is made here of the finiteness of a graph, either in terms of its associated objects (vertices) or arrows (edges). Indeed, it is entirely reasonable to define categories whose graphs contain an infinite number of edges. A simple example is the group $\mathbb{Z}$ of integers under addition, which can be represented as a single object, denoted $\{\bullet\}$ and an infinite number of morphisms $f : \bullet \to \bullet$, each of which represents an integer, where composition of morphisms is defined by addition. In this example, all morphisms are invertible. In a general category with more than one object, a *groupoid* defines a category all of whose morphisms are invertible.

As our paper focuses on the use of category theory to formalize causal inference, we interpret causal changes in terms of the concept of isomorphisms in category theory. We will elaborate this definition later in the paper.

Definition 2. *Two objects X and Y in a category $\mathcal{C}$ are deemed* **isomorphic**, *or $X \cong Y$ if and only if there is an invertible morphism $f : X \to Y$, namely f is both* left invertible *using a morphism $g : Y \to X$ so that $g \circ f = \mathbf{id}_X$, and f is* right invertible *using a morphism h where $f \circ h = \mathbf{id}_Y$. A* **causally isomorphic change** *in a category is defined as a change of a causal object Y into $\hat{Y}$ under an intervention that changes another object X into $\hat{X}$ such that $\hat{Y} \cong Y$, that is, they are isomorphic. A* **causal non-isomorphic effect** *is a change that leads to a non-isomorphic change where $\hat{Y} \ncong Y$. An alternate definition would be to define a causally isomorphic change as a change that is an isomorphism in the category whose morphisms are causal changes.*

In the category **Sets**, two finite sets are considered isomorphic if they have the same number of elements, as it is then trivial to define an invertible pair of morphisms between them. In the category $\mathbf{Vect}_k$ of vector spaces over some field k, two objects (vector spaces) are isomorphic if there is a set of invertible linear transformations between them. As we will see below, the passage from a set to the "free" vector space generated by elements of the set is another manifestation of the universal arrow property.

Functors can be viewed as a generalization of the notion of morphisms across algebraic structures, such as groups, vector spaces, and graphs. Functors do more than functions: they not only map objects to objects, but like graph homomorphisms, they need to also map each morphism in the domain category to a corresponding morphism in the co-domain category. Functors come in two varieties, as defined below.

Definition 3. *A* **covariant functor** *$F : \mathcal{C} \to \mathcal{D}$ from category $\mathcal{C}$ to category $\mathcal{D}$, and defined as the following:*

- *An object FX (also written as $F(X)$) of the category $\mathcal{D}$ for each object X in category $\mathcal{C}$.*
- *An arrow $F(f) : FX \to FY$ in category $\mathcal{D}$ for every arrow $f : X \to Y$ in category $\mathcal{C}$.*
- *The preservation of identity and composition: $F\, id_X = id_{FX}$ and $(Ff)(Fg) = F(g \circ f)$ for any composable arrows $f : X \to Y, g : Y \to Z$.*

Definition 4. *A* **contravariant functor** *$F : \mathcal{C} \to \mathcal{D}$ from category $\mathcal{C}$ to category $\mathcal{D}$ is defined exactly like the covariant functor, except all the arrows are reversed.*

3.1. Universal Arrows

This process of going from a category to its underlying directed graph embodies a fundamental universal construction in category theory, called the *universal arrow* [35]. It lies at the heart of many useful results, principally the Yoneda Lemma that shows how object identity itself emerges from the structure of morphisms that lead into (or out of) it. The Yoneda Lemma codifies the meaning of universal causality, as it implicitly states that any change to an object must be accompanied by a change to its presheaf structure. Consequently, we can model UC in a representation-independent manner using the Yoneda Lemma.

Definition 5. *Given a functor $S : D \to C$ between two categories, and an object c of category C, a* **universal arrow** *from c to S is a pair $\langle r, u \rangle$, where r is an object of D and $u : c \to Sr$ is an arrow of C, such that the following universal property holds true:*

- *For every pair $\langle d, f \rangle$ with d an object of D and $f : c \to Sd$ an arrow of C, there is a unique arrow $f' : r \to d$ of D with $Sf' \circ u = f$.*

Above we used the example of functors between graphs and their associated "free" categories and graphs to illustrate universal arrows. A central principle in the UCLA architecture is that every pair of categorical layers is synchronized by a functor, along with a universal arrow. We explore the universal arrow property more deeply in this section, showing how it provides the conceptual basis behind the Yoneda Lemma, and Grothendieck's category of elements. In the case of causal inference, universal arrows enable mimicking the effects of causal operations from one layer of the UCLA hierarchy down to the next layer. In particular, at the simplicial object layer, we can model a causal intervention in terms of face and degeneracy operators (defined below in more detail). These in turn correspond to "graph surgery" [5] operations on causal DAGs, or in terms of "copy", "delete" operators in "string diagram surgery" of causal models defined on symmetric monoidal categories [25]. These "surgery" operations at the next level may translate down to operations on probability distributions, measurable spaces, topological spaces, or chain complexes. This process follows a standard construction used widely in mathematics, for example group representations associate with any group G, a left $\mathbf{k}$-module M representation that enables modeling abstract group operations by operations on the associated modular representation. These concrete representations must satisfy the universal arrow property for them to be faithful. A special case of the universal arrow property is that of universal element, which as we will see below plays an important role in the UCLA architecture in defining a suitably augmented category of elements, based on a construction introduced by Grothendieck.

Definition 6. *If D is a category and $H : D \to \mathbf{Set}$ is a set-valued functor, a* **universal element** *associated with the functor H is a pair $\langle r, e \rangle$ consisting of an object $r \in D$ and an element $e \in Hr$ such that for every pair $\langle d, x \rangle$ with $x \in Hd$, there is a unique arrow $f : r \to d$ of D such that $(Hf)e = x$.*

Example 1. *Let E be an equivalence relation on a set S, and consider the quotient set S/E of equivalence classes, where $p : S \to S/E$ sends each element $s \in S$ into its corresponding equivalence class. The set of equivalence classes S/E has the property that any function $f : S \to X$ that respects the equivalence relation can be written as $fs = fs'$ whenever $s \sim_E s'$, that is, $f = f' \circ p$, where the unique function $f' : S/E \to X$. Thus, $\langle S/E, p \rangle$ is a universal element for the functor H.*

3.2. The Grothendieck Category of Elements

We turn next to define the category of elements, based on a construction by Grothendieck, and illustrate how it can serve as the basis for inference at each layer of the UCLA architecture. This definition is a special case of a general construction by Grothendieck [40].

Definition 7. *Given a set-valued functor $\delta : C \to \mathbf{Set}$ from some category C, the induced* **Grothendieck category of elements** *associated with δ is a pair $(\int \delta, \pi_\delta)$, where $\int \delta \in \mathbf{Cat}$ is a category in the category of all categories* **Cat**, *and $\pi_\delta : \int \delta \to C$ is a functor that "projects" the category of elements into the corresponding original category C. The objects and arrows of $\int \delta$ are defined as follows:*

- $Ob(\int \delta) = \{(s, x) | x \in Ob(C), x \in \delta s\}$.
- $\mathbf{Hom}_{\int \delta}((s, x), (s', x')) = \{f : s \to s' | \delta(f)(x) = x'\}$

Example 2. *To illustrate the category of elements construction, let us consider the toy climate change causal model shown in Figure 6. Let the category C be defined by this causal DAG model, where the objects Ob(C) are defined by the four vertices, and the arrows $\mathbf{Hom}_C$ are defined by the four edges in the model. The set-valued functor $\delta : C \to \mathbf{Set}$ maps each object (vertex) in C to a set of instances, thereby turning the causal DAG model into an associated set of tables.*

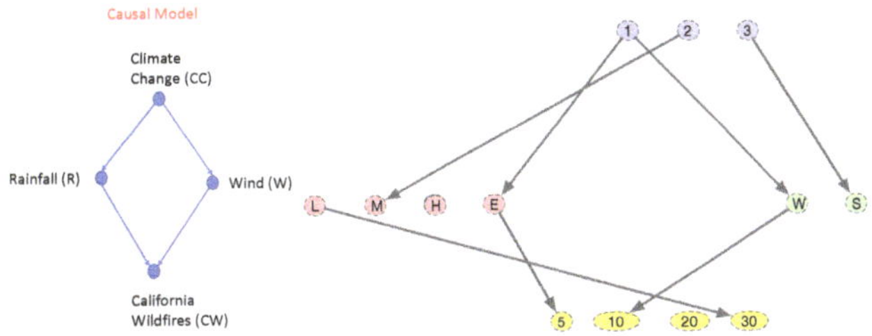

Figure 6. A toy causal DAG model of climate change to illustrate the category of elements construction. **Climate Change** is a discrete multinomial variable over three values 1, 2, and 3. For each of its values, the arrow from **Climate Change** to **Rainfall** maps each specific value of **Climate Change** to a value of **Rainfall**, thereby indicating a causal effect of climate change on the amount of rainfall in California. **Rainfall** is also a multinomial discretized as low (marked "L"), medium (marked "M"), high (marked "H"), or extreme (marked "E"). **Wind** speeds are binned into two levels (marked "W" for weak, and "S" for strong). Finally, the percentage of California wildfires is binned between 5 and 30. Not all arrows in the category of elements are shown, for clarity.

Later in the paper, we give an application of the category of elements construction to relational causal models, where in particular, it gives a rigorous semantics for ideas such as *relational skeleton* and the *ground graph* proposed in [21,32].

3.3. Yoneda Lemma

The Yoneda Lemma plays a crucial role in UC because it defines the concept of a representation in category theory. We first show that associated with universal arrows is the corresponding induced isomorphisms between **Hom** sets of morphisms in categories. This universal property then leads to the Yoneda Lemma.

Theorem 1. *Given any functor $S : D \to C$, the universal arrow $\langle r, u : c \to Sr \rangle$ implies a bijection exists between the* **Hom** *sets*

$$\mathbf{Hom}_D(r, d) \simeq \mathbf{Hom}_C(c, Sd)$$

While this is a well-known result whose proof can be found in [35], the crucial point here is its implication for causal inference. As we will see later, often in the modeling of causal inference using symmetric monoidal categories [25,29,30], a correspondence is set up between two categories, for example the symmetric monoidal category representing the structure of a causal DAG model, and the category of stochastic matrices that defines the DAG semantics. The universal arrow theorem above shows how the morphisms over the symmetric monoidal category can be synchronized with those over the stochastic matrices, enabling causal interventions to be tracked properly. A special case of this natural transformation that transforms the identity morphism $\mathbf{1}_r$ leads us to the Yoneda Lemma.

$$\begin{array}{ccc} D(r,r) & \xrightarrow{\phi_r} & C(c,Sr) \\ \big\downarrow{\scriptstyle D(r,f')} & & \big\downarrow{\scriptstyle C(c,Sf')} \\ D(r,d) & \xrightarrow{\phi_d} & C(c,Sd) \end{array}$$

As the two paths shown here must be equal in a commutative diagram, we get the property that a bijection between the **Hom** sets holds precisely when $\langle r, u : c \to Sr \rangle$ is a universal arrow from c to S. Note that for the case when the categories C and D are small, meaning their **Hom** collection of arrows forms a set, the induced functor $\mathbf{Hom}_C(c, S-)$ to **Set** is isomorphic to the functor $\mathbf{Hom}_D(r, -)$. This type of isomorphism defines a universal representation, and is at the heart of the causal reproducing property (CRP) defined below.

Lemma 1. **Yoneda Lemma**: *If $H : D \to \mathbf{Set}$ is a set-valued functor, and r is an object in D, there is a bijection that sends each natural transformation $\alpha : \mathbf{Hom}_D(r, -) \to K$ to $\alpha_r \mathbf{1}_r$, the image of the identity morphism $\mathbf{1}_r : r \to r$.*

$$y : \mathbf{Nat}(\mathbf{Hom}_D(r, -), K) \simeq Kr$$

The proof of the Yoneda Lemma follows directly from the below commutative diagram, a special case of the above diagram for universal arrows.

$$\begin{array}{ccc} D(r,r) & \xrightarrow{\phi_r} & Kr \\ \downarrow{\scriptstyle D(r,f')} & & \downarrow{\scriptstyle C(c,Sf')} \\ D(r,d) & \xrightarrow{\phi_d} & Kd \end{array}$$

3.4. The Universality of Diagrams and the Causal Reproducing Property

We state two key results that underly UC, and while both these results follow directly from basic theorems in category theory, their significance for causal inference is what makes them particularly noteworthy. The first result pertains to the notion of diagrams as functors, and shows that for the functor category of presheaves, which is a universal representation of causal inference, every presheaf object can be represented as a colimit of representables through the Yoneda Lemma. This result can be seen as a generalization of the very simple result in set theory that each set is a union of one element sets. The second result is the causal reproducing property, which shows that the set of all causal effects between two objects is computable from the presheaf functor objects defined by them. Both these results are abstract, and apply to any category representation of a causal model.

Diagrams play a key role in defining UC and the UCLA architecture, as has already become clear from the discussion above. We briefly want to emphasize the central role played by universal constructions involving limits and colimits of diagrams, which are viewed as functors from an indexing category of diagrams to a category. To make this somewhat abstract definition concrete, let us look at some simpler examples of universal properties, including co-products and quotients (which in set theory correspond to disjoint unions). Coproducts refer to the universal property of abstracting a group of elements into a larger one.

Before we formally the concept of limit and colimits [35], we consider some examples. These notions generalize the more familiar notions of Cartesian products and disjoint unions in the category of **Sets**, the notion of meets and joins in the category **Preord** of preorders, as well as the least upper bounds and greatest lower bounds in lattices, and many other concrete examples from mathematics.

Example 3. *If we consider a small "discrete" category $\mathcal{D}$ whose only morphisms are identity arrows, then the colimit of a functor $\mathcal{F} : \mathcal{D} \to \mathcal{C}$ is the* categorical coproduct *of $\mathcal{F}(D)$ for D, an object of category D, is denoted as*

$$Colimit_{\mathcal{D}} F = \bigsqcup_{D} \mathcal{F}(D)$$

In the special case when the category C is the category **Sets**, *then the colimit of this functor is simply the disjoint union of all the sets $F(D)$ that are mapped from objects $D \in \mathcal{D}$.*

Example 4. *Dual to the notion of colimit of a functor is the notion of* limit. *Once again, if we consider a small "discrete" category $\mathcal{D}$ whose only morphisms are identity arrows, then the limit of a functor $\mathcal{F} : \mathcal{D} \to \mathcal{C}$ is the* categorical product *of $\mathcal{F}(D)$ for D, an object of category D, is denoted as*

$$limit_{\mathcal{D}} F = \prod_{D} \mathcal{F}(D)$$

In the special case when the category C is the category **Sets**, *then the limit of this functor is simply the Cartesian product of all the sets* $F(D)$ *that are mapped from objects* $D \in \mathcal{D}$.

Pullback and Pushforward Mappings

Universal causal models in UC are defined in terms of *universal constructions*, which satisfy a universal property. We can illustrate this concept using pullback and pushforward mappings. These notions help clarify the idea of the Grothendieck category of elements, which plays a key role in the UCLA architecture.

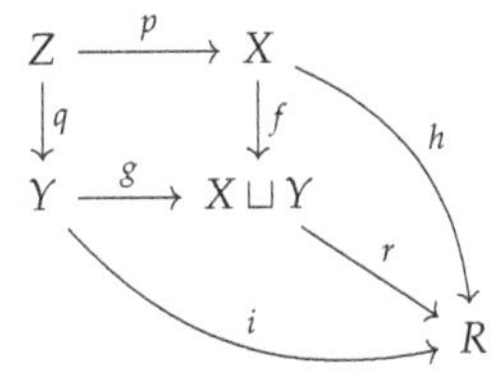

An example of a universal construction is given by the above commutative diagram, where the coproduct object $X \sqcup Y$ uniquely factorizes any mapping $h : X \rightarrow R$, such that any mapping $i : Y \rightarrow R$, so that $h = r \circ f$, and furthermore $i = r \circ g$. Co-products are themselves special cases of the more general notion of co-limits. Figure 7 illustrates the fundamental property of a *pullback*, which along with *pushforward*, is one of the core ideas in category theory. The pullback square with the objects U, X, Y and Z implies that the composite mappings $g \circ f'$ must equal $g' \circ f$. In this example, the morphisms f and g represent a *pullback* pair, as they share a common co-domain Z. The pair of morphisms f', g' emanating from U define a *cone*, because the pullback square "commutes" appropriately. Thus, the pullback of the pair of morphisms f, g with the common co-domain Z is the pair of morphisms f', g' with common domain U. Furthermore, to satisfy the universal property, given another pair of morphisms x, y with common domain T, there must exist another morphism $k : T \rightarrow U$ that "factorizes" x, y appropriately, so that the composite morphisms $f'\ k = y$ and $g'\ k = x$. Here, T and U are referred to as *cones*, where U is the limit of the set of all cones "above" Z. If we reverse arrow directions appropriately, we get the corresponding notion of pushforward. So, in this example, the pair of morphisms f', g' that share a common domain represent a pushforward pair. As Figure 7, for any set-valued functor $\delta : S \rightarrow$ **Sets**, the Grothendieck category of elements $\int \delta$ can be shown to be a pullback in the diagram of categories. Here, $\mathbf{Set}_*$ is the category of pointed sets, and π is a projection that sends a pointed set $(X, x \in X)$ to its underlying set X.

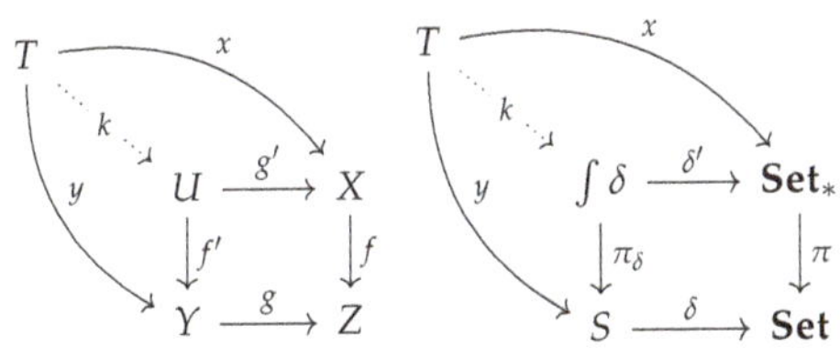

Figure 7. (**Left**) Universal Property of pullback mappings. (**Right**) The Grothendieck category of elements $\int \delta$ of any set-valued functor $\delta : S \rightarrow$ **Set** can be described as a pullback in the diagram of categories. Here, $\mathbf{Set}_*$ is the category of pointed sets $(X, x \in X)$, and π is the "forgetful" functor that sends a pointed set $(X, x \in X)$ into the underlying set X.

In the category **Sets**, we know that every object (i.e., a set) X can be expressed as a coproduct of its elements $X \simeq \sqcup_{x \in X}\{x\}$, where $x \in X$. Note that we can view each element $x \in X$ as a morphism $x : \{*\} \rightarrow X$ from the one-point set to X. The categorical generalization of this result is called the *density theorem* in the theory of sheaves [36]. First, we define the key concept of a *comma category*.

Definition 8. *Let $F : \mathcal{D} \to \mathcal{C}$ be a functor from category $\mathcal{D}$ to $\mathcal{C}$. The* **comma category** *$F \downarrow C$ is one whose objects are pairs (D, f), where $D \in \mathcal{D}$ is an object of $\mathcal{D}$ and $f \in \mathbf{Hom}_{\mathcal{C}}(F(D), C)$, where C is an object of $\mathcal{C}$. Morphisms in the comma category $F \downarrow C$ from (D, f) to (D', f'), where $g : D \to D'$, such that $f' \circ F(g) = f$. We can depict this structure through the following commutative diagram:*

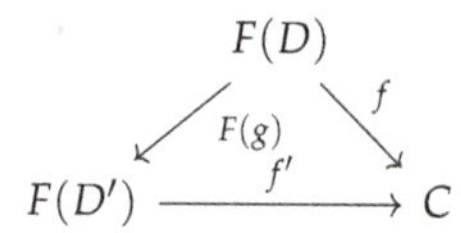

We first introduce the concept of a *dense* functor [40]:

Definition 9. *Let D be a small category, C be an arbitrary category, and $F : \mathcal{D} \to \mathcal{D}$ be a functor. The functor F is* **dense** *if for all objects C of $\mathcal{C}$, the natural transformation*

$$\psi_F^C : F \circ U \to \Delta_C, \quad (\psi_F^C)_{(\mathcal{D},f)} = f$$

is universal in the sense that it induces an isomorphism $Colimit_{F \downarrow C} F \circ U \simeq C$. Here, $U : F \downarrow C \to \mathcal{D}$ is the projection functor from the comma category $F \downarrow C$, defined by $U(D, f) = D$.

A fundamental consequence of the category of elements is that every object in the functor category of presheaves, namely contravariant functors from a category into the category of sets, is the colimit of a diagram of representable objects, via the Yoneda Lemma. Notice this is a generalized form of the density notion from the category **Sets**, as explained above.

Theorem 2. Universality of Diagrams in UC*: In the functor category of presheaves $\mathbf{Set}^{\mathcal{C}^{op}}$, every object P is the colimit of a diagram of representable objects, in a canonical way [36].*

To explain the significance of this result for causal inference, note that UC represents causal diagrams as functors from an indexing category of diagrams to an actual causal model (as illustrated earlier in Figure 3). The density theorem above tells us that every presheaf object can be represented as a colimit of (simple) representable objects, namely functor objects of the form $\mathbf{Hom}_{\mathcal{C}}(-, c)$.

Reproducing Kernel Hilbert Spaces (RKHS's) transformed the study of machine learning, precisely because they are the unique subcategory in the category of all Hilbert spaces that have representers of evaluation defined by a kernel matrix $K(x, y)$ [42]. The reproducing property in an RKHS is defined as $\langle K(x, -), K(-, y) \rangle = K(x, y)$. An analogous but far more general reproducing property holds in the UC framework, based on the Yoneda Lemma. The significance of the Causal Reproducing Property is that presheaves act as "representers" of causal information, precisely analogous to how kernel matrices act as representers in an RKHS.

Theorem 3. Causal Reproducing Property: *All causal influences between any two objects X and Y can be derived from its presheaf functor objects, namely*

$$\mathbf{Hom}_{\mathcal{C}}(X, Y) \simeq \mathbf{Nat}(\mathbf{Hom}_{\mathcal{C}}(-, X), \mathbf{Hom}_{\mathcal{C}}(-, Y))$$

Proof. The proof of this theorem is a direct consequence of the Yoneda Lemma, which states that for every presheaf functor object F in $\hat{\mathcal{C}}$ of a category $\mathcal{C}$, **Nat(**$\mathbf{Hom}_{\mathcal{C}}(-, X), F) \simeq FX$. That is, elements of the set FX are in $1-1$ bijections with natural transformations from the presheaf $\mathbf{Hom}_{\mathcal{C}}(-, X)$ to F. For the special case where the functor object $F = \mathbf{Hom}_{\mathcal{C}}(-, Y)$, we get the result immediately that $\mathbf{Hom}_{\mathcal{C}}(X, Y) \simeq$ **Nat(**$\mathbf{Hom}_{\mathcal{C}}(-, X)$,$\mathbf{Hom}_{\mathcal{C}}(-, Y)$). □

In UC, any causal influence of an object X upon any other object Y can be represented as a natural transformation (a morphism) between two functor objections in the presheaf category $\hat{C}$. The CRP is very akin to the idea of the reproducing property in kernel methods.

3.5. Lifting Problems

The UCLA hierarchy is defined through a series of categorical abstractions of a causal model, ranging from a combinatorial model defined by a simplicial object down to a measure-theoretic or topological realization. Between each pair of layers, we can formulate a series of lifting problems [17]. Lifting problems provide elegant ways to define basic notions in a wide variety of areas in mathematics. For example, the notion of injective and surjective functions, the notion of separation in topology, and many other basic constructs can be formulated as solutions to lifting problems. Database queries in relational databases can be defined using lifting problems [4]. Lifting problems define ways of decomposing structures into simpler pieces, and putting them back together again.

Definition 10. *Let C be a category. A* **lifting problem** *in C is a commutative diagram σ in C.*

$$\begin{array}{ccc} A & \xrightarrow{\mu} & X \\ \downarrow{\scriptstyle f} & & \downarrow{\scriptstyle p} \\ B & \xrightarrow{\nu} & Y \end{array}$$

Definition 11. *Let C be a category. A* **solution to a lifting problem** *in C is a morphism $h : B \to X$ in C satisfying $p \circ h = \nu$ and $h \circ f = \mu$ as indicated in the diagram below.*

$$\begin{array}{ccc} A & \xrightarrow{\mu} & X \\ \downarrow{\scriptstyle f} & \overset{h}{\nearrow} & \downarrow{\scriptstyle p} \\ B & \xrightarrow{\nu} & Y \end{array}$$

Definition 12. *Let C be a category. If we are given two morphisms $f : A \to B$ and $p : X \to Y$ in C, we say that f has the* **left lifting property** *with respect to p, or that p has the* **right lifting property** *with respect to f if for every pair of morphisms $\mu : A \to X$ and $\nu : B \to Y$ satisfying the equations $p \circ \mu = \nu \circ f$, the associated lifting problem indicated in the diagram below.*

$$\begin{array}{ccc} A & \xrightarrow{\mu} & X \\ \downarrow{\scriptstyle f} & \overset{h}{\nearrow} & \downarrow{\scriptstyle p} \\ B & \xrightarrow{\nu} & Y \end{array}$$

admits a solution given by the map $h : B \to X$ satisfying $p \circ h = \nu$ and $h \circ f = \mu$.

Example 5. *Given the paradigmatic non-surjective morphism $f : \emptyset \to \{\bullet\}$, any morphism p that has the right lifting property with respect to f is a* **surjective mapping**. .

$$\begin{array}{ccc} \emptyset & \xrightarrow{\mu} & X \\ \downarrow{\scriptstyle f} & \overset{h}{\nearrow} & \downarrow{\scriptstyle p} \\ \{\bullet\} & \xrightarrow{\nu} & Y \end{array}$$

Example 6. *Given the paradigmatic non-injective morphism $f : \{\bullet, \bullet\} \to \{\bullet\}$, any morphism p that has the right lifting property with respect to f is an* **injective mapping**. .

$$\begin{array}{ccc} \{\bullet,\bullet\} & \xrightarrow{\mu} & X \\ \downarrow{\scriptstyle f} & \overset{h}{\nearrow} & \downarrow{\scriptstyle p} \\ \{\bullet\} & \xrightarrow{\nu} & Y \end{array}$$

4. Universal Conditional Independence in Categories

Before proceeding to further detail the UCLA architecture, we discuss the special role played by conditional independence in causal inference. Causal models can be abstractly characterized by their underlying conditional independences. A number of previous axiomatizations such as *graphoids* [5,16], *integer-valued multisets* [8], and *separoids* [10] can be subsumed under the category-theoretic notion of universal conditional independence [15]. Conditional independence structures have been actively studied in AI, causal inference, machine learning, probability, and statistics for many years. Dawid [10] define separoids, a join semi-lattice, to formalize reasoning about conditional independence and irrelevance in many areas, including statistics. Pearl [16] introduced *graphoids*, a distributive lattice over disjoint subsets of variables, to model reasoning about irrelevance in probabilistic systems, and proposed representations using directed acyclic graphs (DAGs). Studeny [8] proposed a lattice-theoretic model of conditional independences using integer-valued multisets to address the intrinsic limitations of DAG-based representations.

In particular, we want to show how it is possible to define *universal conditional independence* [15], a representation of conditional independence in any category. We build specifically on the notion of *separoids* [10], an algebraic characterization of conditional independence. Recent work by Fritz and Klingler [30] has proposed a symmetric monoidal category representation of DAG type causal models, and an associated categorical probabilistic representations of d-separation. Our goals are to construct a more abstract representation of conditional independence based on non-graphical representations, like separoids [10] as well as integer-valued multisets [8].

Conditional independence plays a key role in causal discovery as it is often used as an oracle in causal discovery from data. Consider the problem of causal discovery as inferring a directed acyclic graph (DAG) $G = (V, E)$ from data, where the conditional independence $\perp\!\!\!\perp$ property is defined using the graph property of d-separation [16]. A given DAG G can be characterized in two ways: one parameterization specifies the DAG G in terms of the vertices V and edges E, which corresponds to specifying the objects and morphisms of a category defining the DAG. The second way to parameterize a DAG is by its induced collection of conditional independence properties, as defined by d-separation. For example, the serial DAG over three variables, $A \rightarrow B \rightarrow C$, can be defined using its two edges $A \rightarrow B$ and $B \rightarrow C$, but also by its conditional independences, namely $A \perp\!\!\!\perp C|B$ using the theory of d-separation. We are thus given two possibly redundant parameterizations of the same algebraic structure. However, multiple DAG models can define the same conditional independences. For example, the serial model $A \rightarrow B \rightarrow C$, as well as the "diverging" model $A \leftarrow B \rightarrow C$ and the "reverse" serial model $A \leftarrow B \leftarrow C$ all capture the same conditional independence property ($A \perp\!\!\!\perp C|B$). This non-uniqueness property arises because Bayes rule can be used to map any one of these three DAGs into the form represented by one of the other DAGs.

4.1. The Category of Separoids

A separoid $(\mathcal{S}, \leq, \perp\!\!\!\perp)$ [10] is defined as a semi-lattice $\mathcal{S}$, where the join $\vee$ operator over the semi-lattice $\mathcal{S}$ defines a preorder $\leq$, and the ternary relation $\perp\!\!\!\perp$ is defined over triples of the form $(x \perp\!\!\!\perp y|z)$ (which are interpreted to mean x is conditionally independent of y given z). We show briefly how to define a category for universal conditional independence, where each object is a separoid, and the morphisms are homomorphisms from one separoid to another. It is possible to define "lattice" objects in any category by interpreting an arrow $f : x \rightarrow y$ as defining the partial ordering [36].

Definition 13. *A* **separoid** *[10] defines a category over a preordered set $(\mathcal{S}, \leq)$, namely $\leq$ is reflexive and transitive, equipped with a* ternary *relation $\perp\!\!\!\perp$ on triples (x, y, z), where $x, y, z \in \mathcal{S}$ satisfy the following properties:*

- **S1:** *$(\mathcal{S}, \leq)$ is a join semi-lattice.*
- **P1:** $x \perp\!\!\!\perp y \mid x$

- **P2:** $x \perp\!\!\!\perp y \mid z \quad \Rightarrow \quad y \perp\!\!\!\perp x \mid z$
- **P3:** $x \perp\!\!\!\perp y \mid z$ *and* $w \leq y \quad \Rightarrow \quad x \perp\!\!\!\perp w \mid z$
- **P4:** $x \perp\!\!\!\perp y \mid z$ *and* $w \leq y \quad \Rightarrow \quad x \perp\!\!\!\perp y \mid (z \vee w)$
- **P5:** $x \perp\!\!\!\perp y \mid z$ *and* $x \perp\!\!\!\perp w \mid (y \vee z) \quad \Rightarrow \quad x \perp\!\!\!\perp (y \vee w) \mid z$

A **strong separoid** *also defines a categoroid. A strong separoid is defined over a lattice $\mathcal{S}$ has in addition to a join $\vee$, a meet $\wedge$ operation, and satisfies an additional axiom:*

- **P6**: *If $z \leq y$ and $w \leq y$, then* $x \perp\!\!\!\perp y \mid z$ *and* $x \perp\!\!\!\perp y \mid w \quad \Rightarrow \quad x \perp\!\!\!\perp y \mid z \wedge w$

To define a category of separoids, we have to define the notion of a homomorphism between separoids [10]:

Definition 14. *Let $\langle \mathcal{S}, \leq, \perp\!\!\!\perp \rangle$ and $\langle \mathcal{S}', \leq', \perp\!\!\!\perp' \rangle$ be two separoids. A map $f : \mathcal{S} \to \mathcal{S}'$ is a* **separoid homomorphism** *if:*

1. *It is a join-lattice homomorphism, namely $f(x \vee y) = f(x) \vee' f(y)$, which implies that $x \leq y \to f(x) \leq' f(y)$.*
2. $x \perp\!\!\!\perp y \mid z \to f(x) \perp\!\!\!\perp' f(y) \mid f(z)$.
3. *In case both S and S′ are strong separoids, we can define the notion of a strong separoid homomorphism to additionally include the condition: $f(x \wedge y) \to f(x) \wedge' f(y)$.*

With this definition, we can now define the category of separoids and a representation-independent characterization of universal conditional independence as follows:

Theorem 4. *The category of separoids is defined as one where each object in the category is defined as a separoid $\langle \mathcal{S}, \leq, \perp\!\!\!\perp \rangle$, and the arrows are defined as (strong) separoid homomorphisms. The category of separoids provides an axiomatization of universal conditional independence, namely that it enables a universal representation through the use of universal arrows and Yoneda Lemma.*

Proof. First, we note that the category of separoids indeed forms a category as it straightforwardly satisfies all the basic properties. The (strong) separoid homomorphisms compose, so that $g \circ f$ as a composition of two (strong) separoid homomorphisms produces another (strong) separoid homomorphism. The universal property derives from the use of the Yoneda Lemma to define a category of presheaves that map from the category of separoids to the category **Sets**. □

4.2. Adjoint Functors in Causal Discovery

First, we need to review the basic concept of adjoint functors, which will be helpful in modeling several aspects of causal inference in this paper.

Definition 15. *A pair of* **adjoint functors** *is defined as $F : \mathcal{C} \to \mathcal{D}$ and $G : \mathcal{D} \to \mathcal{C}$, where F is considered the right adjoint, and G is considered the left adjoint,*

$$\mathcal{D} \underset{F}{\overset{G}{\underset{\leftarrow}{\overset{\rightarrow}{\top}}}} \mathbf{C}.$$

must satisfy the property that for each pair of objects C of $\mathcal{C}$ and D of $\mathcal{D}$, there is a natural transformation between the two sets of morphisms

$$\phi_{C,D} : \mathbf{Hom}_{\mathcal{C}}(C, G(D)) \simeq \mathbf{Hom}_{\mathcal{D}}(F(C), D)$$

An important property of adjoint functors is connected to the concepts of limits and colimits reviewed above.

Theorem 5. *If F and G are a pair of adjoint functors*

$$\mathcal{D} \underset{F}{\overset{G}{\underset{\longleftarrow}{\overset{\longrightarrow}{\top}}}} \mathbf{C}.$$

then the functor G preserves colimits and the functor F preserves limits.

Notice the similarity of this definition to the one earlier where the universal arrow property induced a bijection of **Hom** sets that then led to universal elements, Grothendieck category of elements, and the Yoneda Lemma.

We now introduce the perspective of adjoint functors for causal discovery (see Figure 8). Many causal discovery algorithms [27] that use a conditional independence oracle to query conditional independence properties from a dataset can be viewed in this perspective as using adjoint functors between the category of separoids and the category of the causal model itself. We can design functors that map from the category of all separoids into the category of causal models (in particular, for example, the category of graphs, or the category of integer-valued multisets [8]). Shown in the figure is one particular separoid object with a single conditional independence property stating that A and B are dependent conditional on knowing the value of C), which can realized in two ways: one using a collider DAG $A \rightarrow C \leftarrow B$, and the other as a integer-valued multiset. These pair of functors are an example of the general case of adjoint functors between "forgetful" and "free" functors [40]. To make this more precise, let us define the "forgetful" functor R between a causal model on the right to its underlying set of conditional independences on the left, so that $R(M)$ is the separoid object that represents the conditional independence in a causal model M. Note that R is a "forgetful" functor, in that it "throws away" structural information, including for example, whether the causal model is a causal DAG or an integer-valued multiset. On the other hand, the "free" functor $L(M)$, its left adjoint, maps a given separoid object to any of its associated "free" objects, namely causal models that represent it, irrespective of their formalism. Within the category of causal models, morphisms enable translation between different representations.

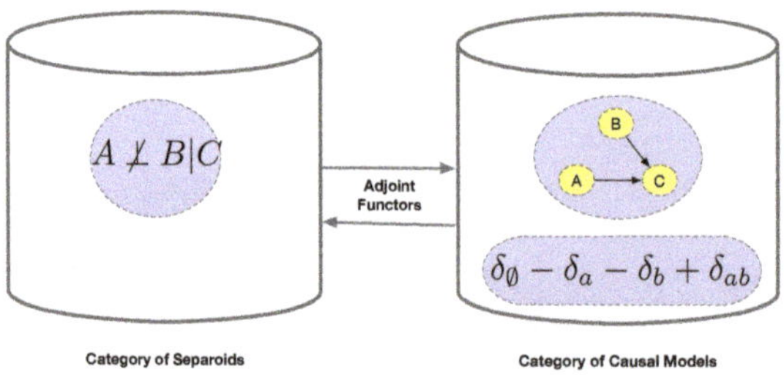

Figure 8. Adjoint functors between the category of separoids and the category of causal models. Here, a causal "collider" DAG over three random variables A, B, and C, and its associated integer-valued multiset, can both be viewed as "free" objects associated with a separoid conditional independence object, whereas the latter can be viewed in terms of a forgetful functor that throws away the causal DAG or integer-valued multiset structure.

5. Layers 1 and 2: Category of Causal Interventions over Simplicial Objects

We now discuss Layers 1 and 2 in UCLA architecture, describing the top simplicial objects layer, and how it interacts with the causal category structure (layer 2). Simplicial sets are higher-dimensional generalizations of directed graphs, partially ordered sets, as well as regular categories themselves. Importantly, simplicial sets and simplicial objects form a foundation for higher-order category theory [13,14]. By using simplicial sets and objects at the top layer, UCLA enables a powerful machinery to define a higher-order category for representing a rich class of causal interventions over a very expressive set of causal models, including relational causal models [32], and perform abstract "diagram surgery", for example "graph surgery" [5] or "string diagram surgery" [25].

Simplicial objects have long been a foundation for algebraic topology [12,39], and more recently in higher-order category theory [13,14,43]. The category Δ has non-empty ordinals $[n] = \{0, 1, \ldots, n\}$ as objects, and order-preserving maps $[m] \to [n]$ as arrows. An important property in Δ is that any many-to-many mapping is decomposable as a composition of an injective and a surjective mapping, each of which is decomposable into a sequence of elementary injections $\delta_i : [n] \to [n+1]$, called *coface* mappings, which omits $i \in [n]$, and a sequence of elementary surjections $\sigma_i : [n] \to [n-1]$, called *co-degeneracy* mappings, which repeats $i \in [n]$. The fundamental simplex $\Delta([n])$ is the presheaf of all morphisms into $[n]$, that is, the representable functor $\Delta(-, [n])$. The Yoneda Lemma [35] assures us that an n-simplex $x \in X_n$ can be identified with the corresponding map $\Delta[n] \to X$. Every morphism $f : [n] \to [m]$ in Δ is functorially mapped to the map $\Delta[m] \to \Delta[n]$ in $\mathcal{S}$.

Any morphism in the category Δ can be defined as a sequence of *co-degeneracy* and *co-face* operators, where the co-face operator $\delta_i : [n-1] \to [n], 0 \leq i \leq n$ is defined as:

$$\delta_i(j) = \begin{cases} j, & \text{for } 0 \leq j \leq i-1 \\ j+1 & \text{for } i \leq j \leq n-1 \end{cases}$$

Analogously, the co-degeneracy operator $\sigma_j : [n+1] \to [n]$ is defined as

$$\sigma_j(k) = \begin{cases} j, & \text{for } 0 \leq k \leq j \\ k-1 & \text{for } j < k \leq n+1 \end{cases}$$

Note that under the contravariant mappings, co-face mappings turn into face mappings, and co-degeneracy mappings turn into degeneracy mappings. That is, for any simplicial object (or set) X_n, we have $X(\delta_i) := d_i : X_n \to X_{n-1}$, and likewise, $X(\sigma_j) := s_j : X_{n-1} \to X_n$.

The compositions of these arrows define certain well-known properties [12,40]:

$$\begin{aligned} \delta_j \circ \delta_i &= \delta_i \circ \delta_{j-1}, \; i < j \\ \sigma_j \circ \sigma_i &= \sigma_i \circ \sigma_{j+1}, \; i \leq j \\ \sigma_j \circ \delta_i(j) &= \begin{cases} \sigma_i \circ \sigma_{j+1}, & \text{for } i < j \\ 1_{[n]} & \text{for } i = j, j+1 \\ \sigma_{i-1} \circ \sigma_j, \text{for } i > j+1 & \end{cases} \end{aligned}$$

Example 7. *The "vertices" of a simplicial object C_n are the objects in C, and the "edges" of C are its arrows $f : X \to Y$, where X and Y are objects in C. Given any such arrow, the degeneracy operators $d_0 f = Y$ and $d_1 f = X$ recover the source and target of each arrow. Also, given an object X of category C, we can regard the face operator $s_0 X$ as its identity morphism $\mathbf{1}_X : X \to X$.*

Example 8. *Given a category C, we can identify an n-simplex σ of a simplicial set C_n with the sequence:*

$$\sigma = C_o \xrightarrow{f_1} C_1 \xrightarrow{f_2} \ldots \xrightarrow{f_n} C_n$$

the face operator d_0 applied to σ yields the sequence

$$d_0 \sigma = C_1 \xrightarrow{f_2} C_2 \xrightarrow{f_3} \ldots \xrightarrow{f_n} C_n$$

where the object C_0 is "deleted" along with the morphism f_0 leaving it. The "edge intervention" model in [44] effectively can be viewed as deleting the vertex from which the edge originates.

Example 9. *Given a category $\mathcal{C}$, and an n-simplex σ of the simplicial set $\mathcal{C}_n$, the face operator d_n applied to σ yields the sequence*

$$d_n\sigma = C_0 \xrightarrow{f_1} C_1 \xrightarrow{f_2} \dots \xrightarrow{f_{n-1}} C_{n-1}$$

where the object C_n is "deleted" along with the morphism f_n entering it. Note this face operator can be viewed as analogous to interventions on leaf nodes in a causal DAG model.

Example 10. *Given a category $\mathcal{C}$, and an n-simplex σ of the simplicial set $\mathcal{C}_n$ the face operator $d_i, 0 < i < n$ applied to σ yields the sequence*

$$d_i\sigma = C_0 \xrightarrow{f_1} C_1 \xrightarrow{f_2} \dots C_{i-1} \xrightarrow{f_{i+1}\circ f_i} C_{i+1} \dots \xrightarrow{f_n} C_n$$

where the object C_i is "deleted" and the morphisms f_i is composed with morphism f_{i+1}. Note that this process can be abstractly viewed as intervening on object C_i by choosing a specific value for it (which essentially "freezes" the morphism f_i entering object C_i to a constant value).

Example 11. *Given a category $\mathcal{C}$, and an n-simplex σ of the simplicial set $\mathcal{C}_n$, the degeneracy operator $s_i, 0 \leq i \leq n$ applied to σ yields the sequence*

$$s_i\sigma = C_0 \xrightarrow{f_1} C_1 \xrightarrow{f_2} \dots C_i \xrightarrow{\mathbf{1}_{C_i}} C_i \xrightarrow{f_{i+1}} C_{i+1} \dots \xrightarrow{f_n} C_n$$

where the object C_i is "repeated" by inserting its identity morphism $\mathbf{1}_{C_i}$.

Definition 16. *Given a category $\mathcal{C}$, and an n-simplex σ of the simplicial set $\mathcal{C}_n$, σ is a* **degenerate** *simplex if some f_i in σ is an identity morphism, in which case C_i and C_{i+1} are equal.*

5.1. Simplicial Subsets and Horns

We now describe more complex ways of extracting parts of causal structures using simplicial subsets and horns. These structures will play a key role in defining suitable lifting problems.

Definition 17. *The* **standard simplex** *Δ^n is the simplicial set defined by the construction*

$$([m] \in \Delta) \mapsto \mathbf{Hom}_\Delta([m],[n])$$

By convention, $\Delta^{-1} := \emptyset$. The standard 0-simplex Δ^0 maps each $[n] \in \Delta^{op}$ to the single element set $\{\bullet\}$.

Definition 18. *Let $S_\bullet$ denote a simplicial set. If for every integer $n \geq 0$, we are given a subset $T_n \subseteq S_n$, such that the face and degeneracy maps*

$$d_i : S_n \to S_{n-1} \quad s_i : S_n \to S_{n+1}$$

applied to T_n result in

$$d_i : T_n \to T_{n-1} \quad s_i : T_n \to T_{n+1}$$

then the collection $\{T_n\}_{n\geq 0}$ defines a **simplicial subset** *$T_\bullet \subseteq S_\bullet$*

Definition 19. *The* **boundary** *is a simplicial set $(\partial\Delta^n) : \Delta^{op} \to$* **Set** *defined as*

$$(\partial\Delta^n)([m]) = \{\alpha \in \mathbf{Hom}_\Delta([m],[n]) : \alpha \text{ is not surjective}\}$$

Note that the boundary $\partial\Delta^n$ is a simplicial subset of the standard n-simplex Δ^n.

Definition 20. *The* **Horn** $\Lambda_i^n : \Delta^{op} \to$ **Set** *is defined as*

$$(\Lambda_i^n)([m]) = \{\alpha \in \mathbf{Hom}_\Delta([m],[n]) : [n] \not\subseteq \alpha([m]) \cup \{i\}\}$$

Intuitively, the Horn Λ_i^n can be viewed as the simplicial subset that results from removing the interior of the n-simplex Δ^n together with the face opposite its ith vertex.

5.2. Example: Causal Intervention and Horn Filling of Simplicial Objects

Let us illustrate this abstract discussion above by instantiating it in the context of causal inference. Figure 9 instantiates the abstract discussion above in terms of an example from causal inference. We are given a simple 3 variable DAG, on which we desire to explore the causal effect of variable A on C. Using Pearl's backdoor criterion, we can intervene on variable A by freezing its value $do(A = 1)$, for example, which will eliminate the dependence of A on B. Consider now the lifting problem where we want to know if there is a completion of this simplicial subset Λ_2^2, which is a "outer horn".

Figure 9. Causal interventions can be related to horns of a simplicial object.

We can view the causal intervention problem in the more abstract setting of a class of lifting problem, shown with the following diagrams. Consider the problem of composing 1-dimensional simplices to form a 2-dimensional simplicial object. Each simplicial subset of an n-simplex induces a a *horn* Λ_k^n, where $0 \leq k \leq n$. Intuitively, a horn is a subset of a simplicial object that results from removing the interior of the n-simplex and the face opposite the ith vertex. Consider the three horns defined below. The dashed arrow $\dashrightarrow$ indicates edges of the 2-simplex Δ^2 not contained in the horns.

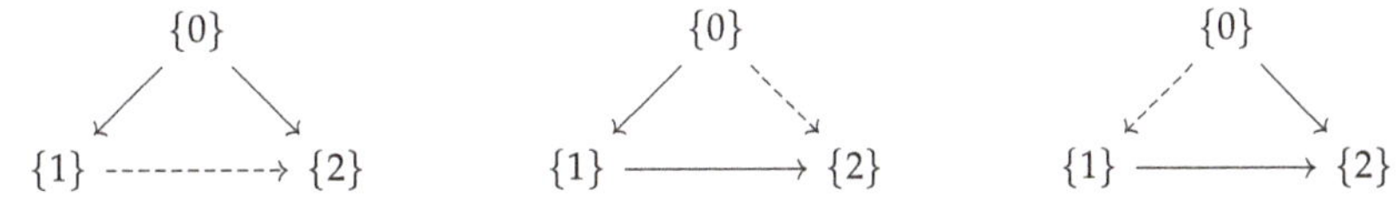

The inner horn Λ_1^2 is the middle diagram above, and admits an easy solution to the "horn filling" problem of composing the simplicial subsets. The two outer horns on either end pose a more difficult challenge. For example, filling the outer horn Λ_0^2 when the morphism between $\{0\}$ and $\{1\}$ is f and that between $\{0\}$ and $\{2\}$ is the identity **1** is tantamount to finding the left inverse of f up to homotopy. Dually, in this case, filling the outer horn Λ_2^2 is tantamount to finding the right inverse of f up to homotopy. A considerable elaboration of the theoretical machinery in category theory is required to describe the various solutions proposed, which led to different ways of defining higher-order category theory [13,14,43].

5.3. Higher-Order Categories

We now formally introduce higher-order categories, building on the framework proposed in a number of formalisms [13,14,43]. We briefly summarize various approaches to the horn filling problem in higher-order category theory.

Definition 21. *Let $f : X \to S$ be a morphism of simplicial sets. We say f is a* **Kan fibration** *if, for each $n > 0$, and each $0 \leq i \leq n$, every lifting problem.*

$$\begin{array}{ccc} \Lambda^n_i & \xrightarrow{\sigma_0} & X \\ \downarrow & \overset{\sigma}{\nearrow} & \downarrow f \\ \Delta^n & \xrightarrow{\bar{\sigma}} & S \end{array}$$

admits a solution. More precisely, for every map of simplicial sets $\sigma_0 : \Lambda^n_i \to X$ and every n-simplex $\bar{\sigma} : \Delta^n \to S$ extending $f \circ \sigma_0$, we can extend σ_0 to an n-simplex $\sigma : \Delta^n \to X$ satisfying $f \circ \sigma = \bar{\sigma}$.

Example 12. *Given a simplicial set X, then a projection map $X \to \Delta^0$ that is a Kan fibration is called a* **Kan complex**.

Example 13. *Any isomorphism between simplicial sets is a Kan fibration.*

Example 14. *The collection of Kan fibrations is closed under retracts.*

Definition 22 ([14]). *An ∞-category is a simplicial object $S_\bullet$ which satisfies the following condition:*

- *For $0 < i < n$, every map of simplicial sets $\sigma_0 : \Lambda^n_i \to S_\bullet$ can be extended to a map $\sigma : \Delta^n \to S_i$.*

This definition emerges out of a common generalization of two other conditions on a simplicial set S_i:

1. **Property K**: For $n > 0$ and $0 \le i \le n$, every map of simplicial sets $\sigma_0 : \Lambda^n_i \to S_\bullet$ can be extended to a map $\sigma : \Delta^n \to S_i$.
2. **Property C**: for $0 < 1 < n$, every map of simplicial sets $\sigma_0 : \Lambda^n_i \to S_i$ can be extended uniquely to a map $\sigma : \Delta^n \to S_i$.

Simplicial objects that satisfy property K were defined above to be Kan complexes. Simplicial objects that satisfy property C above can be identified with the nerve of a category, which yields a full and faithful embedding of a category in the category of sets. Definition 22 generalizes both of these definitions, and was called a *quasicategory* in [13] and *weak Kan complexes* in [43] when C is a category. We will use the nerve of a category below in defining homotopy colimits as a way of characterizing a causal model.

5.4. Example: Simplicial Objects over Integer-Valued Multisets

To help ground out this somewhat abstract discussion above on simplicial objects and sets, let us consider its application to two other examples. Our first example comes from a non-graphical representations of conditional independence, namely integer-valued multisets [8], defined as an integer-valued multiset function $u : \mathbb{Z}^{\mathcal{P}(\mathbb{Z})} \to \mathbb{Z}$ from the power set of integers, $\mathcal{P}(\mathbb{Z})$ to integers $\mathbb{Z}$. An imset is defined over partialy ordered set (poset), defined as a distributive lattice of disjoint (or non-disjoint) subsets of variables. The bottom element is denoted $\emptyset$, and top element represents the complete set of variables N. A full discussion of the probabilistic representations induced by imsets is given [8]. We will only focus on the aspects of imsets that relate to its conditional independence structure, and its topological structure as defined by the poset. A *combinatorial* imset is defined as:

$$u = \sum_{A \subset N} c_A \delta_A$$

where c_A is an integer, δ_A is the characteristic function for subset A, and A potentially ranges over all subsets of N. An *elementary* imset is defined over $(a, b \perp\!\!\!\perp A)$, where a, b are singletons, and $A \subset N \setminus \{a, b\}$. A *structural* imset is defined as one where the coefficients can be rational numbers. For a general DAG model $G = (V, E)$, an imset in standard form [8] is defined as

$$u_G = \delta_V - \delta_\emptyset + \sum_{i \in V} (\delta_{\mathbf{Pa}_i} - \delta_{i \cup \mathbf{Pa}_i})$$

The space of all possible imset representations over n variables defines a lattice [8], where the top of the lattice corresponds to the "discrete" causal model with no non-trivial morphisms, and the bottom of the lattice corresponds to the complete model with morphisms between every pair of objects. Each candidate imset defines a *causal horn*, a simplicial subobject of the complete simplex, and the process of causal structure discovery can be viewed in terms of the abstract horn filling problem defined above for higher-order categories.

5.5. Example: Simplicial Objects over String Diagrams

We now illustrate the above formalism of simplicial objects by illustrating how it applies to the special case where causal models are defined over symmetric monoidal categories [25,29,30]. For a detailed overview of symmetric monoidal categories, we recommend the book-length treatment by Fong and Spivak [1]. Symmetric monoidal categories (SMCs) are useful in modeling processes where objects can be combined together to give rise to new objects, or where objects disappear. For example, Coecke et al. [45] propose a mathematical framework for resources based on SMCs. We focus on the work of Jacobs et al. [25]. It is important to point out that monoidal categories can be defined as a special type of Grothendieck fibration [40]. We discuss one specific case of the general Grothendieck construction in the next section construction, and refer the reader to [40] for how the structure of monoidal categories itself emerges from this construction.

Our goal in this section is to illustrate how we can define simplicial objects over the SMC category CDU category $\mathbf{Syn}_G$ constructed by Jacobs et al. [25] to mimic the process of working with an actual Bayesian network DAG G For the purposes of our illustration, it is not important to discuss the intricacies involved in this model, for which we refer the reader to the original paper. Our goal is to show that by encapsulating their SMC category in the UCLA framework, we can extend their approach as described below. In particular, we can solve an associated lifting problem that is defined by the functor mapping the simplicial category Δ to their SMC category. They use the category of stochastic matrices to capture the process of working with the joint distribution as shown in the figure. Instead, we show that one can use some other category, such as the category of **Sets**, or **Top** (the category of topological spaces), or indeed, the category **Meas** of measurable spaces.

Recall that Bayesian networks [16] define a joint probability distribution

$$P(X_1, \ldots, X_n) = \prod_{i=1}^{n} P(X_i | \mathrm{Pa}(X_i)],$$

where $\mathrm{Pa}(X_i) \subset \{X_1, \ldots, X_n\} \setminus X_i$ represents a subset of variables (not including the variable itself). Jacobs et al. [25] show Bayesian network models can be constructed using symmetric monoidal categories, where the tensor product operation is used to combine multiple variables into a "tensored" variable that then probabilistically maps into an output variable. In particular, the monoidal category **Stoch** has as objects finite sets, and morphisms $f : A \rightarrow B$ are $|B| \times |A|$ dimensional stochastic matrices. Composition of stochastic matrices corresponds to matrix multiplication. The monoidal product $\otimes$ in **Stoch** is the cartesian product of objects, and the Kronecker product of matrices $f \otimes g$. Jacobs et al. [25] define three additional operations, the copy map, the discarding map, and the uniform state.

Definition 23. *A CDU category (for copy, discard, and uniform) is a SMC category* ($\mathbf{C}$, $\otimes$, I)*, where each object A has a copy map $C_A : A \rightarrow A \otimes A$, and discarding map $D_A : A \rightarrow I$, and a uniform state map $U_A : I \rightarrow A$, satisfying a set of equations detailed in Jacobs et al. [25]. CDU functors are symmetric monoidal functors between CDU categories, preserving the CDU maps.*

The key theorem we are interested in is the following from the original paper [25]:

Theorem 6. *There is an isomorphism (1-1 correspondence) between Bayesian networks based on a DAG G and CDU functors* $F : \mathbf{Syn}_G \rightarrow \mathbf{Stoch}$.

The significance of this theorem for the UCLA architecture is that it shows how the SMC category of CDU objects can be defined as Layer 2 of the UCLA hierarchy, whereas the category **Stoch** can be viewed as instantiating the Layer 3 of the UCLA hierarchy. Notice that this theorem in effect defines a universal arrow between the CDU category and the category of stochastic matrices, which is a central unifying principle in UC.

5.6. Nerve of a Category

An important concept that will play a key role in Layer 4 of the UCLA hierarchy is that of the *nerve* of a category [40]. The nerve of a category $\mathcal{C}$ enables embedding $\mathcal{C}$ into the category of simplicial objects, which is a fully faithful embedding.

Definition 24. *Let* $\mathcal{F} : \mathcal{C} \rightarrow \mathcal{D}$ *be a functor from category* $\mathcal{C}$ *to category* $\mathcal{D}$. *If for all arrows* f *the mapping* $f \rightarrow Ff$

- *injective, then the functor* $\mathcal{F}$ *is defined to be* **faithful**.
- *surjective, then the functor* $\mathcal{F}$ *is defined to be* **full**.
- *bijective, then the functor* $\mathcal{F}$ *is defined to be* **fully faithful**.

Definition 25. *The* **nerve** *of a category* $\mathcal{C}$ *is the set of composable morphisms of length* n, *for* $n \geq 1$. *Let* $N_n(\mathcal{C})$ *denote the set of sequences of composable morphisms of length* n.

$$\{C_o \xrightarrow{f_1} C_1 \xrightarrow{f_2} \dots \xrightarrow{f_n} C_n \mid C_i \text{ is an object in } \mathcal{C}, f_i \text{ is a morphism in } \mathcal{C}\}$$

The set of n-tuples of composable arrows in C, denoted by $N_n(\mathcal{C})$, can be viewed as a functor from the simplicial object $[n]$ to $\mathcal{C}$. Note that any nondecreasing map $\alpha : [m] \rightarrow [n]$ determines a map of sets $N_m(\mathcal{C}) \rightarrow N_n(\mathcal{C})$. The nerve of a category C is the simplicial set $N_\bullet : \Delta \rightarrow N_n(\mathcal{C})$, which maps the ordinal number object $[n]$ to the set $N_n(\mathcal{C})$.

The importance of the nerve of a category comes from a key result [40], showing it defines a full and faithful embedding of a category:

Theorem 7. *The* **nerve functor** $N_\bullet$: **Cat** $\rightarrow$ **Set** *is fully faithful. More specifically, there is a bijection* θ *defined as:*

$$\theta : \mathbf{Cat}(\mathcal{C}, \mathcal{C}') \rightarrow \mathbf{Set}_\Delta(N_\bullet(\mathcal{C}), N_\bullet(\mathcal{C}'))$$

Using this concept of a nerve of a category, we can now state a theorem that shows it is possible to easily embed the CDU symmetric monoidal category defined above that represents Bayesian Networks and their associated "string diagram surgery" operations for causal inference as a simplicial set.

Theorem 8. *Define the* **nerve** *of the CDU symmetric monoidal category* (**C**, $\otimes$, I), *where each object* A *has a copy map* $C_A : A \rightarrow A \otimes A$, *and discarding map* $D_A : A \rightarrow I$, *and a uniform state map* $U_A : I \rightarrow A$ *as the set of composable morphisms of length* n, *for* $n \geq 1$. *Let* $N_n(\mathcal{C})$ *denote the set of sequences of composable morphisms of length* n.

$$\{C_o \xrightarrow{f_1} C_1 \xrightarrow{f_2} \dots \xrightarrow{f_n} C_n \mid C_i \text{ is an object in } \mathcal{C}, f_i \text{ is a morphism in } \mathcal{C}\}$$

The associated **nerve functor** $N_\bullet$: **Cat** $\rightarrow$ **Set** *from the CDU category is fully faithful. More specifically, there is a bijection* θ *defined as:*

$$\theta : \mathbf{Cat}(\mathcal{C}, \mathcal{C}') \rightarrow \mathbf{Set}_\Delta(N_\bullet(\mathcal{C}), N_\bullet(\mathcal{C}'))$$

This theorem is just a special case of the above theorem attesting to the full and faithful embedding of any category using its nerve, which then makes it a simplicial set. We can then use the theoretical machinery at the top layer of the UCLA architecture to manipulate causal interventions in this category using face and degeneracy operators as defined above.

Note that the functor G from a simplicial object X to a category $\mathcal{C}$ can be lossy. For example, we can define the objects of $\mathcal{C}$ to be the elements of X_0, and the morphisms of $\mathcal{C}$ as the elements $f \in X_1$, where $f : a \to b$, and $d_0 f = a$, and $d_1 f = b$, and $s_0 a, a \in X$ as defining the identity morphisms $\mathbf{1}_a$. Composition in this case can be defined as the free algebra defined over elements of X_1, subject to the constraints given by elements of X_2. For example, if $x \in X_2$, we can impose the requirement that $d_1 x = d_0 x \circ d_2 x$. Such a definition of the left adjoint would be quite lossy because it only preserves the structure of the simplicial object X up to the 2-simplices. The right adjoint from a category to its associated simplicial object, in contrast, constructs a full and faithful embedding of a category into a simplicial set. In particular, the nerve of a category is such a right adjoint.

6. Layers 2 and 3 of UCLA: The Category of Elements in Causal Inference

Next, we turn to describe the second (from top) and third layers of the UCLA architecture, which pertain to the category of causal models (for example, a graph or a symmetric monoidal category), and the database of instances that support causal inferences. Drawing on the close correspondences between between categories and relational database schemes (see [4] for details), we can view causal queries over data as analogous to database queries, which can then be formulated by corresponding lifting problems. That is, each object in the model, e.g., a variable indicating a patient, maps into actual patients, and a variable indicating outcomes from COVID-19 exposure, maps into actual outcomes for that individual. The causal arrow from the patient variable into the exposure variable then maps into actual arrows for each patient. Causal queries of exposure to COVID-19 then become similar to database queries. In the next section, we will generalize this perspective, showing that we can map into a topological category and answer more abstract questions relating to the geometry of a dataset, or map into a category of measurable spaces to answer probabilistic queries. The structure of the lifting problem remains the same, what changes are the specifics of the underlying categories.

6.1. Grothendieck Category of Elements in Relational Causal Models

The Grothendieck category of elements is related to the notion of ground graphs used in relational causal models [32]. Using the example in their papers, we are given three generic objects, **Employee**, **Product**, and **Business-Unit**, and several morphisms, including **Develops**, **Funds**, **Salary**, **Competence**, **Revenue** and **Budget**. We can view a relational schema as shown as a category, following the approach shown in [46,47]. Note each object, such as **Employee**, maps using a functor into the category **Sets** into actual employees, such as **Paul** or **Sally**. Each morphism in the category, for example **Develops** must accordingly also be mapped by this functor into a set-valued function. So, as illustrated, we have that **Sally** is involved in developing a **Laptop**, and **Paul** is involved in developing a **Case**, both of which of course are instances of **Product**. The GCE for this relational causal model is strongly related to the so-called *relational skeleton* and *ground graph* explored in relational causal models [21,32].

A full discussion of these connections is beyond the scope of this paper, but there are some interesting differences to be noted. In their approach, relations such as **Develops** are depicted as undirected, whereas in our case, we model these as directional properties (which seems natural in this example). Ahsan et al. [32] develop a notion of *relational d-separation* in their work, and it would be interesting to construct a categorified version of that notion, an interesting problem for future work. We turn instead to discuss how GCE plays a key role in lifting problems associated with causal inference in UCLA. These provide a rigorous semantics to their use in relational causal models as well, which might be a fruitful avenue to explore in subsequent work.

6.2. Lifting Problems in Causal Inference

Many properties of Grothendieck's construction can be exploited (some of these are discussed in the context of relational database queries in [4]), but for our application to causal inference, we are primarily interested in the associated class of lifting problems that define queries in a causal model.

Definition 26. *If S is a collection of morphisms in category $\mathcal{C}$, a morphism $f : A \to B$ has the* **left lifting property with respect to S** *if it has the left lifting property with respect to every morphism in S. Analogously, we say a morphism $p : X \to Y$ has the* **right lifting property with respect to S** *if it has the right lifting property with respect to every morphism in S.*

We now turn to sketch some examples of the application of lifting problems for causal inference. Many problems in causal inference on graphs involve some particular graph property. To formulate it as a lifting problem, we will use the following generic template, following the initial application of lifting problems to database queries proposed by Spivak [4].

$$\begin{array}{ccc} Q & \xrightarrow{\mu} & \int \delta \\ \downarrow f & \overset{h}{\nearrow} & \downarrow p \\ R & \xrightarrow{\nu} & \mathcal{C} \end{array}$$

Here, Q is a generic query that we want answered, which could range from a database query, as in the original setting studied by Spivak [4], but more interestingly, it could be a particular graph property relating to causal inference (as illustrated by the following two examples), but as we will show later, it could also be related to the combinatorial category of simplicial objects used to model causal intervention, and finally, it could also be related to questions relating to the evaluation of causal models using a measure-theoretic or probability space. By suitably modifying the base category, the lifting problem formulation can be used to encode a diverse variety of problems in causal inference. R represents a fragment of the complete causal model $\mathcal{C}$, and δ is the category of elements defined above. Finally, h gives all solutions to the lifting problem. Some examples will help clarify this concept.

Example 15. *Consider the category of directed graphs defined by the category $\mathcal{G}$, where Ob($\mathcal{G}$) = {V, E}, and the morphisms of $\mathcal{G}$ are given as* $\mathbf{Hom}_{\mathcal{G}}$ *= {s, t}, where $s : E \to V$ and $t : E \to V$ define the source and terminal nodes of each vertex. Then, the category of all directed graphs is precisely defined by the category of all functors $\delta : \mathcal{G} \to$* **Set***. Any particular graph is defined by the functor $X : \mathcal{G} \to$* **Set***, where the function $X(s) : X(E) \to X(V)$ assigns to every edge its source vertex. For causal inference, we may want to check some property of a graph, such as the property that every vertex in X is the source of some edge. The following lifting problem ensures that every vertex has a source edge in the graph. The category of elements $\int \delta$ shown below refers to a construction introduced by Grothendieck, which will be defined in more detail later.*

$$\begin{array}{ccc} V(\bullet) & \xrightarrow{\mu} & \int \delta \\ \downarrow f & \overset{h}{\nearrow} & \downarrow p \\ \{E(\bullet) \xrightarrow{s} V(\bullet)\} & \xrightarrow{\nu} & \mathcal{G} \end{array}$$

Example 16. *As another example of the application of lifting problems to causal inference, let us consider the problem of determining whether two causal DAGs, G_1 and G_2 are Markov equivalent [48]. A key requirement here is that the immoralities of G_1 and G_2 must be the same, that is, if G_1 has a collider $A \to B \leftarrow C$, where there is no edge between A and C, then G_2 must also have the same collider, and none others. We can formulate the problem of finding colliders as the following lifting* *problem. Note that the three vertices A, B and C are bound to an actual graph instance through the category of elements $\int \delta$ (as was illustrated above), using the top right morphism μ. The bottom left morphism f binds these three vertices to some collider. The bottom right morphism ν requires this collider to exist in the causal graph $\mathcal{G}$ with the same bindings as found by μ. The dashed morphisms h finds all solutions to this lifting problem, that is, all colliders involving the vertices A, B and C.*

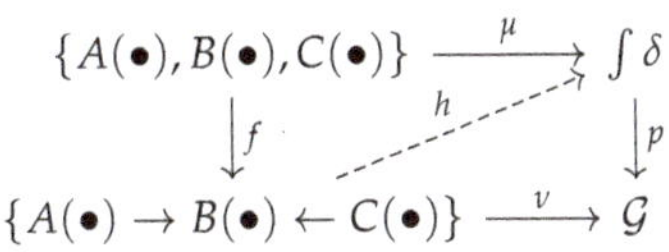

If the category of elements is defined by a functor mapping a database schema into a table of instances, then the associated lifting problem corresponds to familiar problems like SQL queries in relational databases [4]. In our application, we can use the same machinery to formulate causal inference queries by choosing the categories appropriately. To complete the discussion, we now make the connection between universal arrows and the core notion of universal representations via the Yoneda Lemma.

6.3. Modeling Causal Interventions as Kan Extension

It is well known in category theory that ultimately every concept, from products and co-products, limits and co-limits, and ultimately even the Yoneda Lemma (see below), can be derived as special cases of the Kan extension [35]. Kan extensions intuitively are a way to approximate a functor $\mathcal{F}$ so that its domain can be extended from a category $\mathcal{C}$ to another category $\mathcal{D}$. Because it may be impossible to make commutativity work in general, Kan extensions rely on natural transformations to make the extension be the best possible approximation to $\mathcal{F}$ along $\mathcal{K}$. We want to briefly show Kan extensions can be combined with the category of elements defined above to construct causal "migration functors" that map from one causal model into another. These migration functors were originally defined in the context of database migration [4], and here we are adapting that approach to causal inference. By suitably modifying the category of elements from a set-valued functor $\delta : \mathcal{C} \to$ **Set**, to some other category, such as the category of topological spaces, namely $\delta : \mathcal{C} \to$ **Top**, we can extend the causal migration functors into solving more abstract causal inference questions. We explore the use of such constructions in the next section on Layer 4 of the UCLA hierarchy. Here, for simplicity, we restrict our focus to Kan extensions for migration functors over the category of elements defined over instances of a causal model.

Definition 27. *A* **left Kan extension** *of a functor $F : \mathcal{C} \to \mathcal{E}$ along another functor $K : \mathcal{C} \to \mathcal{D}$, is a functor $Lan_K F : \mathcal{D} \to \mathcal{E}$ with a natural transformation $\eta : F \to Lan_F \circ K$ such that for any other such pair $(G : \mathcal{D} \to \mathcal{E}, \gamma : F \to GK)$, γ factors uniquely through η. In other words, there is a unique natural transformation $\alpha : Lan_F \implies G$.*

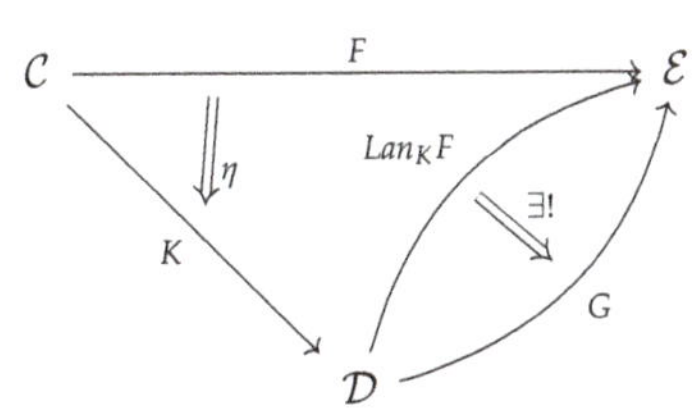

A **right Kan extension** can be defined similarly. To understand the significance of Kan extensions for causal inference, we note that under a causal intervention, when a causal category S gets modified to T, evaluating the modified causal model over a database of instances can be viewed as an example of Kan extension.

Let $\delta : S \to$ **Set** denote the original causal model defined by the category S with respect to some dataset. Let $\epsilon : T \to$ **Set** denote the effect of a causal intervention abstractly defined as some change in the category S to T, such as deletion of an edge, as illustrated in Figure 10. Intuitively, we can consider three cases: the *pullback* Δ_F along F, which maps the effect of a causal intervention back to the original model, the *left pushforward* Σ_F and the *right pushforward* $\prod_F$, which can be seen as adjoints to the pullback Δ_F.

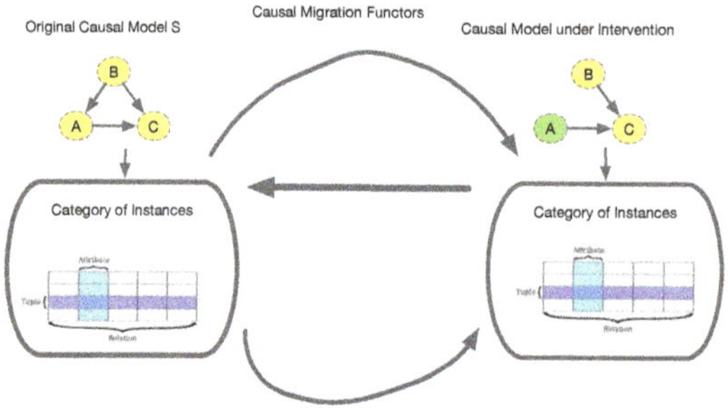

Figure 10. Kan extensions are useful in modeling the effects of a causal intervention, where in this example of a causal model over three objects A, B, and C, the object A is intervened upon, eliminating the morphism into it from object B.

Following [4], we can define three *causal migration functors* that evaluate the impact of a causal intervention with respect to a dataset of instances.

1. The functor $\Delta_F : \epsilon \to \delta$ sends the functor $\epsilon : T \to \mathbf{Set}$ to the composed functor $\delta \circ F : S \to \mathbf{Set}$.
2. The functor $\Sigma_F : \delta \to \epsilon$ is the left Kan extension along F, and can be seen as the left adjoint to Δ_F.
   The functor $\prod_F : \delta \to \epsilon$ is the right Kan extension along F, and can be seen as the right adjoint to Δ_F.

To understand how to implement these functors, we use the following proposition that is stated in [4] in the context of database queries, which we are restating in the setting of causal inference.

Theorem 9. *Let $F : S \to T$ be a functor. Let $\delta : S \to$ **Set** and $\epsilon : T \to$ **Set** be two set-valued functors, which can be viewed as two instances of a causal model defined by the category S and T. If we view T as the causal category that results from a causal intervention on S (e.g., deletion of an edge), then there is a commutative diagram linking the category of elements between S and T.*

$$\begin{array}{ccc} \int \delta & \longrightarrow & \int \epsilon \\ \downarrow{\scriptstyle \pi_\delta} & & \downarrow{\scriptstyle \pi_\epsilon} \\ S & \xrightarrow{F} & T \end{array}$$

Proof. To check that the above diagram is a pullback, that is, $\int \delta \simeq S \times_T \int \delta$, or in words, the fiber product, we can check the existence of the pullback component wise by comparing the set of objects and the set of morphisms in $\int \delta$ with the respective sets in $S \times_T \int \epsilon$. □

For simplicity, we defined the migration functors above with respect to an actual dataset of instances. More generally, we can compose the set-valued functor $\delta : S \to \mathbf{Set}$ with a functor $\mathcal{T} : \mathbf{Set} \to \mathbf{Top}$ to the category of topological spaces to derive a Kan extension formulation of the definition of a causal intervention. We discuss this issue in the next section on causal homotopy.

7. Layer 4 of UCLA: Causal Homotopy

Finally, we turn to discuss the role of the causal homotopy layer. To understand the reason for considering homotopy in causal inference, note that causal models can only be determined up to some equivalence class from data, and while many causal discovery algorithms assume arbitrary interventions can be carried out, e.g., on separating sets [27], to discover the unique structure, such interventions are generally impossible to do in practical applications. The concept of *essential graph* [48] and *chain graph* [49] are attempts to formulate the notion of a "quotient space" of graphs, but similar issues arise more generally for non-graph based models as well. Thus, it is useful to understand how to formulate the notion of equivalent classes of causal models in an arbitrary category. For example, given the conditional independence structure $A \perp\!\!\!\perp B|C$, there are at least three different symmetric monoidal categorical representations that all satisfy this conditional independence [25,29,30], and we need to define the quotient space over all such equivalent categories.

In our previous work on causal homotopy [41], we exploited the connection between causal DAG graphical models and finite topological spaces [50,51]. In particular, for a DAG model $G = (V, E)$, it is possible to define a finite space topology $\mathcal{T} = (V, \mathcal{O})$, whose open sets $\mathcal{O}$ are subsets of the vertices V such that each vertex x is associated with an open set U_x defined as the intersection of all open sets that contain x. This structure is referred to an *Alexandroff* topology [52]. An intuitive way to construct an Alexandroff topology is to define the open set for each variable x by the set of its ancestors A_x, or by the set of its descendants D_x. This approach transcribes a DAG graph into a finite topological space, upon which the mathematical tools of algebraic topology can be applied to construct homotopies among equivalent causal models. Our approach below generalizes this construction to simplicial objects, as well as general categories.

7.1. The Category of Fractions: Localizing Invertible Morphisms in a Category

A principal challenge in causal discovery is that models can be inferred from data only up to an equivalence class. We can view the morphisms between equivalent causal models as "invertible" arrows, which defines a construction called an "essential" graph [48]. The problem of defining a category with a given subclass of invertible morphisms, called the category of fractions [53], is another concrete illustration of the close relationships between categories and graphs. It is also useful in the context of causal inference, as for example, in defining the Markov equivalence class of directed acyclic graphs (DAGs) as a category that is localized by considering all invertible arrows as isomorphisms. Borceux [54] has a detailed discussion of the "calculus of fractions", namely how to define a category where a subclass of morphisms are to be treated as isomorphisms. The formal definition is as follows:

Definition 28. *Consider a category $\mathcal{C}$ and a class Σ of arrows of $\mathcal{C}$. The* **category of fractions** *$\mathcal{C}(\Sigma^{-1})$ is said to exist when a category $\mathcal{C}(\Sigma^{-1})$ and a functor $\phi : \mathcal{C} \to \mathcal{C}(\Sigma^{-1})$ can be found with the following properties:*

1. *$\forall f, \phi(f)$ is an isomorphism.*
2. *If $\mathcal{D}$ is a category, and $F : \mathcal{C} \to \mathcal{D}$ is a functor such that for all morphisms $f \in \Sigma$, $F(f)$ is an isomorphism, then there exists a unique functor $G : \mathcal{C}(\Sigma^{-1}) \to \mathcal{D}$ such that $G \circ \phi = F$.*

A detailed construction of the category of fractions is given in [54], which uses the underlying directed graph skeleton associated with the category. The characterization of the Markov equivalent class of acyclic directed graphs is an example of the abstract concept of category of fractions [48]. Briefly, this condition states that two acyclic directed graphs are Markov equivalent if and only if they have the same skeleton and the same immoralities. In our previous work [41], we explored constructing homotopically invariant causal models over finite Alexandroff topological spaces, which can be seen as a special case of the UCLA framework since finite topological (Alexandroff) spaces define a category [52].

7.2. Homotopy of Simplicial Objects

We will discuss homotopy in categories more generally now. This notion of homotopy generalizes the notion of homotopy in topology, which defines why an object like a coffee cup is topologically homotopic to a doughnut (they have the same number of "holes").

Definition 29. *Let C and C' be a pair of objects in a category $\mathcal{C}$. We say C is* **a retract** *of C' if there exists maps $i : C \to C'$ and $r : C' \to C$ such that $r \circ i = id_C$.*

Definition 30. *Let $\mathcal{C}$ be a category. We say a morphism $f : C \to D$ is a* **retract of another morphism** *$f' : C \to D$ if it is a retract of f' when viewed as an object of the functor category* **Hom**$([1], \mathcal{C})$*. A collection of morphisms T of $\mathcal{C}$ is* **closed under retracts** *if for every pair of morphisms f, f' of $\mathcal{C}$, if f is a retract of f', and f' is in T, then f is also in T.*

Definition 31. *Let X and Y be simplicial sets, and suppose we are given a pair of morphisms $f_0, f_1 : X \to Y$. A* **homotopy** *from f_0 to f_1 is a morphism $h : \Delta^1 \times X \to Y$ satisfying $f_0 = h|_{0\times X}$ and $f_1 = h_{1\times X}$.*

7.3. Singular Homology

Our goal is to define an abstract notion of a causal model in terms of its underlying classifying space as a category, and show how it can be useful in defining causal homotopy. We will also clarify how it relates to determining equivalences among causal models, namely homotopical invariance, and also how it sheds light on causal identification. First, we need to define more concretely the topological n-simplex that provides a concrete way to attach a topology to a simplicial object. Our definitions below build on those given in [14]. For each integer n, define the topological space $|\Delta_n|$ realized by the object Δ_n as

$$|\Delta_n| = \{t_0, t_1, \dots, t_n \in \mathbb{R}^{n+1} : t_0 + t_1 + \dots + t_n = 1\}$$

This is the familiar n-dimensional simplex over n variables. For any causal model, its classifying space $|\mathcal{N}_\bullet(\mathcal{C})|$ defines a topological space. We can now define the *singular* n-simplex as a continuous mapping $\sigma : |\Delta_N| \to |\mathcal{N}_\bullet(\mathcal{C})|$. Every singular n-simplex σ induces a collection of $n-1$-dimensional simplices called *faces*, denoted as

$$d_i\sigma(t_0, \dots, t_{n-1}) = (t_0, t_1, \dots, t_{i-1}, 0, t_i, \dots, t_{n-1})$$

Note that as discussed above, a causal intervention on a variable in a DAG can be modeled as applying one of these degeneracy operators d_i. The above definition shows that every such intervention has an effect on the topology associated with the causal model. Define the set of all morphisms $\mathrm{Sing}_n(X) = \mathbf{Hom}_{\mathbf{Top}}(\Delta_n, |\mathcal{N}_\bullet(\mathcal{C})|)$ as the set of singular n-simplices of $|\mathcal{N}_\bullet(\mathcal{C})|$.

Definition 32. *For any topological space defined by a causal model $|\mathcal{N}_\bullet(\mathcal{C})|$, the* **singular homology groups** *$H_*(|\mathcal{N}_\bullet(\mathcal{C})|; \mathbf{Z})$ are defined as the homology groups of a chain complex*

$$\dots \xrightarrow{\partial} \mathbf{Z}(Sing_2(|\mathcal{N}_\bullet(\mathcal{C})|)) \xrightarrow{\partial} \mathbf{Z}(Sing_1(|\mathcal{N}_\bullet(\mathcal{C})|)) \xrightarrow{\partial} \mathbf{Z}(Sing_0(|\mathcal{N}_\bullet(\mathcal{C})|))$$

where $\mathbf{Z}(Sing_n(|\mathcal{N}_\bullet(\mathcal{C})|))$ denotes the free Abelian group generated by the set $Sing_n(|\mathcal{N}_\bullet(\mathcal{C})|)$ and the differential ∂ is defined on the generators by the formula

$$\partial(\sigma) = \sum_{i=0}^{n} (-1)^i d_i\sigma$$

Intuitively, a chain complex builds a sequence of vector spaces that can be used to construct an algebraic invariant of a causal model from its classifying space by choosing the left $\mathbf{k}$ module $\mathbf{Z}$ to be a vector space. Each differential ∂ then becomes a linear transformation whose representation is constructed by modeling its effect on the basis elements in each $\mathbf{Z}(\mathrm{Sing}_n(X))$.

Example 17. *Let us illustrate the singular homology groups defined by an integer-valued multiset [8] used to model conditional independence. Imsets over a DAG of three variables $N = \{a, b, c\}$ can be viewed as a finite discrete topological space. For this topological space X, the singular homology groups $H_*(X; \mathbf{Z})$ are defined as the homology groups of a chain complex*

$$\mathbf{Z}(Sing_3(X)) \xrightarrow{\partial} \mathbf{Z}(Sing_2(X)) \xrightarrow{\partial} \mathbf{Z}(Sing_1(X)) \xrightarrow{\partial} \mathbf{Z}(Sing_0(X))$$

where $\mathbf{Z}(Sing_i(X))$ denotes the free Abelian group generated by the set $Sing_i(X)$ and the differential ∂ is defined on the generators by the formula

$$\partial(\sigma) = \sum_{i=0}^{4}(-1)^i d_i\sigma$$

The set $Sing_n(X)$ is the set of all morphisms $\mathbf{Hom}_{Top}(|\Delta_n|, X)$. For an imset over the three variables $N = \{a, b, c\}$, we can define the singular n-simplex σ as:

$$\sigma : |\Delta^4| \to X \text{ where } |\Delta^n| = \{t_0, t_1, t_2, t_3 \in [0,1]^4 : t_0 + t_1 + t_2 + t_3 = 1\}$$

The n-simplex σ has a collection of faces denoted as $d_0\sigma, d_1\sigma, d_2\sigma$ and $d_3\sigma$. If we pick the k-left module $\mathbf{Z}$ as the vector space over real numbers $\mathbb{R}$, then the above chain complex represents a sequence of vector spaces that can be used to construct an algebraic invariant of a topological space defined by the integer-valued multiset. Each differential ∂ then becomes a linear transformation whose representation is constructed by modeling its effect on the basis elements in each $\mathbf{Z}(Sing_n(X))$. An alternate approach to constructing a chain homology for an integer-valued multiset is to use Möbius inversion to define the chain complex in terms of the nerve of a category (see our recent work on categoroids [15] for details).

7.4. Classifying Spaces and Homotopy Colimits

Building on the intuition proposed above, we now introduce a formal way to define causal effects in our framework, which relies on the construction of a topological space associated with the nerve of a category. As we saw above, the nerve of a category is a full and faithful embedding of a category as a simplicial object.

Definition 33. *The* **classifying space** *of a causal model defined as a category $\mathcal{C}$ is the topological space associated with the nerve of the category $|N_\bullet\mathcal{C}|$.*

To understand the classifying space $|N_\bullet\mathcal{C}|$ of a causal model defined as a category $\mathcal{C}$, let us go over some simple examples to gain some insight.

Example 18. *For any set X, which can be defined as a discrete category $\mathcal{C}_X$ with no non-trivial morphisms, the classifying space $|N_\bullet\mathcal{C}_X|$ is just the discrete topology over X (where the open sets are all possible subsets of X).*

Example 19. *If we take a causal model defined as a partially ordered set $[n]$, with its usual order-preserving morphisms, then the nerve of $[n]$ is isomorphic to the representable functor $\delta(-, [n])$, as shown by the Yoneda Lemma, and in that case, the classifying space is just the topological space Δ_n defined above.*

Example 20. *In our earlier work on causal homotopy [41], we associated with any finite causal DAG $\mathcal{G}$, a finite Alexandroff topological space, where the open sets of the topology corresponding to* the down sets or upsets *of descendants or ancestors, respectively. Since any causal DAG model $\mathcal{G}$*

induces a partial ordering, we can then define the classifying space of a causal DAG in terms of the topological space associated with the nerve of the DAG, namely $|N_\bullet \mathcal{G}|$.

Example 21. *Witsenhausen [6] defined a measure-theoretic notion of causality called the* intrinsic model. *An intrinsic model* $\mathcal{M} = (\alpha, U_\alpha, \mathcal{I}_\alpha)_{\alpha \in A}$, *where the parameters of the intrinsic causal model over n variables A are defined in terms of a collection of measurable functions over each variable's information field* $\mathcal{I}_\alpha$ *(a subfield of the product* σ*-algebra over all variables upon which it depends), where* U_α *is the space over which* α *takes its values. Heymann et al. [7] showed recently that Witsenhausen's intrinsic model generalizes Pearl's d-separation condition, and can be used to define a rich set of causal models that includes cycles and feedback, as well as more refined notions of conditional d-separation. The definition of causality in an intrinsic model is based on structuring the information fields of every variable in such a way that it is possible to sequentially order them for any particular instance of the underlying sample space. It is possible to define a topology on the underlying variables (which Witsenhausen referred to as* agents*), by defining* subystem *of variables* $B \subseteq A$ *such that every variable* $\alpha \in B$ *has an information field that only depends on the information fields of members in its subset B, that is* $\forall \alpha \in B$, *the condition states that* $\mathcal{I}_\alpha \subseteq \mathcal{F}_B$, *where* $\mathcal{F}_B$ *is the induced product information field over the subset of variables B. Witsenhausen proves that the collection of subsystems forms a finite topology on A. We can then define the classifying space of an intrinsic causal model to be the topological space associated with the nerve of an intrinsic model* $\mathcal{M}$, *namely* $|N_\bullet \mathcal{M}|$.

We now want to bring in the set-valued functor mapping each causal category $\mathcal{C}$ to the actual experiment used, e.g., in a clinical trial [9], to evaluate average treatment effect or quantify the effect of a **do** calculus intervention [5] We can then compute the topological space prior to intervention, and subsequent to intervention, and compare the two topological spaces in terms of their algebraic invariants (e.g., the chain complex, as described below).

Definition 34. *The* **homotopy colimit** *of a causal model defined as nerve of the category of elements associated with the set-valued functor* $\delta : \mathcal{C} \to$ **Set** *mapping the causal category* $\mathcal{C}$ *to a dataset, namely* $N_\bullet(\int \delta)$.

In general, we may want to evaluate the homotopy colimit of a causal model not only with respect to the data used in a causal experiment, but also with respect to some underlying topological space or some measurable space. We can extend the above definition straightforwardly to these cases using an appropriate functor $\mathcal{T}$: **Set** $\to$ **Top**, or alternatively $\mathcal{M}$: **Set** $\to$ **Meas**. These augmented constructions can then be defined with respect to a more general notion called the *homotopy colimit* [40] of a causal model.

Definition 35. *The* **topological homotopy colimit** $hocolim_{\mathcal{T} \circ \delta}$ *of a causal model associated with a category* $\mathcal{C}$, *along with its associated category of elements associated with a set-valued functor* $\delta : \mathcal{C} \to$ **Set**, *and a topological functor* $\mathcal{T}$: **Set** $\to$ **Top** *is isomorphic to topological space associated with the nerve of the category of elements, that is* $hocolim_{\mathcal{T} \circ \delta} \simeq |N_\bullet(\int \delta)|$.

Example 22. *The classifying space* $|N_\bullet \mathcal{C}_{CDU}|$ *associated with CDU symmetric monoidal category encoding of a causal Bayesian DAG is defined using the monoidal category* (**C**, $\otimes$, *I*), *where each object A has a copy map* $C_A : A \to A \otimes A$, *and discarding map* $D_A : A \to I$, *and a uniform state map* $U_A : I \to A$, *is defined as the topological realization of its nerve. As before, the nerve* $N_n(\mathcal{C})$ *of the CDU category is defined as the set of sequences of composable morphisms of length n.*

$$\{C_o \xrightarrow{f_1} C_1 \xrightarrow{f_2} \dots \xrightarrow{f_n} C_n \mid C_i \text{ is an object in } \mathcal{C}, f_i \text{ is a morphism in } \mathcal{C}\}$$

Note that the CDU category was associated with a CDU functor $F :$ **Syn**$_G \to$ **Stoch** *to the category of stochastic matrices. We can now define the homotopy colimit* $hocolim_{\mathcal{F}}$ *of the CDU causal model associated with the CDU category* $\mathcal{C}$, *along with its associated category of elements* *associated with a set-valued functor $\delta : \mathcal{C} \rightarrow$* **Set**, *and a topological functor $\mathcal{F}$:* **Set** $\rightarrow$ **Stoch** *is isomorphic to topological space associated with the nerve of the category of elements over the composed functor, that is hocolim$_{\mathcal{F}\circ\delta}$.*

7.5. Defining Causal Effect

Finally, we turn to defining causal effect using the notion of classifying space and homotopy colimits, as defined above. Space does not permit a complete discussion of this topic, but the basic idea is that once a causal model is defined as a topological space, there are a large number of ways of comparing two topological spaces from analyzing their chain complexes, or using a topological data analysis method such as UMAP [2].

Definition 36. *Let the classifying space under "treatment" be defined as the topological space $|N_\bullet \mathcal{C}_1|$ associated with the nerve of category $\mathcal{C}_1$ under some intervention, which may result in a topological deformation of the model (e.g., deletion of an edge). Similarly, the classifying space under "no treatment" be defined as the $|N_\bullet \mathcal{C}_0|$ under a no-treatment setting, with no intervention. A* **causally non-isomorphic effect** *exists between categories $\mathcal{C}_1$ and $\mathcal{C}_0$, or $\mathcal{C}_1 \not\cong \mathcal{C}_0$ if and only if there is no invertible morphism $f : |N_\bullet \mathcal{C}_1| \rightarrow N_\bullet(\mathcal{C}_0|$ between the "treatment" and "no-treatment" topological spaces, namely f must be both* left invertible *and* right invertible.

There is an equivalent notion of causal effect using the homotopy colimit definition proposed above, which defines the nerve functor using the category of elements. This version is particularly useful in the context of evaluating a causal model over a dataset.

Definition 37. *Let the homotopy colimit hocolim$_1 = |N_\bullet(\int \delta_1)|$ be the topological space associated with a causal category $\mathcal{C}_1$ under the "treatment' condition be defined with respect to an associated category of elements defined by a set-valued functor $\delta_1 : \mathcal{C} \rightarrow$* **Set** *over a dataset of "treated" variables, and corresponding "no-treatment" hocolim$_0 = |N_\bullet(\int \delta_0)|$ be the topological space of a causal model associated with a category $\mathcal{C}_0$ be defined over an associated category of elements defined by a set-valued functor $\delta_0 : \mathcal{C} \rightarrow$* **Set** *over a dataset of "placebo" variables. A* **causally non-isomorphic effect** *exists between categories $\mathcal{C}_1$ and $\mathcal{C}_0$, or $\mathcal{C}_1 \not\cong \mathcal{C}_0$ if and only if there is no invertible morphism $f : |N_\bullet(\int \delta_1)| \rightarrow |N_\bullet(\delta_0)|$ between the "treatment" and "no-treatment" homotopy colimit topological spaces, namely f must be both* left invertible *and* right invertible.

We can define an equivalent "do-calculus" like version of the causal effect definitions above for the case when a causal model defined as a graph structure is manipulated by an intervention that deletes an edge, or does some more sophisticated type of "category" surgery.

8. Contributions of Our Paper

We summarize the principal contributions of our paper. Our principal contribution is the development of the notion of "universal causality", a representation-independent definition whose goal is to elucidate the "universal' properties of causal inference. Our work is inspired by other work, for example separoids [10] elucidates the concept of conditional independence in a representation-independent manner, which applies to conditional independence in probability theory, statistics, and geometry. Another example is the concept of *Grothendieck topology* [36], which defines topology abstractly in the context of any category. Implicit in these constructions is the abstraction of a specific construct—conditional independence or topology–in a manner that lets it be studied across a wide range of representations. Similarly, UC is intended to be an abstract characterization of causality.

1. **Universal Arrow:** We used universal arrows as a unifying principle in UC, which allows synchronizing causal changes at different levels of the UCLA hierarchy. Universal arrows set up a correspondence between a "forgetful" functor and its left adjoint"free" functor. In the application to causal inference, universal arrows, for example, define forgetful and free functors between the category of conditional in-

dependence structures, such as separoids, from the category of actual causal models (e.g., as symmetric monoidal categories of causal DAG models [25,29,30]).

2. **Causal reproducing property:** The universal arrow property leads to the powerful Yoneda Lemma, which provides the foundational result embodied in the causal reproducing property. The CRP implies that all causal influences between two objects X and Y in a category $\mathcal{C}$ are representable in the functor category of presheaves, namely

$$\mathbf{Hom}_{\mathcal{C}}(X,Y) \simeq \mathbf{Nat}(\mathbf{Hom}_{\mathcal{C}}(-,X), \mathbf{Hom}_{\mathcal{C}}(-,Y))$$

3. **Causal interventions as a higher-order category:** Most causal discovery algorithms require a sequence of interventions, which naturally compose to form a category. We introduced the framework of higher-order category theory using simplicial sets and objects to define a category over causal interventions. Simplicial objects provides an elegant and general way of extracting parts of a compositional structure, and its associated lifting problems define when a partial fragment of a causal model can be "put back" together into a complete model.
4. **Nerve of a causal model:** We used the nerve construction to set up a functor between a casual category and its associated simplicial object, which is a fully faithful embedding of any category as a simplicial object. Its left adjoint functor, which maps a simplicial set into a category, is a lossy representation that only preserves structure up to $n \leq 2$ simplices. Simplicial sets suggest a way to define higher-order causal models, a topic for future work.
5. **Relational causal models:** The Grothendieck category of elements is closely related to the notion of *ground graphs* in relational causal models [32], which gives a rich source of applications of causal inference. Any relational database defines a category [4], and our paper shows how to formulate causal inference in the rich space of relational enterprise datasets.
6. **Lifting Problem:** Associated with each pair of layers of the UCLA hierarchy is a lifting problem over a suitable category of elements, from simplicial category of elements, to a category of elements over a dataset, to a category of elements over a topological space. In general, the Grothendieck category of elements is a way to embed each object in a category into the category of all categories **Cat**. This construction has many elegant properties, which deserves further exploration in a subsequent paper.
7. **Homotopy colimits and Classifying Spaces:** We defined causal effect in terms of the classifying space associated with the nerve of a causal category, and with the homotopy colimit of the nerve of the category of elements. These structures have been extensively explored in the study of homotopy in category theory [40], and there are many advanced techniques that can be brought to bear on this problem, such as *model categories* [55].

9. Future Work

There are many directions for future work, and we summarize a few of them below.

1. **Higher-order causality:** Our use of simplicial sets and objects suggests a way of defining higher-order causality, as simplicial sets generalize directed graphs, categories, and partial orders. Simplicial sets permit modeling the interaction between groups of objects, which naturally applies to cases of causal inference with *interference*, where the stable unit treatment value assumption (SUTVA) [9] is violated. Zigler and Papadogeorgou [33] explores an application to causal interference, where the treatment units (e.g., power plants) and response units (e.g., people living close to power plants) have a complex set of interactions, where a particular treatment may affect many individuals. These types of problems can be studied using higher-order degeneracy operators over oriented n-simplexes.
2. **Causal Discovery from Conditional Independence Oracles:** The problem of causal discovery can then be rigorously formulated as a lifting problem as well, where the

conditional independence oracle is defined as a solution to a lifting problem. More specifically, it is possible to define a Grothendieck category of elements for a functor F: **Graph** $\rightarrow$ **Separoids** mapping the category of directed graphs into the category of separoids, which define its equivalent set of conditional independence statements. The Grothendieck fibration in this case maps the category of elements, combining conditional independence properties and graph objects, into the category **Graph**. Algorithms proposed in the literature, such as [27], can be seen as queries in a lifting problem, analogous to the lifting problems defined for the UCLA hierarchy. This approach can be extended to causal discovery over higher-order categories.

3. **Grothendieck Topology:** Analogous to the representation-independent definition of conditional independence using separoids, our longstanding goal has been to define causality purely in terms of a categorical structure. The Grothendieck topology $\mathcal{J}$ for any category, which leads to the concept of a *site* [36], is defined such that for any object c in $\mathcal{C}$, a *sieve* S is a family of morphisms, all with co-domain c such that

$$f \in S \rightarrow f \circ g \in S$$

for any g where the composition is defined. A Grothendieck topology $\mathcal{J}$ on category $\mathcal{C}$ defines a sieve $J(c)$ for each object c such that the following properties hold: (i) the maximal sieve $t_c = \{f | cod(f) = c\}$ is in $J(c)$. There is an additional stability condition and a transitive closure condition. An interesting problem for future work is to define causal inference over sheaves of a site, using the concept of Grothendieck topologies. Any causal intervention that, for instance, deletes an edge, would change the Grothendieck topology embodied in the structure of sieves.

4. **Gröbner Causal Models:** Another direction for future work is to construct Gröbner representations of causal categories. Sam and Snowden [56] define a general **Gröbner** representation for combinatorial categories, which apply to causal models as well. Specifically, denote $\mathbf{Rep_k}(\mathcal{C})$ as the category of representations of a causal model $\mathcal{C}$, where $\mathbf{k}$ is a non-zero ring, and $\mathrm{Mod}_\mathbf{k}$ is the category of left-$\mathbf{k}$ modules. Thus, we can define a **representation** of a causal category $\mathcal{C}$ as a functor $\mathcal{C} \rightarrow \mathrm{Mod}_\mathbf{k}$. Let x be an object of $\mathcal{C}$. Define a representation P_x of $\mathcal{C}$ as a left $\mathbf{k}$-module, where $P_x(y) = \mathbf{k}[\mathbf{Hom}_\mathcal{C}(x,y)]$, that is, $P_x(y)$ is the free left $\mathbf{k}$-module with basis $\mathbf{Hom}_\mathcal{C}(x,y)$. For any particular morphism $f : x \rightarrow y$, let e_f denote the corresponding element of $P_x(y)$. Broadly speaking, this approach generalizes the work on modeling graphical models as algebraic varieties [20,57,58], and ideals on partially ordered sets (posets) [59]. The intuitive idea is that a representation of a category can be defined as an abstract Gröbner basis over an ideal defined on a module whose basis is defined using the free algebra generated by the set of all morphisms out of an object. This approach provides an alternative way of parameterizing causal models defined as combinatorial categories.

10. Summary

In this paper, we proposed a framework called Universal Causality (UC) for causal inference using the tools of category theory. Specifically, we described a layered hierarchical architecture called UCLA (Universal Causality Layered Architecture), where causal inference is modeled at multiple levels of categorical abstraction. At the top-most level, causal inference is modeled using a higher-order category of simplicial sets and objects, defined as contravariant functors from the category of ordinal numbers Δ, whose objects are the ordered natural numbers $[n] = \{0, \ldots, n\}$, and whose morphisms are order-preserving injections and surjections. Causal "surgery" is then modeled as the action of a contravariant functor from the category Δ into a causal model. At the second layer, causal models are defined by a category consisting of a collection of objects, such as the entities in a relational database, and morphisms between objects can be viewed as attributes relating entities. The third categorical abstract layer corresponds to the data layer in causal inference, where each causal object is mapped into a set of instances, modeled using the category of sets and morphisms are functions between sets. The fourth layer comprises of additional structure imposed on the instance layer above, such as a topological space, a measurable space or a probability space, or more generally, a locale. Between every pair of layers in UCLA are functors that map objects and morphisms from the domain category to the co-domain category. Each functor between layers is characterized by a universal arrow, which defines an isomorphism between every pair of categorical layers. These universal arrows define universal elements and representations through the Yoneda Lemma, and in turn lead to a new category of elements based on a construction introduced by Grothendieck. Causal inference between each pair of layers is defined as a lifting problem, a commutative diagram whose objects are categories, and whose morphisms are functors that are characterized as different types of fibrations. We defined causal effect in the UCLA framework using the notion of homotopy colimits associated with the nerve of a category. We illustrate the UCLA architecture using a diverse set of examples.

Funding: This research was supported by Adobe Corporation.

Data Availability Statement: Not applicable.

Conflicts of Interest: The author declares no conflict of interest.

References

1. Fong, B.; Spivak, D.I. *Seven Sketches in Compositionality: An Invitation to Applied Category Theory*; Cambridge University Press: Cambridge, UK, 2018.
2. McInnes, L.; Healy, J.; Melville, J. UMAP: Uniform Manifold Approximation and Projection for Dimension Reduction. *arXiv* **2018**, arXiv:1802.03426.
3. Carlsson, G.E.; Mémoli, F. Classifying Clustering Schemes. *Found. Comput. Math.* **2013**, *13*, 221–252. [CrossRef]
4. Spivak, D.I. Database queries and constraints via lifting problems. *Math. Struct. Comput. Sci.* **2013**, *24*, e240602. [CrossRef]
5. Pearl, J. *Causality: Models, Reasoning and Inference*, 2nd ed.; Cambridge University Press: Cambridge, MA, USA, 2009.
6. Witsenhausen, H.S. The Intrinsic Model for Discrete Stochastic Control: Some Open Problems. In Proceedings of the Control Theory, Numerical Methods and Computer Systems Modelling, Rocquencourt, France, 17–21 June1974; Bensoussan, A., Lions, J.L., Eds.; Springer: Berlin/Heidelberg, Germany, 1975; pp. 322–335.
7. Heymann, B.; de Lara, M.; Chancelier, J.P. Causal Information with Information Fields. In Proceedings of the Neural Inforamtion Processing Systems Workshop on Causal Discovery and Causality-Inspired Machine Learning, Online, 11 December 2020.
8. Studeny, M. *Probabilistic Conditional Independence Structures*; Information Science and Statistics; Springer: London, UK, 2010.
9. Imbens, G.W.; Rubin, D.B. *Causal Inference for Statistics, Social, and Biomedical Sciences: An Introduction*; Cambridge University Press: Cambridge, MA, USA, 2015.
10. Dawid, A.P. Separoids: A Mathematical Framework for Conditional Independence and Irrelevance. *Ann. Math. Artif. Intell.* **2001**, *32*, 335–372. [CrossRef]
11. Lewis, D. Counterfactuals and comparative possibility. *J. Philos. Log.* **1973**, *2*, 418–446. [CrossRef]
12. May, J. *Simplicial Objects in Algebraic Topology*; University of Chicago Press: Chicago, IL, USA, 1992.
13. Joyal, A. Quasi-categories and Kan complexes. *J. Pure Appl. Algebra* **2002**, *175*, 207–222. [CrossRef]
14. Lurie, J. *Higher Topos Theory*; Annals of mathematics studies; Princeton University Press: Princeton, NJ, USA, 2009.
15. Mahadevan, S. Categoroids: Universal Conditional Independence. *arXiv* **2022**, arXiv:2208.11077.
16. Pearl, J. *Probabilistic Reasoning in Intelligent Systems—Networks of Plausible Inference*; Morgan Kaufmann Series in Representation and Reasoning; Morgan Kaufmann: San Francisco, CA, USA, 1989.
17. Gavrilovich, M. The unreasonable power of the lifting property in elementary mathematics. *arXiv* **2017**, arXiv:1707.06615.
18. Darwin, C. *The Effect of Cross and Self-Fertilization in the Vegetable Kingdom*; John Murray: London, UK, 1876.
19. Wright, S. Correlation and causation. *J. Agric. Res.* **1921**, *20*, 557–585.
20. Beerenwinkel, N.; Eriksson, N.; Sturmfels, B. Evolution on distributive lattices. *J. Theor. Biol.* **2006**, *242*, 409–420. [CrossRef]
21. Maier, M.; Marazopoulou, K.; Arbour, D.; Jensen, D. A Sound and Complete Algorithm for Learning Causal Models from Relational Data. *arXiv* **2013**, arXiv:1309.6843. https://doi.org/10.48550/ARXIV.1309.6843.
22. Mahadevan, S. Universal Decision Models. *arXiv* **2021**, arXiv:2110.15431.
23. Nagurney, A. *Network Economics: A Variational Inequality Approach*; Kluwer Academic Press: Dordrecht, The Netherlands; Boston, MA, USA, 1999.
24. Hansen, J.; Ghrist, R. Opinion Dynamics on Discourse Sheaves. *arXiv* **2020**, arXiv:2005.12798.
25. Jacobs, B.; Kissinger, A.; Zanasi, F. Causal Inference by String Diagram Surgery. *arXiv* **2018**, arXiv:1811.08338.
26. Muandet, K.; Kanagawa, M.; Saengkyongam, S.; Marukatat, S. Counterfactual Mean Embeddings. *J. Mach. Learn. Res.* **2021**, *22*, 1–71.

27. Kocaoglu, M.; Shanmugam, K.; Bareinboim, E. Experimental Design for Learning Causal Graphs with Latent Variables. In Proceedings of the Advances in Neural Information Processing Systems 30: Annual Conference on Neural Information Processing Systems 2017, Long Beach, CA, USA, 4–9 December 2017; pp. 7018–7028.
28. Addanki, R.; Kasiviswanathan, S.P.; McGregor, A.; Musco, C. Efficient Intervention Design for Causal Discovery with Latents. *arXiv* **2020**, arXiv:2005.11736.
29. Fong, B. Causal Theories: A Categorical Perspective on Bayesian Networks. *arXiv* **2012**, arXiv:1301.6201.
30. Fritz, T.; Klingler, A. The d-Separation Criterion in Categorical Probability. *J. Mach. Learn. Res.* **2023**, *24*, 1–49.
31. Mahadevan, S. Unifying Causal Inference and Reinforcement Learning Using Higher-Order Category Theory. *arXiv* **2022**, arXiv:2209.06262.
32. Ahsan, R.; Arbour, D.; Zheleva, E. Relational Causal Models with Cycles:Representation and Reasoning. *arXiv* **2022**, arXiv:2202.10706.
33. Zigler, C.M.; Papadogeorgou, G. Bipartite Causal Inference with Interference. *arXiv* **2018**, arXiv:1807.08660.
34. Lauritzen, S. *Graphical Models*; Oxford University Press: Oxford, UK, 1996.
35. MacLane, S. *Categories for the Working Mathematician*; Springer: New York, NY, USA, 1971; Volume 5, p. ix+262.
36. MacLane, S.; Moerdijk, I. *Sheaves in Geometry and Logic: A First Introduction to Topos Theory*; Springer: Berlin/Heidelberg, Germany, 1994.
37. Riehl, E. *Category Theory in Context*; Aurora: Dover Modern Math Originals; Dover Publications: New York, NY, USA, 2017.
38. Joyal, A.; Nielsen, M.; Winskel, G. Bisimulation from Open Maps. *Inf. Comput.* **1996**, *127*, 164–185. .: 10.1006/inco.1996.0057. [CrossRef]
39. May, J. *A Concise Course in Algebraic Topology*; Chicago Lectures in Mathematics, University of Chicago Press: London, UK, 1999.
40. Richter, B. *From Categories to Homotopy Theory*; Cambridge Studies in Advanced Mathematics, Cambridge University Press: Cambridge, UK, 2020.
41. Mahadevan, S. Causal Homotopy. *arXiv* **2021**, arXiv:2112.01847. [CrossRef]
42. Schölkopf, B.; Smola, A.J. *Learning with Kernels: Support Vector Machines, Regularization, Optimization, and Beyond*; MIT Press: Cambridge, MA, USA, 2002.
43. Boardman, M.; Vogt, R. *Homotopy Invariant Algebraic Structures on Topological Spaces*; Springer: Berlin/Heidelberg, Germany, 1973.
44. Janzing, D.; Balduzzi, D.; Grosse-Wentrup, M.; Schölkopf, B. Quantifying causal influences. *Ann. Stat.* **2013**, *41*, 2324–2358. [CrossRef]
45. Coecke, B.; Fritz, T.; Spekkens, R.W. A mathematical theory of resources. *Inf. Comput.* **2016**, *250*, 59–86. [CrossRef]
46. Spivak, D.I. Simplicial Databases. *arXiv* **2009**, arXiv:0904.2012.
47. Spivak, D.I.; Kent, R.E. Ologs: A Categorical Framework for Knowledge Representation. *PLoS ONE* **2012**, *7*, e24274. [CrossRef]
48. Andersson, S.A.; Madigan, D.; Perlman, M.D. A characterization of Markov equivalence classes for acyclic digraphs. *Ann. Stat.* **1997**, *25*, 505–541. [CrossRef]
49. Lauritzen, S.L.; Richardson, T.S. Chain graph models and their causal interpretations. *J. R. Stat. Soc. Ser. B* **2002**, *64*, 321–348. [CrossRef]
50. Barmak, J.A. *Algebraic Topology of Finite Topological Spaces and Applications*; Lecture Notes in Mathematics; Springer: Berlin/Heidelberg, Germany, 2011.
51. Stong, R.E. Finite topological spaces. *Trans. Amer. Math. Soc.* **1966**, *123*, 325–340. [CrossRef]
52. Alexandroff, P.S. *Combinatorial Topology*; Graylock Press: Toronto, ON, Canada, 1956; Volume 1.
53. Gabriel, P.; Gabriel, P.; Zisman, M. *Calculus of Fractions and Homotopy Theory*; Calculus of Fractions and Homotopy Theory; Springer: New York, NY, USA, 1967.
54. Borceux, F. *Handbook of Categorical Algebra*; Encyclopedia of Mathematics and Its Applications; Cambridge University Press: New York, NY, USA, 1994; Volume 1.
55. Quillen, D.G. *Homotopical Algebra*; Springer: Berlin/Heidelberg, Germany, 1967.
56. Sam, S.; Snowden, A. Gröbner methods for representations of combinatorial categories. *J. Am. Math. Soc.* **2016**, *30*, 159–203. [CrossRef]
57. Beerenwinkel, N.; Eriksson, N.; Sturmfels, B. Conjunctive Bayesian networks. *Bernoulli* **2007**, *13*, 893–909. [CrossRef]
58. Geiger, D.; Meek, C.; Sturmfels, B. On the toric algebra of graphical models. *Ann. Stat.* **2006**, *34*, 1463–1492. [CrossRef]
59. Hibi, T. Distributive lattices, affine semigroup rings and algebras with straightening laws. *Commut. Algebra Comb.* **1987**, *11*, 93–109.

entropy MDPI

Article

Conducting Causal Analysis by Means of Approximating Probabilistic Truths

Bo Pieter Johannes Andrée [1,2]

[1] Analytics and Tool Unit, Development Economics Data Group, World Bank, 1818 H St NW, Washington, DC 20433, USA; bandree@worldbank.org or b.p.j.andree@vu.nl

[2] Department of Spatial Economics, School of Business and Economics, VU University Amsterdam, De Boelelaan 1105, 1081 HV Amsterdam, The Netherlands

Simple Summary: The current paper develops a probabilistic theory of causation and suggests practical routines for conducting causal inference applicable to new machine learning methods that have, so far, remained relatively underutilized in this context.

Abstract: The current paper develops a probabilistic theory of causation using measure-theoretical concepts and suggests practical routines for conducting causal inference. The theory is applicable to both linear and high-dimensional nonlinear models. An example is provided using random forest regressions and daily data on yield spreads. The application tests how uncertainty in short- and long-term inflation expectations interacts with spreads in the daily Bitcoin price. The results are contrasted with those obtained by standard linear Granger causality tests. It is shown that the suggested measure-theoretic approaches do not only lead to better predictive models, but also to more plausible parsimonious descriptions of possible causal flows. The paper concludes that researchers interested in causal analysis should be more aspirational in terms of developing predictive capabilities, even if the interest is in inference and not in prediction per se. The theory developed in the paper provides practitioners guidance for developing causal models using new machine learning methods that have, so far, remained relatively underutilized in this context.

Keywords: causality; Bitcoin; inflation; yield spreads; approximation theory; Hellinger distance; Kullback–Leibler divergence; correct specification; misspecified models

Citation: Andrée, B.P.J. Conducting Causal Analysis by Means of Approximating Probabilistic Truths. *Entropy* **2022**, *24*, 92. https://doi.org/10.3390/e24010092

Academic Editor: Kateřina Hlaváčková-Schindler

Received: 22 September 2021
Accepted: 27 December 2021
Published: 6 January 2022

1. Introduction

Philosophers have debated at length whether causality is a subject that should be treated probabilistically or deterministically. This resulted in the development of different inferential systems and views on reality. Pure logic dealt with inferences about deterministic truths [1,2]. Probabilistic reasoning has been developed to allow for uncertainty in inferences about deterministic truths [3,4], to make inferences about probabilistic truths [5,6], or to imply the existence of associated deterministic truths [7–11]. Probabilistic theories about causality were developed throughout the 20th century, with notable contributions by Reichenbach, Good, and Suppe [12]. At the same time, however, the classical model of physics maintained its position as a role model for other sciences, which led researchers, including those concerned with human behavior and economic systems, to reject ideas about probabilistic causation, opting, often, to reason probabilistically about deterministic truths.

In modern physics, the standard equations of quantum mechanics suggest that reality is, in fact, better described by probability laws [13]. The outcome of the Bohr–Einstein debates settled on the assertion that these probability laws are a result of a real indeterminacy and that reality itself is probabilistic (One may also argue that this is simply a correct *exposition of the theory* and not necessarily of the physical world, as more complete theories may yet be discovered). Ref. [14] provides an alternative interpretation of quantum physics in which the probability laws are statistical results of the development of completely determined, but hidden, variables. At a macroscopic level, deterministic laws and contingencies induce associated probabilistic laws (Contingencies is a term used by Ref. [14] to refer to independent factors that may exist outside the scope of what is treated by the laws under consideration, and which do not follow necessarily from anything that may be specified under the context of these laws). In particular, by broadening the context of the processes under consideration, new laws that govern some of the contingencies can be found. This inevitably leads to new contingencies: a process that repeats indefinitely. For this reason, any theory about reality that embraces either of deterministic law or chance, to the exclusion of the other, is inherently incomplete. Regardless of one's position on real indeterminism, it holds, according to this logic, that any natural process that arises deterministically must also satisfy statistical laws that are more general, and so any complete theory about interesting real-world phenomena must be probabilistic.

In a probabilistic view of reality cause and consequence are related by probability laws rather than laws of logical truths. A theory about probabilistic causality can, therefore, be stated in terms of the properties of the *true* measure that describes a process stochastically. The theory of causation developed here is that a causal relationship exists if there exists a *true* probability measure that produces a non-empty stochastic sequence that describes the directly caused effects from perturbations in one variable in terms of the responses in another. The paper shows that ideas about causality, including the direction, statistical significance, and economic relevance of effects, may be tested by formulating a statistical model that correctly describes observed data, and evaluating its dynamic properties. In practice, this means that the inference is conducted with a best approximation of the true probability measure. It is the position of the paper that in order to demonstrate that causality runs from a potential causal variable to the target variable, one requires developing the best approximation of the true probability measure using the potential causal variable and a best approximation of the true probability measure without the potential causal variable. The analysis should then (1) conclude whether the first modeled measure is closer to the true measure, and (2) test that the two modeled measures are not equivalent. Practical routines to do so shall be discussed and an example is provided using random forest (RF) regressions and daily data on yield spreads. The application tests how uncertainty around short- and long-term inflation expectations interact with spreads in the daily Bitcoin price, a digital asset with a predetermined finite supply that has been characterized as a new potential inflation hedge. The results are contrasted with those obtained with standard linear Granger causality tests. It is shown that the suggested approaches do not only lead to better predictive models, but also to more plausible parsimonious descriptions of possible causal flows.

The focus on approximating a correct stochastic representation of the DGP (data generating process) as a means of learning about true causal linkages is different from the approaches that try to simulate laboratory conditions by testing for statistical differences in control groups, such as described by [15,16]. The focus on obtaining a correct functional representation of the data is also different from attributing the presence of causal relationships directly to the values of parameters representing averages in treatment groups, see for instance [17–19] on this approach. Placing emphasis on the need for accurate statistical models for the full data distribution when conducting causal analysis introduces an obvious weakness: it is generally accepted that all empirical models will be mis-specified to a certain degree and that empirical models are likely never correctly specified. The *true* process, after all, is unknown in practice. This is the reason to conduct analyses in the first place. The aim to develop correct models can therefore be seen as an idealistic idea that is difficult to put into practice. However, it is still valuable to understand the role of the correct-specification assumption in causal analysis. It is commonly taught that mis-specification leads to residual dependencies that violate the assumptions made by general central limit theorems needed to obtain correct standard errors, see for example chapter 2 in [20]. However, more general estimation theory for dependent processes, as those developed and discussed for instance by [21–25], may help correct standard error estimation but do not remedy the issue that the structural response of the model is incorrect [26]. These are theories to correct the variance estimator when the underlying model is wrong, and do not address the issue that the structural response of the model does not correctly describe the data.

The paper builds on contributions of others in the following lines of research. The views on causality developed in the paper are related to the information theoretic view on testing causal theories, as discussed by [27–30], which, as here, emphasizes model parsimony. The line of reasoning is inspired by the work of [31,32], who emphasized the importance of a probabilistic formulation of economic theories and warned against the use of statistical methods without any reference to a stochastic process. The paper also emphasizes the importance of the overall model response, and, thus, on focusing on system behavior, rather than on isolated parameters that make no reference to a wider economic system. This has previously been advocated by [33]. The main result of the paper is that convincing statements about partial causal linkages must be underpinned by an accurate model of broader reality, even if the interest is in inference and not prediction per se. In order to do so, researchers must, as shall be discussed, pay due attention to distinguishing between direct causal impacts and system memory and take note of developments in the field of predictive modeling.

The plan of the paper is as follows. Section 2 develops definitions for probabilistic causality in terms of true probability measures using a flexible type of dynamical system that covers many processes observed in economics, physics, finance, and related fields of study. Section 3 discusses approximating this true probability measure as an act of minimizing divergence between the modeled probability measure and the true probability measure, while section 4 forges the link between statistical divergence and distance. This draws the connections between distance-minimization and the use of maximum likelihood criteria. Section 5 provides practical considerations and applies the theory. Finally, Section 6 concludes. Proofs are provided in the Appendix A.

2. Causality in Terms of True Probability Measures

Notation will be as follows.

Notation 1. $\mathbb{N}$, $\mathbb{Z}$ *and* $\mathbb{R}$, *respectively denote the sets of natural, integer, and real numbers. If* $\mathcal{A}$ *is a set,* $\mathfrak{B}(\mathcal{A})$ *denotes the Borel-*σ *algebra over* $\mathcal{A}$, *and* $\times_{t=1}^{t=T}\mathcal{A}$, *alternatively denoted as* $\mathcal{A}_T$, *is the Cartesian product of* T *copies of* $\mathcal{A}$. *Definitional equivalence is denoted* $:=$, *which is to be distinguished from* $\equiv$ *denoting equivalence, for example in the functional sense. For two maps,* f *and* g, *their composition arises from their point-wise application and is denoted* $f \circ g := f(g)$ *and* f^{-1} *is the inverse function of* f. *The tensor product is denoted* $\otimes$. *The notation* $\mu \ll \nu$ *is used to indicate that* μ *is absolutely continuous with respect to* ν, *i.e., if* μ *and* ν *are two measures on the same measurable space* $(X, \mathcal{A})$, μ *is absolutely continuous with respect to* ν *if* $\mu(A) = 0$ *for every set* A *for which* $\nu(A) = 0$, *or, as an example, if* ν *is the counting measure on*$[0, 1]$ *and* μ *is the Lebesgue measure, then* $\mu \ll \nu$. *It is also said that* ν *is* dominating μ *when* $\mu \ll \nu$, *see for instance ([34] p. 574). Finally, the empty set* $\emptyset$ *is also used in the context of an empty sequence, which sometimes would be notated as* $()$ *in the literature.*

Directional causality is interesting when at least two sequences are considered. Specifically, when the focus is on a T-period sequence $\{\mathbf{x}_t(\omega)\}_{t=1}^{T}$, that is a subset of the realized path of the $n_{\mathbf{x}}$-variate stochastic sequence $\mathbf{x}(\omega) := \{\mathbf{x}_t(\omega)\}_{t\in\mathbb{Z}}$ for events in the event space $\omega \in \Omega$. (That is, $\mathbf{x}_t(\omega) \in \mathcal{X} \subseteq \mathbb{R}^{n_{\mathbf{x}}}\ \forall\ (\omega, t) \in \Omega \times \mathbb{Z}$. The random sequence $\mathbf{x}(\omega)$ is a Borel-σ $\mathcal{F}/\mathfrak{B}(\mathcal{X}_\infty)$-measurable map $\mathbf{x} : \Omega \to \mathcal{X}_\infty \subseteq \mathbb{R}^{n_{\mathbf{x}}}_\infty$. In this, $\mathbb{R}^{n_{\mathbf{x}}}_\infty := \times_{t=-\infty}^{t=\infty}\mathbb{R}^{n_{\mathbf{x}}}$ denotes the Cartesian product of infinite copies of $\mathbb{R}^{n_{\mathbf{x}}}$ and $\mathcal{X}_\infty = \times_{t=-\infty}^{t=\infty}\mathcal{X}$ with $\mathfrak{B}(\mathcal{X}_\infty) := \mathfrak{B}(\mathbb{R}^{n_{\mathbf{x}}}_\infty) \cap \mathcal{X}_\infty$, and $\mathfrak{B}(\mathbb{R}^{n_{\mathbf{x}}}_\infty)$ denotes the Borel-σ algebra on the finite dimensional cylinder set of $\mathbb{R}^{n_{\mathbf{x}}}_\infty$, see Theorem 10.1 of [35], p. 159). As always, the complete probability space of interest is described by a triplet $(\Omega, \mathcal{F}, \mathbb{P})$, with $\mathcal{F}$ as the σ-field defined on the event space. $\mathbb{P}$ is used here informally as a placeholder for a collection of probability measures, as we shall introduce the exact probability measures of interest shortly.

If $\mathbf{x}$ is considered as a univariate sequence independent from causal drivers, then for every event $\omega \in \Omega$, the stochastic sequence $\mathbf{x}_t(\omega)$ would live on the probability space $(\mathcal{X}_\infty, \mathfrak{B}(\mathcal{X}_\infty), P^{\mathbf{x}})$ where $P^{\mathbf{x}}$ assigns probability to all elements of $\mathfrak{B}(\mathcal{X}_\infty)$. In a similar fashion, one can consider $\{\mathbf{y}_t(\omega)\}_{t=1}^{T}$ as the subset of the realized path of the $n_{\mathbf{y}}$-variate stochastic sequence $\mathbf{y}(\omega) := \{\mathbf{y}_t(\omega)\}_{t\in\mathbb{Z}}$ indexed by identical t for events $\omega \in \Omega$ (i.e., $\mathbf{y}_t(\omega) \in \mathcal{Y} \subseteq \mathbb{R}^{n_\mathbf{y}}\ \forall\ (\omega, t) \in \Omega \times \mathbb{Z}$ and the random sequence $\mathbf{y}(\omega)$ is a Borel-σ $\mathcal{F}/\mathfrak{B}(\mathcal{Y}_\infty)$-measurable map $\mathbf{y} : \Omega \to \mathcal{Y}_\infty \subseteq \mathbb{R}^{n_\mathbf{y}}_\infty$.) If $\mathbf{y}$ would live similarly isolated from outside influence, then for every $\omega \in \Omega$, the stochastic sequence $\mathbf{y}_t(\omega)$ would operate on a space $(\mathcal{Y}_\infty, \mathfrak{B}(\mathcal{Y}_\infty), P^{\mathbf{y}})$ where $P^{\mathbf{y}}$ assigns probability to all the elements of $\mathfrak{B}(\mathcal{Y}_\infty)$. We have a system of two unrelated sequences (This naturally covers to most common auto-regression case, only stated for $\mathbf{y}_t$ here, $\mathbf{y}_t = f^{\mathbf{yy}}(\mathbf{y}_{t-1}) + \varepsilon_t$, where ε_t is unobserved. The linear auto-regression case is obtained when $f^{\mathbf{yy}}$ is a scaled identity function.):

$$\begin{array}{l} \mathbf{x} := \{\mathbf{x}_t = f^{\mathbf{xx}}(\mathbf{x}_{t-1}), t \in \mathbb{Z}\} \\ \mathbf{y} := \{\mathbf{y}_t = f^{\mathbf{yy}}(\mathbf{y}_{t-1}), t \in \mathbb{Z}\} \end{array}. \tag{1}$$

As we shall see, an important aspect of causal analysis is to rule out that the observed data is not generated by Equation (1). As such, it is important to comment on a number of properties. First, in this system of equations, the functions $f^{\mathbf{xx}}$ and $f^{\mathbf{yy}}$ are intentionally not indexed by t. This does not imply that these functions cannot posses complex time-varying properties; it only limits the discussion to observation-driven models (to the exclusion of parameter-driven models), in which time-varying parameters arise as nonlinear functions of the data. An example would be the threshold models considered by [36,37], in which parameter values are allowed to differ across regimes in the data. The choice to restrict the discussion is made because it is intuitively easier to conceive of causal effects in an observation-driven context where observations represent verifiable values describing different states of real-world phenomena. At the same time, it has been shown that parametric observation-driven models can produce time-varying parameters of a wide class of nonlinear models [38] and that the forecasting power of such models may be on-par with parameter-driven models, even if the latter are correctly specified [39]. Moreover, Refs. [20,40,41] show how observation-driven models may be used to not only investigate how observations impact future observations, but also future parameter values, which may empirically be interesting if those parameters carry an economic interpretation. Finally, many popular machine learning algorithms, such as neural networks, can be reduced to equations that show how parameter values change according to levels in the data [42].

While the dynamics in Equation (1) may be nonlinear, the notation is too restrictive to nest long-memory processes. In particular, the state at time t is only a function of the previous state at time $t-1$, or $t-p$ if the model would be generalized to p-order lags, but not of the full history. Vanishing dependence, implied under contraction conditions [43], is often key to verifying irreducibility and continuity [44] and proving the ergodicity of time series [45]. Proving the ergodicity of a model is needed to obtain an estimation theory under an assumption of correct specification [20,24]. Later, multivariate models will be considered, in which case long-memory properties may arise, for example, when time-varying parameters in one of the functions are a function of past data as well as of past values of those time-varying parameters.

If interrelated stochastic sequences are at the center of inference, additional building blocks are required to describe the processes. This increases the potential complexity of $P^{\mathbf{x}}$ and $P^{\mathbf{y}}$, but it also allows to distinguish between causality, non-causality, and feedback. Consider the stochastic system:

$$\begin{array}{l} \mathbf{x} := \{\mathbf{x}_t = f^{\mathbf{xx}}(\mathbf{x}_{t-1}) + f^{\mathbf{xy}}(\mathbf{y}_{t-1}), t \in \mathbb{Z}\} \\ \mathbf{y} := \{\mathbf{y}_t = f^{\mathbf{yx}}(\mathbf{x}_{t-1}) + f^{\mathbf{yy}}(\mathbf{y}_{t-1}), t \in \mathbb{Z}\} \end{array}. \tag{2}$$

In this multivariate context, $f^{\mathbf{xy}}$ and $f^{\mathbf{yx}}$ will be referred to as the direct causal maps, while $f^{\mathbf{xx}}$ and $f^{\mathbf{yy}}$ control the memory properties within each channel.

When $\mathbf{x}$ and $\mathbf{y}$ are analyzed individually, the properties of $f^{\mathbf{xx}}$ and $f^{\mathbf{yy}}$ are of key interest. They carry information on the future positions of $\mathbf{x}_{t+1}$ and $\mathbf{y}_{t+1}$, and provide predictability without considering outside influence directly. However, correct causal inference around the interdependencies of $\mathbf{x}$ and $\mathbf{y}$ may be preferred over developing predictive capabilities that can result from many configurations within the parameter space that are associated with untrue probability measures. The properties of $f^{\mathbf{xy}}$ and $f^{\mathbf{yx}}$ determine the direction in which effects move. Verifying their properties is central to causality studies. The functions $f^{\mathbf{xx}}$ and $f^{\mathbf{yy}}$, on the other hand, play a central role in the system's responses to external impulses by shaping memory of the causal initial impact of a sequence of interventions, even after that sequence turns inactive.

The functions that control memory properties within channels in some sense determine how the past reverberates into the future, and specifying correct empirical equivalents to $f^{\mathbf{xx}}$ and $f^{\mathbf{yy}}$ is as crucial to the inference about the causal interdependencies as is specifying mechanisms for the action of interest (it would be more general to write Equation (2) with $\mathbf{x} := \{\mathbf{x}_t = f^{\mathbf{xx}}(\mathbf{x}_{t-1}; \mathbf{w}_{t-1}) + f^{\mathbf{xy}}(\mathbf{y}_{t-1}; \mathbf{w}_{t-1}), t \in \mathbb{Z}\}$ and $\mathbf{y} := \{\mathbf{y}_t = f^{\mathbf{yx}}(\mathbf{x}_{t-1}; \mathbf{w}_{t-1}) + f^{\mathbf{yy}}(\mathbf{y}_{t-1}; \mathbf{w}_{t-1}), t \in \mathbb{Z}\}$ and with $\mathbf{w}_t = (\mathbf{x}_t, \mathbf{y}_t)$. In this case, for instance, the dependence of $\mathbf{x}_t$ on its own past, $\mathbf{x}_{t-1}$, is allowed to vary based on the levels in past data. However, under this notation, one could at any point in time, decompose the change in one variable into effects attributed to memory and outside influence separately, which the simplified notation in Equation (2) is intended to focus on). In fact, as Ref. [46] point out, systems may be dominated by memory and the influence of the causal components may be small on the overall process in which case predictive power can be obtained without specifying any causal maps and focusing solely on memory. Inversely, this also suggests that one must obtain a model for the memory process to isolate the causal impacts themselves, suggesting that long-memory applications in which causal inference is of interest must develop a high degree of predictive power, even if prediction is not needed for policy purposes. This can be made more clear by considering the following:

$$\begin{array}{l} \mathbf{x}^0 := \{\mathbf{x}_t^0 = f^{\mathbf{xy}}(\mathbf{y}_{t-1}), t \in \mathbb{Z}\} \\ \mathbf{y}^0 := \{\mathbf{y}_t^0 = f^{\mathbf{yx}}(\mathbf{x}_{t-1}), t \in \mathbb{Z}\} \end{array}, \tag{3}$$

with $\mathbf{x}^0$ and $\mathbf{y}^0$ defined as $\mathbf{x}_t^0 = \mathbf{x}_t - f^{\mathbf{xx}}(\mathbf{x}_{t-1})$ and $\mathbf{y}_t^0 = \mathbf{y}_t - f^{\mathbf{yy}}(\mathbf{y}_{t-1})$. Given the realized sequences $\mathbf{y}(\omega)$ and $\mathbf{x}(\omega)$ generated by Equation (2), the sequential system of Equation (3) moves forward in time as the one-step-ahead directly caused parts of $\mathbf{y}$ and $\mathbf{x}$ that are filtered from the reverberating effects of $f^{\mathbf{xx}}$ and $f^{\mathbf{yy}}$. More specifically, while $\mathbf{y}$ partially consists of memory, there is a part, $\mathbf{y}^0$, that, at any point, is directly mapped from the previous state of $\mathbf{x}$, while, at the same time, $\mathbf{x}$ consists partially of memory and a part $\mathbf{x}^0$ directly generated from the last position of $\mathbf{y}$. In this view, directional causality can be stated in terms of whether (3) produces any values, i.e., diagnosing if there is any statistically significant signal from initial causal impulses left after all memory properties have been stripped from the data. Importantly, the system reveals that by the definitions of $\mathbf{x}_t^0$ and $\mathbf{y}_t^0$, obtaining appropriate estimates for $f^{\mathbf{xy}}$ and $f^{\mathbf{yx}}$ involves $f^{\mathbf{xx}}$ and $f^{\mathbf{yy}}$ being modeled correctly as $\mathbf{x}_t^0$ and $\mathbf{y}_t^0$ are not observed and only result as functions from the observable processes $\mathbf{y}$ and $\mathbf{x}$. Moreover, if $\mathbf{y}(\omega)$ and $\mathbf{x}(\omega)$ are triggered by an event, then it is possible, by process of infinite backward substitution, to write Equation (3) as an infinite chain initialized in the infinite past. Plugging in the equalities $\mathbf{x}_t = \mathbf{x}_t^0 + f^{\mathbf{xx}}(\mathbf{x}_{t-1})$ and $\mathbf{y}_t = \mathbf{y}_t^0 + f^{\mathbf{yy}}(\mathbf{y}_{t-1})$ and defining the random functions $f_{\mathbf{y}}^0(\mathbf{y}_t^0, \mathbf{y}_{t-1}) = f^{\mathbf{xy}}(\mathbf{y}_t^0 + f^{\mathbf{yy}}(\mathbf{y}_{t-1}))$ and $f_{\mathbf{x}}^0(\mathbf{x}_t^0, \mathbf{x}_{t-1}) = f^{\mathbf{yx}}(\mathbf{x}_t^0 + f^{\mathbf{xx}}(\mathbf{x}_{t-1}))$, one can write

$$\begin{array}{l} \mathbf{x}^0 := \{\mathbf{x}_t^0 = f_{\mathbf{y}}^0(\mathbf{y}_{t-1}^0, \mathbf{y}_{t-2}), t \in \mathbb{Z}\} \\ \mathbf{y}^0 := \{\mathbf{y}_t^0 = f_{\mathbf{x}}^0(\mathbf{x}_{t-1}^0, \mathbf{x}_{t-2}), t \in \mathbb{Z}\} \end{array}. \tag{4}$$

Repeating infinitely, and extending infinitely in the direction $T \to \infty$,

$$\begin{array}{l} \mathbf{x}^0 := \{\mathbf{x}_\infty^0 = (f_{\mathbf{y}}^0)^\infty(\mathbf{y}_1^0, \mathbf{y}_1), t \in \mathbb{Z}\} \\ \mathbf{y}^0 := \{\mathbf{y}_\infty^0 = (f_{\mathbf{x}}^0)^\infty(\mathbf{x}_1^0, \mathbf{x}_1), t \in \mathbb{Z}\} \end{array}. \tag{5}$$

$(f_{\mathbf{y}}^0)^\infty$ and $(f_{\mathbf{x}}^0)^\infty$ are the maps that generate $\mathbf{y}^0$ and $\mathbf{x}^0$ infinitely after $\mathbf{y}$ and $\mathbf{x}$ have been generated into infinity. Subscript $_1$ has been used, here, to mark the initialization points. This shows that $\mathbf{x}^0$ can be written as a sequence of iterating functional operations that are all defined on $\mathbf{y}$, and $\mathbf{y}^0$ defined on $\mathbf{x}$ in a similar way (Equation (5) reveals that the sequences that constitute the directly caused parts of $\mathbf{x}$ and $\mathbf{y}$ are ultimately dependent on the values at which the observable process has been initialized. That is, the entire causal pathway depends on the initial impact. In practice, one cannot observe all impacts—including those that occurred in the infinite past—and assurance is required that the initialization effect of the causal pathway must, asymptotically, be irrelevant). For ease of notation, let us write

$$\begin{aligned} \mathbf{x}^0 &:= \{\mathbf{x}_t^0 = \mathbf{f}_{\mathbf{y}}^0(\mathbf{y}_{-\infty:t}), t \in \mathbb{Z}\} \\ \mathbf{y}^0 &:= \{\mathbf{y}_t^0 = \mathbf{f}_{\mathbf{x}}^0(\mathbf{x}_{-\infty:t}), t \in \mathbb{Z}\} \end{aligned} . \tag{6}$$

where bold-faced $\mathbf{f}^0$ is used to refer to the entire sequence of functional operations f^0 up to t, starting in the infinite past $t = -\infty$. This highlights that generating the unobserved quantities $\mathbf{x}^0$ and $\mathbf{y}^0$ from the observed quantities $\mathbf{x}$ and $\mathbf{y}$ by back substitution eventually involves the unobserved quantities $\mathbf{x}_1$ and $\mathbf{y}_1$. This means that some feasible form of approximation is needed, since time series data in practice area almost never recorded since the beginning of the process.

Note first that $\mathbf{f}_{\mathbf{y}}^0 : \mathcal{Y} \to \mathcal{X} \subseteq \mathbb{R}$ is a $\mathfrak{B}(\mathcal{Y})/\mathfrak{B}(\mathcal{X})$-measurable mapping, and $\mathbf{f}_{\mathbf{x}}^0 : \mathcal{X} \to \mathcal{Y} \subseteq \mathbb{R}$ is a $\mathfrak{B}(\mathcal{X})/\mathfrak{B}(\mathcal{Y})$-measurable mapping. The sequence $\mathbf{x}^0$ thus lives on $(\mathcal{X}_\infty, \mathfrak{B}(\mathcal{X}_\infty), P_0^{\mathbf{x}})$, where $P_0^{\mathbf{x}}$ is induced according to $P_0^{\mathbf{x}}(B_{\mathbf{x}}) = P^{\mathbf{y}} \circ (\mathbf{f}_{\mathbf{y}}^0)^{-1}(B_{\mathbf{x}}) \; \forall \; B_{\mathbf{x}} \in \mathfrak{B}(\mathcal{X}_\infty)$, and $\mathbf{y}^0$ lives on $(\mathcal{Y}_\infty, \mathfrak{B}(\mathcal{Y}_\infty), P_0^{\mathbf{y}})$, where $P_0^{\mathbf{y}}$ is induced according to $P_0^{\mathbf{y}}(B_{\mathbf{y}}) = P^{\mathbf{x}} \circ (\mathbf{f}_{\mathbf{x}}^0)^{-1}(B_{\mathbf{y}}) \; \forall \; B_{\mathbf{y}} \in \mathfrak{B}(\mathcal{Y}_\infty)$, see [47] p. 118 and [48] p. 115. The notation shows that the probability measures underlying the stochastic causal sequences result from the functional behavior of the entire system. In particular, the causal sequences can be written as recursive direct effects from another variable that itself consists of memory and causal effects, and the probability measures underlying the causal sequences are thus induced by the functional relationships that describe all dynamical dependencies. This is important to the extent that many causal studies focus on one single marginal dependency, while, from the measure-theoretic perspective developed here, the wider system within any one single process operates, is of importance to the analysis. This suggests that researchers must pay attention to referencing the workings of a broader system when designing their models for inference, something [33] has also argued. Moreover, it has been argued (see [49] for discussion) that probabilistic definitions of causality are not strictly causal in the sense that they do not provide insight in the origin of the probability law that regulates the process of interest, and that a (correct) time-series model only describes (correctly) the probabilistic behavior as the outcome of that unknown causal origin. The notation, here, shows, however, explicitly the relation between the functional behavior of a system and its induced probability measure that assigns probability to all possible outcomes. This suggests that such critiquing views, rather, relate to disagreements around the level of detail in the structure of a model, which in turn would be guided by the research question of interest and the availability of detailed data. Particularly, dynamical systems in economics are often modeled using aggregate macro-economic data that do not have the same granularity as micro-economic data containing information about the behaviors of individual economic agents.

In many cases, a researcher is not able to observe all the relevant variables. When a third, possibly unobserved external variable, $\mathbf{z}$, with effect $f^{\mathbf{z}}(\mathbf{z})$, is considered, the researcher is confronted with the situation that

$$\begin{aligned} \mathbf{x} &:= \{\mathbf{x}_t = f^{\mathbf{xx}}(\mathbf{x}_{t-1}) + f^{\mathbf{xy}}(\mathbf{y}_{t-1}) + f^{\mathbf{xz}}(\mathbf{z}_{t-1}), t \in \mathbb{Z}\} \\ \mathbf{y} &:= \{\mathbf{y}_t = f^{\mathbf{yx}}(\mathbf{x}_{t-1}) + f^{\mathbf{yy}}(\mathbf{y}_{t-1}) + f^{\mathbf{yz}}(\mathbf{z}_{t-1}), t \in \mathbb{Z}\} \end{aligned} . \tag{7}$$

If $\mathbf{z}$ is unobserved, it can still be approximated as a difference combination of $\mathbf{x}$ and $\mathbf{y}$. To obtain an approximated sequence of the *true* $\mathbf{z}$ sequence to condition empirical counterparts for $f^{\mathbf{xz}}$ and $f^{\mathbf{yz}}$ on, one can work with:

$$\begin{aligned} \mathbf{z} &:= \{\mathbf{z}_t = f^{\mathbf{z}|\mathbf{xy}}(\mathbf{x}_{t+1} - (f^{\mathbf{xx}}(\mathbf{x}_t) + f^{\mathbf{xy}}(\mathbf{y}_t))), t \in \mathbb{Z}\} \\ \mathbf{z} &:= \{\mathbf{z}_t = f^{\mathbf{z}|\mathbf{yx}}(\mathbf{y}_{t+1} - (f^{\mathbf{yx}}(\mathbf{x}_t) + f^{\mathbf{yy}}(\mathbf{y}_t))), t \in \mathbb{Z}\} \end{aligned} . \tag{8}$$

Equation (8) suggests to write Equation (7) in terms of $\mathbf{y}$ and $\mathbf{x}$ only by defining $\mathbf{z}$ as a difference combination of $\mathbf{x}$ and $\mathbf{y}$ (Apart from stability conditions imposed on the endogenous process, one requires also that the exogenous impacts enter the system in some suitable manner, which, for example, requires that $f^{\mathbf{xz}}$ and $f^{\mathbf{yz}}$ are appropriately bounded. Following the same arguments that resulted in Equation (5), the initialization of the exogenous impacts $\mathbf{z}_1$ should similarly not carry information influential in the empirical estimates of $f^{\mathbf{xy}}$ and $f^{\mathbf{yx}}$, conditional on partial information). This allows us to define the spaces and measures in terms of $\mathbf{x}$ and $\mathbf{y}$ when the multivariate process includes further variables, in this case, $\mathbf{z}$. If the process is invertible, one can write, by aggregating the functions:

$$\begin{aligned} \mathbf{x} &:= \{\mathbf{x}_t = f^{\mathbf{xx}}(\mathbf{x}_{t-1}) + f^{\mathbf{xy}}(\mathbf{y}_{t-1}) + f^{\mathbf{xz}}(\mathbf{x}_t, \mathbf{x}_{t-1}, \mathbf{y}_{t-1}), t \in \mathbb{Z}\} \\ \mathbf{y} &:= \{\mathbf{y}_t = f^{\mathbf{yx}}(\mathbf{x}_{t-1}) + f^{\mathbf{yy}}(\mathbf{y}_{t-1}) + f^{\mathbf{yz}}(\mathbf{y}_t, \mathbf{x}_{t-1}, \mathbf{y}_{t-1}), t \in \mathbb{Z}\} \end{aligned} . \tag{9}$$

$$\begin{aligned} \mathbf{x} &:= \{\mathbf{x}_t = f^{\mathbf{x}}(\mathbf{x}_{t-1}, \mathbf{y}_{t-1}), t \in \mathbb{Z}\} \\ \mathbf{y} &:= \{\mathbf{y}_t = f^{\mathbf{y}}(\mathbf{x}_{t-1}, \mathbf{y}_{t-1}), t \in \mathbb{Z}\} \end{aligned} . \tag{10}$$

$$\begin{aligned} \mathbf{x} &:= \{\mathbf{x}_t = f^{\mathbf{x}}(\mathbf{w}_{t-1}), t \in \mathbb{Z}\} \\ \mathbf{y} &:= \{\mathbf{y}_t = f^{\mathbf{y}}(\mathbf{w}_{t-1}), t \in \mathbb{Z}\} \end{aligned} . \tag{11}$$

For every $t \in \mathbb{Z}$, the map $f^{\mathbf{x}} \circ (\mathbf{y}_{t-1}, \mathbf{x}_{t-1}) : \Omega \to \mathcal{X}$ is $\mathcal{F}/\mathfrak{B}(\mathcal{X})$-measurable and $\mathbf{x}(\omega)$ lives on the space $(\mathcal{X}_\infty, \mathfrak{B}(\mathcal{X}_\infty), P^{\mathbf{x}})$ where the probability measure $P^{\mathbf{x}}$ is induced by $f^{\mathbf{x}}$ on $\mathfrak{B}(\mathcal{X}_\infty)$ according to the point-wise application of $P^{\mathbf{w}}$ and the inverse of $f^{\mathbf{x}}$. ($P^{\mathbf{x}}(B_{\mathbf{x}}) = P^{\mathbf{w}} \circ (f^{\mathbf{x}})^{-1}(B_{\mathbf{x}}) \,\forall\, (B_{\mathbf{x}}) \in \mathfrak{B}(\mathcal{X}_\infty)$). Similar arguments follow for $P^{\mathbf{y}}$. This tells us that, in the general case of multivariate dependencies and in the presence of possibly unobserved variables, the probability measures underlying the individual sequences are possibly a result of those of the other sequences. This means the space of empirical candidates for the probability measure $P^{\mathbf{w}}$ that underlies the joint process $\mathbf{w} := \{\mathbf{w}_t = (\mathbf{y}_t, \mathbf{x}_t), t \in \mathbb{Z}\}$ operates on $(\mathcal{W}_\infty, \mathfrak{B}(\mathcal{W}_\infty), P^{\mathbf{w}})$. (The sequence realizes under the events $\omega \in \Omega$, $\mathbf{w}_t(\omega) \in \mathcal{W}$, where $\mathcal{W} := \mathcal{Y} \times \mathcal{X}$ and $\mathbf{w}(\omega) \in \mathcal{W}_\infty$, with $\mathcal{W}_\infty := \mathcal{Y}_\infty \times \mathcal{X}_\infty \subseteq \mathbb{R}_\infty^{n_{\mathbf{x}}+n_{\mathbf{y}}} := \times_{t=-\infty}^{t=\infty} \mathbb{R}^{n_{\mathbf{x}}+n_{\mathbf{y}}}$, and the probability measure of the joint process $P^{\mathbf{w}}$ is thus defined on the product σ-algebra $\mathfrak{B}(\mathcal{W}_\infty) = \mathfrak{B}(\mathcal{X}_\infty \times \mathcal{Y}_\infty) = \mathfrak{B}(\mathcal{X}_\infty) \otimes \mathfrak{B}(\mathcal{Y}_\infty) := \mathcal{W}_\infty \cap \mathfrak{B}(\mathbb{R}_\infty^{n_{\mathbf{x}}+n_{\mathbf{y}}})$ (see, [47] p. 119)).

Regardless, the measure $P^{\mathbf{w}}$ is induced by functional relations of Equation (2), which, as was shown, can be decomposed into memory and causal subsystems. One can thus state causality conditions, based on the measures that describe the directly caused effects represented by Equation (6). In particular, one can keep the focus on $P_0^{\mathbf{x}}$ and $P_0^{\mathbf{y}}$, bearing in mind that they are lower-level constituents of $P^{\mathbf{w}}$ on which, in turn, the complete estimation objective will be defined.

Definition 1 (Non-causality). *The stochastic sequences $\mathbf{x}(\omega)$ and $\mathbf{y}(\omega)$ are not causally related if $P_0^{\mathbf{x}}$ and $P_0^{\mathbf{y}}$ are null measures, such that $\mathbf{x}^0(\omega) \in \varnothing \,\forall\, (\omega, t) \in \Omega \times \mathbb{Z}$ and $\mathbf{y}^0(\omega) \in \varnothing \,\forall\, (\omega, t) \in \Omega \times \mathbb{Z}$.*

Definition 2 (Uni-directional Causality). *Causality runs uni-directionally from the stochastic sequence $\mathbf{x}(\omega)$ to another stochastic sequence $\mathbf{y}(\omega)$ (visa versa), if $P_0^{\mathbf{x}}$ is a null measure, and $P_0^{\mathbf{y}}$ is a non-null measure, such that $\mathbf{x}^0(\omega) \in \varnothing \,\forall\, (\omega, t) \in \Omega \times \mathbb{Z}$ and $\mathbf{y}^0(\omega) \in \mathcal{Y} \,\forall\, (\omega, t) \in \Omega \times \mathbb{Z}$ (visa versa).*

Definition 3 (Bi-directional Causality). *The stochastic sequence $\mathbf{x}(\omega)$ is causal with respect to $\mathbf{y}(\omega)$ and $\mathbf{y}(\omega)$ is causal with respect to $\mathbf{x}(\omega)$, if $P_0^{\mathbf{x}}$ and $P_0^{\mathbf{y}}$ are both non-null measures, such that $\mathbf{x}^0(\omega) \in \mathcal{X} \,\forall\, (\omega, t) \in \Omega \times \mathbb{Z}$ and $\mathbf{y}^0(\omega) \in \mathcal{Y} \,\forall\, (\omega, t) \in \Omega \times \mathbb{Z}$.*

Respectively, conditioning on impacts in $\mathbf{x}$, these probabilistic causality definitions can thus be understood broadly as:

1. Whenever an intervention in $\mathbf{x}$ occurs, there is no chance that $\mathbf{y}^0$ reacts as a result of that.
2. Whenever an intervention in $\mathbf{x}$ occurs, there is positive chance that $\mathbf{y}^0$ reacts as a result of that.
3. Whenever an intervention in $\mathbf{x}$ occurs, there is positive chance that $\mathbf{y}^0$ reacts as a result of that. Subsequently there is positive chance that $\mathbf{x}$ reacts to this initial reaction, a probabilistic process that repeats recursively.

Remark 1. *With null-measures, it is meant that the stochastic sequence describing the directly caused effects from one variable to the other takes values in the empty set with probability 1. This is because the functions that induce the probability measure cancel out, hence, they can be removed from the equations resulting in a probability measure that is not induced by any remaining rule or relationship. In practice, one can test whether* $P^{\mathbf{x}}|f^{\mathbf{xx}} \equiv P^{\mathbf{x}}|f^{\mathbf{xx}}f^{\mathbf{xy}}$ *or* $P^{\mathbf{x}}|f^{\mathbf{xx}} \not\equiv P^{\mathbf{x}}|f^{\mathbf{xx}}f^{\mathbf{xy}}$*, where* $P^{\mathbf{x}}|f^{\mathbf{xx}}$ *here denotes the probability measure induced by the functional relationships in Equation (1) and* $P^{\mathbf{x}}|f^{\mathbf{xx}}f^{\mathbf{xy}}$ *denotes the probability measure induced by the functional relationships in Equation (2), to test whether* $P_0^{\mathbf{x}}$ *exists. A practical test is a Kolmogorov–Smirnov-type test.*

3. Limit Divergence on the Space of Modeled Probability Measures

The definitions of causality, in terms of the lower-level components of $P^{\mathbf{w}}$, suggest that correct causal statements can be obtained empirically by extracting relevant counterparts to $P_0^{\mathbf{x}}$ and $P_0^{\mathbf{y}}$ from a relevant counterpart to $P^{\mathbf{w}}$, and investigating the stochastic sequences produced by these modeled measures. For such an approach to be of relevance in an empirical context, one must ensure that the concepts introduced adequately transfer over from the *true* measure $P^{\mathbf{w}}$ to a modeled measure $P^{\hat{\mathbf{w}}}$. The focus is therefore shifted towards detailing how $P^{\hat{\mathbf{w}}}$ can be approximated as a minimally divergent measure relative to $P^{\mathbf{w}}$, and draw on approximation theory to construct equivalence around the *true* measure under an axiom of correct specification.

For some event $\omega \in \Omega$, a realized T-period sequence $\mathbf{w}_T(\omega) := (\mathbf{y}_T(\omega), \mathbf{x}_T(\omega))$ consisting of sequences $\{\mathbf{y}_t(\omega)\}_{t=1}^{t=T}$ and $\{\mathbf{x}_t(\omega)\}_{t=1}^{t=T}$ can be observed. The *true* function $f^{\mathbf{w}}$, consists of our main functions of interest $f^{\mathbf{x}}$ and $f^{\mathbf{y}}$ that in turn are composed of $f^{\mathbf{xy}}$ and $f^{\mathbf{yx}}$ that are of particular interest to the researcher focused on causality, but possibly also functions $f^{\mathbf{xx}}$ and $f^{\mathbf{yy}}$ that shape the responses of an initial causal effect. The exact properties are generally unknown to the observer, but one can design a parameterization mapping that learns the behavior of $f^{\mathbf{x}}$ and $f^{\mathbf{y}}$ when exposed to sufficient data. To learn from the data an approximation of $f^{\mathbf{x}}$ and $f^{\mathbf{y}}$, one can postulate a model

$$\hat{\mathbf{w}} := \{\hat{\mathbf{w}}_t = f(\mathbf{w}_{t-1}; \boldsymbol{\theta}), \boldsymbol{\theta} \in \Theta, t \in \mathbb{Z}\}, \tag{12}$$

with $f{:}\mathcal{W} \times \Theta \to \mathcal{W}$ as our postulated model function and $\hat{\mathbf{w}}$ as the modeled data. In the context of parametric inference, the parameter space Θ is of finite dimensionality, but also in the nonparametric case, the vector $\boldsymbol{\theta} \in \Theta$ indexes parametric models nested by the nonparametric model, each inducing its own probability measure, and Θ indexes families of parametric models, each inducing a space of parametric functions generated under Θ. In this discussion a compact set of potential hypotheses is considered, limiting the inference to parametric models. The arguments can be extended to the nonparametric case, by focusing on a compact subset $\Theta_s \subset \Theta$ of solutions (For example, by letting Θ_s grow as $T \to \infty$, hence focusing on the case $\Theta_{s1} \subset \Theta_{s2} \ldots \subset \Theta_{s\infty} \subseteq \Theta$, see for example [50]). For example, by using priors or penalties that discard $\Theta \setminus \Theta_s$ such that any solution of the criterion necessarily falls within a compact subset space, see [20] p. 210 and [24]. Let f be $\mathfrak{B}(\mathcal{W})$-measurable $\forall\, \boldsymbol{\theta} \in \Theta$ so that $f(\mathbf{w}_t; \boldsymbol{\theta}) : \Omega \to \mathcal{W}$ is $\mathcal{F}/\mathfrak{B}(\mathcal{W})$-measurable $\forall\, \boldsymbol{\theta} \in \Theta$ and $t \in \mathbb{Z}$. $F_\Theta := \{f(\cdot; \boldsymbol{\theta}), \boldsymbol{\theta} \in \Theta\}$ is our space of parametric functions defined on $\mathcal{W}$ generated under Θ under the injective $f_{\mathcal{W}} : \Theta \to F_\Theta(\mathcal{W})$ where $f_{\mathcal{W}}(\boldsymbol{\theta}) := f(\cdot; \boldsymbol{\theta}) \in$

$F_\Theta(\mathcal{W})\ \forall\ \boldsymbol{\theta} \in \Theta$. Under any *true* probability measure $P^{\mathbf{w}}$, every potential parameter vector included in the parameter space $\boldsymbol{\theta} \in \Theta$ induces a probability measure $P^{\hat{\mathbf{w}}}_{\boldsymbol{\theta}}$ indexed by $\boldsymbol{\theta}$ on $\mathfrak{B}(\mathcal{W}_\infty)$, according to $P^{\hat{\mathbf{w}}}_{\boldsymbol{\theta}}(B_{\mathbf{w}}) = P^{\mathbf{w}} \circ f^{-1}(B_{\mathbf{w}}, \boldsymbol{\theta})\ \forall\ (B_{\mathbf{w}}, \boldsymbol{\theta}) \in \mathfrak{B}(\mathcal{W}_\infty \times \Theta)$. Thus, for every potential parameter vector included in the parameter space $\boldsymbol{\theta} \in \Theta$, there is a triplet $(\mathcal{W}_\infty, \mathfrak{B}(\mathcal{W}_\infty), P^{\hat{\mathbf{w}}}_{\boldsymbol{\theta}})$ that describes the probability space of modeled data under $\boldsymbol{\theta}$. The triplet $(\mathcal{W}_\infty, \mathfrak{B}(\mathcal{W}_\infty), P^{\hat{\mathbf{w}}}_{\boldsymbol{\theta}})$ is, thus, itself an element of the measure spaces indexed by $\boldsymbol{\theta}$ across all Θ. Given the *true* probability measure $P^{\mathbf{w}}$ on $\mathfrak{B}(\mathcal{W})$, this process is summarized by a functional $\mathfrak{P} : F_\Theta(\mathcal{W}) \to \mathcal{P}^{\hat{\mathbf{w}}}_{\Theta}$, that maps elements from the space of parametric functions generated by the entire parameter space $F_\Theta(\mathcal{W})$, onto the space $\mathcal{P}^{\hat{\mathbf{w}}}_{\Theta}$ of probability measures defined on the sets of $\mathfrak{B}(\mathcal{W}_\infty)$ generated by Θ through $f(\cdot;\boldsymbol{\theta})$.

Now, $f^{\mathbf{w}}$ is generally not only unknown, but for a finite Θ there is no guarantee that $\exists \boldsymbol{\theta}_0 \in \Theta : P \circ f_{\mathcal{W}}(\boldsymbol{\theta}_0) = P^{\mathbf{w}}$, implying that, in many empirical applications, one is concerned with the situation where $P^{\mathbf{w}} \notin \mathcal{P}^{\hat{\mathbf{w}}}_{\Theta}$. However, if $\exists P^{\mathbf{w}} \in \mathcal{P}^{\hat{\mathbf{w}}}_{\Theta}$, one can learn all about $P^{\mathbf{w}}$ by uncovering the properties of f, given that a sufficient amount of observations is available. (As discussed in the literature on miss-specification, even when the axiom of correct specification is abandoned, f may converge to a function that produces the optimal conditional density, which may reveal properties of $f^{\mathbf{w}}$). Let

$$\hat{\boldsymbol{\theta}}_T := \arg\min_{\boldsymbol{\theta} \in \Theta} Q_T(\mathbf{w}_T; \boldsymbol{\theta}), \tag{13}$$

$\hat{\boldsymbol{\theta}}_T : \Omega \to \Theta$, be the extremum estimate for $\boldsymbol{\theta}_0$ as judged by the criterion $Q_T : \mathcal{W}_T \times \Theta \to \mathbb{R}$. Trivially, $\mathcal{W}_T := \mathcal{Y}_T \times \mathcal{X}_T$ and $\mathbf{w}_T(\omega) \in \mathcal{W}_T$. To see that under correct specification it is possible to approximate the *true* function $f^{\mathbf{w}}$ in terms of equivalence (in the sense of function equivalence [51] p. 288), one can write the criterion function also as a function of the *true* function and the postulated model $Q_T(f^{\mathbf{w}}(\mathbf{w}_T), f(\mathbf{w}_T; \boldsymbol{\theta}))$ in which it is made use of the fact that $f^{\mathbf{w}}(\mathbf{w}_T) := \{f^{\mathbf{w}}(\mathbf{w}_t)\}_{t=1}^T := \mathbf{w}_T$ and $f(\mathbf{w}_T; \boldsymbol{\theta}) := \{f(\mathbf{w}_t; \boldsymbol{\theta})\}_{t=1}^T := \hat{\mathbf{w}}_T$.

The discussion further evolves toward showing that the element in $\mathcal{P}^{\hat{\mathbf{w}}}_{\Theta}$ that is closest to $P^{\mathbf{w}}$ minimizes a divergence metric that results from a transformation of the limit criterion that measures the divergence between the *true* density and the density implied by the model. Note that $\mathcal{P}^{\hat{\mathbf{w}}}_{\Theta}$ is induced by the proposed candidates for $P^{\mathbf{w}}$; studies on causality thus rely on flexible model design as the researcher determines which hypotheses are considered in a study by exerting control over Θ. Naturally, if $\Theta_1 \subset \Theta_2$, then Θ_2 produces a larger $\mathcal{P}^{\hat{\mathbf{w}}}_{\Theta_2} \supset \mathcal{P}^{\hat{\mathbf{w}}}_{\Theta_1}$. This suggests that minimizing this divergence metric over a large as possible $\mathcal{P}^{\hat{\mathbf{w}}}_{\Theta}$ results in selecting $P^{\hat{\mathbf{w}}}$ at a point in $\mathcal{P}^{\hat{\mathbf{w}}}_{\Theta}$ that attains equivalence to $P^{\mathbf{w}}$ only when Θ is large enough to produce a correctly specified hypothesis set. Note that the definition of $F_\Theta := \{f(\cdot;\boldsymbol{\theta}), \boldsymbol{\theta} \in \Theta\}$, as our space of parametric functions generated under Θ, under the injective $f_{\mathcal{W}} : \Theta \to F_\Theta(\mathcal{W})$ and the functional $\mathfrak{P} : F_\Theta(\mathcal{W}) \to \mathcal{P}^{\hat{\mathbf{w}}}_{\Theta}$ that induces the space of probability measures, is defined on the sample space $\mathcal{W}$. This highlights that the correct specification argument, $P^{\mathbf{w}} \in \mathcal{P}^{\hat{\mathbf{w}}}_{\Theta}$, not only stresses flexible parameterization in the sense that parameterized dependencies can take on many values, but also in the sense of using correct data (Indeed, the potential parameters that would interact with data that is not used are essentially treated as zero, so the focus on using correct data is implicitly already contained in the standard statements of correct specification that focus directly on the dimensions of Θ. The distinction is nevertheless useful because nonparametric models are often popularized as methods to reduce miss-specification bias as Θ becomes infinite dimensional, but this does not imply that $P^{\mathbf{w}} \in \mathcal{P}^{\hat{\mathbf{w}}}_{\Theta}$ if important data is missing). When little is known about f, one is thus not only concerned with flexibility in terms of the type of parametric functions generated under Θ, but also the variables on which the modeled measures are defined. When these concerns are appropriately addressed, testing for causality is deciding based on the approximation $P^{\hat{\mathbf{w}}}$ whether the best approximation of the *true* model suggests (1) that $\mathbf{x}$ and $\mathbf{y}$ live in isolation, (2) unidirectional causality, or (3) that $P^{\mathbf{w}}$ produces feedback.

To turn this problem into a selection problem that can be solved by divergence minimization w.r.t. the *true* measure, first introduce the limit criterion by taking $T \to \infty$ and working with the modeled data as the minimizer of the criterion. Specifically, let the limit criterion be $Q_\infty(\boldsymbol{\theta}) := Q_T(f^{\mathbf{w}}(\mathbf{w}_T), f(\mathbf{w}_T; \arg\min_{\boldsymbol{\theta}\in\Theta} Q_T(\mathbf{w}_T;\boldsymbol{\theta})))$ evaluated at $T \to \infty$ with $Q_\infty : \Theta \to \mathbb{R}$ and $Q_\infty(\boldsymbol{\theta}) = Q_\infty^{\mathcal{P}}(P^{\mathbf{w}}; P_{\boldsymbol{\theta}}^{\hat{\mathbf{w}}})\ \forall\ \boldsymbol{\theta} \in \Theta$ with the criterion $Q_\infty(\boldsymbol{\theta}) = Q_\infty^{\mathcal{P}}$ as a measure of divergence $d_{\mathcal{P}}$ on the *true* probability measure and the modeled measure. More specifically, $d_{\mathcal{P}} \equiv Q_\infty^{\mathcal{P}} : \mathcal{P}_\Theta^{\hat{\mathbf{w}}} \times \mathcal{P}_\Theta^{\hat{\mathbf{w}}} \to \mathbb{R}_{\geq 0}$. By definition of $Q_\infty^{\mathcal{P}}$ as a divergence on the space that contains $P^{\mathbf{w}}$ and $P_{\boldsymbol{\theta}}^{\hat{\mathbf{w}}}\ \forall\ \boldsymbol{\theta} \in \Theta$, the element $\boldsymbol{\theta}_0$ is thus the minimizer of that divergence.

Moreover, arg min in the parameter sense, arg min in the function sense (in terms of a divergence metric on the *true* function), and arg min in the measure sense (in terms of a divergence metric on the *true* probability measure), are equivalent limits under the same consistency result. To see this, it is convenient to focus once more on the target and write $\boldsymbol{\theta}_0 = \arg\min_{\boldsymbol{\theta}\in\Theta} Q_\infty^{\mathcal{P}} \equiv \arg\min_{\boldsymbol{\theta}\in\Theta} Q_\infty^{F}(f^{\mathbf{w}}, f_{\mathcal{W}}(\boldsymbol{\theta}))$, with $Q_\infty^{F} : F(\mathcal{W}) \times F(\mathcal{W}) \to \mathbb{R}_{\geq 0}$, to make clear that the criterion establishes a divergence d_F on $F(\mathcal{W}) \times F(\mathcal{W})$, which is, in turn, induced by $d_{\mathcal{P}}$ through $\mathfrak{P}$ according to $d_F(f^1, f^2) = d_{\mathcal{P}}(P(f^1), P(f^2))\ \forall\ (f^1, f^2) \in F(\mathcal{W}) \times F(\mathcal{W})$. This ensures that our statement on the probability measure is relevant under standard consistency results that are focused on the convergence of an estimated parameter vector toward $\boldsymbol{\theta}_0$, while, equivalently, the impulse response functions (IRFs) converge to the *true* IRFs at $\boldsymbol{\theta}_0$. This implies that deciding between Definitions 1–3 can be read from the responses produced by the IRF that minimizes divergence w.r.t. the *true* IRF

Not necessary, but convenient for a proof that holds easily in practical situations, is to assume the existence of a strictly increasing function $r : \mathbb{R} \to \mathbb{R}_{\geq 0}$ that ensures the existence of a transformation of the limit criterion into a metric, $d_{\mathcal{P}}^* \equiv r \circ d_{\mathcal{P}}$, with r being a continuously and strictly increasing function. For convenience, all assumptions are summarized in Assumption 1.

Assumption 1. *For a limit criterion $Q_\infty : \Theta \to \mathbb{R}$ of the form $Q_\infty(\boldsymbol{\theta}) \equiv Q_\infty^{\mathcal{P}}(P^{\mathbf{w}}, P_{\boldsymbol{\theta}}^{\hat{\mathbf{w}}})\ \forall\ \boldsymbol{\theta} \in \Theta$, $d_{\mathcal{P}} \equiv Q_\infty^{\mathcal{P}} : \mathcal{P}^{\mathbf{w}} \times \mathcal{P}^{\mathbf{w}} \to \mathbb{R}_{\geq 0}$ is a divergence. Assume there exists a continuous strictly increasing function $r : \mathbb{R} \to \mathbb{R}_{\geq 0}$ such that $d_{\mathcal{P}}^* \equiv r \circ d_{\mathcal{P}}$ is a metric. The functional $f_{\mathcal{W}} : \Theta \to F_\Theta(\mathcal{W})$ is injective and $\boldsymbol{\theta}_0 \in \Theta$.*

Proposition 1. *Assume 1, then the following are equivalent limits:*

1. $\boldsymbol{\theta}_0$,
2. $\arg\min_{\boldsymbol{\theta}\in\Theta} Q_\infty(\boldsymbol{\theta})$,
3. $\arg\min_{\boldsymbol{\theta}\in\Theta} d_F^*(f^{\mathbf{w}}, f^{\hat{\mathbf{w}}}(\cdot, \boldsymbol{\theta}))$,
4. $\arg\min_{\boldsymbol{\theta}\in\Theta} Q_\infty^{\mathcal{P}}(P^{\mathbf{w}}, P_{\boldsymbol{\theta}}^{\hat{\mathbf{w}}})$,
5. $\arg\min_{\boldsymbol{\theta}\in\Theta} d_{\mathcal{P}}^*(P^{\mathbf{w}}, P_{\boldsymbol{\theta}}^{\hat{\mathbf{w}}})$.

Remark 2. *Dropping the axiom of correct specification implies $\hat{\boldsymbol{\theta}}_\infty \neq \boldsymbol{\theta}_0$, hence, the equivalences of 3–5 are now w.r.t. item 2.*

The equivalences in Proposition 1 not only ensure that for a correctly specified model $\exists \boldsymbol{\theta}_0 \in \Theta$, the element $\boldsymbol{\theta}_0$ results in functional equivalence between the model and the *true* model (item 3), but also in zero divergence between the probability measures $P^{\mathbf{w}}$ and $P_{\boldsymbol{\theta}}^{\hat{\mathbf{w}}}$ (item 4). Moreover, it follows that at $\boldsymbol{\theta}_0$, the empirically estimated probability measure $P^{\hat{\mathbf{w}}}$ is equivalent to $P^{\mathbf{w}}$ in the sense that there is zero distance between the two (item 5).

Remark 3. *Proposition 1 is applicable to a large class of extremum estimators, even those not initially conceived as minimizers of distance. In particular it is often possible to find a divergence on the space of probability measures. For example, method of moments estimators are naturally defined in terms of features of the underlying probability measures. In Section 4 and example is given, using Kullback–Leibler divergence, for which penalized likelihood is an estimator. In this case squared Hellinger distance can be shown to be a lower bound.*

Corollary 1 now delivers that our definitions, set on the *true* measures, transfer to modeled probability measures in the limit for correctly specified cases. It is well-known that standard consistency proofs apply also to approximate extremum estimators, therefore, assuming additionally that $\sup_{\theta\in\Theta}|Q_T(\mathbf{w}_T;\boldsymbol{\theta}) - Q_\infty(\boldsymbol{\theta})| \to 0$ *a.s.*, is sufficient for a consistency result together with the uniqueness of $\boldsymbol{\theta}_0$ within the compact hypothesis space Θ (Note that, under the axiom of correct-specification, consistency results require suitable forms of stability defined on the process rather than the data. While we have loosely remarked on the fact that the non-parametric case of an infinite dimensional Θ is easily allowed, stability of highly nonlinear multivariate time series is a difficult separate topic. Regardless, Refs. [44,45] provide Ergodicity results for a large class of nonlinear time series that include non-parametric ones. The conditions require the nonlinearities to be sufficiently smooth. Specific stability results have also been established for certain neural network models, for example by [52]). This implies that our causality conditions on the *true* measures do not only transfer to the approximate in the limit, but also for large T under standard regularity conditions. Essentially, this is the setting considered by Ref. [11]. Summarized:

Corollary 1. *Given a* true *probability measure* $P^{\mathbf{w}}$*, and an equivalent modeled probability measure* $P^{\hat{\mathbf{w}}}$ *in the sense that* $d^*_{P^{\hat{\mathbf{w}}}} = r \circ d_{\mathcal{P}}(P^{\mathbf{w}}, P^{\hat{\mathbf{w}}}_\theta) \sim 0$*, there are four possibilities for causality:*

1. *There is no causation if* $P^{\hat{\mathbf{x}}}_0$ *and* $P^{\hat{\mathbf{y}}}_0$ *adhere to Definition 1.*
2. $\mathbf{x}$ *causes* $\mathbf{y}$ *if the probability measure* $P^{\hat{\mathbf{y}}}_0$ *adheres to Definition 2.*
3. $\mathbf{y}$ *causes* $\mathbf{x}$ *if the probability measure* $P^{\hat{\mathbf{x}}}_0$ *adheres to Definition 2.*
4. *There is bi-directional causality if* $P^{\hat{\mathbf{x}}}_0$ *and* $P^{\hat{\mathbf{y}}}_0$ *adhere to Definition 3.*

Finally, in the case of a miss-specified model, Proposition 2 implies that the divergence between the optimal probability measure as judged by the criterion and the *true* probability measure attains a minimum at a strictly positive value $d^*_{P^{\mathbf{w}}} > 0$. In this case, the quantity $d^*_{P^{\hat{\mathbf{w}}}}$ determines how "close" the empirical claim is to the *true* hypothesis about causality. While it is difficult to make claims about this quantity, it is evident that minimizing $d^*_{P^{\hat{\mathbf{w}}}}$ may involve widening $\mathcal{P}^{\hat{\mathbf{w}}}_\Theta$ in the direction of $P^{\mathbf{w}}$ by increasing the dimensionality of Θ and allow flexibility while investigating a wide range of data. Disregarding the value of $d^*_{P^{\hat{\mathbf{w}}}}$, the following holds.

Proposition 2. *If* $\boldsymbol{\theta}_0 \notin \Theta$*, then* $P^{\mathbf{w}} \notin \mathcal{P}^{\hat{\mathbf{w}}}_\Theta$*. However,* $\hat{\boldsymbol{\theta}}_\infty$ *is still the pseudo-*true *parameter that minimizes* $r \circ d_{\mathcal{P}}(P^{\mathbf{w}}, P^{\hat{\mathbf{w}}}_\theta)$ *over* Θ*. Therefore,* $P^{\hat{\mathbf{w}}}$ *is the probability measure minimally divergent from* $P^{\mathbf{w}}$ *within* $\mathcal{P}^{\hat{\mathbf{w}}}_\Theta$*. As such, it follows that, from all the potential probability measures in* $\mathcal{P}^{\hat{\mathbf{w}}}_\Theta$*, the measure closest to* $P^{\mathbf{w}}$ *is supportive of one out of* $1-4$ *in corollary 1 based on the properties of* $P^{\hat{\mathbf{x}}}_0$ *and* $P^{\hat{\mathbf{y}}}_0$ *as the best approximations.* $P^{\hat{\mathbf{w}}}$ *provides the best approximation of the* true *causal measure across all the hypotheses considered.*

This leads to the following collection of results.

Corollary 2. *Given a* true *probability measure* $P^{\mathbf{w}}$*, and a non-equivalent, but pseudo-*true *modeled probability measure,* $P^{\hat{\mathbf{w}}}$*, in the sense that* $d^*_{P^{\mathbf{w}}} = r \circ d_{\mathcal{P}}(P^{\mathbf{w}}, P^{\hat{\mathbf{w}}}_\theta)$ *has attained a non-zero minimum, there are four possible optimal hypotheses about causality, as judged by the criterion:*

1. *There is no causation if* $P^{\hat{\mathbf{x}}}_0$ *and* $P^{\hat{\mathbf{y}}}_0$ *adhere to Definition 1.*
2. $\mathbf{x}$ *causes* $\mathbf{y}$ *if the probability measure* $P^{\hat{\mathbf{y}}}_0$ *adheres to Definition 2.*
3. $\mathbf{y}$ *causes* $\mathbf{x}$ *if the probability measure* $P^{\hat{\mathbf{x}}}_0$ *adheres to Definition 2.*
4. *There is bi-directional causality if* $P^{\hat{\mathbf{x}}}_0$ *and* $P^{\hat{\mathbf{y}}}_0$ *adhere to Definition 3.*

Respectively, conditioning on interventions in $\mathbf{x}$, the results can be understood as:

1. Whenever an intervention in $\mathbf{x}$ occurs, our best hypothesis is that there is no chance that $\mathbf{y}$ reacts as a result of that.

2. Whenever an intervention in $\mathbf{x}$ occurs, our best hypothesis is that there is positive chance that $\mathbf{y}$ reacts as a result of that.
3. Whenever an intervention in $\mathbf{x}$ occurs, our best hypothesis is that there is positive chance that $\mathbf{y}$ reacts as a result of that, and these interactions continue to repeat with positive probability.

4. Limit Squared Hellinger Distance

Both Corollaries 1 and 2 assume that an appropriate transformation of the limit criterion exists that provides us with a metric or norm. This assumption allows us to make use of the classical theorems on existence and uniqueness of best approximations that have been naturally obtained for metric, normed, and inner product spaces [53]. While this retains the simplicity of the argument, it also shows that a direct interpretation of Corollaries 1 and 2 can be obtained within the framework of maximum likelihood. Let us first define the criterion function as the maximum likelihood estimator:

$$\arg\min_{\theta\in\Theta} Q_T(\mathbf{w}_T;\boldsymbol{\theta}) := \arg\max_{\theta\in\Theta} \sum_{t=1}^{T} \ln p_t(\mathbf{w}_t|\boldsymbol{\theta}). \tag{14}$$

Note that this is conforming to $Q_\infty(\boldsymbol{\theta}) := Q_T(f^{\mathbf{w}}(\mathbf{w}_T), f(\mathbf{w}_T;\arg\min_{\theta\in\Theta} Q_T(\mathbf{w}_T;\boldsymbol{\theta})))$ with $T \to \infty$ and $Q_\infty : \Theta \to \mathbb{R}$. It can be shown that, under this definition with $Q_\infty(\boldsymbol{\theta}) = Q_\infty^{\mathcal{P}}(P^{\mathbf{w}}; P_{\theta}^{\hat{\mathbf{w}}})\ \forall\ \boldsymbol{\theta} \in \Theta$, the criterion $Q_\infty(\boldsymbol{\theta}) = Q_\infty^{\mathcal{P}}$ is a measure of divergence $d_{\mathcal{P}}$ on the *true* probability measure and the modeled measure. Specifically, we can introduce a divergence $d_{\mathcal{P}} \equiv Q_\infty^{\mathcal{P}} : \mathcal{P}^{\mathbf{w}} \times \mathcal{P}^{\mathbf{w}} \to \mathbb{R}_{\geq 0}$ as follows. Let $p^{\mathbf{w}}(\mathbf{w}_t|\boldsymbol{\theta}_{\mathbf{w}})$ and $p^{\hat{\mathbf{w}}}(\mathbf{w}_t|\boldsymbol{\theta}_{\hat{\mathbf{w}}})$ be, respectively, the *true* density evaluated under the *true* parameter and a modeled density at $\hat{\boldsymbol{\theta}}$, evaluated under the estimated parameter, both at time t, with respect to the Lebesque measure (such that they are probability density functions); then the following is a divergence from the true probability measure to the modeled probability measure (Kullback–Leibler divergence, see [54]):

$$KL(P^{\mathbf{w}}(\mathbf{w}|\boldsymbol{\theta}_{\mathbf{w}})||P^{\hat{\mathbf{w}}}(\mathbf{w}|\boldsymbol{\theta}_{\hat{\mathbf{w}}})) = \begin{cases} \int_{-\infty}^{\infty} p^{\mathbf{w}}(\mathbf{w}|\boldsymbol{\theta}_{\mathbf{w}}) \ln \dfrac{p^{\mathbf{w}}(\mathbf{w}|\boldsymbol{\theta}_{\mathbf{w}})}{p^{\hat{\mathbf{w}}}(\mathbf{w}|\boldsymbol{\theta}_{\hat{\mathbf{w}}})} d\mathbf{w} & \forall\ p^{\mathbf{w}}(\mathbf{w}|\boldsymbol{\theta}_{\mathbf{w}}) \ll p^{\hat{\mathbf{w}}}(\mathbf{w}|\boldsymbol{\theta}_{\hat{\mathbf{w}}}) \\ \infty & \text{otherwise} \end{cases}. \tag{15}$$

Naturally, $KL(P^{\mathbf{w}}(\mathbf{w}|\boldsymbol{\theta}_{\mathbf{w}})||P^{\hat{\mathbf{w}}}(\mathbf{w}|\boldsymbol{\theta}_{\hat{\mathbf{w}}})) \geq 0$ with equality if and only if $p^{\mathbf{w}}(\mathbf{w}|\boldsymbol{\theta}_{\mathbf{w}}) = p^{\hat{\mathbf{w}}}(\mathbf{w}|\boldsymbol{\theta}_{\hat{\mathbf{w}}})$ almost everywhere, i.e., when the probability measures are the same (this is known as Gibb's inequality and can be verified by applying Jensen's inequality).

Kullback–Leibler divergence is not a distance metric, as was used in Corollaries 1 and 2 to establish equivalences by partitioning into classes of zero-distance points. In particular, it is asymmetric

$$KL(P^{\mathbf{w}}(\mathbf{w}|\boldsymbol{\theta}_{\mathbf{w}})||P^{\hat{\mathbf{w}}}(\mathbf{w}|\boldsymbol{\theta}_{\hat{\mathbf{w}}})) \neq KL(P^{\hat{\mathbf{w}}}(\mathbf{w}|\boldsymbol{\theta}_{\hat{\mathbf{w}}})||P^{\mathbf{w}}(\mathbf{w}|\boldsymbol{\theta}_{\mathbf{w}})), \tag{16}$$

and the triangle inequality is also not satisfied. However, it has the product–density property

$$KL(P^{\mathbf{w}}(\mathbf{w}|\boldsymbol{\theta}_{\mathbf{w}})||P^{\hat{\mathbf{w}}}(\mathbf{w}|\boldsymbol{\theta}_{\hat{\mathbf{w}}})) = \sum_{t}^{T} \ln KL(p_t^{\mathbf{w}}(\mathbf{w}_t|\boldsymbol{\theta}_{\mathbf{w}})||p_t^{\hat{\mathbf{w}}}(\mathbf{w}_t|\boldsymbol{\theta}_{\hat{\mathbf{w}}})), \tag{17}$$

for $p^{\mathbf{w}}(\mathbf{w}|\boldsymbol{\theta}_{\mathbf{w}}) = p_1^{\mathbf{w}}(\mathbf{w}_1|\boldsymbol{\theta}_{\mathbf{w}}) \cdot p_2^{\mathbf{w}}(\mathbf{w}_2|\boldsymbol{\theta}_{\mathbf{w}}) \dots p_T^{\mathbf{w}}(\mathbf{w}_T|\boldsymbol{\theta}_{\mathbf{w}})$, and $p^{\hat{\mathbf{w}}}(\mathbf{w}|\boldsymbol{\theta}_{\hat{\mathbf{w}}})$ defined similarly. Hence, the MLE is an unbiased estimator of minimized Kullback–Leibler divergence:

$$\begin{aligned} \arg\min_{\theta\in\Theta} Q_T(\mathbf{w}_T;\boldsymbol{\theta}) &:= \arg\max_{\theta\in\Theta} \sum_{t=1}^{T} \ln \frac{p^{\mathbf{w}}(\mathbf{w}_t|\boldsymbol{\theta}_{\mathbf{w}})}{p^{\hat{\mathbf{w}}}(\mathbf{w}_t|\boldsymbol{\theta}_{\hat{\mathbf{w}}})} \\ &= \arg\min_{\theta\in\Theta} KL(P^{\mathbf{w}}(\mathbf{w}|\boldsymbol{\theta}_{\mathbf{w}})||P^{\hat{\mathbf{w}}}(\mathbf{w}|\boldsymbol{\theta}_{\hat{\mathbf{w}}})). \end{aligned} \tag{18}$$

Note that under standard assumptions, a law of large numbers can be applied to obtain the convergence, hence, by maximizing log likelihood, we minimize Kullback–Leibler divergence. Now, we need to either find a continuously scaling function, r, to ensure that it also minimizes distance between the *true* measure and the modeled measure so that we may reach zero at $d^*_{p^{\hat{\mathbf{w}}}} = r \circ d_{\mathcal{P}}(P^{\mathbf{w}}, P_\theta^{\hat{\mathbf{w}}}) \sim 0$. Alternatively, we find the distance metric directly. We argued above that Kullback–Leibler divergence is not a proper distance (in particular, it is not symmetric and does not satisfy the triangle inequality). However, notably useful is specifying $d^*_{p^{\hat{\mathbf{w}}}}$ directly as the Hellinger distance between a modeled probability measure and the true probability measure [55]:

$$H\Big(P^{\mathbf{w}}(\mathbf{w}|\boldsymbol{\theta}_{\mathbf{w}}), P^{\hat{\mathbf{w}}}(\mathbf{w}|\boldsymbol{\theta}_{\hat{\mathbf{w}}})\Big) = \sqrt{\frac{1}{2}\int\Big(\sqrt{p^{\mathbf{w}}(\mathbf{w}|\boldsymbol{\theta}_{\mathbf{w}})} - \sqrt{p^{\hat{\mathbf{w}}}(\mathbf{w}|\boldsymbol{\theta}_{\hat{\mathbf{w}}})}\Big)^2 d\mathbf{w}}. \tag{19}$$

Specifically, the squared Hellinger distance provides a lower bound for the Kullback–Leibler divergence. Therefore, maximizing log likelihood implies minimizing Kullback–Leibler divergence, which implies minimizing the Hellinger distance. This is easily seen by the following:

Proposition 3. *The squared Hellinger distance provides a lower bound to Kullback–Leibler divergence:*

$$\Big(H(P^{\mathbf{w}}(\mathbf{w}|\boldsymbol{\theta}_{\mathbf{w}})||P^{\hat{\mathbf{w}}}(\mathbf{w}|\boldsymbol{\theta}_{\hat{\mathbf{w}}}))\Big)^2 \leq KL(P^{\mathbf{w}}(\mathbf{w}|\boldsymbol{\theta}_{\mathbf{w}})||P^{\hat{\mathbf{w}}}(\mathbf{w}|\boldsymbol{\theta}_{\hat{\mathbf{w}}})).$$

Remark 4 below highlights that these notions do not just apply to the standard real-valued time series settings considered by Granger, but can apply to the explicit probability modeling of binary outcomes as well. Remark 4 further clarifies a result that has so far only been presented implicitly—that the probabilistic truth identified at the discussed zero-distance point may allow for a base level of entropy to exist even when all functional relationships in the process have been accounted for in a model.

Remark 4. *While the paper has implicitly alluded to modeling continuous real-valued processes though the notational conventions, the connections between true probability and modeled probability are also easily made by focusing on an explicit binary outcome problem. Define cross-entropy for two discrete probability distributions p and q with the same support $\mathcal{X}$:*

$$H(p,q) = \mathbb{E}_p[-\ln q] = H(p) + \mathcal{D}_{KL}(p||q) = -\sum_{x\in\mathcal{X}} p(x)\ln q(x),$$

in which $\mathcal{D}_{KL}$ is Kullback–Leibler divergence, or the relative entropy of q with respect to p, and $H(p)$ is the entropy of p. Now if $p \in \{y, 1-y\}$ and $q \in \{\hat{y}, 1-\hat{y}\}$, we can rewrite cross-entropy:

$$H(p,q) = -\sum_{x\in\mathcal{X}} p_x \ln q_x = -y\ln\hat{y} - (1-y)\ln(1-\hat{y}),$$

or, for predictions generated under a set of parameters $\boldsymbol{\theta}$ and a predictor x, as

$$H(y,x;\boldsymbol{\theta}) = -\sum_{t=1}^{T} y_t \ln p_{\boldsymbol{\theta}}(y|x_{t-1}) - (1-y_t)\ln(1-p_{\boldsymbol{\theta}}(y|x_{t-1})).$$

Remember that the maximum likelihood estimator maximizes the likelihood of the data under some probabilistic model. The correct likelihood in the case of binary classification is Bernoulli:

$$p(y|\pi) = \Pi_{t=1}^T \pi_t^{y_t}(1-\pi_t)^{1-y_t},$$

which results in the likelihood function

$$p(y|x;\boldsymbol{\theta}) = \Pi_{t=1}^T p_{\boldsymbol{\theta}}(y|x_{t-1})^{y_t}(1-p_{\boldsymbol{\theta}}(y|x_{t-1}))^{1-y_t}.$$

Taking logs then gives the following log likelihood function

$$L(\boldsymbol{\theta}; x, y) = \sum_{t=1}^{T} y_t \ln p_{\boldsymbol{\theta}}(y|x_{t-1}) + (1 - y_t) \ln(1 - p_{\boldsymbol{\theta}}(y|x_{t-1})).$$

This shows that negative log likelihood is proportional to Kullback–Leibler divergence and differs by the basic entropy in the data, which is constant. Maximizing the likelihood of a binary model can, thus, be understood as minimizing statistical distance toward a true probability measure; the minimum value is determined by the entropy in the observed data.

5. Application

5.1. Practical Considerations

We continue this section first with some notes on practical considerations. Let $L_T(\boldsymbol{\theta})$ denote the sample log likelihood at $\boldsymbol{\theta} \in \Theta$. Naturally, if $\Theta_s \subset \Theta$, it follows that $\mathcal{P}_{\Theta}^{\hat{\mathbf{w}}} \supset \mathcal{P}_{\Theta_s}^{\hat{\mathbf{w}}}$. In the limit, this means that maximizing likelihood minimizes Hellinger distance over both $\mathcal{P}_{\Theta}^{\hat{\mathbf{w}}}$ and $\mathcal{P}_{\Theta_s}^{\hat{\mathbf{w}}}$. Following Corollary 1, if $\boldsymbol{\theta} \in \Theta_s$, this results in selecting $P^{\hat{\mathbf{w}}}$ at a point in $\mathcal{P}_{\Theta_s}^{\hat{\mathbf{w}}}$ that attains equivalence to $P^{\mathbf{w}}$. In practice, when finite data is used, two different points, one in $\mathcal{P}_{\Theta}^{\hat{\mathbf{w}}} \setminus \mathcal{P}_{\Theta_s}^{\hat{\mathbf{w}}}$ and one in $\mathcal{P}_{\Theta_s}^{\hat{\mathbf{w}}}$, may be obtained because the finite sample log likelihoods $L_T(\hat{\boldsymbol{\theta}}_{sT})$ and $L_T(\hat{\boldsymbol{\theta}}_T)$ that are available are both asymptotically biased estimators of the expected log likelihood $\mathbb{E}L_T(\boldsymbol{\theta}_0)$. This is easily shown by using a quadratic expansion [20,40]

$$\lim_{T\to\infty} \mathbb{E}\Big(L_T(\hat{\boldsymbol{\theta}}_T) - \mathbb{E}L_T(\boldsymbol{\theta}_0)\Big) = \lim_{T\to\infty} \mathbb{E}\sqrt{T}(\hat{\boldsymbol{\theta}}_T - \boldsymbol{\theta}_0)' \frac{1}{T} L_T''(\boldsymbol{\theta}_T) \sqrt{T}(\hat{\boldsymbol{\theta}}_T - \boldsymbol{\theta}_0) \neq 0. \tag{20}$$

Under considerably restrictive conditions, the original work by [56,57] showed that the right hand-side approaches the dimension of $\hat{\boldsymbol{\theta}}_T$ and, hence, an asymptotically unbiased estimator of $\mathbb{E}\ell_t(\boldsymbol{\theta}_0)$ is given by $\frac{1}{T}\sum_{t=2}^{T} \ell_t(\hat{\boldsymbol{\theta}}_T) - k$. Akaike also proposed the well-known AIC given by AIC$= 2T\big(k - \frac{1}{T}\sum_{t=2}^{T} \ell_t(\hat{\boldsymbol{\theta}}_T)\big)$. Several authors have shown that the AIC can be used to consistently rank models according to Kullback–Leibler divergence in considerably more general settings, including the mis-specified case and have suggested further finite sample improvements [58–60]. The AIC is also valid to decide between economic theories for which no test statistics can be found [27]. This highlights that, while maximizing log likelihood over Θ is not the same objective as minimizing Kullback–Leibler divergence in finite samples, working with a complexity-penalized log likelihood (i.e., minimizing the AIC) does select the model that attains the lowest KL-bound of all considered models generated under Θ. Hence, in practice, a researcher can minimize the AIC as the practical objective to minimize Hellinger distance, and use specification tests to diagnose which of Corollaries 1 and 2 is more relevant. Since in-sample fits typically overfit data, a form of regularization would usually allow better out-of-sample results; see, for instance the (supplementary) discussion of [61] or the work of [62,63].

The challenge remains, however, that the AIC cannot be computed for all models as the degrees of freedom used in the correction is generally not a well-defined quantity for non-parametric models. As opposed to relying on in-sample corrections, cross-validation may instead be used to obtain unbiased estimates of $\mathbb{E}\ell_t(\boldsymbol{\theta}_0)$ in a setting that is more attuned to machine learning approaches, see for example [64]. Tests have been developed by [20,40,65] by following the general strategy of [66] adapted to the log likelihood case. The work has shown that choosing the model with the highest out-of-sample log likelihood equals choosing the model configuration that has achieves the highest probability of being the model that has lower Kullback–Leibler divergence. As the training T and validation data $\tilde{T}$ grows $T, \tilde{T} \to \infty$, this strategy chooses the model that has achieved the lowest Kullback–Leibler divergence, with probability converging to one.

5.2. Application to Treasury Yield Spreads and Bitcoin Spreads

The developed theory is now put into practice using daily data from short-term and long-term Treasury yield spreads and Bitcoin spreads. This is an interesting problem because each of these three assets has an important relation to inflation expectations. Rising inflation is also an acute problem, see [67,68].

The empirical strategy is as follows. First, standard linear Granger causality tests are performed as a benchmark. Next, non-parametric models will be fit in an effort to obtain an accurate-as-possible description of the true probability measure. The focus will be on maximizing out-of-sample log likelihood to minimize KL-divergence. Finally, Definitions 1 to 3 show that our conclusions about causality should be supported by a study of the probability measure that describes the causal effects. In particular, it must be decided whether this measure is a null-measure or produces real-valued data. This will be done by taking the best approximation of the true probability measure using the potential causal variable and the best approximation of the true probability measure without the potential causal variable, and (1) concluding whether the first achieves a lower KL-bound, and (2) testing whether the first is not stochastically equivalent to the latter. Section 5.2.1 first describes the data.

5.2.1. Data

Dynamic interactions between spreads in short-term and long-term bond yields can naturally be expected to occur in the data. In the absence of any credit risk, the net value of future bond payments is a function of the return required based on the inflation expectation used to discount the cash stream. Each of the Treasury securities typically caries a different yield, depending on maturity, the ratio between short and long-term treasury yields signals how investors feel about the economy in the short versus long term. If the yields vary substantially throughout the day, the market is uncertain about its expectations. Investigating the flow of causality between long-term and short-term yields and the interactions with other variables has been the objective of a large number of studies. To name a few, refs. [69,70] investigate causality between bonds and credit default swaps, while [71–75] investigate how financial distress propagates throughout connected bond markets.

Proponents of Bitcoin have argued that it is an important hedge due to its predetermined finite supply. While Bitcoin, as an asset class, has only recently attracted the public attention of large institutional investors, many researchers have already analyzed the time-series behavior of Bitcoin prices. An overview of recent developments and more discussion on forecasting Bitcoin prices is by [76]. They investigate a large set of covariates that cover nearly all important classes of financial assets, except bonds. They conclude that the intra-day distribution of daily returns follows a nonlinear memory process better captured by machine learning methods than conventional econometric models, which is further supported by a large body of literature that has documented related modeling exorcises [77–83].

If investors treat Bitcoin as an inflation hedge, then the spreads may causally interact with the U.S. yield spreads. Moreover, spreads in U.S. Treasury yields will arise predominantly from uncertainty in the expectations about the U.S. economy. Bitcoin, on the other hand, as a global asset that can be exchanged peer-to-peer by individuals without the need of a financial intermediary, might react to economic uncertainty in non-U.S. economies that may have the potential to spill over. Bitcoin also trades 24 h a day, every day of the year, and so may react to turmoil that happens outside U.S. trading hours and pass it on when the markets open. At the same time, Bitcoin is a relatively small market and the large institutional investors that dominate the bond market may not be active in the Bitcoin market. Causality from Bitcoin to the bond market could, then, be unlikely. Similarly, since Bitcoin trades non-stop, information assimilates rapidly, and so it may be likely that there is no causal influence of bond spreads at the daily time frame. The different hypotheses about the causal flows will be tested first using standard Granger causality tests.

5.2.2. Estimation Results

The following general system will be considered.

$$\begin{aligned} s(\mathbf{T}_t) &= f^1(L(\mathbf{T}_t, \mathbf{Q}_t, \mathbf{B}_t, \mathbf{S}_t)) \\ s(\mathbf{Q}_t) &= f^2(L(\mathbf{T}_t, \mathbf{Q}_t, \mathbf{B}_t, \mathbf{S}_t)) \\ s(\mathbf{B}_t) &= f^3(L(\mathbf{T}_t, \mathbf{Q}_t, \mathbf{B}_t, \mathbf{S}_t)) \end{aligned} \tag{21}$$

In which L is a lag operator, s is a function that calculates the spread between daily highs (h_t) and lows (l_t) as the log difference $o(\log(1 + h_t) - \log(1 + l_t))$ where 1 is added to account for negative rates. The function o is a simple outlier replacement function that replaces the largest observed spread (the Corona-crash) with the second largest value. The matrices $\mathbf{T}_t$, $\mathbf{Q}_t$, $\mathbf{B}_t$ are, respectively, the daily data of the ten-year bond, Quarterly bond, and Bitcoin price at time t, and $\mathbf{S}_t$ is SP500 price data used as a control. The data used in the analysis runs from 1 January 2017 to 20 December 2021 and were obtained from Yahoo finance using ticker symbols ^TNX, ^IRX and BTC-USD and ^GSPC.

First, a linear VAR model is considered with lags selected using the AIC. All of the maximums of 10 considered lags were selected, and stability was confirmed by verifying that the largest eigenvalue of the companion matrix remained below 1 (The largest eigenvalue was approximately 0.95, indicating that the process was stable but strongly dependent. Results were also generated using differenced data, which resulted in stronger causal linkages. Results are implemented in the code available with the paper but not shown here for compactness. see Supplementary Materials). Conditional Granger tests for causality are calculated by applying an F-test to the squared residuals of the model with and without the lags of a variable of interest in the presence of the autoregressive lags and the other control variables. The table below reports the p-values.

There are two important results in Table 1. First, the AIC, as an in-sample estimator of KL-divergence, selects a very large number of lags. The BIC is not an estimator of KL-divergence, see [84], but is a closely related Bayesian alternative to the AIC that is widely used. It places a larger penalty on the number of parameters and, as such, behaves somewhat similar to the corrected AIC in finite samples. The table shows that with this alternative criterion, a vastly different model is chosen. As Equation (20) showed, and the discussion after mentioned, the in-sample estimator of log likelihood is a biased estimator of expected log likelihood and, in practice, it is difficult to determine the appropriate penalty. In Table 1, two vastly different results are obtained. In both cases, however, the p-values of all causality tests are small. Both models suggest that there are strong causal linkages between spreads in all three markets. The statistical significance is somewhat dubious: the VAR(AIC) suggests that the causal flow of financial distress spills over in all directions. Moreover, Table 1 shows that, by adding more lags the significance of the causality tests increases, while it is likely that with 10 lags the model is trying to approximate a nonlinear process and the extremely high number of parameters involved in this approximation are likely over-fitting the data.

Table 1. p-values for Granger causality tests using VAR methods. Columns indicate the dependent variables, rows correspond to exogenous lags tested for causality. Each linkage is tested in the presence of lagged SP500 spreads as a control. Note that the BIC is not an estimator of KL-divergence, but it is widely used as a Bayesian alternative that places a higher penalty on dimensionality. Blank entries are intentionally left so, as they refer to endogenous linkages.

	AIC (lags = 10)			BIC (lags = 3)		
	$s(\mathbf{T}_t)$	$s(\mathbf{Q}_t)$	$s(\mathbf{B}_t)$	$s(\mathbf{T}_t)$	$s(\mathbf{Q}_t)$	$s(\mathbf{B}_t)$
$L(s(\mathbf{T}_t))$		0	0.0225		0	0.2207
$L(s(\mathbf{Q}_t))$	0		0.0021	0.0183		0.0450
$L(s(\mathbf{B}_t))$	0.0142	0.0083		0.1093	0.0635	

The section will now use an RF model to better approximate (f^1, f^2, f^3). The implementation used is that of [85], all possible tuning parameters are considered. The consistency of the RF in a time-series context under the assumption of data generated by a nonlinear autoregressive process is developed by [86]. As the previous sections detailed, the out-of-sample estimate of log likelihood is proportional to KL-divergence but RF models are typically not estimated using an in-sample log likelihood approach. A log likelihood function can nevertheless still be specified for out-of-sample predictions. To retain simplicity of the example, the commonly used Gaussian formulation is used:

$$\ell(v_t, \mu_t, \sigma_t) = \sum_t^T \frac{1}{2}(2\pi\sigma_t^2) - \frac{(v_t - \mu_t)^2}{2\sigma_t^2} \tag{22}$$

In this function, v_t are holdout validation samples at time t and μ_t is the mean parameter, which will be substituted by the conditional means predicted on the holdout data by the model. Note that σ_t, the variance parameter, is allowed to be time-varying. This is important because spread data is not homoskedastic, and the variance varies over the time dimension [87,88]. The log likelihood function thus allows for heteroskedasticity, the standard literature is followed and σ_t estimated using an ARMA-GARCH model. (The algorithm is as follows. Consider the time-varying density $F_t = (\mu_t, \sigma_t, \vartheta)$, where μ_t is a conditional mean process. For simplicity, it is defined as an ARMA $(1,1)$ process

$$\mu_t = c + \phi\mu_{t-1} + \theta\varepsilon_{t-1} + \varepsilon_t, \tag{23}$$

and the conditional variance, again for simplicity, is specified as a GARCH process of order $(1,1)$:

$$\sigma_t^2 = \omega + \alpha\varepsilon_{t-1}^2 + \beta\sigma_{t-1}^2 \tag{24}$$

with σ_t^2 as the conditional variance, ω an intercept, and L the back-shift operator. The vector ϑ specifies any remaining parameters of the distribution, in this case, the log likelihood is estimated using the Gaussian distribution in line with the validation criterion).

The RF models use three lags of the spread data so that the BIC-selected VAR model is nested. Several other features are added that may help describe the long-term dependencies captured by the AIC-selected model more accurately. In particular, a relative strength index (RSI) of all close values, including the SP500 close, is calculated. This is a standard indicator on $[0, 100]$, described in many resources that compare average upward movement to average downward movements over a look-back period. The standard period of 14 days is used along with a look-back of 14 weeks. The latter is also calculated using the spread data. This way, the model may learn different dependencies in periods of sustained decline, increase, or stability, in spreads and prices. The bootstrap sampling algorithm of the RF allows for case weights, effectively increasing the probability that highly weighted cases are over-represented in the random base learners, see [85]. This is exploited; σ_t^2 is standardized in the training data to be used as case-weights so that observations during more volatile periods feature more frequently in the sampling scheme.

The out-of-sample log likelihood is cross-validated using Equation (23), using 20 folds so that each validation sample has approximately 60 observations. The splits are generated using a stratified sampling approach that conditions on the RSI of the SP500. In other words, validation samples are chosen so that each validation sample equally represents days of under-bought, over-bought, and neutral stock market territories. The split is generated once and kept identical for each model so that the results can be directly compared. In total, an out-of-sample log likelihood value is generated for each observation so the sum of the log likelihood is taken to obtain an estimate of total out-of-sample log likelihood.

The results in Table 2 show the following. First, the nonlinear autoregressive models (indicated by the rows that apply a lag operator to the dependent variable listed in each column) all out-compete the VAR model that used all variables. According to the theory of the paper, the causal results obtained using the linear Granger causality tests in Table 1 should thus be discarded in favor of the theory that each variable follows a nonlinear autoregressive process that only makes possible reference to the SP500 but not the other variables of interest. For instance, the VAR of the ten-year Treasury yield spreads reach an out-of-sample log likelihood of 3916.77, while the nonlinear RF model reached a log likelihood of 3932.78 without using the lagged quarterly yield spreads or Bitcoin spreads. The differences in log likelihood are even larger for the models for quarterly Treasuries spreads and Bitcoin spreads.

Table 2 contains only evidence for two possible causal linkages. First, the model for the spreads on the ten-year that reached the lowest KL-bound used the lags of the quarterly yield data. This suggests that causality, in financial distress, may run from the short-term bonds to the long-term bonds. This is sensible; acute economic fears may impact short-term expectations more heavily, and the reaction in the short-term yields may trigger further fears about longer-term economic expectations. The second causal link could run from the Bitcoin market to the quarterly bonds. This is not far-fetched: Bitcoin trades non-stop and so any event globally can impact the Bitcoin market immediately, whereupon the increased fear in the Bitcoin market could then trigger further reactions in the short-term bond market, which would be more susceptible to short-term economic fears. However, the point increase in log likelihood that backs this hypothesis is small compared to the model that only used endogenous lags and control data.

Table 2. Cross-validated log likelihood for different models. Columns indicate the dependent variables, rows correspond to exogenous lagged data that are used by the models in addition to the control data. For each dependent variable, the model that achieved the lowest KL-divergence is marked by *.

	$s(\mathbf{T}_t)$	$s(\mathbf{Q}_t)$	$s(\mathbf{B}_t)$
VAR	3916.77	4084.68	2204.91
RF			
All	3989.14	4239.42	2251.06
$L(s(\mathbf{T}_t))$	3932.78	4230.44	2251.68
$L(s(\mathbf{Q}_t))$	3991.24 *	4240.54	2251.46
$L(s(\mathbf{B}_t))$	3932.90	4242.67 *	2251.84 *

Recall Remark 1: to test whether the evidence for causality is strong enough; it is important to test whether the probability measures that achieved the lowest KL-bound are stochastically different from those that exclude the causal linkages. A Kolmogorov–Smirnov test, under the null of distributional equivalence against a two-sided alternative, is computed. For the ten-year yield spread model, the p-value is 0, so the null is overwhelmingly rejected. The analysis, thus, concludes that the best possible hypothesis is that disruptions in the short-term bond market cause further disruption in the longer-term bond market. The test for distributional equivalence between the model with and without Bitcoin data has a p-value of 0.8591. In other words, the null of equivalence cannot be rejected and, while the model that used Bitcoin data reached the lowest KL-bound, the analysis does not find significant evidence for a causal flow from the Bitcoin market to the short-term Treasuries as the modeled probability measure is not significantly distinguishable from the competing non-causal measure. This suggests that the probability measure that describes the causal effects in Definition 2 is not distinguishable from that of Definition 1, and so Corollary 1 or 2 remain inconclusive. The final conclusion that causal flows are thus parsimonious is far more likely than the result obtained with the VAR, which suggested that causality flows significantly in all directions.

6. Concluding Remarks

This paper has developed a probabilistic theory of causation using measure-theoretical concepts. It discussed how probabilistic truths can be approximated by minimizing distance to the true probability measure over a space of measures in which each element is associated with a probabilistic theory about causation. This notion is flexible and has allowed for a wide range of models to be used for causal inference, including linear and nonlinear dynamical models. The theory has been applied using daily data on yield spreads to test how uncertainty around short-term and long-term expectations about future inflation interact with uncertainty in the daily Bitcoin price. The results were contrasted with those obtained using standard linear Granger causality tests. While linear Granger causality relies on models that assume a constant causal influence from one variable onto another, specified by static parameters, the analysis has shown that time-varying properties of the auto-regressive process provides a better description of the data. While the linear Granger causality tests finds significant causal influence in all directions, the suggested measure-theoretic approach to causality testing, using, in this example, a random forest model, found only one significant causal link that ran from financial distress in the short-term bond market to uncertainty in the long-term bond market.

As with Granger's approach, a convincing theory of how causes produce effect is not necessarily a prerequisite to making correct causal inferences. Clear hypotheses about causal relations may, however, help guide the inference by helping design better models. However, whereas Granger's definition "is based entirely on the predictability of some series" [5], the ideas of the current paper start with the notion that true probabilistic laws exist and can, and should, correctly be approximated to infer causal structures from data. A conclusion from this is that researchers interested in causal analysis should aim to develop strong out-of-sample predictions, as Granger's techniques applied to inaccurate models may provide an overly enthusiastic description of causal linkages.

The general ideas of the paper differ from the linear Granger tests in terms of result, but share a similarity in thought process. Granger's statement about causality followed from the premises that causes occur before effects and that causes contain unique information about their effect, and so that any causal variable must help forecast outcomes after other variables have been used first. For this reason, many refer to Granger causality as predictability. This paper defined causality directly in terms of the probability measures that define a stochastic process. This, in turn, places the emphasis on finding the best approximation of that probability measure. The theory developed here shows that minimizing KL-divergence implies minimizing distance between a model and the true probability measure and shows that maximizing out-of-sample log likelihood implies minimizing KL-divergence. This does not require parametric models or the degrees of freedom to be known. Instead, the KL-ranking of competing models can be directly read from the out-of-sample log likelihood. The stochastic equivalence, or difference, between probability measures that are induced by causal flows, or from autoregressive properties only, can subsequently be tested. The theory provides practitioners guidance for developing causal models using new machine learning methods that have, so far, remained relatively underutilized in this context.

Supplementary Materials: The following supporting information can be downloaded at: https://www.mdpi.com/article/10.3390/e24010092/s1.

Author Contributions: The work, and any possible error contained therein, is solely my own. Useful suggestions from two anonymous referees have been integrated into the paper. All authors have read and agreed to the published version of the manuscript.

Funding: The research did not receive any external funding.

Institutional Review Board Statement: Not applicable.

Informed Consent Statement: Not applicable.

Data Availability Statement: Code to reproduce the analysis is available along with the paper or can alternatively be requested from the author. The data is taken from Yahoo, the code calls the data from their API.

Acknowledgments: An earlier version containing sections of this work was shared for discussion [89], parts of which have been improved and replicated here for the special issue on "Causal Inference for Heterogeneous Data and Information Theory". I thank the two anonymous referees for their instructive comments and for help correcting and improving parts of the work. Any remaining errors are my own.

Conflicts of Interest: The author declares no conflict of interest.

Abbreviations

The following abbreviations are used in this manuscript:

DGP	data-generating process
MLE	maximum likelihood estimator
IRF	impulse response function
VAR	vector auto-regression
RF	random forest
RSI	relative strength index

Appendix A. Proofs

Appendix A.1. Proof for Proposition 1

Proof. By construction of the criterion, as stated in Assumption 1, $\arg\min_{\theta\in\Theta} Q_\infty(\theta)$ is its minimizer, and, by assuming $\theta_0 \in \Theta$, it is also equal to θ_0. Hence, item 2 is equivalent to item 1 by definition under correct specification.

The equivalence of the deterministic limit criterion (item 2) as a function describing the divergence of the underlying probability measures of $\mathbf{w}$ and $\hat{\mathbf{w}}$ (item 4) is assumed, however, given a limit criterion function $Q_\infty : \Theta \to \mathbb{R}$ and a flexible definition of divergence (e.g., a pre-metric, such as the KL-divergence), it is often possible to find a divergence $d_\mathcal{P} : \mathcal{P}_\Theta \times \mathcal{P}_\Theta \to \mathbb{R}_{\geq 0}$ on the space of probability measures satisfying $\arg\min_{\theta\in\Theta} d_\mathcal{P}(\mathcal{P}^{\mathbf{w}}, \mathcal{P}_\theta^{\hat{\mathbf{w}}}) = \arg\min_{\theta\in\Theta} Q_\infty(\theta)$. The KL-divergence example is provided in this paper in the context of the maximum likelihood criterion.

By the assumption that r exists, the deterministic limit criterion that minimizes divergence, is also the minimizer of a distance metric $d_\mathcal{P}^*(P^{\mathbf{w}}, P_\theta^{\hat{\mathbf{w}}})$, hence item 4 is also equivalent to item 2.

Finally, since $f_\mathcal{W} : \Theta \to F_\Theta(\mathcal{W})$ is injective, $(P^{\mathbf{w}}, P_\theta^{\hat{\mathbf{w}}}) \equiv d_F^*(f^{\mathbf{w}}, f(\cdot,\theta))\ \forall\, \theta \in \Theta$ and d_F^* is a metric on $F_\Theta(\mathcal{W})$, θ_0 is also the minimizer of $d_F^*(f^{\mathbf{w}}, f(\cdot,\theta))\ \forall\, \theta \in \Theta$ so that item 3 is equivalent to item 2.

□

Appendix A.2. Proof for Proposition 2

Proof. The result follows immediately by the arguments used in proposition 1 dropping only the first equivalence. □

Appendix A.3. Proof for Proposition 3

Proof. First, Hellinger distance is

$$H(P^{\mathbf{w}}(\mathbf{w}|\theta_{\mathbf{w}}), P^{\hat{\mathbf{w}}}(\mathbf{w}|\theta_{\hat{\mathbf{w}}})) = \sqrt{\frac{1}{2}\int\left(\sqrt{p^{\mathbf{w}}(\mathbf{w}|\theta_{\mathbf{w}})} - \sqrt{p^{\hat{\mathbf{w}}}(\mathbf{w}|\theta_{\hat{\mathbf{w}}})}\right)^2 d\mathbf{w}},$$

hence,

$$(H(P^{\mathbf{w}}(\mathbf{w}|\theta_{\mathbf{w}}), P^{\hat{\mathbf{w}}}(\mathbf{w}|\theta_{\hat{\mathbf{w}}})))^2 = \frac{1}{2}\int\left(\sqrt{p^{\mathbf{w}}(\mathbf{w}|\theta_{\mathbf{w}})} - \sqrt{p^{\hat{\mathbf{w}}}(\mathbf{w}|\theta_{\hat{\mathbf{w}}})}\right)^2 d\mathbf{w}.$$

Now, the R.H.S. can be written as

$$\frac{1}{2}\int p^{\mathbf{w}}(\mathbf{w}|\theta_{\mathbf{w}})d\mathbf{w} + \frac{1}{2}\int p^{\hat{\mathbf{w}}}(\mathbf{w}|\theta_{\hat{\mathbf{w}}})d\mathbf{w} - \int \sqrt{p^{\mathbf{w}}(\mathbf{w}|\theta_{\mathbf{w}})p^{\hat{\mathbf{w}}}(\mathbf{w}|\theta_{\hat{\mathbf{w}}})}d\mathbf{w}.$$

The integral of a probability density over its domain equals 1, hence the sum of the first two terms is 1, hence this can be rewritten as

$$1 - \int \sqrt{p^{\mathbf{w}}(\mathbf{w}|\theta_{\mathbf{w}})p^{\hat{\mathbf{w}}}(\mathbf{w}|\theta_{\hat{\mathbf{w}}})}d\mathbf{w}.$$

This has an upper bound, provided by the inequality

$$1-\int\sqrt{p^{\mathbf{w}}(\mathbf{w}|\boldsymbol{\theta}_{\mathbf{w}})p^{\hat{\mathbf{w}}}(\mathbf{w}|\boldsymbol{\theta}_{\hat{\mathbf{w}}})}d\mathbf{w}\leq-\ln\int\sqrt{p^{\mathbf{w}}(\mathbf{w}|\boldsymbol{\theta}_{\mathbf{w}})p^{\hat{\mathbf{w}}}(\mathbf{w}|\boldsymbol{\theta}_{\hat{\mathbf{w}}})}d\mathbf{w}.$$

Write R.H.S. as $-\ln\int\left[\sqrt{\frac{p^{\hat{\mathbf{w}}}(\mathbf{w}|\boldsymbol{\theta}_{\hat{\mathbf{w}}})}{p^{\mathbf{w}}(\mathbf{w}|\boldsymbol{\theta}_{\mathbf{w}})}}p^{\mathbf{w}}(\mathbf{w}|\boldsymbol{\theta}_{\mathbf{w}})\right]d\mathbf{w}$ and to obtain the upper bound

$$-\ln\int\left[\sqrt{\frac{p^{\hat{\mathbf{w}}}(\mathbf{w}|\boldsymbol{\theta}_{\hat{\mathbf{w}}})}{p^{\mathbf{w}}(\mathbf{w}|\boldsymbol{\theta}_{\mathbf{w}})}}p^{\mathbf{w}}(\mathbf{w}|\boldsymbol{\theta}_{\mathbf{w}})\right]d\mathbf{w}\leq-\int\left[\ln\sqrt{\frac{p^{\hat{\mathbf{w}}}(\mathbf{w}|\boldsymbol{\theta}_{\hat{\mathbf{w}}})}{p^{\mathbf{w}}(\mathbf{w}|\boldsymbol{\theta}_{\mathbf{w}})}}p^{\mathbf{w}}(\mathbf{w}|\boldsymbol{\theta}_{\mathbf{w}})\right]d\mathbf{w},$$

by applying Jensen's inequality, which can be applied to the integral case, since any random variable whose distribution admits a probability density function has the expected value represented by the integral over the full range of the density.

Finally, define the R.H.S. as

$$E\int\left[\ln\frac{p^{\mathbf{w}}(\mathbf{w}|\boldsymbol{\theta}_{\mathbf{w}})}{p^{\hat{\mathbf{w}}}(\mathbf{w}|\boldsymbol{\theta}_{\hat{\mathbf{w}}})}p^{\mathbf{w}}(\mathbf{w}|\boldsymbol{\theta}_{\mathbf{w}})\right]d\mathbf{w}=-\int\left[\ln\sqrt{\frac{p^{\hat{\mathbf{w}}}(\mathbf{w}|\boldsymbol{\theta}_{\hat{\mathbf{w}}})}{p^{\mathbf{w}}(\mathbf{w}|\boldsymbol{\theta}_{\mathbf{w}})}}p^{\mathbf{w}}(\mathbf{w}|\boldsymbol{\theta}_{\mathbf{w}})\right]d\mathbf{w},$$

and conclude that the last expression is equivalent to the Kullback–Leibler divergence by an elementary row operation.

$$E\int\left[\ln\frac{p^{\mathbf{w}}(\mathbf{w}|\boldsymbol{\theta}_{\mathbf{w}})}{p^{\hat{\mathbf{w}}}(\mathbf{w}|\boldsymbol{\theta}_{\hat{\mathbf{w}}})}p^{\mathbf{w}}(\mathbf{w}|\boldsymbol{\theta}_{\mathbf{w}})\right]d\mathbf{w}\equiv KL(P^{\mathbf{w}}(\mathbf{w}|\boldsymbol{\theta}_{\mathbf{w}})||P^{\hat{\mathbf{w}}}(\mathbf{w}|\boldsymbol{\theta}_{\hat{\mathbf{w}}})).$$

□

References

1. Sundholm, G. A century of judgement and inference,1837–1936: Some strands in the development of logic. In *The Development of Modern Logic*; Oxford University Press: New York, NY, USA, 2009. [CrossRef]
2. Sundholm, G. "Inference versus consequence" revisited: Inference, consequence, conditional, implication. *Synthese* **2012**, *187*, 943–956. [CrossRef]
3. Pearl, J. *Causality: Models, Reasoning, and Inference*; Cambridge University Press: Cambridge, UK, 2000; p. 384.
4. Neuberg, L.G. Causality: Models, Reasoning, and Inference, by Judea Pearl, Cambridge University Press, 2000. *Econom. Theory* **2003**, *19*, 675–685. [CrossRef]
5. Granger, C.W.J. Investigating Causal Relations by Econometric Models and Cross-spectral Methods. *Econometrica* **1969**, *37*, 424. [CrossRef]
6. Granger, C.W. Testing for causality: A personal viewpoint. *J. Econ. Dyn. Control* **1980**, *2*, 329–352. [CrossRef]
7. White, H.; Chalak, K. Settable Systems: An Extension of Pearl's Causal Model with Optimization, Equilibrium, and Learning. *J. Mach. Learn. Res.* **2009**, *10*, 1759–1799.
8. White, H.; Lu, X. Granger Causality and Dynamic Structural Systems. *J. Financ. Econom.* **2010**, *8*, 193–243. [CrossRef]
9. White, H.; Chalak, K.; Lu, X. Causality in Time Series Linking Granger Causality and the Pearl Causal Model with Settable Systems. *JMRL Workshop Conf. Proc.* **2011**, *12*, 1–29.
10. White, H.; Xu, H.; Chalak, K. Causal discourse in a game of incomplete information. *J. Econom.* **2014**, *182*, 45–58. [CrossRef]
11. White, H.; Pettenuzzo, D. Granger causality, exogeneity, cointegration, and economic policy analysis. *J. Econom.* **2014**, *178*, 316–330. [CrossRef]
12. Williamson, J. Probabilistic theories of causality. In *The Oxford Handbook of Causation*; Chapter Probabilistic Theories; Beebee, H., Menzies, P., Hitchcock, C., Eds.; Oxford University Press: Oxford, UK, 2009; pp. 185–212.
13. Bohm, D. *Quantum Theory*; Dover Publications, Inc.: New York, NY, USA, 1951; p. 646.
14. Bohm, D. *Causality and Chance in Modern Physics*; University of Pennslyvania Press: Philadelphia, PA, USA, 1999; p. 170.
15. Rubin, D.B. Estimating causal effects of treatments in randomized and nonrandomized studies. *J. Educ. Psychol.* **1974**, *66*, 688–701. [CrossRef]
16. Heckman, J.J. Econometric Causality. *Int. Stat. Rev.* **2008**, *76*, 1–27. [CrossRef]
17. Heckman, J.J.; Vytlacil, E. Structural equations, treatment effects, and econometric policy evaluation. *Econometrica* **2005**, *73*, 669–738. [CrossRef]

18. Mogstad, M.; Santos, A.; Torgovitsky, A. Using Instrumental Variables for Inference About Policy Relevant Treatment Parameters. *Econometrica* **2018**, *86*, 1589–1619. [CrossRef]
19. Parbhoo, S.; Wieser, M.; Wieczorek, A.; Roth, V. Information Bottleneck for Estimating Treatment Effects with Systematically Missing Covariates. *Entropy* **2020**, *22*, 389. [CrossRef]
20. Andrée, B.P.J. *Theory and Application of Dynamic Spatial Time Series Models*; Rozenberg Publishers and Tinbergen Institute: Amsterdam, The Netherlands, 2020; pp. 1–374.
21. White, H. A Heteroskedasticity-Consistent Covariance Matrix Estimator and a Direct Test for Heteroskedasticity. *Econometrica* **1980**, *48*, 817. [CrossRef]
22. White, H. Maximum Likelihood Estimation of Misspecified Models. *Econometrica* **1982**, *50*, 1–25. [CrossRef]
23. Domowitz, I.; White, H. Misspecified models with dependent observations. *J. Econom.* **1982**, *20*, 35–58. [CrossRef]
24. Pötscher, B.M.; Prucha, I.R. *Dynamic Nonlinear Econometric Models*; Springer: Berlin/Heidelberg, Germany, 1997. [CrossRef]
25. Driscoll, J.C.; Kraay, A.C. Consistent Covariance Matrix Estimation with Spatially Dependent Panel Data. *Rev. Econ. Stat.* **1998**, *80*, 549–560. [CrossRef]
26. Freedman, D.A. On the So-Called "Huber Sandwich Estimator" and "Robust Standard Errors". *Am. Stat.* **2006**, *60*, 299–302. [CrossRef]
27. Granger, C.; King, M.L.; White, H. Comments on testing economic theories and the use of model selection criteria. *J. Econom.* **1995**, *67*, 173–187. [CrossRef]
28. Hlaváčková-Schindler, K.; Paluš, M.; Vejmelka, M.; Bhattacharya, J. Causality detection based on information-theoretic approaches in time series analysis. *Phys. Rep.* **2007**, *441*, 1–46. [CrossRef]
29. Hlaváčková-Schindler, K. Equivalence of Granger Causality and Transfer Entropy: A Generalization. *Appl. Math. Sci.* **2011**, *5*, 3637–3648.
30. Hlaváčková-Schindler, K.; Plant, C. Heterogeneous Graphical Granger Causality by Minimum Message Length. *Entropy* **2020**, *22*, 1400. [CrossRef]
31. Haavelmo, T. The Statistical Implications of a System of Simultaneous Equations. *Econometrica* **1943**, *11*, 1–12. [CrossRef]
32. Haavelmo, T. The Probability Approach in Econometrics. *Econometrica* **1944**, *12*, 115. [CrossRef]
33. Kalman, R. Identifiability and Modeling in Econometrics. *Dev. Stat.* **1983**, *4*, 97–136. [CrossRef]
34. Schervish, M.J. *Theory of Statistics*; Springer Series in Statistics; Springer: New York, NY, USA, 1995. [CrossRef]
35. Billingsley, P. *Probability and Measure*, 3rd ed.; Wiley Series in Probability and Mathematical Statistics; Wiley-Interscience: New York, NY, USA, 1995.
36. Tong, H. *Threshold Models in Non-Linear Time Series Analysis*; Lecture Notes in Statistics; Springer: New York, NY, USA, 1983; p. 323. [CrossRef]
37. Dijk, D.; Teräsvirta, T.; Franses, P. Smooth transition autoregressive models—A survey of recent developments. *Econom. Rev.* **2002**, *21*, 37–41. [CrossRef]
38. Creal, D.; Koopman, S.J.; Lucas, A. *A General Framework for Observation Driven Time-Varying Parameter Models*; Global COE Hi-Stat Discussion Paper Series; Institute of Economic Research Hitotsubashi University: Tokyo, Japan, 2009.
39. Jan Koopman, S.; Lucas, A.; Schart, M. Predicting time-varying parameters with parameter-driven and observation-driven models. *Rev. Econ. Stat.* **2016**, *98*, 97–110. [CrossRef]
40. Andrée, B.P.J.; Blasques, F.; Koomen, E. *Smooth Transition Spatial Autoregressive Models*; Tinbergen Institute Discussion Paper; Tinbergen Institute: Amsterdam, The Netherlands, 2017. [CrossRef]
41. Blasques, F.; Koopman, S.J.; Lucas, A.; Schaumburg, J. Spillover dynamics for systemic risk measurement using spatial financial time series models. *J. Econom.* **2016**, *195*, 211–223. [CrossRef]
42. Andrée, B.P.J.; Kraay, A.; Chamorro, A.; Spencer, P.; Wang, D. *Predicting Food Crises*; World Bank Policy Research Working Papers; World Bank: Washington, DC, USA, 2020. [CrossRef]
43. Straumann, D.; Mikosch, T. Quasi-maximum-likelihood estimation in conditionally heteroscedastic time series: A stochastic recurrence equations approach. *Ann. Stat.* **2006**, *34*, 2449–2495. [CrossRef]
44. Cline, D.B.H.; Pu, H.M.H. Verifying irreducibility and continuity of a nonlinear time series. *Stat. Probab. Lett.* **1998**, *40*, 139–148. [CrossRef]
45. Cline, D.B.H.; Pu, H.M.H. Geometric Ergodicity of Nonlinear Time Series. *Stat. Sin.* **1999**, *9*, 1103–1118.
46. Amador, L.D.R.; Lovejoy, S. Long-Range Forecasting as a Past Value Problem: Untangling Correlations and Causality with Scaling. *Geophys. Res. Lett.* **2021**, *48*, e2020GL092147. [CrossRef]
47. Dudley, R.M. *Real Analysis and Probability*; Cambridge University Press: Cambridge, UK, 2002; p. 555.
48. Davidson, J. *Stochastic Limit Theory*; Oxford University Press: Oxford, UK, 1994. [CrossRef]
49. Hendry, D.F. Granger Causality. *Eur. J. Pure Appl. Math.* **2017**, *10*, 12–29.
50. Geman, S.; Hwang, C.R. Nonparametric Maximum Likelihood Estimation by the Method of Sieves. *Ann. Stat.* **1982**, *10*, 401–414. [CrossRef]
51. Kolmogorov, A.N.; Fomin, S.V. *Introductory Real Analysis*; Dover Publications: New York, NY, USA, 1975; p. 403.
52. Leisch, F.; Trapletti, A.; Hornik, K. Stationarity and Stability of Autoregressive Neural Network Processes. *Neural Comput.* **2000**, *12*, 2427–2450.
53. Cheney, E.; Respess, J. Best Approximation Problems in Tensor-Product Spaces. *Pac. J. Math.* **1982**, *102*, 437–446.

54. Kullback, S.; Leibler, R.A. On Information and Sufficiency. *Ann. Math. Stat.* **1951**, *22*, 79–86. [CrossRef]
55. Hellinger, E. Neue Begründung der Theorie quadratischer Formen von unendlichvielen Veränderlichen. *J. Reine Angew. Math.* **1909**, *1909*, 210–271. [CrossRef]
56. Akaike, H. Information Theory and an Extension of the Maximum Likelihood Principle. In *Information Theory: Proceedings of the Second International Symposium*; Petrov, B.N., Csaki, F., Eds.; Akadémiai Kiado: Budapest, Hungary, 1973; pp. 267–281.
57. Akaike, H. A new look at the statistical model identification. *IEEE Trans. Autom. Control* **1974**, *19*, 716–723. [CrossRef]
58. Hurvich, C.M.; Tsai, C.L. Regression and time series model selection in small samples. *Biometrika* **1989**, *76*, 297–307. [CrossRef]
59. Hurvich, C.M.; Tsai, C.L. Bias of the corrected AIC criterion for underfitted regression and time series models. *Biomelrika* **1991**, *78*, 499–509. [CrossRef]
60. Sin, C.Y.; White, H. Information criteria for selecting possibly misspecified parametric models. *J. Econom.* **1996**, *71*, 207–225. [CrossRef]
61. Andrée, B.P.J.; Chamorro, A.; Spencer, P.; Koomen, E.; Dogo, H. Revisiting the relation between economic growth and the environment; a global assessment of deforestation, pollution and carbon emission. *Renew. Sustain. Energy Rev.* **2019**, *114*, 109221. [CrossRef]
62. Zou, H. The Adaptive Lasso and Its Oracle Properties. *J. Am. Stat. Assoc.* **2006**, *101*, 1418–1429. [CrossRef]
63. Friedman, J.; Hastie, T.; Tibshirani, R. Regularization paths for generalized linear models via coordinate descent. *J. Stat. Softw.* **2010**, *33*, 1–22. [CrossRef]
64. Bergmeir, C.; Hyndman, R.J.; Koo, B. A note on the validity of cross-validation for evaluating autoregressive time series prediction. *Comput. Stat. Data Anal.* **2018**, *120*, 70–83. [CrossRef]
65. Diks, C.; Panchenko, V.; van Dijk, D. Likelihood-based scoring rules for comparing density forecasts in tails. *J. Econom.* **2011**, *163*, 215–230. [CrossRef]
66. Diebold, F.X.; Mariano, R.S. Comparing Predictive Accuracy. *J. Bus. Econ. Stat.* **1995**, *13*, 253–263. [CrossRef]
67. Andrée, B.P.J. *Estimating Food Price Inflation from Partial Surveys*; Policy Research Working Paper; World Bank: Washington, DC, USA, 2021; Volume 9886. [CrossRef]
68. Andrée, B.P.J. Monthly food price estimates by product and market. In *WLD_2021_RTFP_v02_M*; Version 2021-12-02; World Bank Microdata Library: Washington, DC, USA, 2021. [CrossRef]
69. Blanco, R.; Brennan, S.; Marsh, I.W. An empirical analysis of the dynamic relation between investment-grade bonds and credit default swaps. *J. Financ.* **2005**, *60*, 2255–2281. [CrossRef]
70. Delis, M.D.; Mylonidis, N. The chicken or the egg? A note on the dynamic interrelation between government bond spreads and credit default swaps. *Financ. Res. Lett.* **2011**, *8*, 163–170. [CrossRef]
71. Matei, I. Contagion and causality: An empirical analysis on sovereign bond spreads. *Econ. Bull.* **2003**, *30*, 1885–1896.
72. Gómez-Puig, M.; Sosvilla-Rivero, S. Granger-causality in peripheral EMU public debt markets: A dynamic approach. *J. Bank. Financ.* **2013**, *37*, 4627–4649. [CrossRef]
73. Gómez-Puig, M.; Sosvilla-Rivero, S. Causality and contagion in EMU sovereign debt markets. *Int. Rev. Econ. Financ.* **2014**, *33*, 12–27. [CrossRef]
74. Corsi, F.; Lillo, F.; Pirino, D.; Trapin, L. Measuring the propagation of financial distress with Granger-causality tail risk networks. *J. Financ. Stab.* **2018**, *38*, 18–36. [CrossRef]
75. Balcilar, M.; Usman, O.; Gungor, H.; Roubaud, D.; Wohar, M.E. Role of global, regional, and advanced market economic policy uncertainty on bond spreads in emerging markets. *Econ. Model.* **2021**, *102*, 105576. [CrossRef]
76. Chevallier, J.; Guégan, D.; Goutte, S. Is It Possible to Forecast the Price of Bitcoin? *Forecasting* **2021**, *3*, 377–420. [CrossRef]
77. Lee, K.; Ulkuatam, S.; Beling, P.; Scherer, W. Generating Synthetic Bitcoin Transactions and Predicting Market Price Movement Via Inverse Reinforcement Learning and Agent-Based Modeling. *J. Artif. Soc. Soc. Simul.* **2018**, *21*, 5. [CrossRef]
78. Pele, D.T.; Mazurencu-Marinescu-Pele, M. Using High-Frequency Entropy to Forecast Bitcoin's Daily Value at Risk. *Entropy* **2019**, *21*, 102. [CrossRef]
79. Cohen, G. Forecasting Bitcoin Trends Using Algorithmic Learning Systems. *Entropy* **2020**, *22*, 838. [CrossRef] [PubMed]
80. Kim, Y.B.; Kim, J.G.; Kim, W.; Im, J.H.; Kim, T.H.; Kang, S.J.; Kim, C.H. Predicting fluctuations in cryptocurrency transactions based on user comments and replies. *PLoS ONE* **2016**, *11*, e0161197. [CrossRef]
81. Valencia, F.; Gómez-Espinosa, A.; Valdés-Aguirre, B. Price Movement Prediction of Cryptocurrencies Using Sentiment Analysis and Machine Learning. *Entropy* **2019**, *21*, 589. [CrossRef]
82. Lahmiri, S.; Bekiros, S. Randomness, Informational Entropy, and Volatility Interdependencies among the Major World Markets: The Role of the COVID-19 Pandemic. *Entropy* **2020**, *22*, 833. [CrossRef]
83. García-Medina, A.; Luu, T.; Huynh, D.; Schinckus, C.; Stanley, H.E. What Drives Bitcoin? An Approach from Continuous Local Transfer Entropy and Deep Learning Classification Models. *Entropy* **2021**, *23*, 1582. [CrossRef]
84. Burnham, K.P.; Anderson, D.R. Multimodel inference: Understanding AIC and BIC in Model Selection. *Sociol. Methods Res.* **2004**, *33*, 261–304. [CrossRef]
85. Wright, M.N.; Ziegler, A. Ranger: A fast implementation of random forests for high dimensional data in C++ and R. *J. Stat. Softw.* **2017**, *77*, 1–17. [CrossRef]
86. Davis, R.A.; Nielsen, M.S. Modeling of time series using random forests: Theoretical developments. *Electron. J. Stat.* **2020**, *14*, 3644–3671. [CrossRef]

87. Clark, E.; Baccar, S. Modelling credit spreads with time volatility, skewness, and kurtosis. *Ann. Oper. Res.* **2018**, *262*, 431–461. [CrossRef]
88. Kim, J.M.; Kim, D.H.; Jung, H. Estimating yield spreads volatility using GARCH-type models. *N. Am. J. Econ. Financ.* **2021**, *57*, 101396. [CrossRef]
89. Andrée, B.P.J. Probability, Causality and Stochastic Formulations of Economic Theory. 2019. Available online: https://ssrn.com/abstract=3422430 (accessed on 21 September 2021). [CrossRef]

MDPI
St. Alban-Anlage 66
4052 Basel
Switzerland
Tel. +41 61 683 77 34
Fax +41 61 302 89 18
www.mdpi.com

Entropy Editorial Office
E-mail: entropy@mdpi.com
www.mdpi.com/journal/entropy